UNDERSTANDING VYGOTSKY:
A QUEST FOR SYNTHESIS

UNDERSTANDING VYGOTSKY:

A QUEST FOR SYNTHESIS

René van der Veer and Jaan Valsiner

BLACKWELL
Oxford UK & Cambridge USA

The right of René van der Veer and Jaan Valsiner to be identified as authors of
this work has been asserted in accordance with the Copyright, Designs and
Patents Act 1988.

First published 1991
First published in paperback 1993

Blackwell Publishers
238 Main Street
Cambridge, Massachusetts 02142
USA

108 Cowley Road
Oxford OX4 1JF
UK

Library of Congress Cataloging in Publication Data

Veer, René van der, 1952–
    Understanding Vygotsky: A Quest for synthesis / René van der Veer
and Jaan Valsiner
        p.   cm.
    Includes bibliographical references and index.
    ISBN 0–631–18955–6 (pbk.)
    1. Vygotski, L. S. (Lev Semenovich), 1896–1934.
    2. Psychologists — Soviet Union.   I. Valsiner, Jaan.   II. Title.
    BF109.V95V44   1991
    150'.92—dc20   90–19342
                                                                              CIP

A CIP catalogue record for this book is available from the British Library.

Typeset in 10 on 12 pt Sabon
by Acorn Bookwork, Salisbury, Wiltshire
Printed in Great Britain by T.J. Press Ltd, Padstow, Cornwall
This book is printed on acid-free paper

Contents

Illustrations

Preface

In writing this book we have reached a milestone in the development of our understanding of how scientific ideas migrate between countries by way of the intellectual pursuits of individual persons embedded in their cultural contexts. The understanding of the major ideas of Lev Vygotsky that emerges from the pages of this book is the result of years of effort to make sense of the complex, fascinating and, at times, capricious creativity of that Russian/Jewish literary scholar (turned psychologist). For one of us, (René van der Veer), understanding Vygotsky has been a long-term project which has delved deeply into the intricacies of the Russian language and literature to produce an understanding of Vygotsky's contributions (Van der Veer, *Cultuur en Cognitie*, Groningen: Wolters-Noordhoff, 1985). For the other author, (Jaan Valsiner), work on this book has helped to review some aspects of his intellectual and social backgrounds which (since 1980) he has been developing. The Introduction and Epilogue, and chapters 2, 6, 8 and 12 were written by Valsiner; the remainder of the book is by Van der Veer. But the final product is more than the sum of our individual efforts. Our personal differences in focus and style have worked well in complementing each other: while one of us has been nearly over whelmed by microscopic details, the other's instinctive urge for generalizations has kept the project in focus; and when one of us has impatiently rushed to make far-reaching general statements about the state of affairs in psychology, the other has taken him (or her – a tribute to APA-style equality!) back to the details. This combination of personal perspectives has helped us to write a treatise on the life and work of Vygotsky which (we hope) will reveal the intricacies of the history of his ideas without the need for the reader of this book to take a "Vygotskian perspective" while trying to make sense of our (sometimes very detailed) analyses. In any science, it is usually the ardent followers of some interesting theoretical system who render such a system a dogmatic orthodoxy. As a result the freshness of the original ideas may disappear as the unquestioned orthodoxy is accepted. Our aim in this book is to restore the freshness of Vygotsky's ideas by way of revealing the ways in which his thinking borrowed concepts from his predecessors and contemporaries, to analyze these ideas, and to suggest new solutions to the problems he raises. In order to preserve this aim (one might call it an attempt at an archaeology of ideas) we have deliberately decided to avoid overviewing the myriad of interpretations of Vygotsky's work in the past few decades. That task is a different challenge worthy of a separate volume.

The work on this book was made possible only by generous assistance from a number of people who helped us to obtain different original material about Vygotsky, and copies of his original publications. First and foremost, the trust and friendship of Gita L'vovna Vygodskaja is to be acknowledged with deep gratitude. She (and her relatives) received Van der Veer most kindly, gave him access to the family archives, and answered many of our questions. In addition, she gave permission to use part of Vygotsky's correspondence annotated by A. A. Puzyrej. Andrej Puzyrej himself – one of the greatest authorities on Vygotsky's work – was extremely helpful in making a number of rare publications and unpublished materials available and by sharing his insights with us. Elena Aleksandrovna Luria, too, received Van der Veer in a most friendly fashion and allowed him to work with the family archives. Also I. M. Arievich, A. G. Asmolov, G. Blanck, V. V. Davydov, N. Elrod, T. M. Lifanova, L. Mecacci, L. A. Radzikhovsky, A. Stetsenko, P. Tulviste, Ju. A. Vasil'eva, and F. Vidal helped out in the tedious process of locating rare materials, and Nadia Zilper of the University of North Carolina Library was helpful in building up a good collection of Russian/Soviet psychology texts in the US. S. Jaeger provided us with several of Luria's letters to W. Köhler and S. F. Dobkin and P. Ja. Gal'perin gave their personal views of Vygotsky in conversations with Van der Veer. G. Blanck and G. L. Vygodskaja provided us with the photographs of Vygotsky shown in this book. In compiling the list of references we made ample use of T. M. Lifanova's valuable list of Vygotsky's writings published in the Soviet edition of his collected works. Kurt Kreppner brought our attention to the remarkable similarities between the ideas of Vygotsky and some key notions of William Stern. The full extent of that connection remains to be analyzed and is beyond the scope of this book. Madlena Maksimova gave helpful comments on an earlier draft of the book.

We also want to express our gratitude to NWO (Nederlandse Stichting voor Wetenschappelijk Onderzoek) for their financial support, which allowed Van der Veer to spend three months in Chapel Hill, North Carolina, in 1986 and which made it possible for Valsiner to visit the University of Leiden in the summer of 1988. However, we have both sustained a remarkably tenacious search for our own synthesis of an understanding of the life and work of Lev Vygotsky. Thus, nobody but ourselves can take responsibility for the analyses the reader will find in this book.

Researching this book has been an exercise in detective work. Repeatedly we came across alterations to the history of Vygotsky's work in psychology – sometimes deliberate, sometimes unintentional. Not surprisingly, we reacted vehemently to each unsubstantiated myth, and the reader will sense these reactions in a number of places in this book. On reflection we wonder why we were so agitated when we discovered the ways in which Vygotsky has been painted as a "guru"-figure of Soviet (and some international) psychology. After all, histories are written (and re-written) after the fact in order to be functional for the needs of the present time and place. Nevertheless, the realization that a productive historical figure involved in the genesis of psychology is valued by succeeding generations merely in a declarative manner is cause for concern. This concern is sharpened when one considers the myriad of Vygotsky's half-developed ideas which could be highly productive for contemporary psychology only if they were developed and not accepted unquestioningly. It is our hope that this book will stimulate readers to look beyond Vygotsky's intellectual heritage to his consistently developmental approach to all psychological phenomena.

René van der Veer
Jaan Valsiner
Leiden and Chapel Hill

Every inventor, even a genius, is always the outgrowth of his time and environment. His creativity stems from those needs that were created before him, and rests upon those possibilities that, again, exist outside of him. That is why we notice strict continuity in the historical development of technology and science. No invention or scientific discovery appears before the material and psychological conditions are created that are necessary for its emergence. Creativity is a historically continuous process in which every next form is determined by its preceeding ones.

Lev Vygotsky, Voobrazhenie i tvorchestvo v detskom vozraste

Introduction

This book is a case study of the history of a person's scientific ideas in the context of a rapidly changing society. The life and work of Lev Vygotsky have increasingly become a focus for contemporary psychology's social discourse — he constitutes an interesting case for the analysis of intellectual interdependence (see Van der Veer and Valsiner, 1988) between scientists, for a number of reasons. First, wide-ranging claims about the "genius"-like nature of Vygotsky have been made in recent decades — a good means of advertising but perhaps not conducive to an understanding of the content and implications of the ideas of the "genius". Secondly, with the burgeoning of "neo-Vygotskian" fashions in contemporary psychology, the historical focus of Vygotsky and his ideas has receded into the background (with some notable exceptions; see Kozulin, 1990a). For instance, Vygotsky is credited with "being 50 years ahead of his time", for ideas that he himself credited to his predecessors of the 1890s and early 1900s. Of course, this discrepancy is not surprising since the contemporary psychology of the 1990s is increasingly becoming historically myopic. It now resembles a "factory of data production" under the spell of conveniently "theory"-labeled fashions, most of which merely reiterate common-sense knowledge (see Smedslund, 1978, 1979). The development of ideas about psychological issues has become obscured by that feverish and highly compulsive activity, and impasses of psychological thinking of the past become enthusiastically repeated in the present. After all, if the current social consensus of psychologists is used to determine the meaning of "progress" within that discipline, then what is termed as being such is fully under the control of social estimations by psychologists of the present who are guided by the fashions of the day.

Last — but not least — Vygotsky was unique. In his case we have to face an instance of how a "novice" turned into an "expert." Vygotsky had no formal education in the discipline, nor any "training" in the empirical science that dominates psychology departments in our time. However, his literary scholarship and knowledge of the history of philosophy equipped him with the tools to tackle new disciplines. Of course, this background is not sufficient to explain his success – he was lucky to enter psychology at a particularly opportune time (and under coincidental conditions, as we show in this book). His achievements in psychology are framed by larger social changes in that discipline as well as in the society at large. It is often beneficial for a scientific discipline to "import" scholars from other areas to enrich their otherwise in-bred realm of ideas. Often such imput works well (for instance, consider the entrance of a number of physicists into biology after the Second World War; see Crick, 1988), but their actual long-term impact depends largely on the social processes that organize scientific progress.

The nature of Vygotsky's personal background – he was a young Jewish literary scholar hampered by recurrent illness, a passionate talker enraptured by the fine arts, and an equally passionate critic of the mediocre thinking of his contemporary psychologists – encourages an in-depth analysis of his ideas. In short, the present book describes the intricate developmental course of Vygotsky's ideas in order to demonstrate the links between these ideas and the web of other ideas available to him. We trace these links in the hope that specific knowledge of the roots of particular ideas helps us to appreciate Vygotsky's intellectual creativity in its context.

The book is organized in a way that preserves the continuity of Vygotsky's life-course while emphasizing different thematic areas of his intellectual pursuits at different periods. Since it is somewhat artificial to separate a persons life-course into stages, we have chosen a loose structure within which to work: many themes of intellectual pursuit that are dealt with at a late stage have their roots earlier, and there is a remarkable (but not complete) continuity in Vygotsky's ideas, from the time when he was a young idealistic literary scholar (see chapter 2) to the paedological period of his life in the early 1930s. Furthermore, the thematic areas dealt with in separate chapters within a given lifecourse period complement one another, and may seem at times somewhat redundant. Of course, the redundancy is already there in Vygotsky's own writings as he tackled questions of different psychological issues from the same meta-theoretical perspective. It is this meta-theoretical perspective – a consistent (which means redundant) emphasis on viewing all psychological phenomena as those which are undergoing development – from which contemporary psychology can learn. An analysis of Vygotsky's personal (but socially rooted) construction of the developmental paradigm in psychology thus has value for our own similar pursuits in the 1990s.

It is here that the reasons for Vygotsky's current popularity may be found – his constant search for a developmental perspective is fascinating, especially if we consider the practical demise of developmental perspectives in post-Second World War psychology, at least in its mainstreams (see Benigni and Valsiner, 1985; Cairns, 1986). The present efforts of developmentalists to think along developmental lines can benefit from the intellectual successes and failures of Vygotsky and his contemporaries. The reader of this book may want to undertake an excursion into history for the sake of our present research in psychology, and for its future. Or, to paraphrase Vygotsky's recurrent reiteration of a maxim by Pavel Blonsky, *the state of affairs in contemporary psychology can be understood only as the history of that psychology.*

1
Lev Vygotsky

Childhood and Youth

Lev Semyonovich Vygodsky[1] was born on November 5, 1896 in Orsha, a provincial town in the vicinity of Minsk. Little has been published about his childhood and youth. The few things we know have been related by his childhood friend Dobkin and his daughter Gita L'vovna Vygodskaja. (The latter is currently, together with T. M. Lifanova, preparing a biography of her father which will update all the biographical material so far published (cf. Vygodskaja and Lifanova, 1984; 1988).) Meanwhile, in this chapter and in the introduction to the different sections of the book the currently available biographical material will be presented.

Vygotsky was the second child in a family of eight children. His parents were highly educated members of the Jewish community in Gomel', the father working as a department chief at the United Bank and as a representative of an insurance company. The Vygodskys, apparently, could afford to give their children an excellent education. The availability of a fine library, the fact that the family lived in a very large apartment, and the fact that the children had private tutors: all these circumstances indicate that the Vygodskys were a relatively well-to-do family.

Although the Vygodskys were not very religious they held to the Jewish traditions. Thus young Lev Vygotsky received a traditional Jewish education, reading the Torah in Hebrew, delivering a speech at his Bar Mitsva, and so on. The rather frequent references in his work to the Bible can be understood in this context. He was interested in Jewish culture and folklore and identified to some extent with the history of the Jewish people (cf. his

[1]Lev Vygodsky changed his name into Vygotsky, because he believed – after some research of his own – that his family originally came from a village, called Vygotovo. The authors have been unable to establish its location.

discussion of Belyj's "anti-semitism"; Vygotsky, 1916a), and external circumstances encouraged this interest and identification. Among other things, under the Tsarist government Jews were not allowed to live outside the Pale of Settlement, a region in Russia where, until 1907, pogroms were a common occurrence. In his native town, Gomel', Vygotsky himself must have experienced pogroms in 1903 – fortunately repulsed by an organized Jewish defence (Pinkus, 1988, p. 29) – and 1906 (Gilbert, 1979). He also witnessed the ignominious return of the Jewish members of the Russian army there. They had been sent back to their home towns after the rumor had been spread that Jewish soldiers were not to be trusted in war-time.

Notwithstanding the pogroms, Russia's war with Germany and Austria, the civil war, and other disasters, Vygotsky attempted to lead a normal life. As a young boy his favorite hobbies were stamp-collecting, chess, and corresponding in Esperanto (Levitin, 1982, p. 27). Somewhere in Iceland a very old man – or, more likely, his bewildered children – may now and then skim through a collection of incomprehensible letters sent many years ago by a Russian penfriend.

Vygotsky's friend Dobkin (in Levitin, 1982, p. 26) has related that as an adolescent Vygotsky actively participated with a circle of friends in discussing such highly abstract subjects as Hegel's philosophy of history and the role of the individual in history. He also seems to have loved poetry, in particular Pushkin and Heine – later Gumilyov, Mandel'shtam and Pasternak – and frequented the performances in the local theatres. Early reading of Potebnja's "Thought and Language" (1922) may have quickened his interest in psychology.

It was David Vygodsky, a cousin several years older, who had introduced Vygotsky to the Esperanto movement. The cousins were close and corresponded for years after David left for Petrograd in 1919. Part of this correspondence has been preserved in the family archives. David Vygodsky was himself a man of more than average abilities. He became a competent poet, by profession he was a linguist and philologist, and personally he was close to Roman Jakobson and Viktor Shklovsky (Levitin, 1982, p. 27). He also knew several foreign languages and became well known as the translator of Russian poetry into Spanish and Hebrew literature into Russian. During the civil war in Spain he served as the intermediary between the Soviet authorities and the anti-Franco movement. Shortly after Franco's victory he was arrested on unknown charges. As is well known, in those dark years the indictments could be based on almost anything. In the case of David Vygodsky the charge of espionage seems the most likely. After all, he had been involved in the Spanish civil war – unexpectedly lost by the leftist allies – and he had been very active in the suspect Esperanto movement. (Philatelists and Esperantists were arrested in great numbers by the end of the thirties. It was assumed that these groups had used their seemingly innocent contacts with foreign citizens as a cover for more sinister practices. See Medvedev, 1974, p. 681.) The writer Marietta Shaginjan has related the unusual and brave attempts of David's literary friends to get him released from prison. Such celebrities as Fedin, Lavrenev, Shklovsky, Slonimsky, Tynjanov, and Zoshchenko wrote to the authorities, declaring David Vygodsky's innocence and demanding his release. The attempts of these Leningrad writers failed, however (Shaginjan in Medvedev, 1974, p. 806), and David Vygodsky was eventually sent to a concentration camp (some letters from there have survived), where he died in 1942 or 1943.

Education

Vygotsky received his first education from private tutors, and later joined the two highest classes of the private Jewish *Gymnasium* in Gomel', graduating with a gold medal in 1913. His further education was influenced by the fact that he was a Jew. In the first place, Tsarist Russia enforced a quota for the admission of Jews to institutions of higher education. The quota for the universities of Petersburg and Moscow was three per cent. In practice, this meant that gold medalists were assured of admission. However, when Vygotsky was taking his examinations, the minister of education issued a circular letter declaring that Jewish students were to be enrolled by casting lots. This was a serious blow to Vygotsky, whose gold medal had now become virtually worthless. Fortunately, he was one of the lucky few and he started taking courses at Moscow University. The choice of subject was again influenced by his Jewish origin. History and philology were unattractive options, as they usually led only to the position of teacher at a secondary school, and since Jews were not allowed to be government officials, the only position available was that of teacher at a private Jewish *Gymnasium*. There were two more attractive possibilities: law and medicine. Law offered the opportunity to become an attorney and attornies were allowed to live outside the Pale. Medicine guaranteed a modest if uneventful and secure future. At the insistence of his parents Vygotsky applied to the medical department, but after one month he switched to law. He also took other courses and majored in history and philosophy at the Shanjavsky People's University, which was not officially endorsed. However, this was an institute of some quality, since after a strike at the Imperial University many renowned specialists had started teaching there (Levitin, 1982, pp. 29–30).

During his last two years at university in Moscow Vygotsky shared a room with his younger sister Zinaida, who had entered the Non-Credit

Vygotsky's student card at Moscow University. At the time he studied law and still spelled his name with "d".

Woman's University Courses in 1915. Zinaida Vygodskaja was to become a prominent linguist and co-author of several foreign language dictionaries (e.g. Achmanova and Vygodskaja, 1962). It may have been Zinaida – together with David – who kept her brother well-informed of all the developments in linguistics and philology. She also shared an interest in the philosophical writings of Spinoza with Vygotsky.

During his university years Vygotsky maintained his early interests in literature and art. As an adolescent he had started studying Shakespeare's *Hamlet* and had written several drafts of an analysis of it (Vygotsky, 1915a), and his Masters thesis (Vygotsky, 1916d) was the result of this long-standing interest (see chapter 2). A later paper, an analysis of Dostoevsky's writings entitled "Dostoevsky and anti-semitism" seems to have been lost (Radzikhovsky, personal communication, May 1990). Vygotsky's interests broadened to include psychological and pedagogical problems during this period. A course on "The internal form of the word" given by the Humboldtian scholar Shpet (Shpet, 1927; cf. Mitjushin, 1988) must have encouraged within Vygotsky and his sister, who also took the course, a sensitivity to the internal, psychological aspects of language (see also chapter 15). Around this time Vygotsky also started reading the available international psychological literature. It is said that the reading of James' remarkable study *The Varieties of Religious Experience* (1902/1985), and Freud's *Zur Psychopathologie des Alltagslebens* (1904/1987) particularly impressed him. These books, incidentally, made a rather odd and unequal pair: first, because the intellectual sophistication of James' fascinating study is well beyond that of Freud's single-minded quest for the id in human daily behaviour; second, because James' devastating criticism of the sexual "explanation" of religious feeling applied to part of Freud's thinking. In fact, James' critique (see James, 1902, pp. 10–12) of what he called "medical materialism" anticipated much of Soviet psychology's future criticisms of Freudian theory (see chapter 5).

It can be argued that Vygotsky's liking for these books revealed an interest in the extreme layers of mind and – in the case of Freud's book – a predilection for speculative studies. It could also be said to form a continuation of his interest in *Hamlet*, whose "other worldliness" and hidden subjective motives were particularly stressed by the young Vygotsky (see chapter 2). Be that as it may, it is clear that Vygotsky's views at the time were still far from the reactological, objectivist views he was to espouse some years later (see chapters 3 and 6).

Formative Years

Having finished his university studies in 1917 Vygotsky returned to his native town Gomel' where, following the Revolution, he was allowed to teach in state schools. It is this period of Vygotsky's life – from 1917 until his move to Moscow in 1924 – that causes the greatest problems for his biographers. What we do know, on the basis of archival documents and reminiscences of contemporaries, is that Vygotsky held many and various positions in the cultural life of Gomel' and became one of its most prominent cultural leaders. What we know very little about is the content of his thinking at this time. This lack of knowledge is caused by an enormous and puzzling gap in the currently known list of Vygotsky's published writings. Indeed, the twenty-year-old Vygotsky had already published four literary reviews in 1916 and approximately twice as many papers in 1924, yet we find virtually no publications in the seven-year-period in between. The most recent list of Vygotsky's publications (in Vygotsky, 1984b; compiled by T. M. Lifanova) gives only two literary reviews and two unpublished manuscripts for this whole period, while – given Vygotsky's production in other years – one would expect at least thirty or so papers. Although four more literary reviews have been unearthed recently (Vygotsky, 1923a–d), we are still faced with an empty period in Vygotsky's publication history that has to be explained. Observing this same phenomenon Joravsky (1989, p. 255) has suggested that Vygotsky's disciples have refrained from describing this period adequately and from republishing his articles for political reasons. He suggests that "Vygotsky may have consorted with non-Bolsheviks in 1917, for he published in a Jewish periodical (*Novyj Put*) and in one edited by Gorky (*Letopis*) which was critical of the new dictatorship and was soon shut down by it." Although anything is possible, of course, this seems to the present writers not to be the most likely explanation of the gap in Vygotsky's publication history. First, a handful of literary reviews in these same two journals were documented in Vygotsky (1984b) and, moreover, it is not very clear why a former Jewish periodical might not be mentioned in the 1980s. Secondly, there is a more likely candidate for the explanation of the publication gap: the atrocities of the civil war and the occupation by the Germans. At the time Gomel' and its surroundings were harassed by groups of Red and White soldiers, the German army, and bands of local bandits. It is quite possible that one of the battles caused the destruction of local newspaper offices and other archives, as Soviet students of Vygotsky have indeed claimed. If this explanation is the correct one, then our only hope of completing Vygotsky's publication record is that papers will be found in private archives or unexplored public ones.[2]

While most of Vygotsky's papers of this period are probably still missing, it is possible to get an idea of his life between 1917 and 1924 by analyzing his organizational activities in the cultural life of Gomel' (cf. Fejgina, 1988). It is known that Vygotsky taught at various institutes; among them were the Soviet Labor School (Russian: *Sovetskaja Trudovaja Shkola*) where he taught with his cousin David, and the Gomel' Teacher College (*Pedagogicheskoe Uchilishche*). The latter institute was to play a major role in Vygotsky's development as a scientist, for it was in this institute that Vygotsky set up a small psychological laboratory where students could do simple practical investigations. In this laboratory he performed his own first

[2]This hope has now been realized: recently T. M. Lifanova and G. L. Vygodskaja found fifty articles in an archive in Leningrad. All of these were reviews of plays staged in the theatres of Gomel' during the period 1921–3 and published in the local newspapers *Nash Ponedel'nik* and *Polesskaja Pravda* (Lifanova, personal communication, February 24, 1991).

experiments on dominant reactions and respiration that provided the material for his talk on reflexological and psychological investigation (Vygotsky, 1926b; see the introduction to Part II and chapter 2). Working at the Gomel' Teacher College he also started preparing one of his first major books: *Pedagogical Psychology* (see chapter 3). The fact that Vygotsky in this period gave talks about the teaching of literature, and investigated the effect of repeated translations on the content of texts, also testifies to his growing pedagogical and psychological interests (Vygotsky, 1922a; 1923e). Other institutes where Vygotsky taught in this period included the Evening School for Adult Workers, the Rabfak (a faculty where those labourers willing to go to the university took a preparatory course), and the Preparatory Courses for Pedagogues: *Kursy Podgotovki Pedagogov*). The subjects Vygotsky taught varied from Russian literature and language to logic, psychology, and pedagogy.

Vygotsky gave talks at various other institutes on esthetics, the history of art, and the above-mentioned subjects, and co-organized the so-called "literary Mondays" where the work of modern and classic poets and writers was presented and discussed. During these nights the writings of Shakespeare, Goethe, Pushkin, Chekhov, Mayakovsky, and Esenin were discussed, as well as some of the hotly debated topics of the day, such as Einstein's theory of relativity. Vygotsky's brilliant lectures attracted large audiences (Kolbanovsky, 1934c, p. 388).

He was also the co-founder of the publishing house Ages and Days – together with his friend Dobkin and his cousin David – and of the literary journal *Heather*. Both undertakings were short-lived, though: the publishing house published only two books, one of them with poems by Ehrenburg. The ventures came to an abrupt halt because of a problem that haunts the Soviet Union up to the present day: a shortage of paper (although there has always been enough paper to publish millions of copies of the obtuse works of the leading ideologists).

Vygotsky headed the theater section of the Gomel' department of People's Education (*Narodnoe Obrazovanie*), co-operating with one of its organizers, I. I. Danjushevsky, who would later invite him to Moscow to work in the field of defectology. Vygotsky took an active part in the selection of the repertoire, the choice of the setting, and the directing. He edited the theater section of the local newspaper *Polesskaja Pravda*, where the recently found reviews of Belorussian literature, work by Serafimovich, John Reed's *Ten Days that Shook the World*, and a theater performance by Maximov were published. He never lost his interest in theater, regularly met stage-managers and directors (such as Eisenstein) and near the end of his life published a paper on the psychology of the actor (cf. Vygotsky, 1936d).

One may conclude, then, that Vygotsky was an active and prominent member of the cultural life of Gomel' and that diverse activities in this field led him to meet other cultural figures, both in Gomel' and in other cities. It is known, for instance, that Vygotsky was in some way acquainted with the poet Mandel'shtam in the early 1920s. In his library a copy of the poet's *Tristia* was found, which was dedicated to Lev Vygotsky (see also chapter 15). As the dedication was printed, it can be dated exactly to 1922, the year of publication of the collection. Of course, Vygotsky may not have known Mandel'shtam very well at that time but in later years he would be a regular guest of the Mandel'shtams for some period. In Nadezhda Mandel'shtam's (1970, p. 241) memoirs we suddenly catch a glimpse of Vygotsky's later private life. She mentions that in 1933 they "also regularly met ... with Vygotsky, a man of great intellect, a psychologist, the author of the book *Language and Thought*. Vygotsky was fettered to some extent by the rationalism common to all scientists of that period ..." This perspicuous observation is to some extent confirmed by analysis of Vygotsky's work (see chapters 3 and 9) and by the excerpts from his correspondence given below.

In the meantime, Vygotsky's private circumstances in Gomel' had gradually deteriorated. In the first place, the general situation in Russia was almost hopeless. Because of the civil war, the war with the Western allies, and the first land reforms (see chapter 10) the economy of the country had rapidly deteriorated and it was difficult to get enough food. Moreover, the Vygodsky family was struck by tuberculosis (a disease that was said to be typical of Western bourgeois societies; see chapter 5). For Vygotsky's younger brother Dodik the disease proved fatal and in 1920 Vygotsky himself – who had been looking after his brother – fell seriously ill for the first time and was sent to a sanatorium. His condition became very serious and, expecting to die, he asked the literary critic Yuly Aikhenwald, one of his former professors at the Shanjavsky People's University, to publish his writings posthumously. Fortunately, Vygotsky recovered from this first serious attack of tuberculosis, but the disease was to plague him for the rest of his life, causing remittent attacks, and his death in 1934.

One might wonder why, under these desperate circumstances, Vygotsky did not try to leave for Moscow. Moscow was definitely a center of major cultural and scientific activities, a fact that must have been important to a young man so interested in the theater, art, and literature. In addition, Vygotsky must have made many friends during his years at university there. The explanation given by Dobkin is probably the most accurate (Levitin, 1982, p. 37): Vygotsky did not want to leave his parents during this difficult period, and his reluctance to leave for Moscow may, thus, have been connected with the unstable political situation in the Gomel' area. We have seen how Gomel' was in the crossfire of several armies and groups of bandits roaming the country. Apart from that it was, of course, difficult to get permission to settle in Moscow and, finally, a love affair may have played its role: in 1924 Vygotsky married Roza Smekhova from Gomel' and left for Moscow.

Summarizing, one may conclude that the Gomel' period marks the origin of Vygotsky's psychological thinking. It was in Gomel' that he performed his first psychological experiments (see chapter 2) and gave his first talks on subjects related to education and psychology. It also was in Gomel' that Vygotsky started to absorb the available psychological, educational, and paedological literature. This reading enabled him to give a course on psychology to his students and to prepare large parts of the textbook *Pedagogical Psychology* (1926i; see chapter 3). The major part of his dissertation, "The psychology of art" (1925j), was also written in Gomel' (see chapter 2), the topic of this book being in line with his fascination for art and theater.

One may conclude, then, that Vygotsky's shift in interest towards problems of psychology, paedology, and education was a very gradual one, but one that had taken place to a considerable extent before he started working at Kornilov's Institute of Experimental Psychology in Moscow. It would be slightly misleading, therefore, to consider him to have been a "school teacher from a provincial town" who, in 1924, suddenly made his début into psychology (see Luria, 1979 and many other Cinderella-type accounts).

The Man and his Cause

As we have seen Vygotsky's life was not always easy and his living conditions were not always conducive to creative scientific work. In the last years of his life the situation grew worse, becoming almost intolerable. To illustrate this, the conditions in which Vygotsky composed his books are revealing. First, he, his wife, and two daughters lived in one room of an overcrowded apartment – conditions he shared with millions of his compatriots. Secondly, in order to earn his living Vygotsky took upon himself an enormous amount of editorial work for publishing houses and a heavy teaching load, the latter involving travel back and forth from Moscow to Leningrad and Kharkov. Thirdly, Vygotsky suffered from recurrent attacks of tuberculosis. Several times the doctors told him that he would die within a few months and many times he had to suffer exhausting and painful treatments. Operations were repeatedly planned and then postponed again, and the regular periods in overcrowded hospitals and sanatoriums could be intrinsically horrific. Vygotsky's analysis of the crisis in psychology (see chapter 7), for example, was started under the following conditions.

I have already been here a week – in large rooms for six severely ill patients, [there is] noise, shouting, no table, etc. The beds are ranged next to each other without any space between them, like in barracks. Added to this I feel physically in agony, morally crushed, and depressed. (Vygotsky in a letter to Sakharov, dated February 15, 1926)

Recovering in a sanatorium one month later he added:

around me there was such a situation all the time, that it was shameful and difficult to take a pen in the hand and impossible to think quietly . . . I feel myself outside of life, more correctly: between life and death; I am not yet desperate, but I have already abandoned all hope. (Vygotsky in a letter to Luria, dated March 5, 1926)

Fourthly, from about 1931 articles critical of his ideas started being published in the major psychology and paedology journals, within the context of a carefully orchestrated attack on his cultural-historical theory. Vygotsky and his colleagues were, of course, well aware of what was going on and the planning of possible replies to these critical articles, the talks with influential persons to assess the hidden meaning and danger of attacks etc., took immense amounts of time (see chapter 16). Finally, Vygotsky was deeply hurt by the "desertion" of several of his co-workers and students, who left him and his ideas to form the so-called Kharkov group (see the introductions to parts II and III). From very early in his professional life he had seen the development of a new science of man as his cause, a cause he took extremely seriously and to which he dedicated all his energy. Reading his letters to his co-workers and students one gets the impression that Vygotsky and his group formed an almost quasi-religious movement, so overwhelming was the conviction that they were on the right track towards the development of the new science and so great was the respect for Vygotsky as the group's leader. This feeling of a common cause that was worth fighting for, despite pressure, criticism, and indifference from the outside world, had already developed by 1926, as becomes clear from one of Vygotsky's letters to Luria. "I very much deplore the fact that in this difficult time of crisis I am not with you at the institute . . . How seriously we have to think about our [scientific] fate and the fate of the cause that we undertook, when KN [Kornilov] and the other 'bosses' do not wish to think about it." (Vygotsky in a letter to Luria, dated March 5, 1926)

In a later letter to five of his students and collaborators (Bozhovich, Levina, Morozova, Slavina, and Zaporozhec) Vygotsky related his amazement about the fact that first Luria and then Leont'ev started following him on this difficult road towards a new science:

I had a feeling of enormous surprise when A. R. [Luria] in his time was the first to follow this road, and when A. N. [Leont'ev] followed him. Now to the surprise joy is added, that by the detected signposts the big road is visible not only to me, not only to the three of us, but to another five persons. The feeling of the immensity and massiveness of the contemporary psychological work (we live in a period of geological cataclysms in psychology) is my main emotion. But this makes the situation of those few who follow the new line in science (especially in the science of man) infinitely responsible, serious to the highest degree, almost tragic (in the best and real, and not in the pathetic meaning of this word). A thousand times one has to put oneself to the test, to check [oneself], to stand the ordeal before deciding, for it is a very difficult road that requires the whole person. (Vygotsky in a letter to his five students, dated April 15, 1929)

Vygotsky often repeated this theme of total dedication to the common cause and he felt irritated and hurt when collegues, such as Zankov and Solov'ev, hesitated to embark on this new path in psychology (Vygotsky in letters to Leont'ev, dated August 11 and 23, 1929).

It was his rare charm and personal warmth that enabled Vygotsky to make other people join the project. Kolbanovsky (1934c) has related his kindness, responsiveness, sensitivity, and tenderness as a young boy and the modesty and tactfulness evident in his dealings with others less talented than himself. In later years he gave fascinating lectures that attracted large audiences and had a truly mesmerizing effect on most people.[3] One of his pupils described them like this:

It is hard to determine what exactly attracted us in the lectures of Lev Semyonovich. Apart from their deep and interesting content we were charmed by his genuine sincerity, the continual striving upwards with which he captivated his listeners, [and] the beautiful literary expression of his thought. The sound of his soft baritone itself, flexible and rich in intonation, produced a sort of esthetic delight. You very much wanted to experience the hypnotizing influence of his speech and it was difficult to refrain the involuntary feeling of disappointment when it stopped. (Quoted by Kolbanovsky, 1934c, p. 388)

---

[3]Gal'perin (in Haenen, 1989, p. 16) has claimed that Vygotsky's verbal gift verged on pathology. To explain: Seeing a picture Vygotsky could not well understand it. He could tell what he saw, but the sense, meaning, and quality of it eluded him. However, telling another person about the same picture Vygotsky could tell more than this person would see himself and only then did the picture start becoming intelligible for him as well. Gal'perin concluded that everything was focused on speech for Vygotsky, a conclusion strengthened by Vygotsky's own words ("You remember, I always talk – about chimeras and ideas") in a letter to Leont'ev, dated July 11, 1929.

One should not think, however, that Vygotsky was merely a warm, sensitive, and deeply serious person. He also had a keen sense of humor, appreciated the lighter side of life (in a letter to Luria, dated July 26, 1927, he urged him to drink much of the excellent southern wine) and at times could be very sarcastic and sharp. Moreover, he was no dreamer, but a person who was acutely aware of what was going on in the Soviet Union and a keen observer of the personal degradations and dramas it entailed. When he felt betrayed or treated unfairly by people – as in the case of Leont'ev and Luria (see the introduction to part III) – he reacted with vigor and decisively, treating the culprits with severity and not accepting any apologies. But on the whole he seems to have had a surprising talent to avoid personal quarrels, in-group fighting, etc. Whilst being a very sensitive person[4] in terms of inter-personal relations, at the same time he seems to have been detached in some way, an observer at the sideline of an on-going situation. Somehow he distanced himself from turmoil and watched with great objectivity what was going on, trying to find its hidden meaning.

It is tempting to explain his fascination with Spinoza by reference to this personality trait. A rational, cultivated person should "not give way to amazement, not laugh, not cry, but understand" as Vygotsky paraphrased his favorite philosopher in the preface to "The Psychology of Art" (Vygotsky, 1925l/1986, p. 18). One should always attempt to control one's emotions and to subject them to the control of the intellect ("Even about oneself one should not judge subjectively," Vygotsky in a letter to Leont'ev, dated July 31, 1930). One should never give way to the lower passions, but rather climb the rational ladder and be more refined and detached in one's judgements. This life-attitude also comes out in the cultural–historical theory (see chapter 9) and in Vygotsky's personal letters to his students and colleagues. In a reply to Morozova, for example – who had written to him about her depressed state of mind – he stated that "with such moods you have to fight and it is possible to cope with them. Man overcomes nature outside himself, but also in himself, this is – isn't it – the crux of our psychology and ethics" (Vygotsky in a letter to Morozova, dated July 29, 1930). In a second letter he elaborated on this theme telling Morozova that one should never become the victim of one's moods and passions. "The rule

---

[4]Kolbanovsky (1934c, pp. 394–5) has related a somewhat absurd consequence of this sensitivity. Although having an excellent command of several foreign languages Vygotsky refused to speak them and used interpreters to correspond with foreign visitors. To Kolbanovsky's question why he refrained from speaking foreign languages Vygotsky replied: "Even an excellent knowledge of a foreign language cannot safeguard you against an incorrect accent. My speech, even if correct by content and form, will pain the ear of the foreigner listening to me and may because laughter or other inadequate emotions. Out of politeness my interlocutor will try to suppress them. This will make him suffer. Why should I torture him?"

here – in a mental struggle and in the submission of unruly and strong opponents – is the same as in all submission: *divide et impera*, that is, divide and rule ... You have to divide them [the feelings and moods] ... To surmount them – that is probably the most correct expression for the mastering of emotions ... to find a way out is simply a question of mental effort" (Vygotsky in a letter to Morozova, dated August 19, 1930).

Accepting Nadezhda Mandel'shtam's claim that Vygotsky was some sort of a rationalist it should be added that he was not the type of a rationalist who denies any meaning or sense to life. Vygotsky seems to have been convinced that the creative struggle, called life (see chapter 3), had some inner meaning and that life's appearance and its essence do not coincide. A letter to his student Levina best exemplifies this basic conviction:

> Now about another theme about which you write. About inner disharmonies, the difficulty of living. I have just finished reading (almost by chance) Chekhov's *Three Years*. Perhaps, you too should read it. That is life. It is deeper, broader than its external expression. Everything in it changes. Everything becomes otherwise. The main thing – always and now, it seems to me – is not to identify life with its external expression and that is all. Then, lending an ear to life (this is the most important virtue, a somewhat passive attitude in the beginning), you will find in yourself, outside yourself, in everything, so much that none of us can accommodate it. Of course, you cannot live without spiritually giving a meaning to life. Without philosophy (your own, personal, life philosophy) there can be nihilism, cynicism, suicide, but not life. But everybody has his philosophy, of course. Apparently, you have to grow it in yourself, to give it space inside yourself, because it sustains life in us. Then there is art, for me – poems, for another – music. Then there is work. What can shake a person looking for truth! How much inner light, warmth, support there is in this quest itself! And then there is the most important – life itself – the sky, the sun, love, people, suffering. Those are not simply words, it exists. It is real. It is interwoven in life. Crises are no temporary phenomena, but inner life's road. When we pass from systems to fates (pronouncing this word is terrifying and joyful at the same time, knowing that tomorrow we will investigate what is hidden behind it), to the birth and downfall of systems, we see it with our own eyes. I am convinced of it. In particular, all of us, looking at our past, see that we dry up. That is correct. That is true. To develop is to die. It is particularly acute in critical epochs – with you, in my age again. Dostoevsky wrote with horror about the drying up of the heart. Gogol still more horrifying. It is really "a small death" inside ourselves. And that is the way we have to accept it. But behind all this is life, that is, movement, travel, your own fate (Nietzsche taught the *amor fati* – the love of your fate). But I started philosophizing... (Vygotsky in a letter to Levina, dated July 16, 1931).

To understand the hidden meaning behind "the sky, the sun, love, people, suffering," to understand the travel towards death. That may have been Vygotsky's ultimate goal throughout his intellectual life, from his analysis of *Hamlet* to his development of the cultural–historical theory, and further on. In his cultural–historical theory he attempted to sketch how cultural man attempts to overcome the "stikhia" (Greek: *stoicheion*), the elemental chaos of nature, through the creation of cultural instruments. Deeply appreciating the finest artifacts of culture Vygotsky persisted in believing that the "stikhia" would be overcome by culture and that a new human society would be its result.

The End

Despite his generally detached attitude and his Spinozist philosophy Vygotsky must have suffered from the growing ideological pressure, the disintegration of his group of collaborators, and the personal betrayals that took place towards the end of his life. His friend Dobkin remembers visiting Vygotsky during the last year of his life. Apparently, Vygotsky was in a bad physical condition and a depressed state of mind, and contemplating accepting a position at the primate center of Sukhumi. Vygotsky's close collaborator Zeigarnik (1988, p. 179) – in an interview published by Jaroshevsky – has recently confirmed Dobkin's account, claiming that Vygotsky "did everything not to live" in the last years of his life. Both accounts are emphatically denied by Vygotsky's daughter, G. L. Vygodskaja, who distinctly remembers that her father was full of energy and new plans during his (apparent) recovery in the final month of his life (personal communication, 1989). Apparently, toward the end of his life Vygotsky was offered the possibility of setting up and heading a section within the All-Union Institute of Experimental Medicine in Moscow. He was very enthusiastic about this plan as it offered the possibility of picking his own research team and carrying out his new research plans. There is no way of knowing which of these versions is accurate, nor is there any need. For it may well be that Vygotsky worked extremely hard at times – giving the impression that he was careless about his health but perhaps trying to accomplish as much as possible before his death (that, after all, was announced several times) – and was occasionally deeply depressed but still managed to find the energy to make new plans in the final month of his life.

Be that as it may, after repeated haemorrhages – on May 9, May 25, and during the night of June 10–11 – in the early morning of June 11, 1934 Lev Semyonovich Vygotsky died in the Serebrannyj Bor Sanatorium of tuberculosis, the disease he had suffered from for fourteen years. He was buried at the Novodevichy cemetery in Moscow. Vygotsky left behind a handful of books, many articles, and drawers full of unpublished manuscripts. Above all, he left behind a loving family and a devoted group of students who would do everything to protect Vygotsky's heritage in the difficult years to come and to promote his ideas. Now, more than fifty years after his death, Vygotsky's ideas are becoming well known in the scientific world − a process that is still insufficiently understood.

2
Literature and Art

As we saw in the previous chapter, a consistent interest in issues of literature, theatre, art, and literary criticism constituted the social/personal context within which Vygotsky's move into the field of psychology took place. The better-known part of his endeavours in the area of literary analysis and theory is his book *The Psychology of Art*, which was first finished in 1925 as his dissertation, and only later published in different versions in Russian (Vygotsky, 1965, 1968, 1986, 1987) and other languages (Vygotsky, 1971).[1] In order to complete the picture of Vygotsky's literary research one needs to turn to a series of short articles (mainly book and theater reviews) which preceded the final version of the monograph on the psychology of art (Vygotsky, 1916a–c; 1917a–d; 1923a–d), as well as to the handful of articles by him that appeared later (e.g., Vygotsky, 1928z). We can say that the whole period of Vygotsky's life during which he gradually entered psychology (i.e., the years 1922 to 1925) was colored by his continued interest in issues of literature and art, from which questions of psychology gradually emerged. Vygotsky's first sketches in the area of psychology were grounded in his interests in literature.

How, then, did psychological issues become integrated into Vygotsky's thinking about literature and art? How did Vygotsky's psychological theory emerge from the context of his relationship with the art world of his time? And why did he make the move into the field of psychology at all, even starting some laboratory experiments of his own? Despite generally scanty

---

[1]Contrary to what has been suggested by Soviet scholars in later years, Vygotsky wished to publish the book and at one time even reached an agreement with a publisher (Vygotsky in a letter to Sakharov, dated February 15, 1926). Why the book was not published remains unclear, but the fact that some parts of the book were rather close to the formalism current in literary criticism, which was attacked by the leading ideologists of the time, may have played its role (see also the introduction to part I and chapter 15).

evidence of Vygotsky's work prior to his becoming recognized as a psychologist in Soviet sources on the history of psychology, it is possible to reconstruct a part of that transition process. The purpose of the present chapter is to demonstrate how the foundations for Vygotsky's later theorizing were laid during his "formative years" from 1915 to 1925.

Sources for the Analysis: The Architecture of the *The Psychology of Art*

Vygotsky's first major writing in the area of literary analysis – "The tragedy of Hamlet, the Prince of Denmark, by Shakespeare" – dates from the period August 5 to September 12, 1915 when he wrote the first (draft) version while living in Gomel'. The second version of this manuscript is dated February 14 to March 28, 1916 and was completed in Moscow (Ivanov, 1986, p. 500). It is this second version of the text that appears as an appendix to the third Russian edition of *The Psychology of Art* (Vygotsky, 1925l/1986, pp. 336–491), while a separate chapter (8) in the main text of the book constitutes a summary and re-organized version of the earlier analysis of *Hamlet*. Other chapters in the main core of the book are devoted to critical evaluation of Vygotsky's contemporary literary theories (chapter 2 – "Art as cognizing"; chapter 3 – "Art as a means"; chapter 5 – "The analysis of the fable"), as well as psychological theories that were influential in the literary criticism of his time (chapter 1 – "The psychological problem of art"; chapter 4 – "Art and psychoanalysis"). In the *The Psychology of Art* two domains of knowledge – literary criticism and psychology – occur side by side, illustrating the ways in which Vygotsky started to move from the former to the latter in the years 1923 to 1925.

As well as *The Psychology of Art*, a number of book reviews that appeared in the period 1916 to 1917 are relevant. Interestingly, the books he reviewed all belonged to the symbolic end of Russian literary spectrum of the second decade of this century: Andrej Belyj (Vygotsky, 1916a, 1916b), D. Merezhkovskii (Vygotsky, 1917a), and V. Ivanov (Vygotsky, 1916c) all created symbolically highly complex literature which puzzled quite a few readers at the time. However, the young Vygotsky was well educated in the intellectual context of the "Silver Age" of Russian literature, and developed a keen interest in the complexity of literature in that era of symbolism, soul-seeking, and a seemingly regressing world. Vygotsky's standpoint in the literary context of his time illustrates his active effort to break free of the theoretical and ideological impasses in which he saw the contemporary literary world entangled. Of course, to offer an alternative view of the world was no easy task for a 20-year-old. Nevertheless, Vygotsky proceeded to try to do so – first in the field of literary analysis, and later in psychology and defectology.

The Lonely Socialite: Vygotsky's analysis of *Hamlet*

It is probably no coincidence that in 1915 and 1916 Vygotsky made an active effort to analyze *Hamlet*, returning to the issue in *The Psychology of Art* manuscript in the early 1920s. In some ways, the persona of Hamlet may have had a strong intuitive appeal to young Vygotsky. The simultaneous aloofness from other people on the one hand and interaction with them on the other that is central in Shakespeare's tragedy, has been said to have been characteristic of Vygotsky himself (see chapter 1). However, our goal here is not to confirm Vygotsky as a Hamlet-like personality, but rather to trace the development of his view of the human psyche which can be seen in his early writing on the play to his return to the subject matter in the textbook nine years later: the two pieces are substantially different. It was clearly the case that Vygotsky's return to *Hamlet* in 1924/25 had a discourse function that differed considerably from that of 1916.

"My Hamlet" – Vygotsky's Analysis of 1916

In his analysis of 1916, Vygotsky followed the lines of "idealist aesthetics" (rather than "half-materialist psychology"), to use the terms applied by contemporary Soviet efforts to understand the role of *Hamlet* in Vygotsky's development (see Jaroshevsky, 1987, p. 293). Nevertheless, Vygotsky's "idealist esthetics" was already dialectical in its focus – not surprisingly given that his interest in Hegelian philosophy went back to his *Gymnasium* days (see chapter 1). Vygotsky was discovering the opposing sides within the same whole and within this dialectical reasoning, Vygotsky's developmental world view gradually became established.

Vygotsky viewed the "puzzle" of the nature of Hamlet in terms of the concurrent presence of two interdependent forces – of "night" and "day", of "action" and "inaction," and of the external events and internal psychological processes. In rather poetic terms, he described the transition between these opposing states:

> There is, in the daily completing circle of time, in the endless chain of light and dark hours, a boundary between the night and the day that is very difficult to grasp. Before sunrise there is an hour when the morning has already arrived, but the night continues to exist. There is nothing more mysterious and

unintelligible, puzzling and darker, than that transition from night to day. The morning has come – but it is still night; the morning is as if embedded in the night that is still around, it swims in that night. In that hour, which may last only a fraction of a second, everything – all objects and persons – have as it were two different existences *or one disunited existence*, nightly and daily, in the morning and in the night. (Vygotsky, 1925l/1986, pp. 356–7, emphasis added)

The unity of the opposites – Hamlet's inaction and action, hesitancy and impulsiveness, "craziness" and "scheming", etc. – was very much on the young Vygotsky's mind when he was writing his subjective analysis of the tragedy. Dialectical unity of opposites could be found between the external (dialogic) and internal (monologic) forms of discourse: "In parallel with the external, real drama, another, internal, deep drama takes place – which proceeds in the silences (the first – external – proceeds in words), and for which the external drama serves as a framework. Behind the external, audible dialogue one can sense an internal, silent one (Vygotsky, 1925l/ 1986, p. 359).

Vygotsky's analysis of 1916 is full of youthful exclamations of fascination with different sides of the tragedy (e.g. "that link is so deep that one gets dizzy"; Vygotsky, 1925l/1986, p. 439). At the same time, the inevitable movement of the tragedy towards its conclusion was analyzed by Vygotsky in Hegelian terms of "restoration of the discrete unity, the disjunction is overcome" (Vygotsky, 1925l/1986, p. 488) concerning the opposite facets of life and death, day and night, speech and silence, and action and inaction.

In that analysis, Vygotsky explicitly claimed that he was trying to make sense of the tragedy as a myth (Vygotsky, 1925m/1987, p. 347). From his subjective viewpoint, the understanding of such a myth included a mysterious moment, which, however, could be captured by the human recipient of the myth (e.g. see Vygotsky, 1925l/1986, pp. 365–6). Even as early as 1916, in his analysis of *Hamlet* Vygotsky's emphasis on the *pragmatic* aspect of literary texts (the ways in which these texts are interpreted by the recipients) was present. As we will see below, in 1925 that focus became the core of his literary analysis, which led him into psychology.

Hamlet, of course, is a highly sophisticated tragedy which had long puzzled critics, and would continue to puzzle them long after the young Vygotsky wrote his impassioned analysis. One of the myth-like aspects in the tragedy is the appearance of the Ghost. Vygotsky appreciated the *reality* of the appearance of the Ghost in the tragedy – as the messenger from the life-after-death world linking the two opposite sides of the same whole (life and death; see Vygotsky, 1925l/1986, p. 375). It is interesting to note that the idea of the interdependence of life and death as dialectical opposites, which was present in 1916, resurfaced in his analysis of Freud's work in mid-1920s. At that time, he claimed that Freud's Thanatos-instinct must have some credibility, since life and death should be seen as biologically opposite sides of the same whole (Vygotsky, 1982a, pp. 335–6; see also chapters 5 and 7).

Obviously, Vygotsky developed in the literary climate of his time – the pre-1917 creative search of Russian writers and poets, many of whom were fascinated by mysticist writings and discussions of the occult. Perhaps his involvement with a school of thought that encouraged him to speculate in possibilities ensured Vygotsky did not rationalize the tragedy of Hamlet, but rather openly acknowledged that there exists a mystical and religious moment in the tragedy (e.g. Vygotsky, 1925l/1986, pp. 424, 480).

Finally, the compositional structure of the tragedy allowed Vygotsky to analyze the *resolution* of the battle of the opposing forces that were active (and, notably for *Hamlet*, also actively non-active!) during most of the play. Vygotsky saw clearly how all the actions and inactions in the course of the play lead to its inevitable conclusion:

> The whole play is filled with *inactivity*, which is saturated by the mystical rhythm of the internal movement of the tragedy towards the catastrophe. Here, all the failed plans, coincidences, talks, feebleness, languor, blindness, torture – lead to the minute that solves all, that *does not* emerge from the plans of the acting personae, their actions, but *captures* these and *reigns over* them. The knot that was tied before the beginning of the tragedy is being extended and delayed, until it is untied at the right moment. (Vygotsky, 1925l/ 1986, p. 479, emphases added)

The important moment in Vygotsky's analysis of the resolution in the tragedy is the emerging *new quality* which does not merely "come out" from the lines by which actions in the play develop, but "jumps" to a higher level: the resolution "captures" the lines of action and "surrenders" them, rather than merely constitutes a "logical" conclusion in the sense of Aristotelian formal logic. This emphasis on the new quality that results from the interaction of opposites is of course part of the Hegelian scheme that is appropriately applied to the compositional structure of the play. However, it is also the very first appearance of the "shadow" of a developmental focus that was to follow Vygotsky's reasoning all the way in this transition from literary criticism to general psychology. That transition can be traced by looking at Vygotsky's return to the analysis of *Hamlet* in his book on the *psychology* of art.

The Use of *Hamlet* in *The Psychology of Art*

Vygotsky's return to his subject was clearly "captured" by his developing thought about the dynamic structure of literary texts, and by his developing interest in the ways in which "the psychology of art" subordinates the recipient, forces him to feel, breathe, and think in a pre-determined direction, and leads to catharsis. The 1925 version of Vygotsky's analysis is consequently free from youthful and poetic exclamatory statements about the strength of different episodes in the play, and the recognition of the "mystic element" in the play has disappeared. However, the major lines of analysis – the interdependence between Hamlet's actions and inactions, the role of the conclusion in creating a new quality of feeling – are well in place. The reason for the unity of continuity *and* discontinuity between the 1916 and 1925 analyses can be understood as the development of Vygotsky's thought to a new, more general, level at which *Hamlet* became only part of the wider picture. Let us analyze this wider picture and its relevance for Vygotsky's entry into psychology – a discipline that was in turmoil reflecting the conditions prevalent in the Soviet Union.

The Task for a Psychology of Art: The Study of the Message

Vygotsky followed a radical path in his early work on criticism, a path that defined his standpoint on issues of art – the central focus of Vygotsky's analysis in *The Psychology of Art* was the psychological structure of the message (as seen from the perspective of the recipient). The recipient in Vygotsky's analyses sometimes took the role of himself, but at other times was given in the sense of a "generic other." Vygotsky declared that the study of the psychological processes that had led to the creation of an aesthetic message was impossible (since it requires reconstruction of all the complexity of the artists's conscious and unconscious processes, and of the situation):

> as long as we limit our analysis to processes that take place in consciousness, we are unlikely to find answer to the most fundamental problems of the psychology of art. We cannot know from the poet, nor from the reader, what the essence of that experience [*perezhivanie*] is that links them with art. And, as is easy to see, the most relevant aspect of art is that both the processes of its creation and of its use appear to be as if non-understandable, unexplainable, and hidden from the consciousness of those who have to deal with them. (Vygotsky, 1925l/1986, p. 91)

As is evident here, Vygotsky was also pessimistic about the possibility of a full understanding of art by the recipients in their subjective worlds. By denying the possibility of an analysis of the subjective processes of encoding and decoding of the message, what remained possible to analyze, of course, was the message itself. The structure of the artistic message provided the direction for the development of one (rather than another) kind of feeling in the recipient. Each individual, of course, would react to art in his particular (subjectively idiosyncratic) way, but all those individual ways were united by some fundamental structure that the message itself provided. It is not difficult to discern the issue of literary criticism behind this forceful viewpoint of Vygotsky, who was on the one hand unhappy with the highly subjective and often superficial statements of literary critics of his time, and on the other hand was himself interested in literary criticism. Furthermore, the wholesale import of contemporary psychological explanations into literary criticism (e.g. the "easy" use of Freudian explanations by literary critics) led Vygotsky to try to understand how art messages can be thought to be influential in the lives of human beings as social actors: "art can never be fully explained on the basis of the small circle of personal life, but it immediately demands explanation from the wide circle of social life" (Vygotsky, 1925l/1986, p. 110).

Vygotsky's analysis of the fable (chapter 5 in *The Psychology of Art*) provided an empirical demonstration of his route towards the new, "objective" understanding of literature. Undoubtedly, Vygotsky relied strongly on the "formalist school" of literature and literary criticism. However, a more relevant facet of his analysis was the emphasis on the dynamics of the way in which a certain affective experience is gradually generated by the structure of the message.

How to Study the Message: Vygotsky's Analysis of the Fable

The fable is a literary genre that falls between prose and poetry, and as such, its existence was something of a puzzle for leading literary theorists of the past. Vygotsky scrutinized the ideas of Potebnya and Lessing on the subject; they looked upon the fable as "imperfect prose." Vygotsky, in contrast, set out to prove that fables belong to the genre of poetry (Vygotsky, 1925l/ 1986, p. 117), which would explain the otherwise seemingly "unnecessary" development of subsidiary themes in fables, and the often dramatic contrast of the final moral message with the main text.

Vygotsky's main idea in the analysis of the psychological structure of the fable was quite simple: the fable-writer constructs a story where two opposing (moral, emotional, etc.) events (or characters) are mutually interdependent: any description of one feeds into the intensification of the other in the reader's mind, and the intensification of that other in its turn feeds into the intensification of the first. The dynamics of these two "lines" allow for the build up of the foundation for the conclusion (resolution, or *pointe*), which usually goes beyond the previous image, hence creating a discrepancy effect. That contrast of the *pointe* with the preliminary work, otherwise classifiable as "discontinuity" of the "morale" with the "story", was seen as creating a new psychological quality in the (generic) reader.

As we mentioned in chapter 1, as early as his *Gymnasium* days Vygotsky was fascinated by Hegel's dialectical philosophy. It is possible to trace the Hegelian scheme of "thesis – antithesis – synthesis" in Vygotsky's analysis of the fable. First, the separate (oppositional) affective strands built into the fable can be seen as thesis and antithesis (which are dialectically related within the same whole), leading to the emergence of new quality (synthesis) at the *pointe* of the fable. The dialectical leap in the quality of the meaning of the fable story is prepared by the interdependence of the opposing affective lines:

> it becomes very clear that, if those two lines in the fable about which we speak, are carried out and described with the strength of all the poetic means, then there exists not only logical but, more generally, an affective contradiction. The experience of the reader of the fable is fundamentally the experience of contradictory feelings, which develop with equal strength, but are fully linked to each other. (Vygotsky, 1925l/1986, p. 176)

This "affective contradiction" develops in the reader of the fable, until it reaches the culmination point, or "catastrophe of the fable" (Vygotsky, 1925l/1986, pp. 180–1):

> The final part of the fable is that "catastrophe" or *pointe* in which both plans are united in one act, episode, or phrase, disclosing their opposition and bringing the contradictions to the apogee, with that – discharging that duality of feeling that was accumulating during the whole fable. It is as if a "shortcircuit" of two opposing electric charges takes place, in which the whole contradiction explodes, burns up, and solves itself. This is the way in which affective contradictions are resolved in our reaction. (Vygotsky, 1925l/ 1986, p. 181)

Later in the book, while discussing the psychological mechanisms of catharsis (chapter 9), Vygotsky elevated that affective development to the level of *the general law of esthetic reaction* (Vygotsky, 1925l/1986, p. 269). He also traced it into areas of art outside of literature – to the visual arts, architecture, etc. However, these extensions were extremely brief in comparison with his analysis of literature. This seems to have fit with Vygotsky's personality – his predominant orientation toward words and limited understanding of music or the visual arts can be seen appearing in his treatise on "Psychology of Art." Or, perhaps, the title of that book constituted a generalization for which Vygotsky himself was not ready.

It is interesting to note that Vygotsky's understanding of the dialectic dynamics of feelings in the reading of the fable contradicted his own proclaimed principle of the study of the message in itself. The message was analyzed through the perspective of the reader – a clear remnant of Vygotsky's earlier position (from 1915/16) that it is only individual versions of the message that can be experienced. It is perhaps sufficient to think of Vygotsky's emphasis not in terms of the semantics of the message, but rather in terms of its pragmatics: the writer has written a text that the reader reads and tries to understand. The text has some structure created by the author for the reader to interpret. How the reader interprets that structure can take a multiplicity of forms, but there still exist some basic structurally generated directions that guide the reader's reactions in some (rather than other) directions.

There were other, rather more commonplace reasons for Vygotsky's increased interest in the understanding of the dynamics of feelings in reading (and reciting) literature and poetry. From the time of return to Gomel' after 1917 until his departure for Moscow in 1924, Vygotsky taught literature in Gomel' (see chapter 1), and the issue of his students' understanding of literature became important. He dealt with the issue by delivering a talk at a local conference on the methods of teaching literature (Vygotsky, 1922a). It was in 1922/3 that he extended his analytic interest in the study of the reception of literature to the experimental realm, organizing some psychological experiments on that topic at the Gomel' Pedagogical College. The link between his pragmatic-analytic and experimental psychological work can be found in his efforts to understand the means by which Ivan Bunin's short story "Easy breathing", or "Gentle breath"[2] ("*Legkoe dykhanie*") evokes a reaction in the recipient – a reaction that is contradictory to the prevailing descriptive material in the short story. Perhaps in the case of "Easy breathing" even more than in his analyses of the fables, Vygotsky's main idea that the *form* and *content* of a literary text are in contradiction with one another, can be seen.

[2]We prefer to translate *legkoe dykhanie* as "easy breathing", even though it has been rendered "Gentle Breath" in the English translation of Vygotsky (1971, pp. 145–56). Vygotsky's emphasis was clearly on the process of breathing, not "breath".

Complexity of Composition: "Easy Breathing" in the Midst of a Life Full of Hopes, Drama, and Tragedy

Bunin's short story was published in 1916, four years before its non-communist author left Soviet Russia for France. It constituted a highly complicated and dense narrative, in terms of the organization of described events, the author's selection of some rather than other events for description, and, finally, an episode in conclusion from which the novella got its name.

The short story by Bunin covers a fixed set of events in the life of a young girl Olya Meshcherskaja, as well as in the life of an unnamed teacher of hers (*klassnaya dama*) whose brother (a friend of Olya's father) took Olya's virginity. From a sub-plot we learn that the brother also supported the *klassnaya dama* until he died. Furthermore, the *klassnaya dama* – who learns about the fact of her brother's role in making Olya a woman while trying to scold Olya for her hairdo – becomes strongly attached to Olya after the girl is shot by an officer whom Olya had promised to marry but later told that she had never seriously considered marrying, giving him her diary to read as a proof of her infidelity. After reading the diary the officer shoots Olya in a crowded railway station. If we were to look at the short story as a mere reflection of life, all this could be seen as a rather mundane narrative about the fall and tragic death of Olya, and of the sequence of imaginary attachments in the *klassnaya dama*. However, by narrating (through the memory of the *klassnaya dama*) an episode overheard by her earlier – of Olya's discussion with a friend about female beauty – the whole story acquires a new meaning. Bunin, starting from a girlish description of "what female beauty should be like" (dark eyes, black eyelashes, small feet, small breasts, etc.; Vygotsky, 1925l/1986, p. 335), introduces the idea of "easy breathing" (*legkoe dykhanie*) through a brief description of Olya's childish words, followed by the final *pointe* of the whole story:

> "But the main thing is, you know what? – Easy breathing. But I do have it – do listen how I breathe, true, isn't it?" Nowadays that easy breathing again scatters around in the world, in that cloudy sky, in that cold spring wind . . . (Bunin, 1916/1984, p. 265; quoted in Vygotsky, 1925l/1986, p. 335)

It can be seen that the connection of Olya's words with *that* "cloudy sky" and *that* "spring wind" creates the dialectical leap from the meaning of the story as it had unfolded before, to a state of emotional and philosophical complexity which does not succumb to rational analysis. Vygotsky explicitly analyzed the role of "that" in making the generalization:

"*Legkoe dykhanie! A ved' ono u menya est', – ty poslushai, kak ya vzdykhaiu – ved' pravda, est'?*" It is as if we hear the very inspiration [*vzdokh*], and in this story that sounds comical and is written in a funny style we suddenly discover a very different sense when we read the final, catastrophic words of the author: "Nowadays that easy breathing again scatters around in the world, in that cloudy sky, in that cold spring wind . . ." These words close the circle, bring the end to meet the beginning. How much a small word can mean and what immense plangency it can bring to a literary phrase. In this present phrase, carrying all the catastrophe of the story, the key role is held by the word "*that*" easy breathing. "*That*" refers to the air that is just mentioned, to the easy breathing that Olya Meshcherskaja asked her girlfriend to listen to, and further again lead to the catastrophic words "in that cloudy sky, in that cold spring wind." These three words make the idea of the story concrete and united. The story begins from a description of cloudy sky and cold spring wind. It is as if the author with the final words summarizes the whole story: that everything that took place, all that constituted life, love, murder, death of Olya Meshcherskaja – all that in essence is only one event – *that* easy breathing again disseminated in the world, in *that* cloudy sky, in *that* cold spring wind. And all the description of the grave, of April weather, of grey days, and cold winds that the author gave earlier, as if concentrated into one point, included and introduced in the story: the story suddenly acquires new sense and new expressive meaning . . . (Vygotsky, 1925l/1986, pp. 200–1)

This long quotation illustrates how Vygotsky analyzed the language used by Bunin to lead the reader of "Easy breathing" to the formation of a holistic complex of feelings that encompass the world. By moving the concept of "easy breathing" from the context of an adolescent girl's chatter to the context of a world in which people love and murder, the author created a powerful artistic generalization effect. That effect, as depicted by Vygotsky, was similar to the emotional synthesis produced by fables.

Vygotsky tried to analyze the time structure of the depicted events of "*Legkoe dykhanie*". He was obviously fascinated by the way in which Bunin was capable of giving the story a *pointe* that (as with fables) leads the reader to an affective conclusion that is qualitatively more complex than the interdependent feelings that escalate during the story, as it moves back and forth between the present and the past.

Vygotsky's main puzzle in the case of the story about Olya Meshcherskaja was that, by virtue of the brief *pointe*, the story was no longer a story of the life of Olya and her tragic fate, but about *something else*. It creates a highly complex affective resolution in the reader, which seemed to fascinate Vygotsky as a curious puzzle that as a dedicated literary critic he found hard to solve. The importance of "Easy breathing" for Vygotsky can be seen in the fact that he included the full text of the short story in the appendix of his

The Psychology of Art. Bunin was one of Vygotsky's favorite writers from the time of his youth, so his concentration on this short story should not be seen as an episodic case.

Furthermore, the *idea* of "easy breathing" became connected with Vygotsky's life-course in another significant way: it was the connection of that idea with Blonsky's (1922) assertion that the literary text is emotionally received by the reader on the basis of the breathing rhythm while reading, that led Vygotsky into his first experimental study of the reception of literature. Blonsky, obviously, was not the first to come up with the idea that "we feel like we breathe:" the idea was present in Santayana (1896; see Ivanov, 1986, p. 516) and fitted well with the somatic-origin viewpoint of emotions. However, Vygotsky's particular interest in the breathing rhythms while reading literature was linked to his idea that the author's construction of the text leads to the necessity of reading the text with a particular rhythm of breathing, which in its turn leads to the production of a corresponding feeling in the reader:

> the psychic mechanism of poetry can be described by the following three points: 1 the speech rhythm of the text creates a corresponding rhythm and nature of breathing. Every poem or part of prose has its own system of breathing because of the immediate adaptation of breathing to speech. The writer creates not only the rhythm of words, but also rhythms of breathing. When we read Dostoevsky we breathe different from when we read Chekhov. The tone of the narrator is the rhythm of our breathing . . . *the person breathes in the way in which he reads.* 2 For each breathing system and rhythm there exists a specific organization of emotions, that creates the emotional background for the perception of poetry, specific for each work. *"The person feels like he breathes"* (Blonsky). 3 That emotional background of poetic experience is the same or at least similar to the one that the author has at the moment of creating, since in the writing of his speech his breathing rhythm becomes fixed. From here – the "infectious nature" of poetry. *The reader feels like the poet since he breathes in the same way.* (Vygotsky, 1926e, p. 172–3)

Vygotsky felt that "Easy breathing" had an underlying breathing rhythm which would create the emotional background of *easy* breathing. It is here that Vygotsky advanced his major general point about the relationship between form and content in literary writings: the breathing style that leads to the feelings of "ease" is connected in Bunin's short story with the horrors of murder and death. However, as Vygotsky pointed out:

> And instead of tortuous tension we experience almost *painful easiness.* This is the nature of, in any case, that affective contradiction, of that conflict of two opposite feelings, which seem to constitute the surprising psychological law of the short story. I say surprising because in all our traditional aesthetics we are

prepared for exactly the opposite understanding of art: in the course of centuries aestheticians claim the harmony of the form and the content, and that the form illustrates, complements, accompanies the content; and suddenly we discover that this is the greatest misunderstanding. Instead, the form is at war with the content, fights with it, *overcomes it*, and that in this *dialectical contradiction* between the content and the form the real psychological sense of our aesthetic reactions is hidden. (Vygotsky, 1925l/1986, p. 204, emphases added)

Vygotsky here continued his Hegelian–dialectical line of emphasis on the creation of a new emotional quality as a result of the dynamics of relationships of form (breathing style, narrowly defined) and content. His use of dialectical reasoning here (we can date the writing of this passage, at least in its first version, to 1922/23 in Gomel', to the time where his first experimental work was started) predates the "dialectization" of Soviet psychology which occurred later, and in which Vygotsky happened to be a participant. His introspection from reading "*Legkoe dykhanie*" as producing "almost painful easiness" shows how a sensitive intellectual was struggling with the high level of complexity of the literary constructions used by authors to generate very sophisticated feelings in the readers. However, by 1922 Vygotsky had moved from the role of a literary critic (who had the "luxury" of relying upon his own feelings in the process of reading or attending theater performances), to that of a teacher (who, inevitably, had to deal with the inter-individual differences in the ways in which the very same literary text was understood). His first experimental study involved asking a number of subjects in the Gomel' Pedagogical School (N = 9 subjects) to read "Easy breathing" (of which they had had no previous experience) in different ways (aloud and silently), and to listen to the same story as it was read to them by another person. With the help of the pneumograph, the breathing patterns of the subjects were recorded (Vygotsky, 1926e). The same subjects were also tested with another text ("A terrible revenge" by Gogol). After moving to Moscow in 1924, Vygotsky replicated his experimental results while working at Kornilov's Institute.

It is interesting to note that Vygotsky's empirical publication which was supposed to present "the data" about the breathing rhythms of different subjects (Vygotsky, 1926e) was not at all thorough in presenting those findings. None of the original "breathing curves" can be found in his paper (Vygotsky, 1926e). Instead, Vygotsky excuses himself for the lack of detailed analysis of the data by reference to the small number of experiments (ibid., p. 171), following that excuse immediately by an assertion that the few data that were collected supported the author's prediction. In some way (which he does not specify), he measured the correspondence of the breathing curves and the "structure of speech" (determined by the rhythm of the text), and found that 92 per cent of the obtained curves showed correspondence to the speech structure (Vygotsky, 1926e, p. 171). Different texts were claimed to have led to different breathing rhythms (Bunin versus Gogol), and the conditions of reading by oneself (aloud or silently) were seen to differ from that while listening (ibid., p. 171). It was obvious that Vygotsky's transition from the literary world (where his analysis of the text was always done in depth and with great vigor) to the (new to him) arena of empirical research in psychology (with all of its consensual expectations for the number of subjects, etc.) was not a simple one. Vygotsky, contrary to official Soviet historiography, did not "come and conquer" the new discipline. He gradually moved into it, becoming involved in the social discourse of reactologists at the Institute that had been taken over by Kornilov, and developing further in his own ways, neither following anybody slavishly nor dismissing them without a thoughtful analysis. He had no desire to become a psychologist who produced only meticulous and careful empirical analysis of experimental phenomena. He remained a philosopher/methodologist at heart, who enjoyed discussing empirical projects and giving advice, but who would not divert his energy into particular projects as such (see chapter 1). Nevertheless, it was exactly this, more empirically-oriented, social discourse at Kornilov's Institute in which Vygotsky would become an active participant (see also chapter 6).

From the Dominant Features in the Text to the Study of Dominant Reactions

Given Vygotsky's early concern with the theme of catharsis in encounters with art, it is understandable that his first research topic in psychology in 1924 at Kornilov's Institute was that of "dominant reactions" (see chapter 6). The issue that interested Vygotsky – how can qualitatively new emotional complexes arise in the course of reading? – continued in the more laboratory-oriented domain of dominant reactions. As in a fable or a short story (where a *pointe* that is disjunctive with the previous lines of feelings can "catastrophically" lead the person to a new complex feeling), so in the realm of ordinary reactions, where some reactions of low absolute intensity may suddenly lead to a state of affairs where the *whole complex* of reactions becomes dominated by them and acquires a new quality as a result.

Vygotsky's work on dominant reactions was not merely founded on an idea borrowed from literary analysis, for the study had become a "hot topic" in the discourse of Russian psychologists, due to the publications by Ukhtomsky (1924; 1927) and other physiologists and psychologists who were also involved in related research. Vygotsky entered the discussion with his publication. "The problem of dominant reactions" (1926d). To support his theory the synthesis of new emotional "wholes" while experiencing art, Vygotsky sets out to criticize Pavlov's reduction of the complexity of psychological processes to the accumulation of conditional reflexes. Ukhtomsky's idea of the dominant – the nervous center that at any given time coordinates the unity of an organism's behavior – was far more appealing to Vygotsky (see Vygotsky, 1926d, p. 103). This is not surprising, since Ukhtomsky's conception of the "dominant" – that of *integration* of the nervous processes *into a whole* that may be *novel* relative to previous history of the organism – has a structure similar to Vygotsky's "general law of emotional reaction". However, in his article on the dominant, Vygotsky developed his "general law," and set up the problem of the study of the dominant in ways that would soon lead him to emphasize the instrumental role of psychological processes in the development of the person. He stated:

> Up to now, reaction has usually been studied as a response as such, to a certain stimulus. Or, at best, the conditions of the dynamics of reaction in relation to two or more other reactions have been studied. *Here we needed to look at the reaction from a completely different side, study it in a new aspect – not in the role of a response to stimulation, but in a new role – that of diverting, inhibiting, amplifying, directing, and regulating the dynamics of other reactions.* (Vygotsky, 1926d, p. 105, emphasis added)

Ukhtomsky's "dominant" was interesting for Vygotsky as a means of linking his own theories of emotional synthesis in art reception to the triggering of new holistic functional units in the human psyche as a whole. Ukhtomsky's demonstration of the dominant at the level of the functioning of the nervous system supported Vygotsky's theoretical notion of the synthesis (in the same publication, he stated that he considered the reduction of psychological phenomena to nerve processes "lethal" for psychology, and then went on to discuss Ukhtomsky; Vygotsky, 1926d, p. 101). In this publication, Vygotsky presented empirical data (in the form of reaction times and patterns by individual subjects) that emerged as a result of his involvement, together with other young co-workers (G. Gagaeva, L. Zankov, L. Sakharov, and I. Soloviev), in the laboratory study of reactions (see also chapter 6). The important theme in the conclusions that Vygotsky drew from these experiments emphasized the relevance of *conscious* processes in the human psychological functioning along the lines of the "dominant": a weak reaction, *under conditions of conscious direction*, can become a "dominant" in the psychological sphere. As Vygotsky noted (1926d, p. 123), "we are at the doorstep of conscious behavior" when we encounter the ways in which consciousness can re-organize the psychological functioning by "biasing" some reactions to be dominant over others. He had effectively moved into the wonderland of psychology where the understanding of consciousness, its relations with affectivity, etc., have always been a formidable problem. To solve it, he extended his scheme that was earlier developed in the domain of emotional reaction to include that of the interdependence of conscious actions and the affective domain. In this respect, it is obvious that Vygotsky's interests in the domain of art served as the basis for his development in the realm of psychology.

Summary: Vygotsky's Understanding of the Dynamics of Reaction to Literature

During the period of his active interest in issues of art reception Vygotsky moved from the position of literary critic, who would claim the relevance of the recipient's subjective understanding of the message, to that of a scientist, who is concerned with discovering general laws by which a human being encounters such a complex cultural invention such as literature. It is interesting that in his efforts to connect art with life in general (see chapter 11 in *The Psychology of Art*), he gave art a cathartic role in the lives of people in the everyday world. Art could provide the "trigger" for the synthesis of a person's revised world-view, as the person experiences catharsis in his encounter with art. Vygotsky refused to accept two contemporary opposing viewpoints on art – that of mere decoration of life versus "method of building life" (Vygotsky, 1925l/1986, p. 328). Rather, he saw the role of art in the construction of the "new man."

In terms of scientific discipline, Vygotsky's endeavors in the study of the psychology of art went beyond the thematic domain itself. As Vygotsky (1926m/1982) himself noted later, he saw his own analysis of the psychology of art as an effort to devise laws of general psychology on the foundation of the analysis of the structure of relevant materials:

> I tried to introduce . . . a method into conscious psychology, to derive laws of the psychology of art on the basis of the *analysis* of one fable, one short story, and one tragedy. I started from the idea that developed forms of art provide a key to [understanding] the undeveloped ones, as human anatomy does with the anatomy of the ape. Thus, the tragedy by Shakespeare explains the puzzles of primitive art to us, and not vice versa. Furthermore, I speak about *all art* and do not test my conclusions on the [material from] music, painting, etc. Further still: I do not test them on the basis of *all* or the majority of the *kinds* of literature; I take *one* short story, *one* tragedy. By what right? I studied not the fables, the tragedies, and even less so *that* fable or *that* tragedy. In those, I

studied that which constitutes the foundation of all art – the nature and mechanism of the aesthetic reaction . . . the task of the investigation of art lies in . . . the *analysis of the processes in their essence*. (Vygotsky, 1926m/1982, p. 405)

Vygotsky was thus led from his theorizing about the psychology of art to the study of general psychology. His Hegelian–dialectical approach was there from the very beginning. However, particular conditions or specific objects of analysis (e.g. "Easy breathing"), as well as changes in Vygotsky's personal life (e.g. his move to Moscow and his immersion in the social discourse of reactologists at the Kornilov Institute) were instrumental in the further development of his ideas. Vygotsky's move from the analysis of catharsis to that of the dominant had a developmental logic of its own. It prepared him for the next step – the analysis of the role of psychological processes in the life organization of a person – and for remedial instruction for children with developmental difficulties (see also chapter 4). By moving from art to psychology, Vygotsky could test his theoretical constructions derived from one complex domain on another. His work in art enabled him to tackle complex psychological problems and – the present authors would like to claim – far more rigorously than investigators trained as psychologists *per se*, in his time or ours. It was to Vygotsky's benefit – rather than detriment – that he moved to psychology from literary criticism and education. It is no doubt a tribute to that background that his eloquent, even if sometimes mystical, ideas continue to fascinate us in our search for our own synthesis of ideas.

PART I

The First Years in Moscow
1924–1928

Introduction

Vygotsky's Entrance into Institutional Psychology

The story of Vygotsky's entrance into institutional psychology has been recounted many times, but unfortunately, none of the existing accounts gives an accurate version of the events. The standard version runs more or less as follows: in 1924 an unknown school teacher named Lev Vygotsky from a provincial town called Gomel' delivered a talk at the Second Psychoneurological Congress in Leningrad that left the audience speechless. Vygotsky supposedly boldly and persuasively argued that psychologists should study consciousness, an argument in flat contradiction to the prevailing ideas of the time. Kornilov or Luria (here the story varies: some sources claim that Luria heard the talk, was extremely impressed by it and persuaded Kornilov to invite Vygotsky to Moscow, others state that Kornilov himself took the initiative) heard the talk and the decision to admit Vygotsky to the staff of the Institute of Experimental Psychology was immediately taken. Vygotsky moved to Moscow and very soon a troika of psychologists, Vygotsky, Luria, and Leont'ev, evolved. Working at the Institute of Experimental Psychology this troika developed the cultural-historical theory, which quickly became the dominant theory in psychology, making Vygotsky one of the most well-known psychologists of his time (see the introduction to part III).

Unfortunately, this story is untrue (see also chapter 6). First, Vygotsky was no ordinary school teacher. As we have seen, he had set up his own psychological laboratory, had performed psychological experiments, was the author of numerous articles in various journals and newspapers, and had been a very prominent cultural figure in Gomel' (a provincial town in the literal sense of the word, yet possessing a rich cultural life). This in itself makes it unlikely that Vygotsky was totally unknown in the scientific and cultural circles of the Moscow of that time. In addition, Vygotsky had studied and lived for four years in Moscow, which makes it probable that he had his friends and acquaintances there both in and outside the scientific world. He must also have visited the capital on a regular basis (recall his acquaintance with Mandel'shtam). We would like to suggest, therefore, that Vygotsky was not totally unknown in Moscow, that he may have met some of the leading psychologists, and, it is possible, that he may have been invited to give his talk for precisely these reasons. This would adequately explain the presence of a teacher from a provincial town at a conference dominated by professional psychologists, physiologists, and physicians of various orientation (mostly Bekhterevians), a conference which attracted few pedagogues or teachers.

Furthermore, it was not only Vygotsky's plea for the study of consciousness that resulted in the invitation to work at the institute of Kornilov, but also the fact that he criticized Pavlov's and Bekhterev's reflexology, demonstrates a reactological, Kornilovian spirit. To support this argument (see also chapter 6), let us look at Vygotsky's presentations at the congress. (In the standard version of the events of the conference, only one of his presentations is mentioned – and this often misidentified – whilst the other two are retrospectively ignored.)

Presentations at the 1924 Congress

Perhaps because of Luria's (1976, pp. 38–9) rather vague description of the content of Vygotsky's talk, several investigators of Soviet psychological history (e.g. Joravsky, 1989, pp. 258–63) have believed that at the Second Neuropsychological Congress Vygotsky spoke on "Consciousness as a problem of the psychology of behavior" (published as Vygotsky, 1925g). In fact, this talk was presented later that year – on October 19, 1924 – at an "open conference" (*otkrytaja konferencija*) at the Institute of Experimental Psychology in Moscow (see Kornilov, 1926a, p. 248). The real topic of the talk that Luria was alluding to was "The methods [*metodika*] of reflexological and psychological investigation" (presented on January 6, 1924 and published as Vygotsky, 1926b). Although these talks have several themes in common – e.g. the plea for an objective study of consciousness; the references to the similar approach of Watsonian behaviorism – they were clearly different.[1]

Apart from his paper on reflexological and psychological methods Vygotsky presented two other papers at the congress. One was presented on the same day (January 6, 1924) and was entitled "How we have to teach

[1]Wertsch (1985, p. 8, n. 6) was, therefore, incorrect in identifying them.

psychology now" and the other was presented several days later (January 10, 1924) as "The results of a survey on the mood of pupils in the final classes of the Gomel' schools in 1923" (personal communication by Gita Vygodskaja, April 5, 1989). We can see, then, that two of Vygotsky's papers were based on his experiences as a teacher in Gomel'. Unfortunately, as far as we know, no printed accounts of these presentations exist (see also Dajan, 1924).

The third presentation was published and deserves our careful attention as it may provide some clue as to why Vygotsky was invited to come and work at Kornilov's Institute (see chapter 6). Vygotsky's main strategic goal in this paper was to show that reflexology as conceived by Bekhterev and Pavlov had no right to assume the status of an independent school of thought within psychology. It had shown results in the study of lower organisms and processes, but had failed to produce anything interesting about human beings (at the conference many followers of Bekhterev and Pavlov presented their findings and Vygotsky polemically spoke of "the poverty of their results at this congress;" see Vygotsky, 1926b, p. 38). As a result reflexology's declarative statements that all human conduct could be conceived as combinations of conditional reflexes remained unconvincing. Vygotsky argued that reflexology's main shortcoming was that it shied away from the study of consciousness because of its inadequate conception of acceptable research methods. Quoting from various works of Bekhterev and Pavlov he showed that these researchers acknowledged the important role of "subjective experience" (consciousness) in daily life, but deemed the scientific study of this role impossible. Vygotsky went on to argue that reflexologists who wished to be consistent should study these processes, but with an adjusted research method. However, if they were to do so their methods would mirror those of objective psychology and therefore the need for a separate reflexological discipline would be obviated. In sum, Vygotsky's talk combined a sharp attack against reflexologists and a plea for an objective study of consciousness.

To date, Vygotsky argued, reflexologists had refrained from the study of consciousness as the study implied reliance on the subjects' introspectional accounts of their subjective experience. In his view, however, this fear was unfounded: it was possible to consider the subjects' replies to the experimenter's questions as reflexes in themselves, as objective verbal utterances that reflected other, unobservable reflexes (that is, thought or consciousness). After all, reflexologists (Sechenov, Bekhterev) had argued that thought was inhibited speech. So why, then, not study these inhibited reflexes indirectly, through the objective verbal reflexes they caused? In this way, starting from the assumption that the human mind is a conglomerate of reflexes, Vygotsky argued that it would be an adequate reflexological method to conduct interviews (*opros*) with subjects. Of course, such a method would come dangerously close to the method of introspection used by "subjective psychology." Vygotsky (1926b, pp. 34–5) made it very clear, however, that he did not consider the subjects' verbal utterances to be reliable accounts of their subjective experience, but as objective reactions (cf. Watson's "verbal behavior"; Watson's view was discussed by Vygotsky on November 17, 1924 at one of the closed conferences of the Institute; see Kornilov, 1926a, p. 249), which should be studied as such by the experimenter. In his view the subjects were not privileged observers of some internal world: their verbal reactions were simply reactions to internal reflexes induced by the experimenter. Or, to put it in Vygotsky's words: the subjects are not witnesses testifying of a crime that took place before, rather they are the criminals themselves at the moment they are committing their crime. To rely on the criminals' (suspects') statements would be foolish, but it would be equally foolish to ignore them (ibid., p. 45). It was in this context that Vygotsky approvingly referred to Watson and Lashley who independently came to similar conclusions (Vygotsky, 1926b, p. 43; 1925g, p. 198). At the same time, his view of consciousness relied heavily on James' paper "Does consciousness exist?". The idea that verbal reactions were acceptible as scientific data rested on James' idea that each reflex in itself formed the stimulus for a new reflex in the same or another system. The degree of consciousness of behavior – and, therefore, the possibility of verbalizing it – would depend on the degree of "translatability" of reflexes from one system into another: unconscious reflexes, in this view, were reflexes not transmitted to other systems. Consciousness, Vygotsky repeated after James, is the experience of experience, as experience is the experience of objects.

It is interesting to see Vygotsky (1926b, pp. 40–1) pointing out that Watson's and Bekhterev's view led to a form of dualism: by ignoring the reflex nature of consciousness they became materialists in the very restricted domain of lower psychophysiological processes but idealists in the domain of the psyche. This was the same argument he would use several years later in his analysis of the crisis in psychology (see chapter 7).

Thus, we have seen how Vygotsky, taking a consistent reflexological point of view ("being more of a reflexologist than Pavlov himself"), came to the conclusion that consciousness could be studied objectively by interrogating the subject. However, such a method would mirror that of an objective (behaviorist-like) psychology. Consequently, there was no need for two different sciences – reflexology and psychology – of human behavior (Vygotsky, 1926b, p. 42; see also 1925g).

It is not all difficult to see why this talk would appeal to Kornilov, Luria, and the other psychologists working at the Institute. Firstly, Vygotsky argued for a monistic and objective study of the conscious mind. This was clearly the ideologically suggested approach and one that was subscribed to by Kornilov and the various Freudo-Marxists (e.g. Luria). Secondly, Vygotsky's method of studying consciousness was clearly in harmony with Kornilov's own reactology (see chapter 6). Thirdly, Vygotsky attacked the competing discipline of reflexology. By doing so, he temporarily mitigated the dangerous possibility that leading Party ideologists (e.g. Bukharin) would view reflexology as *the* science of human behavior (see Joravsky, 1989, pp. 258–61).

We may conclude, then, that the story of Vygotsky's entrance into psychology is far more complicated than traditional Soviet and Western accounts would have it.

The Institute of Experimental Psychology

By the end of 1924 Vygotsky and his wife had moved to Moscow where they temporarily took residence in the basement of the Institute, accommodation in the city being scarce. The Moscow Institute of Experimental Psychology (formerly the Psychological Institute) had been founded by Chelpanov, who headed it until 1923, when he was accused of being an "idealist." As a result he and other members of staff were dismissed, and the Institute was re-organized (see chapter 6). The new director, Kornilov, invited new people to come and work with him – among them Luria – and developed new research plans on the basis of his reactological world-view. The idea was to study objectively the systems of reactions that constitute the complex behavior of man (see Kornilov, 1925a, p. 244). The first task, however, was to bring some order to the laboratory, which had suffered from the years of economic disasters. Luria's account of these events suggests that they should not be taken too seriously: "we were moving the furniture from one lab to another. I remember very well that as I carried tables up and down the stairs, I was sure that this would make a change in our work, and we would create a new basis for Soviet psychology" (in Levitin, 1982, p. 155). Luria's ironic description of the imbroglio at the Institute shows one side of the picture. The darker side has been pointed out by Graham (1987, pp. 8–9), when he observes that institutional reforms often brought about the tragic dismissal of personnel who were often replaced by young Communists eager for self-advancement. Moreover, he suggests that these replacements were frequently people of inferior scholarship whose enthusiasm for social reconstruction led to their appointments. Whether this was true at the Institute is difficult to decide, of course. It must be said that some of the relatively unexperienced men invited by Kornilov did become prominent members of Soviet psychology. It is difficult to decide, also, which people Kornilov actively wished to invite. Luria, for instance, was invited in late 1923 together with some of his fellow psychoanalysts from Kazan'. At the time he was primarily a psychoanalyst with a bias towards objective studies of the mind (see chapter 4). Others may have been invited because they – like Vygotsky – seemed to share Kornilov's reactological approach.

The research program of the Institute was explicitly reactologist and most research topics were rephrased in reactological terms. In later years Luria sketched the naivety of the whole approach:

> If my memory serves me well, perception was renamed "reception of a signal for reaction;" memory – "retention with reproduction of reaction;" attention – "restriction of reaction;" emotions – "emotional reactions;" in short, we inserted the word "reaction" wherever we could, sincerely believing that we were doing something important and serious. (Levitin, 1982, p. 154)

In practice, this approach left room for the study of a wide range of subjects. Thus, the research projects included objectivist investigations into the inhibition of associative reactions (Leont'ev, under the guidance of Luria); the associations of conditional reactions; the rhythm of reactions in relation to a person's constitution; an objective study of the sensitivity to pain; and an investigation into the periodicity of women's reactions. But the objective study of more subjective phenomena was also possible: Zalkind, Fridman, and Luria, for example, were very much interested in psychoanalysis and read lectures about its possible association with Marxism, among other things (see chapters 4 and 6).

The Institute undoubtedly played an important role in the development of Vygotsky's scientific thinking. For one thing, working at the Institute enabled him to meet several of the most prominent psychologists of his time. He also had an excellent library and equipment at his disposal, in fact he was literally living in the library. As lodgings were difficult to find in Moscow at the time, Vygotsky with wife and child had for the time being settled in a room in the basement of the Institute, a room which also happened to contain the archives of the Institute's philosophical section (Levitin, 1982, p. 37). One should not forget, however, that the majority of the scientific collective of the Institute had been invited to join before his arrival. Vygotsky was thus something of an outsider, conducting many of his activities outside the Institute. These activities were the study of the psychology of art, problems of defectology, pedagogical psychology, and (later) paedology.

Defectology

Judging both by the number of publications and other criteria it can be said that one of Vygotsky's most important areas of interest during this period was defectology (see chapter 4). I. I. Danjushevsky, now working in the Commissariat of Enlightenment at the Department for the Social-juridical Protection of Children, had asked Vygotsky to occupy himself with the social education of blind and deaf children. This work soon led to the publication of a reader on defectology, edited and introduced by Vygotsky (1924d–f). He also participated in the founding of the Institute of Defectology, the director of which was Danjushevsky. Vygotsky was appointed "scientific leader" of this Institute, his task being to inspire the doctors, defectologists, and psychologists connected to the Institute, to coordinate their activities, and to give them theoretical advice. Many informal seminars and congresses were organized (see chapter 4).

It was in connection with his study of defectology that Vygotsky made his one and only trip outside the Soviet Union. In July 1925 Vygotsky traveled to Berlin, Amsterdam, Paris, and London, giving a lecture in London about his defectological work (Vygotsky, 1925c; cf. Brill, 1984, pp. 87–9, for an account of his talk). It was unusual to receive permission to travel abroad, although far more common than it would become in later years. Vygotsky, however, traveled well-prepared. It is instructive to see to what extent the government wished to control the daily pursuits of scientists at that time. Vygotsky received a document, signed by the Commissar – a rank equivalent to minister – of Education Lunacharsky, and dated July 7, 1925. The document (now in the family archives) contained detailed "instructions to the delegate of the People's Commissariat of Education comrade L. S. Vygotsky." Comrade Vygotsky was to participate actively in the conference and to give his lecture "indicating the connections between our system and the general principles of social education, as well as the scientific-technical merits and methodological details of our system." He was allowed to participate in the discussions "both for a better acquaintance with the principles advocated by himself and for the matter-of-fact and principled critique of other systems." He was to protest against the fact that he had not been invited to the conference of the All-German Union of specialists working with deaf children – in case this decision would not be revised – and was to point out the harmful consequences such a decision would have for the international cause of deaf–blind children and the conference itself. He was also to state that the RSFSR was willing to join the international society of deaf pedagogists suggested by French psychologists "if such a society would not contradict the main principles of pedagogical work in the

RSFSR." With regard to all other questions, such as the possibility of the RSFSR taking part in an international society for the deaf—blind and the foundation of an international commission for the education of the deaf—blind, Vygotsky should gather all possible information and declare that he would inform his government, which would answer in a short time any question about the possibility of the RSFSR taking a role in these institutions. Vygotsky received permission to type a summary of the lecture and to distribute it among the psychologists attending the conference. Finally, Vygotsky was urged to present a report on his activities to the Peoples' Commissariat of Education immediately after his safe return to the Soviet Union.

The Psychology of Art

The long and fatiguing train trips may have exhausted Vygotsky, for soon after his return to the Soviet Union his health unexpectedly took a turn for the worse. In the summer of the same year – 1925 – he was to defend his dissertation, *The Psychology of Art* (see chapter 2), but because of his suddenly deteriorating state of health this was postponed and, finally, had to be cancelled. However, *The Psychology of Art* was accepted as a dissertation by the scientific board (protocol dated October 5, 1925) with the following words: "To acknowledge the right to teach in institutes for higher education. In view of illness exempt from public defence of dissertation" (Vygodskaja, personal communication, December 19, 1988) and thus Vygotsky became one of the very few receiving the title of doctor of psychology without having defended a dissertation.

For reasons which are unclear Vygotsky's personal copies of *The Psychology of Art* were lost – perhaps they were not returned by the publisher (see below). Fortunately, many years later a manuscript of the book was found in the private archive of the film director Eisenstein, a personal friend of both Luria and Vygotsky (see also chapter 10), and it is this manuscript which has served as the basis for the various republications of Vygotsky's dissertation. It has been suggested (e.g. Joravsky, 1989, p. 257) that these republications are not fully reliable and the actual original may have contained quotations from Trotsky and Bukharin which have been suppressed by the editors. This seems quite likely – the list of errors and falsifications in the republications of Vygotsky's writings is extremely long and quite impressive – and it would partially explain the fact that the book was not published at the time. Until now it has repeatedly been claimed by Soviet scholars (e.g. Leont'ev, 1986, p. 11; Jaroshevsky, 1985, p. 502) that Vygotsky would not publish his book because he had fundamentally changed his line of thinking.

But this story is untrue: the copy of a contract with a publisher has been found in Vygotsky's private archive (Vygodskaja, personal communication, May 1990) and from the related correspondence it becomes clear that he counted on its publication. It is far more likely that Vygotsky's dissertation was not published for ideological reasons (see also chapter 2).

Other Areas of Interest

In the spring of 1926 Vygotsky suffered another serious attack of tuberculosis. Recovering in the hospital and sanatorium he managed to write his other major manuscript of this period, the analysis of the crisis in psychology. This manuscript showed a thorough knowledge of the psychological literature of the time and prepared the way for the development of the cultural-historical theory (see chapter 7). At approximately the same time his *Pedagogical Psychology* was published, a book summarizing much of his research activities from the Gomel' period (see chapter 3). It was this manuscript that may have stimulated Kornilov's decision to hire a provincial school teacher.

Concurrently with these activities, Vygotsky developed his interest in the origin of consciousness and the instrumental method as one of the key concepts with which to study it. By 1927 the first ideas for the later cultural-historical theory were appearing (e.g. Vygotsky, 1927f; see part II).

3
Pedagogical Psychology

The development of our reactions is the history of our life. If we had to find the most important truth that modern psychology can give the teacher it would be simply: the pupil is a reacting apparatus

Vygotsky, *Pedagogical Psychology*[1]

The textbook *Pedagogical Psychology. A Short Course* (Vygotsky, 1926i) was the first of his few books that Vygotsky would see in print. Although the book was published in 1926 there are reasons to believe that it was written several years earlier. First, the way Vygotsky discussed several issues (e.g. the role of reflexes in human conduct) and thinkers (e.g. Pavlov and Freud) does not accord with the views espoused in his writings and lectures which we know were written around 1926. Secondly, when Vygotsky started work at the People's Commissariat of Public Education in July 1924 he filled out a form and listed under the heading of publications "A brief outline of pedagogical psychology. At the State Publisher's at present" (see Jaroshevsky, 1989, p. 72). It is very likely that Vygotsky was referring to *Pedagogical Psychology* and it was already completed in some form by 1924.

The Basic Idea of the Book

The aim of *Pedagogical Psychology* was to present psychology's most recent findings to students wishing to become teachers at the secondary school. It dealt with a variety of subjects thought to be relevant for the profession of a teacher. Vygotsky informed the reader about such widely different subjects as the function of internal secretion; the nervous system; evolutionary theory; classical conditioning; attention; memory; the origin of instincts;

---

[1] A motto taken from Hugo Münsterberg's *Psychology and the Teacher*.

moral and esthetic education; the advantages of mixed schools; the need to inform children about sexual matters; and the origin of language. In the selection of subjects and the level of treatment, the book did not differ greatly from modern textbooks used in introductory psychology courses. As is often the case today, the text dealt with several subjects that seem of questionable relevance for the teachers' daily practical work, but in general Vygotsky gave a well-balanced overview of the latest psychological findings and his practical advice seems well-founded and sound. It is quite hard to say which sources Vygotsky used in writing the book as it contains very few references. Undoubtedly, he made ample use of the pedagogical writings by his teacher and later colleague Pavel Blonsky (e.g. Blonsky, 1916; 1922). Further, his general reactological world-view harmonized with that of Kornilov (see chapter 6) and made ample use of the findings of Pavlov, Sechenov, and Ukhtomsky. Finally, an important Western source of inspiration was — as is evident from frequent quotations, references, and the motto given above — Hugo Münsterberg's "Psychology and the Teacher" (1909).

Despite the fact that *Pedagogical Psychology* was a textbook, its general approach, as well as several of the subjects it deals with, is particularly relevant for a proper understanding of the development of Vygotsky's thinking. Below we shall deal with various themes discussed in the book, such as the role of education; the function of speech; psychoanalysis; and the creation of the "new man" in the new Soviet society. First, however, we present the general approach to psychological problems advocated in *Pedagogical Psychology*.

Vygotsky began his book by stating that psychology was in a state of turmoil, lacking a unified approach and common concepts. This was a very popular theme at the time and one that Vygotsky himself was to elaborate several years later (see chapter 7). Acknowledging the fact of psychology's crisis, Vygotsky said that nevertheless in his opinion a solution for many problems was within reach: Pavlov's doctrine of the conditional reflexes would provide us with the firm basis on which a new psychology could be built. At the same time Vygotsky realized that many problems still had to be solved. While Pavlov's theory could explain relatively simple human behaviors, Vygotsky argued, the more complex psychological processes were hard to describe in reflexological terms. For this reason he felt obliged to continue using some of traditional psychology's concepts (Vygotsky, 1926i, pp. 8–9). It is clear, however, that he thought this to be but a temporary compromise: at the time of writing Vygotsky seemed convinced that all human behavior consists of (chains of) reflexes and that ultimately it would be possible to translate psychology's old concepts into reflex terminology. This conviction was obvious from his account of the origin and development of human behavior.

The Nature of Human Behavior

All human behavior finds its origin in reactions to stimuli coming from the external world, as Vygotsky bluntly stated (Vygotsky, 1926i, p. 22). These reactions have three parts: (1) stimulus reception; (2) processing of the stimulus; and (3) responding to the stimulus. Although this scheme was akin to the reflex scheme, Vygotsky – following Kornilov – preferred to speak of "reactions". In his opinion reaction was the more general term – applicable also to animals without a nervous system, and to plants – and should preferably be used in order to emphasize the fact that human beings share the reactive nature of their behavior with more primitive forms of life (Vygotsky, 1926i, p. 25). In practice, however, Vygotsky very frequently referred to "reflexes" and relied heavily on Pavlov's theory of the conditional reflexes.

How can one explain human behavior making use of the concept of "reaction?" To Vygotsky children were equipped with inborn, innate reactions. These were (1) unconditional reflexes (e.g. the sucking reflex), and (2) instincts (e.g. drinking; for birds, nest-building). The latter differed from unconditional reflexes in that they seemed relatively "environment invariant" and did not seem to require an eliciting stimulus to trigger the behavior. They were intricate, "built-in" series of coordinated behaviors and, thus, had a more complex nature than simple reflexes (Vygotsky, 1926i, p. 28). Both unconditional reflexes and instincts, Vygotsky stated, had evolved naturally. He fully accepted Darwin's account of the mechanism of variation and natural selection – adding to it the recently discovered fact of mutations – to explain the origin of these innate reactions.

Starting from innate reactions one could explain all human behavior. With the innate unconditional reflexes and instincts the newborn child has, in principle, at his disposal all the materials needed for even the most complex forms of behavior. Combinations of these innate reactions "led to the detection of spectral analysis, to Napoleon's campaigns, or to the discovery of America" (Vygotsky, 1926i, pp. 33–4). To Vygotsky it was Pavlov who gave us the key to understanding how adult behavior develops from these modest, innate beginnings, for the latter's great achievement was to detect that each and every unconditional reflex (innate reaction) can be linked with environmental stimuli, thus producing conditional reflexes. Many years later he would return to this issue stating that, "whereas Darwin explained the origin of species, Pavlov detected the origin of individuals" (see chapter 9). It is the conditional reactions, acquired in personal experiences, that give our behavior its extraordinary flexibility. Because the innate reactions in themselves have been determined by environmental influences in the course of evolutionary adaptation, Vygotsky considered the association of these innate behaviors with environmental factors to be equivalent to "multiplying environment by itself" Vygotsky (1926i, p. 33).

For Vygotsky all human behavior had in principle a reflex nature. Several times in his book he made the additional claim that the reactions have a motor nature. Perception, in this view, was based on eye-movements, thinking was inhibited talking, and emotions were changes in the state of internal organs (Vygotsky, 1926i, p. 15/39). He tended to believe – with Sechenov and Watson – that thinking was based on muscle activity, and claimed that "Imagining a complete paralysis of all muscles, one comes to the natural conclusion that all thinking would come to a complete stop" (Vygotsky, 1926i, p. 169).

It is unclear, however, to what extent he consistently believed in the motor nature of all human behavior. In other passages of the book – analyzing other mental processes – Vygotsky referred to processes of internal secretion and other chemical processes as the ultimate foundation of human behavior (ibid., pp. 50–5). Such an attitude probably boils down to making the more general and less provocative – or profoundly uninstructive, as James (1902/1985, p. 12) would have it – claim that all mental processes have a material substrate.

Vygotsky was well aware of the reductionist tenor of these claims. One might think, he wrote, that having established the motor and reflex nature of thinking, any difference between intelligent and conscious thinking on the one hand, and reflexes and instincts on the other hand, has disappeared. In this view the human being would be a mechanistic automaton, reacting to environmental stimuli (Vygotsky, 1926i, p. 173). Surprisingly, he wished to oppose this point of view.

How, then, did Vygotsky retain the idea of the special nature of human thinking and behavior in general? In our view, during this period of his scientific development he was not particularly clear on this important issue. One line of his reasoning was developed to show the differences between animal and human behavior. According to Vygotsky animal behavior could be entirely explained by reference to (1) innate reactions; and (2) conditional reflexes (which were themselves combinations of innate reactions and personal experience) (Vygotsky, 1926i, p. 40). But human beings – and here Vygotsky heavily relied on Marxist thought – differed in fundamental ways from animals: they have a collective social history and do not adapt passively to nature. Moreover, they actively change their nature according to their design. This transformation of nature is reached by making use of tools in the process of labor. Through this reasoning – which was to reappear (and in more elaborate form) to underpin his writings time and again (see chapter 9) – Vygotsky developed the following explanation of human behavior; human behavior can be fully explained only by taking into account (1) innate reactions; (2) conditional reflexes; (3) historical experience; (4) social experience; and (5) "doubled" (*udvoennyj*) experience. This last term needs some clarification. Vygotsky quoted Marx's spider passage (in which Marx compared spiders and bees with human beings and concluded that the distinguishing characteristic was not the quality of their constructions, but the ability to foresee the result; see Marx, 1890/1981, p. 193) to illustrate the concept that human beings consciously plan their activities and foresee the results. Apparently, he felt the need to reconcile Marx's idea with the general reflexological approach and sought for a reflexological basis of planning activities and free will. The concept of *udvoennyj* experience was to serve this function. It implied that the organism reacts twice: the first time to external events, and the second to internal events. The (internal) plan of building a house would be a stimulus for the actual process of building, whereas the plan itself arose as the result of some reaction to an external event. In this way, conscious activities are (1) really reactions to internal stimuli that (2) arose as reactions to external stimuli. They, therefore, have a "double" nature and may be termed "doubled experience."

In putting forward a reflexological approach, Vygotsky felt constrained to explain the phenomenon of unity in human behavior: human beings do not seem to be at the mercy of myriads of incoming stimuli but show in their behavior a degree of coherence and stability that suggests selective and coordinating mechanisms at work. To explain this apparent coherence Vygotsky had recourse to Ukhtomsky's concept of dominant reactions (see also chapter 2). The environmental stimuli – compared by Vygotsky (1926i, p. 45) to a crowd of scared people wishing to enter through the narrow doors of some public building – compete for the motor areas (*dvigatel'noe pole*) in the brain and only one stimulus will succeed and become the dominating one. All energy from the surrounding parts of the brain will flow to this field, thus making the organism subordinate all other activities to this one dominating stimulus and creating the impression of coherent, well-organized activity.

Despite the general reflexological and reactological flavor of Vygotsky's work at this time its importance should not be overemphasized. When discussing the various aspects of teaching he seldom referred to the underlying reflexological framework and one gets the distinct impression that the choice of subjects for the book and their general treatment was hardly influenced by his methodological stance.

Education

Vygotsky's view of the relationship between education and development as expressed in *Pedagogical Psychology* was hardly original at this time, for he made frequent reference to, among others, Blonsky's works. This view was also different from the views he would espouse in the 1930s and for which he was to become famous. His main tenet around 1924 was that pupils in some fundamental way are really educating themselves, as it is new personal experience that leads to the formation of new reactions (Vygotsky, 1926i, p. 336), and one wonders whether it reflected his own experiences in school (see chapter 1). The only thing caretakers and teachers can do is to arrange the environment in which children and pupils are situated in such a way as to maximize the possibilities of the formation of new reactions. Vygotsky emphasized the need for pupils to learn from their own activities: their role should not be reduced to one of passively receiving accepted knowledge.

Whilst highlighting the importance of personal, private experience, Vygotsky was opposed to the so-called "free education" movement prevalent in the Soviet Union at that time (see Kozulin, 1984). Children should not be left to themselves when acquiring new knowledge and wisdom, as this was equivalent to not educating them at all, leaving their development to the obnoxious forces of the "street." Bringing up children necessarily means restricting their freedom of action, Vygotsky reasoned, sometimes in the interest of the child himself, sometimes in the interest of the collective (1926i, p. 242). The role of parents and teachers is and should be enormous: in forming part of the children's environment and organizing this environment they will steer the children's mental development to a considerable extent. This emphasis was also clearly expressed in the definitions of education Vygotsky provided. Early in his book he defined the educational (*vospitatel'nyj*) process as the "process of social reform [*perestrojka*] of biological forms of behavior" (Vygotsky, 1926i, p. 10). Later on he preferred Blonsky's similar definition of education/upbringing as the "planned, goal-directed, intentional, conscious influencing of and interference in the child's natural growth processes" (1926i, p. 67).

One catches a glimpse of Vygotsky's personal philosophy of life when reading *Pedagogical Psychology*. He argued that teachers should be professionals stimulating the child to take an active approach to life, for life is a continual struggle and the teacher should be a fighter as well as an artist. Ideally, human life is creative labor, Vygotsky claimed. The person will be transformed in this process of creative labor reaching new levels of insight and understanding.

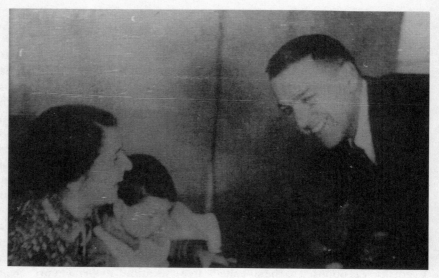

Vygotsky, his daughter Gita, and his wife Rosa Smekhova during a filmed psychological experiment.

The Plasticity of Man

There was some tension between the revolutionary pathos of those days about the creation of a "new man" and the scientific findings Vygotsky presented. On the one hand, he claimed that child behavior is not a plaything of environmental forces: the development of the child, Vygotsky argued, is always the result of a dialectical struggle between "man and the world," where the role of hereditary constitution is not smaller than that of environment (1926i, p. 62). This and similar remarks seem to indicate that Vygotsky saw definite limits to the possibilities of transforming human beings by societal reforms and was by no means an extreme environmentalist.

On the other hand *Pedagogical Psychology* was by far Vygotsky's most ideological book and contained many references to the prospects of the new classless society and the possibilities of reforming human nature. Among other things, Vygotsky referred to Marx's and Engels' analysis of economic substructures in society. He also reiterated the idea of the class character of the social environment and its ideology and spoke of the class nature of the stimuli that fashion the behavior of each child. All education, then, in his opinion, had its class background, a fact that was clearly supported by examining a capitalist society, where children were taught a bourgeois mentality and morality. Fortunately, it was possible to "perform revolution's music" thereby creating a new society (Vygotsky, 1926i, p. 215–27).

One gets the impression that Vygotsky sincerely believed the utopian statements of leading Soviet ideologists and politicians about the future communist state (see also chapter 4). He repeated, for example, the idea that, having created the new society, communist man would live without conflict. It was through societal reforms that the blessed transformation of mankind would come true. "The revolution undertakes the re-education of all mankind," Vygotsky stated (1926i, p. 345), approvingly quoting Trotsky on the possibilities of transforming the human being. Voicing a blend of eugenic ideas and progressive political thought (also advocated by some of the Western leftist intellectuals of that time, among them George Bernard Shaw (Gould, 1981; Kevles, 1985, p. 86)) Vygotsky added that we should not "bend for the dark laws of heredity and blind sexual selection" (1926i, p. 347). The unlimited plasticity of human material could be exploited by organizing the social environment in the right way. The final passage of *Pedagogical Psychology* (pp. 347–8) testifies to an almost unlimited faith in the possibility of the improvement of man and deserves to be quoted at length.

Man will finally take seriously the idea of harmonizing himself. He will set himself the goal of bringing into the movement of his own organs – during work, during walking, during play – the utmost precision, expediency, economy, and, thereby, beauty. He wishes to master the half-unconscious and, after that, also the unconscious processes in his own organism: breathing, circulation of the blood, digestion, impregnation – and within the necessary boundaries to submit them to the control of reason and will. The human species, which crystallized in the form of *homo sapiens*, will again be radically re-cast and will master the set of intricate methods of artificial selection and psychophysical training. This is entirely in accord with the developments. Man first banished the dark element [*stikhija*] from production and ideology, supplanting barbarous routine by scientific technique and religion by science. He then expelled the unconscious from politics by overturning monarchy and class-ridden society by democracy, by rationalist parliamentarianism and, after that, by the fully articulated Soviet dictatorship. The dark element [*stikhija*] was most strongly ensconced in the economic relations, but from there, too, man will destroy it through the socialist organization of economy. Finally, in the deepest and darkest corner of the unconsciousness, the uncontrolled [*stikhijnyj*], the subterranean, the nature of man himself lay hidden. Is it not clear that the greatest efforts of scientific thought and creative initiative will be directed there? The human species will not stop crawling on all fours before god, Tsars and capital only to bend obediently before the dark laws of heredity and blind sexual selection! Liberated man will wish to reach a greater equilibrium in the work of his organs, a more even development and wear of his tissues. By this alone he will bring the fear of death within the limits of an adequate reaction of the organism to danger, for there can be no doubt that precisely the extreme anatomical and physiological disharmony of man, the exceedingly unevenness of the development and wear of organs and tissues give the life instinct the morbid, frustrated, hysterical form of a fear of death. It [the disharmony] obscures reason and nourishes stupid and degrading phantasies about an existence beyond the grave. Man will set himself the goal of mastering his own feelings, of raising the instincts to the height of awareness, to make them transparent, of laying wires from the will to the hidden and the subterranean and thereby raise himself to a new level – to create a "higher," societal biological type, if you wish – a superman.

This quotation shows to what extent Vygotsky was carried away by the prevailing ideology and the revolutionary zeal of the time. It also shows how far he had evolved from the dreamy young boy analyzing Hamlet's meetings with ghosts. The quoted piece voices an ideal of rational man which was probably nourished by Vygotsky's frequent reading of Spinoza (see chapters 9 and 14).

The fact that in sketching his utopia Vygotsky once referred to Trotsky and the fact that he borrowed Nietzsche's concept of Superman – as Shaw did in his *Man and Superman* (see Kevles, 1985, pp. 86–91) – to sketch the qualities of the "new man" have so far prevented the re-issue of this little-known book in the Soviet Union.

Freud

As in the manuscript of *The Psychology of Art* (see chapter 2) in *Pedagogical Psychology* Vygotsky frequently referred to Freudian theory. The difference between them is that in *Pedagogical Psychology* there was no indication of a critical attitude towards the ideas of the Viennese magician. Vygotsky seemed to accept Freud's ideas fully and, among other things, suggested to future teachers that Freud had discovered the existence of child sexuality and the origin of sexually-based neuroses. He also embraced Freud's theory of defense mechanisms and devoted several pages to a discussion of the concept of sublimation (1926i, pp. 79–84). Finally, in a section of the book entitled "The Ego and the Id" Vygotsky presented Freud's personality model (1926i, pp. 179–80). It thus would seem that Vygotsky at the time – around 1924 – accepted uncritically a large part of Freud's thinking. Another possibility is that he simply wished to present to future teachers an unbiased overview of the contemporary currents of psychology and deliberately refrained from giving his judgement.

Speech

Given that Vygotsky would later become famous for, among other things, his view of speech, it is of some interest to look at his treatment of this subject in *Pedagogical Psychology* (pp. 175–9). Vygotsky claimed that philologists had established three stages in the development of every language. These stages were, apparently, also present in child development. In the first stage, speech is equivalent to the reflexive cry, connected with emotion and instincts. In the second stage children detect their own cry and its result: the appearance of the mother. Frequent combination of cry and mother will lead to a conditional reflex: the act of the organism is now connected with the meaning it has. Vygotsky claimed that "The cry of the child already has significance, because it expresses something understandable to the child himself and the mother" (1926i, p. 176).

But in the second stage we still cannot speak of human speech, as the meanings are strictly individual or restricted to a few child–caretaker dyads. Vygotsky subscribed to the idea that originally in each language there was a clear logical connection between the sound of a word and its meaning. In that (mythical) period every individual understood why things were called the way they were. Gradually this understanding got lost and only the sound and the meaning rested. The disappearance of the logical link was caused by the fact that many more people started using the words: gradually people forgot, for example, that ink was originally black. The third stage, then, was characterized by the fact that all meanings were shared by all members of a speech community.

The function of language, Vygotsky claimed, is two-fold: it is (1) a means of social coordination of the actions of various people; and (2) a tool of thinking. The two functions seem linked in Vygotsky's thinking of that time, for he claimed that we always think verbally: thinking is talking to oneself. Generally speaking, we organize our behavior internally as we organize our behavior externally towards others. Our thinking thus has a social character, and our personality (*lichnost'*) is organized like social interaction (*obshchenie*). This reasoning led Vygotsky to claim that:

> In this way, the child first learns to understand others and only afterwards, following the same model, learns to understand himself. It would be more exact to say that we know (*znaem*) ourselves to the extent that we know others, or, even more exact, that we are conscious of (*soznaem*) ourselves only

to the extent that we are another for ourselves, that is, a stranger (*postoron-nyj*). (1926i, p. 179)

This is the reason, Vygotsky concluded, why speech, the tool of social interaction, is at the same time the tool of intimate interaction with oneself. This general idea formed a consistent theme in Vygotsky's writings and was quite probably based on Vygotsky's reading of Janet, and – through Janet – ultimately on Baldwin's thinking (see Van der Veer and Valsiner, 1988; Valsiner and Van der Veer, 1988).

Mental Tests

In 1936 Vygotsky was to be posthumously accused of abusing intelligence tests by referring children to special schools on the basis of low test scores (see chapter 16). In several chapters of this book it will be seen that this accusation was patently false. In fact, in *Pedagogical Psychology* one can see Vygotsky arguing for a cautious use of mental tests. Having explained the underlying principle of Binet-Simon's and Rossolimo's mental tests, Vygotsky immediately made some critical comments. Although these tests can provide us with some insights they have definite drawbacks, Vygotsky argued. In the first place there is no such thing as general giftedness: Chekhov may have been a brilliant writer but he was a rather mediocre medical doctor. Likewise, some children are gifted intellectually while others may become creative artists. One, therefore, should be wary of referring children to special forms of education solely on the basis of these assessments of their intellectual capacities. This reasoning was in line with Vygotsky's general plea for a well-rounded education, including the stimulation of moral, emotional, and esthetic development. He argued against a one-sided intellectual training, stating that it is possible to discern not only gifted thinking, but also "gifted feeling" (1926i, p. 115). In the second place, Vygotsky advanced an ecological argument stating that the results of mental tests are obtained in an artificial situation. There is, therefore, no guarantee that they will be valid under the circumstances of everyday life (1926i, p. 331). This line of reasoning was in accord with his general thinking about the utility of tests and examinations in schools. In general, he was against formal examinations because these tend to give us a distorted picture of the true level of the child's knowledge and abilities (1926i, p. 74) by making the child nervous and therefore the child performs suboptimally.

Conclusions

In the preceding paragraphs some of the themes dealt with in *Pedagogical Psychology* have been presented. It is clear that Vygotsky was greatly influenced by Pavlov's thinking at the time, but clearly saw its limits. In chapter 6 it will be seen that Vygotsky's views of this period were close to Kornilov's reactological world-view. His utopian ideas about the new man in the new Soviet society, his sympathetic discussion of Freud's hypotheses, his materialistic approach to psychological issues, and his claim that man was fundamentally different from animals were in complete harmony with the general ethos of the time. The fact that Vygotsky had finished his manuscript of *Pedagogical Psychology* by 1924 may, therefore, have greatly facilitated his entrance to academic psychology (see chapter 6). It would be only several years later – when developing the cultural-historical theory – that Vygotsky developed a distinctly novel perspective in psychology.

4

Defectology

The term "defectology" was traditionally used for the science studying children with various mental and physical problems ("defects"). Among those studied were deaf–mute, blind, ineducable, and mentally retarded children. Ideally a defectological diagnosis of a particular child and the prognosis for his or her (partial) recovery would be based on the combined advice of specialists in the field of psychology, pedagogy, child psychiatry, and medicine.

Vygotsky's interest in problems of defectology probably came into being during his work as a teacher in Gomel' but only became evident in 1924 with his first publications in this field. These writings reflected the work he was doing at the subdepartment for the education of defective children of the Narkompros, which he combined with his activities at Kornilov's Institute of Experimental Psychology. Gradually he became active as a consultant for the diverse specialists working with "defective children" in various institutes (see chapter 1) and started investigating the children himself. Luchkov and Pevzner (1981, p. 66) have commented that once a week the most interesting clinical cases were diagnosed in a collective meeting of psychiatrists, psychologists, pedagogues, students, and other interested people. These meetings were conducted under the guidance of Vygotsky and are said to have attracted up to 250 people. It would seem, then, that Vygotsky and his co-workers were following the grand psychiatric tradition of diagnosing and demonstrating patients in public. The diagnostic protocols of these clinical sessions were preserved for some time by Vygotsky's collaborator L. Geshelina, but, unfortunately, they seem to have been lost during the war and after Geshelina's death (Luria, 1979, p. 53). Although, according to several contemporaries (e.g. Bejn, Vlasova, Levina, Morozova, and Shif, 1983, p. 340) Vygotsky himself was a very skilled clinician, this is not shown in his writings, which as a rule lacked any clinical detail. Thus, in contrast to other writers in this domain (e.g. Janet,

1926, 1929; and Wallon, 1925), Vygotsky seldom gave case histories to illustrate his point of view, but stuck to presenting what he considered to be important theoretical lessons to be learned from the practical work in this field.

We do know that Vygotsky did invariably include among the subjects who participated in the many experiments he supervised a number of "abnormal" persons, such as deaf or blind children, persons suffering from aphasia, or people diagnosed as schizophrenic. Feeble-minded children, for example, were asked to solve the forbidden color task (see chapter 9) and a number of feeble-minded children and schizophrenics participated in the concept-formation experiments (see chapter 11). But nowhere in Vygotsky's work can one find a clear and exhaustive discussion of the experimental results of these "deviant" subjects. For an indirect account of several of the experiments performed the reader should consult Zankov (1935a), who faithfully followed Vygotsky's approach and dedicated his book to his former teacher.

We may conclude, therefore, that Vygotsky's defectological writings – although of potential importance for the practical work with "defective" children – are of a rather general and theoretical nature.

It is important and interesting to study Vygotsky's defectological writings from several points of view. First, they have some intrinsic value and supposedly greatly influenced the development of defectology in the Soviet Union (Bejn, Vlasova, Levina, Morozova, and Shif, 1983, pp. 333–41; Luchkov and Pevzner, 1981, pp. 64–7). Secondly, they are closely linked to his other work and – sometimes – provide a clue to an understanding of the development of his thinking as a whole. Finally, a discussion of his work in this field will show the various phases in his work. Starting from 1924 Vygotsky tried to formulate his own view of the "defective" child – a task that was never completed and lasted until his death in 1934.

Early Writings: The Importance of Social Education

Vygotsky's first writings in the field of defectology (Vygotsky, 1924f; 1925b–d; 1925i) concentrated on the problems of deaf–mute, blind, and retarded children, and culminated in his trip to Germany, Holland, England, and France in the summer of 1925 (see the introduction to part I).

A common characteristic of these first writings is their emphasis on the importance of the social education of handicapped children and on the children's potential for normal development. This emphasis was closely linked to Vygotsky's analysis of the role of any physical defect in the child's life. He argued that every bodily handicap – be it blindness, deaf–muteness, or a congenital mental retardation – first and foremost affected the children's social relations, rather than their direct interactions with the physical surroundings. The organic defect inevitably manifests itself as a change in the child's social standing. Thus, parents, siblings, and peers will treat the handicapped child very differently from the other children, be it in a positive or negative way.

To Vygotsky this social fact was in its turn a manifestation of the principal difference between human beings and animals. He reasoned that for human beings – in contrast to animals – a physical defect will never affect the subject's personality directly. For between human beings and the physical world stands their social environment which refracts and transforms their interactions with the world (1924i, p. 63). Therefore, in Vygotsky's view, it was the social problem resulting from a physical handicap that should be seen as the principal problem. To substantiate this view he quoted the statement by a contemporary author that blind children do not originally realize their blindness as a psychological fact. It is only realized as a social fact, a secondary, mediated result of their social experience (1924i, p. 68; 1925f, p. 52).

Starting from these premises Vygotsky reasoned that the social education, based on the social compensation of their physical problems, was the only way to a satisfactory life for "defective" children. In his opinion the special schools of that time did little to provide such a social education. Being influenced by religious and philanthropical ideas – remnants of a bourgeois mentality that originated in the Western world – they emphasized the children's unfortunate fate and the need to bear their cross with resignation. In contrast, Vygotsky argued for a school that refrained from isolating these children but, rather, integrated them as far as possible in the society. The children should be given the opportunity to live with normal subjects. To this end Vygotsky argued for the necessity of carrying out an experiment examining the results of joint education of blind and normal subjects (1924i, p. 74). Emphasizing the fact that these defective children were 95 per cent healthy and had a potential for normal development he passionately pleaded for the walls of the special schools to be pulled down and for these children to participate in the *komsomol*, where they could be trained to participate in normal fulfilling labor activities. By participating in the pioneer movement the deaf–mute and blind children would live and feel like the rest of the country. Their pulses "would beat in unison with the pulse of the huge masses of the people" (1924i, pp. 75–6; 1925b, pp. 112–13).

There were clear utopian undertones in his defectological writings of that time. Echoing the general rhetoric and emotion of the 1920s he claimed that "The social education that arose in the greatest epoch of the final reform of mankind is called upon to realize that of which mankind has always dreamt

as a religious miracle: that the blind would see and the deaf would hear"
(1924i, p. 71).

By participating in social life in all its aspects children would – in a
metaphorical sense – overcome their blindness and deafness. Vygotsky had
no doubts that such a social education was sorely needed. He repeatedly
stated that the old idea of there being some automatic, biological compensation for certain defects had been proved wrong. Thus, it had been shown
that blind subjects did not as a rule have enhanced hearing. In so far as they
outperformed normal subjects it was the result of their special circumstances and training.

The clearly optimistic tenor of Vygotsky's writings of these years was not
exceptional, nor were his ideas very original. The researchers present at the
Second Meeting on the Social-judicial Protection of Minors held in 1924
accepted resolutions that stated that the education of handicapped and
normal children was to become combined to a great degree and underlined
the idea that the first category should be trained to become socially valued
workers (Bejn, Levina, Morozova, 1983, p. 348). Vygotsky (1925f) was one
of the speakers at this meeting. The new ideas in the Soviet Union in
themselves reflected research developments and changing attitudes towards
"defective children" in the West, the only principal difference being –
according to Vygotsky (1925f, p. 62) – that in the West it was a matter of
"social charity," while in the Soviet Union it was a matter of "social
education."

Talking about the special problems of blind and deaf children Vygotsky
made some statements that were particularly relevant to the understanding
of the development of his thinking. Several times he reasoned that to learn
the Braille script does not in principle differ from learning normal script, for
the learning of both types of literacy is based on the multiple pairing in time
of two stimuli. Seen from the physiological point of view, in both cases
literacy was based on the formation of conditional reflexes, the sole difference being that different receptive organs were conditioned to different
environmental stimuli. Blindness and deafness, therefore, to Vygotsky
were nothing other than the lack of one of the possible roads to the formation of conditional reflexes with the environment (1924i, p. 66; 1925b,
p. 102; 1925f, p. 53). The remedy was simply the replacement of the traditional road by another, and consequently, no special theory for the
treatment of deaf and blind children was needed. Ultimately, Vygotsky
reasoned, the eye is nothing else than a tool serving a certain activity that
can be replaced by another tool (1924i, p. 73). Accepting an idea put
forward by Birilev (1924), he stated that for the blind the other person can
act in the role of instrument, like a microscope or telescope. The step to the
other person – the cooperation with others, transcending the boundaries of

individualistic pedagogics – was the vital foundation for any special pedagogics.

It follows from this that in the case of blind children the task for the defectologist amounts to the connecting of symbolic systems and signals to other receptive organs (e.g. skin, ear). In principle, this would change nothing. Whether one reads gothic letters, roman letters, or Braille script does not change the idea of reading. Therefore, Vygotsky could claim, that "Important is the meaning, not the sign. We will change the sign [and] retain the meaning" (1924i, p. 74). The task of special schools or special teachers was the training of these special symbol systems.

Deafness, Vygotsky claimed, is a less serious defect than blindness. It has, however, more serious consequences: the lack of speech deprives deaf children of social contacts and social experience. This is most unfortunate, "For speech is not only a tool of communication, but also a tool of thinking, consciousness develops mainly with the help of speech and originates in social experience" (1924i, p. 78).

Referring to Natorp and using an idea first formulated by Baldwin and Janet, Vygotsky emphasized that a human being taken in isolation is only an abstraction. Even thinking for ourselves we retain the fiction of communication. In other words, without speech there would be no consciousness, nor self-consciousness.

During these years Vygotsky was of the opinion that special teachers had to teach deaf–mute children oral speech, which in his opinion was the only speech that could lead to the development of abstract concepts. Neither mimics nor sign language were, therefore, to be allowed by the teacher. The learning of oral speech should be promoted by making the task interesting for the children, by creating an atmosphere in which the children felt the need to speak (1925f, p. 55). He therefore strongly advised the integration of the teaching of speech with the playing of all sorts of games that elicited oral speech in a natural way. In this way the child's interest in using speech would be promoted. This position was a reaction to the methods used at the time, which emphasized the technical sides of oral speech without taking on board the idea that speech for deaf–mute children should be an instrument of communication which they would like to use. Thus, by endlessly rehearsing the right pronunciation of particular words the children did not learn to use speech as an instrument of social interaction, preferring mimics or sign language to communicate their ideas. In Vygotsky's words, they learned "pronunciation, not speech." In a talk given on May 25, 1925 during a meeting of the Pedagogical Council of the Scientific State Council he presented a detailed plan for the comparative investigation of various methods that were in line with his thinking (1925c).

Taking the right approach we can create a new land for our handicapped children, Vygotsky concluded. Reiterating his idea that defectiveness itself is but a social evaluation of some physical variation, he asked the reader to imagine a land where blindness or deaf–muteness were highly valued. In such a country these handicaps would not exist as a social fact. In a similar way, the introduction of social education which would encourage handicapped children to become socially valued workers, would eliminate the idea of defectiveness as a social fact in the new society (1924i, p. 84).

These ideas give an insight to an understanding of the development of Vygotsky's thinking. In the first place, it is evident that Vygotsky at this time was still largely thinking in terms of reflexology. As we have seen, he considered learning to read to be nothing other than the establishment of conditional reflexes. Secondly, it can be seen that several ideas that were to become of primary importance in later years are already being espoused. Thus, Vygotsky mentioned the idea of the eye and speech as "tools" for the carrying out of some activity (reading or thinking, respectively). In connection with this we can see the first formulation of the idea of mediation – human beings having no direct contact with the physical surroundings and having to rely on social others or tools. Also remarkable was his explicit distinction between signs and meanings and his emphasis on the latter concept. This attitude seems to contradict a claim often made, namely that Vygotsky developed from a period during which he concentrated exclusively on signs to a more mature understanding of the relevance of word meanings. Although there is definitely some truth in this claim, the present account of Vygotsky's very early defectological ideas shows that the distinction was well known to Vygotsky and that he did not hesitate to opt for the concept of meaning.

Flirtations with Adler

It was in 1927 that Vygotsky's views on defectological problems underwent a sudden change. Under the influence of the third edition of Adler's *Praxis und Theorie der Individualpsychologie* (1927) he started emphasizing the possibility of compensation and even supercompensation for children's physical defects (Vygotsky, 1927c; 1928a; 1928u; 1928ab; 1928ae).

Adler (1927) had observed that we cannot really understand a person's behavior unless we know its function and purpose. All organisms strive after a certain goal and the task of the psychologist is to find this goal. It is only after finding an imaginary line that can be drawn through the different aspects of an organism's behavior that this behavior will start to become intelligible to the observer. This imaginary line links all different aspects of behavior – makes the organism into an individual – and points like an arrow to some future goal. This idea of goal-directedness or finality of behavior Adler opposed to the idea of causality and reflex chains. Reasoning that having only the knowledge of the causes of behavior would never enable us to understand the unity and future course of behavior, he argued for the functional, goal-directed point of view. Without the guideline of the directional goal the organism would not be able to "master the chaos of future" and all action would be a blindly "groping around" (1927, p. 2). Knowing a person's intentions, however, one can more or less predict his or her behavior, Adler reasoned. To support this view he gave the example of a man contemplating suicide. Knowing his goal it is quite easy to foresee that he would reply with the word "rope," when asked to quickly respond to the word "tree." But without this knowledge of his intentions it would be virtually impossible to predict the answer. All psychological phenomena, therefore, should be understood as the preparation for some future goal. Adler went on to posit that the – mostly unconscious – goal of all persons is to be superior to others and to reach a superior position in social life. This striving to be superior – or God-like in Adler's terms – is in itself ridiculous, but suffices to explain the actions of individuals and their development. Each inability or incapacity is subjectively felt as a serious obstacle on the road to perfection that should be overcome at all costs. This is particularly true for children, who are surrounded by adults who surpass them in almost every possible area. The feeling of inferiority to adults is the child's most powerful motive to develop, Adler argued (1927, p. 9). More important than their real capabilities – which may be relatively poor or excellent – is their subjective assessment of these capabilities, which usually results in a feeling of inferiority. Both handicapped and normal children are motivated by the single goal to become adult-like, and later – having become adults themselves – to become God-like. They are constantly striving for a future perfection, a future that will compensate them for their current sense of inferiority. The whole possibility of the child's upbringing and development depends on this feeling of inferiority (1927, p. 9). Characteristic for Adler, then, was the positing of a striving for perfection which was caused by an initial feeling of inferiority which in its turn was evoked by very real differences between children and adults. In chapter 7 of his book he summarized this idea by saying that one can deduce "a psychological law of the dialectical leap from organ inferiority through the subjective feeling of inferiority to the psychological striving for compensation or supercompensation" (1927, p. 57). The result of the striving for compensation might be successful – normal development or even superior development – or might result in failure. In the latter case, neuroses – which Adler considered to be unsuccessful attempts at compensation for felt inferiority – would develop.

In several ways this theory harmonized with Vygotsky's earlier ideas regarding the problems of defectology. First, Adler's view was moderately optimistic in that it posited that inferiority ("defects") might be overcome, and that the struggle for compensation might even result in supercompensation. Secondly, Adler's emphasis on the struggle for social position was at least compatible with the view that for "defective" children it was of vital importance to attain a position in the "collective" or society as a whole. Thirdly, and connected with the first two points, Adler's theory de-emphasized the idea of an organic disposition for inferiority, underlining the idea of future compensation. Elaborating on this theme he called his own theory a "positional" theory – because of the emphasis on social position – as opposed to the "dispositional" theories that stressed organic dispositions (Adler, 1927, p. 56). Similarly, Adler's future-oriented theory posited a welcome alternative to Freud's emphasis on the relevance of past experience (Vygotsky, 1927c, p. 37; 1928v, p. 161).

These and other ideas were enthusiastically welcomed by Vygotsky. At first he particularly liked the idea that the compensatory tendencies would automatically, naturally originate in the "defective" child. The defect in itself formed the primary stimulus for the development of the personality and the educational process could make use of these natural tendencies (Vygotsky, 1927c, pp. 40–1; 1928ae, p. 183).

> What a liberating truth for the pedagogue: the blind develops a psychological superstructure on the failing function, that has a single task – to replace vision; the deaf with all means develop means to overcome the isolation and seclusion of muteness! . . . [We] did not know that a defect is not only psychological poverty, but also a source of richness, not only weakness, but also a source of strength. (Vygotsky, 1927c, pp. 40–1)

The use of the word "superstructure" is, of course, hardly accidental. Vygotsky deliberately chose this term to suggest an analogy with Marx's economic and sociological points of view.

There is no doubt that Vygotsky at first fully believed in the existence of (super)compensation and in the correctness of Adler's view on these matters. Time and again he repeated the account of Adler's theory given above, quoted parts of it (using mainly chapters 1 and 7 of Adler's book) and argued its vital importance. Giving the example of vaccination and the resulting "superhealth" of the child he claimed that supercompensation by the organism was an omnipresent phenomenon in biology that had been scientifically established beyond any reasonable doubt (Vygotsky, 1927c, p. 34). He did realize, again following Adler, that for "defective" children the attempts to compensate for a defect might lead to failure, but stressed that the possibility of supercompensation in itself showed "like a beacon" the road educational efforts should take (Vygotsky, 1927c, p. 46).

It is interesting to see how Vygotsky tried to integrate Adler's theory with his own still partially reflexological thinking and with Marxist ideology. We have seen above how he defined education as the establishment of conditional reflexes and saw no distinction in principle between the education of defective and other children in this respect. By 1927 he still claimed this – and on the basis of this idea even posited the "complete re-educability of human nature" (Vygotsky, 1928v, p. 155) – but at the same time stated that this was only one side of the matter and began to emphasize the deeply unique nature of each defective child, which called for a special system of education (1927c, p. 43; 1928ae, p. 182).

Vygotsky considered Adler's emphasis on the goal-directed nature of all behavior to be in line with Pavlov's concept of the goal reflex (*refleks čeli*) and he repeatedly remarked that Adler had referred to Pavlov in this respect (Vygotsky, 1927c, p. 44; 1928a, p. 96; 1928v, p. 158; 1929m, p. 11). Vygotsky even went as far as to claim that his own earlier research of the phenomena of dominant reactions (1926d) could likewise be explained with the help of the concept of supercompensation (1927c, p. 45). His conclusion was, that "If the doctrine of conditional reflexes sketches the horizontal aspect of the person, then the theory of supercompensation gives his vertical" (1927c, p. 49). Here he was paraphrasing the words of the emigré philosopher Semyon Frank as Jaroshevsky (1989, p. 125) pointed out.

The possible reconciliation of Adler's individual psychology with Marxist thinking was at first rather an open question to Vygotsky. If anything, he thought that they might be integrated. Thus, he noted that Adler was active in the socialist movement and had regularly referred to the writings of Marx and Engels. Repeating approvingly the lines by Adler quoted above in the short sketch of his theory, he argued that individual psychology was dialectical, because of its claim that defects would result in their opposite and for its emphasis on the continuous development towards a future goal (Vygotsky, 1928v, p. 157). Adler's theory was also decidedly social in its emphasis on the socially felt inferiority and the striving for a socially satisfactory position. Moreover, Adler underlined an idea of social struggle that Vygotsky found compatible with the thinking of Darwin and Marx. He found the idea that an organism that is fully adjusted to its environment would have no need to develop characteristic of both Adler and Darwin. It is precisely the state of not being adjusted that causes species or individuals to develop and leaves potential for development and education (1927c, p. 37–8; 1928a, p. 96; 1928v, p. 162). By 1928, however, Vygotsky's position had changed slightly. While still presenting Adler's theory with enthusiasm he now added that Adler's main philosophical positions were marred by their metaphysical elements and that it was only his practice that was interesting (Vygotsky, 1928v, p. 156). Theoretically speaking he now considered Adler's individual psychology to be a curious mixture of the natural-scientific approach, on the one hand, and the idealist approach on the other hand (Vygotsky, 1928v, pp. 164–5; see also chapter 7).

The acceptance of Adler's general theoretical views did not change all of Vygotsky's views on more specific defectological problems. He continued to see speech as the liberating factor in the life of blind children, claiming that "blindness would be overcome by the word" (1928a, p. 95; 1928ae, p. 184) and still insisted that speech exercises should be made interesting for deaf children, thereby creating an inner need to speak orally (Vygotsky, 1927c, p. 47). His rhetoric, too, was still there and led Vygotsky to evoke the slightly grotesque image of "the new blind man" in the new society (1928a, p. 100).

However several concepts had definitely changed in Vygotsky's thinking. For instance, his adoption of a more structural view of personality. Previously Vygotsky had claimed that blindness was nothing other than the loss of one instrument that could simply be replaced by another, but he now realized that to this "horizontal" truth should be added a "vertical" truth and stated that "blindness is not only the lack of vision ... it causes a deep restructuring of all the forces of the organism and the personality" (1928a, p. 86/89). He now believed that a handicap such as blindness causes a reorganization of the whole mind, involving the use of other ways, instruments, and means to reach the same goals (1929m, p. 12). These views constituted a first step towards his later structural views regarding the inter-functional connections.

The Cultural-Historical Approach

From 1928 the general direction of Vygotsky's defectological writings changed. A paper published the next year (1929m) clearly marked the transition from Adlerian theory to the cultural-historical approach. It combined the last complete discussion of Adlerian ideas with the presentation of a whole new set of ideas, such as those of instruments, of lower and higher functions, of primitivism etcetera, all of them characteristic of what was to be called the cultural-historical theory (see chapter 9).

That is not to say that Adlerian ideas vanished from Vygotsky's writings without leaving a trace. Elements of Adler's theory were still present in later years (see Vygotsky, 1928ah, pp. 176–9 with a reference to the Society for Individual Psychology, 1928ab, p. 172; 1929y, pp. 139–41), but they were presented without the earlier emphasis and enthusiastic quotations, and without, in fact, even mentioning Adler's name. The definitive break from Adler's views was only articulated in Vygotsky (1931o, pp. 119–21), when he claimed that the objective opportunities present in the child's collective were more important for the possibility of compensation than the child's subjectively felt inferiority.

Nor do we wish to say that clues to the cultural-historical approach had not surfaced in Vygotsky's writings during or even before his flirtation with Adler: several elements of a cultural-historical approach seemed to be present before its actual formulation. To give an example, we find the idea that human psychological functions are "artificial, social, technical" as early as 1928 (Vygotsky, 1928c, p. 95). It may well be that the origins of Vygotsky's and Luria's cultural-historical theory can be found, to a great extent, in the domain of defectological research. It was not only facts like the existence of the Braille script that may have led Vygotsky to think of psychological functioning as tool-use, but there was also a body of writings in this field that may have stimulated his thinking towards the formulation of the cultural-historical theory. An example would be the writings by Petrova (1925) and Vnukov (1925) on "primitive" children (see below).

In a paper given in 1929, having first presented Adler's ideas Vygotsky referred extensively to Petrova (1925) and presented the outlines of a cultural-historical conception of defectological issues (Vygotsky, 1929m). Here we will only give the bare outlines of this theory in so far as it is necessary for an understanding of Vygotsky's new understanding of defectological problems, leaving a detailed discussion of the cultural-historical theory for chapter 9.

Vygotsky now reasoned that the problems of "defective" children resulted from a mismatch between their deviant psycho-physiological organization and the available cultural means. For normal children the assimilation or "ingrowing" (*vrastanie*) in their culture would constitute no problem. Studying these children it is difficult to distinguish between their mastering of culture and the maturational processes. For normal children the natural and cultural spheres (*plany*) intertwine and merge, forming a single social-biological sphere of development.

Vygotsky reasoned that for the model child, development can be seen as a process of armament and rearmament (see chapter 9). The child masters different cultural means (arms) only to discard them later on for the mastering of other, more powerful cultural instruments. To him the development of the natural functions (e.g. natural memory) was insignificant and could never fully explain the great differences between adult and child. This view implied that developing children become not more but rather otherwise developed, making use of another set of instruments. Vygotsky, consequently, opposed all diagnostic procedures that were based on a purely quantitative approach.

An example of the use of a cultural instrument would be the counting procedures we use. When asked to state which of two groups contains more objects, instead of assessing the amounts directly, we start an elaborate counting procedure. This intermediate operation can take various forms, e.g. one can use one's fingers or count mentally, but always involves cultural, roundabout ways of reaching the goal (1928ab, pp. 166–7).

All cultural instruments, sign and tool alike, are fundamentally societal or social means (1928ab, p. 166). They originated in the history of mankind as the product of living together in groups and will have to be mastered again by each child in social interaction. In a way, Vygotsky reasoned, these techniques are directed at controlling our own behavior, like tools are destined to control nature. The most important cultural tool is speech and, therefore, the fate of the child's whole cultural development depends on whether he or she masters the word as the main psychological tool (1929m, p. 26).

Vygotsky's combination of the idea of mastering tools with the idea of the social origin of higher psychological functions relies on Janet's law that psychological functions appear twice in the life of a subject: first, as an interpersonal function, then as an intrapersonal function (Vygotsky, 1931g, p. 197). His favorite example to illustrate this was that of speech, which first serves an interpersonal, communicative function and then starts to be used as an intrapersonal instrument of thinking (1931g, pp. 198–202). Tools, therefore, can be called social in two senses: they were developed in the history of mankind by groups of collaborating people and they have to be mastered by each individual child again in a process of social interaction. This reasoning led Vygotsky to conclude that

> The development of higher psychological functions is only possible along the roads of their cultural development, whether it proceeds along the line of the mastering of external cultural means (speech, writing, arithmetic) or along the line of internally making perfect the psychological functions themselves (elaboration of voluntary attention, logical memory, abstract thinking, concept-formation, freedom of will, etcetera). (1928ab, p. 173)

The distinction between a natural line of development and a cultural line of mastering socially originated instruments seemed to be confirmed by the examples of children who had difficulties in mastering culture. One result of not having "ingrown" sufficiently into human culture was the case of "child primitivism", a concept which, according to Vygotsky, met with no resistance at that time, although he acknowledged that it was somewhat contentious. To Vygotsky a child-primitive (*rebenok-primitiv*) was a child that did not go through his or her cultural development, or, to be more precise, found him- or herself on the very lowest rungs of cultural development.

The notion of the child-primitive was taken from various studies of that time, notably one by Petrova (1925). Petrova – who in her turn took inspiration from the well-known studies done by Lévy-Bruhl and Thurn-wald (see chapter 9) – had essentially done with children what Luria would do six years later with Uzbek peasants. She had presented the children with syllogisms, used the method of free association, and had asked the children to find common properties between several objects, to give the generic name for them, etcetera. On the basis of this approach she distinguished between primitive and non-primitive children (Petrova, 1925, p. 60). Primitive children reacted in much the same way as Luria's subjects, that is, they refused to draw conclusions from premises describing situations they did not know personally, judged from their own limited experience, and they gave "poor," concrete definitions of objects; in general they knew very little of the world. For Petrova this type of primitivism or *nekul'turnost* was especially prevalent among the peasantry who, more than others, had suffered from the feudal system (1925, p. 63). Discussing the answers of several children in great detail she concluded that primitivism was in itself not necessarily tied to a low degree of giftedness – indeed, it sometimes manifested with high intelligence – and could be overcome by the right type of education (1925, p. 91). From this description it can be seen that Petrova used "primitive" in the sense of "uneducated." Children without the benefit of a good education would reason poorly, give insufficiently sophisticated answers, lack important cultural knowledge, in other words, would be "primitive."

This reasoning was in line with Vygotsky's ideas and he praised Petrova for her fascinating study. What he particularly liked was the distinction between feeble-mindedness and primitivism, taking them as reflecting the natural and cultural lines of development. The child-primitive was perfectly healthy and in this respect differed from the feeble-minded. Feeble-mindedness Vygotsky considered to be the result of an organic defect that hindered natural intellectual development and consequently prevented cultural development. The natural development of the child-primitive might have been quite normal, only he or she stayed outside cultural development. Gradually he would elaborate this conception, pointing out the need for distinguishing between the primary (natural) and secondary (cultural) results of organic defects (Vygotsky, 1931f, p. 3).

If feeble-mindedness and primitivism are different categories with quite different prognoses, then we should try to differentiate between them using the right diagnostic techniques. It may be true, Vygotsky said (1929m, p. 25), that generally primitivism and feeble-mindedness go together, or better, that feeble-mindedness causes primitivism. Nevertheless, they remain two different phenomena – primitivism can exist without organic defects and defects will not automatically cause primitivism – that should be carefully distinguished.

In general Vygotsky saw primitivism as the inability to use certain cultural tools. Petrova's subjects, consequently, constituted exemples of isolated (partially) natural development. The subject who, when presented with a syllogism, would not decide an answer on the basis of words alone demonstrated that she was capable of using words as a means of communication but not as a means of thinking. She was, therefore, blocked in her cultural development and in need of special education (Vygotsky 1929y, p. 147).

The children with some organic defect constituted a much more serious case. For these children the process of assimilating into human culture was quite different, there was no easy merging of the natural and cultural lines of development. Taking an idea from Krünegel (1926), Vygotsky stated that the defective child was not congruous with the structure of the existing cultural forms. This was understandably so, because human culture was created under the conditions of a more or less stable biological type and therefore, its material tools and adjustments, its social-psychological apparatuses and institutes were adapted to their normal psycho-physiological organization (1928ab, p. 170; 1929m, p. 22). The defect, calling for a more or less complete reorganization of the child's mind, ruined the process of assimilating into human culture. Vygotsky reasoned that the blind and deaf–mute constituted, as it were, an experiment of nature showing that the cultural development of behavior was not necessarily tied to one or the other organic function (1928ab, p. 171; 1929j, p. 334). This natural experiment enabled us to see the conventionality and flexibility of the cultural forms of behavior (1928ab, p. 172).

If the distinction between primitivism as cultural subdevelopment and dysfunctioning as the result of an organic defect is valid, then we need fine-tuned instruments to make the right diagnosis. Vygotsky considered quantative method's like Binet's to be insufficient (Vygotsky, 1928ah, p. 175; 1929y, pp. 144–8), but he was very interested in various studies of that time investigating children's ability to use tools. He mentioned favorably the work done by Bacher (1925), who – using Ach's concept-formation method (see below and chapter 11) – had investigated children's ability to use words as instruments for the elaboration of concepts (Vygotsky, 1928ah, p. 176) and the work done by Lippman and Bogen (1923) applying Köhler's method (see chapter 9) to the study of retarded children (Vygotsky, 1929y, p. 146).

The consequences of these new ideas for Vygotsky's treatment of more specific defectological issues were actually rather modest. He now claimed that the potential for the development for defective children should be sought in the area of higher psychological functions (1931f, pp. 4–6), arguing that the lower functions are less educable, because they more directly depend on organic factors. Because the higher functions develop in social interaction through the use of cultural means, we should concentrate our efforts on adjusting these means to the different needs of defective children. A defect does not automatically lead to higher psychological dysfunctioning but this occurs through the intermediary of the collective (tools) that we can manipulate. Primitivism can therefore be corrected by teaching children the use of specially designed means, such as the Braille script and sign language (1928ab, p. 173; 1929m, pp. 24–9). Referring to Eliasberg, Vygotsky also argued that the special schools should not restrict their efforts to the teaching of simple skills relying on teaching with visual aids, but should also try to teach the children the beginnings of abstract thinking (1929m, p. 33; 1929y, p. 149). The compensation for an organic defect was to be found in the learning of concepts acquired in the collective (1928ah, p. 177; 1931f, p. 11). Of course, these views to a great extent only reiterated Vygotsky's earlier point of view that defects had to be overcome by the word.

In addition, Vygotsky's introduction of various cultural-historical points of view such as the natural and cultural line of development and primitivism, was not at all clear and proved to be controversial. The concept of primitivism implied a reference to an evolutionary point of view of human culture, which not everybody was ready to accept (see chapters 9 and 16). Furthermore, it was not clear what Vygotsky's point of view was about the relation between natural and cultural development and how they were to be defined: in one paper he stated that the deaf child left to itself would never learn to speak, but a page later he claimed that the child left to itself, even without any education, would spontaneously enter the road towards cultural development (1928ab, pp. 171–2). This latter seemed in clear contradiction with his new emphasis on restructuring, "feed-back" effects of the mastering of cultural instruments. Arguing for the profound effects mastery of cultural tools would have on the natural functions of the child, he claimed that their old, natural ways of thinking would be pushed aside and destroyed. There, thus, was a "deep conflict" and no smooth transition between the natural and cultural line of development (1928ab, p. 169). It is clear, therefore, that Vygotsky's view at this time was not without its loose ends and contradictions (see also chapter 9).

There was one minor idea in this period of Vygotsky's writings that deserves some attention: the idea of mixed-level groups as a condition promoting cognitive development. Referring to a study by Krasussky which had shown that when left to themselves retarded children formed groups of mixed intelligence, Vygotsky concluded that the feeble-minded find their "living source of development" in social interaction with others who are on a higher level than themselves. "This diversity of intellectual levels forms an important condition of the collective activity," he concluded (1931f, pp. 7–9). This idea anticipates the concept of the zone of proximal development as traditionally understood (see chapter 13).

The Final Period: The Turn to Clinical Psychology

In the final period of his life Vygotsky became increasingly interested in and knowledgable of the domain of deviant adult behavior. He read widely in the field of psychiatry and clinical psychology and his topics of interest now came to include, among other things, the study of aphasia, schizophrenia, Alzheimer's disease, Parkinson's disease, and Pick's disease. His preferred authors were, among others, Head, Kretschmer, and Lewin. Of course, Vygotsky's writings in this field do not fall under the heading of defectology. Nevertheless, some of them are mentioned here. The reason is that Vygotsky's work in the domain of clinical psychology was intimately connected with his developmental studies. Seen against this background all classifications of his work as "defectological," "paedological," "psychological," "pedagogical" etcetera, are relative: he was a synthetic thinker who defies such classifications.

Vygotsky's first excursion into the discipline of clinical psychology of adults was probably his study of schizophrenia with the help of Ach's method of studying concept-formation (this study will be discussed in chapter 11 in connection with his concept-formation research). Suffice it to say here that Vygotsky discerned dynamic similarities between the developing conceptual thinking of children and the disintegrating conceptual thought of schizophrenics. The key to understanding both children and adult patients he considered to be the study of word meanings.

The topic of word-meaning recurred in the study of Pick's disease published in 1934 (Samukhin, Birenbaum, and Vygotsky, 1934). This study was untypical of Vygotsky, because of its wealth of clinical facts: two patients suffering from Pick's disease (a form of dementia) were described in detail. The article gave their full life-history, details of the progression of their disease, answers to the psychologist's questions and tests, etcetera. The authors attempted to find the rationale behind all the patients' symptoms and in doing so relied heavily on Kurt Lewin's notions of field dependence, *Aufforderungscharacter*, and the like (see chapter 8). In general, in this period of his life — between 1932 and 1934 — Vygotsky drew on Lewin's work quite frequently, possibly because of his close collaboration with

Lewin's former pupils, Zeigarnik and Birenbaum (see the introduction to part III).

Conclusion

It has been shown that Vygotsky's defectological writings formed an important and integral part of his whole theoretical approach, and as such they reflected the several changes that his thinking underwent. Of course, many of Vygotsky's ideas were far from original. He was both following in the footsteps of experts in the field of "defectology" from the past and dependent on the views that were characteristic of his time.

His pedagogical optimism regarding the development of blind and deaf children may serve as an illustration. On the one hand, Vygotsky was clearly defending the view that the possibly harmful effects of a physical defect such as blindness or deafness could be fully overcome by creating alternative but equivalent roads for cultural development. Blind and deaf subjects had a potential for normal mental development – they might, perhaps, be seen as variations and not as aberrations of the human blueprint – and it was possible for them to become valued and fully integrated members of our society.

In defending this view Vygotsky was pursuing an ancient and respected tradition. Plato, after observing deaf people, had remarked in *Cratylus* that meaning could be signified by the hands, head, and other parts of the body. Diderot (1749/1972) in his famous *Letter about the Blind* underlined the normal potential for mental development of blind–deaf children and suggested that it should be possible to teach them language "if one would trace on their hands the same characters that we trace on the paper." Diderot's contemporaries De l'Epeé and the philosopher Condillac became convinced that deaf children could be effectively taught sign language. In the nineteenth century this idea had grown into a general conviction and Sicard, the great reformer of the education of the deaf, emphasized that the chief problem for deaf children is their lack of "symbols for fixing and combining ideas . . . that there is a total communication gap between him and other people" (quoted by Sacks, 1989, p. 15). In Sicard's view the teaching of sign language would restore the communication gap and enable the deaf child to lead a completely normal and fulfilling life.

Thus, the possibility of cultural development, via sign language for the deaf and tactile language for the blind, had been foreseen by several brilliant thinkers of the past and is now generally accepted by modern research. Some of Vygotsky's eminent precursors also claimed that such alternative routes were equivalent to our normal spoken language. In this sense, then,

Vygotsky was following in the footsteps of several visionary thinkers of the past.

The same is true for Vygotsky's utopian view of a society where deaf and blind people would be fully integrated and where their "defect" would not be seen as such. This view, anticipated by Sicard, fell from favour by the end of the nineteenth century but is once more being passionately defended by researchers such as Sacks (1989). Sicard's own words (quoted from Lane, 1984, pp. 89–90) illustrate the continuity of this idea:

> Could there not be in some corner of the world a whole society of deaf people? Well then! Would we think that these individuals were inferior, that they were unintelligent and lacked communication? They would certainly have a sign language, perhaps a language even richer than ours.

Clearly, then, Vygotsky's pedagogical optimism formed part of a powerful tradition in European thinking. This tradition could be easily combined with the prevailing Soviet ideology of the plasticity of human beings and the idea of the "new man."

On the other hand, his ideas were, of course, peculiar to his own time. For example, whilst defending the principal equivalence of different routes towards cultural development, Vygotsky nevertheless was opposed to teaching deaf children (only) sign language and advocated the teaching of oral speech, reasoning that sign language would not allow the child to develop conceptual, higher forms of thinking. At the time this was a generally held view. Recently, modern researchers have claimed that a sign language such as American Sign Language (ASL) has all the properties of normal oral speech and will in no way disadvantage the child learning it. Children learning ASL would reach the same level of conceptual thinking as children learning vocal speech (Sacks, 1989, p. 20). This would imply that the years of very difficult training that the task of learning oral speech for deaf children entails would only serve the goal of enhancing the questionable possibilities of integration in the "normal" society.

In conclusion we may say that Vygotsky's defectological work formed an integral part of his thinking in other domains and underwent the same theoretical evolution. Unfortunately, his defectological writings were of a rather general nature and a composite picture of Vygotsky as clinical practitioner cannot be reconstructed. In general, however, it seems that his theoretical views – such as the cultural-historical approach (see chapter 9) – did not result in innovations in clinical practice. However, they did encourage a view of deviant (child) development from a certain – optimistic – perspective and as such formed part of a similar, long-standing tradition in European thinking.

5

The Role of Psychoanalysis

Few scientists have stirred the imagination of both scientists and laymen as Freud did. For a time, the topic of the Oedipus and Electra complexes dominated civilized conversation throughout Europe. The Russian intelligentsia was no exception to this and practically all of Freud's books were swiftly translated into Russian. However, after 1930 psychoanalysis became a *scientia non grata* in the Soviet Union and Freud's books turned into bibliographic rarities for which the interested Soviet intellectual happily paid (even in 1990) the equivalent of a month's salary. The emergence of the psychoanalytic movement in Russia, its demise in the 1930s, and its partial resurrection in the 1980s is one of the tragi-comic stories of Russian intellectual history (the first part of which has recently been described by Miller, 1986, 1990; Kätzel, 1987 and Angelini, 1988).

Psychoanalysis in the Soviet Union: The First Years

Russian interest in psychoanalytic theory first became evident around 1908, when several psychiatrists and physicians in both Moscow and Odessa started to study and popularize Freud's work. The pioneers of the psychoanalytic movement were N. E. Osipov, M. O. Feltsmann, N. A. Vyborov, and M. Wulff (Luria, 1925c). Osipov had been studying in Switzerland under the direction of Carl Jung and had visited Freud in Vienna, corresponding with him for a long time (Miller, 1986, p. 126). Together with Feltsmann he published a series of books in Moscow, entitled "The Psychotherapeutic Library," which included translations of Freud's *Three Essays on the Theory of Sexuality*; *Five Lectures on Psychoanalysis*; *On Dreams*; and *The Analysis of a Phobia in a Five-Year-Old Boy*. Wulff, later the President of the Russian Psychoanalytic Society, returned to his native Odessa at that time having finished his medical studies and an analysis with Karl Abraham in Berlin (Miller, 1986, p. 126). He also published a series of psychoanalytic books, including, among other things, Freud's *Gradiva*. In the following years several more of Freud's books, including *The Interpretation of Dreams*, were translated and Vyborov published many translations of articles by Freud, Jung, and Adler in *Psychotherapy*, the journal he edited. Other prominent Russian psychoanalysts have been mentioned by Miller (1986), including Drosnes, who referred one of his patients (later to be known in the scientific literature as "the wolfman") to Freud for analysis and Sabina Shpil'rejn, whose remarkable career we will summarize below.

After the revolution and the civil war the interest in Freudian theory revived and in various parts of the country psychoanalytic discussion groups and societies were founded. For our purpose the history of the Moscow Psychoanalytic Society and the Kazan Psychoanalytic Society is the most interesting. Luria took an active part in both of these societies and it is no exaggeration to say that the institutional history of psychoanalysis in the Soviet Union was to a substantial degree determined by his efforts. In the following a first and still incomplete description of the activity of the two societies will be given.

The Kazan Psychoanalytic Society: Luria's Venture into Psychoanalysis

The history of the Kazan Psychoanalytic Society is, to a large extent, the history of Luria's early involvement in Freudian theory. Having graduated in 1921 with a degree based mainly on the biological and social sciences, Luria founded the Kazan Psychoanalytic Society (or Circle) in the late summer of 1922. The twenty-year-old Luria took the liberty of informing Freud about this major event in psychological history and – much to his surprise – received a kind reply (Luria, 1979, p. 24). From 1921 to 1923 Luria completed his formal schooling at both the Kazan Medical and Pedagogical Institutes, while at the same time directing his psychoanalytic discussion group.

The activities of the Kazan Psychoanalytic Society can be substantially reconstructed. Luria mentioned part of his psychoanalytic activities in his scientific autobiography, revealing, for instance, that in these early years the members of the Society analyzed patients in the psychiatric clinic in Kazan, one of whom appeared to be Dostoevsky's granddaughter (Luria, 1979, p. 24; 1982, p. 11). Acting as the Secretary of the Society Luria made meticulous notes of the meetings, which can still be consulted in the archives of the Luria family. Also he immediately started sending short reports on the activities of the Society to the *Internationale Zeitschrift für Psychoanalyse*, the journal founded and edited by Freud. Each issue of this journal contained a section "About the psychoanalytic movement" (*Zur psychoanalytischen Bewegung*), which published short accounts of the activities of psychoanalysts in various countries, written by the local representatives of the movement. In 1922 the journal received a note stating that a psychoanalytic society in Kazan had been founded (Luria, 1922a). Its author – probably Luria – promised to send a report of the first meetings of the society. This brief announcement meant the beginning of Luria's long affiliation with the journal, first as the secretary of the Kazan Society, later as the secretary of its counterpart in Moscow.

From the archives we learn that the Society met 17 times between September 7, 1922 and September 4, 1923 and that the number of people present at the meetings varied from six to 12 people. The majority (15) of the 20 members of the Society were medical doctors, some of them students, Luria himself being practically the only person with some training as a social scientist. A substantial number of the circle's members were Jewish, which is hardly surprising in view of the fact that Kazan at the time was one of the principal Jewish towns outside the Pale, and in view of the fact that the medical profession was one of the few intellectual professions open to Jews. In general, Luria was the principal driving force of the Society, acting as its secretary, taking minutes during the meetings, and delivering half a dozen talks. It will be of some interest to present a short summary of some of the society's meetings. This will bring out the degree of Luria's involvement in the psychoanalytic movement more clearly and will give us an impression of the type of research that was practiced.

Luria's first account for the *Internationale Zeitschrift für Psychoanalyse* of the activities of the society (Luria, 1922b) was very typical of the many reports to follow: it stated with meticulous attention to detail the exact dates of the presentations given, their subject, the names of the speakers and of those who joined the discussion, the names of the people attending the meeting, etc. We thus learn that in the first meeting, on September 7, 1922, Luria gave an address on the "Present state of psychoanalysis," stating that it was now already a classic approach to the study of personality. At the same meeting R. Averbukh gave a rather doubtful talk on the behavior of an arrested professor, who (following the appeal by the patriarch Tikhon) had resisted the attempts by the authorities to confiscate church properties. On the flimsy basis of an article in *Pravda* the accused's defense during the trial was interpreted as betraying his personal sexual preoccupations.

During the second meeting, on October 21, 1922, Luria gave a talk on the psychoanalysis of the way people dress, arguing that women's clothing represents passive sexual motives, whilst men's dress represents active ones, a subject he was to return to in January, 1923 at the All-Russian Congress on Psychoneurology in Moscow (Luria, 1923c, p. 114). But before the young Luria made this trip to the capital the Kazan Psychoanalytic Society had several more meetings on November 2 and 23, December 10 and 24, 1922 (Luria, 1923c). During the meeting on December 10, Luria again delivered a speech, this time on "the present currents in Russian psychology." Distinguishing five different schools he put special emphasis on the ideas of the reflexological school of Bekhterev, which were "close to those of psychoanalysis." This meeting was also of interest, because it saw the first appearance of B. D. Fridman, who was to play a prominent role both in the Kazan Society and in the attempts to found a Freudo-Marxist psychology later on.

After two more meetings, on January 21, and February 4, 1923, Luria again gave two talks during a meeting on February 18. He first talked about "some principles of psychoanalysis," claiming that psychoanalysis was teleological rather than mechanistic, that it gave an explanation rather than a description of behavior, and that it was firmly based on an organic, biological explanation of psychological processes. In his second presentation he gave a psychoanalytic interpretation of Leonid Andreev's play *Savva*.

The Kazan Psychoanalytic Society now met practically every two weeks (Luria, 1923d). On March 5, Luria gave a talk, entitled "Psychoanalysis in the light of the main tendencies of modern psychology," giving an overview of the psychological currents akin to psychoanalysis, such as functional psychology, behaviorism, English neo-Freudism, and Russian reflexology. Surprisingly, in his view all these currents tried to study man as a whole and gave attention to his drives and reflexes. The 50 pages of the text of this lecture constituted the first publication of the society's publishing house, the second was to be an authorized translation of Freud's *Mass Psychology and Ego Analysis* (Luria, 1923e). On March 18, Luria argued that the phantasies one has just before falling asleep – when conscious control has weakened, but full sleep and dreaming have not yet set in – are of some importance. Reflecting the unconscious mental machinery, these phantasies can nevertheless be successfully analyzed by the person him- or herself. The next meetings of the society were on April 22 and 29, and on May 6 and May 31. The latter meeting is of some interest as it was fully devoted to the discussion of the writings of the Russian novelist and philosopher V. V. Rozanov – whose ideas seem to have been rather close to those of Freud.

To the best of our knowledge the seventeenth meeting of the Society, on September 7, 1923, was the last – it is the last to be documented in the Luria archives – since by the end of the year Luria and several of his most active colleagues had moved to Moscow. This did not mean the end of Luria's activities in the psychoanalytic movement, however. Working at Kornilov's Institute of Experimental Psychology he was soon performing exactly the same organizational role in the Russian Psychoanalytic Society in Moscow.

The Russian Psychoanalytic Society

The Russian Psychoanalytic Society had been founded several years earlier, in 1921, by Ermakov and Wulff. The first mention of its existence was made in an announcement sent to the *Internationale Zeitschrift für Psychoanalyse* (1922, pp. 236–7) by a Soviet correspondent whose name was not mentioned, possibly Ermakov. It stated the intention of a group of scientists in Moscow formally to found a psychoanalytic society. The Society was to be the beginning of a broad psychoanalytic movement in the Soviet Union. Fortunately for the historian of science the anonymous correspondent listed the 15 people who had thus far joined the society. It included the names of several prominent scientists, some of whom were to play a major role in the psychoanalytic movement. Thus, we find several of Vygotsky's future colleagues at the Institute of Experimental Psychology, such as Bernshtein, then professor of psychiatry and head of the Psychoneurological Institute in Moscow, and Blonsky, then professor of psychology and pedagogics. We also find Gabrichevsky, professor of the history of art and aesthetics, Il'yin, professor of philosophy and psychology, and the Schmidts. The latter couple were to play a prominent role in the Soviet psychoanalytic movement. Otto Schmidt was a professor of mathematics and, more importantly, head of the State Publishing House. His wife, Vera, was to run a psychoanalytic kindergarten (see below). Finally, there were the names of the founders, Ermakov and Wulff. Ermakov, a professor of psychiatry, was the first president of the Society. Moshe Wulff, a medical doctor, would later be the president and was at the same time a prolific translator of Freud's books. In 1927 he emigrated to Palestine where his archives can still be found (Miller, 1986, p. 126). The same report states that the State Publishing House had decided to institute a special section for psychoanalytic literature in view of the great demand for Freud's writings from both specialists and laymen. The editors of this section were Ermakov and Wulff.

The Society apparently flourished, and soon it was divided into two sections, one, headed by Wulff, dealing with medical problems, the other, headed by Shatsky, "one of the most prominent pedagogues of Russia" dealing with pedagogical problems (see Luria, 1923f). The first volume of Freud's lectures, translated by Wulff, had sold out its 2,000 copies within one month, a second volume had just been published, and several volumes were in preparation. Another indication of the growing popularity of Freudian thinking is the fact that at the All-Russian Congress for Psychoneurology in Moscow (January 10–15, 1923) 11 of the presentations started from psychoanalytic assumptions. One of them was Luria's talk on the psychoanalysis of clothing mentioned before.

In the Fall of 1923 the Russian Psychoanalytic Society underwent several important changes, a detailed account of which has been given by Luria (1924a) – already the secretary – for the *Internationale Zeitschrift für Psychoanalyse*. First, the society was joined by several new and capable members: three of the most active participants in the Kazan Psychoanalytic Society moved to Moscow and became members of the Society. These were Luria himself, R. Averbukh and B. D. Fridman. Another new member of the society was Sabina Shpil'rejn, formerly member of the Swiss Psychoanalytic Society. Shpil'rejn – who also started working at Kornilov's Institute of Experimental Psychology – was originally from Rostov-on-the-Don. She went to Vienna in 1911 and became a member of the local Psychoanalytic Society. Having been analyzed by Carl Jung, she spent several years as a practising analyst in Switzerland (Miller, 1986, p. 127). One of her patients was Jean Piaget, who at that time was a member of the Swiss Psychoanalytic Society (cf. Carotenuto, 1984; Vidal, 1986, 1987, 1988a, 1988b). This injection of new blood gave the Society fresh impetus for its activities.

Secondly, the society decided to organize its activities on a more grand scale. Thus far it had:

1   Organized scientific meetings where members delivered lectures and discussed topics of interest.
2   Published a series of books entitled "The Psychological and Psychoanalytic Library." By the end of 1923 six volumes, mostly containing translations of Freud's writings, had been published and nine more were scheduled (cf. Ermakov, 1923).
3   Been involved in the State Psychoanalytic Institute.

This Institute has been founded in the Fall of 1922 and at first involved only a psychoanalytic kindergarten annex laboratory headed by Vera Schmidt, whose goal was to study empirically the behavior of children starting from psychoanalytic premises. The history of this kindergarten is in itself of some interest. It had been opened on August 19, 1921 and was located on the first floor of a magnificent art nouveau building located in 25 Vorovsky Street, Moscow. Earlier this building (designed by Fjodor Shekhtel) had been the property of the banker Ryabushinsky and after the kindergarten had been closed (see below) it became the residence (from

1931 to 1936) of the Soviet writer Maxim Gorky. As the building nowadays houses the Gorky Museum, its beautiful rooms and the location of the psychoanalytic kindergarten can still be seen.

Initially the kindergarten housed thirty children ranging from one to five years' old.[1] But only several months after the kindergarten's opening rumors spread in Moscow that the staff of the kindergarten stimulated the children's sexual development (Schmidt, 1924, p. 4). As a result the authorities ordered a scientific commission of inquiry to investigate the case. After a thorough investigation of several months the votes of the members of the commission were equally divided on the issue. The People's Commissariat for Education (as the Ministry of Education was called then) thereupon decided to cease funding the kindergarten project. Shortly after the Psychoneurological Institute also ordered an inquiry that likewise resulted in a very negative judgement. The kindergarten now lost the support of the Psychoneurological Institute too and would have had to close had it not been for the unexpected assistance offered by a representative of the German Miners' Union. This person happened to be in Moscow for a congress and offered help on behalf of the German and Russian Miners' Unions. From April 1922, then, the German miners provided the kindergarten's food supplies, while the Russian miners took care of the heating of the building. This odd history explains the otherwise incomprehensible name of the kindergarten, "International Solidarity." In the new and financially more constrained situation the kindergarten had to fire some of the personnel and could only afford to take care of 12 children between two and four years of age (Schmidt, 1924, pp. 3–6). The kindergarten project kept meeting with disapproval and was finally closed in 1928 (Miller, 1986, p. 131).

During the early 1920s the personnel of the laboratory observed the behavior of the children, paying close attention to their play, speech, and sexual inclinations. Part of the findings have been published by Vera Schmidt in *Psychoanalytische Erziehung in Sowjetrussland* (1924), but Luria (1925c) claimed that the greater part of them were still in the archives of the Institute. Among them diaries with observations of every individual child noting their language development, creativity etcetera.

By 1923 it was decided that the Institute should broaden its activities considerably. The Institute started to function as an educational center, organizing many courses and seminars on different levels and for different groups of students. Luria, for instance, gave a seminar on the study of complexes. In addition a Psychoanalytic Policlinic for both adults and

[1]Jaroshevsky (1989, p. 131) has claimed that Stalin's son Vasily was among these children. The authors have not been able to check this far-fetched claim.

children, headed by Ermakov (the president), Shpil'rejn, and Wulff, was instituted. The administration of both the Society and the Institute was in the hands of these three, together with Luria (secretary to the chairman) and Otto Schmidt. Quite probably, the members of the Society also started meeting on a more regular basis.

In the following years it would be Luria who would cover these meetings for the *Internationale Zeitschrift für Psychoanalyse*. These reports (see also Ermakov, 1924) enable us to reconstruct the Society's activities reasonably accurately as was the case for the Kazan society. It is interesting to see, for instance, how the Russian Psychoanalytic Society used the opportunity to establish and improve its international contacts. Thus, at the meeting of October 18, 1923 the Schmidts presented the things they learned during a trip to Germany and Austria (Luria, 1924a). Apparently, they had met Freud, Otto Rank, and Karl Abraham, all of whom had shown a lively interest in the Moscow kindergarten project and had given practical advice. The reports also show Luria's continuing involvement: he not only performed his duties as the society's secretary but also frequently participated in the discussion (the Society met about every two weeks) and presented various talks. It was on May 29, 1924 (see Luria, 1925a; 1926b), for instance, that he gave a talk, entitled "Psychoanalysis as a system of monistic psychology," later to be published in Kornilov (1925a). This talk was very typical of his thinking of the time and, as such, would be criticized by Bakhtin (see below).

Recurrent subjects of the society had been the psychology of art, the possibility of a psychoanalytic upbringing, and problems of psychotherapy (Luria, 1925c, p. 396). This interest in the psychology of art – directly inspired, of course, by Freud's own writings – led to several talks at the meetings of the society and to a seminar at the Psychoanalytic Institute given by Ermakov. Against this background it should come as no surprise to find an invited speaker on this subject present during the meeting on December 4, 1924. It was Luria's colleague at the Institute of Experimental Psychology, Lev Vygotsky, who talked about "the use of the psychoanalytic method in literature" (Luria, 1925b), probably raising the same issues he discussed in chapter 4 of *The Psychology of Art*. Vygotsky may have been invited by Luria, who was of course well aware of the ideas of his colleagues, but this is not certain. In general, one should realize that there was a substantial overlap between the people working at Kornilov's Institute of Experimental Psychology on the one hand, and those involved in the Russian Psychoanalytic Society and the Psychoanalytic Institute on the other hand. Looking through the names of the people working at Kornilov's Institute in 1924 (see Luria in Kornilov, 1926a), for instance, one finds that at least eight of them had been members of the Russian Psychoanalytic Society at one time or another. It is important to note, however, that at the time of his first presentation (see Luria, 1925d) Vygotsky was not a member, but a guest.

In 1925 Luria presented three talks. On March 26, he discussed "The affect as a non-abreacted reaction", on April 16, he talked about the "Experimental study of the phantasies of a boy" (Luria, 1926b), and on November 12, on "The use of experiments for psychoanalytic goals" (Luria, 1926c).

In 1926 he actively participated in the discussions, performed his duties as a scientific secretary, but gave no talks. It was probably by the end of that year that Lev Vygotsky became an ordinary member of the Russian Psychoanalytic Society, judging by the membership list published in the *Internationale Zeitschrift für Psychoanalyse* in 1927 (see Luria, 1927a) that included for the first time Lev Vygotsky, 17 Serpukhovskaya Street, Moscow.

By 1927, then, both Luria and Vygotsky were participating in the Society. Luria's talk on February 23, 1927 on "The experimental study of children's primitive thinking" was followed by Vygotsky's presentation on "The psychology of art in Freud's writings" on March 10 of the same year. The following week, on March 17, Luria continued with a discussion of Bykhovsky's book on Freud's metapsychology. One month later, however, he asked to be relieved of his duties as a secretary, and was replaced by Vera Schmidt (Schmidt, 1927). According to Cole (in Luria, 1979, pp. 210–11), this step was the result of the increasingly critical attitude towards Freud in articles in both *Pravda* and theoretical journals. This interpretation is doubtful, however. In the first place Luria continued to be an ordinary member of the society until 1929 or 1930. Secondly, really strong ideological and political pressure started only around 1930. Articles and books critical of Freudian theory published before that year (e.g. Jurinets, 1925; Sapir, 1926; Bakhtin, 1927/1983) formed part of the ordinary scientific discourse. Thirdly, Vygotsky's becoming a member of the society at approximately the same time Luria resigned as a secretary seems to cast doubt on Cole's assessment of the situation.

Luria the Psychoanalyst: 1920–1930

By now it has become clear that Luria's early fascination with the writings of Freud, Adler, and Jung – facilitated by the fact that he was fluent in German (Vocate, 1987, p. 5) – led to a prolonged period of intense involvement with Freudian theory and the psychoanalytic movement. In fact, it is no exaggeration to say that Luria played one of the most prominent roles in the growth of the psychoanalytic movement in the Soviet Union. Through his work as a secretary of both societies, through the frequent talks on psychoanalytic topics, and through the reports he wrote for the *Internationale Zeitschrift für Psychoanalyse* he promoted psychoanalytic ideas in his country and helped to establish important international contacts. Apart from these reports he also published several reviews (Luria, 1923a; 1923b) and on two occasions more theoretical articles (Luria, 1925c; 1926a) in the same journal.

The young Luria also continued corresponding with Freud for some time and even managed to obtain Freud's authorization for R. A. Averbakh's translation of *Mass Psychology and Ego Analysis* in a letter dated October 6, 1922 written from Berggasse 19, Vienna. One year later he received yet another letter (dated July 3, 1923 and written from Badgastein in the Alps) from the founder of psychoanalysis. Both of these handwritten letters – not written in Gothic script as Luria remembered half a century later (1979, p. 24; 1982, p. 11) – can be found in the Luria family archives. It is not inconceivable, of course, that an interested reader might likewise find Luria's letters in the Freud archives.

It would be wrong, however, to think that Luria was only theoretically and organizationally involved in psychoanalysis. There was a more practical side to his interest too. At the Kazan Psychiatric Hospital he started analyzing psychiatric patients, an activity that probably did not come to an end in Moscow. In addition to his activities as a therapist he performed intriguing empirical psychoanalytic investigations, some of which have been reported on in his *The Nature of Human Conflicts* (Luria, 1932c). Very curious, for instance, was his experimental verification of Freud's dream theory. Luria would hypnotize subjects, make them live in their imagination through a traumatic event, and suggest to them they forget all about the hypnosis as far as their conscious mind was concerned. In this way he could experimentally manipulate the latent content of dreams and – having collected their manifest forms – establish the changes produced by the dream-work. It was found that if one suggests to subjects they dream about very traumatic events (the latent content of the dream) they tend to change the description of these events (the manifest content) through the use of symbolism.[2] The British psychologist Hans Eysenck (1985, pp. 129–31) tried to replicate these experiments and found exactly the same results, without seeing them, however, as any evidence for the validity of Freud's theory.

---

[2]Luria seems to have been unaware of Klaus Schrötter's similar experiments, which antici-pated his own by some 20 years (see Hobson, 1990 p. 55).

Looking back, Luria first and foremost remembered that psychoanalysis seemed "a scientific approach that combined a strongly deterministic explanation of concrete, individual behavior with an explanation of the origins of complex human needs in terms of natural science" (1979, pp. 23–4). However, he finally had to conclude "that it was an error to assume that one can deduce human behavior from the biological 'depths' of mind, excluding its social 'heights.' " We now know that it took him approximately a decade to reach this conclusion.

We may conclude that Luria's involvement in the psychoanalytic movement lasted for approximately ten years, an involvement that led him to analyze patients, conduct experimental research, give presentations, write articles and books, and in general play a very active organizational role in the psychoanalytic movement. One can hardly say, therefore, that this period in Luria's scientific development is of little significance. It would be wrong, also, to suppose that Luria's interest in psychoanalytic theory disappeared without trace after 1930. For instance Mecacci, a scholar of Luria, has argued that Luria's way of diagnosing individual patients was strongly influenced by his clinical psychoanalytic experience (Mecacci, personal communication, September 1988).

From Luria to Vygotsky and Further: The Growing Criticism of Freudo-Marxism

To this point, the content of Luria's views and their development during the 1920s has not been discussed. The development in his thinking cannot be separated from the discussions in Soviet psychology about the correct foundation for a Marxist psychology and the role of psychoanalytic theory in it. The potential compatibility between a Marxist psychology and psychoanalysis was not on the agenda until 1924 to 1925, when the ever-increasing interest in it began to peak around 1930. Kätzel (1987, pp. 108–9) has suggested several reasons for the growing criticism of Freudian theory and attempts at a Freudo-Marxism in the Soviet Union. First, one should realize that the first attempts at formulating a Freudo-Marxist blend of theory (by Bykhovsky, 1923; Luria, 1923e; 1925a; and Fridman, 1925) emphasized firm physiological underpinning of psychoanalysis and its compatibility with objective psychology (e.g. reflexology). These psychologists felt that psychoanalytic theory, therefore, could justifiably be called a materialist theory. Outlining their points of view they propagated what was later to be known as "mechanical materialism," an ideology that came under attack in the second half of the 1920s. Secondly, there was a development in the nature of Freud's writings itself which made a confrontation with Marxist-oriented thinkers inevitable. In several of his later writings, e.g. *Mass Psychology and Ego Analysis*, Freud claimed that the social behavior of man could be understood by reference to biological drives and instincts. Other writings, such as *Beyond the Pleasure Principle*, showed the influence of the philosophy of life (see Kätzel, 1987). Taken together, these later books claimed that societal problems were caused by the nature of man, a claim that ran counter to the optimistic claims being made by leading Soviet ideologists and intellectuals of the time about the new man in the new society. Thirdly, Kätzel points to an "inflation" of psychoanalytic thinking in the 1920s. Psychoanalysts, or people claiming to have a good knowledge of psychoanalytic theory, increasingly tried to explain the most widely varying phenomena with ever more bold speculations. In so doing they displayed an "imperialistic" approach that naturally elicited reactions from researchers otherwise oriented (see also Vygotsky's reasoning to be discussed in chapter 7). Fourthly, several ideologues of the social democratic movement (see Kätzel, 1987) had embraced Freudian theory, which, in the context of the time, meant that a bona fide communist should regard it with some suspicion. Fifthly, the popularity of psychoanalysis was not confined to a small group of enthusiastic physicians; Freudian thinking influenced a growing number of Marxist philosophers and psychologists. This growing influence, actively fostered by the Russian Psychoanalytic Society, made psychoanalysis more "visible" as a psychological science that had to be investigated with respect to its compatibility with a genuine Marxist science.

What, then, were Luria's original theoretical views of psychoanalytic theory in this period and how did he try to combine psychoanalysis with the general Marxist world-view? Let it first be said that there is no such thing as a science of Marxism or psychoanalysis in the sense of a complete body of indisputable statements. On the contrary, the interpretations of various aspects of both world-views abound and even "official" interpretations are subject to regular changes (there are clear parallels here with the establishment of religious dogma, as has been pointed out by, among others, Russell, 1946). Since the beginning of psychoanalysis, psychology has seen many diverse attempts to formulate Freudo-Marxist theories, a situation that continues until the present day. In the West there have been the brilliant writings of Politzer (1969; 1974) and the works of Reich (see below), Fromm, and Marcuse. In the Soviet Union there were the attempts of Bykhovsky, Zalkind, Luria, and various of his colleagues at the Institute of Psychology (e.g. Fridman). Each of these authors made his own blend of various elements of both world-views.

For Luria, as for many others, psychoanalysis was a new promising current opposing the old "idealistic" psychology. That idealistic psychology (e.g. the ideas of Wundt, Chelpanov and others) was naively empirical, made use of contrived experiments, and led to an atomistic and dualistic view of man (Luria, 1925a). Psychoanalysis, however, was monistic, attempted to study the whole personality in the drama of everyday life (cf. Politzer), was refreshingly anti-bourgeois in its emphasis on sexual behavior, and, above all, pointed to the physiological background of all psychological processes. For, while Luria (1925a, p. 50) emphasized that any satisfactory view of man should rest on the findings of both biology and sociology, it is evident that in his opinion a convincing account of the supposedly biological nature of human conduct was the most important. Thus, we read that

> psychoanalysis is primarily an organic psychology of the personality; and its major objectives are: to trace the determining factors of all aspects of the concrete individual, living under definite sociocultural conditions, and to explain the more complex structures of that individual's personality in terms of more basic, deeper lying, unconscious motives. (Luria, 1925a, p. 58)

Luria agreed with psychoanalytic theory that these unconscious motives or drives – like all other psychological functions – depend on organic stimuli. He considered the strength of psychoanalytic theory to be its emphasis on the biological underpinning of all conduct, its "organic character" (Luria, 1925a, p. 68). Psychoanalytic theory points out the "deeper organic tendencies" that the person tends to follow and, in doing so, lays bare the hidden dynamics of human behavior. In a way, then, Freud's theory transforms psychological causality into organic causality (ibid., pp. 70–1). It is true that Luria also mentioned that man is a social or class being and by the end of his article he stated that psychoanalysis should incorporate the system of social influences adding, in a footnote, that only then it would make the step from mechanical to dialectical materialism. This only shows, however, that he was well aware of the subtleties of the on-going debates in the Soviet Union as to the true nature of dialectical materialism. But these remarks cannot take away the impression that the "sociological" aspect of psychological processes was far less integrated in Luria's thinking. Declaring that the social or class nature of individuals was important and conceiving society simply as a conglomerate of external stimuli he went on to study the psychoanalytic – to him biological – background of human conduct. He felt justified in doing so because of the supposedly monistic character of psychoanalytic theory. The energy conception of psychoanalysis, the energy taking either psychic or somatic forms, seemed to demonstrate an essential organic unity. The concept of drive constituted, in Luria's view, "a tremendous step" towards a monistic psychology.

In taking this point of view Luria was hardly original. Kätzel (1987) has pointed out that Bykhovsky (1923) also stressed Freud's quest for an organic foundation of the psyche and his monism. Unlike Luria, however, and in anticipation of Vygotsky, the latter claimed that conscious processes should be studied in their own right. How this was to be done remained unclear. Apparently Bykhovsky thought that a combination of Freudian theory and reactology would suit the purpose.

We may repeat, then, what has been said before: the first defenders of Freudian theory in the Soviet Union (e.g. Luria, Bykhovsky, Fridman, Zalkind) considered this theory to be a healthy antidote against the old "idealistic" psychology, and stressed its compatability with various brands of objective psychology such as behaviorism, reactology and reflexology. As a result, their writings have a definite reductionist flavor: the ultimate explanation of human behavior was to be sought in the deep, biological roots of the mind.

Criticism of Freudo-Marxism: Jurinets' View

One of the first critics of this conception of Freudo-Marxism was Jurinets (1924), a philosopher about whom Luria complained in the *Internationale Zeitschrift für Psychoanalyse* that he was "unfortunately utterly incompetent in the domain of the natural sciences" (1925c, p. 397). Jurinets' criticism of psychoanalysis in the leading theoretical journal *Under the Banner of Marxism* (*Pod Znamenem Marksizma*) led to several public debates in the Soviet Union. In the spring of 1925, during a meeting in the Moscow "House of the Press" that lasted two evenings, Jurinets crossed swords with many adherents of psychoanalytic theory, most of them members of the Russian Psychoanalytic Society (e.g. Wulff, Zalkind, Fridman, Luria, Rejsner). Another debate was soon held in the Communistic Academy and concerned the topic of psychoanalysis and the psychology of art (Luria, 1925c, p. 397).

Jurinets' article was an almost amusing mixture of valid criticism of Freudian theory, (possibly deliberate) distortions, and plain mistakes. The author used various rhetorical devices − not all of them very subtle − to substantiate his claim that the origin of psychoanalysis was yet another token of the continuing disintegration of Western bourgeois society. Thus we read that "Born in Vienna and Budapest, in a country . . . that is flourishing without much effort by trampling on the Croatian, Slovenian, Dalmation, and Serbian peasants who are sucked out to the bone marrow, Freudian theory took much of the spirit of this capitalism" (Jurinets, 1924, p. 52). Jurinets observed that this pernicious doctrine was infiltrating the

"Marxist camp" and suspected that its growing popularity was due to a lack of knowledge and insufficient understanding of its fundamental ideas. He, therefore, set out to explain and criticize the basic tenets of Freudian theory (1924, p. 53).

In the first place, Jurinets argued, Freudian theory is not materialist. Despite his frequent references to the nervous system Freud did not give matter its due role in his system. As an example Jurinets quoted Freud's statement in *Beyond the Pleasure Principle* about the psychological results of severe traumatic experiences (e.g. mechanical concussions, wars). In Freud's view the resulting mental state, called by him traumatic neurosis, often could not be attributed to organic lesions of the nervous system brought about by mechanical force (Freud, 1920/1984, pp. 281–3). To Jurinets this meant that Freud saw mental processes as being independent from brain structures, a view that he could not accept as it seemed to contradict a materialist conception of the mind. In addition he tried to argue that Freud's view of the psyche – a psyche that existed beyond time and space – was similar to Bergson's, making Freud guilty of philosophical idealism by association.

Jurinets went on to argue that Freud's theory was not monistic. Unfortunately, he did not take this term in its ordinary philosophical meaning and, instead, seems to have understood by "monism" something like consistency or coherence. Consequently, he set himself the rather trivial task of pointing out inconsistencies and contradictions in Freudian thinking by comparing books from different periods and texts written by different psychoanalytic authors. In itself it was, of course, quite legitimate to ask how Freud or Freudians would reconcile earlier viewpoints with later revisions – and Jurinets asked some good questions – but these questions were irrelevant to the issue of monism as such. The same could be said of Jurinets' claims that Freud proposed a dualistic theory. It might well be argued that he did, but Jurinets' arguments were largely irrelevant. Among other things, he (Jurinets, 1924, p. 69) argued that Freud distinguished ego drives and sexual drives, which is true, of course, but hardly makes a convincing argument for dualism in the normal philosophical sense of the word.

The weakest point of Freudian theory in Jurinets' eyes was its social psychology or sociology. Freud's theory of the origin of primitive society – the idea of the first patricide and its results – was dismissed as pure phantasy and as contradicting the doctrine of primitive matriarchy (accepted by Marxists through Engels' reading of Morgan, see chapter 9), and his sociology accused of lacking the idea of class, thus making it utterly sterile. In addition Jurinets noticed that Freud – following Le Bon – had a rather low opinion of the masses, seeing them as regressive and potentially dangerous phenomena. This was, of course, unacceptable to Jurinets, who shared – at least rhetorically – the belief in the sound judgement of the vast flag-waving masses of daily workers as opposed to, for instance, the small minority of unconvinced "culturally refined intellectuals" (Jurinets, 1924, p. 63). Jurinets (1924, p. 82), moreover, astutely observed that psychoanalysis had nothing to say in the field of politics or, more specifically, agricultural reforms, concluding that "consequently, psychoanalysis cannot say anything in those domains that Marxists consider the core of history."

Jurinets concluded his article with a sharp attack against the psychoanalyst Kolnaj (1920), who had tried to interpret communism and Bolshevism themselves as pathological phenomena in human history, and who had uncovered, among other things, the hidden homosexual agenda behind the famous communist slogan "Workers of the world, unite!"

Jurinets' article should not be dismissed as being totally without value as a serious criticism of Freud and his followers. Concentrating on Freud's latest books – *Beyond the Pleasure Principle* (1920) and *The Ego and the Id* (1923) – Jurinets pointed out some inconsistencies in Freud's thinking and highlighted its increasingly speculative nature. He was also one of the first to point out various influences on Freud's thinking of the work of philosophers such as Schopenhauer, Nietzsche, Bergson, and Simmel. But overall Jurinets did not substantiate his criticisms and failed to give a fair account of Freud's views, and his incorrect interpretation of philosophical terms such as "monism" and "dualism" made his paper unfit to be a conclusive demonstration of Freudian theory's incompatibility with Marxism. Freud's initials may well indicate the genre to which his writings belong and his ideas may well be incompatible with Marxism, but Jurinets simply failed to demonstrate this.

Criticism of Freudo-Marxism: Bakhtin's View

The most complete and convincing critique of Freudian theory from the Marxist point of view has undoubtedly been given by Bakhtin (1927/1983). His *Freudian Theory: A Critical Essay* provided a complete overview of psychoanalytic theory in its different states of development and argued its essential incompatibility with dialectical materialism. The structure of Bakhtin's essay – written under the pen-name of V. N. Voloshinov (see chapter 15) – was as follows. First, psychoanalysis was situated among the other psychological currents of the time and provisionally characterized as just another variant of subjective psychology. Secondly, an overview was given of the main themes of psychoanalysis, its concepts and its methods. Thirdly, and lastly, it was argued that a theory thus conceived was alien to a principled Marxist point of view. This third part also contained as a last chapter a devastating critique of the attempts at designing a Freudo-Marxist theory by people like Bykhovsky (1923), Luria (1925a), Fridman (1925), and Zalkind (1924a; 1927b).

What reasons did Bakhtin give for his claim that psychoanalysis was a subjectivist approach? His main criticism was directed at what he saw as the basic, underlying theme of psychoanalysis, that is, the idea that essential for the explanation of human behavior is not class, nation, or the historical period in which they live, but their age and sex. He found the idea that "Man's consciousness is determined not by his historical, but by his biological being, the most important part of which is sexuality" (Bakhtin, 1927/1983, p. 13) characteristic of Freudian theory.

In itself, or so Bakhtin argued, this theme was not new at all; Freud had simply joined the company of different philosophers of life, such as Bergson, Simmel, and Scheler. The views of these diverse philosophers (and Bakhtin included among them also James) he summarized in three points (1927/ 1983, p. 17). They (1) have a biological conception of human life and conceive of man as an isolated organic unity; (2) undervalue consciousness and attempt to diminish its role in the creation of culture to an absolute minimum; and (3) try to replace all objective social economic factors by subjective psychological or biological ones. Thus, Bergson stressed the instinct-like *élan vital* to explain human culture and James tried to reduce all forms of cultural creativity to the biological processes of adaptation (this same argument has always been used by Soviet scientists to criticize Piaget's view). In general, then, these researchers went "beyond the historical and social" (Bakhtin, 1927/1983, p. 21) to look for the underlying organic causal factors of human conduct. For Bakhtin their views were just harmful abstractions: conceiving of the human being in isolation from his immediate surroundings, his milieu, class, and society one could never explain his conduct.

Psychoanalysis, then, should be seen against the background of the various existing philosophies of life. But this was not the whole story, Bakhtin argued. Dividing all psychological currents into two broad categories – objective and subjective psychology (see Vygotsky's similar procedure in chapter 7) – it was clear to him that psychoanalysis belonged to the category of subjective approaches.

What did Bakhtin have in mind when he wrote of subjective and objective psychology? Generally speaking, he argued, psychology has only two sources of information about the workings of the human mind, namely introspection and observation. Subjective psychologists (he mentioned Wundt, James, and Chelpanov) rely on the first source, checking it against other – external – evidence through experiments. For Bakhtin this use of experiments did not change the fundamental idea of subjective psychology:

the final word was spoken by the subject. In his opinion, the combination of the subject's introspectional account of his inner experience with the observational evidence obtained by the researcher resulted in a curious and dualistic mixture of incompatible data. Bakhtin (1927/1983, p. 33) argued that one should limit oneself to the study of the materialized aspects of human behavior. In the case of inner experience this implied that it can only be studied in so far as it can be translated into the language of external experience. The inner experience of the subject materializes in his verbal utterances, his account of the things felt. These verbal reactions (the verbal behavior as Skinner would have it), their sound, physiological background, and meaning, can be studied objectively. Bakhtin argued that even the subject's inner speech, is material and can, therefore, be objectively studied (cf. chapter 15). Not surprisingly Bakhtin referred to Watson for a similar view on the status of inner experience. What is more interesting is that he also referred to Vygotsky's (1925g) paper "Consciousness as a problem of the psychology of behavior," discussed in the introduction to part I. These cross-references confirm that both Vygotsky and Bakhtin were close to a behaviorist world-view at that time, and Bakhtin's reference demonstrates that he was aware of at least one of Vygotsky's writings. Likewise, it has been claimed (see Radzikhovsky, 1982, p. 489) that Vygotsky read at least one of Bakhtin's works, namely his "Marxism and the Philosophy of Language" (1930/1972), but in chapter 15 we suggest that this is doubtful.

So, what Bakhtin proposed was a conceptual change: the object of study is not the subject's "inner experience," but its verbal equivalent in the form of inner and outer speech. By using such an approach the conceptual unity of our psychological analysis is retained, for both observational evidence and inner and outer speech belong to the realm of material reality. The dualistic position of subjective psychology, therefore, can be avoided. However, whilst defending this behaviorist-like position Bakhtin stressed one major potential danger of behaviorism and other objective currents of thought prevalent in psychology, namely their tendency to be silent about the social aspects of behavior. It was at this point that he propounded the idea of an objective analysis of the social origin of word meanings. For him it was clear that "The most vague thought, even if unspoken, as well as the most complex philosophical movement both presuppose the organized communication between individuals" (Bakhtin, 1927/1983, p. 42).

Ultimately, this position implied that all utterances, theories, etc. are determined by the class the speaker or author belongs to. In Bakhtin's view, then, thoughts and words were double mirrors, reflecting not only the object spoken of but also the knowing subject and, ultimately, his class, society, and historical period (Bakhtin, 1927/1983, pp. 44–5). It was from this position – elaborated in Bakhtin's later writings, e.g. "Marxism and the

Philosophy of Language" (1930/1972) – that Bakhtin criticized Freudian theory.

Bakhtin substantiated this definition of psychoanalysis as having an essentially subjectivist approach with several additional arguments. Among other things, he argued that although psychoanalysis claimed to provide an organic foundation for behavior, in reality the bodily processes were only discussed in so far as they surfaced in the accounts of patients. In Bakhtin's opinion Freud never provided a convincing account of the biological and physiological background of, for example, erogenous zones or drives. These concepts were founded entirely on the quicksand of introspectional evidence without any reference to physiological data. Bakhtin argued that Freud "psychologized" biology. Likewise, he "subjectivized" the important sociological factors playing a role in the origin of human behavior. To support the latter claim Bakhtin pointed to Freud's theory of personality. The subdivision of the human mind into ego, superego, and id in Freud's view reflected deep natural forces in the human mind. Not so, according to Bakhtin. In his opinion the struggle between ego, superego, and id was the struggle between different ideological motives, each having their counterpart in the reality of a certain society. More specifically, the patient's utterances did not only reflect his individual psyche, but also a genuine struggle between the different ideologies of doctor and patient. Freud's psychodynamics, therefore, did not reflect a strictly individual struggle but rather a dispute between two persons. It was Freud's mistake to project these complex social relationship into the patient's individual mind.

Bakhtin accepted that Freud was right to state that the conscious motivation of our behavior cannot always be trusted. Consciousness is the commentary that every adult person applies to each of his acts (Bakhtin, 1927/1983, p. 171) and, as such, can be incorrect. But the same holds true, Bakhtin argued, for our unconscious commentaries. For the so-called unconscious motives are also utterances that are objectively determined and reflect a proximal social event, the event of communication, of speaking to another person. The origin of these utterances we will never find within the boundaries of the unique, individual person. "Experiencing [*Osoznavaya*) myself, I try as it were to look at myself through the eyes of the other person, the other representatives of my social group, my class" (Bakhtin, 1927/1983, p. 175).

If we call the inner and outer speech that imbues all of our behavior our "everyday ideology", then it is true that this ideology does not always coincide with the official group ideology – although in a healthy collective it does (1927/1983, p. 180). When there is an especially large gap between these two ideologies it may even become very difficult for the individual to verbalize his private everyday ideology. Such was the case for sexuality,

Bakhtin argued, in the society of that time. It provided Freud with the opportunity to claim that the everyday ideological motivations were strictly private reflections of deep wishes and drives. Starting from the adults' accounts and their present ideological motivation of events that had supposedly taken place decades earlier he "sexualized" family life. "All this is a projection into the past of those ideological interpretations of behavior that are characteristic only of the present. Freud nowhere transcends the boundary of a subjective construction" (Bakhtin, 1927/1983, p. 167).

Reading these reflections by Bakhtin – which are in themselves open to dispute – it comes as no surprise to learn that he condemned the Russian Freudo-Marxist attempts at unification. In the final chapter of his book Bakhtin sharply criticized the few Freudo-Marxist attempts he took more or less seriously. Here we will only summarize his criticism of Luria's paper "Psychoanalysis as a system of monistic psychology" (Luria, 1925a).

Bakhtin took Luria's main argument to be that Freud supposedly offered a non-atomistic account of the whole personality. This he countered by pointing out that (1) Freud retained the familiar faculties of the mind (volition, feeling, and rational thought) that had been put forward earlier by traditional psychology; and (2) one cannot give an account of the whole personality confining oneself to the individual seen in isolation from his social surroundings. Neither did Bakhtin accept Luria's claim that Freud provided an organic basis for human behavior, repeating his by now familiar argument that the organism for Freud was only a secondary phenomenon whose description was based entirely on introspectional accounts. Ironically, as a result of the foregoing, there was one of Luria's arguments that Bakhtin accepted, namely the claim that Freud offered a monistic account of human conduct. But to Bakhtin this was a monism of the idealist, spiritual kind. However cautious – and inconsistent – Freud may have been in talking about the relation between body and mind, the method he used betrayed the fundamental nature of his framework: a theory built on the projection into the past of ideologies obtained through adults' introspection was bound to end up in idealism of the purest order.

Criticism of Freudo-Marxism: Vygotsky's View

Judging by his manuscript on psychology's crisis, Vygotsky was as critical of Luria's attempts to reconcile Marxism and psychoanalysis as was Bakhtin. In this analysis he sharply criticized his co-worker's supposedly atheoretical approach (Vygotsky, 1926m/1982). Discussing the general issue of the spread of scientific ideas (see chapter 7), Vygotsky mentioned the same attempts at combining Marxism and psychoanalysis as were discussed by

Bakhtin. Most of the time, he argued, the authors would declare Marxism to be monistic, materialistic, dialectic, etc. Then they would find the same monistic, materialistic, etc. approach in Freudian theory and conclude that both systems coincided. In the process the most glaring contradictions were rendered void by declaring parts of Freudian theory superfluous, exaggerations and the like. Thus, some Soviet theorists ignored pansexualism as it did not agree with Marxist philosophy. But removing pansexualism from Freudian thinking, Vygotsky argued, meant removing its soul, the central part of the whole system. "For Freudian theory without the doctrine of the sexual nature of the unconscious is equivalent to Christianity without Christ or Buddhism with Allah" (Vygotsky, 1926m/1982, p. 329). This approach was theoretically naive and careless, Vygotsky claimed, and led to grotesque distortions of both Marxist and Freudian thinking. As an edifying example he took Luria's paper (1925a) on psychoanalysis as a monistic system. Vygotsky argued that Luria could only conclude that Marxism and Freudian theory were compatible by distorting both systems of thought and he tried to point out some of Luria's mistakes. In the first place he objected to Luria assuming that the theories of Darwin, Kant, Pavlov, Einstein, and Marx were similar to those systems that constituted the methodological foundation of modern science. The role of each of these thinkers was fundamentally different and listing them together suggested the author believed that the fact that they had all made fundamental contributions to science sufficed to conclude that they represented the same theoretical position. The basic scientific approach would then consist of the sum of their contributions. This Vygotsky considered to be impossible in view of the deeply contradictory philosophical nature of various systems and he sarcastically remarked that "Here, that is, on the first page, we might conclude our reasoning" (Vygotsky, 1926m/1982, p. 330). Of course, all the theories had their value, but they could not be easily reconciled without distorting their nature. Freud would be amazed, Vygotsky stated, to learn that psychoanalysis was a monistic system and that he "followed historical materialism," as Fridman (in Kornilov, 1925a, p. 159) had claimed. Freud never declared himself to be a monist, materialist, dialectician, nor a follower of historical materialism, and Vygotsky went on to prove that he was none of these. He concluded that one can only come to these conclusions by considering superficially some of the characteristics of Freud's doctrine without seriously analyzing it. Luria's attempt at combining Marxism and Freudian theories involving a "series of most naive transformations of both systems" (Vygotsky, 1926m/1982, p. 330), constituted a fine example of such a theoretically careless approach.

Despite this harsh judgement Vygotsky did not argue that everything in psychoanalysis contradicted Marxism – in fact, he was not sure it did

(Vygotsky, 1926m/1982, p. 334) – but he did claim that to argue so one had to make an extensive and deep analysis of Freudian theory. The more so as psychoanalytic theory constituted, in his opinion, not an *a priori* finished system, but a spontaneously evolved conglomerate of insights and facts:

> like Pavlov, Freud discovered too many things to create an abstract system. But like Molière's hero without suspecting it himself all his life was speaking prose, Freud the investigator created a system: introducing a new word, making one term agree with another, describing a new fact, drawing a new conclusion, he everywhere in passing, step by step created a new system. This only means that the structure of his system is deeply original, obscure and complex, and very difficult to understand... That is why psychoanalysis requires an extremely careful and critical methodological analysis and not a naive superposition of the features of two different systems. (Vygotsky, 1926m/1982, p. 333)

In this passage one feels that Vygotsky was intrigued by Freud's original and often speculative ideas and that he felt his writings deserved careful and critical study. Both aspects – fascination plus critical distance – came out even more clearly in Vygotsky's earlier references to Freud. Leaving the textbook *Pedagogical Psychology* aside these can be found in his and Luria's preface to Freud's *Beyond the Pleasure Principle* and in his *The Psychology of Art* (Vygotsky and Luria, 1925a; Vygotsky, 1925j).

Vygotsky's Earlier Views on Freud and Freudo-Marxism

By far the most positive evaluation of Freud can be found in the preface to *Beyond the Pleasure Principle*. In this preface – which preceded another preface by Moshe Wulff – Vygotsky praised Freud as having "one of the most courageous minds of this century" (Vygotsky and Luria, 1925a, p. 3). He argued there that Freud's fantastic speculations about the death drive, *Thanatos*, were speculations based on hard facts. Freud's truly original ideas made him comparable to Columbus: both discovered a new continent and neither provided us with a fully reliable map of the newly discovered land (Vygotsky and Luria, 1925a, p. 13). Emphasizing the fact that Freud wished to be a materialist thinker, Vygotsky welcomed *Beyond the Pleasure Principle* as a valuable step towards the creation of a dialectical and monistic psychology. That Vygotsky's views on Freud underwent a clear evolution can be seen from his judgement about the possibility of developing a Freudo-Marxist approach. At that time he still considered the attempt to find "a synthesis between Freudian theory and Marxism with the help of the doctrine of the conditional reflexes and to develop a system of 'reflexological Freudian theory' " to be "new and original" (Vygotsky and Luria, 1925a, p. 4).

For *The Psychology of Art* Vygotsky analyzed other parts of Freudian thinking. Looking for a theory that would give an adequate explanation of the creation and experience of artistic creations it was impossible to avoid discussing Freud's ideas and in the fourth chapter of the text he tried to come to terms with them. He started his analysis of psychoanalytic theory by immediately postulating the need for some concept of the unconscious to explain the fundamental issues of a psychology of art. By restricting ourselves to the analysis of conscious processes we will hardly find any answers, for experience shows that neither the producer nor the audience of artistic creations can fully explain the aesthetic feelings they experience. But does the Freudian explanation of unconscious processes and the role they play in the creation and reception of art satisfy the accepted standards of scientific reasoning? Freud claimed that at the basis of artistic creativity is an unsatisfied, often sexual drive. The artist's sublime creations are in effect disguised unconscious wishes and the connoisseur admiring his work is secretly satisfying his basic – again unconscious – needs. Psychoanalysts will not, therefore, draw a sharp line between works of art, dreams, and neuroses, since all of them represent the workings of the unconscious forces of the mind. The function of art is easily explained by the Freudian theorist: it allows both artist and connoisseur to satisfy their primitive needs without violating the standards of (Western) society. Art is a protection against rape and murder.

Vygotsky (1925l, p. 98) argued that the most flawed aspect of a theory thus conceived is its understanding of the role of the form artistic creations can take. According to psychoanalysts the role of the form is to mask the primitive content of the story, like the manifest form of dreams masks their latent content. At the same time the form has to allude in subtle ways to the real pleasure behind the conscious scenery. The function of the form, then, is to prepare for the unconscious satisfaction of basic needs. Vygotsky concluded that for psychoanalytic theory the form is really a façade hiding the real pleasure that is explained by the content. This implies that the different forms and styles of art and their historical development are in reality left without any explanation (Vygotsky, 1925l, p. 102). To explain the form of dreams and neuroses by referring to primordial drives may make sense, Vygotsky stated, but art and its development are far more determined by social factors: "art can never be fully explained from the restricted sphere of personal life" (1925l, p. 110). It is one thing to claim that products of art have an unconscious background that is transformed into socially accepted forms, but it is another thing to explain just how these transformations in the social sphere take place. Psychoanalysis, in Vygotsky's opinion, failed to provide this last explanation and he saw two reasons for this failure. The first mistake was to try to reduce all psychological phenomena to sexual drives. Secondly, by so doing psychoanalysts actually went to the extreme of reducing the role of conscious processes to that of a blind tool in the hands of unconscious drives, effectively reducing their role to zero (1925l, p. 104). Using an ever-growing catalog of sexual symbols they were able fully to explain any work of art, whether created by Michelangelo or Dostoevsky. To Vygotsky these "explanations" only showed the "extreme poverty" of the method, its sterility, and arbitrariness. He would not accept that all creative processes could be explained by the Oedipus complex and that, therefore, "man was a slave of his childhood." How would one explain the different styles and qualities of novels, how would one explain the different trends in music? The implication of such psychoanalytic theorizing was that any distinction between the conscious, social activity of artists and the unconscious activities of neurotics disappeared.

Vygotsky concluded that the valid, practical application of psychoanalysis in the domain of aesthetics still awaited its realization. The concept of the unconsciousness was undoubtedly of fundamental importance but this should not make us blind to the active role of conscious processes: art as the unconscious is only the problem; art as the social solution of the unconscious – that is its most likely answer (Vygotsky, 1925l, p. 110).

Vygotsky on Freud: Conclusions

While being increasingly critical of many of Freud's concepts, Vygotsky still deeply valued his work. His early interest in *Hamlet* – emphasizing the drama's mystical and religious aspects – his fascination with James' *Varieties of Religious Experience*, his wide reading of speculative "non-materialist" thinkers, all show that Vygotsky preferred original (be they speculative) conceptions to stale ideas that conformed to the accepted world-view. His interest in Freud fits this basic feature of his thinking and the present authors are inclined to see his interest in Freudian theory as perfectly consistent with his early fascination with the hidden motives explaining Hamlet's behavior (see chapter 2).

That Vygotsky continued to appreciate the original, speculative side of Freud's writings is clear in an intriguing passage in his study of psychology's crisis (Vygotsky, 1926m/1982, pp. 335–6). Referring to his and Luria's earlier preface to *Beyond the Pleasure Principle* he repeated his judgement that, although Freud's theses definitely have a speculative nature and the empirical corroboration of the claimed facts is hardly convincing, and although his ideas show dazzling contradictions and paradoxes, his idea of a death drive (Thanatos) was valid for the biological science of the time. Science clarified the idea of life to a great extent, Vygotsky added, but cannot yet explain the concept of death. Death is generally understood as the negation of life, its denial, but according to Vygotsky

> death is a fact that has its positive sense too. It is a special type of being and not only not-being ... it is impossible to imagine that this phenomenon is in no way represented in the organism, that is, in the processes of life. It is hard to believe that death would have no sense or would only have a negative sense. (Vygotsky, 1926m/1982, pp. 335–6)

Referring to Engels (1925/1978, p. 554) he expressed his belief that a dialectical understanding of life would provide an underpinning of the idea that "to live means to die" (cf. his letter to Levina quoted in chapter 1).

It is hard to understand what Vygotsky exactly meant by this passage. Of course, these words were written when Vygotsky felt that he was "between life and death; I am not yet desperate, but I have abandoned all hope" (Vygotsky in a letter to Luria, dated March 5, 1926). But a reference to his delicate health and the recurrent attacks of tuberculosis can only partially explain why he apparently had given the issue a good deal of thought and came to this conclusion. It is quite clear, however, that he appreciated Freud's contribution to this domain. Borrowing a metaphor from Lev Shestov he judged Freud's theory of Thanatos to be "no big highway in science or a road for everyone, but an Alpine path above the abysses for those free of vertigo" (ibid., p. 336). Science, in Vygotsky's opinion, was in need of such books: they did not provide the truth, but were instrumental in finding it. They did not provide all answers, but asked the right questions. The asking of such questions, Vygotsky declared, requires more creativity than is needed for the umpteenth observation of some phenomenon according to some accepted cliché:

> there are problems that one cannot approach flying, but that have to be approached on foot, limping and ... in these cases it is no shame to limp. But he who only sees the limping is methodologically blind. For it would not be difficult to show that Hegel is an idealist, the crows proclaim that from the house-tops; it needed genius to see in this system an idealism that stood materialism on its head, that is, to sever the methodological truth (dialectics) from the factual lies, to see that Hegel, limping, was approaching the truth. (Vygotsky, 1926m/1982, p. 336)

What Vygotsky implied – borrowing Freud's (1920/1984, p. 338) metaphor about limping towards the truth – was that Freud's writings constituted an important step towards the truth. However speculative, paradoxical, and often simply wrong they may have been, they raised important questions that a genuine Marxist psychology could not avoid.

The Demise of Psychoanalysis in the Soviet Union: The Reich–Sapir Debate

In 1929 the well-known psychoanalyst and Communist Wilheim Reich visited Moscow to lecture at the Communist Academy on the problem of fusing Marxism and Freudian theory (Miller, 1986, p. 132). Rather surprisingly Reich was allowed to publish this lecture in an article in *Under the Banner of Marxism* (Reich, 1929). The publication, however, was part of a carefully orchestrated scheme. Reich's paper was published together with a note by the editorial board declaring that the fact that the article was published did not imply that the editorial board shared the author's views. In addition, the Party official I. D. Sapir was given the German text of Reich's lecture and was asked to write a reaction to it. Sapir's sharp criticism of Reich's views was published in the same journal issue and virtually marked the end of the public debate on psychoanalysis in the Soviet Union (Sapir, 1929).

Reich's Version of Freudo-Marxism

Reich's paper was in part a reaction to Jurinets' attack on Freudian theory (Jurinets, 1924; published in *Unter dem Banner des Marxismus* – the German version of *Under the Banner of Marxism* – as Jurinetz, 1925). He began by distancing himself from authors like Kolnaj and by accepting the validity of two types of criticism that had been repeatedly raised by Jurinets and others. First, Reich admitted, psychoanalysis can never be a world-view on a par with Marxism. Instead, it should be considered a psychological method providing the description and explanation of mental life on a natural scientific basis. Psychoanalysis, therefore, was a specific scientific method applicable to a limited domain of scientific study. With this tactical retreat Reich tried to avoid a conflict with Marxism as the sole provider of the right world-view. Secondly, Reich added, the real subject of psychoanalytic theory is the mental life of societal man. The problems of mass movements, politics, agricultural reform, etc. can indeed never be studied through its methods. Marxism, therefore, should study societal phenomena, while psychoanalysis should study societal man. The two scientific methods could compensate and enrich each other.

Reich did not accept the criticism that psychoanalysis as a method was incompatible with Marxist thinking. Specifically, he countered the arguments that (1) psychoanalysis was the product of a disintegrating bourgeois society – the argument used by Jurinets (1924; 1925); and (2) that it was idealistic. In his first argument he essentially said that the origin of an argument says nothing about its validity and he shrewdly observed that Marx's theory itself had been developed in a bourgeois society. Neither was psychoanalysis idealistic in Reich's view but here he did not yet provide any arguments, and just claimed that critics had unfairly concentrated on various psychoanalysts' views not taking into account that these views differed fundamentally from Freud's.

Before setting out to explain the main concepts of psychoanalytic theory as he saw them, Reich made one remark about the materialist notion of the psyche. Referring to different passages in the works of Marx and Engels he explained that the mind is a material phenomenon, which, however, should be studied at its own level. Reducing the mind to its organic properties would not enhance our understanding one bit, he claimed (Reich, 1929, p. 184). To do so would be to commit the fallacy of "mechanistic materialism," a point of view that had been condemned by Marx, Engels, and Lenin. Reich wisely refrained from giving a detailed description of the exact nature of the mind's material being, nor did he explain in any detail why it could not be reduced to organic factors. Instead he set out to explain the principle ideas of psychoanalytic theory and the way he thought they were compatible with the Marxist world-view.

The core of psychoanalytic theory is the doctrine of drives, Reich (1929, p. 186) stated. In his opinion the sexual drive (libido) and the drive for self-preservation had a clear organic origin, but Reich admitted having some problems with Freud's later detection of the death instinct (Thanatos). Seeing the destructive tendencies as the secondary result of the non-satisfaction of the libido, however, one might be able to retain the essentially organic, material basis of Freud's drive theory, Reich argued. But the expression of these organic drives is heavily determined by societal factors. The instinctual life is regulated by the reality principle, which is in essence a function of the demands made by a given society, and, in the end, therefore, of its economic structures. Reich (1929, p. 187) stated that: "All this is rooted in the economic conditions; the ruling class claims a reality principle, that serves the interests of its preservation of power." Reich ventured as his opinion that the anal drives – traditionally associated with avarice – would be more prevalent in bourgeois circles, while the proletariat would be more inclined to engage in procreative activities (1929, p. 188). The meaning of the reality principle, therefore, was heavily dependent on the existing society and would change in time.

A person's unconscious, too, was heavily influenced by the society in which he lived, for only those forces that are unacceptable are suppressed in a given society. The censure exercised over the expression of unconscious drives would be different in different cultures and in different time periods, as would be the content of the unconscious. To illustrate the latter statement Reich reminded the reader of the "interesting clinical finding" that at that time many female patients had started dreaming of giant zeppelins (1929, p. 188). Both the suppression and sublimation of unconscious drives from the id were intimately connected with the values and norms of the specific society. Reich was able to conclude, therefore, that "psychoanalysis cannot imagine a child without a society; it knows the child only as a societal being" (1929, p. 189). It went without saying that the superego was fully determined by society: the superego of the child is a product of the rules and precepts prevalent in his family, a family that in its turn is dependent on strictly economic conditions of living. The ego takes an intermediate position, in trying to negotiate between the demands of the biological drives from the id, on the one hand, and the societal demands of the superego, on the other hand, it is often the plaything of these other parts of the dynamic personality system. Reich concluded that the ego was half- and the superego fully determined by the society in which the person lived. There could be no doubt, then, that psychoanalysis gave due credit to both social and biological factors in human development. Moreover, psychoanalysis could complete Marxism in the sense that it could provide an analysis of the ways the ideology of a specific society could influence a specific individual person. Through the prism of the nuclear family – the dynamics of which were explained by Freud by concepts such as the Oedipus complex – the contemporary child internalized the prevailing ideology (1929, p. 191).

Reich continued by listing all the "laws" of dialectics and demonstrating their objective presence in the psychoanalytic practice. Thus the continuous stimulation of erogenous zones is only pleasant up to a certain moment, which shows that the quantitative build-up of sexual energy suddenly gives rise to a qualitatively different feeling (1929, p. 195). Likewise, psychoanalytic practice had seen many examples of feelings that turned into their opposites – e.g. the sadistic child turning into a surgeon (1929, p. 198) – thus demonstrating yet another of the basic tenets of dialectic thought. Moreover, psychoanalysis gives us an insight into the dialectical fact that many human actions are rational and irrational at the same time. A peasant plowing the soil, for example, is at the same time symbolically having an incestuous relationship with mother earth. Reich was convinced, however, that in the end many seemingly irrational acts could be interpreted in a rational way.

Reich raised the question of whether the Oedipus complex as such is also dependent on the type of society in which it is exhibited. Referring to Jones, who had argued that the Oedipus complex had always existed in the same form in human history, and to his opponent Malinowski, Reich opted for the latter's point of view. In his opinion the whole Oedipus complex was, in the end, determined by economic structures and would disappear in a socialist society (Reich, 1929, pp. 201–2). It is true, Reich admitted, that Freud in *Totem and Taboo* considered the Oedipus complex the cause of sexual repression. This was probably because Freud did not take into account the original matriarchical organization of human society, relying on a Darwinian account of primitive society. We now know, however – following Bachofen, Morgan, and Engels (see Kuper, 1988 and chapter 9) – that it is possible to interpret the Oedipus complex as a result of societal sexual repression, Reich reasoned. This would mean that the Oedipus complex, or at any rate its expression, was tied to specific societies (Reich, 1929, p. 202). Thus, we can see Reich correcting Freud in order to bring the latter's theory of the original tribe in accord with the Marxist canons.

Finally, Reich discussed the phenomenon of psychoanalysis from a sociological point of view. In his view the emergence of a bourgeois mentality led to the repression of sexual instincts, which in its turn led to an alarming increase in the number of mental disorders. Everybody denied the sexual nature of these disorders until Freud raised his voice, and vilified and ridiculed he had to fight against the ruling bourgeois mentality in the scientific world. However, Freud's uncovering of sexual repression was fundamental: the phenomenon of sexual repression was more long-standing than that of the exploitation of one class by the other. Moreover, sexual repression was not limited to one specific class, although it did take different forms in different classes. Reich was gloomy about the prospects for Freud's theory: the ruling bourgeois mentality could not accept the shocking ideas about the role of libido and the desirability of sexual freedom, and both the expert and the layman did everything to deny or distort the theory. Already former allies such as Jung, Adler, and Rank had dissented and to Reich this showed that in a bourgeois society the demise of psychoanalysis was unavoidable. Its future would lie in a socialist society: Marxist reforms would bring about the necessary social revolution which would eliminate the factors hampering the free expression of sexual drives. In this new society, the task of psychoanalysis would be threefold: (1) to elucidate mankind's history through the analysis of myths; (2) to take care of sexual and mental hygienics; and (3) to assist in the sound upbringing of the new generation (Reich, 1929, p. 206).

Sapir's Reply

Reich's view of utopia was not shared by Sapir, who flatly denied the scientific validity of psychoanalytic theory as a whole and its compatibility with the Marxist world-view. To begin with, Sapir did not accept "comrade Reich's" modest claim that psychoanalysis was no more than a psychological method for the description and explanation of individual societal man, a method that was of no use in the domain of mass movements, politics, etc. For Sapir the claims of psychoanalysis were much more pretentious. Referring to Freud's *Mass Psychology and Ego Analysis*, *Totem and Taboo*, and *The Future of an Illusion*, he remarked that Freud had definitely made excursions into the realm of sociology. As a tool for sociological or social psychological explanation, however, the value of psychoanalysis was close to zero. Drawing heavily on Marx, Engels, and Plekhanov, Sapir gave the following account of the relationship between society, social psychology, and individual psychology.

The task of social psychology was to study the social psyche or ideology that forms the intermediate link between the individual psyche and various socio-economic phenomena. Forming part of a collective the person receives the accepted ideology of this collective. Although the person is not passive in this respect – he also is a co-creator of the ideology – the individual properties of people are relevant for the sociologist only in so far as they have an objective relation to the class struggle in all its forms. For, although the laws of the individual psyche can conflict with the tasks of the collective or its psyche, in the end they can always be explained by societal forces. Therefore, psychological laws applying to the individual are always "superseded" in the system of the societal whole. It is true, Sapir reasoned, that a minor role for these individual laws is present, as in the case of the personal properties of a leading political figure – Lenin? – but "hardly anyone will deny that this is no more than a rippling on the waves of societal-economic development" (Sapir, 1929, p. 217). What Sapir was presenting, then, is a "top-down" model, in which socio-economic factors determine social psychological phenomena, which in their turn determine the individual psychological processes. Form and content of individual acts are, therefore, in the end determined by socio-economic factors. From this point of view it is useless to point to the biological background of human motivation, for this background has always been there and, thus, cannot explain the specific differences between different social systems and epochs (1929, p. 218). The methods of psychoanalysis – pointing to biological drives – and Marxism – pointing to socio-economic laws – therefore, are simply not at the same level and should not be juxtaposed.

In Sapir's opinion Reich could not counter the above views. Reich could explain something of the way in which an individual came to believe a certain ideology, but not very much. Religious feelings, for example, do not have to find their origin in sexual drives, Sapir reasoned. He suggested that the beliefs of a rational theologian or a traditional believer are founded on different grounds. Sapir concluded that (1) even on the level of the individual psychoanalysis ignores the rich variety of internal motives; (2) behavior is much more determined by social factors than by biological ones; (3) the biological recedes completely in conscious acts; and (4) no matter what the internal motives are, they form part of an objective social process that explains them. "Let different people believe on different grounds – sociologically speaking what matters is the fact that this specific religion with this specific content is determined by certain societal forces" (1929, p. 220).

To strengthen his argument for the importance of a socio-economic approach – as opposed to a purely biological one – Sapir mentioned the beneficial effect on people's health of participating in the revolutionary movement. The situation was different in the lower strata of bourgeois society where the conditions – such as mass unemployment – for the spreading of various diseases were excellent. This explained the fact that diseases like tuberculosis and arteriosclerosis were especially widespread in Western Europe and the United States. Sapir rightly concluded that even in the field of medicine a purely biological approach is misguided. He did not give credence to Reich's explanation of the prevalence of mental disorders in bourgeois society. Taking the psychoanalytic point of view, a massive repression of sexual drives might as well have led to the flourishing of bourgeois culture through the mechanism of sublimation, which in Sapir's view again showed the utter emptiness of psychoanalytic explanations of social phenomena.

Sapir was more positive about psychoanalysis as a theory of individual psychology, although also here he expressed serious criticism. He looked approvingly at psychoanalysis' account of the mind as a dynamic system consisting of different subsystems, one of which is the unconscious. Arguing that quite probably these psychological processes formed the expression of various psychological processes, he nevertheless stated that they could not be reduced to elementary neurodynamic processes. Sapir expressly stated the limitations of Pavlov's work with conditional reflexes. In his view these inhibitory and excitatory processes took place in the "morpho-functional" structure of the brain that developed during the history of the life of the individual. Whether a stimulus would lead to a specific reaction – such as a neurosis – would, therefore, depend on the structure of the brain that developed during this individual's lifetime. Without taking this morpho-functional structure into account the talk of conditional reflexes would be empty (1929, p. 228). Sapir concluded this intriguing reasoning with the suggestion that brain structures differ for the conscious and unconscious parts of the dynamic personality system and that the elementary neurodynamic processes are determined by them. We can see, then, that Sapir opts for a non-mechanistic, dialectic materialism, where the elementary physiological properties are becoming "superseded" in the process of development. This view is also evident in his comments on the notion of the unconscious. He acknowledged that often people have motives for their acts that they do not wish to admit. However, in Sapir's opinion these deep motives were (1) not always unconscious; (2) not always very powerful; (3) rarely biologically based; and (4) lost all their power under favorable circumstances. For Sapir psychoanalysis greatly exaggerated the role of libido in human development, in not seeing that there are secondary, social motives, that may have evolved genetically from the primary sexual motives but that eventually acquired independence. Sexual motives do play a role, but are fully controlled by the higher social motives that originated from them. It is only when the latter are weakened (e.g. in the case of alcohol abuse) that the primary motives come into play. Their role is very limited, however, and in general the biological forces only indicate possibilities for development, whereas economic forces will determine its direction (1929, p. 233). We may conclude, then, that also in the domain of individual psychology psychoanalytic theory was accused of overemphasizing the role of biological factors to the detriment of the social ones.

Summarizing Sapir's critique of Reich's views we may say that they were a restatement of several well-known themes. In the first place, no scientific theory – whether psychoanalysis or any other – could compete with Marxist thought when dealing with problems that had a clearly social psychological or sociological impact. The excursions of different psychoanalytic authors into this area highly irritated the ideological gatekeepers of dialectical and historical materialism. Secondly, any theory that directly or indirectly called into doubt the possibilities of social reform or progress – for instance, by pointing to biological factors that limited these possibilities – by the same token proved its unscientific approach. The supposedly ubiquitous drives of human behavior posited by psychoanalytic theory were of no relevance for its explanation. Real explanations had to be sought in the socio-economic factors outlined by the theoreticians of Marxism.

The debate about psychoanalysis in the Soviet Union now had virtually come to an end. Former psychoanalysts had changed their views (e.g. Zalkind and Luria; although the latter still mentioned Vera Schmidt's work in Vygotsky and Luria, 1930a, pp. 135–43) or left the country (as Wulff did). Against all hope the Psychoanalytic Society tried to continue its work, now with Kannabikh as its chairman. Vera Schmidt (1928a; 1929b) continued to cover the meetings of the society for the *Internationale Zeitschrift für Psychoanalyse*, but not for very long. Her last report appeared in 1930 and covered the period from January 7, up to March 27, 1930. Thereafter no more reports were received and the membership lists published in the journal up to 1935 seem not to have been updated. Miller (1986, p. 131) reports that Schmidt's school for the psychoanalytic treatment of disturbed children was closed in 1928 (see also Kozulin, 1984, p. 94) and that the Psychoanalytic Society was officially closed in 1933.

General Conclusions

Like all psychologists of the beginning of this century, Vygotsky and Luria took a great interest in psychoanalytic theory. Luria's role in Soviet psychoanalysis was far more prominent than Vygotsky's, who was at best a fascinated outsider. In fact, the development of Luria's thinking cannot be understood without a thorough study of the internal Soviet debates on Freud and his followers. Part of this historical context – with all its comic and tragi-comic aspects – has been reconstructed in this chapter. The history of the origin, flowering, and demise of psychoanalysis in the Soviet Union forms an instructive example of the way the new Soviet state would eventually solve intellectual debates: by dictating the right world-views from above. As such, the history of the psychoanalytic movement in the Soviet Union was not at all unique. As Kozulin (1984, p. 94) has remarked: "Psychoanalysis simply shared the common fate of all independent psychological movements. After the appropriate 'methodological' or 'ideological' discussions, all major groups of Soviet psychologists – reflexologists, reactologists, personalists, and pedologists – were silenced, their journals ceased publication, and all translations of 'bourgeois' psychologists were banned."

Meanwhile, the differences between Vygotsky's and Luria's attitudes towards psychoanalysis is interesting to observe. Broadly speaking, one might say that Vygotsky – being always very critical of Freudian thinking – never condemned the system as a whole but rather stressed its fundamental contributions to psychological science. Luria, on the other hand, was an ardent follower of Freud's ideas up to the late 1920s, when he turned away from psychoanalysis and in later years he tended to ridicule his early enthusiasm for psychoanalytic theory. Vygotsky's approach seems to have been both intellectually more demanding and ideologically more dangerous, for after Freud's writings fell into disrepute harsh criticisms of his thinking were welcomed as a shibboleth of the right world-view. Such unqualified condemnations, however, are not to be found in Vygotsky's writings. Vygotsky's indifference to the general ideological climate may again reflect one of the basic dialectics of his personal life: a relative ideological independence based on a generally hopeless physical condition.

6

Konstantin Kornilov and His Reactology

While Vygotsky was analyzing and writing about the psychological processes of reacting to literary texts in 1922–3, another intellectual was becoming involved in slightly different processes of reaction. That man was Konstantin Kornilov, a recently promoted professor at Moscow University's Institute of Experimental Psychology. Born in 1879, Kornilov had been associated with the Institute since 1907, first as an assistant to its director, Georgi Chelpanov (until 1915), then as a *Privatdozent* (until his promotion to professorship in 1921; see Murchison, 1929, p. 557). For all his career from 1910, Kornilov had been active as a meticulous experimenter in the laboratory, studying the different kinds of reactions and adult subjects and publishing some reports (Kornilov, 1913a, 1913b, 1914; Korniloff, 1922) as well as a book *The Theory of the Reactions of Man* (*Uchenie o reaktsiakh cheloveka*) (Kornilov, 1922a). In the years 1922–4, Kornilov extended his activities to experimenting with reactions other than those of his laboratory subjects – who were colleagues at the Institute and officials of the State – to the "stimuli" involving Marxist dialectical philosophy in conjunction with psychology. As a result, the ground for entrance of a number of the representatives of the "young generation" into psychology was prepared. Vygotsky happened to be one of those brought into psychology by the sequence of social actions and reactions set in motion by Kornilov.

The Psychology of Reactions: Development of Kornilov's Ideas

Like many of the psychologists of the 1920s, Kornilov's ideas developed in the course of the 1910s. As he himself says (Kornilov, 1922a, p. 7), his ideas acquired independence in 1913 when he started to study the dynamic nature of reactions, looking particularly at the "energy expenditure" during different kinds of reactions in laboratory settings. He claimed to have completed twelve separate experimental investigations in the decade 1910–20.

The Meaning of "Reaction"

On the basis of studies of reaction time in psychology, Kornilov conceptualized "reactions" in a way that was unique in two respects. First, he was interested in the process of the form of reaction (rather than a mere registration of reaction times). This interest in reaction as a process was, he claimed, the result of studying the "psychodynamics" of the Danish psychophysiologist Alfred Georg Ludwig Lehmann (1858–1921), particularly his *Elements of Psychodynamics* (*Elemente der Psychodynamik*) (Lehmann, 1905). Kornilov's interest in the form of the reaction emphasized the wholeness of the reaction process: "The reaction, as a primarily given experience [*perezhivanie*] in the course of immediate experience is a certain completed whole, from which we extract separate moments through analysis and abstraction, giving them specific names" (Kornilov, 1922a, p. 13).

Life according to Kornilov, constitutes of reactions, each of which a multitude involves interaction between the living organism and its environment. Each reaction, aside from the measurable latency time (reaction time = time from the stimulus to the onset of reaction), has both specifiable form (the behavior of the subject in the course of reaction) and intensity. Turning to real-life phenomena, Kornilov illustrated the relevance of the reaction dynamics by way of differences between people in their behavior:

> some, while greeting you, briefly and feebly shake your hand, while others, on the contrary, do it unhurriedly and vigorously. Waiting for admittance one person will give an abrupt and penetrating ring, quickly and forcefully pushing the electric button, while others produce a weak and hesitant bell-ring by a slow and feeble touch of the button – in time you may be able to guess correctly who is coming to visit you. However, where this speed and power of movements of the subject is characterized most clearly is in the style of piano playing. While for some it is characteristic to strike the keys quickly and forcefully, others, in contrast, produce the sound through a slow and light touch of the instrument, and that differential pattern of the temporal and dynamic moments creates the characteristic imprint of the style of different musicians. (Kornilov, 1922a, p. 20)

Secondly, through the idea of organism–environment interaction, Kornilov linked his reaction concept with the energy concept. Reaction was considered to be "nothing else but the transformation of energy and constant violation of the energetic balance between the individual and the surrounding environment" (1922a, p. 13). Furthermore, these energetic processes were viewed as producing the subjective side of the psychological processes (1922a, p. 14). Kornilov toyed with the idea of a special kind of energy – psychic energy – which would be as real as its physical counterparts (1922a, p. 141),[1] since it is based on the time, intensity, and form of the discharges of brain cells in response to external stimulation. Kornilov's emphasis on the dynamic side of the reaction process – evident in his emphasis on the intensity and the form of the reaction as opposed to mere reaction speed – made it possible for a number of his co-workers in the 1920s to fit their psychodynamic (e.g. Freudo-Marxists, see chapter 5) or sociodynamic (e.g. Vygotsky, Reisner, Beliaiev) approaches to the general framework. Furthermore, the well-known theory of N. A. Bernstein (*fiziologia aktivnosti*: physiology of activity) was also linked with Kornilov's reaction-dynamic theorizing in the 1920s.

Variety of Reactions: From Simple to Complex

Kornilov's experimental program (carried out in 1910–21) included the study of seven types of reactions, which constituted a profile of measures for his analysis of behavior (1922a, pp. 22–3):

1   the natural reaction was described as putting the subject into conditions in which he can react to the stimulation in the most comfortable ways;
2   the muscular reaction: the subject must make a movement as soon as the stimulus is sensed, the attention is primarily concentrated on the movement;
3   the sensory reaction: the subject must make a movement only after clear perception of the stimulus. Attention is thus mostly concentrated on the stimulus;
4   the differential reaction (*reaktsia razlichenia*): the subject is presented two (simple differentiation) or more (complex differentiation) previously known stimuli. Movement follows only after their clear differentiation;
5   the choice reaction: the subject receives two previously known stimuli, and has to react to one of them and not to the other (choice between movement and no-movement). Alternatively the subject may be given more than two stimuli, and to each of them he has to

---

[1]Kornilov was certainly not original in his reliance on the energy notion. That notion widely entertained among European scientists at the turn of the century, and in Russian psychology had already been used by Bekhterev (1904; see also Bekhterev, 1921/1922).

respond by a specific movement (choice between various movements);

6 the recognition reaction: the subject must react only to a given stimulus in the array of many;

7 the associative reaction: the movement must follow only after the stimulus has triggered a first association in the mind (free association), or after the stimulus has evoked an image that stands in a specific logical connection with the stimulus (logical association).

These seven reaction types cover the range from the most simple (1) to the highly complex (7). By way of this range of reactions studied by Kornilov it becomes apparent how the consciousness-oriented behaviorism – which Kornilov's "reactology" in the 1920s was, in contrast with Pavlov's and Bekhterev's reflexological reductionism – could emerge under his leadership. The reaction types can be viewed as qualitatively different from one another, and so Kornilov did not have to compromise his thinking in order to incorporate dialectical Marxism within it in 1922–3, when he began his fierce fight for "Marxist psychology" to be accepted. The range of reaction types was seen as a profile of the reactions of the subject, which led Kornilov to the formulation of the "general law" of human behavior: the "principle of monophasic energy expenditure" (*printsip odnopoliusnyi traty energii*). On the other hand, the reaction profiles of different subjects became linked with Kornilov's speculation on the nature of work habits, which in their turn were instrumental in the vicious criticism of his work by the ideological critics of the early 1930s (see below).

The Principle of the Monophasic Energy Expenditure

Kornilov defined this main principle of his theory in the following way: "the reasoning activity and external expression of movements are in a reverse relationship to each other: the more complex and intense the thinking process becomes, the less intense becomes the external expression of movement" (1922a, p. 122).

Thus, Kornilov's basic law of reaction is quite simple: "energy" becomes "expended" either externally (in observable behavior) or internally (in mental reactions in the mind). Furthermore, Kornilov's principle is developmental in its nature. The emphasis on "becoming" in his formulation cannot be interpreted merely as a phrasing to illustrate a formal correlational relationship. Rather, Kornilov's principle set up the developmental sequence of reactions as proceeding from the external to the internal (in a sense this emphasis constituted a very fitting context for Vygotsky's later emphasis on the internalization of external functions). Kornilov stressed the primacy of the external side of reactions over the internal ones:

> to be alive, to possess psyche – that means first of all to express oneself in action. If living beings only possessed intellect and emotions, but would not express themselves in actions, there would be no life in the world, and consequently no psyche ... Only external appearance creates life, only through those expressions can we make conclusions about the presence of intellect and emotions. (1922a, p. 127)

Kornilov's argument in favor of the active organism as the condition for the emergence of psychological functions was set up to counter Meumann's (1908) strong emphasis on the role of intellect in human psychology. This argument also antedates the main standpoint of the so-called "activity theory" (e.g. Leont'ev, 1975), which became a catchword in Soviet psychology much later.

The Roots of Intellect in the Process of History

Kornilov viewed the development of intellect as "an *inhibited* will-process that is not turned into action" (1922a, p. 128, added emphasis). Again, countering the "cognitive primacy" that Meumann's ideas included, Kornilov emphasized the *developmental* nature of all intellectual processes. Thus, the capability of setting goals and making them conscious (*predstavlenie čeli*) could not be seen as a starting point for intellectual processes, but rather as an end-state of psychological development (1922a, p. 127) which enables the organism to relate to its environment in qualitatively novel ways. The idea that the inhibited nature of will leads to the development of cognitive functions aligns Kornilov's theorizing with Freud's emphasis on sublimation, paving the way to the emergence of "Freudo-Marxism" in Kornilov's Institute in the mid-1920s (see chapter 5).

Kornilov's argument against Meumann in the realm of primacy of the activity over intellect (and will) took an interesting historicistic turn. Kornilov argued first that if Meumann's position was correct, then all human life would historically develop towards the minimum of external activity and maximum of intellectual efforts (which are not observable). This would be equal to the "merging with God" as the highest and ultimate goal of the "all world process." Declaring this view of history "anti-historical" (1922a, p. 133), Kornilov argues that human history reflects a tendency toward overcoming the disharmony between intellect and will, both in the minds of individuals and in the psychology of whole social classes. He views this synthesis (equilibration) of will and intellect in the achievement of "reasonably acting will" (*razumno deitsvuiushchaia volia*) that is seen as the historical (and desired) future goal both for individuals and whole societies (cf. 1922a, p. 134). In the case of individuals, the "reasonably acting will" would allow the person to benefit from new (higher) cognitive functions in the area of intentional action, and novel intentional actions can "feed into" the intellectual processes. In terms of dialectical thought, Kornilov implied that the "qualitative leap" of the "intellect → will system" belonged to a higher level of interdependence. It was the application of this synthesis of will and intellect at the level of societies which enabled Kornilov to admit the possibility of a social utopia – the new Soviet state, which proclaimed the building of a fair and qualitatively unsurpassed new society of equality, freedom, and work.

Applied Implications: For Work Processes and Education

Kornilov's proclamation of his "reactology" as the direction for psychology to take in the 1920s was explicitly linked with issues of application of that reactology in the social praxis of the changing society. He saw two main areas of applicability of his theory and experimental techniques: in the optimization of work (in the context of a subdiscipline that was labeled "psychotechnics" in the 1920s), and in the complex study of child development in the context of "paedology."

In his analysis of the process of work (1922a, pp. 143–52; 1922b), Kornilov attempted to characterize seven different types of work by the kinds of reactions (see p. 114) that are necessarily involved in the process and give the process its main emphasis. For instance, the natural type of work processes (based largely on reaction type (1) is the case of work in which:

> the person in the process of work is in a more or less unpressured state and fulfills the task without special tension, since it fits his nature. He focuses his attention more or less equally between the object of work and his movements. The professions that belong to this type do not demand either intense reasoning activity or intensive muscular activity. Such are most small jobs in home management, the work of technical personnel in institutions: the doorman, watchman, errand boy, maid, janitor, etc. (1922a, p. 145)

In contrast, the most complex work-type – work processes of the association type – involved all the intellectual professions. In cases of this type, the more the task (demands) in terms of the required associations to link it with other knowledge, the longer the time the task takes, and the lesser the energy expenditure in the peripheral "work organ" (1922a, p. 149). Following his principle of monophasic energy expenditure, Kornilov argued that

the transition from peripheral expenditure of energy to central energy expenditure is more complicated than the reverse process. That is equal to the fact
that the transition from mental to physical work always takes place more
easily, than the reverse process of change from physical work to mental work.
In its applied meaning this implies that to create a representative of physical
work from the intellectual person is an easier task than to create an intellectual
person out of a professional of physical work. (1922a, p. 151)

This contrast between two directions of change in professions turned out
to be prophetic in two ways. First, the idea of the difficulty of turning
physical workers into intellectuals was embodied in the fate of Kornilov's
own future when (around the time of the forceful entrance of the "proletarian intellectuals" into academic positions) his critics made active use of this
"bourgeois superstition" of his. The Party's task was to create trustworthy
academics out of people of proletarian background and dubious education
– exactly the transition that Kornilov had declared difficult. Secondly,
Kornilov's explanation of the easy transfer from intellectual work to "re-
education" though manual labor became a widespread practice as more and
more "old intellectuals" were assigned to such enforced change of the type
of work by the State in the form of labor camps.

The paedological application of reactology as seen by Kornilov extends
the discourse of "work reactology" into the developmental process of
children in the context of education. He evoked the slogan of the Soviet
State – synthesis of physical and mental work (as it was widely propagated
in the context of the "labor school" (*trudovaia shkola*)) – and advocated the
exact study of "pedagogical reactions" of children (1922a, p. 157). The
synthesis of mental and physical work was proclaimed to be the criterion of
"harmonious education", which, however, was declared to be impossible in
capitalist class society (1929, p. 158). The implementation of the principle
of synthesis of the physical and mental work in child development was
supposed to lead to a new form of relationship between central and
peripheral energy expenditure: moving from the monophasic to biphasic
(central–peripheral) expenditure (1922a, p. 159). This synthesis linked
Kornilov's dynamic psycho-reactology with his acceptance of dialectical
materialism that became the ordinary social discourse theme of Soviet
sciences in the early 1920s.

Kornilov and Dialectical Materialism: The Next Step

Kornilov's work in the area of reaction dynamics provided a sound foundation for links to be built with the dialectical thought system which became

widespread in the Soviet Union in the early 1920s. However, ideas do not usually exist independently of actions (Kornilov's own point!) and Kornilov's shift to dialectic philosophy was mirrored in his actions in the context of the establishing of psychology. He began by usurping his mentor Georgi Chelpanov (the founder and Director of the Institute of Psychology at Moscow University) and forcing him into retirement (not an impossible task, as Chelpanov was 60 years old in 1922). Going beyond the provincial context of Moscow, Kornilov's encouraged institutional self-actualization which led to his taking a leading role in the newly started "fight for Marxist psychology." Of course Kornilov had to accept the tenets of dialectical thinking and Marxist terminology relatively quickly in order to satisfy this wider ambition.

Kornilov's newly adopted role as an "activist for a Marxist psychology" was first mooted during his presentation on January 14, 1923 at the First All-Russian Congress of Psychoneurology (Kornilov, 1923a). Eager to develop a Marxist psychology (and to become the Director of the Institute where he was working), Kornilov gave a strong vindication of his theories of reactology in opposition to Chelpanov's "idealist psychology." He did not hesitate to use rhetorical means meant to discredit Chelpanov's thinking from the point of view of the newly dominant social ideology of the Soviet state. So, Chelpanov's school of thought was declared to be "a servant" of idealist philosophy which for its part was seen as a "servant of religion" (Kornilov, 1923b, p. 86). On other occasions (e.g. in his bitter dispute with Struminsky (1926), a leftist speculative Marxist, Kornilov, by this time Director of the Institute, defended his own position by pointing to the similar stance taken by other psychologists at the Institute, so presenting a unified "front." His detractors were accused of "anti-dialecticalness" and "revisionism" in their thinking (Kornilov, 1926c, p. 186). Thus, by being involved in the conception of the institutionalization of early Soviet psychology, Kornilov quickly became a deft politician, whose manoeuvres in the Institute involved the strategic use of ideology to further the development of his own research and science.

In his efforts to "fight" the Chelpanovian "speculative psychology" (*umozakliuchitel'naia psikhologia*) Kornilov tried to enlist potential allies from the different corners of psychology who would be antagonistic to Chelpanov's introspection-oriented psychology. First, psycoanalytic traditions were evoked as useful for building a "new psychology." Psychoanalysts' methodology of the study of hidden psychological processes by way of external reactions (Kornilov explicitly used the metaphor of an iceberg – the study of nine-tenths of it by way of external signs, or the remaining one-tenth; 1923a, p. 45) was similar in its structure to Kornilov's reactology. Like reactological methods, psychoanalytic methodology was perceived as diminishing the dominant role of introspectionist methodology. In a strange marriage, psychoanalysis became a bedfellow to Russian behavioristic approaches to behavior (see chapter 5). The latter became a topic of discourse in 1923, as Bekhterev's *General Foundations of Reflexology* and Pavlov's collection of papers *Twenty Years of Experience in the Study of Higher Nervous Activity* were published that year. However, the highly "materialistic" physiological emphases of Bekhterev and Pavlov were not well suited to Kornilov's goals. He attacked Bekhterev's use of the energy concept, claiming that by the central role of that concept Bekhterev left "materialism" behind (Kornilov, 1923b, p. 90). In order to highlight the differences between his own use of the energy concept and that of Bekhterev, he claimed allegiance with Lenin's maxim of psychic processes being features of matter.

Pavlov's emphasis on the reduction of all psychological processes to "conditional reflexes" was rebutted by Kornilov in a different context. Pavlov's opposition to the new regime in Russia which had emerged as a result of a war, revolution, and famine, was clear-cut (see Joravsky, 1985, 1989, chapter 7). In his text of 1923 Pavlov made a revealing comment about the times he lived in, calling for the need to explain the complexity of the human psyche, which, being "led by dark forces" inflicts upon itself "unexpressable miseries through wars and revolutions" the horrors of which replicate "inter-animal relationships." Pavlov called for the establishment of an objective science of human nature, which could "bring it out from the contemporary darkness in the field of interpersonal relations" (Pavlov, 1923, p. 128). Kornilov did not hesitate in pointing to Pavlov's opinion of the social changes in Russia, and on several occasions he reiterated Pavlov's phrase in his paper (Kornilov, 1924b, pp. 93, 94–5). It should be remembered, however, that in these efforts to discredit Pavlov's reputation, Kornilov was merely aligning himself with Bukharin (1924a) and Zinoviev (1923), who had started the campaign a year previously.

In the 1920s ideological in-fighting slowly became the characteristic of most of Russian psychology, and became the dominant means of Soviet psychological discourse in the 1930s. Still, apart from the efforts to discredit his opponents, Kornilov's acceptance of the newly popular ideology of "dialectical materialism" was founded on his earlier reasoning about reaction dynamics. It was the nature-philosophical dialectics of Friedrich Engels (which became increasingly widespread in Soviet Marxist philosophy by the mid-1920s) that served as Kornilov's starting point for an amalgamation of his "reactology" with Marxist philosophy. Engels' nature-philosophical standpoint was characterized by accepting the principle of development as the kernel of all understanding of the world. In his presentation at the Second Psychoneurological Congress in January, 1924 (that is, shortly after taking over the Directorship of the Moscow Psychological Institute from Chelpanov), Kornilov proceeded to outline an application of the Marxist-dialectical viewpoint to psychology. He did so by emphasizing the relevance of the "law of development of nature, history, and thinking," pointing out to his audience that it is exactly the emphasis on the latter that is a "category of purely psychological kind" (1924a, p. 107). In his characterization of the major "principle of dialectic method," that of "continuous variation," Kornilov argued that "the world must be understood not as a complex of complete things, but as a complex of processes in which things that to us appear constant, as well as thought images (that is, concepts) in our heads, undergo the continuous process of emergence and extinction" (1924a, pp. 107–8).

Furthermore, the principle of the "leaping" transition from quantitative to qualitative (and vice versa) development was important, and was rooted in the Hegelian dialectical methodology that was the starting point for all Marxist philosophy. Application of the idea of qualitative transformation of phenomena to their opposites was not difficult in the realm of psychology:

It is generally known that a qualitatively defined emotion, when it reaches a certain limit in its development, transforms into an emotion that is qualitatively different. Indeed, I am not speaking about the elementary states of satisfaction and dissatisfaction, which at a certain duration and intensity transform into their opposite feelings. If we take more complex emotions we can observe, for instance, that the feeling of [self]-praise, when it reaches a certain key point, transforms into the feeling of self-admiration; the feeling of self-worth into a feeling of pride, economizing becomes stinginess, bravery becomes impudence, etc. (1924a, pp. 110–11)

The dialectical "triad" (thesis – antithesis – synthesis) fitted well into Kornilov's dynamic perspective of psychological phenomena. Furthermore, Kornilov inserted the role of contradictions into the developmental process as its main "engine." Every developmental process takes place as a result of contradictions, the negation of the "thesis" by its "antithesis", which leads to a "synthesis" in the emergence of a novel form in the given development. Kornilov explicitly viewed conscious and unconscious processes as "thesis" and "antithesis" to each other and hence new psychological phenomena were seen as emerging as a synthesis of these two spheres:

Here, in a number of concrete forms we see that what was conscious becomes embedded in the unconscious sphere, in order to emerge again later in a conscious form, richer in content. Such are the processes of remembering, which are followed by unconscious processing and new reproduction in the act of imagination. Such is, by its nature, the act of creation, where from conscious formulation and oftentimes intense work on the given problem, when we do not reach a solution, we will receive it considerably later as a result of intensive work in the unconscious sphere. (1924a, p. 111)

Kornilov's interest in dynamic relationship between conscious and unconscious processes was based on his devotion to the study of the dynamics of reaction parameters under the conditions of increasing task difficulty. The dynamic view of the "principle of monophasic energy expenditure" that Kornilov entertained, followed a similar pattern:

the person who is involved in a certain type of mental work (the central discharge), will expend less energy in the movements of his organs – eyes, limbs (peripheral discharge) – the more complex the mental work is. But if we make that mental work excessively difficult, it inevitably leads, earlier or later, to an explosive, affective expression of inhibited peripheral activity. (1927, p. 203)

Thus Kornilov viewed the dialectical unity of cognitive and affective processes in the context of problem-solving ("reaction tasks") as generating qualitatively different outcomes depending upon the complexity of the task. This parallels the emphasis on interaction between the conscious and unconscious processes in psychoanalytic reasoning. He viewed the "psychoanalytic act" as a synthesis that entails the dialectical reorganization of the "energy expenditure" between the mental and bodily spheres (see 1924a, p. 112). Given this parallel, it was not at all surprising that Kornilov made it possible for a number of young psychoanalytically-oriented investigators (e.g. Averbukh, Luria, and Fridman; see chapter 5) to continue their psychoanalytic studies as part of the activities of the Psychological Institute. Kornilov's holistic view of the reaction processes enabled him to appreciate the complexity of psychological functions and their interdependence with social settings (1925b, p. 22).

Undoubtedly one of the most widespread misunderstandings about Kornilov's psychological credo that the retrospective Soviet official sources on the history of psychology have promoted, is that of the essential similarity of his "reactology" to Bekhterev's "reflexology" and American behaviorism. Ironically, the roots of this myth can be located in the efforts of his former teacher and later adversary Georgi Chelpanov, who declared that a congruence existed between Kornilov's and Bekhterev's "reductionism" of all subjective psychological processes to a system of reflexes (Chelpanov, 1924). Kornilov forcefully rebuked the accusation, pointing to the application of dialectical synthesis on the study of behavioral and psychological aspects of human activity as the basic difference between his and Bekhterev's methodologies (Kornilov, 1925c). His perspective on the mind–body problem was an interactionist one – the mind (subjective psychological processes) is interdependent with the body (physiological and behavioral processes). The psychological processes are *functionally* dependent (*funktsional'naia zavisimost*; Kornilov, 1925b, p. 20) upon the physiological and behavioral processes, but not reducible to the latter, nor separable from them. Furthermore, behavior in itself cannot be studied without taking the subjective psychological side into account:

> if we want to study the actual behavior of a concrete and holistic personality, we must take into account both of these sides, objective and subjective, since in every reaction of the living organism both these sides are inseparable from one another. Such a two-sided, study of human behavior merged into an inseparable unity I call *reactological investigation, since the concept of reaction, differently from reflex, includes both these sides*. And so, exactly that inseparable and organic merge between the subjective and objective sides gives us that *synthesis* that must be at the foundation of Marxist psychology. (1925b, p. 19)

Finally, Kornilov envisaged the use of dialectics in psychology on a large scale, not limiting it only to the explanatory side of psychological constructs but arguing for its introduction as the method of investigation. In the latter application, he stressed the relevance of the "dialectical leap" as the basic principle by which psychological development takes place. Hence the methodology used to study development has to fit that nature of the phenomena – first and foremost, in the study of child development and of the qualitative change in the psychology of people in pathological cases (1924a, p. 113).

In sum, Kornilov's (developing) ideas for a "Marxist psychology" in the years 1923–7 paved the way, in all their aspects, for entrance of Vygotsky to the field of psychology. Both were interested in the Hegelian synthesis as fundamental: Kornilov accomplished that in his fight for the reconstruction of psychology; while Vygotsky moved in a parallel direction in his efforts to understand how recipients of art messages arrive at new feelings. Both were active in trying to understand dynamics of complex processes: for Kornilov these were reactions of subjects under different task conditions; for Vygotsky these were the different receptions of complex literature and theatre performances. Furthermore, Kornilov's (often rhetorical) statements about the kind of psychology he wanted to build espoused themes that later become developed in Vygotsky's (and his colleagues') work. Thus, the call for dialectics as a method of investigation became elaborated in concrete form in the "method of double stimulation" (1927–9) (see chapter 9), and the unity of developmental processes in ontogeny and pathology can be seen in the early 1930s when Vygotsky and Luria became intensively involved in medicine. Under Kornilov's new directorship the Institute of Experimental Psychology in the mid-1920s was an environment that (with the concurrent "fight" for "Marxist psychology") constituted a fertile ground for Vygotsky's development. Of course, Vygotsky's importation to the Institute was part of a major organizational change of that institution under Kornilov's guidance.

Kornilov's "Path to Power" at the Moscow Psychological Institute

Kornilov had been associated with Chelpanov from the time the latter started working at Moscow University (in 1907, after teaching at Kiev University in 1892–1907). He was an active participant in the work of the Psychological Seminary, which served (prior to the establishment of the Psychological Institute) as the major higher educational center for Russian psychologists, and was attached to the Faculty of Philosophy of Moscow University. Among the members of the Seminary, Kornilov appears to have been one of the most active, as were Nikolai Rybnikov (a child psychologist who continued his work in parallel to Kornilov throughout the 1920s), and Pavel Blonsky. From the Fall of 1909, Kornilov was the leader of one of six groups of students who studied reaction types in the framework of the laboratory "practicum" in experimental psychology and this group continued to conduct research under his leadership for years (see "*Otchet o deiatel'nosti*," 1914).

As one of the first junior assistants to Chelpanov, Kornilov was a participant in the establishment of the Psychological Institute in 1912 (see Chelpanov, 1914, for a detailed history of the Institute), and worked in it from its beginning. In his social-political world-view, Kornilov claimed to have been close to the social democratic movement in Russia since 1905 (see Petrovsky, 1967, p. 56), and this may have encouraged him to become involved in the building of a new science in the context of a "new social order" in the early 1920s. Teplov candidly commented upon the speed of Kornilov's conversion into a "new psychologist:" while in 1921 Kornilov had still been in favor of the separation of psychology from philosophy, he then called for the use of Marxism in order to re-organize psychology in January 1923 (Teplov, 1960, p. 11).

What events took place in the Psychological Institute and its social environment in that short space of time? The events of the early 1920s seem to indicate intellectual and local-political turmoil. Interestingly, among the Russian intellectuals who had been associated with the Psychological Institute in the pre-1917 years, it was not Kornilov but Blonsky who first raised the issues of "Marxist reformation" of psychology (Blonsky, 1920, 1921; see also Joravsky, 1985, 1989). Around the same time, in November 1921, Chelpanov was reappointed to the Directorship of the Psychological Institute (Petrovsky, 1967, p. 59). In March 1922, Lenin's article "On the meaning of militant materialism" was published in the journal *Pod znamenem marksizma* (Lenin, 1922), leading to the upsurge of an active (indeed militant) "fight" for Marxism in the intellectual sphere of society. This took the form of establishing new institutional strongholds for a development of "Marxist" science. Furthermore, in 1921–2 there was a wave of reactions against "bourgeois" intellectuals and scientists, many of whom were sent to exile in the West in 1922 (161 leading scientists in philosophy, sociology, and other areas) (Joravsky, 1985). The exile of these specialists was publicly explained by the need for educating the "proletarian intelligentsia" who would be ideologically fully devoted to the new regime, while being comparable in expert knowledge to the specialists with "bourgeois backgrounds." The latter "could not be trusted ideologically" and were denounced as anti-Soviet "schemers," charges supported by claims that they had concealed their "scheming" by means of their possession of knowledge not available to the proletariat (see *Pervoe predosterzhenie*, 1922, p. 1). The distrust of the "intelligentsia" was phrased in terms similar to the justifications of the expropriation of property of the "bourgeois" classes as a result of the revolution: the proletariat had taken the property, and now the time had come to take privileged knowledge from the bourgeois intelligentsia who possessed it. Of course, knowledge could not be simply and directly expropriated, but only gradually learned from the "old generation," who would be subsequently replaced by the newly learned, ideologically loyal "cadres." It is probably a myth to consider the 1920s in the Soviet Union a time of high freedom in intellectual innovation (cf. Jakhot, 1981). Rather, such a *de facto* freedom may have been a result of the asynchrony between the "takeover" of political and intellectual "power" by the new regime. Having taken over the political power and gradually consolidated it, the regime could afford to allow social discourse which appeared to be unfettered, within limits. The proof of those limits can be seen in the fate of the intelligentisia in August 1922, when some of them were exiled to the West but others were said to have been "sent to the Northern provinces of Russia" (*Pervoe predosterezhenie*, 1922, p. 1), a pattern that antedates the wider "relocation programs" of selected Soviet people in the 1930s.

So, the beginnings of the fight for Marxist psychology in the early 1920s were closely intertwined with the gradual efforts of the Soviet regime to annexe the domains of the scientific and humanitarian knowledge, and exiling the specialists of untrustworthy class backgrounds. Of course, that set two axiomatic conditions for the "new" psychology: it had to declare unquestioningly its allegiance to Marxism, and the issue of the class-determinism of psychological phenomena had to surface in it in some form. Indeed, the Soviet society of the early 1920s became filled with social suggestions and expectations for the conversion into and following of a "Marxist line". Of course, what that "line" should be like, was not (yet) strictly determined, hence it was possible for many different versions of "Marxist psychology" to emerge and compete for dominance in the psychological and philosophical discussions of the 1920s.

As a serious thinker of his time, Chelpanov, much like Pavlov, could not (and would not) remain silent under the upsurge of ideological militant turmoil, calling it openly an "ideological dictatorship of Marxism" in 1922. The timing for this outburst seems to have coincided with the fate of his academic colleagues as they were exiled from the Soviet Union that year. Chelpanov had been the Chairman of the Moscow Psychological Society since its re-opening in 1920 (after a two-year break, due to the war and the death of its first chairman L. M. Lopatin). The Society finished its activities in 1922, "in conjunction with the exile of the most active reactionaries" (!) as one Soviet description put it (Chagin and Klushin, 1975, p. 44).

Chelpanov's public statements about the "ideological dictatorship" evoked defensive and suspicious reactions from the promoters of the new "Marxist science" (see Bukharin, 1924b, p. 133; Frankfurt, 1925). Kornilov's criticism of Chelpanov merely reflected the increasing ideological chasm between the new political regime and Chelpanov. In his first proclamation of a "Marxist psychology" in January 1923, Kornilov devoted only one paragraph to an attack on Chelpanov, reviewing (1923a, p. 43), his position in respect to the "soul" (*dusha*) as an antidote to Lenin's "materialistic emphasis" on the psyche. By the end of that year, his attacks on Chelpanov had become increasingly vicious in their content (e.g. the statement that Chelpanov's "school" – from which Kornilov himself originated – had been "undermining all trust in psychology"; 1923b, p. 86) but remained relatively short, especially in comparison with his lengthy criticisms of Pavlov and Bekhterev. (It seems that the intensity of "Chelpanov-bashing" in Kornilov's publications grew only after he had taken over the Psychological Institute from Chelpanov.) The last major public attack against Chelpanov occurred on October 24, 1923 in *Pravda*. About three weeks later, on November 15, 1923 "it was suggested to Chelpanov that he hand over the Psychological Institute to Professor Kornilov" (Petrovsky, 1967, p. 59). The transition of power had been administratively arranged, and Kornilov rushed to re-organize the Institute along the lines of the new "Marxist psychology" which he had been proclaiming for the past year.

The immediate effects of the Kornilovian takeover of the Psychological Institute was remembered by an active "participant observer" of that process, Alexander Luria, (decades later, March, 1974). He joined the staff of the Institute in the Fall of 1923 and was appointed to be its Academic Secretary at the age of 21:

> I was immediately immersed in the thick of events. Our Institute was supposed to reform the whole psychological science by abandoning Chelpanov's idealistic theory and creating a new materialist one. Kornilov spoke of a Marxist psychology. He believed that one should give up subjective experiments and make an objective study of behavior, notably of motor reactions, which purpose was to be served by a dynamometer. Meanwhile the reform of psychology was proceeding in two forms: first, by way of renaming things, and second, by way of moving furniture. If my memory doesn't fail me, perception was renamed reception of a signal for reaction; memory, retention with reproduction of reaction; attention, restricting of reaction; emotions, emotional reactions; in short, we inserted the word 'reaction' wherever we could, sincerely believing that we were doing something important and serious. At the same time we were moving the furniture from one lab to another. I remember very well that as I carried tables up and down the stairs, I was sure that this would make a change in our work, and we would create a new basis for Soviet psychology. That period was remarkable for our naivety and enthusiasm, but predictably it soon reached a dead end. Differences with Kornilov began almost from the beginning, as we did not like his approach . . . (Levitin, 1982, pp. 154–5)

Luria's eyewitness reconstruction of the enthusiastic devaluation of "old" psychology within the Psychological Institute should not, of course, be taken at its face value. After all, his recollection of the Institute is personal and he is armed with hindsight concerning Kornilov's "fall into disrepute" in the early 1930s. The effort to re-name every aspect of psychology in conjunction with the fashion for "reactology" was of course predictable. Similar re-labelling has occurred since in Soviet psychology (e.g. finding "reflexes" in every psychological phenomenon in the early 1950s, or inserting the term "activity" everywhere in the social context of the Moscow University Psychology Faculty in the 1970s). Likewise, international psychological fashions are not very different. We eagerly speak of the "cognitive revolution" in every area of psychology, while continuing the study of behavior in ways that remind an outside observer of some lax behaviorism. Furthermore, Luria's recollection of Kornilov's interest in the study of behavior in an objective way reflects the official historiographical equation of "reactology" with "reflexology" and condemns both for their "mistakes" or for "lagging behind the progress of science" (see, e.g. Petrovsky, 1967; Smirnov, 1975).

In many accounts, Luria has emphasized that the new personnel which was brought in by Kornilov was very young (see Luria, 1979, p. 31; 1982, p. 18). However, quite a number of psychologists who had been associated with the Psychological Institute before the civil war continued their work there. A brief overview of the structure and activities of the Institute in 1924 illustrates the width of coverage of different areas, as well as the age composition of the co-workers of different sections. The overview is largely based on the report of the Academic Secretary of the Institute (Luria, 1926g), with additional material from a diversity of other sources.

The Institute (from 1924 its official name was "Moscow Institute of Experimental Psychology") consisted of six sections:

(1) General Experimental Psychology. This section was led by Kornilov himself (who was 45 years old in 1924), and included a varied list of associates. First, both Pavel Blonsky (40 years) and Nikolai Bernshtein (28 years) were listed as the co-workers of this Section. Both had the highest official rank within the Institute – "true member" (deistvitel'nyi chlen) – but only Bernshtein was listed as being involved in a research topic. ("The layer of reaction on the form of movement".) Bernshtein's relatively high formal status may have been due to his connection with the Central Institute of Labor, whose Director, Aleksei Gastev, made this Institute a rather important institution in the social context of the 1920s. Blonsky was at that time mostly involved in the activities of the Academy of Communist Education, which he had helped to found in 1919 together with Nadezhda Krupskaia (Sergeeva, 1974), and his work at the Institute in 1924 seems to have been limited to one public lecture and a contribution to the first collection of papers (Blonsky, 1925a). Kornilov's own research topic was given as "The problem of reaction of maximum inhibition." Secondly, Alexander Luria (aged 22) was listed as "scientific co-worker of the first rank", together with a number of others carrying the "second-rank" label: V. A. Artemov (aged 27), Lev Vygotsky (aged 28), G. M. Gagaeva, S. I. Ginzburg, N. F. Dobrynin (aged 34), and Ju. V. Frankfurt. Luria was listed as being very active in organizing research and coordinating research efforts of students and extra-mural co-workers on the topics of "objective symptoms of complex reaction," "study of hypnogenic complexes," "inhibition of associative reactions" (with A. N. Leont'ev who belonged to the category of "extra-mural co-workers" in 1924), and "objective symptoms of complex reactions of erythrophobics." Vygotsky was also reported to have taken upon himself a similarly active role. He was involved in a collective project (with L. S. Sakharov, L. V. Zankov, aged 22, and I. M. Soloviev, all of whom were "extra-murals") to study dominant reactions, and was listed as the advisor of I. M. Soloviev in a study of the influence of subdominant stimuli on rhythmic work. Other co-workers of this section were involved in

their individual topics: Artemov was studying the linkage between conditional reactions, Gagaeva studied the correlation between blood-type and reaction-type, and Dobrynin the processes of attention. Ginzburg and Frankfurt were not listed as being involved in particular experimental work. The latter, of course, was highly prominent in his active "Marxist militant" fight for a new psychology (e.g. Frankfurt, 1925). At the same time, a number of extra-mural co-workers of the Section were described as proceeding with their own specific topics at the Institute. R. V. Volevich had the theme of "objective study of pain"; D. I. Ravkin investigated "reaction rhythm in connection with human constitution"; T. D. Faddeev was interested in the "relation of reaction speed and sensitivity to galvanic electricity"; A. D. Miller (with Kornilov) studied "the dynamic side of reaction to visual and acoustic stimuli"; T. Frenkel studied "movement thresholds"; and E. I. Rubinstein and D. N. Bogojavlensky (with Luria) "chain verbal reactions." Obviously, this Section was the most numerous and active one within the Institute, where the activities of Luria and Vygotsky proceeded in parallel with the experimental and philosophical direction of Kornilov.

(2) Social Psychology. This section was led by the "true member of the Institute," Professor Mikhail. A. Reisner (born 1868, died 1928; 56 years of age in 1924). Reisner, who had been a law professor in St Petersburg in the pre-1917 years (he was one of the first professors appointed to Bekhterev's Psychoneurology Institute, teaching government law there from 1907; Gerver, 1912), had declared his support for the Bolshevik regime in late 1917 (Fitzpatrick, 1970, p. 318), had been one of the founders of the Socialist Academy in October, 1918 (Chagin and Klushin, 1975, p. 50), and worked in Lunacharsky's Narkompros in the years following that. His section included no collaborators designated as first rank, and only two of the second rank (M. I. Ginzburg-Dajan and Sudeikin). No experimental topics were listed as being studied by this Section, so it can be assumed that most of its activities in 1924 were theoretical in their nature, and in line with Reisner's published work of the time, which linked Freudian and Marxist ideas in psychology (Reisner, 1925).

(3) The Applied Psychology (Psychotechnique) Section was led by Professor Isaak Shpilrejn (aged 33), a doctor from the University of Leipiz in 1912 who had moved from Gastev's Central Institute of Labor (where he had been since its beginning in 1921) to the Psychological Institute in 1923 (while retaining the ties with the Commissariat of Labor, and the Communist Academy). He was listed himself as a first-rank co-worker and a member of the Institute's Collegium. His section included only one other first-rank

colleague, S. G. Gellershtein (aged 28), and ten extra-murals. The research topics of this section included the theme of trainability in the study of professions, methods of psychotechnical studies of large groups, the effects of exhibitions on the visitors, and the use of language among Red Army soldiers.

(4) The Psychopathology Section was headed by the member of the Institute Aaron B. Zalkind (aged 35), a medical doctor (who studied at Moscow University in 1906–11 and received his medical degree in 1918, after practising in a military hospital through the war years), who by the early 1920s was a Marxist fighting for the reorganization of psychology (Dajan, 1924), psycho-hygiene (Zalkind, 1924b, 1930c), and pedagogics. Zalkind was closely linked with the Bolshevik Party organization, and with the Communist Academy. His section at the Institute included A. I. Zalmanzon (first-rank co-worker) and B. D. Fridman (second-rank co-worker), with only one listed extra-mural collaborator (somebody called Dr Khachitur-jan). Only one theme of empirical investigation (carried out jointly by Zalmanzon and Fridman) – the human constitution and reactions in con-nections with the reaction rhythm in case of different illnesses – was listed for 1924. The co-workers of this section were active in other ways over 1924: Fridman analyzed psychoanalytic thinking (Fridman, 1925; see chap-ter 5), discussed issues of psychotherapy and Marxism at the internal colloquia of the Institute, and at the Second Psychoneurological Congress in January. It seems that Zalkind was the key connection between Kornilov and the ideological leadership of the Soviet intelligentsia. He, like the leading philosopher of the time – A. M. Deborin – were members of the Institute's Collegium.

(5) The Child Psychology Section was headed by Kornilov's peer from the years of joint studies and work at Chelpanov's Institute (since 1907), Nikolai Rybnikov. Like Blonsky (who had followed Chelpanov from Kiev to Moscow in 1907; see Kozulin, 1984, chapter 6), Rybnikov had the rank of true member of the Institute, but his Section included no listed full-time or part-time co-workers, and the only empirical research topic that was listed for this Section was carried by Rybnikov himself ("Biogenesis of child's speech reactions"). On that topic, Rybnikov gave only one presenta-tion in the Institute's colloquia series in 1924. Rybnikov had been an active investigator in the Chelpanov years (Rybnikov, 1916) and continued so after Kornilov took over the Institute leadership (Rybnikov, 1925, 1926, 1928), but he was obviously very much on the periphery on the "mind-scape" that dominated the Institute in 1924. He did participate actively in the paedology movement in the latter half of the 1920s, but was never seen

to implement any of the reactological philosophy promoted and vigorously defended by Kornilov.

(6) The Animal Behavior Section was headed by Vladimir M. Borovsky (aged 42) who, after getting his doctorate from the University of Heidelberg in 1910, had been working at Saratov University (1918–20) and had moved to Moscow as a Docent in 1920 to work at the First Moscow University. At the Institute, he had the lowest rank (first-rank co-worker) among all section heads in 1924, and his section consisted of only one other first-rank colleague (the preparator of the laboratory, V. V. Troitsky), and of one extra-mural co-worker (B. N. Beliaev). Two topics of empirical work were listed for this section for 1924, both carried out by Borovsky: reactions to monochromatic stimulation in invertebrates, and the study of delayed reactions. Despite the small size of this section, Borovsky could be observed to be rather active in 1924: he gave one general colloqium (on the "mechanistic theory of animal behavior") and five internal colloquia at the Institute. Later, his activities led to the propagation of materialist psychology (Borovsky, 1929a), and to overviewing of the Soviet psychology from Kornilov's perspective (Borovsky, 1929b). A decade later, he was paired with Kornilov in an attempt to attribute different negative characteristics to them (Georgiev, 1937).

This detailed overview of the structure of the Institute in 1924 leads us to think that it was not really such a monolithic fortress of new Marxist psychology as Kornilov himself repeatedly presented it (Kornilov, 1926c, 1927). Indeed, the most numerous section, of General and Experimental Psychology, was devoted to studies other than those of "reactology:" from the philosophical and ideological activities of Kornilov and Frankfurt, to numerous rather traditional-looking laboratory studies of younger co-workers, to the clearly psychodynamically-oriented studies of "complexes" instigated by Luria. At the same time, other sections seem to be either very little touched by the new fashion for "reactology" (e.g. Rybnikov's), or taking their activities in other directions that are only remotely linked with Kornilov's theoretical efforts (Zalkind's psychopathology, Shpilrejn's psychotechnics, Reisner's social psychology). While remaining distant from the "reactological" theories of Kornilov, these three sections and their leaders seem to have linked Kornilov well with other institutions which were involved in the promotion of Marxist science and its administration, that is, the Communist Academy and Narkompros (Reisner), the Communist Party Central Committee and its Agitprop department (Zalkind), and the Commissariat of Labor as well as the Central Institute of Work (Shpilrejn). In this respect, it is not surprising that Luria's eyewitness' account of the life at the Institute captured mostly the work of Kornilov's Section, which was the most numerous and most active part of the re-organized Institute.

A plurality of perspectives is not easily tolerated at Russian academic institutions, the hierarchical organization of which is largely indebted to the German academic traditions. Furthermore, in the social turmoil of the "new society" and its transition from war communism to the New Economic Policy, one would expect a Russian scientific institution to be a rather complex social system. It is not surprising that under the conditions of the revolutionary *glasnost* of the 1920s the Institute was fraught with interpersonal frictions. In the discussions of the Presidium of RANION (*VseRossiiskaia Assotsiasia Nauchno-Issledovatel'skikh Institutov Obshchestvennykh Nauk* – The All-Russian Association of the Research Institutes of Social Sciences) it was noted that the Psychological Institute (which belonged to RANION) included a number of "in-fighting groupings" of researchers from 1926 onwards (Petrovsky, 1967, p. 68). It is therefore probably correct that (as Luria remembered) disagreements within the Institute began almost immediately after its reorganization. Which factions were fighting which remains largely embedded in the folklore of Soviet psychologists, but it is not clear on the basis of the historical published materials that there was any major public break between Kornilov and Luria's (or Vygotsky's) lines of work. Both Luria and Vygotsky were newcomers to psychology whose indebtedness to Kornilov extended beyond mere gratitude (for transferring them to Moscow), to an acknowledgement of his influences on the substantive side of their work; it was therefore hardly in their interests to initiate any schism.

Convergence of Developmental Lines: Vygotsky in Kornilov's Institute

Kornilov's conception of "reaction" retained the qualitative specificity of intra-psychological phenomena, while claiming that their study should take place by way of their external indications (reactions). Vygotsky's thinking in 1924–6 was clearly interdependent with Kornilov's reactology, as we attempt to demonstrate below.

Let us first analyze the project that led to Vygotsky's being invited to work at the Institute, that is, the presentation at the Second Psychoneurological Congress in Leningrad. Vygotsky's presentation – on the topic of reflexological investigation – took place on January 6, 1924, and received a moderately enthusiastic reaction by Dajan (1924) who singled it out as a noteworthy example of psychologists of the "intermediate standpoint" who already "started on the road of scientific objectivism, but did not yet make the decisive step to dialectical materialism" (Dajan, 1924, p. 164). Dajan's account leads us to believe that the invitation to Vygotsky to go to Moscow was motivated purely by ideological personnel needs of Kornilov rather than by any "objective recognition" of Vygotsky as a "living genius" (see the introduction to part II).

After moving to Moscow, Vygotsky published an article that was based on the oral presentation in Leningrad (Vygotsky, 1926b). In the published version, it is argued that the reflexological reductionism of Protopopov, Pavlov, and Bekhterev overlooks the basic issue of psychology – that is, the organization of the system of reflexes where some of those obtain greater importance than others as they become their regulators:

> Reflexes do not exist separately, do not act haphazardly, but unite into complexes, systems, complex groups and formations that determine human behavior. The laws of integration of reflexes into complexes, the types of such formations, kinds and forms of interaction within these systems and between whole systems, all these questions have first-rank relevance for the problems of scientific psychology of behavior. The study of reflexes is only beginning, and all these areas remain yet unexplored. However, already now it is possible to speak, as a fact, about the undoubted interaction of different systems of reflexes, about *reflection* of some systems on others, and even to describe approximately the principle of that reflection ... *Some reflex, in its response part (movement, secretion) itself becomes a stimulus for a new reflex of the same or other system.* (Vygotsky, 1926b, p. 32)

Thus, the idea of psychological regulation of behavior and cognition was expressed by Vygotsky at the time of his first endeavors at the Institute. The instrumental side of the regulation – the construction of means of regulation – was not yet evident in this writing, but the idea of a hierarchical organization of systems of reflexes and the presence of different qualitative features at different levels of the hierarchy were there in the written version of his presentation at the Congress. Vygotsky went on to defend the use of selected versions of introspection against attacks of objectivity-demanding reflexologists, who at the time were propagating human experiments without giving subjects any instructions, and who dismissed all subjective experiences as not being viable research materials. While rejecting the acceptance of subjects' self-description as an objective database (the practice from the Würzburg School), Vygotsky insisted upon acceptance of self-report data for the purpose of the study of hidden reactions (1926b, p. 45). Here, Vygotsky's and Kornilov's ideas coincide: the psychological investigation preserves its qualitative specificity in the domain of the research of complex, delayed reactions, that in principle cannot be studied by immediate, behavioral responses.

In their converging efforts to overcome the reductionism of behavioristic tendencies in Russian and international psychologies, Kornilov and Vygotsky proceeded to enlist the work of Gestalt psychologists to their side Vygotsky's short introductory preface to the Russian publication of Kurt Koffka's article on introspection (Koffka, 1924) in the volume of publications of the Institute (Vygotsky, 1926f) is stylistically interesting. Here, in marked contrast to the other papers by Vygotsky in the same volume (Vygotsky, 1926b, 1926d, 1926e), Vygotsky used quasi-military terminology to describe the historical course of the development of Marxist psychology. For instance, he emphasized the tactical need to "separate oneself from fellow travellers" at a particular time in history, in the "general war against subjectivism and empiricism" (of Chelpanov), and for "the freeing of human psychology from the biological imprisonment" (Vygotsky, 1926f, p. 176). Furthermore, Vygotsky declared that "the fight becomes deeper and enters a new phase" (p. 177). Such military-like terms, phrased in the terminology of Marxist fights in and around the Institute, are very uncharacteristic of the rest of Vygotsky's writings (which, however, are often bitingly polemical but do not use ideological terminology). These features are closer to Kornilov's style of argument in the 1920s, and may indicate Vygotsky's relatively easy (but passing) flirtation with Kornilov's discourse in the beginning of his work at the Institute.

Of course, Vygotsky's early work at the Institute showed greater interdependence with reactology than either stylistic excesses in the presentation of translations, or the use of the term "reaction" in opposition to the reductionism of reflexology demonstrate. Vygotsky became involved in empirical research on the interdependence of reactions with a group of colleagues (Gagaeva, Zankov, Sakharov, and Soloviev) and under Kornilov's acknowledged supervision. The results of this joint project, presented by Vygotsky (1926d), reveal the ways in which he practically integrated the notion of reactions into his reasoning. The experiments were devoted to the analysis of the "principle of the dominant" in subjects' reaction systems. Under specifiable conditions, a given reaction can begin to play an integrative role in respect to other reactions in the given system (hence it becomes dominant), under other conditions another reaction may overwhelm the given system. Arguing against Pavlov's mechanistic atomism in reasoning about the summation of reflexes, Vygotsky relied on the philosophy of Gestalt psychology in describing that summation: "Reflex plus reflex turns out to be not two reflexes, but some new form of behavior" (1926d, p. 102).

In their experimental efforts to study the principle of the dominant in the sphere of reactions, Vygotsky and his colleagues put into practice the first version of the idea that in a complex system of reactions (which includes an internal part, hidden from outside observation), some reactions emerge as regulators of others in the framework of the whole system. The empirical work on the dominant principle supported Vygotsky's argument for an analysis of consciousness.

One of the very first theoretical (polemical) projects of his own that Vygotsky undertook after arriving in Moscow and starting to work at the Institute was the preparation and writing of the article on consciousness (Vygotsky, 1925g). Work on this article must have kept him busy: on that topic he gave a short internal colloquium to the Institute on March 24, 1924, which was followed by the Institute's much larger open colloquium towards the end of that year (October 19, 1924; Luria, 1926g, p. 248). The publications arising from these colloquia show clear signs of a close intellectual interdependence with the social environment of the Institute over 1924. First, the selection of the epigraph from Karl Marx – the reference to the difference between architectural activities of spiders and bees on the one hand, and human beings on the other – seems to follow from the use of that quotation in the everyday professional interaction between the young Marxist psychologists at the Institute. As a result, the very same quotation appears at the conclusion of the article by the Ukranian psychophysiologist Z. Chuchmarev, published in the same volume as was Vygotsky's paper on consciousness (see Chuchmarev, 1925, p. 220). Secondly, the polemical character of Vygotsky's article fits in very well with Kornilov's goals of the time. Vygotsky started from a substantive criticism of the ideas of Bekhterev and Pavlov, for their extension of reflex-based explanations to all psychological phenomena, either in the form of "energetic principles" (Bekhterev) or labelling of complex phenomena as "reflexes" (Pavlov; see Vygotsky, 1925g, pp. 176, 179 as well as p. 183). Invoking the criticism by Vagner of the overextension of the reflex principle, Vygotsky warned against carrying over explanatory concepts from simple to more complex psychological phenomena. Reflexes are the foundation, but from the foundation one cannot say anything specific about the building that is to be erected on it (Vygotsky, 1925g, p. 181; the same idea was also apparent in *Pedagogical Psychology* outlined in chapter 3). It is in this respect that Kornilov's emphasis on the qualitatively different organizational forms of reactions was well aligned with Vygotsky's position. Furthermore, from that alignment it follows quite predictably that Vygotsky would be drawn to structuralistic approaches to psychological phenomena:

consciousness is not to be viewed biologically, physiologically and psychologically, as a second line of phenomena. A place and an interpretation must be found for it in the one line of phenomena [together] with all reactions of the organism. This is the first requirement for our working hypothesis. Consciousness is the problem of the structure of behavior. (1925g, p. 181)

Vygotsky's argument fitted well with Kornilov's intention of establishing a dialectical psychology in terms of qualitative transformation and "centralization" as well as delaying of reactions, once those become more complex. In a way, Vygotsky's acceptance of Kornilov's reactology can be seen as a stepping-stone for his later studies of internalization of experiences that take place in the inter-personal sphere. In the 1925 paper, the link between inter-individual and intra-individual psychological phenomena is forged with the help of a quotation from Paul Natorp's *Social Pedagogics* stating that there is no self-understanding possible without its basis – that is, the understanding of others (Vygotsky, 1925g, p. 196). Interestingly, the reference to Natorp – an idealist philosopher (as well as another reference to Theodor Lipps; 1925g, p. 195) – does not appear in the recent Russian re-publication of the article in the collected works (see Vygotsky, 1925h/1982). Consciousness can be viewed as the "fiction of interaction" (see also Van der Veer and Valsiner, 1988, and Valsiner and Van der Veer, 1988, about similar ideas in the work of Baldwin and Janet and their influence on Vygotsky), that is, a transformation of interactive experience into the realm of the delayed internal reaction structure.

Vygotsky proceeded to link the reactological emphasis with the evolutionary view on animal behavior, stating the necessity to understand the uniqueness of the human relations with the world via labor. Furthermore, Vygotsky evoked the idea of circular reaction (emanating from the work of James M. Baldwin in the 1890s) in the study of consciousness (Vygotsky, 1925g, pp. 187–8). The idea of circular reactions provided some dynamic order for the conceptualization of consciousness as a process. A similar focus is apparent in the preface to the revised edition of A. Lazursky's *General and Experimental Psychology* (Vygotsky, 1924b). The concept of combining reflexes into holistic units (complex reactions) with new qualitative features was presented by Vygotsky as the object of investigation of psychology that the reflexology of Bekhterev and Pavlov overlooked.

In the Psychology of Art – finished while working at the Institute – Vygotsky publicly adopted the same position as Kornilov and dismissed Chelpanov's claim that experimental psychology cannot be built around Marxist ideas as the latter are fitting only for social psychology (Vygotsky, 1925l/1986, p. 26). The intellectual debt to Kornilov is seen in the terminology; for instance, the insistence upon the term "aesthetic reactions" (p. 111 and others). He applied Kornilov's "law of monophasic energy expenditure" to the dynamics of "aesthetic reactions" (p. 263), emphasizing the delayed and modified (transformed) nature of emotional reactions:

A very vivid imagination increases our amorous excitation, but in this case the fantasy is not the expression of the emotion it enhances but rather the discharge of the preceding emotion. Whenever an emotion finds its solution in images of fantasy, this "dreaming" weakness the true manifestation of the emotion; if we expressed our doubts in our fantasy, its external manifestation will be quite weak. We feel that, with reference to emotional responses, all those general psychological laws established with respect to any simple sensory-motor response remains valid. It is an irrefutable fact that our reactions slow down and lose intensity as soon as the central element of the emotion becomes more complicated. We discover that, as the imagination (the central element of the emotional reaction) increases, its peripheral component loses intensity. (Vygotsky, 1971, p. 210; in Russian: Vygotsky, 1925l/1986, pp. 262–3)

The connection between this thought and Kornilov's emphasis on the dialectical transformation of emotions (see above) under the conditions of monophasic energy expenditure, as well as to the ethos of psychodynamic thought, is evident. Furthermore, Vygotsky linked Kornilov's reactological idea with Karl Groos's view on play, as in play, and likewise in aesthetic activity, we deal with the *delay* but *not suppression* of the reaction. The delayed emotional reaction develops dialectically – the emotion develops in two contradictory directions which become negated (overcome) at the end, giving rise to a new emotion – the catharsis effect (Vygotsky, 1925l/1986, p. 269; see also chapter 2).

Vygotsky arrived at the point of questioning Kornilov's reactological ideas by 1926. This is quite interestingly reflected in his manuscript on the crisis in psychology (Vygotsky, 1926m/1982; see also chapter 7). After a positive reference to Kornilov's reactology book (p. 346) and the outlining of his emotional reactions classification alongside those of Bekhterev's and Pavlov's reflex types (p. 350), Vygotsky begins to criticize Chelpanov (p. 358) and to align himself with Kornilov on terminological issues (pp. 360–1). The first signs of the cracks in this alignment surface when he starts to doubt the adequacy of Kornilov's claim of considering psyche the *function* of the brain (p. 368). Vygotsky is on the verge of accepting Chelpanov's criticism of Kornilov's "somewhat mechanistic" way of conceptualizing the mind–body problem, tracing in it the preservation of a dualistic perspective. Furthermore, he moves to a devastating philosophical criticism of Kornilov's solution:

The new theory accepts, after Plekhanov, the doctrine of psychophysical parallelism and full non-reductionism of the psychological to the physical, viewing the latter as a crude, vulgar materialism . . . Kornilov sees a functional relationship between them [mind and body], but with that any *wholeness* is immediately eliminated: two different variables can be in a functional relationship. It is not possible to study psychology in terms of reactions, since *within* the reactions two functional elements, not reducible to unity, are embedded. The psychophysical problem is not solved this way, but transposed to the *interior of each element*... (Vygotsky, 1925m/1982, pp. 398–9)

Vygotsky declared that the problem of mind–body dualism remained unsolved in Kornilov's hands, but did not dwell upon a criticism of him. Instead, Vygotsky proceeded to elaborate a criticism of Frankfurt's analysis of Plekhanov's treatment of the mind–body problem (Frankfurt, 1926). He becomes agitated with Frankfurt's "mixing-up" of controversies on the issue of whether psyche is material or immaterial, and finds that the latter arrives at "horrifying" conclusions for the science of psychology. The issue of relationships of inductive and deductive reasoning in science is outlined in Vygotsky's counter-argument (1926m/1982, pp. 399–407). He emphasizes the need to study processes in their generic essence, using the individual case study as the empirical (inductive) component of an otherwise theoretical endeavor. In contrast to Frankfurt's philosophical rhetoric, Vygotsky cites Pavlov's strict investigation of the reflexes in dogs as an example of the unity of inductive and deductive sides of the scientific process (p. 407). Perhaps this indicates Vygotsky's increasing dissatisfaction with the ideological – philosophical rhetoric in which the Kornilov school of thought and other Marxist psychologists were increasingly involved. Evidence for this emerges a couple of pages later:

> many "Marxists" cannot show a difference between theirs and idealist theory of psychological knowing, since *it does not exist*. After Spinoza we took over our science in a mortally sick state, in search of hopeless medicine; now we see that only the knife of the surgeon can save the day. A bloody surgery is to take place; many textbooks have to be broken into two ... many phrases will lose head or feet, other theories will be cut open exactly in their stomach. We are only engaged by the cut, the line of the break, the line drawn by the future knife. (1926m/1982, p. 411)

This near surrealistic call for future progress in Marxist psychology does not seem to be in agreement with the social discourse of the time at which it was given. In a curious way, this pogrom-metaphor predicted the events of the early 1930s, albeit not as part of progress in psychology. Vygotsky, freeing himself from the burden of all Marxist rhetoric of the time, (re)claimed the way out of the crisis – the dialectical synthesis of the mind–body problem (p. 416) – but without the immediate application of dialectical materialism to the problems of natural sciences and psychology (p. 419). This latter point contradicted Kornilov's argument for the applicability of dialectics as a method in psychology (Vygotsky expressed this very directly in his criticism of Kornilov's textbook; Vygotsky, 1926m/1982, p.

421), and resembled Chelpanov's argument at least in its external form. Furthermore, Vygotsky refused to apply the existing Marxist sociological theory (historical materialism) to history or sociology, calling rather for the development of a special theory of historical materialism that would link abstract laws of dialectics with concrete issues of the day (as opposed to a rhetorical mix of Marxist concepts with social-political issues of the day). At the same time, Vygotsky did not forget the historical indebtedness to Kornilov (p. 423), while actively calling against the use of the label "Marxist" as attached to any particular viewpoint in psychology:

> the specific difficulty of the application of Marxism to new areas: the present particular state of that theory; immense responsibility in the use of that term; political and ideological speculation on its basis; all that does not allow a [person with] good taste to say "Marxist psychology" nowadays. Better let others say about our psychology that it is Marxist, than label it as such ourselves; let's use it [Marxism] in reality and wait with words. After all, *Marxist pyschology does not exist yet*, it has to be understood as a historical task, not as a given. At the present situation it is difficult to do away with the impression of scientific unseriousness and irresponsibility of [the use of] that label. (Vygotsky, 1926m/1982, p. 433)

There was, then, a dramatic change in Vygotsky's attitude: from his enthusiastic agreement with the voices calling for a Marxist psychology in 1924, to the denunciation of the (ever-increasing) cacophony of such a chorus by 1926. The crisis he saw psychology to be in was more than the crisis of "old psychology" or reflexology in the study of higher psychological processes. It was a crisis of the new psychology that was drifting increasingly into the obscurity of scholastic play with terminology borrowed from the classics and in-fighting within the social institutions. In that regard, Kornilov's reactology played a definite, although contradictory, role.

Conclusions: Vygotsky and Reactology 1924–1926

We have tried to demonstrate in this chapter how Kornilov's reactological views served to expedite Vygotsky's entrance into psychology at a time of increasing and often abrasive social discourse about the building of a Marxist psychology. Apart from the advantage of being brought into the emergent new psychology establishment, Vygotsky's thinking in those years developed on the basis of his collaboration with Kornilov's opposition to Bekhterev's and Pavlov's reflexologies and Chelpanov's experimental psychology. In his usual style, Vygotsky never claimed enthusiastic allegiance to Kornilov's camp – in contrast to many other co-workers at the Institute (e.g. Borovsky and Frankfurt). In his analysis and synthesis of ideas, however, Vygotsky began from a foundation that was similar to Kornilov's (with the exception of the latter's ideological rhetorics). His ideas over the years developed in a dialogue with other scholars of the time, in ways that indicate the *de facto* alignment of Vygotsky's ideas with Kornilov's, and the impact those had upon a synthesis of his own. Finally, Vygotsky saw beyond the limitations of the reactological world-view, and moved on to construct the cultural-historical theoretical system (see chapter 9). It is entirely possible that in everyday work Vygotsky's contacts with Kornilov were not very extensive; after all, Kornilov was involved in the administration of the Institute and the supervision of his followers in purely reactological research projects. Still, Kornilov's active support of Vygotsky's work seems to have continued. For example, Vygotsky is one of the most frequently recommended authors in Kornilov's textbook on psychology (Kornilov, 1928b) for further reading. In his 1927 overview of psychology in the USSR, Kornilov wrote of Vygotsky's work in conjunction with his own (Kornilov, 1927, p. 211). It may well be that Vygotsky's health on the one hand, and his extension of research activities from the Institute to other institutional bases on the other hand (especially the Psychological Laboratory of the Academy of Communist Education) diminished the contact between Vygotsky and Kornilov. Nevertheless, Kornilov's ideas served as important catalysts for the development of Vygotsky's thinking over these years.

7

Crisis in Psychology

For me the primary question is the question of method, that is for me the question of truth ... (Vygotsky in a letter to Luria, dated March 5, 1926)

Dissatisfaction with the results of psychological research has taken different forms in different periods, but psychologists have often voiced the opinion that psychology is in a state of crisis. The result of a comparison with the natural sciences may contribute to this feeling, where the sciences were falsely pictured as a monolithic whole without any competing schools and currents of thought. The many different approaches in psychological science would then be seen as a sure sign of its poor status compared to the natural sciences. The quality of the research findings that hardly ever enabled the researcher to formulate general laws of the mind or its development would also play a part, which again was seen as an indication that psychology fell short of being a real science.

Of course, there have been very real causes for the problems that psychology experienced, causes that were there from its inception (Kendler, 1981). One of these is the problem of mind–body dualism, a problem with which Vygotsky was grappling for years (see chapter 14). It was Spranger (1923) who first clearly sketched how this mind–body dualism had resulted in a bifurcation of psychology as a science. In his opinion the unity of psychology had been lost because one group of researchers was oriented towards the natural sciences and their methods, while other groups resorted to hermeneutic, interpretative methods. Although Spranger underlined the great differences between these two approaches (see also Bühler, 1927/1978, pp. 68–82) he did have some hopes that the strong aspects of the natural scientific physiological psychology and the interpretative psychology of the soul and spirit (*Psychologie des Seelisch-Geistigen*) could be combined into a future "biopsychology" (see Scheerer, 1985, p. 18).

Spranger's analysis of the causes for psychology's lack of unity brought some order in a discussion that had been going on for a long time in German psychology and would continue until the present day. Binswanger (1922), Driesch (1926), Jaensch (1923), Münsterberg (1922), Koffka (1924;

1926a), were among others who had written theoretical analyses of psychology's problems. One of the most prominent psychologists to react to Spranger's analysis was Karl Bühler, who in 1927 published his classic analysis *The Crisis in Psychology*. This book – the content of which cannot be analyzed here – was one of the most profound attempts ever undertaken to diagnose psychology's problems. Partially agreeing with Spranger's analysis Bühler developed his doctrine of the three aspects that any psychology should take into account.

It is obvious from the many references in the "The Historical Significance of the Crisis in Psychology" that Vygotsky was well acquainted with many of these writings and that his analyses owe much to the German psychological literature of the time.[1] As always his point of view evolved by partial agreement and disagreement with and selective use of other researchers' theories. Bearing this in mind the reader can make his own assessment of the merits of Vygotsky's analysis. It is likely though, that Vygotsky's was the first coherent attempt to explain the crisis in psychology from a Marxist point of view (Jaroshevsky and Gurgenidze, 1982, p. 449).

The Crisis

Vygotsky agreed with many of his foreign and Soviet colleagues that psychology in the 1920s was living through a period of turmoil. Already in his *Pedagogical Psychology* (see chapter 3) he had mentioned psychology's crisis but at the time he did not attempt to analyze its origin. It was one of the recurrent attacks of tuberculosis, confining him to bed, that enabled him to begin to analyze the reasons for the crisis (see introduction to part I). This analysis resulted in the manuscript "The Historical Significance of the Crisis in Psychology". It is unclear whether this study was meant for publication – it contained rather sharp attacks against some of his colleagues at the Institute (see the criticism of Luria in chapter 5) but in fact it was only published in 1982 (Vygotsky, 1926m/1982). Apparently, Luria tried to get the manuscript published in the mid-1930s, he refers to the paper as "in print" (1935b, p. 226) – but these attempts failed and between 1934 and 1982 and during Vygotsky's lifetime the manuscript in its entirety was known by few people.

In this paper of approximately 140 pages Vygotsky analyzed the psychological currents of his time, traced to what extent they were compatible or

---

[1]In the Soviet edition of Vygotsky's *Collected Works* 1927 is given as the year of completion of the "Crisis" manuscript (Vygotsky, 1982a, p. 469). However, as was already indicated in Vygotsky (1934a, pp. 321–3) and as became clear in the introduction to part I, the manuscript was written and completed in the summer of 1926.

incompatible with the goals of psychology as he saw it, and sought to find materials for a future methodology. Reading the manuscript, the outlines of Vygotsky's own stance with regard to philosophical and epistemological problems become progressively clear. However, this is not the only reason why the essay is of interest. It will become clear in later chapters that Vygotsky's analysis of the "state of art" in psychology can be seen as the prelude of his and Luria's later cultural-historical theory (see chapter 9).

The Argument for a General Psychology

Both Vygotsky's analyses and the conclusions he reached were rather different from those of Bühler (1927). He began the paper by observing the lack of unity and consistency in psychology's research findings. Researchers from different schools had produced facts that seemed to have little in common. It was hard to see, for instance, how to reconcile the psychoanalytic image of man with Pavlov's theory of the higher nervous activity. It seemed impossible to combine Gestalt psychology's ideas with those of Watson's behaviorism. In short, to Vygotsky psychology seemed a hodge-podge of unrelated or contradictory research findings without any unifying idea whatsoever. Vygotsky deplored this state of affairs, arguing – unlike some contemporary researchers – that psychology should be a unified science with a single set of theoretical concepts and explanatory principles. As most empirical researchers were working within the framework of one accepted theoretical approach, trying to work out the details of its world-view, psychology should initiate a separate subdiscipline to study the problem of its theoretical unity. Vygotsky labelled this subdiscipline "general psychology" and he devoted the greater part of his study arguing the need for such a subdiscipline, sketching its tasks, and outlining its agenda.

In Vygotsky's view it would be the task of general psychology to evaluate the findings unearthed in the different research domains, to consider whether they could be reconciled, and to design a consistent theoretical framework. Psychology does not need new fact-finding, Vygotsky argued, but shared concepts or ways to interpret the gathered facts. To him psychology lacked a common frame of reference, or, in other words, a set of common concepts and explanatory principles. Vygotsky argued that psychology was consequently in need of a "methodology," by which he meant a general set of assumptions on what constitute acceptable research methods and a definition of the subject of psychology. The need for general psychology and a shared methodology could be demonstrated by studying the history of psychology, and the study of scientific discovery and its dissemination would be particularly instructive.

From Scientific Discovery to World-View

That psychology is in urgent need of general theoretical concepts explaining and unifying its structure could be seen from the fact that each and every important scientific discovery was soon elevated to the status of such a concept. The development of scientific discoveries into general theoretical concepts can be schematically described, Vygotsky argued, despite the fact that the dynamics of science are determined by a complex whole of factors both external and internal to science as such. Vygotsky distinguished between (1) the general social atmosphere of the epoch; (2) the general laws of scientific knowledge; and (3) the demands of objective reality. His view of the determinants of the dynamics of science is, therefore, a mixture of the internalist and externalist.

How, then, do scientific discoveries grow into general theoretical concepts? Vygotsky gave the following account of the vicissitudes of a scientific discovery. Each discovery goes through five phases. In the first phase, we see a factual discovery in a narrowly defined field of science. Pavlov, for example, demonstrated the conditional reflex with regard to the salivary response of dogs; the notion of Gestalt, on the other hand, arose in the psychology of perception. In the second phase, the influence of the discovery is extended to the adjacent research areas and the idea of the discovery is formulated somewhat more abstractly. Pavlov's procedure, for instance, is now considered to be relevant for other reflexes than the salivary one and for other animals than dogs. The third phase is characterized by the domination of a whole subdiscipline of psychology by the new discovery, which is now already considered to be a principle or idea of more general relevance. The influence of the new idea is felt gradually in other subdisciplines of psychology and it is formulated in a still more abstract way. At the same time its connection with the original empirical, factual basis becomes very loose. Pavlov's idea of conditioning left the circumscribed area of animal psychology and developed into a more general principle applicable to human beings and animals alike. In the fourth phase the idea has grown into a universal principle that can be used to analyze the results of other scientific disciplines, such as sociology and anthropology. The idea now has become a philosophical system or *Weltanschauung* and it turns out that labor, creativity, art, and class struggle can all be explained by referring to the conditional reflex. This marks the transition to the final, fifth phase in which the idea will burst like a soap-bubble, for as *Weltanschauung* it will meet with fierce resistance: "It is only now, when the idea is completely detached from the facts which gave birth to it, developed to its logical boundaries, put to the ultimate consequences, as much generalized as possible, that the idea at last shows its real nature, unmasks its true face" (Vygotsky, 1926m/1982, p. 304).

The social, ideological aspect of the discovery has gradually become more clear and is now at its most vulnerable to the attacks of critics. These critics will refer the idea to its original, factual basis and moreover, they will eventually try to interpret these very facts in the light of a new idea that in itself will gradually grow into a new world-view and, thus, repeat the developmental cycle. Vygotsky describes the transition point as follows:

> The idea manifests its social nature much more easily as a philosophical fact than as a scientific fact; and that is the end of its role: [the idea] is unmasked as a foreign agent dressed up as a scientific fact, and [now] starts its life as an element of a general and open class struggle of ideas. But exactly here, as a tiny part of an enormous whole, it will perish like a raindrop in the ocean, and stop leading an independent life. (1926m/1982, p. 305)

This description of the expansion of scientific discoveries – in which some have seen an anticipation of Thomas Kuhn's ideas – is typical of psychology, Vygotsky claimed. It showed the extent to which the psychology of the 1920s was in need of general ideas: literally any important scientific discovery at any point of time was regarded as the life-saving general principle for psychology. He went on to demonstrate this claim for four psychological approaches: Stern's personalism, Freud's psychoanalysis, Pavlov's theory of conditioning, and Gestalt psychology. The theorizing of each of these schools was originally full of content and meaningful with regard to the original domain of facts. Raised to the status of a world-view, however, "they are absolutely identical, like round and empty zeros." The extension of the idea beyond its original domain brought with it a proportional loss of meaning, Vygotsky concluded.

Having argued the need for general concepts and clarifying principles – and, therefore, indirectly the need for a general pschology – Vygotsky went on to discuss the form general psychology should ideally take.

The Nature of a General Psychology

Vygotsky first discussed Binswanger's (1922) claim that general psychology had to be a logical discipline analyzing abstract concepts, devoid of any content. The need to formulate general psychological ideas and principles, Binswanger had argued, would bring the general discipline into the realm of pure logic. Vygotsky disagreed with Binswanger's contention, arguing that this would imply a sharp break between general psychology and the subdisciplines providing the empirical findings. For him there had to be a gradual transition by necessity. In Vygotsky's view each and every concept, however abstract, ultimately referred to reality and therefore general psychology could never be a purely logical endeavor. The idea that all concepts – whether they are psychological, philosophical or even mathematical concepts – ultimately refer to concrete, empirical reality was based on Engels' *Dialectics of Nature* (1925). Vygotsky agreed with Engels that all "free creations and imaginations of the human mind" ("*freien Schöpfungen und Imaginationen des Menschengeistes*") are an utter impossibility (Engels, 1925/1978, p. 530).

The relation between abstract concepts and theories, on the one hand, and facts (reality), on the other, has, however, a dialectic nature. Although even the most abstract concepts are ultimately based on (factual statements about) objective reality, it is also true that every scientific fact already implies a first abstraction. No perfectly abstract ideas can exist without a material foundation as no perfectly concrete facts can exist without the beginning of abstraction, Vygotsky claimed. In his opinion this state of affairs had often been overlooked by those psychologists wishing to follow the model of the natural sciences. These psychologists falsely assumed that natural science proceeded by a purely objective and direct registration of facts. In Vygotsky's opinion this was a distorted view of natural sciences' procedures. This he attempted to demonstrate in several ways.

It should be understood, Vygotsky argued, that even seemingly purely empirical facts imply abstraction, because (1) we make a selection from the stream of experiences and (2) scientific facts are presented in verbal or symbolic form. With regard to the first point Vygotsky stated that human perception is necessarily selective: an eye that would see everything, would, therefore, see nothing. The scientific equipment we use in research does not change this situation: it, too, can only register part of reality and that in a specific way. "That is why there is a complete analogy between the selection of the eye and the further selection of the instrument: both the former and the latter are selective organs" (1926m/1982, p. 348).

With regard to the second point, Vygotsky noted the following. Scientific findings are always couched in symbolic systems or language. Using language, however, we cannot avoid introducing abstractions and generalizations. Vygotsky claimed that all concepts go "beyond the information given" and using them in describing empirical findings, therefore, implies subscribing to various (proto)theories (1926m/1982, pp. 316 and 358).

Vygotsky further argued the value of theoretical thinking by discussing the relative merits of induction and theoretical analysis. It was his conviction that the "domination of induction and mathematical treatment and the underdevelopment of analysis considerably ruined ... experimental psychology" (1926m/1982, p. 402). Again, this overemphasis on induction and mathematical treatment – which had been observed by various critics (see Bühler, 1927, p. 11) – was based on an indequate understanding of the way the natural sciences proceed. In the natural sciences and in sound psychological research theoretical analysis plays a prominent role and directs induction. As an example of theoretical analysis Vygotsky mentioned Pavlov's research on conditional reflexes. In studying a particular dog's salivation Pavlov in fact studied the conditioning of reflexes in animals in general. This is the general feature of analysis: in studying the representative of a class we do not study the individual as such, but the general properties of all members of the class. From this study of one particular individual we then generalize to all others. Afterwards, of course, we have to find the limits of the general principle. Vygotsky claimed the same held true for his study of the esthetic reactions (see chapter 2). Analyzing only one fable, one short story, and one tragedy he studied the basis of all art, that is, the nature of esthetic reactions. "I did not study the fable, the tragedy and even less the fable in question and the tragedy in question. I studied in them that which constitutes the foundation of all art – the nature and mechanism of the esthetic reaction" (1926m/1982, p. 405).

What Vygotsky is claiming here is that the generic nature of the subject of study can be inferred from the study of one particular case. Because one abstracts from certain features of the subject under study one can advance the claim that certain properties hold for the general case. Vygotsky saw an analogy here with the case of experiments. In that case, too, an artificial combination of conditions is created to reveal the action of some specified law in its clearest form. Theoretical analysis, then, is performing thought experiments, abstracting from certain features to trap one of nature's laws in its clearest form (1926m/1982, p. 406). It is interesting to see that Vygotsky did not share the concern of many contemporary researchers: that the experimental approach gives a distorted picture of events as they take place in reality:

> It might seem that analysis, like the experiment, distorts reality – creates artificial conditions for observation. Hence the demand for the closeness to life and naturalness of the experiment. If this idea is carried further than a technical demand – not to scare away that which we are looking for – it leads to the absurd. The strength of analysis is in the abstraction, like the strength of the experiment is in artificiality. (Vygotsky, 1926m/1982, pp. 406–7)

In chapter 9 it will be seen that this understanding of the value of the experimental approach formed part of Vygotsky's general methodological approach and finally led him to elaborate the idea of formative experiments.

In this way Vygotsky criticized the then-prevalent idea that the natural sciences (and science in general) proceeded by direct, unprejudiced, atheoretical registration of facts. His theoretical position was partly grounded in

Marxist thought. The strength of analysis as compared to induction had been stressed by both Marx and Engels and the idea of analyzing the esthetic reaction in its abstract form is clearly related to Marx' idea of studying the commodity value as the "germ cell" of capitalist society. Moreover, the idea of the material/realistic background of any concept goes back to Engels' claims in *Dialectics of Nature* (Engels, 1925/1978, see pp. 346, 475, 506). Another aspect of Vygotsky's thinking – the idea of all concepts/words as (proto)theories – can clearly be traced to his earlier linguistic studies, particularly to his reading of the work of Potebnya (see chapter 1).

The implication of his reasoning was that the general psychology he was searching for could not be completely separated from the empirical findings unearthed in the various psychological schools. Binswanger's idea of a content-free theoretical psychology was, therefore, ill-founded.

Against Eclecticism

The need for a principled analysis of psychology's basic concepts by a subdiscipline of general psychology was demonstrated by Vygotsky in various ways. The eclectic combinations of principles and ideas coming from different schools (e.g. Freudo-Marxism) would not have been possible had researchers realized the dialectic relation between theory and facts. It was in the context of discussing these eclectic systems that Vygotsky voiced his sharp criticism of Luria's brand of Freudo-Marxism (see chapter 5). In doing so, he more fully outlined his view of the scientific process sketched above.

What eclectic thinkers do not understand, Vygotsky argued, is that in borrowing from other schools of thought or other sciences we also import their underlying ideas. These thinkers conceive of science as a process of collecting and classifying factual givens gathered by direct experience. That Vygotsky disliked the idea of science as the diligent registration of objective facts is clear. He also criticized the idea that direct experience is important in scientific research. In his view science was based on the reconstruction and interpretation of indirectly given phenomena, and in this respect, he saw no fundamental differences between the natural and social sciences and the study of history. Referring to Max Planck and Engels, Vygotsky argued that all of these sciences transcend the directly visible by making use of instruments and making inferences about the unknown. The idea that the direct experience of phenomena is the one and only point of departure for science he considered to be a sensualistic prejudice. In order to know something we do not need our sense organs, for these instruments are no mere extensions of the senses, rather they liberate us from them. That is why blind or deaf persons can be excellent scientists, Vygotsky claimed, a reference to his defectological work (discussed in chapter 4). The reliance on direct experience was present in both subjective and objective psychological approaches. In subjective psychology the direct experience of the subject's conscious thinking in introspection was taken as the starting point of theorizing. Introspectionists believed the data from introspection to be the only or most valid ones. Behaviorists, on the other hand, restricted themselves to the direct registration of external, observable facts. In both cases the researchers did not go beyond the immediately given, believing valid conclusions should be based on direct experience. Vygotsky argued that this belief was based on a misunderstanding; for in each and every interesting scientific investigation we go beyond the information given – in fact, we cannot avoid doing so. Vygotsky's concept of words as (proto)theories, whether psychological research or the natural sciences is the subject, supports this. In none of these branches of science do researchers rely solely on direct facts, rather they all interpret and extrapolate to past and future (1926m/1982, p. 344).

Of course, the indirect, interpretative method – like the method of direct experience – may distort the objective facts, but in Vygotsky's opinion psychology had no choice but to transcend the limitations of the human senses. With a cross-reference to Engels (1925, p. 506), Vygotsky remarked that although we can never see the world through the ant's eyes, we can reconstruct its view of the world. Psychology like the natural sciences has to rely on the indirect method of interpretation. The general theme behind this point of view is the idea that the role of the human observer in scientific research should be minimized. The emancipation from our sense organs is not only a prerequisite for the study of psychology, it will be psychology's liberation and its *salto vitale* (1926m/1982, p. 349).

Having argued that psychologists cannot avoid making inferences about phenomena that have not been experienced directly in their investigations and having shown that (proto)theories are always there to guide our thinking, Vygotsky again warned against the uncritical acceptance of ideas taken from other subdisciplines or sciences. His evaluation of the uncritical import of some methods into psychology – after more than half a century – still deserves to be heard: "Such a *blind* transportation . . . of the experiment, the mathematical method from the natural sciences created in psychology the outward appearances of science, under which, in reality, was hidden a complete powerlessness before the phenomena under study" (1926m/1982, p. 354).

The Role of Praxis

Having discussed the dangers of eclecticism and the need for a thorough analysis of psychology's methodological approach Vygotsky returned to his original theme: the crisis in psychology. He had by now revealed some of its underlying causes. The lack of a general psychology, psychologists' lack of methodological understanding, and the resulting eclectic attitude had contributed to the haphazard collection of seemingly unrelated facts that hampered psychology's development.

But what was it that suddenly caused psychology's crisis to be more acutely felt? The most pressing reason for psychology's crisis, Vygotsky felt, was the rapid development of applied psychology. Applied psychology – or practice – had been the cornerstone ignored by the builders of psychology. This claim he tried to clarify in three ways:

(1) Practice (praxis) is the strictest test for any theory: it very often forces the researcher to reconsider his views and that is exactly what constitutes its value for scientific progress. In former days, Vygotsky reasoned, academic psychology used to look with some contempt at applied psychology. The application of knowledge in practice was seen as a post-scientific endeavour – that is, outside the realm of real science – that need not have immediate repercussions for the theory as such (Vygotsky, 1926m/1982, p. 387). In the 1920s Vygotsky saw a radical change in this situation. The growth of branches of applied psychology, such as psychotherapy, paedology (including intelligence testing), and educational counselling forced researchers to be explicit in their assumptions and to re-examine their theoretical concepts. It was against this background of rapid societal reforms and the need for scientists to contribute to these reforms, that Vygotsky agreed with those who considered practise to be the supreme court of science, the ultimate judge of truth. At the same time his thinking in this respect could be interpreted as showing some affinity with that of Lenin in his *Materialism and Empiriocriticism* (1909). The problem here was – as Boeselager (1975, p. 37) has explained – that Lenin's concept of practice and its relation to theory can be interpreted in many ways and "through its contradictory statements, left open and encouraged many possibilities of further development." It is clear, however, that Vygotsky greatly valued the reforming influence of practice:

> However insignificant the practical and theoretical value of the Binet-scale or other psychotechnical tests, however bad the test in itself may be, as an idea, as a methodological principle, as a task, as a perspective it is very much [valuable]. The most complex contradictions of psychology's methodology are brought to the field of practice and can only be solved there. Here the dispute stops being sterile, it comes to an end . . . That is why practice transforms the whole of scientific methodology. (1926m/1982, p. 388)

(2) The emphasis on applied psychology did not lead Vygotsky to adopt a non-theoretical approach. He considered it to be of the utmost importance

to develop a methodology for applied science. Psychology, in his opinion, was in need of a philosophy of practice guiding the applied investigations. It was the combination of applied research and a good methodology, Vygotsky argued, that might enable us to solve the crisis in psychology. He took care, thus, to emphasize the role of theory in doing applied research, being, evidently, very critical of the then widespread practicism: "despite the fact that it has compromised itself more than once, that its practical meaning is very close to zero, and that a theory is often ridiculous, its methodological meaning is enormous" (1926m/1982, p. 388).

(3) It was Vygotsky's conviction that practice, being an impartial arbiter, would not allow more than one winner in scientific debates. Moreover, he was convinced that applied psychology would favor a certain approach in psychology and show the uselessness of others. Applied psychology (psychotechnics) would, therefore, eventually reform psychology. "It's no good using Husserl's eidetic psychology for the selection of tram-drivers," Vygotsky argued (1926m/1982, p. 389). Ultimately, therefore, the development of applied psychology would lead to the triumph of causal, objective psychology: "Psychotechnics is focused on actions, on practice . . . it has to do solely with causal, with objective psychology; non-causal psychology does not play a role whatsoever for psychotechnics" (1926m/1982, p. 390).

This statement referred to one of the other main themes of Vygotsky's study: the bifurcation of psychology into objective, causal psychology, on the one hand, and subjective, hermeneutic psychology, on the other hand.

The Bifurcation of Psychology

Earlier we referred to the many different currents and schools of thought in psychology. In the 1920s, psychology was divided into, among other things, reflexology, reactology, psychoanalysis, Gestalt psychology, personalism, and behaviorism. Following other researchers (e.g. Dilthey, Wulff, Münsterberg, Kornilov, and – above all – Spranger) Vygotsky stated that the enormous diversity in psychology could be reduced to a dichotomy. Psychology could be conceived of as consisting of two basic types, each with their own conception of what constituted science and with their own methodological approach.

These two types of psychology were causal, explanatory psychology as opposed to descriptive, intentional psychology. Psychologists belonging to the first group considered psychology to be a natural science (*Naturwissenschaft*), emphasizing the experimental approach and the explanation and prediction of human behavior. The second type of psychologists regarded psychology as "science of the soul" (*Geisteswissenschaft*) and sought to understand or describe human psychological processes. They denied the possibility of the natural science approach for the higher psychological processes, arguing that these processes can only be empathically understood. Some representatives of descriptive psychology, however, admitted the possibility of a causal explanation of relatively simple, lower, psychological processes in the style of a natural science. At the same time, many adherents of the natural science approach were reluctant to study the higher psychological processes. These were in their opinion difficult to investigate, or – for some of them – even nonexistent. In this way the following situation evolved: causal, natural science psychology studied the lower processes (e.g. reaction time), and descriptive psychology studied the higher processes (e.g. problem-solving). It is clear from Vygotsky's study that he was not satisfied with such a division of labor. In his opinion objective, materialist psychology should not abandon the higher processes to descriptive psychology. Consequently, he opted for a psychology inspired by the natural sciences that would also study the higher processes (1926m/1982, p. 417). Vygotsky's choice was made on methodological grounds: he preferred objective, causal psychology because of its superior methods, at the same time acknowledging descriptive psychologists' concern with the higher psychological processes. At the same time he was linking up with Lenin's (1909) notion of *partijnost'* (partisanship). One consequence of the idea of *partijnost'* was that in philosophy of science ultimately only two positions were possible: one eventually had the choice between being either a materialist or an idealist (Boeselager, 1975, p. 30). All intermediated positions could be reduced to one of these two extremes according to Lenin. At the time it was unclear, however, what this natural scientific approach to the higher psychological processes would imply. In fact, Vygotsky voiced some doubts as to whether psychology might be a natural science in the strict sense of the word:

> we leave another question open too – whether psychology really is a natural science in the strict sense . . . But this is still a particular and very deep problem – to show that psychology is possible as a materialistic science, but it does not belong to the problem of the significance of the psychological crisis as a whole. (1926m/1982, p. 384)

The cultural-historical theory and the research methods it espoused were intended to clarify this issue (see chapter 9). Another issue Vygotsky left unanswered at the time was the question of the *origin* of psychology's bifurcation. In chapter 14 it will be seen that he traced this dualism to the writings of Descartes and studied Spinoza's writings in depth to find ways to eradicate it.

So far, in discussing "The historical significance of the crisis in psychology" we have concentrated on its theoretical implications. It should not be forgotten, however that it was also partly a discussion of the psychological theories of the time and, as such, reflected Vygotsky's changing ideas in this respect. Many psychologists were the target of Vygotsky's sometimes vitriolic pen. Twice in "The historical significance of the crisis in psychology" he dealt with attempts by contemporaries to construct a Marxist psychology by finding the right quotations in the work of the Marxist classics.[2] In his opinion these writings were mostly of very questionable value: they mostly served a polemic goal and started from wrong premises. These researchers, Vygotsky suggested, were looking (1) in the wrong place; (2) for the wrong thing; and (3) in the wrong way (1926m/1982, p. 397). They were looking in the wrong place, because Marxist thinkers simply had not dealt with psychological issues and – even if they had – could not possibly have solved them readily. Neither Marx, Engels, nor Plekhanov solved the problem of the nature of the human mind, Vygotsky wrote (1926m/1982, p. 421). They were looking for the wrong thing, because they were looking for clear-cut answers to psychological or philosophical questions and not for a methodological approach. It would be a miracle, Vygotsky argued, to find a finished system of psychological thought in Marxist thinking. In fact, it would be like finding a science before starting it oneself. Finally, the so-called Marxist psychologists were looking in the wrong way, because they were hampered by their fear of Marxist authorities. In their search for dogmas they did not critically evaluate the scanty remarks made by Marxist thinkers about psychological problems. Vygotsky did not believe one should look for answers in the writings of Marxist thinkers, nor for clear-cut hypotheses: "I do not want to find out [about the nature of] the psyche for free – by clipping a few quotes – I want to learn from the *whole* of Marx's method how to build a science, how to approach the investigation of the psyche" (Vygotsky, 1926m/1982, p. 421).

Instead Vygotsky pleaded for the creation of a new methodology – or general psychology – sufficiently developed to deal with the phenomena studied. For the creation of such an approach it was "necessary to disclose the essence of the given domain of phenomena, the laws of their change, the qualitative and quantitative characteristics, their causality, to create the categories and concepts adequate to them, in one word, to create one's own *Capital*" (1926m/1982, p. 420).

---

[2]Vygotsky felt that Soviet psychology was "deeply provincial... Who reads us here? Chelpanov in order to count the errors and then to laugh loudly out of delight; Frankfurt to check its loyalty ... I still have the hope that I can force my daughter (from five years on!) to read my articles, but you are childless!" (From a letter to Luria, dated March 5, 1926.)

Conclusions

Both Vygotsky's sketch of psychology's crisis and his analysis of its causes make a surprisingly modern impression. His arguments against an empiricist approach in psychology and his plea for a unified psychological science is echoed even now (Staats, 1983). His description of the dynamics of science and the emphasis on theory fits well into the image of science sketched by post-positivistic philosophers of science. Many of the arguments advanced by Vygotsky have even found their way into introductory textbooks on the philosophy of science (e.g. Chalmers, 1982). It is now considered common knowledge in Western science that positivism – empiricism – was wrong and that "observation statements must be made in the language of some theory" (Chalmers, 1982, p. 28). The charge that researchers select from the multitude of phenomena before conducting their experiments is still heard. Many philosophers of science would agree with the statement that "observations and experiments are carried out in order to test or shed light on some theory, and only those observations considered relevant to that task should be recorded" (ibid., p. 33). In general, it can be said that philosophers of science like Popper, Kuhn, Lakatos, Hanson, and Feyerabend struck at the roots of the positivistic registration-induction model. What is remarkable is that Vygotsky's argument was very similar to and anticipated the ideas of these post-positivistic philosophers of science in several ways. At the same time that Carnap was developing the tenets of logical positivism, Soviet theorists began to develop a fundamentally different view of the dynamics of the scientific enterprise. The historical backgrounds of these divergent developments in the philosophy of science have been analyzed by Boeselager (1975).

We may conclude, then, that in "The historical significance of the crisis in psychology" Vygotsky was trying to integrate the ideas of Marx, Engels, and Lenin into his thinking and at the same time drawing heavily on the writings of prominent Western – mostly German – and Soviet psychologists. The topicality of his ideas of the philosophy of science (e.g. the emphasis on theory) has its background in the curious history of philosophical thought.

8

Vygotsky and Gestalt Psychology

When Vygotsky was appointed to the Moscow Institute in 1924, he began his studies from a clear axiomatic basis which encouraged him to take an interest in the developments in Gestalt psychology. As we saw before (see chapters 1 and 2), Vygotsky's credo in intellectual life – the understanding of synthesis emerging from dialectical oppositions – was well developed before this move. Whilst working at the Institute he emphasized the importance of the study of consciousness, defining it as "the problem of the structure of behavior" (Vygotsky, 1925g, p. 181). Hence, the emphasis on structure was the essential first meeting point between Vygotsky and the ideas of Gestalt psychology.

If Vygotsky's interest in Gestalt psychology was a result of gradual evolution of his ideas, then the growing interest in Gestalt psychology in the Institute was a coincidence of the kind in which social history is rich. The Marxist psychology that Kornilov was promoting at the time was actively engaged in the search for alternatives to traditional psychology, a tradition exemplified in the young Marxists' minds by Chelpanov's professional image (see chapter 6). Gestalt psychology's opposition to the old German associationistic psychology made thus a rather fitting bedfellow for the rumbling and verbose Marxist psychology in the Soviet Union.

Neverthless, although the environment in which Vygotsky developed his interest in Gestalt psychology was heatedly ideological, he managed to synthesize a thorough and relatively unideological analysis of the "new German psychology," and used it to arrive at a synthesis of fundamental importance for psychological methodology: the method of double stimulation. This analysis and synthesis took place within an easily defined period starting in 1924 and ending in the middle of the advent of the fight against menshevizing idealism around 1931. Although Vygotsky kept speaking (and writing) about Gestalt psychology until his death, its importance as a tool for synthesis diminished.

Vygotsky's acquaintance with Gestalt psychology began when he was editing Russian translations of German works, reiterating the basic messages of the new psychology, and meeting some of the Gestalt psychologists during their visits to the Soviet Union (e.g. Gottschaldt, Koffka, Lewin). These personal contacts, however, were not influential in the birth of his interest. He first met Lewin and Koffka, for example, in November 1931 and May 1932 respectively. Rather, it was the new German publications (see Scheerer, 1980) that provided speculative material for Vygotsky and his colleagues.

The Development of Gestalt Psychology and its Presence in Russia

The emergence of Gestalt psychology as one of the schools of thought in German science in the second decade of this century, and its institutional establishment in the early 1920s (by way of establishing the journal *Psychologische Forschung* in 1922) was a natural source of stimulation for psychologists in the Soviet Union. Historically, Russian intellectual life has been most closely connected with that of Germany (see Joravsky, 1989; Valsiner, 1988). In the pre-1917 period, many Russian scientists received their education in Germany, and published in German-language journals. This tendency continued in the 1920s but was ended in the early 1930s by the advent to power of radical tendencies in both the Soviet Union and Germany. Most of the psychologists in the 1920s were fluent in German, able to both read and write in the language.

Vygotsky was at the forefront of the task of editing and translating new German psychology texts into Russian. He wrote the foreward (Vygotsky, 1926f) to the very first Russian translation of a work of Gestalt psychology – that of Koffka (1924, 1926b). In 1930, he edited the translation of Karl Bühler's *Abriss der geistigen Entwicklung des Kindes* and wrote a foreward to that (Vygotsky, 1930ac), as well as to the translation of Wolfgang Köhler's *Intelligenzprüfungen an Menschenaffen* (Vygotsky, 1930s). In 1934, he published his foreword to the Russian edition of Kurt Koffka's *Grundlagen der psychischen Entwicklung* (Vygotsky, 1934k). Practically all the translations of the major works of German *Gestalt* psychologists of the time in Russian were somehow connected with Vygotsky's organizational and explanatory efforts (also: Vygotsky, 1930d; Vygotsky and Luria, 1930a). Together with Vygotsky, Alexander Luria (Luria, 1926f) and V. Artemov (1928) from the Kornilov Institute were active in explaining and applying Gestalt psychology. Beyond the Kornilov Institute, interest was shown in Gestalt psychology by other institutional circles, notably reflexology (Mjasishchev, 1930) and paedology (Abel'skaja and Neopikhanova, 1929, 1932).

Apart from editing translations and writing forewords, Vygotsky kept alive his interest in the contemporary developments in Gestalt psychology by commenting upon current debates in his publications (e.g. the Rignano–Köhler debate (see Köhler, 1928 and Rignano, 1928) was discussed in Vygotsky, 1930d, p. 123; the Köhler–Bühler disagreements were used productively by Vygotsky as well). Last (but not least), Vygotsky wrote a number of descriptive overviews of major Gestalt psychology experiments (Vygotsky, 1930d; Vygotsky and Luria, 1930a). In contrast to the usual style of Vygotsky, who largely evaded experimental and empirical details in most of his other writings, his descriptions of Gestalt psychology experiments are rich in details.

What, then, was the basis for Vygotsky's thorough interest and fascination with Gestalt psychology (as well as the reasons for its criticism)? Vygotsky's general attitude towards Gestalt psychology as a school of thought changed between 1924 and 1934, in ways that are consistent with the development of his own ideas.

Vygotsky's Critical Analyses of Gestalt Psychology

Vygotsky applied to the analysis of Gestalt psychology his characteristic thesis–antithesis–synthesis compositional scheme. In different places – in written or oral form – and dependent upon the function of the message (informative, polemic, or a position statement) the relative importance of each of these compositional components varied. Thus, in texts meant for a general audience and/or students (e.g. Vygotsky, 1930d; Vygotsky and Luria, 1930a) the description of the ideas and experiments of Gestalt psychologists is relatively long and detailed, whereas the element of criticism (antithesis) is rather limited, with some explanation of synthesis. In texts that could be classified as position statements (e.g. Vygotsky, 1926f), the elements of criticism and synthesis dominate, and the descriptive side is minimal. And, of course, in polemic texts, the antithesis and synthesis elements are extensive, while the description of the ideas of Gestalt psychology remain fragmentary. Such a differentiation between texts written for different purposes is hardly surprising, and can be seen as a general functional organization of communicative messages. This distinction in Vygotsky's case should be kept in mind, since in our contemporary retrospective efforts to understand his reasoning, the particular functions of texts are not clearly discernible (e.g. as in the published six-volume series).

That Vygotsky's first connection with Gestalt psychology was deeply embedded in the ideological discourse being conducted in Kornilov's Institute can be deduced from the style of his first discussions of the issues. In his introduction to the Russian translation (Koffka, 1926b) of Koffka's classic paper on the role of introspection in psychology (Koffka, 1924), Vygotsky charted out a programmatic perspective that the nascent Marxist psychology could have on the somewhat older Gestalt psychology (Vygotsky, 1926f). This perspective surfaced also in other texts written (and delivered) by Vygotsky (1926b, 1926d) in his first year at the Institute (1924–5).

The first mention of the relevance of Gestalt psychology in Vygotsky's work appears to be in the published version of his oral presentation at the All-Russian Psychoneurology Conference in Leningrad on January 6, 1924. This text appears to be re-worked for publication, particularly with respect to the separate (end) part which deals directly with the relevance of Gestalt psychology (Vygotsky, 1926b, pp. 43–6). Indications for this come from different sources. First, a contemporaneous commentary of the presentations at the Leningrad Conference (Dajan, 1924) reviews the main points of Vygotsky's presentation on reflexology, but does not mention anything about Vygotsky's comments upon Gestalt psychology in that presentation. Secondly, the end section (which is textually separated from the preceding parts in the original publication) makes use of Koffka's classic article on introspection that was originally Koffka's oral presentation on February 23, 1924 at the united meeting of British and Cambridge Psychological Associations, and which appeared in the written version only by October, 1924 (Koffka, 1924). Vygotsky's comments at the end of the published version of his Leningrad talk are clearly an antithesis and an integrative synthesis in discourse with Koffka (especially in his answer to the issue of how the introspective method can be used; Vygotsky, 1926b, p. 45). Furthermore, Vygotsky returns to the issue of Gestalt psychology in a third publication in the same collection, that on dominant reactions (Vygotsky, 1926d, pp. 100–4), which in its main focus was devoted to the presentation of experimental results obtained in collaborative work at the Moscow Institute in 1924–5.

The initial interest in Gestalt psychology shown at the Institute was clearly charted by Vygotsky (and his colleagues) in terms of an antithesis to the different camps of psychology as those were perceived: those of empirical psychology (of the Chelpanov tradition, following the German traditions of introspectionist reasoning) on the one hand, and behaviorism on the other. The fact of this contrast may explain why the short section on Gestalt psychology was added to Vygotsky's Leningrad presentation for its publication. Let us remind ourselves that Vygotsky's criticism in 1924 was addressed to the reductionist ethos of reflexological (Pavlovian and Bekhterevian) work, which overlooked the dialectical nature of qualitative change. At the same time, Vygotsky reminds us that Gestalt psychology is a new (from his perspective-revolutionary) outgrowth from the German introspectionist psychology. In his characteristically cosmopolitan way, Vygotsky reminded his audience:

> There can be nothing more false than the wish to describe the crisis that breaks the Russian science into two camps as a local Russian crisis. The crisis is going on worldwide throughout psychological science. The emergence of the psychological school of Gestalt-theory, that grows out from empirical psychology, gives vivid evidence about that. (1926b, p. 44)

This idea — of the wider than local (Russian) nature of the crisis in psychology — is repeated by Vygotsky in the same volume (1926f, pp. 176, 177). It is a reference to Chelpanov's counter-argument to Kornilov's efforts, but could be seen also as his personal dislike of the patriotic nature of the ideological fight for Marxist psychology that was going on in the Institute at that time (see chapter 6). The same idea was dominant in his manuscript on the crisis in psychology, where the discomfort with "declarative and fighting Marxism" was expressed more intensely (see chapter 7).

Interestingly, Vygotsky's "grand vision" for the role of Gestalt psychology (in Vygotsky, 1926f) in the further development of psychology as a science was phrased in uncharacteristically ideological terms. It reminds the reader of Bolshevik/Leninist description of tactics of revolution. Thus, Vygotsky narrates that in the beginning of "Russian" psychology's crisis the orientation towards "American militant (*vointsvuiushchii*: that is, the same term as Lenin used in 1922 on the article on militant materialism; Lenin, 1922) behaviorism" was the "correct" one, since it was important to "conquer objective positions in psychology" (*zavoevat' ob'ektivnyie pozitsii v psikhologii*) and "break out of the prison" of "spiritualistic and idealistic subjectivism." However, it was further claimed that Marxist psychology can proceed together with American behaviorism and Russian reflexology "only up to a certain point," at which there will be an historical need to separate from "fellow travelers" and set out on one's own direction (Vygotsky, 1926f, p. 176). The future for the improvement of psychology was described as vulnerable to being "stuck in an idealist swamp" (*zaviaznet v idealisticheskom bolote*, 1926f, p. 177). The use of militant Bolshevik terminology was even more apparent in a general description of the situation:

> Yesterday's *allies in the joint war* against subjectivism and empiricism may possibly turn out to be *our enemies* tomorrow in the *fight* for the establish-

ment of principal foundations for the social psychology of the social human being, for the *freeing* of psychology from *biological imprisonment* and its return to the status of an independent science, rather than a branch of comparative psychology. In other words, as we begin the process of building psychology as a science of the behavior of the social human being, rather than that of a higher mammal, the line of separation from yesterday's *allies* becomes clearly charted out. (1926f, p. 176; emphasis added)

So, Gestalt psychology according to Vygotsky (as he saw it by 1926) was expected to be one of these "fellow travelers" of Marxist psychology, an approach that shared the methodology but in the end failed to compete with the new psychology that Marxist philosophy promised to provide in the new (Soviet) society. Retrospectively we know that promise was an utopian one: neither Marxist psychology nor Soviet society have provided any qualitative breakthroughs in our understanding of human psychology or in the ways of organizing social life. Gestalt psychology, having had some influence on psychologies in different countries following the exodus of the main Gestalists from Germany by the 1930s, has likewise largely been forgotten.

Still, when seen through Vygotsky's eyes in the mid-1920s, Gestalt psychology appeared to be in agreement with the interests of the developing Marxist psychology in two ways. First, it was perceived to be a *monistic psychological system* that tried to unite the internal and external (behavioral) sides of psychological phenomena (Köhler's maxim of "what is internal is also external"), and to be interdisciplinary in its Gestalt-perspective, cutting across boundaries of physics, physiology, and psychology. Gestalt psychology was seen as accepting the dialectical law of transformation of quantity into quality, which thus fitted well with the cornerstone of Marxist dialectical psychology (and Vygotsky's long-established Hegelian world-view). Secondly, Gestalt psychology satisfied Vygotsky's active interest in synthesis, by providing foundations for new methods of investigation where both the external (behavioral) and internal psychological sides were linked but not reduced to each other, a mistake both behaviorism and empirical psychology made. Not surprisingly, the methodological emphasis of Gestalt psychology was described by Vygotsky in terms of Kornilovian reactology: "The new methodology tries to lay the foundation for the functional, subjective–objective method, that would include the descriptive (descriptive-introspectionist) and functional (objective-*reactological*) points of view" (Vygotsky, 1926f, p. 178, emphasis added).

This prediction of a methodology borne out by Vygotsky and his colleagues, to a higher degree that others in the Moscow Institute (see chapter

6). Both Vygotsky's method of double stimulation and Luria's *Methode der abbilden Motorik* developed as descendants of Gestalt psychology.

Among the areas of Vygotsky's disagreement with Gestalt psychology, were his fears that Gestalt psychology would return to vitalistic and mechanistic explanations, the "too close similarity" of problems of its psychology to contemporary physics, the absence of the social perspective on psychological issues, and the "intuitive theory of the mind" (Vygotsky, 1926f, p. 178). He took the emergence and development of Gestalt psychology as a proof of the historical correctness of the direction which Marxist psychology was taking at the time, while reminding the readers that it is not to be expected that a system of Marxist psychology could emerge in "Western science." Apparently, Vygotsky had internalized the values of the Soviet utopian thinking that surrounded him at the time of his transition to psychology (see also chapter 3).

Given Vygotsky's interest in Gestalt psychology, it is surprising that in his next major theoretical text, on the crisis in psychology (Vygotsky, 1926m/ 1982, see also chapter 7) he barely discussed the relevance of Gestalt thinking. Of the 144 printed pages of that text, Vygotsky devotes only one page to a description of the role of Gestalt psychology in the efforts to overcome the crisis (1926m/1982, pp. 395–6). His coverage here is free of the military terminology that could be seen in the texts published in 1926. He merely charts out the basic principles of the Gestalt position, reiterating the primacy and the generality of structural organization of the whole over its parts, and proceeds to ask a short low-key question of whether that system of thought can successfully combine materialistic psychology and phenomenology of behavior. In a cursory remark, Vygotsky doubts that Gestalt psychology will turn out to be a "third way" out of the crisis (1926m/1982, p. 396), but then instead of elaborating this doubt he moves on to discuss William Stern's personalism.

Vygotsky's analysis of Gestalt psychology served as one of the foundations of the cultural-historical theory. The doubts he had begun to express about the role of the new German psychology grew, as his own synthesis of the structural world-view and the dynamics of dialectical study of development proceeded. In that process, Vygotsky at times contrasted Gestalt psychology with other trends in psychology (putting emphasis on the "positive breakthroughs" of Gestalt psychology relative to these others), but at other times he turned increasingly critical of Gestaltists' inability to solve the problem of dialectical synthesis.

A good example of this two-perspective attitude is revealed in Vygotsky's analysis of Köhler's views on the intelligence of anthropoids (Vygotsky, 1929h). The editors of *Estestvoznanie i marksizm*, the Marxist journal arguing for the amalgamation of natural sciences with dialectical materialism, found it necessary to provide a footnote to Vygotsky's discussion of Köhler, explaining that only questions linked with Köhler's experiments, and not the "Marxist analysis" of Köhler's theory, were represented in Vygotsky's article. This seems to have been a means to appease the more militantly Marxist readership of the journal, given Vygotsky's style of discussion in which Marxist philosophers appeared only when they made sense for the substantive discussion.

Vygotsky (1929h) contrasted Köhler's thinking and empirical evidence with those of his critics (Bühler, Lindworsky), and analyzed the connection between Köhler's ideas and those of Vagner. Again, we see Vygotsky being critical of both extremes – the reduction of intellectual functions to a sum of behavioral elements, and the separation of the behavior from the "realm of ideas." He still has much hope in the methodological promises of structural psychology:

> The principle of structure fulfils a double methodological function ... and that carries its true dialectical meaning. On the one hand, that principle *unites* all levels in the development of behavior, eliminates that break that Bühler writes about, shows the continuity in the development of the higher out of the lower, and that the structural characteristics are present already in instincts and habits. On the other hand, that principle also makes it possible to establish all the deep, principal, qualitative difference between one and the other level; the novelty that every new stage brings into the development of behavior, that distinguishes it from the previous one. (Vygotsky, 1929h, pp. 147–8)

Thus structural psychology is seen as capturing the dialectics of development by uniting the opposites ("lower" and "higher" levels) through the emphasis on unity, and distinguishing them by the opposition of qualitative uniqueness of the levels. This can be interpreted more as Vygotsky's instrumental use of Gestalt psychology in his own thinking, rather than as an objective statement about that framework. Vygotsky himself seems to have recognized it, by agreeing with Bühler's description of structural psychology as linked to the philosophy of Spinoza (Vygotsky, 1929h, p. 153).

Vygotsky's multi-sided view of structural psychology subsequently became more critical of the hopes of that trend. In a chapter in a volume overviewing contemporary directions in psychology (Vygotsky, Gellershtejn, Fingert, and Shirvindt, 1930), he went beyond the primary function of explaining the Gestalt psychology movement, and declared that "structural psychology comes to the radical reorganization of all psychological theories of learning and child development" (Vygotsky, 1930d, p. 105). At the same time, he pointed to the dangers inherent in Gestalt thinking once more: the reduction of all phenomena to the notion of structure only. For Vygotsky, "only a dialectically reconstructed notion of structure can become the main tool for psychological investigation" (1930d, p. 119). In that dialectical reconstruction of the notion of structure, the emphasis on the formation of novel structural forms, and the functioning of those forms in the further synthesis of even newer forms, becomes crucial. According to Vygotsky (1930d, p. 124), this dialectical perspective on structural transformation has to be based on a clear understanding of the social factors that lead to the reorganization of structures. Of course from that desired perspective, Köhler's emphasis on the universality of Gestalts in physical and psychological worlds could not be satisfactory to Vygotsky any more. The interdisciplinary claims of Gestalt psychologists that were originally rather favorably received by Vygotsky (1926d, 1926f), by now had lost most of their original charm. By this time his hopes for a synthesis of knowledge to occur in the communication between sciences had been transferred to paedology (see chapter 12).

In *Studies of the History of Behavior* Vygotsky's criticism of the openness to the idea of synthesis emerged most clearly (Vygotsky and Luria, 1930a). In chapter 1, Vygotsky overviewed Köhler's animal experiments in detail. In the whole corpus of Vygotsky's writings, an attention to the empirical details of investigation is quite rare. Of course, Vygotsky used the details to enable the reader to understand the basic principles of structural psychology, so the unique nature of this text may be explained by its dialectic functions. The ideas that were particularly emphasized in this text included the structural organization of the field (pp. 26–7), the plasticity of means–ends linkages in animal (and human) behavior (p. 23), and the qualitatively novel nature of intellectual behavior (in contrast with instincts and conditional reflexes). Vygotsky led the reader, in the course of this chapter, from the dialectical viewpoint of qualitative leaps in the process of evolution to the emergence of new structural forms by way of dialectical reorganization. Doing this he made use of his favorite metaphor of *korotkoe zamykanie* (on pp. 34, 39, 41; see also chapter 2). He concluded by claiming that the principal difference between the intellectual functioning of apes and those of humans is the qualitative difference between the capability of constructing mediating devices (in humans) in the form of signs (p. 47), and the limitation of the chimpanzees to the level of tool use without the parallel presence of labor (p. 50; see also chapter 9). Vygotsky demonstrated his fully Marxist–dialectical understanding of the issues in this chapter, thus criticizing Köhler and the rest of Gestalt psychology for not accepting the dialectical transformation idea.

In his lectures on infancy, Vygotsky (1932o/1984, p. 312) argued that the theory of structural psychology can capture the fundamentals from which development proceeds, but it cannot explain the process of development in the future-oriented direction. The same criticism is repeated when Vygotsky deals with the "crisis of the first year of life." The child discovers the structure of the world that exists as it is, and is not open to further development (Vygotsky, 1933h/1984, p. 324). A more thorough and substantive analysis of the theoretical premises of Gestalt psychology was given in his lecture at the Academy of Communist Education on June 26, 1932, when Vygotsky outlined the underlying structure of Gestalt psychology's claims that it opposes the "mechanistic" and "vitalistic" perspectives in psychology (Vygotsky, 1932e/1960). Returning to Köhler's earlier propositions as well as to more recent arguments by Wertheimer and Koffka, Vygotsky showed that Gestalt psychology's reduction of all phenomenology constitutes another "mechanistic" (in a wider sense) approach that overlooks the development of *new structures*. He viewed Gestalt psychology's emphasis on dynamic change as reflecting the "balance principle" (equilibration), from which basis no new structural states (but rather the reestablishment of the "good form") can follow (Vygotsky, 1932e/1960, p. 477).

Thus, by 1932–3, Vygotsky had started to consider Gestalt psychology a "naturalistic psychology" that in its theoretical core did not differ from reflexology since it reduced meaning to structure (Vygotsky, 1933g/1982, p. 159). The basis for this criticism was Vygotsky's own cultural-historical theory, which had begun to emphasize the role of meanings in reorganization of the structure of psychological phenomena. From that perspective, the strict separation of *homo sapiens* from other primates which Vygotsky had arrived at contradicted the emphasis Gestalt psychologists placed on diminishing the inter-species differences and reifying the overwhelming causal role of the *Gestalten* (see Vygotsky, 1934l/1982). Thus, the great hopes of 1926 of Gestalt psychology freeing psychology "from its biological imprisonment" had failed, as Vygotsky perceived it. Nevertheless, he continued to make active use of specific arguments of Gestalt psychologists on particular issues (see below), but the enthusiasm for this school of thought as a whole was no longer the same as in earlier years. In a way, Vygotsky (1926f) lived up to his prediction that the link with Gestaltism was a temporary and episodic one. In his own development, Vygotsky's increasing emphasis on meaning led him away from the overwhelming emphasis on structure, although the latter remained an unquestionable starting point for all of his psychological work (see Vygotsky, 1934o/1982; 1935m/1983).

Vygotsky's Analysis of Specific Facets of Gestalt Psychology

Vygotsky's relationship with Gestalt psychology was of crucial importance for the development of his own cultural-historical theory and methodology (see chapter 9). Hence tracing which particular aspects of Gestalt psychologists' work captured Vygotsky's attention, and focusing on the way he transformed ideas from Gestalt psychology into new ideas within his own theoretical framework, is worth studying.

The Primacy of Structural Organization: Units of Analysis

From the very beginning of his interest in Gestalt psychology, Vygotsky was interested in the structure of psychological processes. Not surprisingly, it was Gestalt psychologists' actively ideological anti-associationistic and anti-elementaristic stand that Vygotsky at first used in his own disputes with his opponents. The Gestalt emphasis on structural unity happened to coincide with Vygotsky's first year's work on dominant reactions (see chapter 6).

In the introduction to his first (and only) empirical paper on dominant reactions, Vygotsky employed the Gestalt principle against Pavlov's militant elementarism in reducing all phenomena to reflexes and their aggregates (Vygotsky, 1926d). Ukhtomsky's idea of "the dominant" (1924; 1927) (a minor aspect of a physiologically complex process that at a time begins to govern the whole process) was close to Vygotsky's own (see chapter 2). Gestalt psychology's structural holism, which refused to use any summative aggregation idea, fitted Vygotsky's intellectual efforts very well. Thus, to illustrate the problem of the structure of behavior, he polemicizes against Pavlov to point to the integrative-holistic, rather than atomistic (summative), view of reflex actions:

> Already in the experiments of academician Pavlov the investigators had to encounter such forms of behavior, where one reflex comes into conflict with another and the behavior of the animal is no longer determined by the sum of the active stimuli and their corresponding reflexes, but by some facts that emerge from the clash of the two reflexes. Reflex plus reflex turns out not to be two reflexes, but a certain new form of behavior. It is true that these simplest acts are easily interpreted as processes of simple, almost mechanical interaction. "Two reflexes," says academician Pavlov, "are literally the equivalent of the two sides of scales." But the notion of scales is already a certain complex, dynamic whole, that stands closer to behavior than the notion of a chain, i.e. simple mechanical connection. (Vygotsky, 1926d, p. 102)

Here Vygotsky's interest in deciphering the "complex, dynamic whole" which stands behind behavioral phenomena forges a direct link with the focus of Gestalt psychology. That emphasis led him to address (episodically and not always succinctly) the issue of "units of analysis" in psychological research (see Valsiner, 1988, p. 173–9). This concern for units can be traced back to Wolfgang Köhler's focus on similar issues, and is reflected in the discourse about qualities of atoms and molecules in a chemical substance. Briefly narrated, in a complex chemical substance (such as water, H_2O) the constituent elements (atoms) do not possess the same qualities as the holistic structure to which they belong. Thus, using oxygen and hydrogen separately to extinguish a fire is impossible, but their synthesis (water) is well known as the primary aid of firefighters.

The theme of a holistic organization of natural systems was a widespread topic of discussion in the natural sciences and philosophy in Vygotsky's time. Russian intellectual discourse of early twentieth century gave the world the beginnings of general systems theory, in the form of Bogdanov's *tektology* (Bogdanov, 1922). Positive evaluation of Gestalt psychology's emphasis on structural holism was echoed in different contexts (e.g. Agol, 1928, p. 214), and was explicitly linked with the traditions of A. Lazurskii's experimental methodology (Luria, 1926f). The contrast of the quality of the structure of chemical molecules with those of their constituents was frequently referred to in these discussions.

In his writings, Vygotsky used the water molecule versus hydrogen and oxygen atoms example repeatedly to explain his notion of the breakdown of psychological processes to units, rather than elements (Vygotsky, 1926d, p. 104; 1934l/1982, p. 288; 1934o/1982, p. 173; 1935m/1983, p. 248; 1960, p. 129; and other sources). This analogy was widely used in Gestalt psychologists' arguments against associationistic perspectives at that time. Vygotsky's reasoning about the units issue was interestingly symptomatic: it passionately emphasized the need to study the appropriate units as minimal *Gestalts* (structures of the phenomenon that preserve the essence of the phenomenon), and refused to enter the analysis of the breakdown of the units (see Valsiner, 1988, chapter 5 for further discussion of that topic). It was as if Vygotsky was, for some reason, afraid of losing the phenomenon if efforts to study its transformation were made both as it develops (from lower states to a higher form) and as that latter structure may break down (move from a higher to another lower form). In other terms, Vygotsky insisted upon the *principle* of dialectical synthesis but not upon the study of its process mechanisms.

Of course, Vygotsky's own development led him to view different kinds of units in the phenomena he was interested in. If in the middle of the 1920s the unit was to be a structure of reactions united by a dominant, then by the end of his life he began to view word meaning as the relevant unit of analysis (Vygotsky, 1934a, p. 9). Perhaps the largely episodic and vague talk by Vygotsky about the "analysis into units" that resurfaces in his writings and speeches from time to time is better understood as a rhetorical device, that is, as a means to the end of defending a structurally oriented dynamic theoretical stance against the efforts to analyze it into elements. Then it becomes more clear why Vygotsky did not proceed with the study of these units in any productive way, but rather emphasized the need for such study.

Towards a New Method: From Köhlerian Experiments to the Method of Double Stimulation

The role of Köhler's experiments with primates in the development of Vygotsky's cultural-historical theory is analyzed in another chapter (see chapter 9). Here it is of interest to chart the ways in which Vygotsky's specific methodological innovation – called by him (somewhat awkwardly) "the functional method of double stimulation" (Vygotsky, 1929s, p. 430) – was based on Köhler's work. In Köhler's experiments the subject was situated in a structured situation with different possible objects available to be used to reach a goal, the access to which was blocked by the existing structure of the setting. The subject could invent a way for solving the problem, either through bypassing or overcoming the blockage of the goal (e.g. approaching the goal via alternative routes), or by making use of the objects available in the given situation to get to the goal (tool use). Mikhail Basov's co-workers, S. Shapiro and E. Gerke (1930), extended Köhler's methodological idea to the study of children's problem-solving on the basis of social background knowledge. The child who encounters a Köhlerian-type situation brings into it a set of "scripts" that had been established in the course of previous social experience, and with the help of speech. Vygotsky followed the work done in Leningrad by Basov's research group (compare Shapiro and Gerke, 1930, pp. 80–6 and Vygotsky, 1931h, pp. 387–92). He, too, enriched the Köhlerian experimental setting by pointing out that children use their qualitatively higher (in contrast with primates) "level of behavior" in such settings, that is, the use of signs (Vygotsky, 1931o/1983, p. 123). Metaphorically speaking, Vygotsky thus added a "fifth dimension" to the Köhlerian "structure of the field." Beside the three dimensions of space and the fourth of time, Vygotsky inserted into the structural-psychological scheme the notion of meaning (see Vygotsky and Luria, 1930d/1984, p. 48). Meaning is generated by the subject by way of constructing a sign (or using a previously constructed and internalized one), and using signs in communication (speech). The use of that sign in the psychological system of the person thus re-organizes the whole structure of the setting. In this respect, the construction of meanings through the use of signs in an experimental setting provides the synthesis. The person re-organizes the understanding of the situation and (may) act in accordance with this new understanding. On the other hand, when openness to the emergence of such synthesis is not present, the subject may be "stuck" in the experimental situation in which the experimenter expects the subject to construct the meaning of the setting that is intended by the experiment. Thus, Vygotsky argued that the difference between "practical-action" and "cognitive-intellectual" tasks given to mentally retarded children may reveal the accessibility of problem-solving in the former but not in the latter (Vygotsky, 1929y/1983, p. 146). Vygotsky illustrated it with an example from a study by Petrova (1925) in the clinic of M. Gurevich in Moscow (the "primitive child" phenomenon as it was labelled at the time):

> A child who is deeply retarded in her adaptive reactions is being studied. She had been to many children's institutions and was then sent to the psychiatric hospital under the suspicion of psychological pathology. In the hospital no psychological illness was discovered, and the child was transferred to be studied in Gurevich's clinic. The girl is a Tatar who in early childhood changed one unconsolidated language knowledge for another, and learned to speak in the latter. She was completely untaught to think in the new language. The girl was not familiar with the idea that on the basis of a few words it is possible to draw conclusions. The psychologist confronted her with a number of reasoning tasks, in some cases in a practical and in others in verbal form. When confronted with practical tasks, the subject gave positive answers. She responded with full non-understanding and inability to reason when she was given verbal tasks. For instance, the child is told "My aunt is taller than I, and my uncle even taller than my aunt. Is my uncle taller than me?" The girl responds: "I don't know. How can I say, whether the uncle is taller, if I have never seem him?" . . . The child is delayed in her cultural development, in the development of verbal thinking, but she is not mentally retarded [*debil*] . . . (Vygotsky, 1929y/1983, p. 147)

The experimental verbal task given to this child presumes that the child is capable of understanding the task and then solving it. However, the child lacks the "knowledge base" for tackling such tasks of deductive reasoning, and refuses to solve the problem. The child, like the illiterate adults in later "cultural-historical experiments" in Central Asia (Luria, 1974), constructs the meaning of the given situation differently from the ways in which the experimenter interprets it. For Vygotsky, the contrast within the same subject between success in practical reasoning and lack of success in verbal reasoning was indicative of the subject's present level of intellectual development. However, even that contrast in itself did not satisfy Vygotsky's concern with the study of the developmental processes by which the new, higher forms of intellectual functioning emerge. Thus, the experimenter's role in his new methodology was not merely to arrive at a "diagnostic profile" of the higher and lower psychological functions, but actively to promote the transition from the present state of affairs to the new (not yet existing) one. All the experiments within the cultural-historical theory (see chapter 9) and concerning concept-formation (see chapter 11) are similar in this respect: the subject is put in a structured situation where a problem exists (so far that follows the lines of Gestalt psychology) and the subject is provided with active guidance towards the construction of a new means to the end of a solution to the problem. From here Vygotsky's fascination with "teaching experiments" follows, his criticism of Gestalt psychology's inability to study development, and his constant call for the study of psychological functions that have not yet developed but will emerge soon (see chapter 13). It should not be forgotten that Vygotsky was a crusader for handicapped children and their right to social education, a belief he had held long before arriving at the "method of double stimulation" (Vygotsky, 1925c).

For this new task of experimental study of the emergence of higher psychological functions, the old ways of looking at psychological experiments had to be reconsidered. This innovation of experimental methodology – recognition of the meaning-constructing role of the human subjects in the experimental settings – emerged at an intersection of Vygotsky's development of his cultural-historical theory: its experimental basis (see chapter 9) on the one hand, and his interests in the development of concepts on the other (see chapter 11).

Dynamic Relationships of the Parts within the Whole: Lewin

Vygotsky's use of structural-psychological ideas in his own theorizing fits his functionalist emphasis. The differentiated "landscape" of the Gestalt psychology movement made it possible to address relevant psychological issues using different Gestalt authors' viewpoints as means to an end. Thus, as Vygotsky had been constantly interested in the dynamic unity of affect and reasoning (see chapter 2), Kurt Lewin's work in the 1920s and early 1930s was of relevance to him.

A number of issues which were reflected in Lewin's work appealed to Vygotsky. First, Lewin's criticism of the traditional static perspectives in science (Lewin, 1931/1982) followed similar lines of criticism put forward by Vygotsky. Thus, science could be said to need to transcend the "phenomenological" (static emphasis on existing forms) viewpoint to adopt Lewins' "conditional-genetic" perspective (Vygotsky, 1930d, pp. 112–13). Surely that use of Lewin's terminology was a modified version of the earlier

maxim of Blonsky's: "behavior can be viewed only as history of behavior."
How that history could be studied was further revealed by Vygotsky's
analysis of adolescents' needs and interests (Vygotsky, 1931h, pp. 185–95).

Lewin's emphasis on the holistic, structural organization of children's
needs (in contrast to the established associative connections and habits)
was, of course, a favorite idea of Vygotsky's, who never tired of fighting the
non-dialectical reductionism of the psychology of that time. In his commentary on Lewin's theory of interests, Vygotsky argued:

> Human activity is not a mechanical sum of unorganized skills, but it is
> structurally captured and organized by dynamic holistic strivings and
> interests. Together with the establishment of structural relation between
> interest and skill, the new theory comes with logical rigor to a totally new
> perspective on an old problem of inborn and acquired interests; it poses the
> question in ways that were not pursued before . . . Interests are not acquired, but
> they develop – in that introduction of the notion of development into the
> study of interests lies the most important word that the new theory has said on
> the whole problem of interests. (1931h, p. 187)

Vygotsky's favorite theme – dynamic development of higher-level phenomena – is evident here. The kernel of Vygotsky's criticism of Lewin in this
respect is also embedded here: the theme of non-recognition of higher
(historically developed and sign-mediated) interests, and the lack of acceptance of the Hegelian idea of dialectical synthesis in Lewin's work (1931h,
pp. 191–3).

Nevertheless, Lewin's emphasis on the study of the dynamic side of
psychological processes was a forceful ally in Vygotsky's quest for the study
of dialectical synthesis, and he emphasized the relevance of Lewin's
conditional-genetic methodological perspective for the study of developing
phenomena (see Lewin, 1926a, 1931/1981). That methodological stance
called for the study of the processes that take place (and the conditions that
are necessary) as a new structure emerges from an old one. In the environment of the psychology of the 1920s and 1930s this was a powerful contrast
to the tendency to study the outcomes (phenotypic appearances) and to
make entified causal attributions in order to explain development (see
Vygotsky, 1931m/1983, pp. 96–7). All human mental processes (including
the use of language) are aimed at the temporary stabilization of the flow of
experiences – translating that flow into static constructs (entities) – hence
the process of this translation can be called "entification"; and its products
are "entified" attributions, ideas, and other mental static phenomena. This
contrast between developmental and nondevelopmental research orientations is nowadays even more marked, so Vygotsky's alliance with Lewin on
that topic is as fresh as ever. From the emphasis on conditional-genetic

study follows the impossibility of studying development via its static outcomes. In the latter, the conditions that wrought its emergence are usually inadvertently lost, hence development cannot be studied through its outcomes. The outcomes of behavioral development reflect the results of automization of newly developed functions ("fossilized behavior"; *okamenelost' povedenia*; see Vygotsky, 1931m/1983, p. 99), and a study of these behavioral fossils in the outcomes cannot replace the prospective study of the developmental process itself. Of course, Vygotsky went along with Lewin's thinking only in respect to the dynamic and developmental viewpoint, whilst criticizing his perspective for its lack of emphasis on dialectical synthesis.

Finally, Lewin's efforts (e.g. Lewin, 1926a, 1926b, 1926c) to (re)unite affect and cognition were of relevance to Vygotsky, who discovered in a number of Lewinian experiments supporting material for his own position:

> K. Lewin demonstrated in which ways one emotional state is transformed into another, and how the displacement of emotional experiences takes place when an unresolved and uncompleted emotion continues to exist, often in a hidden form. He showed how affect enters into any structure with which it is connected. Lewin's main idea is that it is not possible to encounter affective, emotional reactions in an isolated state (as elements of psychic life that only later become associated with other elements). The emotional reaction is a distinctive result of the given structure of the psychic process. Lewin showed that the triggering emotional reactions can emerge in sports activity both in external movements and mental activity (e.g. chess play). He showed that in these cases different content emerges in coordination with different reactions, but the structural place of emotional processes remains the same. (Vygotsky, 1932i/1982, pp. 433–4)

Vygotsky was particularly enthusiastic about Lewin's experiments in which subjects were put into a meaningless setting and left to wait. In such settings they were observed to accumulate emotiogenic "power" which led to the cognitive reorganization of the subjective situation by construction of some subjective meaning to it. Subjects were also seen to devise action plans in such emotiogenic situations, which would be subsequently put into action in an automatic fashion (Vygotsky, 1932i/1983, pp. 461–3). This connection between emotional stress and cognitive reconstruction of the meaning of the situation, as well as with action-plan construction, conformed with Vygotsky's cultural-historical theorizing in 1930 to 1932. In Lewin's experiments, he could see the unification of affective processes (the increase of emotional agitation) with cognition (construction of new meanings) and action (development of mental action plans that control subsequent action). The acceptance of Lewin's work was linked closely in Vygotsky's thinking with his consistent interest in the philosophy of Spinoza (Vygotsky, 1932i/ 1983, p. 387; e.g. the close link between Zeigarnik's experiments and Spinoza's ideas; also in Vygotsky, 1935m/1983, p. 249).

Lewin's field-theoretical perspective also appealed to Vygotsky because of its emphasis on the unity of the psychological phenomenology with the structure of the (subjectively flavored) environment in which the person is embedded. Lewin's *Aufforderungscharakter* idea (Lewin, 1926a, 1926b) was actively used by Vygotsky (1932p/1984, p. 341), and in his lectures he sketched Lewin's famous film of a child trying to sit onto a stone.

However, Vygotsky explicitly charted his disagreements with Lewin's theoretical system; these disagreements focused on the issue of how human beings control their actions by way of psychological processes. Vygotsky's answer to that question was clear: through acting upon the world and by controlling its stimuli (the process of mediation) one controls one's actions. The role of signs in that process was of central importance for Vygotsky by that time (Vygotsky, 1931m/1983, p. 120).

Vygotsky also found Lewin's thinking congenial to his own in the area of understanding mental retardation, particularly, Lewin's effort to see the roots of mental retardation in the affective-volitional, rather than cognitive processes (see Vygotsky, 1935m/1983, pp. 234–6; also chapter 4). But again, Lewin is criticized for his "anti-dialectical" connection of affect and cognition (Vygotsky, 1935m/1983, p. 242–3). Furthermore, Vygotsky saw Lewin's lack of developmental emphasis in the analysis of the cognitive/ affective complex in the mentally retarded child:

> He [Lewin] does not know the dialectical rule that in the course of develop-ment the cause and the consequence exchange places; that higher psychologi-cal functions that once emerged on the basis of certain dynamic conditions have a feedback influence on the processes that generated them, that in development the lower [processes] are replaced by higher; that in development the physiological functions change by themselves, but first of all the inter-functional links, relations between different processes (in particular between intellect and affect) are changed. Lewin looks at affect outside of development and without linkages with the rest of the psychic life. He posits that the role of affect in the psychic life remains unchanged and constant in the course of the whole development, and thus, consequently, the relation of intellect and affect remains constant. (Vygotsky, 1935m/1983, pp. 244–5)

Thus, again, Vygotsky's criticism of Gestalt psychology concentrated on the issues of development as emergence of qualitatively novel characteris-tics. Of all the Gestalt psychologists among Vygotsky's contemporaries, it was Kurt Koffka who most explicitly made an effort to handle issues of development.

Processes in Development: Vygotsky on Koffka

It was Koffka's work in the 1920s that served as an introduction to psychology for Vygotsky (see above). First, it was relevant for Vygotsky that Koffka stressed the structural nature of learning and development (Vygotsky, 1930d, p. 105). Furthermore, Koffka's acceptance of the inclusion of words in the structure of a setting – in conjunction with tools – was an important idea from Vygotsky's point of view (1930d, p. 111). However, as he himself predicted in 1926, a relationship with Koffka's work in particular and Gestalt psychology in general, had its limits for Vygotsky. He became critical of the axiomatic assumption of equilibrium inherent in Gestalt psychology in general and in Koffka and Wertheimer in particular. "[Gestalt psychology considers] typical for any movement, for any change of the physical structure, that it moves from a rest state through the violation of equilibrium into another rest state. From that follows that the psychic structure is viewed first of all as something that stays in an equilibrium state" (Vygotsky, 1932e/1960, p. 477).

In his lengthy foreword to the Russian translation of Koffka's *Die Grundlagen der psychischen Entwicklung*, Vygotsky gave perhaps the most direct and systematic critical analysis of *Gestalt* psychology that is available in his writings (Vygotsky, 1934k/1982). Vygotsky first views Koffka's effort to apply the principle of structure to developmental phenomena. In contrast, Vygotsky would apply the principle of development to phenomena that Gestalt psychology characterized by way of the structural account (and to that Vygotsky wholeheartedly agreed). The structure of the developmental process includes the relevant contact between teaching and learning (*obuchenie*), but how do the *first novel actions* in the developing organism emerge (Vygotsky, 1924l/1982, p. 242)? Koffka's answer to that question – an explanation by reference to the formation of novel structures – did not satisfy Vygotsky as it did not differentiate the lower and higher psychological processes (1934l/1982, p. 246). This, of course, was a criticism that again originated in the dialectical perspective on development; by not recognizing the qualitative leaps in the developmental processes (both ontogenetic and phylogenetic) Koffka was viewed to overextend the structuralist principles to phenomena which Vygotsky viewed as being qualitatively different from one another. Particularly (along the lines of his own emphasis on meaning), Vygotsky criticizes Koffka for not recognizing the relevance of the semiotic activity as a qualitatively different human characteristic (1934l/1982, pp. 272–5). This criticism remains quite valid – especially as we now know of the close continuity between Koffka's work and the "affordance"-theorizing of the Gibsons and their followers. Vygotsky's example of how different people with varying knowledge bases view the same object illustrated that well:

> Let us compare how a chessboard (with chess pieces on it) is perceived by different people: a person who does not know how to play chess; a person who had just started to learn to play; middle-level; and excellent chess players. Surely it can be said that each of the four people view the chessboard differently. The one who does not know how to play chess perceives the structure of the pieces from the perspective of their external characteristics. The meaning of the pieces and their position on the board fall completely outside of his perspective. That very same chessboard provides a different structure to the person who knows the meanings of the pieces and the moves. For him, some parts of the table become the background, others become the focus. Yet differently will the medium-level and excellent chess players view the board. Something like that takes place in the development of the child's perception. The meaning leads to the emergence of a meaningful picture of the world ... (Vygotsky, 1934l/1982, pp. 277–8)

So, while animals have only perception of the world, humans have a meaningful picture. This idea, borrowed by Vygotsky from Gelb (1934l/1982, p. 280), reflects his core criticism of Gestalt psychology's structuralist reductionism. Vygotsky pointed out that Koffka's structuralist perspective does not allow the emergence of novel forms. His analysis of Koffka's understanding of development served largely as a means towards the end of elaborating the ideas of the zone of proximal development (see chapter 13). Namely, Vygotsky points to the similarity in Koffka's view on development and that of Thorndike (the teaching–learning process = development; 1934l/1982, pp. 285–6), while reducing the complexity of that process to different units (elementary skills versus structures). In an insightful, retrospective passage, Vygotsky summarized the road that Gestalt psychology had traveled. Characterizing Koffka's perspective on development, he noticed that Koffka's structuralist view resembled a "mosaic" of structures developing in parallel and becoming associated with one another:

> At first, separate molecule-structures exist, separately and independently from one another. Their development involves the change of the measures and size of these structures. Thus, again in the beginning of development there is a chaos of unorganized molecules, from which by way of unification a holistic orientation to reality emerges. (Vygotsky, 1934l/1982, p. 288)

This description of development did not differ from Thorndike's only in the size of the units involved (instead of elementary actions Koffka sees structures). Thus, Gestalt psychology replaced development seen as inter-element association formation with inter-structure association formation and, thus, did not overcome the basic difficulty of the associationistic world view. Koffka's inability to explain development was seen by Vygotsky as an indicator of the theoretical impasse of the whole of Gestalt psychology.

Functional Systems: The Development and Breakdown of the Structural Organization of Psychological Processes

In the late 1920s and particularly the early 1930s, Vygotsky developed an interest in the principles by which the human brain functions, an interest sparked possibly by his beginning some form of medical studies around that time (see chapter 1). The continuity of reasoning is quite clear: the dominant in the structure of reactions is a systemic phenomenon and so is any neurophysical phenomenon in the human brain. In the brain, the functional organization of the dominant can be traced in the connections between different parts of the brain in a manner parallel to tracing the systemic organization of higher and lower psychological processes in the holistic psychological structure of an individual. Hence Vygotsky's interest in the functional systems (the labeling of which can be seen to mirror his emphasis on the dynamic and instrumental nature of these structured units):

> In the process of the psychic development of a child . . . not only internal reorganization and improvement of separate functions takes place, but also inter-functional links and relations are qualitatively changed. As a result, new psychological systems emerge that unite in complex coordination a number of elementary functions. These unities of a higher kind, that come to replace homogeneous, elementary functions we tentatively name higher psychic functions. (Vygotsky and Luria, 1930d/1984, p. 81)

The functional systems in the brain, which Kurt Goldstein's holistic perspective had charted out in his neurology, provided Vygotsky with much material for thought. In contrast to his earlier (experimental) efforts to study the dominant in reactions, the study of holistic functional organization of the brain led Vygotsky to use neurological (and psychiatric) case material that had been accumulating in the scientific literature.

Research on the human brain and its functioning is a curious area of study, for in no other fields involving human subjects is research so much dependent on the advancement and use of technology, both military and scientific. Vygotsky's interests in the functioning of the brain benefited *de facto* from the results of the First World War, which brought the issue of brain damage and its compensation to the attention of medical and behavioral scientists. Of course, empirical phenomenology, in and by itself, is blind to new understanding of the general principles by which the brain works. Fortunately, some of the researchers working with patients with war-injuries were basing their research on a structuralistic world-view (Goldstein and Gelb, 1920; Gelb and Golstein, 1925).

Case material from neuropsychology enabled Vygotsky to support his views with evidence. For example, quoted Goldstein's example of an encephalitic patient whose disturbance had blocked the capability to follow abstracted instructions (e.g. "shut your eyes"; the patient could not do it), but who could perform that action when it was embedded in a context (e.g. "show how you go to sleep"; Vygotsky, 1932i/1982, pp. 463–4). In a similar vein, the effects of brain damage on the breakdown of categorical cognition (Gelb and Goldstein, 1925) supported Vygotsky's views on the role of concepts in organizing and re-organizing a person's psychological processes (e.g. Vygotsky, 1931h, pp. 408ff; 1934h, p. 1072). He explicitly argued that cases of color-name aphasia demonstrate a lowering of the person's reasoning from the level of higher processes (capability to reason by way of concepts) to the lower level of reasoning in complexes (Vygotsky, 1931h, p. 412).

The issue of regression leads us to a complicated topic in Vygotsky's thinking where inconsistencies can be found. On the one hand, Vygotsky occasionally seemed to use "regression" in terms of its ordinary meaning (especially when referring to other authors' work), that is, returning to a previous level in a hierarchy of levels or stages. At the same time, this use of the term would be contradictory to his dialectical, synthesis-oriented perspective. If Vygotsky emphasized the dialectical restructuring of organisms in the progressive phase of development, then a similar qualitatively new restructuring should be accepted to be in place at the regressive phases of the process. In other terms, if Vygotsky's idea of developmental dialectical synthesis is followed with rigor it is not possible for any organism to regress to a *previous* stage/state of development. Instead, the organism may become transformed from a higher to a lower state or stage, but that would *not* constitute retracing of a previously traversed path in development. Vygotsky did not express himself clearly in this matter (see also Kozulin, 1990b), but we can point to some of his ideas that are consistent with this more rigorous interpretation of regression.

Vygotsky's interest in the breakdown of psychological functions took two parallel directions in the early 1930s: the psychiatric and the neuropsychological. In the psychiatric domain, he became interested in the breakdown of higher psychological functions in schizophrenic adults (Vygotsky 1932b/1956; see also the slightly modified English translation in Vygotsky, 1934h). This interest was clearly coordinated in his mind with the ontogenetic developmental interest in the move from thinking in complexes to that of concepts in adolescence. When the adolescent moves up from the use of complexes to concepts, the schizophrenic patient shows a move down from concept-based reasoning to that in complexes (which, in that downward movement, at times are masked as "pseudo-concepts:" words that seem to be concepts but can be demonstrated to be mere covers for complexes). The schizophrenic process, according to Vygotsky, starts from the hidden alterations in the meanings of words (Vygotsky, 1932b/1956, p. 486), followed by the downwards development of thinking with the help of pseudo-concepts. The fall from conceptual thinking is characterized by de-coupling (*rascheplenie*), decomposition (*raspad*) and destruction of the higher psychological functions. These three synonyms used for describing the transformation downwards are contrasted to growth (*rost*), development and building of higher levels in ontogeny (Vygotsky, 1932b/1956, p. 482).

In a lecture delivered a month and a half before his death (on April 28, 1934) at the Institute of Experimental Medicine in Moscow, Vygotsky directly addressed the issue of development and decomposition of higher psychological functions (Vygotsky, 1934j/1960). First, he (re)emphasized the construction of qualitatively novel psychological structures in ontogeny, under conditions of social interactions ("development of interaction and generalization go hand in hand"; 1934j/1960, p. 373). The problem of locating with the brain the different developing and decomposing psychological functions began to overwhelm Vygotsky in this (and his very last) text. However, instead of explicitly analyzing how higher brain functions become decomposed, he reiterated the need to analyze the structural organization of the higher processes. In the joint work on empirical case description of Pick and Alzheimer patients' psychological breakdown (Samukhin, Birenbaum and Vygotsky, 1934), the clinical data about the breakdown were explained by reference to seeing dementia as a structural reorganization according to general psychological principles.

In an extract that was prepared for a presentation (made by someone else in June, 1934) at the First Ukranian Congress of Neuropathology and Psychiatry that took place in Kharkov, Vygotsky addressed the issue of localization of psychological functions in the brain (Vygotsky, 1934o/1982; see also Vygotsky, 1965). In that address, Vygotsky clearly recognized the differences between development of the brain <—> psychic functions relationships in children with brain defects on the one hand, and those of adult brain-damaged persons (Vygotsky, 1934o/1982, p. 172). There is no single way in which psychological functions are linked with the work of different parts of the brain in children and adults: similar brain damage (of child and adult) can produce vastly different symptoms in the psychological spheres, while different symptomatic pictures can reflect similar underlying brain damage. Vygotsky, of course, used this as a strong argument against efforts geared towards simple mapping of psychological functions (as elementaristic entities) to different parts of the brain (he cautioned listeners against forgetting that these different parts are systemically linked). He posited the existence of differential quantitative effects of brain damage to different brain centers in the form of a general law: for children with brain damage, the nearest *higher* brain center (relative to the damaged part of the brain) is more affected by the damage in the functional sense, than the brain centers that are *lower* than the damaged area. In contrast, the effects of brain damage in adults were posited to lead to a reverse effect: the nearest *lower* center(s) (relative to the damaged area) are more affected by the damage than the nearest *higher* center (1934o/1982, p. 173). It is interesting that here Vygotsky operated only with quantified ordinal relationships (more functional effects in X than Y), and did not attempt to apply his ever-present dialectical scheme. Of course, behind this general quantitative law his emphasis on the emergence and new quality of higher psychological functions is discernible. In the development of brain-damaged children the damage blocks the emergence of new functions in higher centers while forcing the lower centers to develop compensatory functions (i.e. the higher centers are more damaged than the lower ones). Once the person's brain is damaged in its adult state (which means that the higher centers have become to function in novel, generally controlling ways over lower ones), then the immediate lower centers (those that are controlled by the damaged area) are more impaired than the relatively more flexible (higher) centers which can develop compensations by way of becoming linked to other (non-damaged) centrifugal neural linkages.

Vygotsky did not specify the particulars of the structural-functional breakdown of brain functions. Instead, he proceeded to call for the study of inter-functional relationships, leaving it open to debate what (other than a general principle of dynamic Gestalts of brain activation) that implied and how brain scientists could proceed with such a study. The subsequent work of Luria along these lines has elaborated that direction, and Luria's account of the role of Vygotsky in devising a number of clinical experiments (see Luria, 1982, chapter 7) shows how the issue of brain defects was dealt with in a developmental framework. Indeed, many of the rehabilitation ideas for brain-damaged patients that were put into practise by Luria in the following decades can be traced to Vygotsky's thinking about the method of double stimulation as applied to the re-learning processes of neurologically dys-functional patients.

Kurt Goldstein and the Roots of Vygotsky's Ideas on Inner Speech

One of the theories for which Vygotsky is well known is his treatment of "inner speech," its functions in thinking, and its social origins as he contrasted those functions with Piaget's notion of "egocentric speech" (Vygotsky, 1934a, chapter 7). The issue of inner speech goes back to Wilhelm von Humboldt's language of philosophy (see also chapter 15), and was actively discussed by a number of German neurologists interested in speech (Wernicke, Storch) at the turn of the century. Vygotsky's treatment of the issue of inner speech as a special, transformed form of external speech followed the tradition of Kurt Goldstein (1933) in seeing parallels between the breakdown of inner speech in aphasic patients and children's speech development. Goldstein, a neurologist, provided relevant evidence from the breakdown of higher functions (in aphasia), yet the connection he made between the neurological cases and children's development of inner speech remained non-empirical. In fact, Vygotsky explicitly follows Goldstein in his treatment of inner speech: "In essence, if we were consistent and took Goldstein's point of view to its end, we must agree that inner speech is not speech at all, but thinking and affective-volitional activity, since it includes in itself motives of speech and thought that is expressed in word" (Vygotsky, 1934a, p. 278).

Vygotsky developed his theory beyond Goldstein's perspective, by enriching his idea with the notion of the dialectical transformation of speech when it is transformed from the external to the internal form. The latter transformation is of course socially organized (the idea of internalization that Vygotsky took from Janet; see van der Veer and Valsiner, 1988). The similarity between Vygotsky's elaboration of the issue of inner speech and that of Goldstein's can also be seen in the latter's fascination (see Goldstein, 1948, pp. 94–8; see also chapter 11) with Vygotsky's ideas (after learning about them through the English language publication of chapter 7 of *Myshlenie i rech*; Vygotsky, 1939).

Conclusions: Vygotsky's Dialectical Oppositions with Gestalt Psychology

In this chapter we have demonstrated the intellectual closeness between Gestalt psychologists and Vygotsky. Not surprisingly, the effort of Gestalt psychologists to retain the structural organization of the phenomena was close to Vygotsky's anti-reductionist's heart. Vygotsky borrowed extensively from different Gestalt colleagues of his (Köhler, Koffka, Lewin, Goldstein), whilst criticizing them for their non-dialectical (non-developmental) stand. In his efforts to unite the *principle of Gestalt* and the *principle of development*, Vygotsky made others aware of a possible direction of theoretical thought, still largely unexplored in contemporary psychology – despite the current fashion of mentioning his name in many present-day publications.

Vygotsky's emphasis on the structural dynamics of psychological phenomena went further than Lewin's and reached the already familiar domain of "qualitative synthesis." He was indebted to the Gestalt movement for his experimental methodology as well as his treatment of units of analysis. His ideas on learning were formed during a dialogue with Koffka and, last but not least, the theoretical issue for which he has subsequently become well-known – the theory of inner speech – was an elaboration of Goldstein's similar thoughts, aligned with the German tradition of a philosophy of language, from Wilhelm von Humboldt onwards. The principle of structure became that of dialectical transformation and hierarchical integration of structures in Vygotsky's thought, and the traditional question of regression acquired new characteristics in that context. However, Vygotsky never specified the dialectically transformable structures in any concrete detail, and we are still as far as ever from the realization of an adequate and elaborate methodological work that would bring Vygotsky's structuralism to the instrumentarium of modern-day psychologists.

PART II
The Cultural-Historical Theory 1928–1932

Introduction

Vygotsky's scientific career peaked in the late 1920s and early 1930s. He was teaching paedology and psychology at a number of institutes and doing editorial work for various publishing houses. As a member of the editorial boards of *Psikhologija*, *Pedologija*, *Pediatrija*, and *Psikhotekhnika i Psikhofiziologija Truda* he reviewed countless manuscripts. In addition, from 1931 onwards he was the chairman of the collective of VARNITSO[1] of the Bubnov State Pedagogical Institute in Moscow. Finally, he worked as a deputy in the section concerned with people's education of the Frunze Soviet (Frunze being one of Moscow's districts) after his election by the proletarian students (Kolbanovsky, 1934c, p. 394). Given this background it is remarkable that Vygotsky managed to conduct creative scientific work in those years, but in fact, these years were among the most productive of his life.

Towards 1928 Vygotsky started to develop the outlines of his cultural-historical theory (see chapter 9). His thinking now acquired a different and more original character, whilst remaining very much intertwined with the theories of prominent European thinkers of that time. No doubt, several key concepts were borrowed from the Gestalt school within psychology (see chapter 8) and in chapter 11 it will be seen that Vygotsky's concept-formation research developed in dialogue with the work of Ach and Piaget.

It is commonly thought that the cultural-historical theory was the accomplishment of the *troika* consisting of Vygotsky, Leont'ev, and Luria. Here we should be cautious not to project our current evaluations of cultural-historical theory, its authors, and its value onto the canvas of the diverse and confusing scientific and cultural life of the time. Historically speaking, there was at first no *troika*. Vast differences of opinion and attitude existed

[1] These letters stood for *Vsesojuznaja Associacija Rabotnikov Nauki i Tekhniki dlja Sodejstvija Socialisticheskomu Stroitelstvu v SSSR* (All-Union Association of Workers in Science and Technics for the Furthering of the Socialist Edification in the USSR).

between Vygotsky and Luria, and from 1924 it took four or five years before they really started to cooperate and co-author in a fruitful way. As became clear in chapter 4, until 1930 Luria was greatly influenced by Freudian theory – a theory that was evaluated by Vygotsky much more critically. In general, it can be said that Vygotsky and Luria were very different thinkers – a fact that is very evident also from the few publications they co-authored – Luria representing the typical scientist who clearly and didactically espoused his ideas, faithfully and meticulously referring to his sources, while Vygotsky was the brilliant humanist who suggested sweeping changes in various areas, and who typically did not refer to his sources or did so with supreme carelessness. So, while it took some time before Luria decided to join forces with Vygotsky (see chapter 1), it took even longer for Leont'ev to decide to join the team. Moreover, his role was to be much more modest. Although he did fine work in the field of the experimental confirmation of Vygotskian ideas – see, for instance, the description of his memory research in chapter 9 – he never co-authored a book or article with Vygotsky and was barely visible as a co-founder of the cultural-historical theory at that time. In fact, when critics attacked the basic ideas of the cultural-historical theory in the 1920s and 1930s, they always spoke of the theory developed by Vygotsky and Luria (chapter 16), not mentioning Leont'ev. The idea of the heroic and inseparable three musketeers fighting against traditional psychology is, then, a romantic reconstruction favored by Leont'ev and Luria. As we will see, the myth of the *troika* served the function of obscuring the very real differences of opinion and personal conflicts that would develop between Vygotsky and Leont'ev (and, to some extent, Luria) at a later stage (see the introduction to part III).

It is a distortion, also, to consider the cultural-historical theory as one of the most prominent theories of the time, or that Vygotsky – let alone Luria or Leont'ev – was considered to be a major psychologist by his contemporaries. Many other psychologists, some of them now totally forgotten, were more well known at the time and considered more eminent than the founder of cultural-historical theory. These included Basov, Zalkind, Kornilov, Blonsky, and others (see, for instance, chapter 12). Also, cultural-historical theory as such was not accepted by many scientists when first developed and from its beginnings met with criticism. In fact, the growing (ideological) opposition caused a situation where Vygotsky eventually had very few colleagues sympathetic to his theory and had to rely greatly on the work done by a small circle of devoted young students.

Most of the experiments providing the empirical evidence for the cultural-historical theory were carried out in the Academy of Communist Education, since a special psychological faculty and a laboratory were created there in 1928. Luria became the head of faculty while Vygotsky was the head of the

Psychological Laboratory. During the period Vygotsky was developing the cultural-historical theory his teaching gradually concentrated on paedology (see chapter 12). The result of this teaching formed a series of textbooks on paedology (Vygotsky, 1928t, 1929n, 1929p, 1930p, 1931h).

The Origin of the Kharkov School

When the Psychological Laboratory of the Academy of Communist Education was closed down in 1932 Vygotsky and his collaborators lost an important meeting place where they planned and carried out experiments, held internal conferences, etc. In the increasingly intolerant intellectual climate in Moscow the foundation of the Ukrainian Psychoneurological Academy in Kharkov in 1930 was a most welcome event. The Kharkov founders of the Academy invited researchers from all over the country to come and work there. Among them were the psychiatrist Judin from Kazan', the neurologist Sukhareva from Moscow, and Vygotsky, Luria, Leont'ev, Zaporozheč, and Bozhovič. Here, then, seemed an opportunity to do the experimental work carried out to support the cultural-historical theory. Again, however, the lodgings finding proved very difficult. The Ukrainian Academy could arrange only one room in a communal flat for each scientist and his or her family. Vygotsky preferred to stay in Moscow, while Luria and Leont'ev started living twenty days a month in Kharkov and the rest of the month with their families in Moscow.

It was in Kharkov that the cultural-historical school started to disintegrate. First, Vygotsky's conception of paedology was met with resistance from people like Gal'perin from the very beginning. Vygotsky conceived paedology as an all-embracing science of the child synthesizing the findings of physiology, defectology, psychology, and pedagogy around the key concepts of development and age periods. Gal'perin (see Haenen, 1989, pp. 13–14) has claimed that he opposed this idea arguing that progress in science is made by specializing in and not by combining various branches of knowledge. The fundamental danger for the paedologist, he claimed, was that one cannot possibly be an expert in all of these fields. As a result of such arguments the new collective remained aloof from paedology and the ideological difficulties it increasingly involved. Secondly, Leont'ev started gradually developing his activity approach that was in fundamental contradiction with several of Vygotsky's most cherished ideas (see the introduction to part III).

The ensuing differences of opinion did not immediately result in conflicts. For some time Vygotsky traveled on a regular basis to Kharkov, delivering lectures at the Academy and taking undergraduate examinations at the

Medical Institute. But he gradually shifted his main activities towards Leningrad and started cooperating with a new collective at the Herzen Institute of Education. The Psychoneurological Academy itself did not exist very long, the problem being that it had never been formally founded. The researchers received financial support, but when in 1935 Kiev became Ukraine's capital – instead of Kharkov – the Academy lost its direct contacts with government circles and after some time ceased to exist (Haenen, 1989, p. 11).

9

Cultural-Historical Theory

The Main Sources of the Theory

Between 1928 and 1931 Vygotsky and Luria wrote several accounts of the cultural-historical theory. The first, and surprisingly complete, version of the theory was presented in a concise article published in *Pedologija* (Vygotsky, 1928p). The paper introduced many of the themes which will be dealt with in this chapter (e.g. the instrumental method, mediation, primitivism, different lines of development), but discussed them mainly in the context of child development. Part of the paper (translated into English as Vygotsky, 1929s) was devoted to a discussion of the many experimental investigations that Vygotsky, Luria, Leont'ev, and their students carried out in the Krupskaja Academy of Communist Education between 1925 and 1928.

After 1928 Vygotsky published several papers on the relation between animal and human behavior, and on the ideas regarding the concept of primitivism (a theme that was discussed in chapter 4; e.g. Vygotsky, 1929e; 1929f; 1929h; 1929i). The result of his thinking in this area was also propounded in *The Behavior of Animals and Man* (Vygotsky, 1930q/1960), the first book-length work dealing with several of the cultural-historical themes. Written in the years 1929–30 at the request of the publishing house *Rabotnik Prosveshchenija* it constituted an attempt to write a brochure for the general public about the relation between animal and human behavior in the light of evolutionary theory and Marxist thought. Although the text was well-written and accessible to the educated layman, it was not published at the time.

The next major cultural-historical work was *Studies of the History of Behavior. Ape. Primitive. Child* (Vygotsky and Luria, 1930a). This book was published in 1930[1] and would be the focal point for many of the criticisms that Vygotsky and Luria received in the early 1930s. In the 1990s Soviet students of Vygotsky tend to be silent about this book and the compilers of Vygotsky's completed works excluded it, giving preference to his many unpublished writings. The reason for this reticence can probably be found in the highly debatable content of the book. In the first chapter Vygotsky discussed Köhler's experiments with chimpanzees, in the second he presented the available ethnographic findings (mainly relying on Thurnwald and Lévy-Bruhl) regarding "primitive," non-Western people, and in the final chapter Luria gave an account of child development. The key question is, of course, whether it made sense to present the findings in these different areas in the context of one book. It was not obvious what one would gain by comparing the findings from such diverse scientific fields and many scientists opposed such an approach. This was one of the fundamental questions of psychology in the 1920s and 1930s — similar questions are being asked in the contemporary debate about the application of ethological and sociobiological findings to human beings — and it is of fundamental importance when judging the cultural-historical theory as a whole.

The sequel to *Studies of the History of Behavior* was another book co-authored with Luria, called *Tool and Sign* (Vygotsky and Luria, 1930d/1984). The history of this book is interesting in itself. Written by Vygotsky and Luria in 1930 it was immediately translated into English and submitted for publication in Murchison's *Handbook of Child Psychology*. However, for reasons unknown the manuscript was not accepted for publication and neither the Russian nor the English version of the study were published during Vygotsky's lifetime. The story revived in the 1960s when the Soviet editors of Vygotsky's collected works found that the original Russian version had been lost and had the text translated back into Russian.

Finally, we now have available the most complete discussion of cultural-historical theory, entitled *The History of the Development of the Higher Psychological Functions*. Vygotsky started writing this book around 1929, rewrote it several times (Puzyrej, 1986b), and finally completed it in 1931 (Vygotsky, 1931n/1983). Essentially it constituted another attempt to formulate the framework already described in *The Behavior of Animals and*

---

[1]The first plans for this book date back to early 1927. In it Vygotsky planned to elaborate his ideas about man's development from ape to superman (cf. chapter 3). After completion he would receive 175 roubles from the State Publishing House. Later Luria joined the project. One reason publication was delayed was that Vygotsky was extremely dissatisfied with the first variants of his co-author's chapter on child development. They contained far too many — uncritical — references to the work done by psychoanalysts such as Vera Schmidt, Melanie Klein, and others for his taste (Vygotsky in letters to Luria, dated July 26, 1927 and Leont'ev, dated July 23, 1929).

Man, *Studies of the History of Behavior*, *Tool and Sign*, and the original journal article (Vygotsky, 1928p). Vygotsky even took the paragraph headings from the latter paper, which now served as the titles for the first five chapters of his new study. *The History of the Development of the Higher Psychological Functions*, however, was not simply a restatement of an old theme, but contained new theoretical arguments and far more empirical material. This most complete statement of the cultural-historical theory (it contained more than 300 pages) shared the sad fate of its immediate precursors and of many others of Vygotsky's writings: it was not published during his lifetime.

We may conclude, then, that the present-day reader is probably in a much better position to judge the intricate set of ideas that constituted the cultural-historical theory than Vygotsky's contemporaries. For unless they attended some of Vygotsky's many lectures, or were personally acquainted with the author, they had rather little on which to base their judgement. At any rate, they missed the most detailed exposition of the theory's main themes given in *The History*.

The Theory

To understand any complex human phenomenon we have to reconstruct its most primitive and simple forms, and to follow its development until its present state – in other words, to study its history. This view – here taken from Durkheim (1985, pp. 4–5) – was very common around the turn of the century and led to many fascinating ethnographic, sociological, and psychological studies. Basically, of course, it took much of its inspiration from the ideas formulated by Lamarck, Spencer, and above all, Darwin.

In psychology the evolutionary point of view led to the study of different developmental fields with respect to their relevance for mental processes. It was quite common, for instance, to speculate about the relevance of phylogenetic developments for child development and to relate different brain structures to different periods in phylogenesis. It was equally common to suggest that in cases of pathology – say a brain lesion, or a case of hysteria – a person might regress to phylogenetically older types of behavior, because the phylogenetically newer brain parts had been damaged. Finally, it was very popular to speculate about evolutionary developments in human culture, suggesting that human culture went through a long series of developments from primitive culture to the most supreme form of civilization, that is, the European culture of the twentieth century.

It would be quite impossible to list and discuss the many psychologists from the beginning of this century who addressed these issues. Suffice it to say that Stern (e.g. 1927) speculated about the parallels between human phylogeny and ontogeny; that Werner (1925) devoted a whole book to the comparisons of the different developmental domains listed above; that Bühler (1918) compared children's drawings with those of adults belonging to "primitive" cultures; that Freud in his *Totem and Taboo* (1913) argued that primitive tribes formed a "well-preserved preliminary stage of our own development"; that Kretschmer (1916/1950) devoted much attention to the "geological" structure of the brain; and that Koffka (1925) explicitly discussed the question whether the comparisons between different developmental areas were relevant and useful. It is interesting to follow Koffka's reasoning for a moment, as it is so typical for the time discussed. "We should never forget," Koffka reasoned (1925, p. 1–2) "that the subject that we normally investigate in psychological research is the adult 'educated' Western European, a being that, biologically speaking, stands on the latest rung." He clarified this statement by stating that for psychology it was important to compare (1) man and animal; (2) Western developed culture and non-Western "primitive" culture ("To us the world looks different from the way it looks to a Negro from Central Africa, from the way it looked to Homer too, we speak a different language . . . real translation is impossible . . . "); and (3) adult and child.

All of these authors dealt with the obvious question of whether such comparisons might be misleading and inadmissible, whether they were of little relevance but rather innocent, or whether they provided important and new insights. Although most authors denied that the development in one domain simply repeated the development in other domains, it was generally felt that cross-comparisons were relevant and might provide insights in the general laws of development as such. Indeed, one of the main tasks of the new science of paedology was to study the laws of general development, taking the phenomena established in the different domains as its starting point (see chapter 12).

To the present-day reader the psychological writings of the beginning of this century are both fascinating and unsettling. Fascinating, because these authors so clearly realized that much of psychological theorizing was based on experiments performed with (a limited section of) the Western European population. Describing the mentality of different cultures they showed the limits of European and American psychology and provided the foundation for cross-cultural theory – however wrong their attempts at systematization of the findings may have been. Unsettling, because in so many writings – despite many cautious remarks by the authors – the idea of Western cultural superiority was so evident.

It will be clear, then, that Vygotsky's cultural-historical theory was only one of many theories that tried to give an account of the origin and development of the mental processes of Western educated adults. Vygotsky, too, in his cultural-historical theory compared (1) the psychology of animals and human beings; (2) the psychology of "primitive" man and Western man; (3) the psychology of children and adults; and (4) the psychology of pathological and healthy subjects. In doing so, he relied heavily on the writings of Darwin, Engels, Bühler, Koffka, Köhler, Thurnwald, Lévy-Bruhl, Durkheim, and Kretschmer to mention but a few authors. This is not to say that Vygotsky's theory was simply an amalgam of the ideas formulated by these different authors. Vygotsky essentially presented a theory of man, his origin and coming into being, his present state amidst the other species, and a blueprint for his future. The image of man that derives from this theory is that of man as a rational being taking control of his own destiny and emancipating himself from nature's restrictive bounds. It is an image of man that is partially based on Marxist thinking and partially on the ideas of various philosophers, such as Bacon and Spinoza. But above all, of course, this was an image of man Vygotsky believed in, a belief that was very common among the people of his time and in the country he lived.

Different Influences on Vygotsky from Evolutionary Ideas

To understand cultural-historical theory one should first know Vygotsky's view on the origin of contemporary man – Homo sapiens – and his relative position in comparison to animals. In order to understand this position it is essential to know that Vygotsky – following Marxist thought – distinguished two periods in human's phylogeny. The first part – biological evolution – had been described and explained by Charles Darwin in his theory of evolution. The second part – human history – had been sketched by Marx and, more thoroughly, by Engels. For Vygotsky the greater part of human phylogenesis had been explained by Charles Darwin. He was well acquainted with Darwin's writings and repeatedly praised him for his theory of evolution, which provided the key to our understanding of animal behavior. There is no doubt that Vygotsky was very impressed by Darwin's arrangement of seemingly unconnected pieces of evidence into a coherent genetic account of evolution. Many times in his life he would state that such a type of classification – based on a common origin – was far superior to other type of classifications, mostly based on superficial phenomenal similarities. Darwin was for Vygotsky the founder of a causal-genetic approach in science.

Accepting the Darwinian concepts of "variation" and "natural selection" and the whole account of evolution, Vygotsky was forced therefore to accept several of its implications. Thus, it would seem logical, for instance, to accept the hereditary background of human anatomy, physiology, and (perhaps) behavior, to accept the idea that we have many things in common with animals (e.g. various brain structures), and, in general, to accept a continuity in the development from animals to man. At first sight, Vygotsky did not seem to have any problems here. Indeed, he fully accepted the genetic background of many human physiological and psychological processes. In Vygotsky (1929p), for example, he listed the Mendelian laws of genetics (following Bühler, 1918) – which were still unknown to Darwin himself, of course – and explained their importance. Also, at that time, he was not principally opposed to all forms of eugenics (see also chapter 3). On the contrary, he claimed that seen "From the theoretical and principled side eugenics as a science concerning the amelioration of the human race through the mastering of the mechanism of genetics forms an achievement of modern scientific thinking that is completely beyond doubt..." (Vygotsky, 1929p, p. 11).

It must be acknowledged, however, that he did oppose the form eugenics had taken in the United States and other capitalistic countries. His reasons were clear: (1) the knowledge of genetics was as yet insufficient; and (2) "inherited" traits in capitalistic societies did not really reflect a genetic background. Vygotsky's reasoning seems to have been that in a classless society – where people have the same chances and opportunities – interindividual differences are likely to reflect genetic differences, whereas in a society such as the U.S. this was extremely unlikely. In this connection Vygotsky warned against the hasty conclusions drawn by Pearson and Galton, arguing that the high correlations they found reflected a common environment rather than shared genes (a critique that has been confirmed by Gould, 1981).

Vygotsky also was well aware of and agreed with the discussions of human brain anatomy by, for instance, Edinger (1911) and Kretschmer (1916/1950). He attached great value to the developmental principles that the latter author had outlined in his *Medical Psychology*. These principles were, respectively, (1) the principle that lower brain structures do not simply disappear as other structures develop, but continue functioning in a subordinated position; (2) the principle that during this development the lower functions lose part of their function to the higher ones; and (3) the principle that the lower functions can regain autonomy in case the higher ones are damaged or weakened (Kretschmer, 1916/1950, pp. 46–7). The latter principle was considered to be particularly relevant in discussing various cases of pathology. A careful study of different patients might lay bare the phylogenetic older layers of the human mind. It is clear that Vygotsky was much influenced by these and similar (e.g. Werner, 1925) discussions about the "geological" layers of the human mind, and that these ideas were formed as a direct result of accepting the evolutionary point of view.

In general Vygotsky had also no problem with the idea that the evolution of man from animals was a continuous process. But he did not accept that this was the whole story and resisted Darwin's claim that "the mental faculties of man and the lower animals do not differ in kind, although immensely in degree" (Darwin, 1871/1981, p. 186). On the contrary, Vygotsky claimed that there were fundamental differences between animals and human beings, differences that originated with the onset of human culture. Whereas animals are almost fully dependent on the inheritance of genetically based traits, human beings can transmit and master the products of culture. Mastering the knowledge and wisdom embodied in human culture, they can make a decisive step towards emancipation from nature. The specifically human traits, then, are acquired in mastering culture through the social interaction with others. Arguing in this way, Vygotsky imposed a limited role on biological evolution and the genetic background of human behavior. Behavior did have a genetic background in his opinion, and this background had its origin in biological evolution, but it was restricted to the lower processes. The specifically human, higher processes developed in human history and had to be mastered anew by each human child in a process of social interaction.

Importantly, it was not only the Darwinian version of evolutionary thinking that was relevant to Vygotsky's synthesis of developmental ideas. Equally noteworthy was his reliance on the evolutionary thought of the 1890s which was associated with the work of C. Lloyd Morgan, H. Osborne, and J. M. Baldwin.

Above all it is the direct link with Baldwin's evolutionary thought that becomes evident in a number of Vygotsky's texts. Baldwin's idea of "circular reaction" was described in Vygotsky (1925d, p. 188), and can thus be seen as being one of the roots of the cultural-historical methodology (see also Vygotsky, 1931h/1983, p. 320). Allusions to Baldwin recur throughout Vygotsky's discourse, until his death (see, e.g. Vygotsky, 1934d, pp. 53, 61). Basically, the issues of the sociogenetic origin of cognitive processes (i.e. children's thinking emerges in the context of dispute: Vygotsky, 1931h/1983, p. 141; 1931o; 1935d, p. 16); and the Baldwinian emphasis on the unity of evolution and involution (Vygotsky, 1929m, p. 7; 1931h/1983, p. 178; 1932e/1984, p. 253; 1935d, p. 75) are what one finds consistently reflected in Vygotsky's thinking. Furthermore, Baldwin's idea of personality emerging at the transition from understanding others to that of one's own self was recognized by Vygotsky (1931h/1983, p. 324). Baldwin's close connection with Janet's sociogenetic ideas was of course an additional factor which made Baldwin relevant for Vygotsky. Interestingly, Vygotsky never made any detailed analysis of Baldwin's ideas, which suggests that in his own disputes with his contemporaries Baldwin's ideas were not of the highest relevance at the time. There was little for Vygotsky to criticize in

Baldwin, as the latter's ideas were used in Vygotsky's productive thinking as foundations for developmental science, rather than as areas of debate.

Vygotsky's reliance on the different evolutionary theories was clearly linked with his interest in the emergence of higher psychological functions in phylogeny. That interest led him not only to the classic primatological experiments of Wolfgang Köhler, but also to take notice of a discipline that had emerged at the intersection of evolutionary thinking and animal behavior studies – zoopsychology.

Vladimir Vagner's Zoopsychology as a Foundation for Vygotsky's Theory

Vladimir Aleksandrovich Vagner (Wagner) (1849–1934) was the founder of Russian comparative psychology traditions. His main empirical observations were done on insects and avian species. Despite his empirical interests in behavioral construction (e.g. nest or net-building) among species that were "lower" on the evolutionary classification ladder, his theoretical contributions dealt with the issues of development of intelligent behavior (aside from instincts). This separation of "instinct" and "intellect" ("*razum*") was relevant to Vygotsky, whose indebtedness to Vagner is noteworthy. Vagner was one of the active members of the Psychoneurological Institute in St Petersburg from its inception, and thus had a formative influence on many of Vygotsky's contemporaries.

Vagner emphasized the use of the ontogenetic perspective alongside the phylogenetic comparisons between species in his version of zoopsychology (Vagner, 1901, Part III). While distancing himself from the "anthropomorphizing" tendencies that were present in the animal psychology of the turn of the century, Vagner did not jump to the behavioristic other extreme of denying qualitative differences in psychological functions between species. However, Vagner viewed the development of "instinct" as being highly different from that of "intellect." Whereas in the ontogeny of the latter new formations could build upon previous ones, in the case of "instincts" novelty appears on the scene by way of substitution of one instinct by another. In the case of "instincts", Vagner accepted the idea of a "biogenetic law":

> every stage in the given chronological change of one instinct by other ones in an individual constitutes a stage in the history of development of instincts of the given species; in other words, the ontogenesis of the given instinct of the given individual represents at the same time the phylogenesis of the instinct of the given species. (Vagner, 1901, p. 61)

In other words, experience does not change instinct, but merely regulates its presence or absence, or substitution by another instinct (Vagner, 1910, p. 343). Vagner's concept of instincts included the notion of possible substitutions among parts of the instinct (see Vagner, 1910, p. 268), thus making it different from our contemporary ethological interest in instinctive behavioral chains. However, the whole program of instincts for invertebrate species was seen as a closed, hereditarily predetermined, species-based behavior range. In contrast, at the level of vertebrate species Vagner accepted the idea of learning from experience having a place, and led to the development of "intellect" (*razum*). Furthermore, he posited the development of "instincts" and "intellect" from the reflex basis along parallel lines in phylogenesis (Vagner, 1913, p. 282):

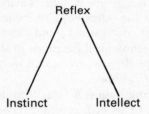

While the development of instincts takes place via a "pure" line (i.e. the previously present instincts are not transformed into new ones), the intellect progresses on the basis of the previous structures (a "combined" line). The relationships between "instinct" and "intellect" were viewed by Vagner as those of gradual subordination of the other by the "intellect" in the course of phylogenesis. In many ways, Vygotsky's (and Luria's) fit of the Marxist idea of control over one's own lower psychological processes by the higher (voluntary) ones proceeds along the same line. Vagner explicitly emphasized the lack of harmony between the "instincts" and "intellect" in the human species, where the suppression of instincts is a major goal (attainable by only a few: Vagner, 1913, pp. 412, 427–8). Vagner rejected Pavlov's efforts to reduce all instincts to reflexes, and to eliminate the subdiscipline of zoopsychology from science (Vagner, 1925, pp. 3–9). Instead, Vagner continued to emphasize the qualitative distinction between psychological functions of different species that are at different evolutionary levels, and claimed that in the case of humans, the specifically novel regulation mechanisms – "collective psychology" – take over from the mechanisms of natural selection, which govern pre-human phylogenesis (Vagner, 1929).

As a zoologist, Vagner was interested in the relationships between morphological and psychological features. He saw the process of development of psychological functions as being loosely coupled between the morphology and behavioral organization: hence the notion of parallel lines in development that was later central for Vygotsky's developmental thinking:

> the change of morphological and psychological characteristics *can take place independently of each other in two parallel lines*: in that the changes in these lines may coincide, but also need not coincide with each other; new features can appear separately, i.e. the morphological [line] remains unchanged but the psychological changes, and vice versa: the psychological [features] change and the morphological ones remain unchanged. (Vagner, 1913, p. 235)

Vagner's ideas concerning development clearly appealed to anybody who was interested in building a non-reductionist theory of psychological development. Vagner's disagreement with Pavlov paralleled Vygotsky's similar arguments against the reflexology of Pavlov and Bekhterev. Furthermore, Vagner's contrast of "instinct" and "intellect" paralleled that of "lower" and "higher" psychological functions in Vygotsky's discourse, and the pairing of onto- and phylogenetic research methodology accorded with Vygotsky's cultural-historical line.

Vygotsky was considering Vagner's ideas from the very beginning of his entrance into psychology. In his *Pedagogical Psychology* Vagner's theory of instincts as separate from reflexes had already been explicitly overviewed (Vygotsky, 1926g, pp. 70–4). And he used Vagner's critique of Pavlov as a supporting source in similar efforts of his own (see Vygotsky, 1925d, p. 181). Vygotsky also used Vagner in his analysis of the crisis in psychology (see Vygotsky, 1927a/1982, pp. 308, 375–7, 418), although criticizing Vagner's way of unifying psychology.

The most interesting confrontation that Vygotsky had with Vagner's ideas was associated with the analysis of the work of Wolfgang Köhler. Vagner's interpretation of Köhler's chimpanzee experiments was characteristically minimalistic (i.e. attributing the behavior of the apes to instinctive mechanisms). Vygotsky argued that Vagner had not understood the relevance of the structure of the operation (performed by the ape) and its coordination with the structure of the task (Vygotsky, 1930i, p. xxi). For Vygotsky, Köhler's Gestalt orientation was a relevant aspect worth defending against the skepticism of Vagner. Interestingly enough, four years later (and in conjunction with his growing dissatisfaction with Gestalt psychology), Vygotsky had no difficulty accepting the conservative evaluation of Köhler's studies in just the way that Vagner had done – chimpanzees whose intellect had become human-like were still developing along the "pure" line of development where the new function remained disjunctive with the previous ones ("... in the experiments of Köhler we have in front of us –

intellectual operations within the system of instinctive consciousness"; Vygotsky, 1934c/1982, p. 258).

In contrast, Vygotsky's developmental theorizing was built on the notion of Vagner's "combined" line of development – on the basis of previous structures, qualitatively new structures come into being as the organism is actively involved in its environment. Phylogenetically that meant the transition from looking at the processes of evolution, to the consideration of human cultural history. In Vygotsky's own social context, it entailed the synthesis of evolutionary and zoopsychological ideas with Hegelian-Engelsian-Marxian notions of history.

Marx and Engels: Human History and Biological Evolution

The distinction Vygotsky made between biological evolution and human history was based on the writings of Marx and, most importantly, Engels. Marx (1890, p. 194) – following Benjamin Franklin – had defined man as "a toolmaking animal" and Engels in his study "The part played by labor in the transition from ape to man" (1925/1978) had elaborated this view. Vygotsky was well aware of Engels' account – first published in the Soviet Union in *Dialectics of Nature* (1925/1978) – and repeatedly referred to it to explain the difference between animals and man.

Engels' account of the origin of *Homo sapiens* was rather crude but not implausible in view of the available evidence (Engels, 1925, pp. 444–5). According to him the history of mankind began when the precursor of man left the trees and developed an upright gait. This was a decisive step towards the transition from animal to man (1925, p. 444). The erect posture freed the hands for the manipulation of objects and enabled the development of finely tuned motor actions together with the development of visual ability. The result was a gradually improving eye–hand coordination and the development of the corresponding brain parts. The hands, sense organs, and brain developed in a complex interaction. Man started to cooperate in labor, which necessitated a means of communication. This, Engels argued, resulted in the development of speech. Labor, then, came first, and created the need for speech (1925, p. 447). It was labor that was defined by Engels to be the defining characteristic of human beings. The origin of labor was the manufacture of the first primitive flint tools by our predecessors. The cooperation in groups, making tools, and communicating with each other through speech, gradually led to the planned, deliberate transformation of nature. Engels acknowledged that animals showed the rudiments of conscious, planned action – acknowledging, as Marx did, a simple tool-use among some animals – but claimed a principal difference between animals and man: animals use nature, whereas human beings control nature.

In sum, Engels emphasized the manufacture and use of tools in the history of mankind and argued that human beings displayed an essentially different relationship with the environment: instead of passively using its facilities, human beings actively transformed nature (often with unforeseen and negative results, as Engels quite keenly observed, far ahead of his time). Vygotsky accepted this account – indeed, one might ask whether there was any room for dissent in this matter in the 1920s – and tried to integrate it into his theory of man. Interestingly enough, he choose to ignore some of Engels' more outlandish statements, such as the claim that parrots understand what they say, the assertion that the eating of meat positively influenced the development of the human brain, and Engels' embracing of one form of the recapitulation thesis.

It is not easy to judge Engels' theory of labor (see Woolfson, 1982, for a sympathetic analysis). Concentrating on the idea of tool-manufacture and its role in anthropogenesis – and accepting the idea of one single feature discriminating between animals and human beings – one might agree with his account. Certainly, the invention and use of tools played a major part in human history, a theory with which many contemporary experts concur (e.g. Richards, 1987; Leakey, 1981). But it should be noted that the distinction between tool-use and labor is rather vague, as is the account of the origin of speech, an account which appears to embody Lamarckian traits. Be that as it may, Vygotsky's taking on-board Engels' theory implied an acceptance of a distinction between biological evolution and human history and the importance of the role of tools and labor in the origin of human culture. One of the major challenges for Marxist psychology would be to demonstrate how tool-use and labor influenced the human mental processes. Some authors have argued that Engels' theory of labor was simply another attempt to argue man's superiority to the animal world and – by reintroducing the original gap – was nothing other than a regression to pre-Darwinian times. This is the opinion of, for instance, Walker (1983, pp. 54–5), who has claimed that Engels' theory gave rise to "a split of almost Cartesian proportions between the mental qualities of ape and those of man," and who has argued, that "accepting Marxist economic determinism tends to result in a theological kind of division between animal and human consciousness." Whether this is a fair assessment will become clear only after discussing the whole cultural-historical framework, but it should be stressed here that a return to a Cartesian notion of animals and man was not the intention of either Engels or Vygotsky, for both fully accepted the idea of Darwinian animal–man continuity, interpreting this continuity, however, in a dialectical way. One might perhaps summarize Vygotsky's view on the relation of animal to human behavior by paraphrasing Darwin: for Vygotsky the difference in mind between man and the higher animals was *both* a matter of degree and of kind. To the naive logician this may seem an odd point of view but, as we will see, for Vygotsky's view of the psychology of animals versus that of man, dialectical logics pretended to provide a solution.

Meanwhile, the marriage of evolutionary theory to Marxist thought did require some dialectic counseling. The first thing that might be asked is whether the characterization of man as a tool-using animal was a fortunate one. Had not Darwin (e.g. 1871/1981, pp. 51–3) already pointed out that the manufacture and use of tools was not at all rare among animals? How then, should we characterize the essential difference between animals and men? And what new light was shed on this issue by the very recent investigations by Yerkes (1916), Köhler (1921), Guillaume and Meyerson (1930; 1931), and others? These were questions that Vygotsky and other Marxist psychologists could not avoid and these questions were not at all easy to answer, taking into consideration the fact that the writings of Marx and Engels had to be accepted as articles of faith. They were also questions that were of genuine interest to any psychologist and it is quite easy to see why Vygotsky devoted so much time and energy to their discussion.

A second problem that was left unsolved by Engels was that of the exact nature of the historical period. Can we reconstruct the history of *Homo sapiens* from primitive cultures to present man? Was it allowed to use cross-cultural evidence in this respect, assuming that current non-Western people were somehow identical or similar to historical primitive man? These were questions that fascinated Vygotsky and his contemporaries – many of whom saw a straight, undeviating development from ape to savage – and that could not be avoided in the grand theory that Vygotsky envisioned. In order to answer them he turned to the available ethnographic evidence provided by Durkheim, Lévy-Bruhl, and Thurnwald.

Finally, one might ask whether biological evolution and human history should be seen as two distinct periods in phylogenesis, or whether they overlap in time. This last question we will try to answer immediately, leaving the answer to the first questions to the following paragraphs of this chapter. To say that biological evolution and human history did not overlap would be equivalent to formulating a so-called "critical-point" theory, that is, a theory that claims that the development of the capacity for acquiring culture was a sudden occurrence in the phylogeny of primates. Accepting this (now discredited view (Geertz, 1973, pp. 62–9)) involves in essence seeing biological development as the precursor of cultural development. It does not seem that Engels' and Vygotsky's theories implied such a point of view. Engels, in his rather cryptic account, seems to avoid a critical-point theory by claiming there is a complex interaction between the development of hand, sense organs, and brain, and by stating that "the hand was not only the tool of labor, but also its product" (Engels, 1925, p. 445). If read in a sympathetic way this view implies that human culture and biology – at least for some indefinite period of overlap – developed in a complex process of interaction. It is quite probable that Vygotsky was of the same opinion, although he sometimes formulated views that were very similar to a critical-point view. Thus, sometimes he wrote that "apparently the biological evolution was finished long before the historical development of man started" (Vygotsky, 1930q/1960, p. 447), but at other times he explained that

> Man's development, as a biological type, apparently, was already mainly finished at the moment that human history started. This, of course, does not mean that human biology came to a stand-still from the moment that historical development of human society started. . . . But this biological change of nature had become a unity dependent on and subordinated to the historical development of the human society. (Vygotsky and Luria, 1930a, p. 54, p. 70)

In general, Vygotsky's writings reflect the conviction that biological changes play a very minor role in the relatively short period that followed the onset of human culture. As we will see in discussing Vygotsky's use of ethnographic literature, this view he saw confirmed by the findings of Thurnwald (1922). Of course, part of the problem of the critical-point theory is that it derives from an inappropriate choice of time scale (Geertz, 1973, p. 65). Another problem might be whether it makes any sense to use "biology" and "culture" as opposite or exclusive terms.

We may conclude that Wertsch (1985, p. 29) was not fully accurate in attributing a critical-point theory to Vygotsky. In so far as he suggested this point of view, it was as a result of his conviction that the "tortoise" of biological evolution was eclipsed by the "hare" of cultural revolution (Barash, 1986).

Animal and Man: Two Points of View

Combining the theories of Darwin and Engels provided a general frame-work for thinking about the origin of the human being, but this framework could not possibly give the answers to all the questions posed by new investigations. One of the key problems was that of the relation of animal intelligence to human intelligence. Could Darwin and Engels enlighten the recent findings in this field? And again: could these perspectives be combined without friction? To answer these and related questions Vygotsky thoroughly investigated the available findings of animal psychology and analyzed the main points of view.

A classical view of the difference between animals and human beings had been formulated by Descartes. Vygotsky criticized the Cartesian idea that animals were no more than living machines and the resulting animal–man dichotomy on many grounds. First, Darwin's findings and his explanation of them seemed to belie any dichotomy. Secondly, accepting with Descartes a crude, mechanistic form of materialism as the appropriate way of describing animal behavior, one is almost forced to introduce idealistic factors for the explanation of human beings. For unless one accepts La Mettrie's (1748/1981) idea that all living beings are automata, Descartes' view leads to the introduction of spiritual, nonmaterial – and thus idealistic – factors to explain specifically human behavior. The introduction of the notion of the soul is, therefore, the logical counterpart of the mechanistic materialism applied to animals, Vygotsky reasoned. To him Descartes' unfortunate animal–human being dichotomy was the almost inevitable result of his nongenetic, nonevolutionary approach. "The denial of a psyche to animals," Vygotsky stated, "prohibits any possibility of a genetic explanation, that is, an explanation from the evolutionary point of view on the development of the human psyche" (1930q/1960, p. 404). Thirdly, Descartes' view contradicted various other empirical findings. Vygotsky claimed – without further arguments – that (1) it was well known that "irritability" formed the start of all psyche, and (2) that the psyche was a function of the brain (1930q/1960, p. 405). The latter point of view was most probably based on Edinger (1911), who had shown that the development of new brain structures was closely tied to the development of new mental processes. To Vygotsky this finding seemed incompatible with the Cartesian notion of an independent psyche or soul.

Having discussed this inadequate view on the relation between animal and human intelligence, Vygotsky, interestingly enough, claimed that American behaviorism in a sense inherited the Cartesial legacy. The most important example of behaviorist animal psychological research constituted Thorndike's experiments with cats and his explanation of their behavior in terms of trial and error. Vygotsky agreed with the very critical discussions of these experiments in the German psychological literature (e.g. Koffka, 1925, pp. 116–32) – discussions that anticipated much of the current criticism (e.g. Walker, 1983, pp. 61–5) – and stated that Thorndike grossly underestimated the capabilities of animals. Following Lloyd Morgan's canon, that said that "in no case may we interpret an action as the outcome of the exercise of a higher psychical faculty, if it can be interpreted as the exercise of one which stands lower on the psychological scale," behaviorists effectively excluded the possibility of a truly genetic explanation (see Walker, 1983, pp. 56–8, for a recent criticism of this canon).

The natural opponent of any dichotomous view was Darwin's theory of evolution. This was the second view of the animal versus human intelligence issue that Vygotsky discussed. Interestingly enough – and in line with the remarks made above about the difficult marriage between Darwin's and Engels' theories – he sided with Darwin against the Cartesian view but did not fully accept the former's ideas. It was Darwin's anthropomorphic discussions of animal behavior that Vygotsky found difficult to swallow. In several places Darwin (1871/1981, pp. 62–9; cf. Graham, 1987; Walker, 1983) had ascribed mental capacities to animals – such as a sense of humor and a belief in supernatural agencies – which seemed difficult to defend on the basis of the available evidence. Vygotsky argued that Darwin and his contemporary Romanes were inclined to exaggerate the capacities of animals by making use of – often amusing – anecdotal evidence (see Walker, 1983, pp. 46–51 for a confirmation of this critique). For Vygotsky this uncritical acceptance of anecdotal evidence was simply inconsistent: by ascribing to animals higher mental faculties that they did not possess Darwin undermined the idea of the evolution of intelligence. Thus, we see a theme repeated: whereas Darwin's theory had accomplished the formidable feat of closing the Cartesian gap between animal and human behavior, in accepting the credibility of anecdotal evidence about animal intelligence Darwin underestimated human beings' qualitative uniqueness.

Vygotsky concluded that there were two opposing views in animal psychology: (1) the view that animals are totally different from human beings, a view defended by Descartes and behaviorism; and (2) the view that animals are not basically different from humans. Vygotsky believed Darwin (somewhat unjustly, see Walker, 1983, pp. 39–51) and Romanes belonged to the latter camp. Neither of these views was acceptable to Vygotsky, who envisioned an evolutionary account which would not lose sight of the qualitative differences between animals and human beings that arise in the course of this evolution. This view became particularly clear in his discussion of the most recent findings unearthed by Köhler and Yerkes.

Animal and Man: Assessing the New Evidence

That Vygotsky attached great value to Köhler's (1921) experiments with chimpanzees is evident in the fact that he extensively discussed the German psychologist's investigations and their best interpretation (e.g. Vygotsky, 1929h; 1930s; Vygotsky and Luria, 1930a), and actively encouraged the translation of Köhler's book into Russian (Köhler, 1930; translated by Vygotsky's collaborators at the Institute of Experimental Psychology, L. V. Zankov and I. M. Solov'ev). The most detailed discussion of Köhler's work can be found in the first chapter of Studies of the History of Behavior. Ape.

Primitive. Child. In fact, it can be said that this chapter is no more than a long commentary on Köhler's experiments – a commentary that was strongly influenced by Bühler (1918) and Koffka (1925) – and an attempt to interpret them in cultural-historical terms.

In general it can be said that Vygotsky completely agreed with Köhler's (1921) and Koffka's (1925) interpretation of the former's findings. Discussing the chimpanzees' solution to detour problems, and their manufacture and use of tools, he agreed with these authors that the Gestalt, or structure of the visual field, was of fundamental importance. Instruments were only taken into account by Sultan[2] and his colleagues when they were in the vicinity of the desired goal and boxes could not be seen as a ladder as long as another chimpanzee was using it as a chair. Such abuse of the boxes apparently changed the whole Gestalt of the boxes, thereby making their use as a tool impossible. It is quite clear that Vygotsky was greatly impressed by Köhler's experimental demonstrations of the laws of *Gestalt*. He enthusiastically related the experiments with chickens (Köhler, 1921, p. 10) showing that these animals can learn to choose the lighter one of any of two shades of gray. In his view this was "a magnificent experimental proof" of the role of *Gestalts* in animal behavior (Vygotsky and Luria, 1930a, pp. 27–8).

Vygotsky also accepted Köhler's conclusion that the chimpanzees displayed genuine insight. As is well known Köhler (1921, pp. 133–62) took great pains to counter the idea that the behavior of Sultan *cum suis* resulted from the slow formation of associations, pointing to, among other things, the chimpanzees' sudden solution of a problem after many fruitless attempts. Vygotsky agreed with this analysis and tended to agree with Bühler (1918, p. 280) that the chimpanzees are confronted with novel situations and experience a sort of "Aha Erlebnis."

Finally, Vygotsky accepted the evidence (Köhler, 1921, p. 26) that the solutions found by the chimpanzees are not dependent on the particular concrete situation and thus can be generalized to other situations. Different objects acquire the functional value (*Funktionswert*) of a tool (Vygotsky and Luria, 1930a, p. 43).

Chimpanzees, then, seemed to demonstrate surprisingly intelligent behavior and no qualitative differences between animal and man whatsoever had been proved. However, Köhler and Bühler had already pointed out various limitations to the performances of the chimpanzees. Thus, Köhler (1921, p. 192) in the concluding paragraphs of his book had argued that the chimpanzees "lack the priceless technical tool" of speech and are very limited in their "most important material of intelligence, the so-called representations." These factors confined the chimpanzees to the immediate situation

---

[2]Sultan was the name of one of Köhler's chimpanzee-subjects.

and prevented "even the slightest beginning of cultural development." Chimpanzees do not make tools for tomorrow, for they lack language and have a limited imaginary power for time, Köhler concluded.

This reasoning gave Vygotsky a first empirical clue as to the qualitative distinction between chimpanzees and human beings: the chimpanzees missed the "priceless technical tool" of speech. It will be seen that Vygotsky considered the role of speech in intelligent behavior to be of the utmost importance. Köhler's findings also demonstrated that, phylogenetically speaking, speech and intellect were initially independent phenomena, an issue that Vygotsky considered to be of fundamental importance and which he often discussed (e.g. 1929e; 1929f).

But what about the chimpanzees' skillful use of tools? Did it not contradict Marxist thinking? Here again Vygotsky could employ one of Köhler's observations. Köhler had noted that tools do not play a significant role in the life of the chimpanzees or other animals for they can easily do without artifacts, and in fact, as Köhler observed, as soon as chimpanzees get into a serious conflict they throw away their sticks and decide the fight without any auxiliary means. Thus, animals do show the beginning of tool manufacture and use, but tools do not play an important role in their adaptation to the environment. What Vygotskyy attempted to bring home here is, that there is a qualitative difference between animal and human tool-use. Quoting Plekhanov he observed that "what exists in embryonic form in one species, can become the defining characteristic of another species" (Vygotsky, 1930q/1960, p. 422).

Elsewhere (Vygotsky and Luria, 1930a, p. 49) he claimed that animals display tool-use, but not labor. We are thus given the following account: animals manufacture and use tools but this tool-use never develops into labor. As animals do not develop labor they cannot possibly develop speech and, in general, culture. The situation is totally different for human beings, who are fully dependent in their daily life on the use of various tools. In an example typical for that time Vygotsky claimed that "The whole existence of the Australian savage depends on his boomerang, like the whole existence of contemporary England depends on its machines" (Vygotsky, 1930s, p. viii).

Human beings' history was for Vygotsky the history of artifacts, of artificial organs. These artifacts allowed humans to master nature as the technical tool of speech allowed them to master their own mental processes.

To some readers this may seem a poor solution to the problem of the relation of animal to human intelligence. The solution rests on the idea that at some point tool-use is transformed into labor according to the dialectical law that says that many quantitative changes may result in a qualitative leap (see Engels, 1925). Thus again Vygotsky (1930q/1960, p. 420) – who stated that "Köhler's investigations lead for the first time to the factual foundation of Darwinism in psychology in its most critical, important, and difficult point" – opted for the dialectical solution that the difference between animals and human beings is both a matter of degree and of kind.

Vygotsky hardly discussed Yerkes' (1916) and Yerkes' and Yerkes' (1928) experiments with monkeys and apes but in connection with this research he made a remark that is of some interest for the issues discussed in this chapter. Vygotsky volunteered to replicate Yerkes' and Learned's (1925) attempt to teach apes language, if the Sukhumi primate center would allow him, but suggested the use of a different method: "Maybe we can teach the chimpanzee to use his fingers, like deaf–blinds do, that is, teach them sign language" (Vygotsky, 1930q/1960, p. 426). This approach adopted by Vygotsky from his defectological work anticipated the idea of the Gardners' experiment with Washoe by some 40 years.

The History of Man: Using the Ethnographic Findings

The claim that Australian aborigines are very similar to European children, or that schizophrenics regress towards an ape-like state, would not be taken very seriously by the experts in the 1990s, but at the turn of the century these ideas were as common as, say, the idea that men were superior to women. Most investigators freely compared the findings of anthropology with those of pathology and investigated the parallels between human phylogeny and ontogeny. Reading the literature of that time one frequently finds the implicit or explicit idea that the developments in these different fields can be summarized under the heading of "progress," a concept that allowed one to understand the findings more or less as one single continuous series of development. Thus, lower animals progressed via apes into prehistoric primitive men. Prehistoric man, in his turn, was surprisingly similar or indeed identical to contemporary non-Western people, whose cultural and mental development had become entrenched at one of the stages Western man had long left behind. Western children somehow repeated this historical-cultural development, which made them initially very similar to non-Western adults. Likewise, adult Western people might regress into child-like or non-Western-like states in cases of severe pathology. This notion of continuous progress and accidental regression was often compounded with ideas about the biological superiority of the white race over the other races and with the idea that the culture of Western educated people was far superior to that of the Western common man. It is against this background of now unacceptable ideas – although many of them are, of course, very much alive in Western cultural discourse – that one should judge Vygotsky's cultural-historical theory and, in particular, his remarks about the latest ethnographic findings.

Durkheim

Vygotsky's understanding of other cultures and of the relation of culture to mental processes was based on his reading of Durkheim, Lévy-Bruhl, and, most importantly, Thurnwald. Although he sometimes referred to Durk-heim quite critically (Vygotsky, 1934a, p. 59), one can see why the ideas of the French sociological school would appeal to him. In the first place, Durkheim – like his contemporary Janet – took an explicitly genetic point of view. As mentioned earlier, Durkheim (1985, p. 5) defended the idea that any real explanation of complex social phenomena rested on the reconstruc-tion of its development. Secondly, Durkheim resisted the idea that a blueprint for complex mental functioning can be arrived at by a study of the individual. In his view each society shared a set of collective representations that imposed themselves (much like Kantian categories) on the individual. These collective representations were the carriers of the accumulated experi-ence of generations of people and could be compared to tools. For Durk-heim they were "clever instruments of thought, that the human groups have . . . forged in the course of centuries and where they have accumulated their intellectual capital" (Durkheim, 1985, pp. 23–7). In his opinion the collective representations were similar to tools, because these too repre-sented accumulated – in this case material – capital (1985, p. 27). Durkheim concluded that "To know from what the conceptions are made that we have not made ourselves, it would not suffice to question our conscience: it is outside ourselves that we have to look, it is history we have to observe" (1985, pp. 27–8).

 It is not at all difficult to see how this conception influenced Vygotsky. Replacing "collective representations" with "higher mental processes" one gets ideas – as will become clear in the remainder of this chapter – that have been voiced by Vygotsky on many occasions. This is not to say, of course, that cultural-historical theory is equivalent to Durkheim's approach. For Vygotsky and his followers Durkheim did not provide an adequate explana-tion of the origin of the collective representations, nor did he give an adequate psychological account of the way individual people acquired them. However, it can be seen that Vygotsky – directly or indirectly through Lévy-Bruhl – adopted much of Durkheim's global approach, a fact that would be exploited by his later critics (see chapter 16).

Lévy-Bruhl

Part of the influence that Lévy-Bruhl exerted on Vygotsky should be attributed indirectly to Durkheim. Lévy-Bruhl (1910/1922, pp. 1–4) shared Durkheim's conception of the collective representations and claimed that the higher mental functions were unintelligible as long as one studied the individual, an idea he traced to Comte. Lévy-Bruhl, however, also provided Vygotsky with many detailed descriptions of primitive thought, descriptions that Vygotsky used in his characterizations of primitive cultures and in his many comparisons of children with primitives.

Lévy-Bruhl's influence is clearest in *Studies of the History of Behavior. Ape. Primitive. Child* (Vygotsky and Luria, 1930a). In the second chapter of this book Vygotsky related many of Lévy-Bruhl's findings and closely followed the latter's organization of the material. In fact, the titles and content of Vygotsky's paragraphs four, five and six are clearly borrowed from the third, fourth, and fifth chapters of Lévy-Bruhl's *Les Fonctions Mentales dans les Sociétés Inférieures* (1910/1922) (translated into English as *How Natives Think*, Lévy-Bruhl, 1966). In the second paragraph Vygotsky related Lévy-Bruhl's dispute with the English School in anthropology. Lévy-Bruhl had criticized Tylor and Frazer for their assumption that the workings of the human mind are identical in every culture (1910/1922, pp. 6–20). He would at least leave open the possibility that the bewildering cultural variety of collective representations corresponded with different mental functions. Vygotsky completely agreed with this reasoning: accepting the English point of view would imply that the human mind had not developed at all during human history. The sole differences between cultures would be in the content of experience but the mechanisms of mind would be identical in every epoch and culture (Vygotsky and Luria, 1939a, p. 60). Vygotsky acknowledged that Lévy-Bruhl was the first to claim that the mechanisms of primitive thinking did not coincide with those of "cultural man." Despite certain inaccuracies Lévy-Bruhl had to be credited for the fact, that

he was the first to pose the problem of the historical development of thinking. He showed that in itself the type of thinking is not a constant unity but one that changes and develops historically. The investigators who have followed the road indicated by him have tried to formulate more precisely on what the difference between the historical types of thinking of cultural and primitive man depends, in what the peculiarity of the historical development of human psychology resides. (Vygotsky and Luria, 1930a, p. 64)

We can see, then, that a fundamental idea of cultural-historical theory, namely the idea that people in different cultures and epochs have different higher mental processes, was present in the work of Lévy-Bruhl. It was this idea that Luria would try to corroborate in his expeditions to Uzbekistan (see chapter 10). The fact that Vygotsky used Lévy-Bruhl's ideas does not imply that he accepted the whole of his theory. Referring to various critics he suggested that Lévy-Bruhl's characterization of primitive collective representations as prelogical was unfortunate: seen from their subjective point of view they were completely logical. Vygotsky added as an additional critical point that the primitive's actions in daily life had to be logical in the objective sense of the word: otherwise they simply would not survive. This criticism – repeated by Luria (1976, p. 8) – was not very convincing, however, for Lévy-Bruhl (1922/1976, p. 141) himself acknowledged this point and made an explicit distinction between the practical thinking in daily life and the mystical thinking about kinship, history, etc.

Durkheim's and Lévy-Bruhl's fundamental idea that the differences in mentality between people living in different cultures was not attributable to their individual capacities had another side to it. It implied, that people living in primitive or "inferior" cultures were not necessarily intellectually inferior to Western people. Lévy-Bruhl, in particular, repeatedly emphasized that the primitives did not suffer from an intellectual indolence (*torpeur intellectuelle*), or a feebleness of spirit (*faiblesse d'esprit*) (Lévy-Bruhl, 1922/ 1976, p. 67). If they might sometimes seem stupid, this was an "apparent stupidity," rooted in the fact that our questions simply did not make sense to them (Lévy-Bruhl, 1922/1976, p. 39). Since the collective representations constituted the world of primitives, they were, one could say, living in another world, a world that in a number of ways did not coincide with ours. As a consequence, many of the questions Western man posed to himself

simply did not apply to them (Lévy-Bruhl, 1922/1976, p. 67). The implication of this view was that one should not confront people from other cultures with tasks taken from one's own culture and then draw conclusions from their possibly poor performance. For this would be judging them by our Western standards and seeing their thinking as a rudimentary form of our own, an approach that Lévy-Bruhl explicitly condemned. One can see, then, that Lévy-Bruhl's approach – despite certain deficiencies (Bunzel, 1966; Thomas, 1976) – led to conclusions that were very valuable to Vygotsky. Indeed, to say that people from different cultures have different higher mental capacities but do not differ essentially in regard to their basic capacities, is only one step from Vygotsky's statement that their higher mental processes differ, but the lower processes are identical. It was, by the way, a point of view that contradicted many of Lévy-Bruhl's contemporaries' who were often inclined to attribute mental differences to innate capacities.

It may be concluded that Lévy-Bruhl provided Vygotsky with a useful way of thinking about the relation of culture to mental processes. In addition he provided Vygotsky with many observations about the way primitive people thought and these ethnographic observations were used by Vygotsky to reconstruct the historical development of human thinking and to draw comparisons with human ontogeny.

Vygotsky accepted, for instance, the findings presented by Lévy-Bruhl (1922/1976, pp. 124–30), that supposedly showed that the thinking of primitive people hardly proceeded via concepts, but had a very concrete character. Primitive thought did not lead to the formation of concepts and scientific knowledge (Lévy-Bruhl, 1922/1976, p. 203), which was reflected in their language, a language that was less developed than our own and which had very few generic terms. However, it had a wealth of concrete names for all sorts of objects (Lévy-Bruhl, 1910/1922, pp. 117–24; 151–203). When primitive people did use generic terms they mostly were of the inadequate family-concept type (described by Wittgenstein), that is, various instances of the concept overlapped, but there was not one feature they all shared (Vygotsky and Luria, 1930a, p. 98). Vygotsky speculated that this feature of primitive thinking might explain the phenomenon of participation described by Lévy-Bruhl. In many cases where we would use abstract concepts or reason, primitive people relied on their prodigious memory (Lévy-Bruhl, 1910/1922, pp. 117–24; 1922/1976, pp. 35–7), a phenomenon which reminded Vygotsky of Western children's behavior. In sum, Lévy-Bruhl and Vygotsky agreed that primitive thinking was very concrete and, therefore, reflected only the immediate situation. It was also more fused with emotions and visual impressions. Vygotsky would probably not have objected had a contemporary said that these features of primitive thinking gave it an intermediate position between the ape's full dependence on the visual field and adult abstract Western thinking. He did compare – following Jaensch (1923; 1925) – the memory of primitive people to that of a Western child.

Nevertheless, Lévy-Bruhl's findings also pointed out that primitive people in backward cultures (Vygotsky, 1931n/1983, pp. 67–8) had recourse to artificially created stimuli in order to control their own behavior. As examples Vygotsky related on several occasions that of the Magololo chief who would solve an issue by dreaming about it (Lévy-Bruhl, 1922/1976, p. 172); the throwing of bones as a decision procedure (1922/1976, pp. 192–5); and the use of body parts in counting (Lévy-Bruhl, 1910/1922, pp. 204–57). All of these examples of various cognitive methods in contemporary non-Western cultures he accepted as indications that historically Western thought had gone through stages in which these methods had been prevalent. Visiting the Australian aborigines the Western ethnographer – most likely a missionary – was visiting the past of his own culture. This conclusion again confronts us with the question whether Vygotsky adopted a simple evolutionary scheme after all and whether his cultural-historical theory was free of ethnocentrist ideas. To settle this question we will turn to his other major source of information about the mental functioning of primitive man: Thurnwald's "Psychologie des primitiven Menschen" ("Psychology of Primitive Man") (1922). Thurnwald's book was published as one of three volumes in a series edited by Kafka. The first volume was written by Kafka himself and dealt with animal psychology. The second volume was Thurnwald's and dealt with primitive man. The third volume was written by Giese and gave an overview of child psychology. Thus, the three volumes covered the three main developmental concerns also distinguished by Vygotsky.

Thurnwald

Thurnwald's basic claim was that the modern mind is superior to that of the prehistoric mind. This superiority could not be explained by differences in biological makeup but rather had cultural origins. The mental superiority of present-day people was due to the invention and accumulation of cultural means and processes. Unfortunately, very little reliable knowledge was available about the culture and mind of prehistoric man and so to illustrate his point of view, Thurnwald proposed therefore to look at various non-Western cultures.

Such an approach raised various questions, as Thurnwald realized only too well. May one resort to the study of present-day people if one's goal is to study prehistoric man? Does the study of the culture – or cultural remnants – of people allow one to draw conclusions about the way these people think (thought)? Is the culture of Western man superior to that of non-Western "natural," or "primitive" man? These were some of the questions that, ideally, had to be answered.

Thurnwald was not very clear about these issues but he made four claims that shed some light on them, at least implicitly. These were the claims, that (1) prehistoric man was the precursor of all present-day human beings; (2) the culture and mind of prehistoric man were similar to that of present-day "natural" man; (3) there was no difference in biological makeup between Western and non-Western, or "natural" man; and (4) the culture and mind of Western man were superior to that of non-Western man. The first claim hardly needs any comments and will not be discussed here. With respect to the second claim Thurnwald defended a cautious point of view, stating that similarities in one cultural feature (e.g. technology) cannot simply lead us to conclusions about similarities in mental makeup but if one found many of these similarities when studying a wide variety of cultural customs and products, then such conclusions seemed justified to him (1922, p. 150). Among the topics discussed by Thurnwald were, among other things, the different types of communities in which people lived; the role of women in these communities; the various sorts of technologies in use; different types of economy; law; moral thinking; music; art; writing and language; counting systems; mythical thinking; and religion. His assumption – an assumption that Vygotsky would turn into one of the cornerstones of his theory – was that culture, as a means of control and knowledge of the surroundings, does not merely imply technological perfection but also the cognitive abilities that coincide with it (1922, p. 154). Of course, Thurnwald touched here on a problem that is still very much alive in present-day cross-cultural psychology (e.g., Cole and Scribner, 1974; Berry and Dasen, 1974; Scribner and Cole, 1981). All in all, Thurnwald did think that it was justified – after careful consideration of many cultural phenomena – to draw conclusions about prehistoric culture and thinking on the basis of the study of present-day natural people. Thurnwald's third claim was relevant to Vygotsky's conception of the lower psychological processes. The question was whether the different cultures of primitive people might not be explained by their different biological makeup. Several findings, such as the early onset of puberty among natives, seemed to indicate that these people indeed belonged to a different biological type. Contrary to many of his contemporaries, however, Thurnwald felt that the evidence here was not conclusive. He did not exclude the possibility that such phenomena were caused by different cultural customs (e.g. food habits) and concluded that the existence of different biological types among present-day people had not been proven. With respect to the fourth claim Thurnwald admitted, that of course there was an enormous variety of present-day "primitive" or "natural" people. Moreover, these people were in no way primitive in the sense of not having any culture at all: they did have their own, all be it poor, culture. In this respect they were much closer to European man than to apes (1922, p. 152). Nevertheless, Thurnwald argued, on the basis of our and their technological-intellectual performance we tend to think that we are culturally "more developed" than they are. We are inclined to call certain cultures "inferior," others "superior," and to discern certain "progressive" developments. The assumption obviously is that our mind historically depends on theirs and that our culture developed from theirs. This would imply that the culture of nonWestern people had come to a standstill in the past millennia. Studying non-Western people we would indeed study our own past.

Thurnwald mentioned the idea that different cultures might be actually incomparable on a linear scale. Rather surprisingly, he tended to agree with this point of view. Theoretically speaking, Thurnwald stated (1922, p. 157), one can only say that human culture branched into different developmental directions but the "accumulation" of knowledge and abilities is experienced subjectively by Western people – from their egocentric point of view – as progress. In practice, Thurnwald himself felt more inclined to the subjective point of view and throughout his book he freely used terms like "poor" and "paltry" to characterize the cultures of non-Western people.

In sum, it is probably fair to say that Thurnwald was a moderate ethnocentrist. He clearly thought that Western cultures were superior to all other cultures, and that these latter cultures represented a stage of mental development Western people had long left behind. On the other hand, he admitted that from some – practically unattainable – objective point of view these different levels of culture might be viewed as equivalent cultural variants. Of course, Thurnwald was by no means the only one to think this way. Gould (1981), in a fascinating study, has shown how many of the great men of psychology's history were prone to ethnocentrist and even racist reasoning. Moreover, positions similar to that of Thurnwald are being defended even today. Barash (1986, p. 36), for example, recently stated that "An aborigine brought from central Australia to Western Europe can leap hundreds if not thousands of generations of cultural evolution within a few years."

It is quite interesting to see which elements from Thurnwald's thinking Vygotsky accepted and which he simply ignored. The first thing to be noticed is that the ethnocentrist position defended by Thurnwald was fully shared by Vygotsky. He agreed with the idea that one can discern different levels of culture and viewed the study of people living in the "uncivilized world" as a legitimate means of obtaining data about the primitive mind of prehistoric man (Vygotsky and Luria, 1930a, p. 58). Vygotsky also accepted Thurnwald's point of view that the cultural inferiority of these people was not necessarily caused by biological factors: their anatomy and physiology were not greatly different from ours. In fact, whereas Thurnwald had written that the evidence was not conclusive, Vygotsky interpreted him as claiming that no biological differences whatsoever did exist. This fact is of some importance as it was the only evidence Vygotsky ever gave for his claim that the lower psychological processes – presumably closely tied to the biological makeup – were identical for all human beings in different cultures and epochs.

Quite different from Thurnwald's, however, was Vygotsky's selection of cultural phenomena in discussing the differences between various cultures. He narrowed down Thurnwald's concept of culture significantly by concentrating on the phenomena of language, counting systems, and writing, ignoring his other subjects, such as the different systems of law, moral thinking, art, religion, etc. There may have been three, interconnected, reasons for this particular selection of relevant cultural phenomena. In the first place, one can make a distinction between social – "soft" – and technological – "hard" – cultural evolution (Barash, 1986, p. 41). Social evolution includes the changes in forms of law and government, economics, family, music, art, and religion. Technology is the discovery and implementation of methods by which human beings can act on their environment. It uncovers the laws of nature and seeks to manipulate them. Keeping this distinction in mind one immediately sees that Vygotsky ignored all cultural phenomena belonging to social evolution. The reason for this selection seems clear: there is very little evidence for progress in this domain of culture (Barash, 1986, p. 42). Baghwan is not clearly a wiser man than Christ was and Homer's creations are not obviously inferior to those of Kundera, Nabokov, or Frisch. The case seems different for the topics Vygotsky selected: writing systems, counting systems, and language. At least to Vygotsky and his contemporaries it seemed obvious that, for example, counting by using body parts was more limited than counting with the use of written numbers. Also, evidence gathered by Lévy-Bruhl and other anthropologists seemed to indicate that the natives' languages were definitely inferior as regards the formation and use of abstract concepts. Thus, Vygotsky selected those aspects of culture that were milestones in human history and with regard to which the notion of cultural progress was intuitively more plausible. Secondly, literacy and counting systems could be thought of as sign systems that served a double function. Counting systems and written and spoken language did not only serve a definite function in the outer world – say, the preservation of tradition in written texts – but also served as instruments for the growing control of human behavior. They were sign systems that transformed our mental functioning as tools transformed the inanimate universe (Vygotsky and Luria, 1930a, p. 54). This double function of sign systems and the comparison with tools will be discussed below. Thirdly, the selection of cultural procedures that might be thought of as tools was, naturally, much effected by Marx's and Engels' account of the history of man. Tool-use and language were considered, as we have seen, as defining characteristics of man (see Bloch, 1983, for an intelligent criticism of Marx's and Engels' anthropological thinking).

Thus, Vygotsky selected technology-like aspects of culture for the comparison of cultures, for technology had radically changed the outlook of Western cultures, while no progress was evident in other aspects of culture.

The choice of these aspects conformed with Marxist anthropology and was also consistent with Vygotsky's fascination with Bacon's writings. It is Bacon who has been called the "master philosopher" of technology (von Wright, 1988). It was Bacon, whose words were used several times by Vygotsky (1928p, p. 76; 1929s, p. 418; Vygotsky and Luria, 1930a, p. 7) to illustrate his view: "Neither the naked hand nor the understanding left to itself can effect much. It is by instruments and aids that the work is done . . ." (Bacon, 1620/1960, p. 39).

This particular selection of cultural phenomena made Vygotsky particularly vulnerable to the tendency – already present in Thurnwald's thinking – to compare different cultures on a linear scale. And in fact, this is what he did in various publications, an approach that would bring him much criticism (see chapter 16). In Vygotsky (1929i), for example, he claimed that the level of societal and cultural development of the national minorities – having in mind, for example, the Islamic culture in Uzbekistan – was "low." Within the next five years – it was the time of the First Five-Year Plan – these cultures had to "take a grandiose leap on the ladder of their cultural development, jumping over a whole series of historical levels." Vygotsky characterized the national minorities as "backwards" and judged a "forced cultural development" to be essential in order to reach "a unified socialist culture" (Vygotsky, 1929i, p. 367).

However, emphasizing culture as such as the underlying cause of mental differences between people belonging to different cultures had its positive aspects. On the basis of the writings of Lévy-Bruhl and Thurnwald, Vygotsky rejected the idea – defended by such contemporaries as Burt, Terman, and Yerkes – that different mental performances could be fully explained by biological factors. He clearly saw that mental tests can never be culture-fair and criticized their use in judging the mental abilities of non-Western people, emphasizing that the mental functioning of people should always be judged against the background of their culture and personal circumstances (e.g. Vygotsky, 1929i, p. 369).

Summarizing, it can be said that Vygotsky was in full agreement with many of his contemporaries in characterizing different cultures as either "superior" or "inferior." The ethnocentrist position he defended and his discussion of relevant cultural findings were greatly influenced by Thurnwald (1922). Vygotsky avoided, unlike many of his colleagues, the mistake of explaining cultural and mental differences by referring to biological or even racial differences, again inspired by Thurnwald. In this respect, his cultural-historical theory constituted a definite step forward in our understanding of people from different cultural backgrounds. The now unacceptable statements about "inferior" cultures should be seen against the background of Vygotsky's sincere wish – a wish that had become a slogan in the

Soviet society of the 1920s – to emancipate all citizens and liberate them from the yoke of the pre-revolutionary "feudal" system.

Thurnwald's study did not only provide Vygotsky with a way of thinking about culture and its relation to thought: as with Lévy-Bruhl's writings it also served as a source of knowledge about other cultures. Most importantly, Thurnwald discussed several findings that Vygotsky could use for his theory that sign systems served a double function and that they were similar in some sense to tools.

Of greatest interest were Thurnwald's discussions of primitive memory aids, counting, and writing systems. With regard to counting systems he noticed (1922, p. 273–5) that primitive counting was very much tied to concrete images and that numerals were frequently seen as names for a concrete set of objects: numerals were often represented by concrete objects or animals – such as a crocodile because of the number of its teeth – and in many cultures counting procedures made use of body parts. In general, then, the counting systems were as little abstract and decontextualized as supposedly the primitive language (1922, p. 269) was. Thurnwald also observed that primitive people would not complete tasks that were far removed from their concrete everyday life experiences. For example, one subject whom Thurnwald asked to count as far as he could using imaginary pigs as a unit, refused to count over 60 as larger numbers of pigs were simply unrealistic (1922, p. 274). Thurnwald concluded that primitives were very much tied to their concrete reality and refused to do abstract tasks, a phenomenon that Luria would observe again in Uzbekistan (see chapter 10), and that Petrova would recognize in "child-primitives" (see chapter 4).

Different memory-aid systems were discussed by Thurnwald (1922, pp. 243–65) in great detail and were considered by him as the origin of our current writing systems. For Thurnwald memory aids originated as individual means to overcome time, which afterwards became conventionalized and began to serve as a means of communication within a community (1922, pp. 243–4). He discussed various systems, mentioning in passing Vygotsky's favorite example of a knot tied in a handkerchief. Four of Thurnwald's illustrations demonstrating various of the most primitive coding systems – such as the Peruvian Quippu system of tying knots in a string (a system of Inca origin nowadays spelled as "khipu;" cf. Alcina Franch and Palop Martínez, 1988, pp. 116–19) – were reproduced by Vygotsky (see figures 31, 32 (p. 244), 33 (p. 245), and 35 (p. 247) in Thurnwald, 1922; and the figures 14, 15 (p. 81), 16 (p. 82), and 19 (p. 86) in Vygotsky and Luria, 1930a). Thurnwald's discussion of various writing systems and the development from pictographic to ideographic systems were retold by Vygotsky and clearly influenced his and Luria's research. Luria's (1929d/1978) study of the development of writing in the child, for example, was an attempt to show that children too go through a picto-graphic and ideographic phase in their symbolic activity.

It is interesting to see that Vygotsky – as a rule – was somewhat more inclined to interpret Thurnwald's ethnographic findings in an evolutionary, developmental way than Thurnwald was himself. An example can best illustrate Vygotsky's reasoning in this respect. Having discussed the "Afri-can habit" of transmitting important messages by a messenger who repro-duces the message word by word, Vygotsky compared this system to the Peruvian khipu system and concluded: "One has only to compare the memory of the African messenger who... makes exclusive use of his natural eidetic memory with the memory of the Peruvian "officer of knots" – whose task it was to tie and read the Quippu – in order to see in which direction the development of human memory goes as culture develops" (Vygotsky and Luria, 1930a, p. 85).

What Vygotsky is implying here is, that very primitive people remem-bered things by retaining the vivid, concrete experience of the event – the mneme (Semon, 1920) – while culturally more advanced people developed technical means to do the same. In doing so they developed a *memoria technica* (cf. Yates, 1984) which replaced natural, eidetic memory and would eventually cause its decay. Of course, the suggestion was that a similar development would be discernible in child development.

Another difference between Thurnwald's and Vygotsky's interpretation of ethnographic findings emerges in their discussion of the origin of memory aids. Whereas Thurnwald suggested that these methods originated as pri-vate means to retain information that later became conventionalized and started to serve the social function of communication, Vygotsky wrote that initially signs were "not so much used for the self as for others, with social goals... [they] only later become signs also for the self" (Vygotsky and Luria, 1930a, p. 86). This direction from outer to inner processes was strongly connected with Vygotsky's growing conviction that many cultural procedures could be seen as analogous to tools.

Tool and Sign

Discussing the performances of Sultan and other chimpanzees, Köhler (1921, p. 192) concluded that they lacked the "priceless technical tool" of speech. Lacking speech and lasting representations they were only able to solve problems when the required tool was introduced into the visual field, thereby changing the whole Gestalt. Several years later Koffka (1925) suggested, that perhaps we might see human speech as analogous to chimpanzees' tool-use. The words used by children might be seen as in a way similar to the stick given to the chimpanzees: their introduction changed the Gestalt and made solution of the task possible (Koffka, 1925, p. 243). Of course, Koffka was only one in a long series of thinkers (e.g. Dewey, 1910, pp. 314–18) who suggested that speech might be seen as an instrument or tool of thinking, but his observation was particularly important to Vygotsky, because it was made in a phylogenetic context and linked several developmental fields that were of vital importance to Marxist anthropology. In addition, the ethnographic findings related by Lévy-Bruhl and Thurnwald – e.g. the throwing of bones as a decision procedure; the use of body parts in counting procedures; and the use of various memory aids and writing systems – suggested that, historically, human beings had developed various cultural instruments to aid their mental performances. Combining these ideas with various suggestions made by Ribot, Binet, Claparède, Durkheim, and others, Vygotsky attempted to elaborate the idea that cultural instruments – most importantly, speech – were in many ways similar to tools. Naturally, a convincing demonstration of the similarity between tools and the uniquely human feature of speech would be yet another marvelous proof of the validity of Marxist thought.

Human behavior, Vygotsky (1930z/1960) reasoned, consists of two types of processes: (1) natural, lower acts that developed in the course of evolution and are shared with (higher) animals; and (2) artificial, instrumental acts that evolved in human history and are, therefore, specifically human. The relation between natural and artificial acts Vygotsky (1928p, p. 63; 1929s, p. 420; 1930z/1960, p. 104; 1931n/1983, p. 111) summarized in his well-known triangle figure (see figure 9.1).

The figure depicts the relation between natural and artificial processes for the case of memory. In natural memory the link between two stimuli A and B is established through the direct process of conditional reflex formation: A and B are coupled one or more times, after which the presentation of A will lead to the expectation of B. This is presumably the way animals remember information. In artificial, or instrumental, memory use is made of an intermediate mnemotechnical aid X, for example, a knot in a handkerchief. Thus, to remember that on a specific day (A) one has to phone a specific person (B) one might simply repeat many times for oneself: "On day A I

FIGURE 9.1   The relationship between natural and artificial memory

have to ring B." This would establish a direct associational link between A and B. However, one might also introduce a third element X into the situation by making use of a knot in a handkerchief, or some other memory aid (X). The link between A and B is then established in a less direct, or mediated way. For A (the fact that it is the specific day) will lead to X (the tying of a knot), and X in its turn (feeling the knot at some point during the day) will elicit phoning B. This type of remembering information that makes use of an intermediate instrument X is presumably specifically human.

Vygotsky repeatedly underlined that there was nothing extraordinary or supernatural to these instrumental acts: each instrumental, artificial, or cultural act – he initially used the term *priem* (method, device, trick), a term much used by his contemporary, the formalist Shklovsky – can be completely decomposed into the composite natural acts. For the complex artificial act (A–X–B) consists of two ordinary conditional reflexes (A–X and X–B) and nothing more. For Vygotsky (1928p, pp. 61–2) the uniqueness of instrumental acts, therefore, resided fully in their structure: they were as much subject to the laws of association as any other, more simple act. He was of the opinion, that "Culture in general does not create anything new over and above what is given by nature, but it transforms nature according to the goals of man" (1928p, p. 61) and claimed that instrumental acts involved the "active use of natural properties of brain tissue" (1930aa/ 1982, p. 104). This point of view he found confirmed in the work of the Danish psychologist Høffding (1892, p. 198), whose statement, "thinking in the real sense of the word cannot free itself from these laws [of association] just as it is impossible to render inoperative the laws of external nature by any artificial machine; but like the physical ones we can steer the psychological laws to serve our goals," Vygotsky quoted approvingly.

By emphasizing the reflex-like nature of the components of instrumental acts Vygotsky attempted to give a firm, natural scientific foundation for the higher functions. It is clear that from the very beginning he tried to give an account of the cultural processes that fitted within a natural-scientific – indeed, in some respects virtually behaviorist – approach and attempted to avoid "free-floating" spiritualist constructions. This attitude remained the same throughout his various discussions of cultural-historical theory, as becomes obvious in the following quotation from the last version of this theory.

As is well-known, the fundamental law of our behavior says that behavior is determined by situations, that the reaction is elicited by stimuli, and therefore, the key to the mastering of behavior lies in the mastering of stimuli. We cannot master our behavior otherwise than through the corresponding stimuli . . . In this respect the behavior of man does not constitute an exception to the general laws of nature . . . (Vygotsky, 1931n/1983, p. 278)

Vygotsky's approach led to a dialectical view of human behavior in which several levels could be discerned, but avoided positing any gaps between them. In later years, following Bühler (e.g. 1919, pp. 7–23, pp. 45–51), he often distinguished three of these behavioral levels. First, we have the behavioral level of inborn reactions, or unconditional reflexes. For Vygotsky these evolved in biological evolution as discussed by Darwin and he often equated them with Bühler's term "instinct." Secondly, we have the behavioral level of conditional reflexes as first discussed by Pavlov. This level of behavior was equivalent to the level called "training" (*Dressur*) by Bühler. Vygotsky reasoned that since the formation of conditional reflexes rests on the association of unconditional reflexes to environmental stimuli and as the latter differ for each individual, Pavlov in a way had given an account of the origin of individual organisms. On many occasions he summarized Darwin's and Pavlov's contribution in this context in the following words: "While Darwin explained the origin of species, Pavlov explained the origin of individuals" (e.g. Vygotsky and Luria, 1939a, p. 11). Thirdly, we have the behavioral level of intellectual processes, equivalent to Bühler's "intellect" (*Intellekt*), that involves the use of instruments. As we have seen, these instrumental acts can be thought of as combinations of conditional reflexes.

Although it was not altogether clear how Vygotsky could combine his own two-level theory – of natural and cultural acts – with Bühler's three-level model, one can understand his reason for doing so. It may be concluded that to him each higher level of behavior could be analyzed into its composite lower parts. The novelty of each new level solely resided in the structural combination of these elements (Vygotsky, 1928p, p. 64; 1930aa/1982, p. 106). Combining Darwin, Pavlov, and Bühler, Vygotsky tried to link the cultural, instrumental acts to the natural processes, thus embedding them in a natural scientific framework.

The mnemotechnical and other aids used by human beings to improve their performance have the character of signs, Vygotsky claimed. They are social artifacts designed to master and thereby improve our natural psychological processes. As examples of signs he listed words, numbers, mnemotechnical devices, algebraic symbols, works of art, writing systems, schemata, diagrams, maps, blueprints, etc. (Vygotsky, 1930aa/1982, p. 103). From this list it is obvious that any stimulus that can signify another stimulus may be seen and used as a psychological instrument or sign. This was indeed Vygotsky's point of view. It is the human being who decides that some stimuli may serve as means to operate upon other stimuli, thereby creating two classes of stimuli: (1) stimuli-means (*stimuly-sredstvy*), or signs; and (2) stimuli-objects (*stimuly-ob'ekty*) (Vygotsky, 1930aa/1982, p. 105). When stimuli-means and stimuli-objects were combined in one act, Vygotsky spoke of instrumental acts.

For Vygotsky the inclusion of signs in the psychological act led to important structural changes. Their use implied that (1) new psychological functions became involved; (2) several natural processes would eventually decay; and (3) such properties of the whole act as its intensity and length would change (1930aa/1982, p. 105). He concluded that "The inclusion of a sign in one or the other behavioral process . . . reforms the whole structure of the psychological operation as the inclusion of a tool reforms the whole structure of a labor operation" (Vygotsky, 1928p, p. 64; 1930aa/1982, p. 103).

Vygotsky argued that the way the introduction of signs – or stimuli-means – changed the whole psychological structure resembled the way tools change labor operations. Both tool and sign form an intermediate link between object and operation, between object and subject. Both labor operations and instrumental acts are mediated acts, that is, they involve a third element that comes between human beings and nature. The essential difference between instrumental psychological acts and labor operations is that signs are intended to control the psyche and behavior of others and the self, whereas tools are employed to master nature or material objects. Another difference is that stimuli, in contradistinction to tools (which are selected because of their material characteristics, such as their flexibility, or hardness) do not become signs because of their intrinsic properties: any · stimulus can signify any other stimulus (Vygotsky, 1930aa/1982, pp. 103–6).

It may be concluded that Vygotsky offered the following peculiar account of the use and significance of cultural instruments in human history: Human beings invented in human history a set of cultural instruments – such as the Inca khipu system – that can be thought of as stimuli-means, or signs. With the help of these signs they mastered their own psychological processes, thereby improving their performance immensely. Such use of external signs to master internal psychological processes means that man masters himself as he mastered nature – that is, from outside. Human history is, then, on the one hand the history of man's growing dominion over nature through the invention of tools and the perfection of technology, and, on the other hand, it is the history of man's gradual control of the self through the invention of "the cultural technique of signs" (Vygotsky, 1928p, p. 76). The optimistic conclusion to be drawn from Vygotsky's account of human history is that one could see definite progress in two respects: modern man surpassed his precursors through (1) his superior dominion over nature through technology, and (2) his improved control over the self through "psychotechnology." It would take the Second World War and the later general environmental pollution to make people seriously doubt these claims.

Evolution and History: Conclusions

The fundamental problem for Vygotsky and other Marxists was to reconcile the Darwinian account of human evolution with the image of man as the self-conscious creator of his own destiny and the new society of prosperity and eternal bliss. Naturally, then, the problem was to give an account of the origin of mankind that acknowledged Darwin's theories but at the same time set apart human beings as something very special in the animal kingdom.

We are now in a position to summarize the way Vygotsky dealt with this problem in his cultural-historical theory. To him anthropogeny could be thought of as consisting of two, overlapping, time periods: the enormously long period of phylogenesis and the relatively short period of human history. In his opinion during phylogenesis biological evolution had led to the development of the species *Homo sapiens*, a species which consequently had many features in common with the higher animals. These common features included similarities not only in anatomy, and physiology but also in behavioral processes. The latter were based on what Vygotsky coined the "natural" or "lower" psychological processes.

The invention of primitive tools marked the onset of human history and triggered a whole set of biological and psychological developments, such as the development of a more thumb-dominated hand and the expansion of the human brain to its present size. These developments were concurrent with the development of external sign systems, such as mnemotechnical aids and speech. The use of various sign systems enabled the control over the human psyche to increase and all contemporary people make use of many of these cultural systems in their mental functioning. When sign systems were included in mental functioning Vygotsky spoke of "instrumental," "cultural," or "higher" psychological processes.

Thus, although some minor evolutionary changes had no doubt occurred during human history, for Vygotsky all contemporary peoples formed part of a single species and, as such, varied anatomically, physiologically, and to some extent psychologically within a very narrow range. It was the "natural" or "lower" psychological processes they all had in common. Nevertheless, their mental functioning differed markedly, depending on the various symbol systems used within the different cultures. Whilst having identical brains and identical lower psychological processes, people from different cultural backgrounds might show deeply different higher psychological – e.g. thought – processes.

Vygotsky argued that the human brain allowed for the processing of different sign systems, each system leading to different higher psychological processes. The sign systems themselves constituted the heritage of each culture and had to be mastered anew by each member of the culture. This process of mastering cultural devices will be described in detail in the paragraphs devoted to human ontogenesis, but some features of this process may be mentioned here. Specific to Vygotsky's thinking was the claim that the cultural devices were accessible for each new potential member of the culture as public sign (or symbol) systems that have to be mastered first through an overt act. Thus, children first learn to read aloud and only afterwards start reading to themselves (a habit that, at least in Western Europe, started only in the Middle Ages, see Geertz, 1973, pp. 76–7). Further, they first count on their fingers and only then "in their heads." They also first use external memory aids, such as knots in handkerchiefs, and only later internal ones, such as words or sentences. In general, then, Vygotsky claimed that cultural sign systems are first mastered in an overt act and only later can start functioning covertly following a complex process of internalization.

This view implied that human thinking – and higher psychological processes in general – are primarily overt acts conducted in terms of the objective materials of the common culture, and only secondarily a private matter (cf. Geertz, 1973, p. 83). The origin of all, specifically human, higher psychological processes, therefore, cannot be found in the mind or brain of an individual person but rather should be sought in the social "extracerebral" sign systems a culture provides.

Thus, Vygotsky's view of cross-cultural differences between people's mental functioning differed from several other well-known positions. Unlike his predecessors Spencer and Stanley Hall he denied the existence of any genetic differences between the members of different cultures. Unlike anthropologists such as Bastian, Tylor, and Frazer (see Klausen, 1984) – and contemporary structuralist thinkers such as Lévi-Strauss (cf. Tulviste, 1988a) – he was of the opinion that the thinking of people belonging to different cultures differed fundamentally. In his opinion both the content and form of human thinking were based on the symbolic systems available.

In so far as Vygotsky ranked the people belonging to different cultures on an imaginary evolutionary ladder it was a ranking based not on genetic or racial differences but on the supposedly different qualities of the respective cultures. He did think – together with many of his contemporaries – that it was possible to compare cultures in a global fashion and to order them on some sort of cultural ladder. Debatable as this view may be, it harmonized with the general optimistic framework of that time: the people belonging to the various "backward" cultures of the Soviet Union might be (re)educated within a relatively short period, perhaps of a few years.

So far exactly how the individual persons belonging to a specific culture master the corresponding sign systems and how these systems become internalized have not been discussed. Nor have we learned how this process effects the human mind and whether one can distinguish different degrees or phases in the "sign control" over the mind. It is these and other questions that will be addressed in discussing Vygotsky's account of child development.

Child Development: Two Lines

Vygotsky's basic claim – presented in Vygotsky, 1928p – was that in the development of each child one can distinguish two lines: the line of natural development, that is, the processes of growth and maturation; and the line of cultural development, or the mastering of various cultural means, or instruments. As was indicated above, that distinction borrowed heavily from Vagner's zoopsychological theory. Although this bifurcation of child development reminds us immediately of the biological and historical periods of development in human phylogeny, Vygotsky denied that child development did strictly mirror this phylogeny, emphasizing the deeply unique character of each of these developmental domains. One way in which the two obviously differed was the fact that children are born into a ready-made culture that they have to accept as they find it (Vygotsky and Luria, 1930a, p. 157).

In practice, it was very difficult to distinguish between the natural and cultural line of development, Vygotsky argued, but fortunately the researcher had some methods at his disposal. First, he might study the special case of "defective" children. In the case of these children we may see the difference between cultural and natural developments with more clarity, since the normal cultural instruments are not adjusted to their abnormal physiological constitution and consequently natural and cultural development will diverge (see chapter 4). Secondly, it was possible to reconstruct the way natural and cultural processes become intertwined in an experimental environment. From the specially designed method of double stimulation developments emerged that formed an excellent model of normal child development (see below).

By far the most important cultural instrument for Vygotsky was speech and he devoted a lot of energy to the study of the integration of speech with other mental processes, most importantly problem-solving, or thinking. But as has been discussed above, cultural instruments might also be maps, diagrams, abstract symbols, and the like. He believed child development was to a great extent equivalent to the mastering of these various cultural tools. In the light of this idea it was not really surprising that Vygotsky and Luria often would claim that the cultural development of the child was anticipated by a period of "natural," or "primitive" development. Apparently, around 1930 both still thought that the early period of the child's life could be largely explained by the natural line of development. Newborns and toddlers in this view had not yet appropriated sufficient cultural means and so lived a life of "primitive," nonsocial reticence. The mastering of each new cultural instrument was anticipated by a period of natural development. As some cultural instruments are mastered relatively late in childhood this led Vygotsky and Luria to characterize the performances of children of, sometimes, seven or eight years' old as testifying to their "natural" development.

This view was particularly clear in Luria's chapter in *Studies of the History of Behavior* (Vygotsky and Luria, 1930a). Referring to the findings of Freud, Piaget, and his old friend Vera Schmidt (see chapter 5), Luria sketched children as initially "organic beings," who retained their reticence for a long time, and who needed protracted cultural pressure to strengthen their tie with the world and replace their primitive, natural thinking by cultural thinking. In his own words:

> But the thing is, that he [the child] is born isolated (*otorvannym*] from [his culture], and is not immediately included in it. This inclusion in cultural conditions is not as simple as putting on new clothes: it is accompanied by profound transformations in behavior, by the formation of its new, fundamental, and specific mechanisms. That is why it is completely natural that each child will necessarily have its precultural primitive period. (Vygotsky and Luria, 1930a, p. 157)

It is evident that Luria was using a concept of culture very similar to that sketched in the discussion on human history above. In the context of the child's intellectual development culture was conceived of as an arsenal of tools, artifices, and devices that enhanced the level of performance. In this sense, Vygotsky and Luria were justified in picturing the young child as precultural: indeed, very young children do not know of the sophisticated cultural tricks Vygotsky and Luria had in mind. But in a broader sense of the word these children were, of course, "cultural" beings. They lived in culturally structured environments, experienced the personal relationships, religion, art, etc., characteristic of their own specific culture.

Rearmament

In the quotation given above Luria stated that the mastering of cultural means was not equivalent to the putting on of clothes. This was an important remark, for the examples he provided might lead one to think that the sole differences between children belonging to different cultures – and between children and adults – was to be found in the different tools they possessed. This impression was strengthened by the metaphors Luria used. In *Studies of the History of Behavior* he talked about the process of acquiring cultural means as of a process of "rearmament." In his point of view children mastered certain cultural means only to discard them as they learned new, more powerful means (the analogy with the arms race is indeed clear). But, notwithstanding these metaphors, Luria and Vygotsky also intended to say something else: people do not only possess mental tools, they are also possessed by them. Cultural means – speech in particular – are not external to our minds, but grow into them, thereby creating a "second nature." What Luria and Vygotsky meant is that mastering cultural means will transform our minds: a child who has mastered the cultural tool of language will never be the same child again (unless brain damage reduces him or her to a precultural state; see below). Thus, people belonging to different cultures would literally think in different ways, and the difference was not confined to the content of thinking but to the ways of thinking as well.

It was not really clear how this view related to the optimistic claims about re-educating primitive people to a level of culture similar to our own, for these people presumably had learnt to think in definite ways within the parameters of their own culture and could not readily give up these ways of thinking. If they could, then culture would indeed be equivalent to clothing and one could undo its influence quite easily. Perhaps here, too, there is hidden a concept of development or progress which implies that whilst one cannot undo the influence of higher cultural means, one can nevertheless easily rid people of primitive tricks and knacks. Thus, there may be some tension between the optimistic claims about the possibility of rapidly re-educating people belonging to different (sub)cultures and the idea that the appropriation of cultural means has deep consequences for the workings of mind.

Sketching the cultural development of the child as a process of armament and rearmament Luria claimed that the degree to which children have mastered cultural tools – arms in this metaphor – indicated their intellectual giftedness or backwardness. Referring to Lipmann's and Bogen's (1923) research, discussed below, Luria stated that mentally retarded children did not use tools and were, in this sense, like primitive beings. The development of higher psychological processes and, therefore, of higher intellect was based on a superior mastery of cultural instruments. This view had optimistic implications: if mental retardation was caused by insufficient tool-use then it might be possible to train these children to use cultural means more effectively, thereby improving their performance (apparently, the inability to make use of cultural means as such was not seen as based on some deep, "organic" deficiency). An implicit assumption also seems to have been that "cultural," "learned" behaviors were more easily changed than innate or genetically based behaviors. Both assumptions can be challenged, of course. Vygotsky's and Luria's approach also suggested a rather original criticism of the existing test practices. If giftedness was essentially the ability to make use of the various cultural instruments then many of the existing intelligence tests missed the point (Vygotsky and Luria, 1930a, pp. 226–31). By measuring lower psychological processes such as reaction-time and knowledge gained in school, researchers did not establish the extent to which children were capable of making use of cultural means.

Summarizing Vygotsky's and Luria's global view of child development (in 1930a) it may be concluded that in their view all children went through a stage of "natural" development, characterized by the child's inability to make use of the available cultural means. Because children of this age do not make use of these tools they could be called "primitive," in the sense of precultural. At a certain point of development, adults will start to give them cultural instruction – surprisingly, Vygotsky and Luria used the "scaffolding" metaphor in this context (1930a, p. 202), thus, anticipating Bruner's later work by several decades – which leads to a radically new way of mental functioning. The cultural means would become incorporated in the fabric of children's minds and the adults would then stop their assistance. The child had now left the "natural," precultural stage and had become a fully fledged member of the society: a cultural being.

This theory of two lines in child development was partly inspired by the Marxist view of anthropogeny sketched above and partly by the findings of psychological research. Particularly important were the findings of developmental psychology that seemed to indicate that the distinguishing trait between primates and human children was speech.

Child and Ape: the Role of Speech

Köhler's investigations of chimpanzees' tool-use had started a whole new tradition of research in child psychology. His own tentative comparisons of children's thinking with that of apes were soon followed by investigations of, among others, Bühler (1918), Lipmann and Bogen (1923), Brainard

(1930), and Guillaume and Meyerson (1930; 1931). These investigations were of paramount importance to Vygotsky, as they provided tentative answers as to the crucial differences between animal and human thinking.

Bühler (1918, pp. 285–7) was one of the first to test a child using a task borrowed from Köhler. A nine-month-old girl, whom he and his wife Charlotte Bühler studied, was encouraged to get a piece of biscuit by pulling a string attached to it, but did not make any progress during one month of testing. Notwithstanding some accidental successes the child clearly did not grasp the situation. Further investigations by Bühler (1919, p. 51) led him to posit a "chimpanzee-like age period" in early childhood. He claimed that the solutions of practical problems by children of approximately 12 months' old were very similar to those of Köhler's chimpanzees. Vygotsky and Luria (1930d/1984, p. 8) found these investigations of principal importance as they seemed to demonstrate the existence of practical, instrumental intelligence in the preverbal period of a child's development. The child's instrumental, practical thinking clearly anticipated its speech development: the act anticipates the word (cf. Wallon, 1942/1970).

The investigations performed by Guillaume and Meyerson (1930; 1931) were carefully replicated and extended versions of Köhler's original research and, thus, were not specifically carried out with the intention of comparing animal and children's thinking. Over a period of four years these investigators presented Köhler-like tasks to many different species of monkeys and apes, arriving at approximately the same results as Köhler did. Summarizing the results of a first series of experiments on detour problems, however, the authors, rather surprisingly, compared the performance of apes with that of some of the patients suffering from aphasia described by Head. Head had asked his patients to play a game of billiards and had noted that many of them were capable of making a simple stroke but failed to make complicated ones involving more balls or cushions. Guillaume and Meyerson concluded:

> To be sure, the billiard movements are in many ways more complex than the detour we have described and analyzed in the case of our apes. But the nature of the problems preventing the subject from clearly perceiving the structure of the situation seems rather analogous. In both cases it is the vision of the whole that lacks or is troubled, it is the signification of the whole that did not appear. One has said of certain patients suffering from aphasia, apraxia, or agnosia that they could not read forms in space and that they spelled them as it were. It seems that one finds something analogous with our animals. (Guillaume and Meyerson, 1930, pp. 235–6)

This conclusion – which, unfortunately, seemed wholly unconnected with the fine experimental work the researchers had done – was enthusiastically cited by Vygotsky. The fact that people who lost their speech regressed to a level that was analogous to that of chimpanzees he found very significant. It constituted indirect proof that speech played an important organizational role in the higher psychological processes of human beings. When the ability to speak was somehow lost, an individual would fall back into a pre-verbal or ape-like state of mental functioning. The intellectual performance of apes was, thus, comparable to that of pre-verbal children or aphasics (Vygotsky, 1930q/1960, pp. 426–7; Vygotsky and Luria, 1930d/1984, p. 13, p. 25).

Unlike the research done by Guillaume and Meyerson, Brainard's (1930) investigation was specifically meant to compare the "mentality of a child with that of apes." The child in question was the author's three-year-old daughter Ruth (Stanford–Binet IQ of 141), who – rewarded by the pieces of chewing gum her father stuck to ceilings and walls as Köhler's chimpanzees had been by bananas – had to solve many of the tasks Köhler presented to his chimpanzees. Brainard concluded, among other things, that

> a three-year-old has approximately the same difficulties in solving the problems as did Köhler's apes. The child has the advantage of speech and understanding of directions, whereas the apes have the advantage of longer arms, greater strength, and more experience in climbing and handling rough objects. (Brainard, 1930, p. 289)

As was to be expected, Vygotsky did not concur with this conclusion. He concluded that Brainard saw speech as a secondary, nonessential factor on a par with factors such as the length of arms. Vygotsky and Luria (1930d/1984, p. 11) argued, that the author did not see that the inclusion of speech into the problem environment was of principal importance and changed its whole psychological structure.

The most elaborate experiments with children – using Köhler's tasks – had been carried out by Bogen (see Lipmann and Bogen, 1923). This author presented children with many practical tasks trying to establish the existence of "practical intelligence" in addition to discursive "gnostic intelligence." The solution of the practical problems required an understanding of the physical structure of the situation and their own bodies, and not necessarily an explicit theoretical knowing (Lipmann and Bogen, 1923, p. 37). In this sense the subjects' knowledge of the physical properties involved was "naive," according to the authors.

Lipmann and Bogen repeatedly observed that the children's performance was not determined by the optical characteristics of the situation – as it was for Köhler's apes – but by their insight into its physical properties and these "naive physics" took priority for the children. So, in essence, the difference between apes and children could be summarized by saying that the behavior of apes was strongly determined by the visual field, whereas the behavior of children was determined by their insight into the physics of the situation and the tools used (Lipmann and Bogen, 1923, pp. 87–9). Nevertheless, Lipmann and Bogen (1923, p. 100) concluded that no *qualitative* differences between the *behavior* of children and apes had been demonstrated in their experiments.

Interestingly enough, the authors also investigated some children with lower discursive intelligence. Although their performance in the eyes of Lipmann and Bogen was sometimes comparable to that of Köhler's apes, the general finding was that children with low IQ might adequately perform practical tasks. For the authors this formed additional evidence for the suggestion that theoretical and practical intelligence were relatively independent intellectual skills (Lipmann and Bogen, 1923, pp. 86–7). It is hard to see, therefore, how Luria could refer to these experiments – in which, again, retarded children sometimes managed to use the available tools quite well – to substantiate his claim that the ability to use cultural tools or signs is indicative of children's general giftedness.

Lipmann and Bogen's book was important to Vygotsky in several ways. In the first place it formed an example of research with the conclusions of which he could not agree. To claim that in the domain of practical intelligence the sole difference between chimpanzees and children was the being determined by, respectively, either the visual field or "naive physics" was unacceptable to Vygotsky. It implied that the authors saw no principal role for speech in the solving of practical problems. For Vygotsky the solution of such problems by children of approximately eight to 12 years had to be tied to their speech development. In his view, Lipmann and Bogen's truth could not possibly be the whole truth, since speech and (practical) thinking become intertwined at a very early age and, therefore, the role of speech in problem-solving is of utmost importance. Secondly, Lipmann's and Bogen's work provided Vygotsky with the notion of a "naive" understanding of some mental process by the subjects. As will be seen below, in the following years Vygotsky would distinguish between several stages of the internalization of signs. The second of these stages – naive psychology – was directly inspired by Lipmann's and Bogen's book.

We may conclude, then, that for Vygotsky the fundamental difference between the intellectual performances of ape and child was caused by the introduction of speech and the ensuing "intellectualization" of practical intelligence. In later years (Vygotsky, 1934l/1982, pp. 264–5) he would say that the child operates neither in a visual nor in a phsyical field, but rather in a "semantic field." It was "the word [that] liberated the child of the slavish dependency Köhler observed with animals."

So far, however, we have not seen any investigations that might substantiate experimentally Vygotsky's point of view of the role of speech – or signs in general – in children's thinking processes. It is to some of these experiments in the domain of developmental psychology that we will now turn.

Mediation: The Case of Memory

One of Vygotsky's favorite examples demonstrating the separate existence of two lines in child development was that of memory. The natural line of memory development was tied to various processes of growth and maturation – the material substrate of this process had been described by Semon (1920) as the mneme – whereas the cultural line of development was tied to the mastering of various cultural tools. His immediate source of inspiration here was Binet's (1894) study of the memory of arithmetic geniuses and chess masters. Binet had found out that some of the people who earned their living by performing arithmetic computations on the stage used simple mnemotechnic tricks, such as the replacement of numbers by letters. He hypothesized that the majority of psychological operations might be simulated this way, that is, replaced by others that were only superficially similar (Binet, 1894, p. 155). This observation led Binet to distinguish between natural memory and artificial memory. The latter form of memory he characterized as the simulation of natural memory and its development Binet called "fictitious," as no "real," natural memory developed.

Vygotsky did not think Binet's choice of terminology very fortunate. In the first place he objected to the use of the term "simulation" as it suggested that cultural memory was some sort of deception. This objection may seem strange in this time of computer simulations of human thinking, but it was not in the 1930s: indeed Binet introduced the concept of mnemotechnics in the context of fraud (1894, pp. 155–8). Vygotsky argued that cultural development was no simple deceit and suggested that Binet would have agreed with him, since Binet himself had suggested the teaching of mnemotechnics in school (1894, p. 164). Secondly, Vygotsky objected to the idea that artificial, cultural development of memory was "fictitious" development. In his eyes it was a very real development, be it of a special type.

It may be noted here that Binet's distinction between "real," natural memory and "artificial," simulated memory and his "condemnation" of the latter bears some resemblance to contemporary discussions about the validity of computer simulations of human thinking. In both cases a phenomenally similar result is reached through various internal means and experts quarrel about the acceptability of these similar results as adequate proofs of ontological identity.

The experimental confirmation of the existence of two lines of memory

TABLE 9.1   Average number of words remembered for different age groups (from Leont'ev, 1931/1983, p. 54)

Age	Series			
	A	B	C	D
4–5	0.2	2.2	2.9	1.7
5–7	1.5	4.7	8.1	5.8
7–12	1.8	6.3	11.4	8.5
10–14	1.9	7.3	11.4	10.7
12–16	3.2	7.9	13.1	11.9
22–28	4.4	10.1	14.3	13.5

development was given by Leont'ev and Luria in a series of investigations carried out in the Krupskaja Academy of Communist Education (see Leont'ev, 1931; Luria, 1979, pp. 85–6; Vygotsky, 1931n/1983, pp. 239–54). The basic set-up of Leont'ev's experiments was as follows. In series A the subjects were read ten nonsense syllables which had to be reproduced immediately afterwards. In series B the subjects were read 15 words which also had to be repeated immediately afterwards. In series C the same procedure was followed, with the sole difference that the subjects were given 30 pictures of objects or scenes with the suggestion to use them in order to facilitate the reproduction process. The pictures did not directly represent the words but links between the pictures and words were relatively easy to establish. (In the terminology already used, the words to be remembered were the object stimuli, while the pictures constituted the means stimuli.) Series D was equivalent to series C, with the difference that a relation between the words and pictures was slightly more difficult to find or construct. Leont'ev (1931/1983) claimed that he and his associates had tested no fewer than 1,200 subjects, but the results given in table 9.1 were based on the performance of "only" 410 subjects (see table 9.1).

If we wish to discuss the differences between direct, "natural" memory and mediated, or "artificial" memory, then we may compare the number of words remembered in series B and C, which leads to the following results (see figure 9.2).

It can be seen that the difference between the number of words remembered in series B and C for young (pre-school) children is very small, it increases with school children and, finally, diminishes somewhat with adults. According to Vygotsky and his colleagues these curves might be explained as follows. Pre-school children were not yet capable of using the

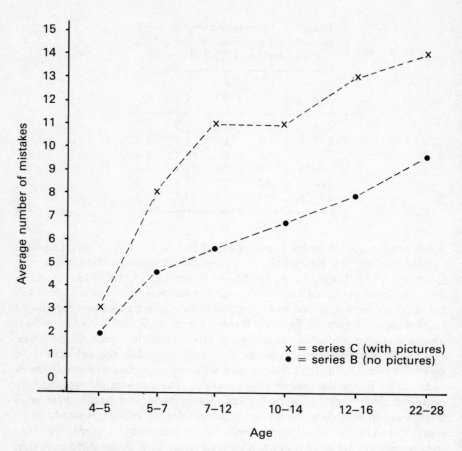

FIGURE 9.2   Direct and mediated memory for different age groups (from Leont'ev, 1931/1983, p. 55)

pictures and for these children both scores, therefore, reflected direct, or natural memory. As children grow older they acquire the ability to use the external means and the number of words remembered grows correspondingly. Finally, the curves of series B and C get closer to each other for adult subjects. This meant, in the view of Vygotsky and his associates, that both curves for adults reflected mediated remembering, the difference being that the result of series B reflected internally mediated remembering and series C externally mediated remembering. In essence, then, Vygotsky claimed that the results of both series B (no pictures) and C (with pictures) reflected unmediated remembering for young children and mediated remembering for adults. This explanation is ingenious, but in need of additional arguments. Vygotsky claimed that observations substantiated the following claims: (1) as subjects grow older they show an increasing preference for mnemotechnical means; (2) in particular adolescents and adults increasingly prefer internal mediation by means of words; and (3) these developments, however, can be encouraged by submitting younger children to a prolonged training with this type of memory tasks. Presumably, all subjects were questioned as to the internal means they used, but, unfortunately, no such data have been provided. We are left, then, with an explanation that may be plausible, but is in need of further confirmation.

In addition, one may raise several methodological objections to the way Leont'ev conducted and interpreted the experiments. One of the crucial claims for the whole reasoning is that the curves for B and C again approach each other in adolescence and adulthood. This tendency in itself was not very clearly present in Leont'ev's findings. But even if the claim is accepted, one might look for other explanations, the most obvious one being a "ceiling effect" for series C. For the performance in series C could hardly be improved – in fact, the mode for adults was 15 – whereas there was clear room for improvement in series B. Leont'ev (1931/1983, p. 60) acknowledged this possible alternative explanation and tried to disprove it, but unsuccessfully in the view of the authors of this book. In essence his reasoning went as follows: It might be suggested that lengthening series C might yield an improvement of the mean or modal performance. But lengthening a series is in a sense equivalent to enhancing its level of difficulty. To assess the possibility of a "ceiling effect" we may, therefore, look at a more difficult series. Fortunately, such a series is present in the form of series D. As the mode of series D for adults, is only 14, it may be concluded that enhancing the level of difficulty – or lengthening the series – does not influence modal performance. Therefore, the possibility of a "ceiling effect" is ruled out. In Leont'ev's eyes this reasoning settled this "strictly methodological" issue.

Another problem with Leont'ev's experiment – and with other cultural-historical experiments of this period – is that the leap from external to internal mediation had not as such been demonstrated. The hypothesized use of internal means by older subjects is not made more plausible by, for instance, discussing introspective data or protocols of subjects' verbal utterances. Finally, Leont'ev's discussion of the findings suffered from a shortcoming that was also typical of Vygotsky's and Luria's research of that period: when picturing the mental processes of children four to five years of age – and sometimes even of seven to eight years of age – as "noncultural," or "natural" they used the word "culture" in a very restricted meaning. It may be true that young children are not versatile in making use of sophisticated mnemotechnics, but they are certainly not "natural" in the sense of noncultural. For one thing, their language development has proceeded considerably at this age. As we argued before, Vygotsky and his associates used the word "cultural," whereas the term "well-educated" seems more fitting to describe the findings they actually observed.

Mediation: The Case of Attention

Vygotsky's view of human attention processes coincided with the viewpoint of Ribot (1888) to some extent. He agreed with Ribot that the attention processes of primitive man were very poorly developed, whereas in modern cultured man they had attained a very considerable degree of perfection (Leont'ev, 1932, p. 60). In Leont'ev's words (whose views at that time fully coincided with those of Vygotsky and Luria): "the transition of the savage from capricious and fitful dissipation of energy to the specific, systematic, and organized labor of man, signifies . . . the transition to a higher form of activity of attention" (Leont'ev, 1932, p. 61).

Human beings had gradually learned to master their attention by invent-ing cultural means – or signs, or instruments – to do so. Each child had to master these cultural instruments anew, a process that might take consider-able time. In Leont'ev's opinion:

> It is only at an advanced stage of individual psychological development that voluntary attention begins to take on that central importance which it possesses in the general system of behavior of the cultured adult. This most important psychological function of a modern man is the product of his social and historical development. It was born in the primitive savage out of the process of his socialization; being a product of labor activity, it is at the same time an indispensable condition for it. In this sense, this function has develo-ped historically, and not biologically. "Each subsequent generation," says Ribot, "*learns* voluntary attention from the preceding one." Thus the develop-ment of voluntary attention means, first of all, that the child acquires a series of *habits of behavior*. (Leont'ev, 1932, p. 63)

This lengthy quotation aptly shows the now familiar cultural-historical reasoning with respect to the process of attention. The experimental con-firmation of this view with regard to ontogenesis was found in several series of experiments conducted by Leont'ev and, maybe, Vygotsky himself (see Vygotsky, 1931n/1983, pp. 205–38; Leont'ev, 1932). We will restrict our treatment of these experiments to a discussion of the so-called "forbidden colors game."

Leont'ev (1932) introduced the method of double stimulation into a well-known European children's game. In the original, folk-form of this game, one child asked another a series of questions to try to make him or her reply with "yes," "no," "black," or "white," all of them "forbidden answers." The game is over (local variations exist) as soon as the person questioned inadvertently uses one of these words and the time past or the number of questions asked may serve as objective measures of the performance. In Leont'ev's version the rules of the game were as follows: the child was (1) not supposed to mention two colors (specified to be different in each series of questions) and (2) not to mention any color name twice. Each series of questions consisted of 18 questions of the following type: What color is grass? Have you been in the forest? Do you like going to school? What color is the flag? The child was asked to answer as fast as possible to these questions. In practice this turns out to be quite a difficult task for children and perfect performance is not even guaranteed in the case of adults (cf. Adams, Sciortino-Brudzynski, Bjorn, and Tharp, 1987; van der Veer, 1991). By asking each subject four series of 18 questions with different couples of forbidden colors Leont'ev (1932) established the average number of mistakes for four age groups. He then introduced a set of auxiliary means, or instruments, into the situation and repeated the whole procedure, thus establishing a level of unaided, "natural" performance (the first series of four) and a level of aided, instrumental performance (the second series of four). The instruments in question were a set of color cards given to the child with the instruction that he or she might use them in order to solve the task. In Vygotsky's (1931n/1983, pp. 208–11; 1931xx, pp. 375–81) analysis in the second part of the experiment the child faced the following situation. The questions of the experimenter formed a first series of stimuli (the object stimuli; see above) and the color cards a second series (the means stimuli; see above). Making use of this second series the child learned to master the task and the number of mistakes rapidly diminished, Vygotsky claimed. Regarding the performance of subjects of various age groups that did not make use of color cards as the "natural" performance and that with color cards as the mediated, "instrumental," or "artificial" performance Leont'ev and Vygotsky found different curves for the development of both types of attention. In fact, they claimed that the two developmental curves again formed the "parallelogram" established in their investigations of memory (see figure 9.2). Naturally, Vygotsky explained the findings along the same lines. The "natural" and "mediated" performances of pre-school children are virtually identical, because these children simply do not use the color cards. In this age group both natural and mediated scores therefore, represent a natural process of attention. School age children start making use of the color cards, so their internal operation of attention becomes externalized, and gradually the mediation procedure becomes increasingly sophisticated. Young school children, for example, will often have recourse to the color cards in a mechanical fashion, turning each color card that has been used upside down and giving color answers irrespective of the questions asked. Thus, they will not hesitate to answer "black" to the question "What color is grass?" if "black" was the next color card to be turned up. Vygotsky acknowledged that this type of mediation diminished the number of mistakes dramatically, but remarked that it went hand in glove with a lower quality of the answers. The reason was, in his opinion, that the younger school children were still dominated by the instruments they used. It was only the older school children who started to use the color cards in a more independent fashion, thus showing full mastery of the cultural instruments. This grasp of cultural means was, moreover, reflected in a still lower number of average mistakes.

Finally, the performance of adults deserves attention. For, whereas the mediated performance of school children was much better than the unmediated one, no such difference was noticeable for adults. Adult "natural," unmediated and "artificial," mediated performances virtually coincided. For Vygotsky this implied that both performances reflected the same process, that is, mediated attention. The sole difference in his view was that the adults who made use of the color cards displayed external mediation, whereas the adults who had no color cards at their disposal displayed internal mediation. This explanation echoed his explanation of the performance of pre-school children. Whereas for pre-school children the similar scores in both conditions (color cards versus no color cards) reflected the same internal process, namely unmediated attention, for adults they reflected mediated attention.

The resulting view of the development of attention was as follows. Young children are not capable of steering their attention towards making use of external means, as they have not mastered their attentional processes and are slaves to external factors. As they grow older they learn to make use of external means to steer their attention. At first this use is imperfect and the children are dominated by the cultural means available, but gradually they learn to use them at will. Finally, the cultural instruments become internalized. The use of external means diminishes and subjects start to rely on their internalized procedures. Superficially their performance now is similar to that of pre-school children, but the processes behind the performance are fundamentally different.

Crucial for this account is the notion of internalization of cultural means. What evidence, if any did Vygotsky have available for this hypothesis? Does the cross-sectional design of Leont'ev's experiments allow us to say anything about the longitudinal development of attention processes? With regard to the latter question Vygotsky argued that single-case studies had established essentially the same developmental order as found in the cross-sectional set-up. That is, he claimed that if one did repeated experiments with a pre-school child that one would observe essentially the same changes in one child within the time frame of one prolonged experiment – as in the case with memory. The child would (1) at first show incomplete and inefficient use of the color cards; (2) proceed to their use and become completely dominated by them; (3) master the efficient use of the color cards; and (4) start ignoring the color cards and relying on internal procedures (Vygotsky, 1931n/1983, p. 210). He concluded that these developmental changes reflected a process of "ingrowing" (vrashchivanie), or internalization. At the same time, however, he posited that the most effective and usual internal means of mediation were words. Adults would most probably control their attention process in the forbidden color game by mentally rehearsing the forbidden color names. This meant that the internally mediated attention process was no simple copy of the externally mediated process transposed to an internal plane. In reality subjects learned to discard the artificial external means (the color cards) and started making use of completely different internal ones (unspoken words). In a sense, then, it was somewhat mislead-ing to speak of an internalization, or "ingrowing" process as in the case of attention no single means of mediation was internalized. In later years Vygotsky would try to show that even in the case where the means of mediation did stay the same – say, in the case of external and internal speech – the fact of its internalization would cause significant transformations of its structure (see chapter 11).

Stages in the Mastering of Mind

In the years that he developed his cultural-historical theory Vygotsky maintained that the cultural development of the child went through four phases (1928p, pp. 68–71; 1929s, pp. 424–8; 1931n/1983, pp. 250–1; Vygotsky and Luria, 1930a, pp. 200–9).

The first stage he coined *the stage of natural, or primitive behavior*. In this stage – characteristic of pre-school children – subjects rely on their natural mental processes and do not use the available cultural means. In the second stage children do use the cultural means presented to them, but do not fully understand their function. Thus, in memory experiments, described above, young school children can make use of the available pictures, provided that there is a simple link between picture and the word to be remembered. Looking at the pictures before them they reproduce the words correctly. However, as soon as there is no such simple link these children are helpless. Not understanding what goes wrong they simply read aloud what they understand to be the content of the picture and assume that it will coincide with the word to be remembered. With these children there never was a real understanding that the pictures might be used actively – that is, by introducing new, nonobvious links – in order to recall the words. This stage Vygotsky called *the stage of naive psychology* by analogy with Lipmann and Bogen's (1923) notion of naive physics (see above). In his view it was a transitory phase that soon was followed by *the stage of external use of cultural means*. In this stage the child understands the possibility of active, instrumental use of cultural means and – in the case of the memory experiment – will invent links between pictures and words, or select the appropriate pictures from a larger set. According to Vygotsky this stage would soon give way for the final, fourth stage of cultural development, that is, *the stage of internal use of cultural means*. In this fourth stage the external use of instruments is replaced by internal mental activity. Thus, in the case of Vygotsky's and Leont'ev's memory experiments children would first use the pictures in order to reproduce a series of words, but as they were asked to reproduce this series again and again they finally stopped consulting the pictures. In Vygotsky's view the whole series of pictures had been internalized and now formed an internal device to recall the series of words, much as for memory experts a well-learned list of words, or a map of some familiar building, may serve as a vehicle for the recall of other material.[3]

However, this type of internalization – where the set of external means is internalized as a whole – formed only one of many types, Vygotsky (1928p, pp. 70–1) claimed. In many motor skills we may observe another type of internalization: the so-called "stitch" type. In choice–reaction-time experiments, for example, where subjects have to press different buttons corresponding with different stimuli, one may observe this type of "ingrowing." At first, subjects will speak appropriate words between stimulus and response in order to facilitate the right choice. After prolonged exercise, these intermediate links fall out, and the reaction becomes automatic. Thus, in Vygotsky's analysis, the intermediate words, or external cultural means, will disappear as the reaction-time process becomes automatic and internalized, much as stitches can be removed after two parts of tissue have grown together.

In his own view (Vygotsky, 1928p, p. 71) the positing of these and other possible forms of internalization, or ingrowing, and the sketch of the four stages of cultural development had only a very provisional character. But he did claim that as a general rule the cultural development of the child would

---

[3]It may be noted that Vygotsky himself used these techniques successfully and displayed his abilities during lectures to his students by memorizing rapidly long lists of numbers (see Puzyrej, 1986a, p. 77).

proceed from no use, via external use, to internal use of cultural means. It would be another Soviet psychologist, Gal'perin, who would devote his long career to the investigation of this claim.

The Control of Mind and Rational Man

With the research of the development of mediated memory and attention Vygotsky attempted to demonstrate one of the basic tenets of cultural-historical theory: man masters his own mental processes by introducing new, artificial elements into a situation. The basic structure of this procedure Vygotsky clarified several times (e.g. Vygotsky, 1931n/1983, p. 67) by discussing the story of Buridan's ass. Supposedly the Dutch philosopher Buridan (1295–1358) had first described the sad situation of an ass caught between two equal bales of hay: not knowing which bale to choose the poor animal died of starvation. However, as Vygotsky rightly remarked, this vignette cannot be found in Buridan's writings. There is the story of a hungry and thirsty dog that does not know what to do first: to drink or to eat. In its turn this situation was most probably borrowed from Aristotle, who described a man finding himself in the same awkward position (Krop, 1988, p. 39).

Vygotsky may have learned about Buridan's ass when reading his favorite philosopher Spinoza, who referred to this problem in his *Ethics* (1677/1955, p. 123). To him the interest of this rather artificial problem of making a rational choice between two identical alternatives – a problem that was also analyzed by Schopenhauer and phrased in poetical terms by Dante in his *Divina Commedia* – was in the way a human being would solve the problem. Contemporary psychological approaches had done little to solve this theoretical problem. Pavlov had restricted his research to animals, experimentally demonstrating that dogs in a similar situation fall into a stage of neurosis or apathy. Behaviorists, according to Vygotsky, would predict starvation for human beings too, as behavior in their view was fully determined by external stimuli and these were of equal strength in a Buridanian situation.[4] Vygotsky found the first indication of the way human beings in reality solve these problems in literature: Tolstoy, picturing Pierre Bezukhov's indecision as to whether to join the army has him play a game of patience, the outcome of which would decide the hero's future. For

---

[4]It is interesting to note that the Buridanian ass already surfaced in Vygotsky's earlier writings (Vygotsky, 1926i, pp. 174–5; Varshava and Vygotsky, 1931, p. 35). In these books, however the problem is only stated and no possible solution for human beings is presented, since Vygotsky had not yet developed the instrumental approach.

Vygotsky (1931n/1983, p. 67) this was an excellent example of human decision-making: human beings take recourse to artificially created stimuli. It is the introduction of some artificial stimulus, or sign, into the situation that tips the balance in favor of one or the other decision. In this connection Vygotsky discussed several of Thurnwald's and Lévy-Bruhl's findings mentioned above (e.g. primitive counting systems and memory aids) in order to show that this tendency had its precursors in the history of mankind.

As was to be expected, Vygotsky attempted to create an experimental analog of the problem of rational choice between two equivalent alternatives, and, also predictably, the description of these experiments was, impossibly vague (see Vygotsky, 1931n/1983, pp. 274–8) and one can only guess to what they really amounted. Apparently, children were encouraged to make a choice between two series of equally attractive or unattractive series of actions. It was then suggested to them that they might cast lots to decide which series of actions to choose. Sometimes, also, Vygotsky waited for the spontaneous throwing of dice or, alternatively, explicitly instructed the children to do this. In all cases he was interested in the psychological differences that the introduction of the dice would bring about. Vygotsky claimed that the experimental data confirmed his theoretical expectation, that is, that the introduction of artificial elements – dice – radically transformed the psychological nature of the choice process. Rather surprisingly, this time he provided no description of possible developmental sequences in the ability to make use of these artificial elements.

It is not difficult to see that Vygotsky's treatment of the development of the higher psychological processes and his emphasis on the growing control of the human mind owed a great deal to Spinoza. Both thinkers displayed a certain degree of rationalism, or intellectualism, that is, both shared the ideal of rational man whose intellectual functions (speech, thinking) controlled to a large degree the whole personality. Spinoza in his *Ethics*, particularly opposed the view of man as a slave to his affects, or passions. Seeking a way for man to control his passions he emphasized the mind's capacity to understand, for when the intellect had clear and distinct knowledge of these passions, it would gradually learn to control them. The initially rather vague and primitive passions would eventually be understood by the intellect and submitted to its control. Spinoza claimed that acting in the real sense of the word implied intellectually understanding of what we are doing. It was this idea of the growing control over the emotions by the intellect and the resulting mastering of our behavior that was also clearly present in Vygotsky's cultural-historical theory. Of course, Vygotsky extended the notion of intellectual control to all other, initially primitive, psychological processes. But his assertion that we should strive for the "intellectualization of all psychological functions" (Vygotsky, 1932i/1982,

p. 415) was essentially in line with Spinoza's thinking. Leont'ev's words quoted above formed a beautiful illustration of this thinking: the "capricious" and "fitful" dissipation of energy by "savages" was opposed to the "organized" and "systematic" labor of rational modern man. Rational man acquired dominion over his primitive mental process by making use of various cultural tools.

The analogy between Spinoza's and Vygotsky's view of man can be extended even further (see Van der Veer, 1984) by pointing out that they shared a notion of the role of tools in the growing dominion over nature and primitive mind. Consider, for example, the following words by Spinoza:

> But as men at first made use of the instruments supplied by nature to accomplish very easy pieces of workmanship, laboriously and imperfectly, and then, when these were finished, wrought other things more difficult with less labour and greater perfection; and so gradually mounted from the simplest operations to the making of tools, and from the making of tools to the making of more complex tools, and freshs feats of workmanship, till they arrived at making, with small expenditure of labour, the vast number of complicated mechanisms which they now possess. So, in like manner, the intellect, by its native strength, makes for itself intellectual instruments, whereby it acquires strength for performing other intellectual operations, and from these operations gets again fresh instruments, or the power of pushing its investigations further, and thus gradually proceeds till it reaches the summit of wisdom. (Spinoza, 1677/1955, p. 12)

Thus, Spinoza combined his ideal of rational man with a notion of intellectual tools that was not unlike Vygotsky's. What was truly original in Vygotsky's investigations was, of course, that he tried to demonstrate empirically how each and every individual child would master this process of the growing intellectualization of his or her primitive behavior.

We may conclude, then, that Vygotsky defended an image of rational man who had learned to submit his primitive drives and emotions to the control of the intellect. Unlike prehistoric man, contemporary "savages," and Western children, the modern well-educated adult had fully mastered his behavior by making use of the means his culture supplied. In chapter 14 we shall see how Vygotsky in later years attempted to elaborate this idea for the case of emotional development relying heavily on Spinoza and arguing against the ideas of the latter's contemporary Descartes.

10
The Expeditions to Central Asia

Vygotsky's and Luria's ample use of the work of foreign ethnographers to develop their cultural-historical theory was described in chapter 9. The central idea that the lower psychological processes would be the same for all living people while the higher psychological processes would differ between persons belonging to different cultures was based on the evidence gathered by Thurnwald, Werner, Lévy-Bruhl, Durkheim, and others (Vygotsky and Luria, 1930a). It was only natural – in view of the sometimes doubtful nature of the ethnographic evidence – that Vygotsky and Luria felt the need to witness these cognitive similarities and differences themselves in a carefully designed psychological study. It was because of this that the idea of a psychological expedition to some "primitive" region of the Soviet Union was born. According to Luria (1971, p. 266; 1974, p. 3; 1976, p. v) the initiative for such an expedition was taken by Vygotsky.[1]

Vygotsky was informed about the expeditions' results through the detailed reports – five of them in the case of the first expedition – and protocols that Luria sent to Moscow. There is no doubt that he was extremely glad with the results that Luria obtained during the first expedition in 1931. In several letters to Luria he expressed his unrestrained enthusiasm exclaiming that the results were "marvelous" and "infinitely important." Vygotsky believed that the new theory now had proven itself in experimental practice (Vygotsky in letters to Luria, dated June 20, and July 11, 1931). To convey to the reader Vygotsky's feelings of joy and triumph we can do no better than to quote a fragment of one of his letters to Luria.

[1]This claim is not really confirmed by their personal correspondence. Vygotsky, for example, wrote to Luria "I consider *your* theme a deeply interesting one, one that can be carried out and that will bring our cause further" (Vygotsky in a letter to Luria, dated June 12, 1931; emphasis added).

I have already written to you in Samarkand and Fergana about the *enormous and incomparable* impression that your reports and protocols made on me. In our investigation this is an enormous, decisive step, a *turning point* towards the new point of view. But in *any* context of European investigations such an expedition would be an *event* (Vygotsky in a letter to Luria, dated August 1, 1931; original emphasis)

Vygotsky himself – probably because of his frail health – did not participate in either of the expeditions and the burden of their organization fully rested on Luria.

It was decided (possibly Vygotsky had made some useful contacts during his earlier stay in Tashkent in 1929; see the introduction to part II) – to visit several remote villages (*kishlaks*) in the Soviet republic of Uzbekistan and during the summers of 1931 and 1932 the expeditions – preceded by lengthy seminars – took place (Luria, 1931b; 1931c; 1932b; 1932d; 1933b; 1934; 1935c). Luria felt that both the choice of the location (small villages that remained "primitive" and "underdeveloped under the influence of the Islamic religion") and the time period (the period of collectivization of Soviet agriculture) were particularly suitable for conducting ethnographic research. Because Luria stressed these aspects of the project (1974, pp. 3–4; 1976, pp. v–vi) we do well to reflect for a moment upon the historical and political situation as it was at the time.

The Historical and Political Background

From 1929 to 1932 the Soviet authorities conducted two operations concurrently that were called "the collectivization of agriculture" and the "elimination of the kulaks as a class." The idea was that "backward individual farming" would be replaced by farming in collective farms (*kolkhozes*) and that the property of independent, "prosperous" farmers (*kulaks*) – who were supposedly exploiting their less prosperous fellow farmers – would be impounded by the state.

That the *kulaks* existed and that they had to be exterminated as a class had been an article of faith in the Soviet state from its inception. Marxist theory seemed to demand the belief that within the peasantry various antagonistic classes were exploiting each other in most inhumane ways. Unfortunately, even the great Lenin was unable to give an even roughly definition of the nature of a *kulak* (Conquest, 1988, p. 44) and Stalin – who intensified the whole monstrous "dekulakization" operation – was no improvement in this respect. It thus remained rather unclear who belonged to the dangerous class of *kulaks*. The concept included, for example, anyone

In the spring of 1929 Vygotsky lectured for several months in Tashkent.

who employed hired labor, but also people who owned some property, such
as a few horses or cows or a house. To make matters simpler the authorities
introduced the concept of *kulak* henchmen (*podkulachniki*) for those who
owned less than was to be expected for an inveterate *kulak* (Heller and
Nekrich, 1986, pp. 234–5). Using this new twin concept virtually everybody belonging to the peasantry could now be accused of being either a
kulak or a *kulak* henchman. Having thus solved all the conceptual difficulties concerning the definition, the authorities, under the firm guidance of
Lenin and Stalin (from 1924) did not hesitate about the right policy to
follow: the *kulaks* were capitalists of some sort and had to be liquidated to
the last man (and woman, and child). This liquidation took various forms:
many were deported and died *en route* or in the uninhabitable places of
relocation; others were shot immediately or died of starvation; still others
fled and were arrested and shot or sentenced to hard labor in concentration
camps; finally, many peasants actively resisted the government policy and
died in armed conflicts with the military (Heller and Nekrich, 1986, pp.
222–44). The result was a genocide of unsurpassed scale – comparable only
to that of the Jews and Armenians – that has only recently been described in

all its monstrous details (Conquest, 1988). It is now estimated that it resulted in the death of approximately 14 million people (Conquest, 1988, pp. 444–6) in the country as a whole and it was the population of Soviet Central Asia which suffered a disproportionately high loss, for many were forced to discontinue their nomadic life of cattle-breeding and to grow grain in soil that was utterly unsuitable for that purpose.

It was the brilliant proletarian writer and supreme humanist Gorky who found the words to justify this mass murder at the time: "If the enemy does not surrender, he must be destroyed" (Heller and Nekrich, 1986, p. 236). The reaction of one of his morally less talented colleagues, the Nobel laureate Pasternak, was rather different: having witnessed the desolation in the *kolkhozes* he fell ill and felt unable to write for a whole year (Conquest, 1988, p. 21). The collectivization and dekulakization not only resulted in the death of millions of people: it also had a disastrous influence on agriculture and it is no exaggeration to state that the country has not yet recovered from the whole collectivization process. Conquest mentions that in Central Asia one-third of the horses, half the cattle, and two-thirds of the sheep and goats died as a result of the collectivization campaign and the ensuing famine (1988, p. 284).

Seen against this background Luria's description of the circumstances under which he conducted his cross-cultural research seems rather insensitive, to say the least. Following the official version of the historical events he remarked that

> Before the revolution, the people of Uzbekistan lived in a backward economy . . . When the socialist revolution eliminated dominance and submission as class relations, people oppressed one day enjoyed a free existence the next . . . Uzbekistan became a republic with collective agricultural production . . . The period we observed included the beginnings of collectivization . . . Because the period studied was one of transition, we were able to make our study to some extent comparative. (Luria, 1976, pp. 13–14)

"A period of transition"! One wonders what Luria was thinking when he wrote these lines. Obviously, when he first published the results of the expeditions to Central Asia in book form (Luria, 1974; 1976) it still was not possible for Soviet citizens to publish realistic descriptions of the events that took place from 1929 to 1932 (or, for that matter, in any other period of Soviet history). But if he really condemned the collectivization and/or dekulakization campaign he might have refrained from publishing his text – publication had already been delayed by more than 40 years! (see below) – or have tried to find more sensitive ways to mention the subject. (It would seem, however, that Luria was not in each and every respect a sensitive man:

years before he had developed a lie detector (Luria, 1928c; 1928e) and, with Leont'ev, tested it during the purge of the students and personnel at the Moscow University (Luria, 1979, pp. 35–36/201–202); he also for many years preserved in his study the brains of a former close friend (in an alcohol jar) because of their interesting form).

It may also be that Luria until 1974 truly believed – as he probably did in the early 1930s (see Koffka's account below) – in the justice and functionality of both collectivization and dekulakization and, thus, embodied a characteristic example of the mixture of blind faith in one's own cherished dogmas and moral insensitivity towards nonbelievers typical of so many religious people in so many, far too many, historical periods.

Koffka's Participation and the Great Wall

From Luria we learn that the following people accompanied him on both expeditions to Uzbekistan: Professor P. I. Leventuev of Samarkand; E. N. Mordkovich and F. N. Shemyakin from Moscow; and Kh. Ashrafi and A. A. Usmanov of the Uzbek State Academy of Education (1931b, p. 383; 1934, p. 255). Different researchers completed this group in the two expeditions to form research groups of 10 to 15.

Luria wanted very much to make the second expedition to Uzbekistan an international undertaking and wrote to the Gestalt psychologists Köhler, Lewin, and Koffka to ask them to participate. He also was thinking of inviting the ethnographer Thurnwald (Luria in a letter to Köhler, dated December 3, 1931). Because Köhler was unable to participate in 1932 Luria decided to organize another big expedition in the summer of 1933, regarding the expedition of 1932 as an opportunity to replicate the results of the first expedition and a preparation for the third (Luria in a letter to Köhler, dated March 6, 1932), but this third expedition never materialized (see also chapter 16) and Köhler, Lewin and Thurnwald did not participate in the second expedition.

Koffka, however, accepted the invitation and his account of the expedition complements Luria's very well. Having travelled to Europe from Northampton in Massachusetts, and having waited in Berlin for the necessary papers Koffka arrived in Moscow at the end of May 1932. He met Kolbanovsky, Luria, Eisenstein, and Vygotsky there. The latter served as his interpreter when, on May 29, Koffka gave his lecture "The overcoming of mechanicism in modern psychology" (published in *Psikhologija*; see Koffka, 1932). Koffka's account of this event – the lecture was attended by approximately 300 people – is rather amusing:

Most of them understood German, but since some did not, Professor Vygotsky, a most charming man, acted as my interpreter. I talked for about 5 or 10 minutes, and then he gave the most fluent translation you can imagine. He talked much more fluently than I, and it seemed to me for a much longer time. (Harrower, 1983, p. 145)

Several days later Koffka and the Moscovite participants of the expedition left by train for Uzbekistan and by the end of June the actual expedition began. Unfortunately, after several weeks of research, Koffka started to suffer from severe attacks of fever — he himself suspected at first that he had malaria — and had to return to Moscow. Only by early August was he well enough to continue his journey to Berlin.

Looking back upon his adventure in the Soviet Union several years later Koffka was, above all, struck by the uniform world-view of his Soviet fellow researchers:

The strongest impression I gained from being with these different people in the train was the amazing uniformity of their outlook. It was as though all of them, my colleagues included, had gone through the same school in which they had learned the same lessons, lessons in history, economics, politics, and philosophy. The fundamental conviction colored their views on all subjects, and this conviction had all the power but also the rigidity of a dogmatic faith. Theirs was the proletarian state heralding the dawn of real culture, while beyond the Soviet border bourgeois civilization was still bending all its efforts, even their science and art, to the profit of capitalism and thereby perverting them ... The uniformity of intellectual and emotional outlook is one of the strongest memories ... It has its great side; it gives to the people a wonderful enthusiasm which is ever willing to make any personal sacrifice. But for a mind like my own, brought up in the tradition of the West, it was not only utterly alien, but actually oppressive. It was not that I had to guard my tongue; on the contrary, I gained the distinct impression that the people with whom I talked liked to get my spontaneous reactions. Neither do I believe that these people said what they were "supposed" to say. I believe I should not have felt the oppression quite so much, and certainly not in the same way, had it been like this. What confounded me was that they all were honest and yet uniform. Talking to them was like running against a stone wall. To have built this wall in a relatively short time is perhaps one of the greatest achievements of the Soviet government — however negatively one may value it. (Koffka, in Harrower, 1983, pp. 159–60)

The Topics of Research and Some Results

The goal of both expeditions was to study the mental processes of the native population during the period of "transition" that was sketched above. The idea was that the higher mental processes would change under the influence of the social reforms carried through – above all under the influence of schooling – whereas the lower processes would remain the same. To test this idea Luria and his colleagues investigated, among other topics, perception, concept-formation, causal thinking, religious thinking, and the ability to perform numerical operations. The first expedition concentrated on adult subjects, whereas the second also included children among the subjects.

It is impossible to summarize the data gathered by the investigators in this paragraph – the first expedition alone resulted in 600 protocols of individual experiments – and, in fact, it is clear that even Luria's own monograph (1974; 1976) dedicated to the two expeditions presents only a fraction of the data. In that book he does not refer at all, for example, to the study of religious thinking that was carried out. We will, therefore, limit ourselves to a concise discussion of only two topics: the perception of illusions and the classification of objects.

Optical Illusions

Luria's study of visual illusions was directly influenced by Gestalt psychology. Gestalt psychologists had claimed that the Gestalt perceptual principles were the result of enduring characteristics of the brain and not bound up with culturally transmitted meanings of objects. However, Vygotsky and Luria – following Rivers (1901) – assumed that at least some of these visual processes partially rested upon semantic, interpretative processes, and would, therefore, differ between subjects belonging to different cultures. Cole has related that Luria in one of their first experiments demonstrated the virtual absence of classical visual illusions, a result that he supposedly wired excitedly to Vygotsky ("The Uzbekis have no illusions!"; Cole in Luria, 1979, p. 213)[2] and reported to his Gestalt colleagues. Reality, however, was slightly more complex that this story suggests. First, the results of the first experiments were rather mixed and Luria's letters to his German colleagues were rather cautious. Secondly, Koffka's experiments in the second expedition disagreed partially with the results found in the first expedition. The question arises, then, as to what evidence with respect to optical illusions Luria and his colleagues really found in the two expeditions.

In a letter to Köhler (dated December 3, 1931) Luria mentioned that one group of visual illusions – e.g. the Müller-Lyer illusion – was present in practically all the subjects tested, whereas other illusions – which Luria

---

[2]From Vygotsky's correspondence we learn that he first heard about the visual illusion results through one of Luria's letters (Vygotsky in a letter to Luria, dated June 20, 1931).

suspected depended upon the interpretation of perspective in the two-dimensional figures – were far less prevalent. The absence of the latter illusions Luria explained by referring to the fact that these people were not familiar with perspective in drawings. Finally, Luria mentioned that some other visual illusions – such as the Poggendorf illusion – "are virtually absent in more primitive subjects." He produced a table (also present in Luria, 1976, p. 44, although with some of the numbers changed) that showed that the tendency to succumb to a number of optical illusions decreased as the degree of "primitivism" of the subjects changed, that is, that less "primitive" people were more prone to succumb to these optical illusions. The table proved in his opinion that some illusions (e.g. the Müller-Lyer illusion) probably have a physiological basis, whereas others depend upon the degree of cultural education of the subject. In his letter to Köhler he added that these results were not yet quite clear to him as various studies by other researchers had demonstrated these illusions "in young children and even in animals".

It is interesting to compare these initial and rather cautious conclusions regarding the cultural basis of optical illusions with the later report by Koffka (in Luria, 1934/1935, p. 257) and Luria's (1974; 1976) own monograph published four decades later. The monograph essentially repeats the conclusions he reached 40 years before (omitting the doubts regarding the data that he had originally) stating that it may be considered proven that "even relatively simple processes involved in perception of colors and geometrical shapes depend to a considerable extent on the subjects' practical experience and their cultural milieu" (Luria, 1976, p. 45). Koffka, however, during his short-lived participation in the second expedition to Uzbekistan, reached a rather different conclusion. In his own words:

> The following results may be considered proved: With very few exceptions the men and women examined by us succumbed to the optical illusions – of which a great variety was shown – just as we do. Quantitative measurements of the Müller-Lyer and Poggendorf patterns yielded a slightly smaller amount of these illusions than control experiments with European psychologists. The exceptions, which were very rare in this expedition, but had been much more frequent in the first, are easily explained by the attitude of the testees toward the experimenter. Naive, social subjects who treated the experimenter on a footing of equality and did not regard the experiment as a test of their ability had the illusion without exception. Only when the subjects were suspicious, staring a long time at the patterns before making their judgments, the illusions failed to appear with some though by no means with all the patterns, in accordance with well-known facts. Similarly, it could be proved with several very simple figures like Mach's book, Necker's cube, Schröder's staircase, that plane perspective drawings may compel the perception of a tridimensional

object. If the pattern is more complex and has greater representative value, the intended tridimensional effect, as a rule, does not appear, although we see these figures as tridimensional. Thus the opposite report of previous investigators can be explained, according to which Uzbeks, not reached by modern culture, cannot perceive perspective. (Koffka in Luria, 1934, p. 257)

We thus see that Koffka on the basis of his data flatly denied Luria's initial conclusions: the "primitive" Uzbekis did succumb to optical illusions like the Poggendorf illusion and were able to see perspective in drawings. It is rather unfortunate – quite apart from the value of both Luria's and Koffka's conclusions about the cultural and physiological basis of illusions – that Luria (1974; 1976) ignored these conflicting interpretations in his monograph. Discussion of Koffka's failure to replicate his initial results might have started an interesting debate on the various ways of conducting this type of ethnographic research – Koffka's remark about the role of the subjects' attitude toward the experimenter, for example, was quite relevant (see Kloos, 1991) – and would have countered the effects of the beautiful but oversimplified story about the Uzbekis not having illusions and the like.

The Classification of Objects

In order to investigate the "primitive" ways of classifying objects Luria essentially followed the same procedure as in the study of perception. Subjects were divided into four groups of different "educational level" or "degree of primitivism" and these groups were presented various tasks. Performance as a function of group adherence was then measured. The following subject groups were discerned by Luria (1976; the designation of these same groups given in his letter to Köhler in 1931 are in parentheses): (1) Ichkari women living in remote villages who were illiterate and not involved in modern social activities ("very backward"); (2) peasants in remote villages, who continued to maintain an individualistic economy [sic], to remain illiterate, and to involve themselves in no way with socialized labor [sic] ("peasants from very primitive villages"); (3) women who attended short-term courses with no formal education and almost no literacy training ("wives of illiterates . . . culturally backward"); (4) Active *kolkhoz* workers ("actively involved in society; mainly from collectivized villages"); and (5) women students admitted to a teachers' training college.

This list of subject groups is rather interesting. It can be seen how in the 1970s Luria carefully avoided using the terms "primitive" and "backward," terms which he used freely in his letters to Köhler and in other publications of the early 1930s, such as his chapter in *Studies of the History of Behavior* (Vygotsky and Luria, 1930a, p. 123; p. 154), where he spoke of Uzbek women as "standing on a low level of cultural development", that is, a "very primitive level."

The list of subject groups and the procedure followed raises also several questions. In the first place, it would be interesting to know how Luria actually ranked his subjects on a "ladder of cultural development" or "primitivism." Nowhere in his book do we find clarification of his assumptions in ranking these groups – although he does mention schooling and participation in the *kolkhoz* as relevant factors – and one only hopes that he did not deduce this ranking from the performances on the various tasks measured. But even supposing that the distinction and ranking of various subject groups were nonproblematic a number of methodological questions remain. It is unclear, for example, whether the groups were matched for possibly relevant intervening variables such as age of the subject. We may also safely assume that the investigators could not follow a double-blind procedure, that is, they surely knew to which group the subjects belonged they were questioning. Finally, it is not altogether clear to what extent the investigators tried to take account of social factors such as the one mentioned by Koffka in the preceding paragraph. In view of these possibly confounding factors, Luria's results at best formed an interesting starting point for further research.

What did Luria and his collaborators find with respect to the classification of objects? The subjects were presented with 19 geometrical figures of varying form. Their first task was to name these figures. Luria distinguished concrete, object-oriented names and categorical names and he found that only the "most culturally advanced" group of subjects named geometrical figures by categorical names such as circle, triangle, etc. (1976, p. 32). The most "primitive" subjects designated all the figures with the names of objects: a circle, for example, would be called a plate, watch, moon, etc. (see table 10.1).

Probably as a result of these different naming attitudes, Luria found quite varying results when he asked the subjects to combine similar figures into

TABLE 10.1   Percentage and type of naming geometrical figures (after Luria, 1976, p. 34)

Group	Number of subjects	Percentage of object-oriented names given
Ichkari women	18	100.0
Women in pre-school courses	35	85.3
Collective-farm activists	24	59.0
Women at teachers' training colleges	12	15.2

TABLE 10.2 Classification of geometrical figures (percentages) (after Luria, 1976, p. 40)

Group	Number of subjects	Failure to classify	Object-oriented names	Classification	
				In terms of individual graphic features	In terms of geometrical categories
Ichkari women	10	21.8	20.4	57.8	0
Women in pre-school courses	35	18.3	8.4	55.0	18.3
Collective-farm activists	24	12.8	11.6	30.8	44.8
Women at teachers' training colleges	10	0	0	0	100

groups. The most "primitive" subjects refused to combine figures belonging to the same geometrical category into one group, seeing them as very concrete objects that had nothing to do with each other. Culturally more "advanced" subjects had no problem whatsoever with this task (see table 10.2).

Luria concluded that these results show

> the extent to which the perception of subjects who have attended school where they employ abstract geometrical concepts differs from that of subjects who have grown up under the influence only of concrete object-oriented practical activities ... The data show how the principle of classifying geometrical figures varies with changing cultural level. (1976, p. 39)

It was accepted, of course, that abstract, categorical classification was superior to and should replace concrete, object-oriented classification – an assumption that was very common in the 1930s, but which is criticized by some researchers today (e.g. Sacks, 1989, pp. 121–2).

The results found by Luria and his colleagues have been replicated by modern research, but the results have been interpreted by various researchers in various ways (Berry and Dasen, 1974; Cole and Scribner, 1974). Cole (in Luria, 1976, p. xv), for instance, does not believe that the Uzbekis in Luria's investigation really acquired new modes of thought, but rather is inclined to interpret the data as the result of "changes in the application of previously available modes to the particular problems and contexts represented by the experimental setting." This seems a view that is far less radical than Vygotsky's and Luria's, who did imply that cultural changes would lead to transformations of both the content and form of thinking (see chapters 9 and 11). The background to Cole's interpretation is that he is skeptical of applying developmental theories cross-culturally. It would seem, however, that one can claim that different cultural practices lead to different modes of thinking – some of which are from some point of view more powerful than others – without succumbing to an "ethnocentrist" view as defended by Vygotsky and Luria (see also chapter 9). Such a point of view, in which the existence of "universals" in the higher realms of the human mind is de-emphasized, has been defended recently in a remarkable book by the Estonian psychologist Tulviste (1988a).

Why the Results Were not Published at the Time

Luria and his fellow researchers conducted their research in the summers of 1931 and 1932 and Luria completed his monograph about the results of the expedition by the end of 1933 or the beginning of 1934 (see Luria, 1974, p. 4, where he mentions that Vygotsky died soon after its completion), but the monograph remained unpublished for forty years. At the time Luria only published some short overviews in foreign journals and publication in the Soviet Union was probably restricted to the transactions of the expedition (Luria, 1931b, p. 383). One wonders why he publication of the results was delayed for such a long period.

One of the main reasons must have been Razmyslov's (1934) paper – more fully discussed in chapter 16 – in which the conclusions drawn on the basis of the expeditions to Uzbekistan were the subject of a violent attack. Although Razmyslov made some critical remarks concerning Vygotsky's views in this respect – Vygotsky did not understand or did not wish to understand that one cannot find the thinking in complexes, established by Lévy-Bruhl in primitive peoples, in contemporary Uzbekis, and in his lecture entitled "On the methodical foundations of the study of culturally unique peoples" he wrongly tried to prove the existence of forms of primitive thinking among the formerly suppressed nationalities (Razmyslov, 1934, p. 82) – he directed his main criticism against Luria, stating that Vygotsky did not take part in the expedition and was not directly involved with the work done (Razmyslov, 1934, p. 84).

Razmyslov's main criticism was that Luria did not adequately describe the enormous progress that had been made in Uzbekistan through the introduction of the social reforms. Instead of emphasizing the creation of the "new man" with his new attitude towards labor and his new communist consciousness Luria tried to show that the members of the kolkhozes were not capable of conceptual thinking and failed to conceive abstracts from concrete situations (Razmyslov, 1934, pp. 82–3). This accusation had some factual background. Indeed, as we have seen (see tables 10.1 and 10.2), Luria had presented data that seemed to prove that even kolkhoz activists still frequently designated geometrical figures as objects and did not always combine these figures into abstract categories. For Razmyslov this was an insult to the politically highly conscious kolkhoz activists. To make things worse he was able to produce some protocols[3] that supposedly showed that Luria and his collaborators deliberately ignored politically highly intelligent answers and denoted these as inferior. Thus, according to one protocol reproduced in Razmyslov (1934, p. 83) an Uzbek subject – and, more importantly, the illiterate president of a kolkhoz – was encouraged to imagine a baj (rich peasant) with miserable cattle. The subject refused to imagine this situation arguing that bajs always had excellent cattle, and that

---

[3]Provided to him by the Moscovite participant in the expeditions, F. N. Shemyakin who thus "betrayed" his colleagues.

if they did not have it, then they had been dekulakized by the Soviet authorities and, consequently, were no longer *bajs*. According to Razmyslov, Luria concluded that this subject refused to accept hypothetical premises and thought concretely (see also chapter 4). Another protocol given by Razmyslov – although less political – showed the same problem: people were designated as "situational" or "concrete" thinkers as soon as they refused to speak about hypothetical situations suggested by the experimenters. In itself such results indeed pose a serious problem – do such refusals betray an (culturally based) inability or rather an (equally culturally based) unwillingness to think hypothetically? But what made Razmyslov's paper politically highly dangerous was that he was able to show how an honest *kolkhoz* president, who reasoned perfectly logically about the (non)existence of *bajs* after the "dekulakization" campaign, could be portrayed as a limited concrete thinker. It would seem that Razmyslov's (and the Communist Party's) concept of cultural advancement – based on the raising of political consciousness – and Luria's concept of cultural development – based on the replacement of situational, concrete thinking by abstract thinking – were at variance here. It will come as no surprise, then, that Razmyslov (1934, pp. 83–4) concluded that Luria's research had been pseudoscientific, reactionary and anti-Marxist.

In our interpretation, then, the point of Razmyslov's paper was not so much that Luria had insulted the Uzbekis or touched on the sensitive issue of national minorities (Cole in Luria, 1976, p. xiv) – indeed the party officials have always defended a crude form of Russian chauvinism – but that he had undermined the sacred idea of collectivization by pointing out that *kolkhoz* activists were not yet capable of abstract thinking. It is ironic that Luria, who even forty years later was still praising collectivization, became the victim of such criticism.

Razmyslov's attack was sufficiently strong to make immediate publication of the results of the expeditions to Central Asia unwise and, perhaps, impossible. Later events in Soviet psychological science – the Paedology Decree of 1936 (see chapter 12) – would prevent publication for several more decades.

11

The Universe of Words: Vygotsky's View on Concept-Formation

Vygotsky's interest in the processes of concept-formation and concept development became apparent around 1927 and continued until his death in 1934. One can discern several phases in his thinking on this subject, notably, a first phase connected with replications and extensions of work done by Ach and his followers, and a second phase connected with replicating and extending the work of Piaget. Vygotsky's writings on concept-formation belong to the better-known part of his work (e.g. Brushlinsky, 1968; Berg, 1970; Rissom, 1985), but they are seldom understood in an adequate historical context and viewed as the heterogenous replication experiments they actually were.

One problem is that current Western researchers know Vygotsky's concept-formation research through translations of *Thinking and Speech* (translated as *Thought and Language*). Leaving apart the continuing translation problems of the existing American editions (Vygotsky, 1962, 1986, 1987; for some examples see Van der Veer, 1987, and chapter 13) it can be said that by reading *Thinking and Speech* one cannot readily reconstruct the chronological order in which Vygotsky's various manuscripts on concept-formation were written. Thus, it is said in the Russian edition of 1982 (faithfully copied in the American edition of 1987) that chapter 5 of *Thinking and Speech* – the chapter that deals with extensions of Ach's approach – is similar in content to that of a talk on "The development of everyday and scientific concepts in school age" that Vygotsky presented on May 20, 1933 (published in Vygotsky, 1935h). This would suggest that Vygotsky's writings on the advantages and disadvantages of Ach's approach and his analysis of his own replications had been written during the time he discussed ideas like "the zone of proximal development" and "sensitive zones," and was rethinking the relation between education and development in general. Nothing could be further from the truth. In reality, chapter 5 was written around 1930 – on the basis of research done in the preceding years by Sakharov, Kotelova, Pashkovskaya, and Vygotsky himself – and published in *The Paedology of the Adolescent* (Vygotsky, 1931h; see paragraphs 5–24 of chapter 10, on pp. 229–89). At that time Vygotsky worked with a set of ideas (e.g. the instrumental approach, the idea of primitivism) that were still rather far from those he would develop in the last one and a half years of his life (e.g. the system approach, the zones of development).

Also it is not easy to understand Vygotsky's endeavors in the domain of concept-formation research by reading chapter 6 of *Thinking and Speech* and its commentaries. Composed in the spring of 1934, this chapter dealt with several issues that fascinated Vygotsky as he worked at the Herzen Pedagogical Institute. As such it reiterates the talks he gave in 1933 (published in Vygotsky 1935h), combining them with an appraisal of Piaget's latest writings and their replications and extensions by Vygotsky's collaborators. Unfortunately, the fact that the chapter was composed by Vygotsky while he was suffering from a strong attack of tuberculosis led to a rather chaotic composition. It should be added that part of the chapter had been written before: pages 163–76 and 256–9 were identical with the pages 3–17 of the preface to Shif (1935). The remaining parts of the chapter were dictated to Sof'ya Davydovna Eremina, a stenographer and long-time friend of the Vygodsky family. One of Vygotsky's daughers, Gita Lvov'na Vygodskaja, vividly remembers how her father walked back and forth in his room dictating the chapters of *Thinking and Speech* that had not yet been written (Vygodskaja, personal communication, October 1989).

The first editor of the book, Kolbanovsky, checked the text of all chapters and may have removed some unwelcome references to "fascist" authors and paedology (replacing the word "paedology" by "school psychology" etc.). Our suspicion that Kolbanovsky may have removed the word "paedology" is based on the fact that Vygotsky freely used it in the lectures that formed the basis for large parts of chapter 6 of *Thinking and Speech*, yet the word is absent in the chapter itself (see Vygotsky, 1935h). Many years later Kolbanovsky (1956, p. 112) was still providing public excuses for Vygotsky's paedological research and mentioned that Vygotsky had "agreed" to give his book the subtitle "A psychological analysis" (see also chapter 16).

An example of the deletion of a reference to a "fascist" author can be found in chapter 5 of *Thinking and Speech*, where Vygotsky speaks of "one of the contemporary authors" (Vygotsky, 1934a, p. 136). In the original text of *The Paedology of the Adolescent* (Vygotsky, 1931h, p. 263) this anonymous author was Felix Krueger, the German psychologist, whose affiliation with the Nazi regime has been well documented (Geuter, 1985).

Kolbanovsky also polished the text of the transcripts, so that the book could be presented as a cohesive whole. Remaining references to the conversation-like nature of the chapter (e.g. Vygotsky, 1934a, p. 239, where he referred to "our conversations") have been removed by the editors of later editions.

This curious history of the origin of *Thinking and Speech* should make us cautious, but we should not jump to the conclusion that the text of all dictated chapters of *Thinking and Speech* is basically untrustworthy. Vygotsky's daughter, Gita Lvov'na Vygodskaja, is of the opinion that the text is fairly reliable, basing this opinion on the fact of the very friendly relation that existed between Kolbanovsky and Vygotsky at that time (Vygodskaja, personal communication, October 1989; see also chapter 16). Be that as it may, chapter 6 of *Thinking and Speech* clearly betrays its conversational origin, for it is full of repetitions, transgressions, and passages that are in need of additional clarification.

One goal in this present chapter, therefore, will be to reconstruct the historical genesis of Vygotsky's thinking in the domain of concept-formation research. The principal writings here are Sakharov (1928; 1930), Vygotsky (1930h; 1931h; 1934a; 1934h; 1935f; 1935h) and Shif (1935). Another goal will be to clarify the way Vygotsky's ideas in this domain were linked with the general nature of his thinking in the respective periods.

Replicating and Extending Ach

Concept-formation Research

The first cultural-historical writings on concept-formation research were linked with the new tradition created by Ach (1921) and were written by Vygotsky's collaborator at the Experimental Institute of Psychology, L. S. Sakharov (Sakharov, 1928; 1930). Sakharov's posthumously published lecture at the Paedological Conference in Moscow on January 1, 1928 – he committed suicide on May 10 of the same year[1] – provides some insight in the way Vygotsky and his collaborators looked at the state of concept-formation research (Sakharov, 1930).

---

[1]A Commission had to investigate the case. In a letter to Sakharov's widow one month after the death of her husband, Vygotsky mentions that the Commission apparently still had not been formed. In this very warm and sensitive letter he also mentions that, overwhelmed by sorrow, he had not yet been able to resume Sakharov's work (Vygotsky in a letter to Sakharova, dated July 17, 1928).

Sakharov began his talk by mentioning two ways of investigating children's conceptual thinking and their disadvantages. The first method is that of asking for a definition: an experimenter lists the features of a concept and asks the child for its name, or he mentions several concepts and asks the child to give the superordinate concept. One problem with this method is that it cannot reveal the development of concepts since one investigates only the qualitative characteristics of concepts the child already has at his disposal. In addition, the method is purely verbal and therefore one cannot see how the child uses these concepts in practical dealing with objects. Finally, one is faced with the problem that children may mean different things by the same words. Sakharov concluded that the method of definition was unsuitable and turned to the second method of investigating conceptual development: the direct method. All versions of the direct method have in common that a subject is presented with a set of objects that may have one or more features in common (cf. Grünbaum, 1908). The task may be to find in subset A an object that resembles another object in subset B, or to group similar objects together, etc. Tasks of this type were presented by Luria to Uzbek subjects in 1931 and 1932 (see chapter 10). In the opinion of Sakharov and Vygotsky, however, these methods had one basic shortcoming: the functional role of words in the abstraction process is excluded (see Ach, 1921, p. 28 for the same point). Using this nonverbal approach one cannot expose the role words play in the formation of concepts and the child's behavior will be fully determined by the objects' characteristics. Thus, while the method of definition attempts to understand the process of concept-formation on a purely verbal plane – in isolation from the concrete objects the concepts refer to – the direct method investigates concept-formation in the purely practical sphere – in isolation from the guiding role of words.

Ach's Search Method

Vygotsky and Sakharov believed that the ideal method of studying concept-formation should involve the simultaneous introduction of both objects and words. A decisive step forwards in this respect was made by Ach in his famous *Über die Begriffsbildung* (1921), in particular with his "search method" (*Suchmethode*). Ach started his investigations from four theoretical assumptions that were very close to Vygotsky's thinking at the time. First, research should study the development of concepts and not its finished products (1921, p. 1). Secondly, the method had to be developmental-synthetic, that is one should study the way words acquire significative meaning, the way they transform into symbols. Therefore, one has to start with words that originally have no meaning, that is, nonsense words, and trace the way they develop into meaningful units (Ach, 1921, pp. 1–2; p. 32). Thirdly, concepts serve a definite function in thinking and man is no passive receiver of impressions as Galton had it (1921, pp. 28–9). Therefore, one has to bring the subjects into a situation where the concepts can play a functional role and are as indispensable as the tools in Köhler's experiments with chimpanzees (1921, p. 32). Ach's new method of investigating children's thinking and the reasoning behind it made an enormous impression on the psychological world and a new research tradition started virtually immediately (e.g. Bacher, 1925; Rimat, 1925; Usnadze, 1924; 1929; 1930).

It is not difficult to see how the new approach accorded with Vygotsky's thinking of the time. As we saw in the preceding chapter, the idea of a genetic approach, the idea of words as tools, and the comparison with Köhler's chimpanzee experiments were all akin to the set of ideas put forward in the cultural-historical theory. However, although Ach's search method constituted a big step forwards in concept-formation research it was not without its faults, according to Vygotsky and Sakharov. It will be remembered that Ach's search method consisted of presenting the subjects (mostly children) with twelve objects of different form (cubes, cylinders, triangles), size (big, small), and weight (heavy, light). Each object had a tag with its name on it according to the following rule: the three heavy and big objects were called "Gazun," the light and big objects "Ras," the heavy and small objects "taro," and the light and small objects "fal." After a training period – during which the child repeatedly had to lift the objects and to read out loud their names – the tags were taken away and subjects had to select the objects with the name specified by the experimenter. In further series the number of objects was enlarged by adding the dimension of color (yellow, red, and blue). Also Ach tested the subjects' understanding of the newly acquired concepts by asking questions like "Is a Gazun bigger than a fal?" etc. It comes as no surprise that several researchers quickly realized the diagnostic value of the search method and developed it into an intelligence test (Bacher, 1925; Rimat, 1925; see also Sakharov, 1928 on Bacher's paper). Vygotsky and Sakharov thought that Ach's search method, although of immense value, had two shortcomings. The first disadvantage of the method was that the subject's mental processes were insufficiently externalized. Having investigated fifteen normal and retarded children in the summer and fall of 1927 Sakharov came to the conclusion that the training period did not allow the experimenter to study the subjects' mental processes. Ach's solution to this problem – which was to rely on the subjects' introspection for this period – was unacceptable to Sakharov. A second disadvantage of Ach's method was that his artificial world of objects was fully symmetrical. To Sakharov this was uncharacteristic of real life and he proposed instead to start with an unorganized set of objects that could only be ordered with the help of words.

The Revised Search Method

On the basis of these considerations Sakharov and Vygotsky developed the revised search method, in which subjects were presented with objects of (1) different colors (yellow, red, green, black; and white); (2) different shape (prisms, parallelopipeds, cylinders); (3) different height (low, tall); and (4) different base surface (large, small). The names of the objects had been written on their underside and were, therefore, invisible. The nonsense words connected with the objects were "bat" (for small and low objects), "dek" (small and tall), "roc" (large and low), and "mup" (large and tall). The twenty to thirty objects were placed in a disorganized fashion on one part of a games board which had various segments. The number of objects belonging to each category was unequal. The experimenter now turned one of the objects upside down, had the child read its name, and put it – with its name visible – in a separate segment of the board explaining that this was the toy of children from another culture and that there were more of these toys among the objects. It was explained that if the child would find the other "toys" he would win a prize. The child was encouraged to work carefully and slowly and the order in which he selected the "toys" was recorded as well as the time used. After the child had made an incorrect selection the experimenter would have him turn one of the objects not selected upside down and read its name. This new instance of the concept was then laid next to the first one and all other objects were put in their original place. The child, thus, had to start the selection process all over again, now having two instances of the concept at his disposal. This – rather frustrating – process continued until the child had correctly finished the task. In between the experimenter would ask the child to explain the reasons for his choice and to give a definition of the concept "toy."

It is clear that this revised search method has many elements in common with Ach's original method but that several important changes had been made. Most importantly the names of the objects are at first invisible and after each attempt at selection the child has one more name on which to base his hypothesis. Sakharov saw the revised search method as a special version of the method of double stimulation where the gradually changing relation between the two types of stimuli – words and objects – is externalized to an extreme degree.

Empirical Results

On the basis of the first experiments with adults and school children (he prepared an investigation of preschool children by replacing the words by colored signs) Sakharov claimed that one could distinguish three stages in concept-formation. At first, children would see the words as individual signs, or proper names. In the second stage the word would become a family name tied to a specific set of objects. Only in the third and final stage it would become an abstract concept (Sakharov, 1930, p. 32). Unfortunately, Sakharov made no attempt to illustrate these supposed stages by reference to the experimental data gathered. In a footnote to Sakharov's paper it was mentioned that the investigations he started had been finished by Vygotsky, Kotelova, and Pashkovskaya and that they had prepared a monograph for publication. This monograph was never published, but one does find a disproportionally long chapter in *The Paedology of the Adolescent* (later published as chapter 5 of *Thinking and Speech*) which deals with these further investigations. It is, therefore, to this chapter we have to turn in order to get an idea of the nature of the experimental findings.

First Vygotsky briefly reiterated the arguments put forward by Sakharov (1930), adding an additional difference between the revised search method and Ach's original procedure: the subjects cannot proceed inductively, but have to work from the top downwards, that is, starting from hypotheses. Having studied "more than 300" subjects (children, adolescents, adults, mental and other patients) Vygotsky concluded that "the development of the processes that later on lead to the formation of concepts is rooted deeply in childhood, but only in adolescence mature, take shape, and develop those intellectual functions that in their unique constellation form the psychological foundation of the concept-formation process" (Vygotsky, 1931h, pp. 240–1; 1934a, p. 114). This conclusion he contrasted with the opinion of contemporaries, such as Charlotte Bühler, who had claimed that the principal mental operations are completed at a very early age and that further mental growth consists purely in acquiring new knowledge. At this time, however, Vygotsky had become convinced that in mental development both form (the mental operations, such as concepts) and content (knowledge) change in an intricate interdependent process, a process which reminds one of the dialectical interplay that Vygotsky envisioned in works of art (see chapter 2). Thus, the mature adult concepts were preceded by various "protoconcepts" that Vygotsky set out to describe in great detail. His leading idea still was that the principal difference between lower and higher types of mental activity is that the latter are operations mediated through signs (Vygotsky, 1931h; p. 245; 1934a, p. 118).

What, then, were the child's ways of classification or generalization that preceded fully grown concepts? Vygotsky distinguished three stages in the child's development towards real conceptual thinking: (1) the stage of syncretism; (2) the stage of the formation of complexes; and (3) the stage of potential concept-formation. In the first, syncretic stage (the term "syncretism" was borrowed from Claparède and Piaget (1923)) objects are grouped together by the child on the basis of irrelevant perceptual factors, such as spatial proximity. The objects grouped together, therefore, do not necessarily have any features in common. One might immediately object that if children did attach words to objects in this singular way then communication with adults would become rather difficult. In this respect Vygotsky relied heavily on Usnadze (1930) who had introduced the notion of "functional equivalents" to clarify this issue. Usnadze – who used Ach's search method and whose investigations of children's way of grouping objects show many similarities to those of Vygotsky and his collaborators – observed that children can communicate with adults in an adequate way while the words they use are still not concepts in a real sense. He then continued by stating that children's words are the "functional equivalents" (Usnadze, 1930, p. 140) of adults' concepts and described their nature in great detail. Communication between adults using real concepts and children using their functional equivalents was considered possible, because adult and child share a common context in the form of the object-world they are referring to. Because of this shared context, their word meanings or concepts will partially overlap (Vygotsky, 1931h, pp. 246–7). The stage of syncretic ordering of the objects was subdivided by Vygotsky into three substages. In the first substage children would work on a "trial and error" basis selecting arbitrary objects and trying arbitrary others when corrected. In the second substage they would select those objects that were spatially close to each other in the original configuration. The third substage is very vaguely described by Vygotsky, but one gets the impression that in this the children selected various syncretic groups, from which they selected several objects to form yet another syncretic group. For Vygotsky, this two-step process was one step further removed from an ordering on the basis of perceptual features and, therefore, he considered it to be a more advanced substage than the two substages mentioned before. Incidentally, it is not easy to see how this ordering behavior would become evident in an experiment using the revised search method.

In the second stage the children will arrange the objects into "complexes," that is, they will select objects on the basis of some concrete, objective feature but the selected feature may seem irrelevant to adults and will anyhow be changed one or more times during the ordering process. The result is that subgroups of objects will share one or more features but it is not possible to find one single feature that is shared by all instances of the "complex." Thus, while the instances of a real concept all have one or more features in common, this is not true for a "complex." Vygotsky – as Sakharov did before – compared complexes to family names: each member of a family has some traits in common with other members but all members do not necessarily share one trait. The thinking in complexes is superior to syncretic thinking as the ordering is now done on the basis of objectively existing object features. Interestingly enough – for it seems to indicate an acceptance of Piagetian concepts – Vygotsky (1931h, p. 248) claimed that a child thinking in complexes "overcomes, to a certain extent, his egocentrism."

The stage of complex formation was subdivided by Vygotsky into five substages:

1　Associative complexes. In this substage the child adds objects to the first object, because they share one (shifting) feature with it. One object may be selected because it shares its color with the starting object, another because it has a similar form, etc. Also contrast may lead to inclusion. Vygotsky (1931h, p. 251) remarked that for the child in this substage words stop being proper names and become family names (cf. Sakharov, 1930).

2　Collections. The idea of collections is that those objects are grouped together that are complementary to one another. Thus, when the starting object is a yellow pyramid the child will add objects with other colors and another form until all forms and colors are represented. Vygotsky observed that such an attitude is based on observing objects together in their concrete functional context (e.g. a fork, a knife, and a plate) and suggests that it is common among adults too, but in particular among the mentally diseased. We might add that Luria (1974) observed a similar tendency among illiterate peasants during his expedition to Uzbekistan also in 1931 (see chapter 10).

3　Chain complexes. In this substage a child who has to start with a yellow triangle (that is, the experimenter has explained to the child that this is a toy of children from a different culture and has asked him to find the other toys) may add all other triangles and then – if the last triangle happens to be blue – add all other blue objects, etc. Thus, the selection criterion changes all the time, but the child is solely inspired by the last object it has selected and has stopped taking into account the original yellow triangle.

4　Diffuse complexes. This type of ordering of the objects is characterized by the fact that the selection criterion itself becomes very diffuse. Thus, starting with a yellow triangle, the child might add a trapezium because its form is vaguely similar to that of a triangle. The trapezium might be followed by a square, again of vaguely similar form, etc. The same tendency may be observed for the color dimension. The substage of the formation of diffuse complexes once again shows a principal trait of complexes: they can be supplemented in any direction and therefore have no boundaries.

5 Pseudoconcepts. The most important trait of pseudoconcepts is that they phenotypically encompass the same objects as a real concept but originate in a quite different way. As an example Vygotsky (1931h, pp. 256–7) mentions that a child may add all available triangles to a given yellow triangle. This behavior might be based on a real understanding of the geometrical concept "triangle," but often is not: the child has relied on some very concrete perceptual features. Vygotsky thus seems to indicate here that a real concept (like "triangle") rests on the understanding of some abstract features that are not given in the perceptual world. Thus, the pseudoconcepts are a perfect example of a case where the word meanings (the application of words to concrete objects) of children and adults coincide but where their understanding is at different levels. In Vygotsky's analysis this phenomenon appears because the adults steer the children's word-use, forcing them to apply the word "triangle" to the same set of objects as an adult would. This joint reference (the extension of the word), however, does insure adequate communication but not the same level of thought. Vygotsky concluded, therefore, that Ach was wrong to equate word-meaning with concept, as the child and adult may refer to the same set of objects (have the same word-meaning) but rely on different psychological operations (concrete features versus abstract definitions). The use of words that refer to common sets of objects enable the adequate communication between adult and child, but the child still has to travel a long road until his understanding of a concept coincides with that of the adult.[2] Vygotsky concluded that the pseudoconcepts form the most prevalent and convincing example of Usnadze's notion of concepts' functional equivalents. Vygotsky thought that it was through verbal interaction with adults – "that powerful motor of the development of children's concepts" – that the pseudoconcepts would develop into real concepts. In one of his characteristic Hegel-like asides Vygotsky concluded that the concept in itself and for others exists before it

---

[2]Unfortunately, Vygotsky used the term "word-meaning" in a very different sense as well. Discussing linguistic research (through Peterson, 1930) he mentioned Husserl's famous example of the "winner at Jena" and the "loser at Waterloo" and accepted the distinction between "word-meaning" (*znachenie*; technically "intension") and "object reference" (*predmetnaja otnesennost*; technically "extension"). He now applied this new terminology to his empirical findings stating that the "object references" of the words used by children and adults coincide while the "word-meanings" they use differ. Using this new terminology he now claimed that we have to investigate the way children's word-meanings change during development. This will also be the sense in which the term will be used in the remaining part of this chapter.

exists for the child himself, that is, the child may apply words correctly before he consciously realizes the real concept.

Having sketched this global development from syncretic thinking up to pseudoconcepts on the basis of his experimental findings, Vygotsky set out to argue that this development also could be shown to coincide with the known psychological findings of the time. In this respect he claimed that his findings harmonized with the facts known about children's language development and about the development of human language *per se* (Vygotsky, 1931h, pp. 264–73). He also claimed that the phenomenon of participation in primitive thinking first observed by Lévy-Bruhl (see chapter 9) could be explained in the light of these findings. In his view, the claim by the Bororo that they were red parrots – an event which led Lévy-Bruhl to introduce the concept of participation – should not be interpreted to mean that they felt they were identical to parrots. Rather, the claim simply implied that these people felt that they and parrots belonged to the same family. Lévy-Bruhl was wrong, then, in interpreting the family complex used by the Bororo as if it were a real concept where all instances share some common feature.

In chapter 10 of *The Paedology of the Adolescent* (and, therefore, also in chapter 5 of *Thinking and Speech*) – Vygotsky concluded his discussion of children's conceptual development by stating that the development he had sketched constituted only one aspect of a complex whole. For in his opinion the formation of syncretic wholes and complexes rested on the combination of similar objects into sets. For analytical purposes, however, the ability to combine objects on the ground of similarity could be distinguished from the ability to analyze, to separate, to abstract from certain features and highlight others. The development of the ability to abstract would partially overlap with the child's growing ability to form sets of similar objects and real concept-formation would demand a complete mastering of both abilities. The third stage preceding the final stage of real concept-formation would combine these abilities and would lead to "potential concepts," a term borrowed from Groos. However, the description of these potential concepts and their difference from pseudoconcepts and real concepts is utterly vague and one feels that Vygotsky's attempt to link his empirically established sequence of stages with the findings of other authors is rather awkward. We also simply have to accept at face value his statement that the transition from thinking in potential concepts to thinking in real concepts only takes place in adolescence (Vygotsky, 1931h, p. 281). The fact that adolescents may have substantial problems in defining the concepts they have formed, led Vygotsky to the statement that the conscious realization

(Claparède's *prise de conscience*) and logical definition of a concept comes after mastering it through practice.

Conclusions

Summarizing, we could say that Sakharov and Vygotsky developed an interesting version of Ach's search method which may have some advantages over the original one. However, a major disadvantage of the revised search method might be that the child has to start the classification process all over again after each attempt. This is a rather frustrating procedure for younger children in particular, as Vygotsky himself would realize some years later (Vygotsky, 1934a, p. 244). The developmental sequence established (in many ways similar to the results found by researchers such as Werner, Usnadze, and Piaget) also deserves careful attention. Several critical remarks, however, can be made. In the first place it is very difficult to grasp the classification process behind the different stages listed by Vygotsky. As happened so often in his work, he did not present the raw material in the form of protocols and he never gave an example of a classification based on a pseudoconcept versus a classification based on a real concept. It is, consequently, rather difficult to understand the difference between pseudo-concepts and real concepts. One gets the impression that what Sakharov and Vygotsky had in mind were, respectively, a classification based on perceptually given features versus a classification based on geometrical properties possibly explicitly stated in the form of a definition. Thus, a child who combined all triangles because "they look alike" operated with a pseudoconcept, whereas an adolescent who combined all triangles because "they are triangles and not squares etc." would operate with a real concept (in particular if the adolescent was able to give a formal definition of the concept "triangle"). This distinction, however, is only inferred from the different available texts and not based on any explicitly stated claims.

Despite these critical remarks one can see why the research done with Ach's revised search method was of fundamental importance to Vygotsky. For the investigations proved the idea – put forward by Usnadze and others – that children, adolescents, and adults may mean different things by the same words. It showed that children's learning of words marks only the onset of a semantic development that may take years to reach its culmination point. In a way, then, children and adults are living in a different semantic universe and the words they use coincide only in that they refer to the same objects. In the final years of his life, Vygotsky investigated how this semantic fabric becomes transformed in the course of the years and what factors are of fundamental importance in determining this transformation process.

Replicating and Extending Piaget

New Themes

Vygotsky's last contributions to the domain of concept-formation can be found in the sixth chapter of *Thinking and Speech* and were dictated by him in the Spring of 1934. By this time themes such as the relation between education and development, the zone of proximal development, and the idea of a formal discipline had been dominating his thinking for some time (see chapter 13) and it is only natural that they were present in his renewed discussion of concept-formation research. Thus, Vygotsky clearly repeated the content of various of the talks he gave in the year before (1933), using the same examples, referring to the same authors, and in general drawing the same conclusions. The content of these talks was transcribed and printed in another posthumously published book, entitled *The Mental Development of Children in Education* (Vygotsky, 1935h; see also chapter 13). However, the sixth chapter of *Thinking and Speech* also contained some new themes: a discussion of a new approach to the study of concept development; and a renewed appraisal of some of Piaget's findings in the light of this approach.

It is interesting to see how Vygotsky evaluated the experiments carried out by himself, Sakharov, Pashkovskaya, and Kotelova five years before, and how he prompted the new turn his concept-formation research had taken. He now believed that the best result one can expect from such artificial experiments is a crude sketch of the different stages of concept development, for one can never understand the way each new stage evolves from the preceding one and is dependent on it (1934a, p. 244). In the investigations using the revised search method "each time in each stage (syncretes, complexes, concepts) we again took the relation of the word to the object, ignoring that each new level in the development of generalization rests on the generalization of the preceding levels." This shortcoming was caused, Vygotsky reasoned, by the set-up of the experiment, which provided neither the explanation of the relation between the different levels of conceptual thinking and the transfer from one level to another, nor the understanding of the relations of generality since, according to the logic of the experiment, the subject had (1) to start all over again after each attempt at grouping the objects, thus annulling the work done and the generalizations found; and (2) to work with concepts of a rather low level. The investigation of real-life concepts was meant to remedy these shortcomings and, in particular, to demonstrate the way the environment might steer the development of children's concepts.

There follows a discussion of Vygotsky's new investigations into children's conceptual thinking and the reasons for Vygotsky's self-critical remarks will be explained. It will also become clear that Vygotsky's later concept-formation research was, above all, an attempt to rethink and extend Piaget's research in this field.

Replicating Piaget

Vygotsky and his collaborators – most importantly Leont'ev – had been trying to replicate Piaget's main findings since approximately 1928. Thus, Pashkovskaya replicated Piaget's (1926) experiments and investigated adolescents' conceptual thinking by clinically interviewing them, asking questions like "What is love?" (see Vygotsky, 1931h, pp. 303–6). Leont'ev translated and adapted Piaget's (1924) questions, which were supposed to demonstrate children's ability to use "although" and "because" conjunctions (see Vygotsky, 1931h, pp. 235–66); and, Leont'ev and Shejn adapted Piaget's investigation of children's understanding of proverbs (1923). Among other things, they observed the interesting finding that children tended to change their answers when asked to explain them. In their view this was caused by the restructuring influence of external speech and to test this idea they asked one group of children to write down the solution to the proverb task and another one to reason aloud. As expected the answers differed substantially (see Vygotsky, 1931h, pp. 327–30). Unfortunately, the references to these investigations – and there were quite probably many more, most of them carried out by students – are few and utterly vague, but we do know that many hundreds of subjects were investigated using Piagetian tasks.

Two Types of Concepts

Piaget's distinction between spontaneous and nonspontaneous concepts and his general conceptualization of the relation between education and development, as expressed in the writings available at the time, were, by 1932, central to Vygotsky's concerns (Piaget, 1921; 1923; 1924; 1926; 1927a; 1927b; 1932; 1933; Piaget and Rossello, 1921; Margaraiz and Piaget, 1925; see also chapter 13).

In his preface to Shif (1935) (also published as part of chapter 6 of *Thinking and Speech*) Vygotsky explained at some length why he was interested in the investigation of both spontaneous and scientific concepts.

By spontaneous concepts he meant concepts that are acquired by the child outside of the context of explicit instruction. In themselves these concepts are mostly taken from adults, but they never have been introduced to the child in a systematic fashion and no attempts have been made to connect them with other, related concepts. Because Vygotsky explicitly acknowledged the role of adults in the formation of these so-called spontaneous concepts he preferred to call them "everyday" concepts, thus avoiding the idea that they had been spontaneously invented by the child. Examples of everyday concepts would be the concepts used by Piaget such as "brother" and "house." By "scientific" concepts Vygotsky meant concepts that had been explicitly introduced by a teacher at school. Ideally such concepts would cover the essential aspects of an area of knowledge and would be presented as a system of interrelated ideas. Thus, in Shif's investigation the area of knowledge studied was the development of Communism in the Soviet Union and the clarifying concepts introduced were, for example, "serfdom," "exploitation," "bourgeois," and "revolution."

The Need to Investigate Scientific Concepts

Vygotsky wondered whether the mastering of these two types of concepts might take different roads and was in favour of the investigation of the development of scientific concepts in particular: Piaget had discarded their investigation since in his opinion they only reflect the mastering of cultural knowledge and do not truly reflect the characteristics of the child's mind. In Vygotsky's view this attitude was the result of several erroneous fundamental assumptions in Piaget's theory. First, it was self-contradictory to claim that theoretical concepts do not reflect the child's way of thinking as Piaget himself had shown that concepts are transformed in the process of mastering them, so there was no reason to restrict this finding to spontaneous concepts. Secondly, in accepting that nonspontaneous concepts do not reflect the characteristics of the child's way of thinking one is forced also to accept that there is an unbridgeable gap between the two types of concepts, which was what Piaget actually did. He did not see the way these concepts are united in the child's mind. Thirdly, these views led to a tension in Piaget's thinking: on the one hand it was claimed that the study of nonspontaneous concepts cannot reveal the characteristics of the child's way of thinking. Their study is, therefore, pointless. On the other hand, one of the pillars of Piaget's system is that the child's thinking is gradually socialized. Schooling is one of the most concentrated forms of socialization. However, in Piaget's view the scientific concepts taught at school are not related to the child's spontaneous concepts. It is difficult to see, therefore, how socialization and spontaneous development are connected in Piaget's thinking. Vygotsky connected this problem to Piaget's more general view of education and development and their relation. According to Vygotsky Piaget saw the child's cognitive development as the replacement or suppression of the original ways of thinking by new ones. In this view the concepts taught at school are incompatible with the child's spontaneous concepts and, as such, their study cannot possibly reveal anything of the child's particular ways of thinking. One has to know the child's spontaneous thinking in order to be able to fight it. Vygotsky fundamentally disagreed with all of these views and the many investigations he supervised in this period were set up to disprove such views. One of the most well-known is Shif's (1935) study of everyday and scientific concepts.

Shif's Study: Teaching a Communist World-View

Shif started her investigation in 1932, trying to combine a theoretical interest with the societal demands of the time. One year before the Party had warned against attempts to teach Soviet children an anti-proletarian world-view (CK VKP(b) September 5, 1931). Apparently, the attempts to teach children a sound communist view of the history of the Soviet Union had not been overly successful. Shif consequently selected the concepts taught in the course on the history of the communist movement in the Soviet Union (*obshchestvovedenie*) as examples of scientific concepts. Following Piaget's format, she constructed questions ending in mid-sentence on "although" or "because" that had to be completed by the children. A successful completion demonstrated a correct use of the concept involved. It is interesting to look at several of the sentences used. The questions regarding everyday concepts had been translated by Leont'ev years before and were of the type: "The girl reads badly, although ...." and "The pilot fell with his airplane because ...." The examples of questions regarding scientific concepts that Shif added now seem slightly more exotic. They were of the type: "The police shot the revolutionaries because ..."; "The capitalists prepare for a war against the USSR because ..."; "There are still workers who believe in god, although ..."; and "*Kulaks* and popes do not have the right to be voted into the Soviets because ....".

Shif and her collaborator Latysheva presented these questions to 36 children from the second class and 43 children from the fourth class. As children were admitted at the Soviet elementary school at the age of seven, this implies that the children's age ranged between seven and 11. The everyday test was the same for both classes but the scientific test differed because of the different curricula the children followed. In the second class all children were interviewed individually. In the fourth class all children

TABLE 11.1   Percentage of correct answers given in scientific and everyday tests for two age groups (after Shif, 1935, p. 48)

Class		Everyday	Scientific
2	"because"	59	80
	"although"	16	21
4	"because"	81	82
	"although"	66	80

wrote down their answers at the same time and were interviewed afterwards. The main quantitative results of Shif's investigation can be summarized as follows (see table 11.1).

Shif noted that the performance of children in the second class was much better when answering the "because" questions concerning "scientific" material than when dealing with material covering everyday knowledge. She ascribed this to the instruction by a teacher: the children simply remembered the right answers. Shif elaborated her study by subdividing both correct and incorrect answers into several subcategories. For example, incorrect answers might be so classified because of the replacement of one conjunction by the other (e.g. "the child fell off his bike, although he was not cautious." The child has replaced "because" by "although"), or might be simply tautological, etc. Correct answers were classified as "schematic" when the child literally repeated what he had been taught at school using stereotypical phrases. Employing these subdivisions Shif found that the answers to "scientific" questions although answered correctly more often, were frequently of a rather schematic nature. The children in the second class were clearly not really understanding what they said – that is, the semantic level of their concepts was low (Shif, 1935, p. 37). The children had mastered the correct use of the concepts but these were still empty for them and not filled with concrete, personal knowledge. The answers to the everyday questions, on the contrary, were never of this schematic, stereotypical nature. On the other hand, tautological answers (e.g. the child fell off his bike, because he fell off his bike) were absent in the scientific test and rather prevalent in the case of everyday questions (14 percent in the case of "because" questions in the second class). Shif was inclined to interpret this phenomenon positively. In her view the need to repeat the scientific material in the classroom, the necessity to answer to questions about this material, and to explain these answers, led the child to the conscious realization of the scientific concepts. It was the lack of such conscious realization that led children to give tautological answers in the everyday test, that is, in the situation Piaget had investigated. We thus can see the positive and negative aspects of everyday and scientific concepts in the second class. In the area of scientific knowledge, that the children apply the concepts correctly more often is a positive factor. They will also explain their answers more frequently. The negative side of scientific concepts in this age group is that the answers and their explanation are frequently of a stereotypical nature. The everyday concepts are strong where the scientific ones are weak, and vice versa. Stereotyped answers are lacking for everyday concepts but the number of correct answers is lower and children have more trouble in explaining their answers.

As can be seen in table 11.1 the results for the "although" questions for this age group were rather different. Shif found no systematic differences between the quality of the children's answers in both areas. The replacement of the conjunction "although" with "because," for example, took place in 39.5 percent and 39.8 percent of the answers to, respectively, everyday and scientific questions. Shif concluded that the results for the scientific and the everyday test were identical. The finding that scientific concepts for "although" conjunctions demonstrated no superiority she explained by referring to the fact that the scientific material was introduced to the children emphasizing causes and corollories. Constructions with "because" would be thus far more prevalent in the classroom. The generally lower number of correct answers to "although" questions demonstrated that this conjunction was more difficult to grasp for younger children.

Of the children in the fourth class Shif pointed out that with "because" questions in both areas we find a high percentage of correct answers (81 percent and 82 percent), indicating that the children have mastered the causal way of thinking. A more detailed analysis of the answers in the scientific area shows that the children's answers have lost their stereotypical character and are full of concrete content. In contrast with the younger children, the children from the fourth class do not simply repeat the memorized material but rather have understood the reasoning behind it. The answers to the "although" questions are somewhat weaker but still largely correct. The results for the scientific area were better, which again indicated to Shif the importance of systematic instruction.

The question now arises how this set of results – which was confirmed in a replication experiment by students of the Herzen Pedagogical Institute in 1933 (see Shif, 1935, p. 43) – could be explained in a developmental perspective. Shif's answer to this question was clearly influenced by the set of ideas Vygotsky adopted in 1933 (she wrote the theoretical part of her dissertation in the spring of 1934). She claimed that explicit instruction in a subject at school leads to the use of certain ways of thinking within specific areas. Gradually these ways of thinking will spread to other areas and elevate the child's thinking to a higher level. Thus, the correct and explained use of "because" conjunctions is first introduced in a scientific context and will only later generalize to everyday thinking. The explicit classroom instruction creates a zone of proximal development for the child (see chapter 13). The same holds true for the use of "although" conjunctions: in the fourth class its use within the scientific area is still superior to its use in everyday thinking but this difference will probably gradually disappear in the next few years of the child's development. Education, therefore, prepares the road for the child's cognitive development.

Shif versus Piaget

Shif's results were in sharp contradiction to the views attributed to Piaget. First, Shif had shown that the grasp of scientific concepts does reflect the child's way of thinking, for the understanding of these concepts was quite different for the two age groups and showed the peculiarities specific to the age groups. This finding also confirmed Vygotsky's earlier claim that the word-meanings develop slowly for children. Secondly, Shif claimed that everyday concepts and scientific concepts are united in the child's mind as the former are presumably brought to a higher level by the teaching of the latter. For both Shif and Vygotsky it followed that that the scientific concepts taught at school and everyday concepts were not incompatible, but rather they were partners in an intricate interrelationship. Of course, Vygotsky reasoned, one cannot teach scientific concepts to a child when his everyday concepts have not reached a certain minimal level. Scientific concepts, therefore, have their foundation in everyday concepts. But as soon as the scientific concepts have been mastered they will start to transform the child's everyday concepts, bringing these to a higher level of understanding. A consequence of this view was that education was seen as one of the factors bringing about cognitive development and not as the provider of finished knowledge that can be swallowed verbatim by the child as soon as he has reached a certain maturational level.

All of these conclusions contradicted the views attributed to Piaget above. Of course, the conclusions were of highly speculative nature. One problem is that it is not very clear how the teaching of scientific concepts, such as "exploitation" and "proletarian" would lead to a better use of "because" and "although" conjunctions. The use of these conjunctions may be more frequent in a curriculum taught at school but in itself there seems no simple logical connection between the "scientific" nature of ideas and the use of these connections. Shif would probably have argued in reply to this criticism that the forms of thinking (the use of conjunctions) cannot be separated from their content (scientific versus everyday knowledge). But the present authors would argue that there is a fundamental ambiguity in Shif's and Vygotsky's reasoning about scientific and everyday concepts. On the one hand one may distinguish between concepts that do (scientific) or do not (everyday) reflect essential properties of the phenomena studied – in Vygotsky's reasoning "essential" would refer to abstract and not perceptually given features. The mastering of one or other type of concept would be reflected in the child's answers to questions, his ways of solving tasks, etc. On the other hand, the scientific concepts are introduced in a very special setting that implies the training of various (meta)cognitive skills. Thus, children are asked to rehearse these concepts, to state them explicitly, to explain them, etc. The training of these (meta)cognitive skills will probably be reflected in the child's way of solving various tasks. Vygotsky never attempted to distinguish these two aspects of mastering scientific concepts and, indeed, his notion of scientific concepts clearly involved the training of (meta)cognitive skills. For it is probably the mastering of these skills that leads to the most important achievements of adolescence, that is, the conscious realization and arbitrary use of mental tools.

Even if all this is accepted, and several methodological objections that might be raised about her investigation ignored, it seems clear to the present writers that Shif's main argument – that the higher number of correct answers to questions concerning everyday knowledge was the result of the preceding teaching of scientific concepts – is still contentious. It was still rather unclear how this reforming influence of the teaching of scientific concepts would come about and it was not without reason, therefore, that Vygotsky devoted much reasoning to this problem in the remaining parts of the sixth chapter of his *Thinking and Speech*.

Conscious Realization and Deliberate Use

To support his arguments for the influence of scientific concepts Vygotsky repeatedly (see Vygotsky, 1934a, pp. 178–80; pp. 235–7) had recourse to an analogy. He said that the mastering of scientific concepts would relate to the mastering of everyday concepts as the learning of a foreign language to the learning of the mother tongue. The mother tongue is learned spontaneously and unsystematically and although children learn to apply the words correctly they usually do not consciously realize what grammatical rules they apply in doing so and could not possibly formulate them. Common to everyday concepts and the mother tongue, then, is that in both cases the child combines a more or less correct use with a fundamental lack of conscious realization of the rules involved. The child chooses the right words and concepts, but cannot yet reflect on and prompt the choices made (cf. Piaget, 1924). A foreign language, however, is learned in a very different way. In this case the grammar is introduced explicitly and children are taught to explain their choice of certain verbs, cases etc. This will necessarily lead to a conscious realization of the rules involved and to their deliberate use. Consequently, children will have less difficulty in explaining their choices than in the case of their own language. In this sense the learning of a foreign language leads to the same beneficial results as mastering scientific concepts: the child can deliberately make choices and can explain them since he can reflect on the rules involved. Vygotsky reasoned that ideally this new ability will carry over to his own language, and he will start seeing his own language as a special case of a larger group of languages that share many properties. Likewise, a child learning algebra will ideally begin to see the rules of arithmetic as a special case of a larger and more general set of rules (Vygotsky, 1934a, p. 235). Vygotsky claimed that a child having learned a foreign language has acquired a set of notions that enables him to reflect on his own language and consciously to realize the rules he had thus far been applying automatically. Vygotsky carried the analogy still further: both scientific concepts and words from a foreign language have a mediated nature, he argued. For the words of a foreign language are learned as translations of words already known and not by ostension. Thus, the native speaker of English will have learned the word "nose" as his mother repeatedly pointed to various noses and pronounced the corresponding word. The Russian word "*nos*", however, he will learn simply as the translation of "nose." Therefore words of our mother language would have a direct tie to the object world, whereas foreign words would be tied to the object world only via the words of our mother tongue. The same would hold true for everyday and scientific concepts, Vygotsky argued. Everyday concepts such as "farmer" and "worker" find their reference in the concrete world of the child, whereas scientific concepts such as "exploitation" and "serfdom" do not. The understanding of the scientific concept "exploitation" assumes the understanding of the everyday concept "worker" and its relation to the concrete world of the child is mediated by it. Both scientific concepts and foreign words, therefore, have a mediated character.

What Vygotsky tried to argue with this and other analogies was, that the explicit and systematic teaching of rules and concepts within one area will perhaps carry over to other areas. The most important results of such teaching in his view were the conscious realization (*osoznanie*, or *prise de conscience*) and deliberate use, or voluntariness (*proizvol'nost*), of the rules underlying the children's behavior. These results only evolved in adolescence and formed the most important achievements (*novoobrazovanie*; *Neuleistung*) of this period in life.

Conclusions

On the basis of the empirical results discussed above and various analogies he drew Vygotsky arrived at the following controversial conclusions. First, one can distinguish between everyday concepts and scientific concepts. These have a different origin, different strengths and weaknesses, and interact in complex ways. Secondly, scientific concepts, that is, concepts introduced in a systematic and explicit fashion, lead the child to the conscious realization and deliberate use of his own mental operations. Thirdly, these results will generalize to the domain of everyday thinking. Fourthly, this proves the fundamental importance of education for mental development. Fifthly, everyday concepts are directly tied to concrete objects in the world and, therefore, generalize objects. The word "house," for example, refers to various houses the child has seen and abstracts from specific features to express the general idea of "house." Scientific ideas, however, do not directly refer to objects but to everyday concepts. In this way they constitute a "generalization of generalizations." The new, higher type of thinking (thinking in scientific concepts) is, therefore, not based on a fundamentally new connection with the object world but on a reconceptualization of existing knowledge.

It is here that Vygotsky saw a fundamental difference with his earlier research based on Ach's revised search method. That series of experiments had suggested that mental development consisted in finding new ways of tying words to objects (syncretic wholes, complexes, etc.) for each age group, after which the ways of thinking displayed earlier were discarded. In each age period, therefore, the child had to reinvent the set of objects a word referred to. He now claimed that the mastering of a higher level of thinking preserved the knowledge acquired before and consisted in seeing the earlier knowledge as a special case of more general rules. Vygotsky seemed to imply, then, that after a course in communist thinking an everyday (lower) concept such as "farmer" would still refer to the same set of objects but would have changed its meaning (intension). The child would now understand that a private farmer is not a man growing corn, etc., but a proletarian misled by the false *kulak* ideology. The feedback effect (Vygotsky, 1934a, p. 246) of higher mental operations does not undo the results of earlier operations but retains them in a peculiar way. Once again, then, Vygotsky found an application for Hegel's concept of "superseding" (cf. Solomon, 1983).

These ideas were thought-provoking but hardly problem-free as Vygotsky realized all too well (see Vygotsky, 1934a, pp. 257–9). One may question the methodological set-up of the experiments (e.g. the fact that they were cross-sectional) carried out by Shif and others of Vygotsky's students, and wonder whether the findings were valid and reliable. One may also doubt, of course, the interpretation of the results. Modern research, for instance, has suggested that is it surprisingly hard to demonstrate the generalization of cognitive skills from one area of thinking to another (Scribner and Cole, 1981). This would imply that while Vygotsky's arguments about the transfer of cognitive skills tied to the teaching of scientific concepts may be plausible, they are in need of additional experimental verification.

From Ach's Revised Search Method to the "Vygotsky Test"

As is well-known, Vygotsky's *Thinking and Speech* only became available to the Western researcher in 1962, in the form of a highly abridged and edited edition (Vygotsky, 1962). The dissemination of his ideas concerning concept-formation could only begin, therefore, in the 1960s (cf. Valsiner, 1988, pp. 150–66). Some of his earlier ideas, however, found their way to the West via a curious detour: the study of schizophrenia (see chapter 3). In 1934 the journal *Archives of Neurology and Psychiatry* published Vygotsky's paper "Thought in schizophrenia" and Kasanin, who translated the text, remarked in a footnote that "For the past five years Vigotsky, together with Professor Luria, had been doing extremely interesting work on the psychology of schizophrenia, utilizing the experimental technic of the *Gestalt* psychology. The article was written at my request over three years ago" (Kasanin in Vygotsky, 1934h, p. 1063).

In this paper Vygotsky remarked that many researchers had seen similarities between the thinking of adolescents and schizophrenics. His own research led him to the conclusion that these similarities were undoubtedly present, but should be interpreted against the background of the quite different dynamic processes that take place in these different groups. Emphasizing these dynamic differences (e.g. growth versus decay) Vygotsky nevertheless thought that the study of adolescent thinking might prove useful for the study of schizophrenic thinking and vice versa. In order to study the thinking of schizophrenics he used the revised search method described above (erroneously called a "*Gestalt* technic" by Kasanin).

Vygotsky described the methodology of his investigation and its results in rather vague terms (as usual), but his fundamental claim was clear: the thinking of schizophrenic patients ("not counting refusals and half-hearted cooperation" and limiting the discussion to "all cases in which the results were definite and clearcut" (Vygotsky, 1934h, p. 1066) could be described in terms of the categories that denote preconceptual thinking in children. That is, the patients' thinking could be classified as thinking in "associative complexes," "chain complexes," etc. (see above). Vygotsky concluded that "my observations show that complex thought observed in patients with schizophrenia is the nearest step to conceptual thought and immediately precedes it genetically. There is some similarity, then, although by no means an identity, between the thought of the patient with schizophrenia and the thought of a child" (1934h, p. 1068) and that "in persons with schizophrenia thought is really regressive" (1934h, p. 1067). A second conclusion was that in schizophrenia it would seem that the meanings of words become changed. The patient reverts to the forms of complex thinking that lay hidden in a subordinate function in the geologically older layers of his mind (see chapter 11). Or, in Vygotsky's own words:

> Associations, as a primitive form of thought, are retained as a substructure in the development of the higher forms of thinking, but they are uncovered and begin to act independently in accordance with their own laws when the whole personality, for some reason, is disturbed. There is reason to believe that complex thought is not a specific product of schizophrenia, but merely an outcropping of the older forms of thought, which are always present in a latent form in the psyche of the patient but which become apparent only when the higher intellectual processes become disturbed by illness ... Each one of us carries schizophrenia in a latent form, i.e. in the mechanisms of thought which when uncovered become the central figure in the drama of schizophrenic thought. (Vygotsky, 1934h, p. 1071)

But if the word-meanings of schizophrenic patients do indeed differ from those of normal adults, then this difference should come out also in other ways, Vygotsky reasoned. Referring to Gelb and Goldstein's (1920; 1925) work on the disturbances of categorical thinking he mentioned various tests used to diagnose the patients' understanding of words in an indirect way. These included tests dealing with the capacity for metaphorical expression (e.g. a ship plows the sea) and Piaget's test requiring the subject to match a specific proverb with another of similar meaning. It was found that the patients – who otherwise seemed to have preserved normal intelligence – could not find the metaphorical sense of expressions unknown to them but were bound by the literal, concrete meaning of the words presented.

Finally, Vygotsky hypothesized that the emotional and perceptual disturbances characteristic of schizophrenic patients had their common origin in the disturbance of conceptual thinking. He also assumed that the patient's sense of self had been disturbed as this was intimately connected with the growth of conceptual thinking in adolescence.

Vygotsky's paper at first received little attention, possibly as a result of its vagueness, but this situation changed several years later when Kasanin and Hanfmann published two articles in which they gave a detailed description of the method of investigation used by Vygotsky and their own suggested revisions (Hanfmann and Kasanin, 1937), and provided some of their empirical results (Kasanin and Hanfmann, 1938). Hanfmann and Kasanin argued that the value of the test was that it allowed a detailed qualitative analysis of the subjects' performance. The steps in the patients' reasoning are nearly always reflected in the manipulations with the objects and their comments. Nevertheless, they suggested the introduction of a scoring procedure – based on the time needed for solution and the number of blocks turned up by the experimenter, that is, the *amount* of help given – in order to make group comparisons possible (Hanfmann and Kasanin, 1937, p. 533; Kasanin and Hanfmann, 1938, p. 40). In addition, they supplied detailed instructions as to which blocks to turn up after a subject's attempt at classification, how to respond to the subjects' questions, etc. Kasanin and Hanfmann (1938) obtained the results of experiments conducted with 50 schizophrenics selected according to their ability to participate in the task. The quantitative results of these patients were compared with those of 45 normal adults and it was found that the achievement of the schizophrenic group was markedly inferior to that of the group of normal adults. The deviation of the patients' performance from that of the normal subjects of the same educational level was especially striking in the group with the highest educational level.

Kasanin and Hanfmann (1938, pp. 45–6) concluded that the results confirmed Vygotsky's view of schizophrenic thinking as a form of regression. They suggested that the test itself might serve as a basis for judging the degree of schizophrenia, at least for patients with a higher educational level. Low performance for patients with an inferior educational level *might* reflect schizophrenia as well as the subjects' poor intellectual level.

Kasanin and Hanfmann's papers were read avidly and discussed by the specialists in the field. It is interesting to see, for example, how Kurt Koffka reacted to their paper published in 1938. In a letter to his collaborator, Harrower, he first wrote that he thought the results to be "clear-cut and significant." But Harrower's reply made him change his mind. She wrote that she and Goldstein were very critical of Vygotsky's procedure and that Goldstein had argued that there really wasn't any guarantee that it touched conceptual thinking at all, as the problems might be solved at a purely sensory level. Harrower, on the basis of her own first experiences with the "Vygotsky test," added that a major ambiguity built into the test was which block to turn up after a subject's first faulty classification. The selection of the block to be turned up was crucial since one choice would help a given individual much more than others. She stated that, in a personal letter to her, Kasanin accepted this criticism, admitting that the kind of help provided by the experimenter was given on intuitive grounds. Finally, Harrower claimed that she had repeatedly found that the subjects did not take into account the nonsense syllables at all: they therefore did not set out to find out the word-meanings. These arguments seem to have convinced Koffka: in a reply to Harrower he wrote that "it has very clearly nothing to do with concept-formation, but with what Hume and Vygotsky thought concept-formation was. It may be a particular kind of abstraction" (see Harrower, 1983, pp. 135–7).

One can easily see how the two paradigms of scientific research clash in this example. On the one hand, we have the clinician Vygotsky, with his interest in a qualitative diagnosis of the *processes* of thinking of the individual and his lack of interest in standardization of research methods. On the other hand, we have Harrower, who was interested in reliable measurements, and who therefore criticized the test's lack of standardized procedures. As such the criticism would reflect a continuing debate in the social sciences (see Van der Veer, Van IJzendoorn, and Valsiner, 1991). Moreover, the claim that classification can be based on an interpretation at a purely sensory level seems to be simply mistaken. It may hold true for the postulation of several types of complexes but, in order to conclude that children or schizophrenics reasoned on a conceptual level, the subjects had to define the concept and to demonstrate their skill in using it while answering various questions (see also Hanfmann, 1941). It is exactly this ability which distinguished conceptual thinking from the more primitive – and perhaps largely sensory – levels of thinking. One would think, then, that this first criticism of the "Vygotsky test" was based on too narrow a view of the procedure: it is only justified when one focuses criticism on the quantitative outcome measures of time and number of blocks turned up.

Bolles and Goldstein (1938, p. 43) in their study of impaired abstract behavior in schizophrenic patients decided not to use the test suggested by "the Russian psychiatrist Vygotsky" and opted instead for the sorting test used by Gelb and Goldstein (1925) as it was "simpler and more adaptable to various situations." The results they found roughly accorded with Vygotsky's, and they concurred with the theory that the characteristic defect of the schizophrenic patients appeared to be an impairment of the capacity "for the type of behavior we call 'abstract behavior' " (Bolles and Goldstein, 1938, p. 65). In an interesting monograph on abstract and concrete behavior Goldstein and Scheerer gave a detailed description of five tests designed to tap the "abstract attitude" of various patients, but although they mentioned Vygotsky's paper and the "Vygotsky test" they chose not to include it, preferring the simpler Weigl–Goldstein–Scheerer Color Form Sorting Test, which does not make use of nonsense syllables (Goldstein and Scheerer, 1941, pp. 110–30).

It does seem that Vygotsky's use of the revised search method to study the thinking of schizophrenics and other mental patients met with little success, for researchers appear to have followed the example of Kasanin and Hanfmann. The same holds true for the use of the "Vygotsky test" as a measure of intelligence (Semeonoff and Laird, 1952; Semeonoff and Trist, 1958). This use of Vygotsky's approach – facilitated by Hanfmann and Kasanin's (1942) introduction of a definite scoring method and their discussions about the educational level of subjects – met with essentially the same objections as the revised search test. As M'Comisky and Worsley (1970, p. 193) remarked, it was difficult to devise "a standardizable set of administration instructions and a more generally acceptable way of scoring performances (both quantitatively and qualitatively) on the test." These authors decided to "simplify" the "Vygotsky test" by omitting the trapezium, hexagon, and semi-circle, which were deemed to be "ambiguous." Administering this simplified version, having also eliminated the "time-help" factor from the scoring system and limited the administration time to 25 minutes, the researchers established "norm data" for three age groups against which future researchers can compare their data.

M'Comisky's and Worsley's simplified Vygotsky test would seem a rather perverted version of the original revised search method and a far cry from Vygotsky's and Sakharov's original qualitative diagnostic procedure. Surprisingly the authors were acutely aware of this problem, as Kasanin and Hanfmann had been before them, and it is instructive to follow their reasoning for a moment:

> The present modification of the Vygotsky test brings up in a pointed way an incompatibility of objective in the use of a test since the addition to it of a quantitative scoring system by Hanfmann and Kasanin (1942). Originally the test was intended by Vygotsky to yield a *qualitative* appraisal of the subject's level of thinking and strategy in tackling the problem which constitutes the test – an aspect of concept-learning research which has for some years now been receiving increased emphasis (Bruner et al., 1956; Pikas, 1966). The addition of a scoring system by Hanfmann and Kasanin (1942) added a second and overriding consideration, *quantitative* appraisal. Since then, two kinds of appraisal of the subject's performance have been possible: a quantitative appraisal based on level of solution, time taken and help given, and a qualitative appraisal based on the subject's general level of conceptualization, strategy and organization in tackling and solving the problem. (M'Comisky and Worsley, 1970, p. 195)

Following this lucid analysis the authors gave a defence of their alterations to the procedure of the original test on the grounds that (1) it made standardization possible; (2) proficiency of administering the test would be easier to attain; and (3) administration time would be shortened. They did not find the loss of qualitative information crucial.

Conclusions

Although many Western researchers who have discussed Vygotsky's revised search method have paid lip-service to the goal of qualitative analysis, the pressure to develop measures for quantitative performance that were indicative of individual abilities has been strong. The promulgation of a scoring method by Kasanin and Hanfmann (1937; 1938; 1942) allowed group comparison but *also* facilitated the introduction of a method allowing for the comparison of individual scores, by regarding them as a reflection of the person's general intelligence. In addition, it was generally felt that the procedure should be standardized and simplified because the administration of the test was "a skill which is not easy to acquire" and took too long to administer (Semeonoff and Laird, 1952, quoted in M'Comisky and Worsley, 1970, p. 196).

In the opinion of the present authors this overriding Western interest in scientific rigor and quantitative outcome measures has, to a great extent, determined the development of the revised search method into the (simplified) Vygotsky test. Vygotsky's clinical qualitative approach was lost in the process and his interest in the *dynamics* of cognitive change was replaced by an emphasis on the comparison of individual and group scores. It is ironic that even these Westernized versions of Vygotsky's procedure met with little success. The claim made by the editors of Vygotsky (1956, p. 502) that his paper on conceptual thinking in schizophrenia met with a "broad response in the psychiatric world literature" is certainly an overstatement. M'Comisky and Worsley's (1970, p. 193) remark that "attempts during the past 30 years to develop the Vygotsky sorting test for diagnostic purposes in clinical psychology have made only limited headway" seems a more accurate description of the reception of Vygotsky's revised search method by Western psychologists.

PART III
Moscow, Kharkov, and Leningrad 1932–1934

Introduction

In the final years of his life Vygotsky's involvement in the activities of the Herzen Pedagogical Institute in Leningrad grew. He had been invited to lecture there by Rubinshtejn, and it is characteristic of Vygotsky that he rapidly gathered a new group of collaborators, including M. A. Levina, G. E. Konnikova, Zh. I. Shif, and D. B. El'konin. His main interests gradually shifted towards the following, interrelated, issues.

1 The semantic structure of consciousness and the relation between affect and intellect. Viewing cognitive development as the development from thinking in complexes towards genuine conceptual thinking, Vygotsky increasingly considered the scientific concept to be the key to explaining various phenomena of consciousness. While cognitive development was dominated by the *development* of genuine (scientific) concepts, various clinical syndromes – such as Pick's disease (cf. Goldstein and Katz, 1937) and schizophrenia – were shown to be connected to a *loss* of genuine conceptual thinking. At the same time, however, Vygotsky developed a deep interest in the relation between the *ratio* and emotions (see chapter 14). This interest can be at least partially attributed to his growing knowledge and appreciation of the seminal work done by Kurt Lewin and his associates (see chapter 8).

It is not widely known that Lewin and Vygotsky knew each other personally and that several of Lewin's students collaborated with Vygotsky. Lewin first visited Vygotsky in November 1931 as a result of an extensive correspondence between the two men that may have started long before. In June 1931, for example, Vygotsky mentioned that he had received from its author Lewin's (1931/1981) newly published brochure on Galilean and Aristotelian thinking in psychology and in August of the same year he mentioned that Lewin planned to come to Moscow in the fall (Vygotsky in letters to Luria, dated June 12, and August 1, 1931). Several years later, and quite unexpectedly, Lewin again visited Moscow (Zeigarnik, 1988). Having visited a congress in the USA in 1933 Lewin wanted to return to Germany via Japan and Moscow. However, it was during this trip that he learned of Hitler's rise to power and, shocked by the turn of political events, Lewin decided to postpone his return to Berlin. From Moscow he consulted his colleagues in Berlin (e.g. Köhler) about the proper way to handle the new situation and as a result Lewin decided to emigrate from Germany as soon as possible. Naturally, during his several weeks stay in Moscow Lewin frequently met his colleague and fellow anti-Nazi, Vygotsky. He visited Vygotsky's home in Serpukhova Street and also gave a talk at the Institute of Psychology, showing his famous film about a child trying to sit on the stone. This film, incidentally, was left in Moscow when Lewin finally left for Germany and is now in the *dacha* of the Luria family. Vygotsky and Lewin appreciated each other's work deeply and when, in 1936, Vygotsky's students and colleagues wished to compose a posthumous *Festschrift* Lewin happily agreed to submit a chapter (Levina and Morozova, 1984). However, as a direct result of the Paedology Decree this *Festschrift* never materialized (Zeigarnik, 1988, p. 179; see chapters 12 and 16).

The personal ties between the Berlin institute and Vygotsky's group were not limited to these contacts between Lewin and Vygotsky. Luria spent some time in Berlin and Vygotsky's collaborators Zeigarnik and Birenbaum both worked for many years in Berlin as Lewin's assistants. Immediately after her return to Moscow Zeigarnik gave several lectures (on June 10 and 13, 1931) on the latest findings of Lewin and his collaborators, lectures which were much appreciated by Vygotsky. Naturally, Vygotsky did not fully agree with Lewin's interpretation of his findings and in various minor experiments he tried to refute his views.

2   The relation between education and development (see chapters 11 and 13). This research was loosely connected with a debate about the appropriate way of teaching in secondary schools. Proponents of the "complex system" (*kompleksnyj*) defended the view that various subjects (e.g. mathematics, geography) had to be taught as an interrelated whole, or complex. The method of "learning by doing" projects was advocated as the appropriate means of acquiring knowledge. Proponents of the "subject system" (*predmetnyj*) argued that each specific subject had to be taught separately in the traditional way. In the early 1930s all "progressive" ideas, including the "complex system" theory, were condemned by the Party as leftist aberrations (Kozulin, 1984, pp. 31–2). Of course, Vygotsky's critics were happy to point out that he had opted for the "wrong" opinion and had allied himself to the ideas of the radical progressive Shulgin, a later Party decision notwithstanding (see chapter 16).

3   The concept of stages ("age periods") and development (see chapter

12). This work was the result of Vygotsky's involvement in paedology. Working at the Faculty of Paedology of Difficult Childhood (as Professor and Head of the Faculty) of the Moscow State Pedagogical Institute, at the Second Moscow Medical Institute (as Head of the Faculty of General and Age Paedology, and as Professor from 15 April, 1931), and at the Herzen Pedagogical Institute in Leningrad, he lectured extensively on paedological topics. (See Vygotsky's own account of his activities, compiled January 14, 1934; here given by his daughter Vygodskaja, personal communication, November 1988).

4   The localization of psychological functions in the brain (see chapter 12). This work was prompted by Vygotsky's study of medicine (he studied medicine in Kharkov and at the Moscow Medical Institute) and his growing interest in adult pathology. Apart from his intrinsic interest in psychopathology, Vygotsky needed, also working in a neurological and psychiatric clinic, the formal status of a physician.

5   The topic of inner speech (see chapter 15). This research was part of Vygotsky's efforts to replicate and refute Piaget's work on children's inability to decenter. In particular, he wished to prove that egocentric speech originated from social, interactive speech and had a regulatory function. The latter point returned to his earlier writings on the relation between thinking and speech.

The Disintegration of Vygotsky's Research Collective

Vygotsky's vision of a large research collective working for a common cause was never realized. At times, it appeared that it might be possible to establish such a collective, but on each occasion Vygotsky was required to move to a new Institute and to work with new colleagues. For example, after graduation his students (e.g. Levina, Morozova) were sent to work in different cities all over the Soviet Union, and so in order for any cohesive program to be developed, they had to travel to Moscow where Vygotsky regularly organized so-called internal conferences. The closing down of the Academy of Communist Education and the resulting relocation of some of Vygotsky's co-workers (Bozhovich, Leont'ev, Luria, Zaparozhec) to Kharkov also compromised the research program. Moreover, in Kharkov, Leont'ev developed his own view of cognitive development in response to ideological criticism. Leont'ev distanced himself from Vygotsky's ideas in an obituary written in 1934 (pp. 188–9) in which he emphasized that mediation processes are rooted in material and social, or rather societal, activity and renamed the cultural-historical theory "societal-historical theory." He also referred to the public debate about the merits of reactology for an assessment of Vygotsky's theory (*Itogi diskussii* . . . , 1931). It is clear that in replacing Vygotsky's emphasis on signs as means of mediation between objects of experience and mental functions with the idea that physical action (labor) must mediate between the subject and the external world, Leont'ev aligned himself with the official ideology. According to the ideological gatekeepers, labor (physical activity) had to take precedence of speech (see also Leont'ev, 1935/1983, and chapter 16).

The growing difference between their opinions did not escape Vygotsky's attention and in August 1933 he wrote Leont'ev, who was by then in Kharkov, a letter about the need to clarify their respective positions.

> I feel already and not for the first time that we stand before a very important conversation, as it were, for which we both, apparently, are not prepared, and the contents of which we can only vaguely imagine – your departure [for Kharkov] – is our serious, maybe irremediable, failure, resulting from our errors and real negligence of the cause that has been entrusted to us. Apparently, neither in your biography, nor in mine, nor in the history of our psychology, will what has happened be repeated. So be it. I am trying to understand all this in the Spinozist way – with sadness but accepting it as something inevitable. In my inner thoughts I deal with it as a fact, as something that happened. The inner fate has to be solved in connection with the outer but – of course – it is not fully determined by it. That is why it [the inner fate] is not clear, is [only] vaguely visible, through a haze – and my concern with this has caused the greatest anxiety that I have experienced in the last years . . . You are right that first of all we have to get rid of the need to dissemble . . . That is why I consider it [your decision] correct, despite the fact that I judge everything that happened with A. R. [Luria] differently (and not happily). But I shall return to that some other time . . . (Vygotsky in a letter to Leont'ev, dated August 2, 1933)

We can see in this letter that Vygotsky felt their positions had diverged so much that their "common cause" (note again the almost Messianic tone of his letter) was threatened. We also see that some undescribed difficulties had arisen between Luria and Vygotsky. Puzyrej – whose notes to the unpublished Soviet edition of Vygotsky's letters we have used throughout this book – has suggested that this passage refers to the fact that Luria at some point had joined the Kharkov group and headed the Psychological Section of the Ukranian Psychoneurological Institute, the section that Leont'ev was to lead later. One can well understand Luria's decision to do this, for the conditions offered to him in Kharkov were excellent. At the Psychological Section – which was to be developed into an independent institute within a few years – he was allocated sixteen rooms, fifteen collaborators, and 100,000 roubles per year! (Luria in a letter to Köhler, dated March 6,

A portrait of Lev Vygotsky.

1932). Still, after much deliberation, Luria left the Kharkov group and concentrated his activities in Moscow once more. To this story should be added the account given by Vygotsky's daughter of the personal relations between the psychologists during that period. According to her (personal communication, September 1989) toward the end of 1933 or the beginning of 1934 Vygotsky and Leont'ev stopped seeing each other. Apparently, Leont'ev had written a letter to Luria in which he stated that Vygotsky's ideas belonged to the past and suggested that Luria started to collaborate with him, without Vygotsky being involved. At first Luria agreed, but then he had second thoughts about the plan, and showed Leont'ev's letter to

Vygotsky. Naturally, Vygotsky was hurt and angry and he wrote a harsh letter to Leont'ev, at which point they stopped seeing each other,[1] although it would appear that they continued to exchange letters about research affairs. Understandably, relations with Luria, too, became somewhat strained after this event.

One can see, then, that in the final period of his life even Vygotsky's staunchest allies of the preceding years, Luria and Leont'ev, were contemplating leaving him and for very understandable reasons, not the least of them being the growing ideological pressure. They no longer felt unconditionally bound to pursue the "common cause," that is, the new psychology of man that Vygotsky envisioned. In view of Vygotsky's attitude towards this cause, he must have had immense problems not construing their behavior as a personal betrayal in this, the most difficult period of his life, but to see them rather as the inevitable outcome of personal, scientific, and ideological developments. Once again, he had an opportunity to think of Spinoza's words in The Ethics (1677/1955, p. 128), where the great philosopher explained that one should not abuse or deride human emotions but try to understand them.

[1] It was only by the end of 1955, when the ban on Vygotsky's writings was about to be lifted, that Leont'ev (with Luria) again paid a visit (his last) to the Vygodsky family. The reason for the visit was to look in the private archives for writings that might be (re)published (Vygodskaja, personal communication, September 1989).

12

Vygotsky the Paedologist

> ... *if synthesis is not an empty word, but denotes a really existing fact in the nature of child development then paedology acquires in the recognition of that fact its eternally objective solid basis* ...
>
> Vygotsky, *"Pedologija i smezhnye s neju nauki"*

The standing of Lev Vygotsky in relation to paedology deserves special attention since it has consistently been overlooked by the majority of the existing expositions on the intellectual heritage he left. The reasons for this oversight are not too difficult to find: the word "paedology" remained an ideologically suspect term for half a century in the Soviet Union (since 1936), and its use in discussions could damn the speaker to be judged as "lagging behind the times" and associate him with "dead pseudo-science" at the least, and could even lead to death. One of the major effects of Stalinism on psychology – the 1936 Decree on Paedology, which outlawed the discipline and eliminated paedologists from the educational institutions – has remained in force (or at least was/has not been officially reversed) even in the years following de-Stalinization. Vygotsky was closely associated with paedology in the last seven years of his life, and – as we will show in this chapter – in a highly intellectually productive way. In conjunction with many Soviet educationalists, he participated in the efforts to make paedology a means that might lead to the goals of creating "the new man" during the social restructuring. Paedology had a wide basis in Soviet society in the 1920s/1930s.

Historical Foundations of Paedology in Russia

The paedology of the 1920s in the Soviet Union had a clear continuity with its counterpart of the pre-1917 Russia. Following the American tradition of "child study" ("paidology"; see G. S. Hall, O. Chrisman) and the German

"experimental pedagogics" (see E. Meumann), Russia had already developed a remarkable paedological tradition long before the 1917 Revolution.
Thus, the First Congress on Experimental Pedagogics in Russia took place
in St Petersburg on January 7–13, 1911. At that Congress a number of
paedological topics, such as Rossolimo's "profiles" of child development
analysis and Lazursky's "natural experiment" as a method, were discussed
(Markarianz, 1911). These topics were still of great interest to Russian
paedologists at the time of Vygotsky's emergence on the paedological scene
in the latter half of the 1920s. In late 1913 (January 1914 by the new
calendar) the Second All-Russian Congress took place in St Petersburg, and
again the uses of the "natural experiment" occupied an important place in
its scientific discussions (Basov, 1914). These congresses continued to be
held, even during the First World War, the Third Congress occurring in
January 1916 (Shchelovanov, 1916). The use of "natural experiments" was
under scrutiny once more (Lazursky and Filosofova, 1916). The study of
paedology in pre-Revolution Russia was well-established, substantial and
well-connected internationally (see Arian' 1912; also Konorov', 1908).

This development of paedology in Russia before 1917 was dependent to a
large degree on the organizational activities of Vladimir Bekhterev, whose
Psychoneurological Institute (founded in 1907) led to the opening of the
Paedological Institute. As early as 1903 Bekhterev had expressed the idea
that the opening of a special institution for paedological studies would be
beneficial. So, in 1907, as a part of his Psychoneurological Institute,
Bekhterev organized the Psycho-Paedological Institute. This Institute, in
contrast to paedological institutions in the rest of the world, which were
oriented towards the study of school-age children, focused its attention on
the paedology of infancy and early childhood. It was planned to function as
a live-in ward, where parents or guardians could leave their infants or young
children to be raised (see "Upravlenie Psikho-Pedologicheskim Institutom",
1908). Being a part of the Psychoneurological Institute, the Paedological
Institute could benefit from the input of the best psychological, physiological and biological researchers in Russia at that time (e.g. K. Povarnin, A.
Griboedov, A. Lazursky, V. Vagner). In 1911 the Institute was given its own
building, but as it relied on private donations to survive it was in financial
trouble constantly. Bekhterev consistently tried to persuade the the Government to fund the Institute. He almost succeeded in late 1916, but the
turmoil of the February 1917 Revolution swept aside the government that
had accepted this plan in principle. Because of the difficult economic and
everyday-life conditions that are the concomitants of any revolution, the
Institute was evacuated to the town of Pensa, where it ceased to function.

Bekhterev never gave up his efforts to re-establish the Institute. Since he
was one of the few Russian intellectuals who accepted the Bolshevik
Revolution of October 1917 without much difficulty (after all, Bekhterev

had for years been opposed to the Tzarist government), it was possible for him to argue his case with the new rulers. The Paedological Institute was eventually restored in 1918 as a part of the Commissariat of Education, and became a state institution. Its budget came out of the Pre-School Division of the Council of Communes of the Northern Province and it was housed in a new building in the center of Petrograd. However, the budget of the Pre-School Division was not very substantial, nor were the priorities of the leaders of that Division fully aligned with those of Bekhterev, and in 1920 the Institute was again dissolved (Shchelovanov, 1929).

However, Bekhterev and his colleagues continued their work in the area of paedology, work which led to new research and organizational results in the early 1920s (Osipova, 1928). So, in 1922 the Paedological Institute was re-opened as a research Institution under the guidance of *Glavnauka* (The Directorate of Science), and as a part of the Psychneurological Academy. The new research Institute included four sections which studied: experimental pedagogics; anatomy and physiology; psychology of childhood (a section led by Mikhail Basov); age and individual variability of constitutional types and behavior (led by N. Shchelovanov). After three years of highly productive research the Institute was reoganized yet again. In 1925, the Leningrad Institute of Scientific Pedagogics was founded, and three sections of the Paedological Institute (except for the infancy section headed by N. Shchelovanov) were transferred to the new Institute.

In the 1920s, the effects of paedological research became visible in different educational and research institutions all over the Soviet Union. Obviously, this led to the proliferation of paedological publications written in Russian, and by the mid-1920s the literature on paedology available to readers in the Soviet Union was extensive (Rybnikov, 1925). In this time a number of major textbooks and treatises on special subjects had appeared which added to the substantial available literature from the pre-1917 period. Almost all of the major European and North American works on child development and child study (e.g. works by Baldwin, Compayré, W. Stern, C. Stern, Groos, Sully, Drummond, Claparède, Binet, Meumann, Bühler, and many others) were available in Russian translations by the mid-1920s, and the efforts to translate these international sources proceeded at an extraordinary pace until the early 1930s. In sum, the reorganization of the educational system (practical pedagogics) in post-1917 Russia took place concurrently with paedological research in different institutions.

Soviet Pedagogics and the Rise of Paedology

The development of paedology in the Soviet Union in the 1920s was undoubtedly fuelled by the educational experiments that the government advocated, indeed enforced. Among the myriad of issues and events that shattered the Russian educational system in the 1920s (see Anweiler, 1964; Fitzpatrick, 1979; Lapidus, 1978; Pinkevich, 1930), two themes proved to be dominant: the radical reconstruction of human personality (the building of the "new socialist man") and the limiting the access of selected social classes to educational opportunities. The educational system was open to all the cross-winds of social movements that blew through the Soviet society, cross-winds which sometimes enabled unqualified, incapable ideologues to assume power, only to blow them back to oblivion, having ajudged them unfit to be the leaders of "progress".

The educational experiments of the 1920s were only partially built upon "Marxist" ideology in their particulars. In fact, there was a remarkable continuity evident between the pre-1917 liberal intelligentsia's educational philosophies (often based on European or American models, and disliked by the Tzarist educational officialdom), and the novelties introduced in the 1920s. For instance, the educational community-based experience propagated by S. T. Shatsky (who was also interested in psychoanalysis, see Chapter 5) in the early 1920s was based on his experience between 1906 and 1908 in running children's communes. Shatsky believed in the social organization of children's natural interests in a community context, where work was a natural part of the everyday life of the commune (an idea liberal educators imported from America at the turn of the century) and for him it was not difficult to accept the communist goal of re-educating the whole society as an all-encompassing utopia (Zen'kovsky, 1960, pp. 22–3). Indeed, many novel educational experiments in America were imported and conducted with remarkable speed by Soviet educationalists in the 1920s. For instance, the Dalton Plan (Parkhurst, 1922; Dewey, 1922) and the Project Curriculum (E. Collings) for organizing children's school lives, and were widely discussed and implemented on a large scale. Of course, as these ideas were imported they were modified to accommodate Russian cultural history. As one celebrated visitor was able to write having briefly visited the Soviet Union in 1928:

> while Russian educators acknowledge here – as in many other things – an original indebtedness to American theory, they criticize many of the "projects" employed in our schools as casual and trivial, because they do not belong to any general social aim, nor have definite social consequences in their traion. To them, an educative "project" is the means by which the principle of some "complex" or unified whole of social subject-matter is realized. Its criterion value is its contribution to some "socially useful work." (Dewey, 1929, pp. 101–2)

Indeed, the socio-political and educational objectives were effectively mirrored in experimentation with new pedagogic methods. The experiments were borrowed not only from America (American experiments, surprisingly, seemed to fit ideologically with the needs of the Soviet educators; see Dewey, 1929, pp. 107–8), but also from continental Europe, and their influence is evident in Russian liberal education. Thus, Paul Natorp's "social pedagogy" and Robert Seidel's "labor school" were popular models in the 1920s, and contributed to much of the ideology of the *trudovaja shkola* (labor school) propagated by Blonsky.

All these educational experiments were studied by Russian pedagogues in the difficult and complicated conditions of the nascent Soviet society. The children whose educational future was at stake as the process of reconstructing society by new education took place, came from families that had been separated by war, famines, terror (both "red" and "white"), and difficult economic conditions. These specific conditions of the 1920s left their traces in the educational and paedological literature of the time. Thus, issues of how to handle the masses of orphaned and neglected children (*bezprizorniki*) and how to structure adults' education for literacy were also major topics in the discourse concerning Soviet education in the 1920s.

As the "new society" tried to create the "new man", this discourse, about the role of school in general, and different forms of schooling in particular, was all-pervasive. The debate was enlivened by the constant friction between different parts of the educational bureaucracy that were constantly fighting for control over educational institutions. The history of this infighting between the Commissariat of Education (*Narkompros*) and its rivals is worth careful investigation in itself (Anweiler, 1964). Likewise, the disputes about the future of the school as a social institution in the "new society" (e.g. V. Shulgin's prognosis for the scaling down of schooling under socialism; see also chapter 16), the method of uniting basic and applied (polytechnic) education, the principles of pupils' self-government in schools, and many other pressing subjects set the stage for paedology to assume the role of an integrative scientific discipline closely linked to educational practice. The development of paedology in the USSR was closely linked with these pedagogical and ideological endeavors. Its history can be divided into three main periods: that of the emergence as a separate socially organized discipline (from about 1922 until 1928; see Zalkind, 1931b); the development of established paedology (1928 until 1931–2); and the period of decline (1932–6).

A number of research institutions of pedagogics which served as a basis for the launching of the paedology movement (see "Spisok . . .", 1929) had come into existence in the 1920s. First, of course, was V. N. Shulgin's *Institut metodov shkol'noj raboty* (Institute of School-work Methods; from 1930 renamed as the Institute for Marxist–Leninist Pedagogics) in Moscow. Founded in 1922, it conducted research on bringing school tasks closer to real-life tasks, and from the utopian perspective of building a "new society" where school and life are united, attacked the *Narkompros* educational policies. By the late 1920s, a number of interesting paedological research topics were being studied at the Institute: development of writing and counting skills, the transfer of skills, and so on. Secondly, the *Institut metodov vneshkol'noj raboty* (Institute of the Methods of Extra-School Work) under the directorship of A. Ja Zaks had been opened in 1923. In this Institute, original work on the organization of externally organized and "spontaneous" groups of children emerged. As was appropriate for an institute with such a name, it concentrated researching the integration of children into their social-economic life settings. In Leningrad the *Institut nauchnoj pedagogiki* (Institute of Scientific Pedagogics; director B. Fingert) was started in 1924–5. It inherited the paedological concerns of Bekhterev's previous Institute (see above), and served as the basis for Mikhail Basov's paedological endeavors. And finally, in 1926 the *Institut nauchnoj pedagogiki* (Institute of Scientific Pedagogics) was also opened in Moscow, at the Second Moscow State University and under the directorship of Albert Pinkevitch (see Anweiler, 1964, p. 308). It was because of the work of this Institute and his teaching of paedology at the Second Moscow State University that Vygotsky moved into the center of the Soviet paedological organization. These pedagogical research institutes enabled the social coordination of activities in paedology on an All-Union basis. The growth of paedology was reflected in the structure of psychological research centers: Kornilov's Institute of Experimental Psychology was re-named, in or around 1930, the Institute of Psychology, Paedology and Psychotechnics (*Institut Psikhologii, Pedologii i Psikhotekhniki*).

The First Soviet Paedological Congress took place in December 1927/January 1928, and argued for the promotion and development of the institutional organization of the paedological movement in the USSR (see Nestjuk, 1929). As was the case with all similar events in the Soviet Union at the time, the Congress unfolded in the context of the call for a Marxist restructuring of the new discipline, as the speeches by Anatoli Lunacharsky (the head of *Narkompros* until 1929), Nikolai Bukharin, and Nadezhda Krupskaja illustrated (see Anweiler, 1964, p. 314). Among the many reports on the work of the Congress (see Nestjuk, 1929) was one by Vygotsky (1928r). As was usual for such gatherings, it ended with the passing of a grandiose (and verbose) "resolution" calling for paedology to be established as a Marxist, dialectical discipline emphasizing the role of social environment in the development of children from lower towards higher psychological functions. This call for a "unified science," in which the main focus would be on development, was in accord with Vygotsky's world-view, although it was other paedologists who would have been responsible for the drafting of this resolution, namely A. Zalkind and S. Molozhavyj.

The First Paedological Congress resulted in the publication the journal *Pedologija* (a decision taken by the People's Commissariat of Education on January 26, 1928). The aim of the journal was to coordinate all the paedological activities in the Soviet Union, and to relate paedological research activities more closely to the needs of the educational system. The popularity of paedology in USSR grew substantially after (and with) the inception of *Pedologija* can be seen by the increase in the number of subscribers. It started in 1928 with 200 subscribers and by the beginning of 1929 there were 800, and by the end of that year 1,500 (of which 30 percent were individuals; see "*Na poroge tretiego goda*," 1929).

Of course, the discipline of paedology was embedded in a complex social context and its research was conducted in an environment of ever-increasing suspicion, as one politician after another became the victim of the uncontrolled growth of Marxist ideology. Indeed paedology itself was eventually made a scapegoat of this growth. For instance, from March 1928, dicussions in Soviet intellectual circles revolved around the Shakhty Trial – the trial of a group of engineers in the coal district of Donbass in the Shakhty region. They were accused of having organized the sabotage of the production lines, and of being "representatives" of former (capitalist) mine owners and "agents of foreign intelligence". In the widely disseminated propaganda campaign conducted well before the opening of the trial (in May, 1928) the calls for vigilance about and distrust of people from non-proletarian class background became very intense (see Fitzpatrick, 1979, chapter 6). So, by the fall of 1928, the expulsion and non-admission of students from this background to institutions of higher learning peaked once more, a situation which occurred throughout the 1920s. A number of *Narkompros* leaders (including Lunacharsky and Krupskaja) protested against this class-based discrimination of students but to no avail.

The anti-intelligentsia and anti-cosmopolitan fears that were cultivated by the Shakhty Trial affected the Soviet educational system (*Narkompros* was criticized for the inefficiency of its educational activities), and thus set the stage for the social disputes about paedology's role in "helping the pedagogical practice." In this situation it was inevitable that the social discourse on paedology precipitated the gradual separation between acceptable Soviet and disenfranchised bourgeois psychoneurology. In November 1929 the Moscow Society of Neuropathologists and Psychiatrists finally surrendered to the demands of the Bolshevizing activists, who never tired of pointing to the "exclusive professionalism" of that Society as the root cause of the "bourgeois remnants" of the uncontrollable clique of specialists. This led to the appointment of "proletarian" specialists to professional organizations, a development which affected many different sciences between 1929 and 1931 (Joravsky, 1989, p. 336). The leading Bolshevizing paedologist Aaron Zalkind spoke of this development with unqualified approbation (see

Zalkind, 1929a, p. 456). His stated goal for paedology – in preparation for the large congress on the study of human behavior in January 1930 – was to "unite different psychoneurological sciences ideologically" and "insert them into the service to practise in the reconstructive period" (1929a, p. 456).

The grandiose First All-Union Congress on the Study of Human Behavior took place in Leningrad from January 26 until February 1, 1930. About 3,000 people were registered as participants, many of them "practical workers" in the disciplines relevant to the issues discussed. About half of the participants were from Leningrad, the other half from Moscow and other areas of the Soviet Union. On the agenda of the Congress was the ideologically driven plan to combine the "practice of the construction of socialism." The plenary session included speeches not only by Zalkind, Kornilov, Spil'rein, Molozhavyj among the psychoneurologists but also by Lunacharsky (who had been dismissed from his post as the Head of *Narkompros* in September, 1929) and the philosophers I. Luppol and N. Karev (see "*Na Pervom Vsesojuznom . . .*", 1930). Only one of the speakers at the plenary session – Molozhavyj – devoted his speech entirely to issues of paedology, calling for the specific application of dialectical thought in paedology (Molozhavyj, 1930a). In fact, paedology constituted only one of the thematic "complexes" discussed at the Congress (the other three being: general problems of the science of behavior; psychoneurology or work and psychotechnique; and pathological psychoneurology). The paedological complex was given a clear developmental definition ("the problem of development in the science of behavior"; see Zalkind, 1930b, p. 1). Vygotsky's name occurred only among the list of those editing the paedology section, along with M. Basov, S. Molozhavyj, and N. Shchelovanov. However, it was Molozhavyj (1930b) who wrote the review of the paedological section at the Congress for *Pedologija*. It becomes quite obvious that the ideological leaders of Marxist paedology at the end of 1920s and early 1930s were Molozhavyj (see analysis of his ideas below) and Zalkind, while Vygotsky – although well known and respected among paedologists – played only a secondary role.

The Paedological Section of the Congress provided a rich cross-sectional overview of paedological research being conducted in the Soviet Union at that time. The issue of the effect of social class on the social development of children emerged in many guises in the presentations. However, more prevalent by far was the subject of the processes of development that the paedological section entailed. It demonstrated the wide range of subjects with which paedology was concerned: from reflexology (Osipova, 1930; Shchelovanov, 1930) to the study of children's world-views (Basov, 1930) and children's collectives (Zaluznyj, 1930; Lange, 1930) to the study of mentally retarded children (Zankov, 1930a). Vygotsky organized a sub-section on the study of cultural development of the child, where in addition to his own lecture (Vygotsky, 1930i), Luria presented a paper on the function of signs in the development of children's behavior (Luria, 1930e), and Leont'ev also spoke about the ways in which stimulus-means mediate the development of voluntary memory (Leont'ev, 1930). As a result of the joint research conducted by these three, in the 1920s, the idea of the *trojka* was born. Furthermore, their three-part presentation was specifically mentioned as a positive example of work having a "good grasp of the dialectic nature of development" in Molozhavyj's evaluative review (1930b, pp. 338–9). As well as this, Vygotsky also gave a presentation on the cultural development of the defective child in the same paedology section (Vygotsky, 1930j).

It should be noted that the activites of Vygotsky and his colleagues were not limited only to the paedology section of this Congress. Vygotsky also participated in the general section of psychology, reflexology and physiology of the nervous system, giving an overview of the "method of double stimulation" (Vygotsky, 1930h), followed by his co-workers' empirical presentations (Solov'ev, 1930; Zankov, 1930b).

The Paedological Section was obliged to conclude its contribution to the Congress by formulating a resolution. The "resolution" formulated the "dialectic-materialistic" focus on child development as entailing the emergence of *qualitatively novel* forms of a social-biological kind. In each aspect of paedology covered by the resolution, the idea of emergence of novelty became encoded in different ways. Thus, under the topic "environment and the problem of development" the resolution declared:

> The social-biological formation of the individual takes place through the dialectical unity of external, environmental and internal immanent factors of development, that grow in the process of active activity of the individual under the condition of the class-production environment [*klassovo-proizvodstvennaja sreda*). ("Rezoljucia . . .", 1930, p. 341)

A couple of lines later, the resolution linked paedology with a class-based ideology even further, declaring that the environment of the child must be studied by taking the "class background" as its basis (1930, p. 341). The importance of the paedological study of the young pioneer movement to enable research on the typology of children's development, was stressed again because that movement "fits our class goals" (1930, p. 343). The research on children's world-views was to follow children as they experience the increasing "class struggle" in the Soviet society (1930, p. 342) and children's collectives were singled out as the subject of paedologo-pedagogical studies on children's work in the society. As a direct result of the Congress, paedology in the Soviet Union moved in two directions, one of which proved productive to science (i.e. the emphasis on development, and dialectical synthesis emerging in the child's encounter with structured and changing environments), and the other contributed to the ideological execution of the discipline itself (the explicit emphasis on the class-basis of developmental research).

The Decline and End of Paedology: No Room for Divergent Social Utopias

The task of explaining the demise of paedology in the Soviet Union is probably too complicated to fulfil simply by making reference to Stalinist purges or the emerging new needs of the education system. Instead, the gradual decline and final collapse of paedology (and the demise of many paedologists) can be seen as a direct result of the very same social process in which they themselves actively participated in the late 1920s – the establishment of the "communist man" by way of radical educational changes. It is predictable that any period of *perestrojka* creates the conditions for an equally radical change of direction. By trying to participate in the "common social goal" of creating the perfect socialist utopia, paedologists were setting the stage for their own elimination and enforced re-education.

Paedology's decline was relatively slow, covering the time from about 1930 until the Decree of 1936. The decline began as a side-effect of the social changes sweeping through Soviet philosophy and other social sciences in 1930–1 (see Valsiner, 1988, pp. 89–95), changes which had a direct impact on paedology. Protected by the shield of Marxist ideology, educationalists could justify the devastation of different research traditions in paedology that were not much to their liking. Naturally, the paedologists themselves were eager to adopt the goal of improving "educational practice." After all, that had been their goal all along. Of course, the same nominal goal can be interpreted in different ways by different groups of people.

As a result of the ideological fight against menshevizing idealism, the tone of the disputes between paedologists suddenly became more strident in 1931. This change can be seen in *Pedologija*, where critical and self-critical statements of paedologists became abundant. Many eminent paedologists of the pre-1930s (Blonsky, Molozhavyj, Zalkind, etc.) had closely identified their thinking with the "discredited" "menshevizing idealists" of Abram Deborin, or with the communist functionary Nikolai Bukharin who fell from grace, and their critics were quick to damn them and their ideas for such collusions. Indeed, the fall-out from the collapse of Deborin's reputation as the main source of "Marxist dialectics" in 1930 had a direct effect on psychology and paedology. In the fall of 1930 Kornilov's Institute was also caught in the cross-fire of criticism from external sources (see Joravsky, 1989, pp. 357–8), when his young activist co-workers in the Party cell of the Institute were moved to condemn Kornilov's reactology and to ban him from the position of Director in 1931 (see "Itogi Diskussii . . .", 1931). The resolution of the general meeting of the Party cell of June 6, 1931 denounced Kornilov, Zalkind, and some others who had organized the Congress on the Study of Human Behavior in Leningrad as the followers of the Spencer–Bogdanov–Bukharin line of mechanistic philosophy and accused them of having been allied with the old leadership of philosophy. Not only Kornilov, who was damned in accordance with all the usual Bolshevik rhetoric, a number of other co-workers at the Institute were also condemned in the resolution, including Vygotsky and Luria (see "Itogi Diskussii . . .", 1931, p. 388) whose "culture-flirting psychology" [kul'tur-nicheskaja psikhologija] was dismissed as ideologically wrong and suspect (cf. chapter 16).

The wave of ideological accusations, whose victims were condemned for their identification with the "menshevizing idealism" of Deborin's dialecti-cal materialist philosophy, swept through the entire paedology establish-ment in 1931. In April of that year, there was a review of the paedological departments of the Academy of Communist Education, which provided a public display of self-criticism. For instance, Pavel Blonsky "acknowledged" his own "mistakes," only to come under further criticism (Gel'mont, 1931). In a desperate effort to maintain his position among the leaders of Soviet paedology, Zalkind took a leading role in this wave of (self)-criticism, surpassing himself in the degree of self-castigation, showing his ideological loyalty to the readers of *Pedologija* (Zalkind, 1931b; 1932). Despite these self-accusations, he continued to advocate the Party line in criticizing others. Thus, he was among the first to label Kornilov's reactology as a non-Marxist, Deborinist enterprise (Zalkind, 1931a, p. 5), and to call upon other paedologists to criticize themselves. Among those singled out for such invited self-criticism were not only Blonsky and Kornilov, but also Molozhavyj, Zaluznyj, Basov, Sokoliansky, Vygotsky, and Luria (Zalkind, 1931b, p. 13). Vygotsky and Luria were encouraged not to wait until they were "attacked" but to come forward and "perform the re-evaluation of their gravest mistakes in the form of self-criticism on the pages of our journal." This "call for initiative" could indicate that Vygotsky was not a major target for ideological ritual purifications in 1931, but that he was by the way of his association with the dialectical orientation in psychology, affected by the "great purge" (of course, a more direct wave of criticism against Vygotsky followed a little later; see chapter 16).

These attacks against all the major figures of paedology in the USSR were not confined to their supposed connection with the former philosophical leadership, but also they satisfied clearly a basic need for Slavophilicism and an anti-cosmpolitan backlash. Almost all of the main paedologists had had an excellent ("bourgeois") Europe-oriented education, were fluent in foreign languages, and well-read in the scientific and philosophical literature. It was this affiliation with the international scientific establishment – however selective and actually critical they may have been of it in individual cases – that became a theme for ideological attacks on paedology. Stalin added his weight to the campaign by writing a letter calling for "vigilance" among paedologists (see "Pis'mo t. Stalina...", 1931), in response to which the editorial board of *Pedologija*, again with the help of Zalkind, specified a number of labels to be used to classify the "grave mistakes" of oneself or one's colleagues. Thus, the labels "mechano-Lamarckianism," "mechano-reflexologism," and "Freudo-Adlerian distortions" came into legitimate use. In early 1932 (still bearing the title of the previous year), *Pedologia* published its frontline-report ("*O polozhenii na pedagogicheskom fronte*," 1931) in which labels were attached in summary fashion to the work of all leading paedologists. Thus, Zalkind was declared to have "linked Freudian-Adlerian idealism with reflexology and Lamarckianism" and to have not sufficiently appreciated the role of Marx and Lenin in paedology. Blonsky was declared to have followed "positivistic basis of age standardization" and the "mechanistic approach to the study of the class nature of pupils' environments." Basov was said to eclectically "play with structures" to combine this approach with "mechanistic biologization" and Lamarckianism. Molozhavyj was accused of Lamarckianism and "bare behaviorism," and Zaluzhny of a reflexological approach to the study of collectives. And the authors of this editorial text were quite explicit about Vygotsky: "Sharply expressed eclecticism can be seen in the works of Vygotsky, who has united in his theory of cultural development behaviorism and reactology with Gestalt-psychology that is idealistic in its roots" ("*O polozhenii...*", 1931, p. 9).

It seems that the efforts of the militant Marxist paedologists to force these authors to make public self-critical statements had little success. The editorial report continues with a lament that many of those criticized had not yet responded (Blonsky, Ariamov, Arkin) or had tried to "get by" with half-hearted confessions (Molozhavyj, Zaluzhnyj; see also "*Za marksistko-leninskuiu pedologiu*", 1931). Finally, in an act of editorial-political granduer, they provided a definition of paedology that is worth mentioning as an interesting bit of evidence of the infiltration of the social ethos into a research area:

Paedology is a social science that studies the regularities of age-based development of child and adolescent on the basis of the regularities of class struggle
and the construction of socialism in the USSR. ("O polozhenii...", 1931,
p. 10)

Pedologija was to become a "fighting tool for Marxist-Leninist paedology" and it was suggested that many "dangerous" books on paedology
should be eliminated from use in paedological work. In sum, the new
leadership of the journal quite enthusiastically implemented the "great
break" in paedology. The new leadership of *Pedologija* (R. Vilenkina
emerged as the general editor, and of the old editorial board, only Zalkind
and Gel'mont remained) published a detailed plan for the future of the
journal ("*Plan zhurnala*", 1932), which, however, was one of the last
declarations of the journal (it ended its existence in 1932). In 1932, a series
of "discussions" on the state of Soviet paedology took place in Moscow
under the auspices of the Communist Academy. In the account of that series
(see "*Diskussija o polozhenii...*", 1932) the active ideologization (under
the pretext of "bringing paedology close to practice") could be seen very
clearly. Again, Zalkind led the fight for the new Marxist paedology, calling
for a critical review of all Western literature that had "ignored" the "class
principle" of human development. He defined the "evil of mechanism" in
paedology as the "class-free conceptualization of the environment" ("*Diskussija...*", 1932, p. 96), and added his contribution to the redefinition of
paedology:

Paedology [is a] social science where the primary [aspect] is the social contents
of child development, the development of the child's personality, its ideological and psychological development, the development of its social-productive
activity... Paedology [is a] science that unites in itself, on the dialectical-
holistic plane, all processes of the study of child development and unites all
study of the child (psychological, physiological, psychotechnical etc.) into a
united paedological system. ("*Diskussija...*", p. 97)

His fierce presentation (on April 24, 1932) was followed by three sessions
of discussions of its contents on May 18, June 2, and June 9. Among the
people who were reported to have discussed Zalkind's programmatic statement were Krupskaja, Molozhavyj, Kolbanovsky (since 1931 the Director
of the Institute of Psychology, Paedology and Psychotechnics) Blonsky, and
Vygotsky. Krupskaja's presentation, with its reference to the authority of
Lenin, was in effect a defense of paedology from the excesses of ideological
criticism, which nevertheless emphasized the need for multi-faceted and
practice-oriented paedological research. An even more clear-cut defense of

paedology against the fervor of reforms was provided by Molozhavyj, and Kolbanovsky suggested that the disputes in paedology should be curtailed and real work recommenced. Kolbanovsky's description of the paedological work that took place in his Institute is interesting in this context, since it may explain his support of Vygotsky's paedological work (as well as its re-labeling as "psychology" in 1934):

> [the leading issue is] "the study of the regularities of the child's psychological development, the history of the child's mental development." This study proceeds without separation from physiology, taking into account the social influence of the environment. If that study of the child is called paedological study by someone, then it is not necessary to dispute this, although he [Kolbanovsky] thinks that such study is not paedological but psychological, based on the directions of the founders of Marxism. ("*Diskussia...*", 1932, p. 107)

Despite the efforts of paedologists to tame the increasingly acrimonious ideoligical dispute in paedology, the social environment of the discipline guided its discourse along the paths of the new (Stalinist) society, which was constructed by the joint efforts of naive believers, communists, and political demagogues. Paedology had been taken over by a new guard which forced it to service the needs of pedagogics. The practical activities of paedologists in schools, as well as research efforts and lecture courses at various institutes continued until the Paedology Decree of July 4, 1936 which eradicated all paedology from Soviet society.

As we can see, Vygotsky's position in Soviet paedology is not easy to define, since the scene of paedology shifted so much under the influence of wider social changes. Perhaps the key to understanding Vygotsky's paedology would be provided by an attempt to understand the development of his paedological ideas in the context of all the changing social ferment of paedology at large.

Vygotsky's Role in Soviet Paedology

Given the rich traditions of paedology in Russia, and the educational experiments in the 1920s, it is not surprising that Soviet paedological discourse served as a relevant context for Vygotsky's development as a psychologist. His interest in issues of special education (defectology) must have played an important role in his move into the paedological arena.

Vygotsky's writing of the textbook *Pedagogical Psychology*, which was written in the early to mid-1920s marked the beginning of his studies of children. (Vygotsky, 1926i; see chapter 3). Also, the Congress on Psycho-neurology in January 1924, where Vygotsky made his first appearance on the scene of psychology, was simultaneously a conference on paedology (its full name was The All-Russian Congress on Paedology, Experimental Pedagogics, and Psychoneurology, although paedology section was not yet the separate discipline that it became later). When his dissertation was accepted as qualifying him for academic teaching (in October, 1925), Vygotsky began to be involved in teaching at different places of higher education. His pedagogical activities in the area of paedology were con-ducted at the Second Moscow State University (later the Moscow State Pedagogical Institute), at which active research and education in paedology had begun around that time. At the same time he was teaching at different other institutions of higher education in Moscow, at the Institute of Paedology and Defectology, the Academy of Communist Education, and the Central Institute of Raising the Qualification of Cadres of Public Education.

Vygotsky was an active participant in the journal *Pedologija* from its inception and his article on the cultural development of the child appeared in the first issue of that journal (Vygotsky, 1928p). This article was the first version of the main English-language publication of his lifetime (Vygotsky, 1929s). From the time of the second issue of the new journal, Vygotsky was listed as a "member of the large editorial board" (*Pedologija*, 1928, no. 2, p. 217), with paedologists like M. Basov, M. Bernshtein, P. Blonsky, A. Griboedov, A. Zalkind, A. Zaluznyj, S. Molozhavyj, N. Rybnikov, I. Sokoliansky, N. Shchelovanov, and others. Notably, Alexander Luria was not listed among the members of that board. From 1929 (issues 3 and 4 of the journal) the name of Vygotsky can be found on the front cover of the journal as a "member of the presidium of the editorial board," which he served until 1931. In contrast, Vygotsky's name appears as a member of the editorial board of *Pedologija*'s sister journal *Psikhologija* (also established in 1928) only a year later, that is, from 1930 (starting with the third volume). This slight asymmetry in time need not be a coincidence. This time lapse can be explained by the shift of Vygotsky's interests from psychology to paedology.

On April 15, 1931, Vygotsky became a Professor of paedology at the Second Moscow Medical Institute (G. L. Vygodskaja, November 19, 1988, personal communication). It is exactly around that time that his work came under attack for its supposed connections ith menshivizing idealist philo-sophers and psychologists. Nevertheless, his paedology appointments con-tinued: towards the end of his life (January, 1934) he listed his teaching affiliations as Professor and Head of the Department of General and Age Paedology of the Second Moscow Medical Institute; and as Professor and Head of the Department of Paedology of Disturbed Childhood at Moscow

State Pedagogic Institute, and mentioned that he had been appointed to a professorship at Herzen Pedagogical Institute in Leningrad.

Vygotsky's Paedology: The Study of Development

It is not surprising that Vygotsky became actively involved in paedology in the late 1920s. As is obvious from his assertions about the nature of paedology, he saw in that discipline the basis for a synthesis of the different disciplines studying children. Vygotsky clearly had his own agenda in what-could-be-called paedology, which found its expression in his lectures on paedology from 1931 onwards, lectures which were delivered to students of Leningrad Pedagogical Institute and published after his death as a small book titled *Foundations of Paedology* (Vygotsky, 1935g) under the editorship of M. A. Levina. After the death of Mikhail Basov in October 1931, the course on general paedology was left without a professor to cover the lectures, and arrangements were made for Vygotsky to travel to Leningrad to deliver lectures at the Herzen Pedagogical Institute.

No doubt as a result of its being a course of introductory lectures in paedology, the transcripts published as *Foundations of paedology* are remarkably clear. In fact, the text shows how Vygotsky was concerned with making his version of paedology clear to his listeners. He explicitly made reference to the difficulty of presentation of his abstract ideas, promising the students that he would clarify these ideas when they began the analysis of case materials (e.g. Vygotsky, 1935b, pp. 20).

Vygotsky's version of paedology differed from that of his contemporaries. While his contemporaries were adamant about emphasizing the "interdisciplinary" nature of paedology in the study of the child, Vygotsky explicitly differentiated paedology from other disciplines by defining it as *the science of children's development*:

> One can study children's diseases, the pathology of childhood, and that would also to some extent be a science about the child. In pedagogics, the upbringing of children can be studied, and that too is to some extent science of the child. One can study the psychology of the child and that too will to some extent be a science about the child. Therefore we must specify from the very beginning what exactly is the object of paedological investigation. That is why it is more exact to state that paedology is the science of the development of the child. *The development of the child is the direct and immediate object of our science.* (Vygotsky, 1935b, p. 1, original emphasis)

Note that there is no trace of a connection between any social class-bound background, as the ideological orthodoxy of the time maintained.

Vygotsky's definition of paedology was that it was fundamentally a science of development. Following this specification of the scope of paedology, Vygotsky immediately recognized that he had confronted his students with a new obstacle to understanding. What, after all, is development? He proceeded to characterize its time-bound nature (declaring development to have "complex organization in time," Vygotsky, 1935g, p. 2), and to provide examples of how "calendar time" ("passport age") does not reflect the development of children. At different periods in children's development, time units that are nominally the same (e.g. an interval of one month) are developmentally very different, since they cover different "intensities" of events in the life-course. So, one month at the age of 15 years may be rather uneventful as far as development is concerned, while the same period during infancy may cover some relevant reorganizations that lead the child to a qualitatively new level of functioning. Thus, Vygotsky emphasized the uneven nature of development: it proceeds "cyclically or rhythmically" and if one wanted to graphically depict it, the depiction could not be made with the help of an exponential straight line (Vygotsky, 1935g, p. 6). All development takes the form of "wave-like curves", both when we look at particular functions (e.g. weight, speech, intellectual development, memory, attention, etc.) and at development in general. For Vygotsky, this is "the first law of development:" development is a process which takes place in time, and proceeds in cyclical fashion. He immediately proceeded to describe the "second law" of development: that different aspects of child development develop in uneven and non-proportional way (Vygotsky, 1935g, p. 7). This "second law" in essence reflected Vygotsky's acceptance of the principle of heterochrony, and harmonized well with the then current structural-dynamic perspective on psychological issues. Here, in the context of paedology, Vygotsky had a more systematic explanation of the structural reorganization of the wholes as those develop from one state to a qualitatively new one. The structure of the child's developing personality changes at each new age period, as different parts of the system of the personality take a dominant role in the developing person at different ages. Evoking Baldwin's emphasis on the unity of evolution and involution (1935g, p. 11), Vygotsky described the *intrasystemic reorganization* in the developing person. Heterochrony leads to the reoganization of dominance patterns between parts of the personality at different ages. This takes the form of the "law of metamorphisis" (Vygotsky, 1935g, p. 12), which of course was another version of the idea of dialectical synthesis that had been the core of Vygotsky's world-view all through his life.

Vygotsky saw paedology's conceptualization of development in clearly interactionist terms. He rejected all preformist perspectives on development (1935g, pp. 14–18) and emphasized the future-oriented process that constructs (synthesizes) novel psychological function structures. In human history, the emergence of specifically human psychological functions (higher psychological functions) is of course the most dramatic evidence of the synthesis of the novelty, as Vygotsky's "cultural-historical" theorizing had claimed already before. However, the application of the principles of development to ontogeny is the crucial aspect of Vygotsky's paedology.

He tried to link the process of synthesizing novelty in development with the present and past of the developing child (e.g. "the past has the most immediate influence on the emergence of the present in the future;" Vygotsky, 1935g, p. 20). In other terms, the child's past experiences guide (but do not determine, otherwise development would not create novelty) the ways in which the child's actions at the present are instrumental in the construction of the "new present" (or, previous "future").

Vygotsky paid a great deal of attention to the issue of methodology of paedology. A whole lecture (lecture 2 in Vygotsky, 1935g, pp. 21–41) was devoted to the issue of methodology, in which his emphasis on the analytic strategy ("analysis into units" as opposed to "analysis into elements") was outlined with great vigor and consistency. In fact, it is in *Foundations of Paedology* (out of all texts) where this facet of Vygotsky's thinking is expressed most extensively, possibly again due to the didactic and oral nature of the original text. Furthermore, Vygotsky emphasized the holistic (*chelostnyj*) and "clinical" nature of paedological methodology. He was careful to point out that the holistic emphasis of paedological methodology did not mean a refusal to analyze the phenomena under study but rather it led to the methodological imperative of the use of "analysis into units." In our contemporary terms, we might find Vygotsky to be a forerunner of the present-day fascination with fractals, minimal *Gestalts* of which complex structures are composed.

Vygotsky's emphasis on the normative status of the "clinical method" as the core of paedology as the science of development deserves careful exposition. "Clinical" was the term used by Vygotsky to contrast the development focus of the method to the "symptomatic" one. As Vygotsky explained (1935g, p. 33), the symptomatic emphasis had dominated medicine in the past (in the form of the detection and classification of patients' symptoms, rather than of the illness that these symptoms were reflecting). In contrast, the "clinical method" implied the analysis of the underlying system of causes that give rise to a set of possible (often seemingly contradictory) symptoms. This method is "conditional-genetic" (Kurt Lewin's term that Vygotsky occasionally used), or "syndrome-analytic" (see Luria and Artemeva, 1970), and integrates a number of traditions from a methodologist's repertoire (observation, experiment, interview, etc.). Thus, Vygotsky's "clinical method" was not in opposition to "experimental" or to any other of our contemporarily "scientific" instruments but merely reflected the need to go beyond the external symptoms (atomistically analyzed behaviors) of the developing organisms and to re-construct the causal system that leads psychological development, a process that is defined by the feature of novelty construction.

Vygotsky recognized the great divide between his version of paedology and that propagated by others: a divide caused by the differing views of methodology:

> At first, paedology was also a symptomatic science. It studied external features of child development, of mental development, development of child speech; it claimed that on that or other year, these and other features emerge in the child. It was, like all symptomatic sciences, primarily descriptive, it could not explain why one or another feature emerges. (Vygotsky, 1935g, p. 33)

This definition of paedology as studying "symptom complexes" of children with which Vygotsky contrasted his synthesis-oriented view, was exemplified by Blonsky (1925b, p. 8). Thus, in a way, Vygotsky was aligned here with the trend of the time that had been critical of Blonsky, but Vygotsky never participated in such highly declarative campaigns. In contrast to traditional paedology's description of age-related psychological changes, Vygotsky's version of paedology was essentially a developmental science interested in the basic mechanisms of development that would provided satisfactory explanation for age-related changes. The example that Vygotsky used to illustrate the separation of the symptomatic and causal-genetic analyses was the one used in conjunction with the introduction of the idea of "zone of proximal development" (see chapter 13), that is, the contrast between the "*Wunderkind*" and "truly igenious" children. At the level of external "complex of symptoms" both kinds of children seem comparably exceptional, whereas in the underlying capability of "turning present into future" the "true geniuses" can develop their capabilities further with the help of instructional support, while "*Wunderkinder*" have reached the plateau in their (overtrained) functions (1935g, pp. 35–6). Of course, Vygotsky had to recognize that the set of symptoms (external features) that is available serves as a starting basis for paedology, but he stressed his conviction that paedology should move from the study of symptoms to that of their underlying processes of development. This perspective on paedology as the study of synthesis in development was contiguous with that of Basov's (see Basov, 1931, p. 18).

In Vygotsky's paedology, the "clinical method" in the study of development implied the use of the *case-study* approach in its *longitudinal* version (1935g, p. 38). Developmentally, the main "control condition" that makes sense is that of the previous state of organization of the same child, rather than of any other child (less so a group of children). Of course, the uniqueness of individual life-courses complicates the process of generalizing from such within-case longitudinal comparisons, so Vygotsky combined it with comparison *between* different longitudinal case descriptions of development (1935g, p. 39). Thus, the primary within-case longitudinal analysis, paired with the secondary between-cases longitudinal comparisons, constituted the core of research design for Vygotsky's paedology as developmental science. Although he recognized the value of knowledge about inter-child differences (the differential-psychological focus), Vygotsky concentrated upon the general-developmental focus as the core of paedology as a science.

The "Nature–Nurture Question:" The Paedological Basis of Psychological Investigation of Twins

In his discussion of the general developmental processes, Vygotsky could not ignore the "nature–nurture controversy" as this issue labeled in our contemporary jargon. It is in this debate that Vygotsky focuses on basic mechanisms. Paedology, according to him, is primarily interested in the ways in which the hereditary bases of development and actual life-course experiences of the children become integrated. Therefore, paedology is interested not in "stable" features (immutably genetically determined features, such as eye color, that undoubtedly vary within a population), but rather in those hereditary features that are themselves open to modification when exposed to experience (Vygotsky, 1935g, p. 44).

The "genetic openness" of a subclass of hereditary features was an important theme in evolutionary thinking in Russia in the 1920s, following Severtsov's theory of adaptation. This approach was widespread in paedology (e.g. see Basov, 1931, chapter 2), and (in an over-ideologized form) served later as the basis for Lysenko's "biology." By the late 1920s, however, the interests of evolutionists, medical scientists, and paedologists were united in the efforts to deal with human genetics and its role in psychological development. A large research program on the investigation of development of twins was started at the Medico-Biological Institute in 1929 (see Levit, 1935), with the immediate participation of Alexander Luria and with input from Vygotsky.

In a number of studies with twins which were conducted at that Institute (Lebedinsky, 1932; Mirenova, 1932; Luria and Mirenova, 1936a; 1936b) results indicated that the higher psychological processes would be the domain of relative autonomy of psychological functions from hereditary control, whereas in the domain of lower psychological functions the hereditary features were found to be dominant. Vygotsky endorsed this finding of the "genetic openness" for the higher psychological functions (1935g, pp. 50, 52). Furthermore, Vygotsky claimed that in the process of development the very *relation* between hereditary and experiential factors *changes*, depending upon the particular function under study. Although for many psychological functions the influence of hereditary factors can be observed to decrease over age, for some (Vygotsky mentions the psychosexual functions here) the link between hereditary and experiential sides may become more pronounced over age. In general, Vygotsky seems to apply the idea of "separate lines" that become linked at some time (borrowed from Vagner here), as it is applied to heredity/experience relationships.

Indeed, the sequence of the studies of twins conducted by Luria and his colleagues at the Medico-Biological Institute provided the basis for Vygotsky's claim that higher psychological functions are qualitatively different from their "lower" counterparts, as these "higher" functions have been assembled in development in ways that have "leaped beyond" the genetic control that limits the "lower" functions. In that process, "genes" and "environment" operated not as additive (or separable) entities but as opposites inherently linked in dialectical opposition.

The series of twin studies involved a number of efforts to contrast higher and lower psychological functions. In the work of N. Morozova (referred to in Luria, 1936, pp. 363–4) roughly 150 pairs of mono- and dizygotic twins (age range 6–14 years) were studied using the "cultural-historical" (stimulus-means mediated) memory experiments (similar to Leont'ev, 1931, 1932). A mediated version of the memory experiment was contrasted with recognition memory for simple geometric figures (tapping into "lower" memory processes). Using the traditional means of establishing the extent of genetic "control" over psychological functions (difference in correlation coefficient between samples of mono- and dizygotic twins in the given function) it was shown that the correlation for lower memory processes in the monozygotic group was high, and for the dizygotic twins low. This was seen as proving the link with "gene control" of the elementary memory functions. At the same time, for the mediated memory tasks the difference between correlation coefficients from mono- and dizygotic groups was absent, which indicated the relative independence of the higher form of memorizing from the direct "genetic control."

It is interesting to note here that Luria (as well as Vygotsky) argued in favor of the "relative freedom" of higher psychological functions from the "genetic control," and this constitutes an interesting mixture of traditional research methodology (comparison of correlations) and the dialectical perspective on the gene–environment relationship. If heredity and environment are two opposing sides of the same dialectically developing whole, then it is in principle impossible to specify whether one or the other of the two opposites was in some quantitatively measurable way "more" or "less" in control over the given function. However, it is exactly that quantitative estimation that was used by Luria and Vygotsky to demonstrate the unity of genes and environment. In short, Vygotsky was unable to apply his dialectical scheme of synthesis to human genetics.

Instead, the relevant empirical issue emphasized by Vygotsky and Luria in the studies of twins was the age-specific difference in the traditionally measured gene–environment relative impact upon different psychological functions. Thus, Luria (1936, pp. 365–6) reported that by the age of 12 to 14 years the relative roles of genotype and environment become changed, as the children use mediated psychological functions, while at an earlier age (five to seven years) mediated memorizing was not demonstrated, which paralleled the demonstration of genotype's dominance over environment as measured through the correlation-comparison technique.

At the end of 1932 (and beginning of 1933), the investigations of psychological functions in twins turned into a new domain that was more specifically fitting with Vygotsky's concerns. The research now turned to selective teaching of each of two monozygotic twins of different strategies of problem-solving, and then studying both twins over longer time period. Luria and Mirenova (1936a) taught five pairs of five to six-year-old twins construction skills, the reconstruction of a visual model out of given blocks. Two kinds of skills – based on holistic units (M) and reconstruction by elements (E) – were taught to the twins over two and a half months. Six months after the beginning of the teaching, the twins were tested for their ways of solving the construction problems. In three pairs, the twin who was taught the reconstruction task in accordance with the holistic strategy (model) was shown to have picked up that strategy, whereas the control twins in these three pairs were demonstrated to use an elements-based reconstruction strategy. The two kinds of strategies involved a different role in relation to internal cognitive activity. The first (M) kind led to reliance on planning before acting, whereas the second (E) implied an external, direct trial-and-error approach. Re-testing the three pairs of twins (the rest – the other two pairs – did not show sufficient teaching effect at this time, and were left out) a year later (Autumn, 1934), Luria and Mirenova (1936a) found remarkable preservation of the "higher" strategy (planned construction based on the holistic model) to be retained. Their final conclusion was characteristically phrased in terms of Vygotsky's idea of the development of novel functions: in the process of teaching/learning, new skills can be developed *which lead to the emergence of qualitatively novel psychological operations*. As the child develops further (without the particular skill being further trained), the skill may gradually disappear but the *psychological operation* (e.g. orientation towards planning while solving a problem) remains, and is applicable to other tasks (Luria and Mirenova, 1936a, p. 504). The qualitative synthesis of psychological operations on the basis of skills that emerge in the inter-individual (teaching/learning) experience, remains as a "gained" mechanism for the control of other psychological processes.

The Nature of "Environment" in Vygotsky's Paedology

As in the work of other paedologists of the time (Basov, Molozhavyj, etc.), the nature of the environment occupied a centrally relevant place in Vygotsky's paedology. He devoted a whole lecture to that issue (lecture 4, in Vygotsky, 1935g, pp. 58–78). In that lecture, Vygotsky integrated the major aspects of his cultural-historical theory (e.g. units of analysis as structured minimal wholes, meanings as units of analysis, development as co-produced by active organism and environment, the primacy of social experience over individual-psychological development) with the notion of structured organization of environment that was present in the thinking of paedologists at large (e.g. Basov, 1931, pp. 74–5). According to Vygotsky, paedology studies the environmental structure as it relates to the psychological organization of the developing child, and is not interested in the environment as it exists in itself. It is that relational emphasis that dominates any study of development: the external structure of the environment (the speech that is used by family members, for instance) may be constant, but how different children of different ages relate to that environment (for instance: children of six months, three years, and ten years of age) differs remarkably. If the infant is only beginning to make sense of the curious world of speech surrounding him, the ten-year-old is already an active participant in the family discourse, with a very different (meaningful) relation to the speech environment than can be seen in the younger siblings. Vygotsky (following William Stern's ideas; see Kreppner, Valsiner, and Van der Veer, forthcoming) emphasized the child's personal experience (*perezhivanie*) of the environmental structure. He illustrated the differential emphasis that children's age-related experiences receive, with an example from a clinical case of an alcoholic mother and her three children:

> The external conditions in this family are the same for all three children. The essence of the situation is very simple. The mother is an alcoholic, and seems to suffer on that basis from some nervous and psychological disturbance. This creates an extremely difficult situation for the children. On one occasion the

mother, while under the influence of drink, tries to throw one of the children out of a window, beats the children, and throws them onto the floor. In short, the children live under appalling conditions in a state of fear. The three children are brought to us [in the clinic]. Each of the three presents a quite different picture of disturbed development, in response to the very same life situation ... In the youngest child we find the pattern that is characteristic in such cases for youngest children. He reacts to the situation neurotically, that is, defensively. He is horrified by what is happening. As a result, he develops fears; enuresis and stuttering are manifestations of these fears, and sometimes he simply remains silent; he loses his voice. In other words, the child is utterly cowed, overwhelmed by a sense of helplessness. In the second child, an extremely tortuous state emerges ... a state of ... inner conflict; this is a frequent state in cases where the child develops contradictory affective relationships towards the mother ... an ambivalent relationship. On the one hand, the mother is an object of strong attachment for the child, but on the other, the mother is the source of all kinds of fear, the most difficult impressions that the child experiences.... Finally, the third, eldest child, revealed a completely unexpected pattern. This turned out to be a child who was not very intelligent, quite shy, but who while manifesting these features showed signs of some kind of early maturity, early seriousness, early caring. He already understood the situation. He understood that the mother was sick, and felt sorry for her. He saw that the younger children were at risk when the mother raged. He takes a special role. He must put the mother to bed, see to it that she does not hurt the younger ones, and comfort the younger ones himself. He is left to be the mature one in the family, the one with responsibility to take care of the others. As a result, the course of all of his development is changed. This was not a typical, boisterous child, with lively and simple interests and activities. This was a child who had drastically changed in his development, a child of a quite different type. (Vygotsky, 1935g, pp. 60–2)

Indeed, the "activity" emphasis of Vygotsky's paedology is present in this example: the different relations of different-aged children within the same social-environmental structure depends upon the roles the children have to play in it. However, for Vygotsky the relevance of the interaction with the structured environment was the utilization of the latter as the *resource* for the child's psychic life-experiences and meanings, that were seen as the intricate link that connected the developing child and the environment into a mutual relation. This clarifies Vygotsky's view on how paedology studies the environment in its relation with the acting, experiencing and developing child. It is the child's experiencing (*perezhivanie*) of the environment, organized by the use of meanings (the socially constructed "stimulus-means") that constitutes the essence of the study of environment for Vygotsky's system of paedology. Of course, the generalization process that is involved in the construction of meaningfulness (*osmyslivanie*) of any given personal experience with an environmental structure has the propensity to prepare the developing child for future encounters with different environments. According to Vygotsky,

> The environment has one or another influence on the child's development that differs at different ages, because the child himself changes and his relationship to the given situation changes as well. The environment has that influence ... through the experiences of the child, i.e., depending upon how the child has worked out in himself the internal relationship towards the tone or any other aspect of one or another situation in the environment. The environment defines one or another development depending upon the level of meaningfulness [*stepen' osmyslenija*] that the child has assembled for the given environment. (Vygotsky, 1935g, p. 68)

So, it is the *personally meaningful experience* that emerges in the child–environment relationship and guides the further process of development. Here Vygotsky linked this theory with the basic "law of sociogenesis" propounded by Baldwin and Janet (Van der Veer and Valsiner, 1988): the higher psychological functions emerge first in the collective behavior of the child, in the form of cooperation with others, and only subsequently become internalized as the child's internal functions (Vygotsky, 1935g, p. 77). However, Vygotsky did not present this "cooperation with others" with the primacy of equal collaborators in mind. Instead, Vygotsky considered the asymmetric relationship in the cooperation between the developing child and his social environment to be the normative case. The child's social environment includes a variety of "ideal forms" of the end-product of development (adult forms), and the developing child starts from the lack of possessing these forms. These "ideal forms" guide the child's experiences with the social world, that is, his "cooperation" with others, and direct the child's construction of meaningfulness in his relationship with the world. Vygotsky stressed the dangers for development in cases where these "ideal forms" are not present (e.g. in the case of deaf children of hearing parents) or are not easily accessible (as in peer-group situations when the children's peer group is left to "cooperate" without adult supervision). The latter case was described by Vygotsky when he contrasted children in day-care centers with children raised in families. Given the greater number of children per care-giver in the center, the accessibility to "ideal forms" of adult speech was claimed to be less than in the home conditions.

Vygotsky's strong belief in the relevance of asymmetric relationships between the "social world" (filled with a instances of the "ideal forms") and the developing child is elaborated when he provides a hypothetical example of language-development in deaf–mute children:

If you study a deaf–mute child, it transpires that the development of speech of the deaf–mute child will proceed along two different lines, dependent upon whether the deaf–mute child is isolated in the family, or whether he is developing together with other deaf–mute children. Investigations show that deaf–mute children develop their own kind of speech, mime, mime language, which is very rich in its development. The child develops an alternative language. The children together in cooperation, in society, create that language. But can we compare the development of that mime language with the development of the language that takes place in interaction with the ideal forms? Of course not. It means that if we have a case where the ideal form is absent from the environment, and we only have the case where the initial forms (*nachal'nyie formy*) interact with one another, then the development has an extremely limited, compressed and impoverished nature. (Vygotsky, 1935g, p. 73)

Vygotsky may have been influenced in his comparative evaluation of the relevance of "ideal forms" and "basis-forms" by some data by McCarthy (1930, pp. 62–3) who showed that normal children who experienced adult speech environments produced generally longer speech samples to an (adult) investigator, than children who either associated with older children, or peers. In other relevant work of his (see chapter 13), Vygotsky credited McCarthy with the empirical demonstration of the role of more experienced "social others" in individual development. Most definitely this idea of language development being linked with "ideal forms" in the environment was substantiated by the work of Luria and Judovich (1956). This work was done on language therapy with twins whose parents had taken minimal care of them, and who had developed their own idiosyncratic communication system which functioned well in their own shared environment, but who demonstrated large delay in the development of adult language. By means of separating the twins from each other and providing each of them with a situation of interaction necessity (in therapy sessions) with an adult, the delay in the verbal language development was overcome quite efficiently.

In sum, Vygotsky's version of paedology united several postulates of his cultural-historical theory with the dynamic, interactionist perspective of environment that was developing in paedology in the USSR at the time. The main distinguishing feature of all Soviet paedology of the time, in contrast with its previous European and North-American counterparts, was the emphasis on the social organization of the environment of the developing child (Rybnikov, 1928, p. 5; Zalkind, 1930c, p. 22). Of course, as we showed above, with the "great break" in paedology in 1931–2 the environment became defined in Soviet paedology as *class* environment. In his lectures Vygotsky largely ignored that ideologically driven emphasis, and remained true to his own theory of development. He combined that theory with the active role of the developing child – the "actor-in-environment" (*dejatel' v srede*; the terminology is Basov's) – in the (characteristically Vygotskian) domain of semiotic activity (construction and use of signs). In this respect, Vygotsky's paedology grew out of his cultural-historical perspective and his educational theories being catalyzed by his acceptance of the "ideal form" that was present in his surroundings (that of the creation of the "new socialist man"), while the "class-based" concept of environment was rejected.

Roots of Vygotsky's Paedology: From "Child Study" to a Science of Development

Vygotsky's *Foundations of Paedology* constituted the (published) end-point of the development of his views in that discipline. As with many of Vygotsky's oral texts, the lectures published in that book were highly contentious, yet poorly substantiated with data. The editorial work on these lecture texts has not improved the inadequate referencing, all the more so by the time the book appeared (1935) the whole paedology movement in the USSR was nearing its extinction, that is, the decree of 1936. Others used Vygotsky's early paedological writings, like *Paedology of the School Age* (1928t) were used to actively criticize his supposedly "bourgeois" and "idealistic" ideas that were seen as slavery to Western thinking (Feofanov, 1932). No doubt, under these conditions adding adequate references to the published version of oral lectures might have endangered the fate of the book, a teaching aid as it was meant to be, at Leningrad Pedagogical Institute.

Thus, in order to trace the development of Vygotsky's version of paedology as a science of development, we need to turn his earlier paedological writings, all of which were either educational aids for extra-mural students (1928t; 1929n; 1930p; 1931h), or provocative presentations about paedology and its organizational problems (Vygotsky, 1929i; 1929j; 1931a; 1931b; 1931c; 1931d; 1933d/1935). Vygotsky's debt to the traditions of "child study" (G. S. Hall, etc.), "experimental pedagogics" (E. Meumann), and his contemporary Russian paedology (P. Blonsky, A. Zalkind, M. Basov) then becomes clear. In his characteristic way, Vygotsky followed none of these authorities but did borrow ideas from each, linking these ideas with principles taken from evolutionary thinking (Baldwin, Severtsov, Vagner), and child psychology (W. Stern, Piaget).

The first part of Vygotsky's *Paedology of the Adolescent* (Vygotsky, 1929p) can be viewed as a good example of a predecessor to his later lectures in Leningrad, published as *Foundations of Paedology*. It had basically the same compositional structure (not surprisingly, given that both were meant for students as learning aids), proceeding from the definition of paedology to its methodology, and to the description of the main stages of child development. Interestingly, in 1929 paedology was not yet defined outright as a science of *development*. Vygotsky stuck to the conventional definition of the discipline as a "science of the child," specifying that the main and primacy aspect of child study is that of development, the "main features" of which we need to study (Vygotsky, 1929p, p. 3). The cyclical and nonlinear nature of development was mentioned but not elaborated (compare Vygotsky, 1929p, pp. 5–6 and 1935g, pp. 2–8); the importance of the principle of metamorphosis was made clear, in conjunction with the stress on evolutionary epistemology (Baldwin) and Stern's convergence principle (Vygotsky, 1929p, pp. 6–7). Vygotsky stressed the necessity to conceptualize development as qualitative transformation taking place against a background of quantitative accumulations, and argued for the unity of biological and social sides of development. In this respect Vygotsky seems to have been fascinated by a rather poetic utopian idea of Zalkind's (1927a), quoting him on the theme of how the future is constructed in the present:

> The historical development of the human type is based upon the functions of the cortex. All that development, mediated from outside, as all psychological and cultural development of the child is likewise determined from outside by social environment, is accomplished in its main in the cortex and via the cortex. "The growing cortical mediatedness of human physiology in the end is of great importance as a progenerative factor." History, changing the human type, depends upon the cortex; the new socialist man will be created through the cortex; upbringing is in general an influence upon the cortex. Zalkind created a brilliant formulation that expresses that meaning of the cortex. "The cortex has joint way with socialism, and socialism with the cortex." That is why, in Marxist paedology, the primacy of social mediation of personality development includes the role of cortex in development as the main question. If the cortex has the central role in child development, then it is exactly the degree of development of the central nervous system that should be the basis of division of childhood into separate stages. "The central nervous system is the main factor that produces from the stimuli of social environment the future of the whole organism," says Zalkind. This feature [i.e. the relevance of the CNS] has "not restorational but progenerative meaning." It [the cortex] is a true carrier, or as it were a special "organ of development." (Vygotsky, 1929p, p. 14)

This, somwhat naive reliance on Zalkind by Vygotsky is not surprising. Zalkind was one of the most active organizers of psychoneurological disciplines in the USSR all through the 1920s. Apart from his major organizational roles, he also played a role in the Marxist reconstruction of social sciences. Vygotsky's contacts with Zalkind must have been quite close in everyday life, as they were both connected with the psychological laboratory of the Academy of Communist Education in the latter half of 1920s (see "*Spisok . . .*", 1929, p. 409).

A careful look at this approbation of Zalkind also brings together a number of threads of intellectual interdependence. First, Vygotsky's later theory that the future-generating role of the present state of development was rooted directly in a socialist utopian belief of the 1920s is first suggested here. Secondly, Vygotsky's and Luria's later neuropsychological interests, and espeically those studying the role of higher parts of the brain in organizing the structure of psychological functions, are reflected in the socialist utopian fascination with the cortex. Vygotsky's earlier work on the "principle of the dominant" in the mid-1920s served as another basis for this interest.

Vygotsky's discourse on the methodology of paedology, in 1929, reveals similar richness of sources for the development of his theories. First, he continued his theme of "crisis" that was his central topic some years earlier (see chapter 7), declaring that "paedology is now, especially in our country, living through a most serious crisis" (Vygotsky, 1929p, p. 19). He had in mind, this time, the crisis of the eclectic combination of knowledge from different disciplines that study children. He saw the synthesis of knowledge as a means of resolving this crisis, rather than the accumulation of "data" from different disciplines. In that quest for synthesis in paedology, Vygotsky called for paedology's methodology to be re-built on dialectical grounds. This is implied in his advocacy of the study of processes of development, as applied in structural-dynamic ways. Turning to methods, Vygotsky advised that the empirical observational techniques of M. Basov and S. Molozhavyj, the "natural experiment" of A. Lazursky, and – last but not least – the clinical interview method of Jean Piaget should be employed. Having pronounced on the study of the dynamics of development and dialectics as the only basis for a scientific paedology, he later declared that "paedology is based on the law of large numbers" (Vygotsky, 1929p, p. 33).

Dialectical Philosophy in Paedology: S. Molozhavyj

While Vygotsky's version of paedology still had not crystallized into its final forms by the late 1920s, other Soviet paedologists were quick to make Soviet paedology a specific Marxist discipline. The work of S. Molozhavyj is particularly relevant in this respect, as his texts (Molozhavyj, 1928a, 1928b,

1929, 1930a, 1930b) were the precursors to Vygotsky's own theories. Molozhavyj also preceded Vygotsky in becoming the prime target of ideological criticisms leveled against all major paedologists in 1931–2.

Molozhavyj's efforts to make paedology dialectical constituted a synthesis of Engels' principles of dialectics and the evolutionary biological thinking which was being widely discussed in the USSR at that time (e.g. Agol, 1928; Serebrovsky, 1928; and others). Molozhavyj argued for the processes of equilibration (as our contemporary readers are familiar with, after Piaget) and disequilibration, in conjunction with the notion of structural holism in development: "Every process becomes resolved in a way that brings [the organism] either to the restoration of balance in its previous structural form, or to the destruction, structural change, reorganization, regrouping – to a new type of connections, to a new coordination that enters the system of elementary moments" (Molozhavyj, 1928a, p. 229).

Since any development is possible by way of organism–environment interaction, Molozhavyj formulated what could be claimed to be (another) original version of Soviet "activity theory" (independently of the Lazursky–Basov tradition but preceeding that of Leontiev and the Kharkov School in the 1930s). The abundance of activity theories in scientific thought in the Soviet Union is not surprising, since such theories could emerge precisely at at the intersection of evolutionary and dialectical thought complexes (from Hegel to Engels). Molozhavyj proceeded to define paedology in ways very close to the developmental emphasis that Vygotsky would give a bit later to that discipline:

> The science of the child is the science of developmental processes, the science of the formation of novel mechanisms that are becoming more complex [vyrabotka novykh usloznjajushchikhsja mekhanizmov] under the influence of new factors; [a science of] the break, reorganization, [and] transformation of functions and material substances that underlie those, under conditions of growth of the child's organism. Advancements of all linked sciences that open for us the process of life, its mechanisms and factors in both simple and complex forms pave the way to the understanding of genetics and formation of man. However, the science of the child, as an independent theoretical science, must be built on the dialectical investigation of specific processes of the formation of the child. (Molozhavyj, 1928a, p. 231)

Molozhavyj continued to emphasize the focus on the *plasticity* of the biological basis for all development. Plasticity makes it possible for development to lead to the formation of new structural forms. The emergence of qualitatively novel psychological mechanisms regulates the organism's relationships with its environment. According to Molozhavyj, child development is characterized by the emergence of novel adaptive mechanisms as a result of disequilibration, rather than by equilibrative return to the previous state of the organism. It is the *environment* that plays the leading role in throwing the growing child off balance when the major changes occur (e.g. as in case of transition from the intra-uterine to the extra-uterine environment). However, the processes that are triggered by the new environmental structure are not merely passive-adaptive, but dialectical in their oppositional relations within the child, and between the child and the structure of the environment. In this respect Molozhavyj criticized Darwin's evolutionary theory for its non-dialectical essence, as he recognizes gradual change by way of adaptation rather than by discontinuous change beyond the immediate needs of adaptation that comes into being from the conflict of opposites (1928, p. 234). To substantiate its arguments Molozhavyj made use of genetic reflexology as demonstrating the ontogenetic sequence of child's adaptation to changing structure of the environment.

Of course, it was the communist social utopia that served as the environmental structure for Molozhavyj's and his colleagues' theories of child development as a dialectical process that is guided by the structure of the environment (Molozhavyj, 1930c). Molozhavyj refers to the need for raising a "new man" (1930c, p. 239; also Molozhavyj, 1930b, p. 329; Molozhavyj and Molozhavaja, 1926, pp. 4–7), and, of course, the scenario for this applied task that emerges from his dialectical view of paedology fits that goal: by re-organizing the structure of the environment of the developing child, the educators can guide the child to the synthesis of qualitatively novel psychological functions. The primacy of the social environment is thus the starting datum of any educational system that attempts to make use of the plasticity of development, whereas an emphasis on "genetic predeterminism" of ontogeny fits the educational systems that are fearful of having control over the minds of the children.

Molozhavyj's main empirical work in the area of paedology dates from 1926, most of which is concentrated on the study of preschool-age children's play (the results of that study program were published as Molozhavyj, 1929) and general expressiveness (Molozhavyj and Molozhavaja, 1930). He was working in parallel with Vygotsky and Luria at the Academy of Communist Education, leading the work of the Preschool Section of the Academy. The central theme of Molozhavyj's work can be seen in the holistic (structural) perspective on the functioning of children's social collectives (Molozhavyj, 1930d; Molozhavyj and Shimkevich, 1926; Molozhavyj and Molozhavaja, 1926). Using mostly naturalistic observation and natural experiment techniques, which in the context of kindergartens and young pioneers' groups were most reasonably applicable methods, Molozhavyj (e.g. see Molozhavyj, 1929, pp. 12–15) analyzed the collective-educational process in which the adult (teacher) can organize the activities of the group (collective) of children in ways that would lead to the achievement of pedagogical goals (for instance, perseverance and interest in work).

It becomes obvious that the general tendency to build paedology in the late 1920s on a Marxist basis was quite widely discussed in the paedological community. Vygotsky was not the only one who was trying to develop paedology as a science of dialectical development of the child.

The Development of Vygotsky's Paedological Ideas

We can date the formative years for Vygotsky's development of his own version of paedology as being roughly 1929 to 1931. During this time a number of planning committees were formed to work out organizational plans for the development of paedology in the USSR (see *Pedologija*, 1929, no. 3). Vygotsky's participation in the work of the five-member committee that worked out an organizational plan for the paedology of "difficult childhood" was substantial (see Vygotsky, 1929j). He (and the whole committee) stressed the need to keep research of "difficult childhood" within the frame of general paedological research and away from the eclecticism of empirical research as well as from "pedagogical anarchy" (1929j, p. 334). Four criteria were stated to be at the foundation of the research of "difficult childhood" (as well as defectology or "curing pedago-gics;" *Lechebnaja pedagogika*): (1) Marxist thought as the basis for paedol-ogy; (2) emphasis on the social mediation of the development of "difficult" children; (3) study of dynamics of development of "difficult" children; and (4) the link between paedological research and the development of Soviet school and educational establishments for "difficult" children (Vygotsky, 1929j, p. 336). Criteria (1)–(3) were consonant with Vygotsky's "cultural-historical" theorizing (see chapter 9).

Vygotsky was also involved in the work of another committee on the organization of paedology of "national minorities" (*natsmen*). In this his Euro-Russocentric world-view, fortified by the acceptance of the idea of socialist reconstruction as a progressive social process, found its clear expression. Vygotsky indeed viewed non-Russian cultures in the USSR as being at a lower level in their historical development, and expressed the sentiment that the building of the "new society" opened new developmental possibilities for them (see chapter 9). He argued for the re-education of the children of "national minorities" as it could be the mechanism of cultural change at large (Vygotsky, 1929i, pp. 367–8). In line with the dialectical emphasis on the study of processes of development, Vygotsky expressed strong reservations about the transfer of Western child psychological tests (and their normative standards) to the realm of paedological investigation of children of "national minorities" in the USSR. However, he was not consistent in his evaluation of the use of tests, claiming that mass investigations might lead to the establishment of norms for tests in the Soviet context. Again, at this time Vygotsky was still eclectically mixing traditions of the "old" child study movement with his own (emerging) agenda for general paedology as the study of developmental processes in the child. That latter focus found its place in the "plan for *natsmen* paedology" in the form of the study of the structure of the *environment* of the developing child. That environment

> mainly determines those means of thinking and behavior with which the child becomes equipped in the process of his development. It [the environment] defines in general these possibilities of exercise and development, that are met by his [child's] hereditary instincts. For example, in Islamic nationalities among whom for centuries any kind of graphic activity, any drawing, was forbidden, it is evident that from children of these nationalities it would be impossible to expect any kind of fully-fledged development of the graphic function [drawing] which is so characteristic of pre-school-aged children of all European countries. Peoples who have never seen a pencil lag behind in the area of written speech. As is known, the main methodical demand that is prescribed for our tests is the requirement that they study independently the abilities of the special forms of exercises, [in terms of] the most general and distributed forms and degrees of exercise, in the given environment. But we must say outright: the specific stage of the cultural development of a whole people and the specific national form of that development give rise to a totally different structure of the whole field of hereditary instincts, developing some, eradicating others, and thus giving rise to a special social-psychological type of child. (Vygotsky, 1929i, pp. 375–6)

Here the traditional (diagnostic) use of child-psychological tests is contrasted with the need for basic study of the processes that organize the cultural development of children in their national environmental contexts. The use of tests is inapplicable to the study of these processes, since the tests merely "diagnose" the status of the child, under the assumption of tapping into some general undifferentiated conditions of the environment which is viewed as having a uniform "effect" on children. In contrast, Vygotsky argued that a culturally structured environment creates a "field of exercisability" for the "hereditary precursors" of child development. This idea was the first poorly formulated argument for the need to study those psychological functions whose hereditary basis is most open to environmental influences, a view Vygotsky would elaborate in *Foundations of Paedology*.

It seems that the crucial breakthrough in Vygotsky's emerging specific formulation of paedology as a developmental science took place in late 1930. On November 21, 1930, he gave a presentation on the relationship between *psikhotekhnika* (psychotechnique) and paedology at a joint session of the sections of *psikhotekhnika* of the Academy of Communist Education and the Psychotechnical Society (1931d). He swiftly moved from the consideration of "psikhotekhnika" to general psychology, and considered paedological general reasoning (implicitly or explicitly) "supports" psychologists' research on children (1931d, p. 177). At the same time, Vygotsky argued for limiting the scope of paedology to the period of childhood development, denouncing the inclusion of adult or old-age developmental issues (1931d, p. 183). Vygotsky argued in favor of the paedologization of psychotechnics in order to bring psychotechnical methods in line with paedological theorizing. The latter was not meant to subsume either psychotechnics or pedagogics (or psychology), but to serve as the framework for all these disciplines. Paedology should not be construed as viewing "pure" development and children's upbringing as mutually exclusive opposites about the role of which either/or questions can be posed. Rather, these are mutually inclusive opposites that lead the process of actual development by way of producing dialectical synthesis.

Together with the presentation on the relations between paedology and psychotechnics, Vygotsky published his analysis of paedology in two articles in *Pedologija* (Vygotsky, 1931a, 1931c), the latter of which was simultaneously published also in *Psikhologija*. These articles enable us to understand Vygotsky's own development in a number of ways. It was here that the focus on paedology as a science of child *development* (instead of a science of *children* who develop) becomes clear. Secondly, Vygotsky here linked the "death of paedology" in Western Europe and North America with methodological empiricism and theoretical eclecticism, arguing that it was only on Marxist (dialectical) foundations that paedology as a science of development could flourish. Thirdly, in his characteristic style, Vygotsky argued against contemporary tendencies of reducing paedology to psychology of child development (Blonsky), and to the study of reactions (*à la* Kornilov), and that of setting paedology up as a discipline that borrows nothing at all from psychology (Molozhavyj). It was here that Vygotsky explicitly criticized Kornilov's reactological reductionism in print (although his use of the reactological terminology had diminished since 1927), at a time when Kornilov had become a target of other critics as well. His critique was based on theoretical issues, free of any of the ideological rhetoric in vogue at the time. Vygotsky went as far as to argue that particular disciplines that study children – child psychology, for instance – can become "sciences in their true sense" only if they became founded on the grounds of paedology (Vygotsky, 1931c, p. 14). This "true science" is seen by Vygotsky to be located in the synthesis of knowledge from different disciplines, and concentrated on the holistic study of emerging syntheses in development (1931c, p. 21).

Conclusions: Vygotsky as a Paedologist

As we have seen, paedology for Vygotsky was not merely a label to denote his varied interests in the cultural development of normal and retarded children, and in education at large. Rather, in the late 1920s (at about 1927, after his analysis of the crisis in psychology and with the growing dissatisfaction with the growth of Marxist jargon in psychology), Vygotsky's interests shifted from psychology to paedology, as the rapidly growing discipline of the time. He redefined paedology – along the lines of a dialectical perspective brought to the discipline by Molozhavyj – as the general study of children's development.

It could be said that those aspects of Vygotsky's *psychology* that we in the 1990s have learned to appreciate – consistent emphasis on the processes of development, on the emergence of novel (higher) organizational forms of psychological processes, and refusal to reduce the dynamic psychological complexity to its constituent elements – were actually perceived by Vygotsky as the core of *paedology*. The "interdisciplinary" (in our contemporary sense) nature of Vygotsky's paedology was in dramatic contrast to the eclectic mixing of data from the different disciplines that peripherally studied children. He would no doubt be interested in the current debate about the need to be interdisciplinary in our study of children, since for him the theoretical core of a science (rather than its empirical coverage) determines the generality of the discipline.

It was because of his contributions to paedology that Vygotsky was damned by the authorities, and any study of his ideas banned in the Soviet Union, between 1936 and 1956; which explains the curious modifications of terminology in later republications of selected parts of his work. Until the 1980s, Russian re-editions of Vygotsky's texts were careful to substitute the term "paedology" in Vygotsky's texts with "school psychology", "child psychology," or merely "psychology." Of course, such amendments distanced Vygotsky from the study of paedology (e.g. Kolbanovsky, 1956, p. 112). But these amendments introduced major historical distortions to Vygotsky's original texts, for it was *exactly* through the paedology of his own making that Vygotsky tried to escape from the provincialism of Marxist psychology as it had developed by the late 1920s. Paedology afforded Vygotsky what he had been looking for during his career: a unification of his interest in the development of novel complex functions with that of the educational needs of normal and retarded children and he defended this new discipline against all criticism.

13

Education and Development

In the final years of his life Vygotsky returned to the problems of teaching in school, focusing on the problem of the relationship between school teaching and cognitive development. His approach to this problem was deeply rooted in the paedological writings of the time and evolved whilst he was lecturing at the Herzen Pedagogical Institute in Leningrad. It was at this Institute that Vygotsky became acquainted with S. L. Rubinshtejn, later to be a leading figure of Soviet psychology. Rubinshtejn asked him to lecture for his students, and Vygotsky invited Rubinshtejn to be an opponent at Shif's defense of her dissertation on concept-formation (see chapter 11).[1]

At the Herzen Pedagogical Institute Vygotsky quickly gathered a new group of students (Arsen'eva, Zabolotnova, Kanushina, Chanturia, Efes, Nejfec, and others) and collaborators (El'konin, Konnikova, Levina, and Shif) and became involved in new research projects. Apart from the problem of the relation between instruction and cognitive development the problem of stages (age periods) in child development was a major research interest and led him to write several chapters for a book on child development (see chapter 12), which was never completed.

Lecturing to the students at the Herzen Pedagogical Institute in Leningrad he raised the problem of the relation between school instruction and cognitive development for the first time in the spring of 1933. The last time he dealt with the issue was in the sixth chapter of *Thinking and Speech*, which was probably written in the early summer of 1934. In these months he gave half a dozen lectures on the subject, applying it to various practical problems and different theoretical themes. The development of Vygotsky's theories is illustrated in the lectures and manuscripts gathered in Vygotsky (1935h; 1933n/1984), and the sixth chapter of 1934a (to give the right chronological order). Read in that order it can be seen how the concept of

[1] In the Soviet Union, as in several other European countries, researchers who have completed their dissertation have to defend it during a public meeting. Under the eyes of worried relatives and smiling fellow members of the scientific staff invited professors from other universities test the researcher's knowledge and quick-wittedness during a ceremony that can last up to two hours.

the zone of proximal development was first used in the narrow context of traditional intelligence testing and was later gradually broadened to encompass the general problem of the relation of education and cognitive development.

The Relation of Teaching to Cognitive Development

On March 17, 1933 Vygotsky raised the issue of the relation between school teaching/learning (*obuchenie*) and cognitive development in a lecture at the Epstejn Experimental Defectological Institute in Moscow (Vygotsky, 1933d/1935). He argued that the various points of view regarding this issue fell into three categories. Psychologists belonging to the first category in essence argued that school teaching should follow development: the child's psychological functions should have reached a certain level of maturity, after which the teaching process can start. The psychological functions are seen to develop in a "natural" way, sometimes because researchers link their development directly to the maturation of brain functions. This organistic view of development Vygotsky ascribed, among others, to Piaget.

The organistic view could be criticized, so Vygotsky believed, on three grounds. First, it led to a pedagogical pessimism. In Vygotsky's view, if a child showed an incapacity to deal with or insufficient understanding of a certain field one should concentrate all efforts exactly on this deficiency to compensate for it. This global conviction quite probably arose as a result of his defectological work and was based on his understanding of Adler's concept of supercompensation (see chapter 4). Secondly, according to Vygotsky it had been established that child development is a highly complex process that cannot be characterized using one single measure. American authors had put forward the idea of a double-level approach. One should not only establish what the child can do now, at this moment, for this would be denying that every process has its history (its embryonic phase), that it develops before it becomes measurable in practice. "Essentially speaking, to establish child development by the level reached on the present day means to refrain from understanding child development" (Vygotsky, 1933d/1935, p. 119). Vygotsky pointed out that Meumann and others had suggested that we should establish at least two levels of child development, namely, what the child can do already and what the child's potential is. Research had shown that we should at least measure these two quantities and that the indicator of the zone of proximal development is the divergence between the level of actual development and the level of proximal development. Vygotsky claimed that the concept of the zone of proximal development was particularly helpful to distinguish between normal and retarded children, a remark that must have been in accord with the beliefs of his audience (see also the discussion of Vygotsky and Luria in chapter 9; also Valsiner and Van der Veer, 1992). Finally, Vygotsky mentioned that the organistic point of view was flawed since the laws of child development are in themselves partially dependent on the fact whether the child attends school and gets instruction or not.

The second point of view on the relation between teaching and cognitive development stated that cognitive development is not based on maturation but teaching is the major force in promoting it. The ultimate consequence of this view is that cognitive development is seen as the shadow of teaching.[2] Vygotsky saw Thorndike as a representative of this point of view, for he developed this idea to its extreme by claiming that teaching and cognitive development actually coincide.

Finally, Koffka represented the third point of view. He tried to reconcile the first two contradictory points of view by claiming that both are partially right. Child development is partly based on maturational processes and partly on teaching.

Vygotsky was fully satisfied with none of the above viewpoints, arguing that teaching and development are distinct processes and should not be confused. Child development cannot be seen in isolation from the teaching process however, since the relation between these two processes is highly complex and is certainly not to be compared to the relation between an object and its shadow. To set out his idea of this complex relation Vygotsky dealt with the processes of learning literacy in school.

Learning to write, Vygotsky argued, brings with it its own peculiar difficulties. It would be wrong to say that writing is equivalent to simply translating the spoken words into signs. Referring to various German scholars (Büsemann, Beringer, Ch. Bühler) he claimed that writing is very different from speaking in many ways. It is different in the sense that the objects referred to are not present and that it lacks intonation. It is also abstract in the sense that there is no other person we are speaking to and that the child often lacks a motivating goal for writing the text. Wundt already had pointed out that writing is connected with conscious and voluntary processes. Vygotsky completely agreed and proposed the idea that the child experiences difficulties in writing because he has to become conscious of his own speaking. In speaking the child's attention is focused on what he is speaking about and not on the grammatical structures of his speech. The latter he has at his disposal as a given. The principal problem of

---

[2]The Russian term *obuchenie* can be translated as "teaching," "instruction," and "training." Vygotsky used the term mostly in the context of schooling and clearly had in mind the teaching and learning of (meta-)cognitive skills. We have, therefore, avoided using "training" preferring "teaching," "instruction," and – sometimes – "schooling" instead.

writing, therefore, is to become conscious of one's own acts. An extra complication for the child is that he has to start from internal speech, which is condensed and of a telegraphic nature. Implicitly referring to Hegel, Vygotsky concluded that the child has to start from speech "for himself" and transform it into speech "for others" (see also chapter 15).

What did this imply, then, for the problem that Vygotsky raised in his lecture, that is, the problem of the relation of teaching to cognitive development? In the first place the abilities the child has to acquire in learning to write, for example (that is, to become conscious of his own acts, to picture objects that are not present), are in no sense directly taught by the teacher. The same example showed that cognitive development is not the direct parallel or shadow of the educational process. Vygotsky concluded, therefore, that teaching enables a series of developmental processes that undergo their own development and that paedologists should carefully analyze these developments.

This led Vygotsky to his main hypothesis: teaching is only effective when it points to the road for development. The school child, he said – again employing Hegelian terms – has to learn to transform an ability "in itself" into an ability "for himself." The process of writing requires functions that are hardly developed in the preschool child. The functions develop in the process of learning how to write – in the process of education. The teacher, therefore, essentially creates the conditions for certain cognitive processes to develop, without directly implanting (*privit*) them in the child:

> To implant [something] in the child ... is impossible ... it is only possible to train him for some external activity like, for example, writing on a typewriter. To create the zone of proximal development, that is, to engender a series of processes of internal development we need the correctly constructed processes of school teaching. (Vygotsky, 1933d/1935, p. 134)

This lecture at the Epstein Experimental Defectological Institute is noteworthy for several reasons. First, Vygotsky clearly indicated that the idea of establishing a zone of proximal development is not original with him but arose in the work of American authors and Meumann and others. Secondly, the idea of a zone of proximal development and the more global idea of schooling – or culture at large – influencing cognitive development were not intimately connected at first. They were raised as separate points by Vygotsky and evolved in different contexts. Finally, the different points of view on the role of teaching in cognitive development – in particular the second and third – were not analyzed in any great detail.

In lectures in 1933 and 1934 (1933c/1935; 1933m/1935; 1934i/1935; 1935n) Vygotsky spelled out the positive and negative sides of the different views more fully and gave a fully-fledged presentation of the concept of the zone of proximal development in the context of traditional intelligence testing. These lectures were delivered at the Herzen Pedagogical Institute, at the Leningrad Pedological Institute, at the All-Russian Conference for Preschool Education, and at the Bubnov Pedagogical Institute. In addition Vygotsky wrote two chapters (Vygotsky, 1933n/1984; chapter 6 of 1934a) in which he elaborated and summarized his ideas. From these lectures and chapters a more adequate picture of the three approaches to the issue of the relation between teaching and cognitive development can be deduced.

Vygotsky's detailed critique of Piaget is particularly relevant. He discussed Piaget's thinking in the context of the debate around the form and content of human thinking. Some researchers were inclined to consider exclusively the content (Vygotsky here mentioned Thorndike), others concentrated on the operations (the Würzburg School) of human thought. Vygotsky claimed that these two aspects of human thinking cannot be separated: the content of thinking determines the operations and vice versa (see chapter 11). He criticized Piaget for concentrating almost entirely on the structural side (the content) of children's thinking to the detriment of the functional (operational) side. After all, Piaget claimed that the functions – such as assimilation – did not change during the course of development (Vygotsky, 1933m/1935, p. 98).

Piaget also studied the cognitive development of children independently of their schooling. The things the child learned in school were uninteresting for him, because they were a mixture of the child's own understanding and the things the child simply took over from adults. The child's own thinking should be studied in isolation from school knowledge, Piaget maintained. He, thus, tried to separate teaching from cognitive development:

> The conclusions and understanding of the child, his representation of the world, [his] interpretation of physical causality, [his] acquirement of logical forms of thought and abstract logics, are seen by the researcher as if these processes proceeded by themselves, without any influence from instruction in school. (Vygotsky, 1935n, p. 4)

Vygotsky explained that the rationale behind Piaget's approach is the idea that we should investigate the child's thinking, excluding all superficial knowledge taken over from adults, and thus laying bare its pure, undistorted development. In his opinion this attitude amounted to claiming that teaching has nothing to do with cognitive development and, ultimately, to the idea that teaching should follow (the maturation of) cognitive development. The consequence of this view is that the claim that children who do not attend any formal school teaching will nevertheless develop all higher forms of thinking can be legitimated (Vygotsky, 1934a). Piaget's attitude is, thus, one that can be seen as a justification for the distinction between aptitude and achievement tests.

The second point of view, that teaching and development are equivalent terms, was also discussed more fully in Vygotsky's later lectures. Referring to Thorndike, James, and Russian reflexology and pointing out their associationist background, Vygotsky argued that this point of view was inevitable for these researchers. If teaching is essentially seen as the formation of conditional reflexes and development too, then there is no sense in distinguishing between the two. At most one could argue that teaching promotes the formation of some conditional reflexes as opposed to others, but the deep structure of both teaching and development remains the same (Vygotsky, 1934a; 1935n). He claimed that both Piaget's view and the view endorsed by Thorndike and Russian reflexology shared the assumption that cognitive development is a naturalistic process based on natural processes (1935n). Their main difference was in the temporal view on education and development: serial in the first case, parallel in the second.

Finally, in 1933 and 1934 Vygotsky gradually gave more credit to the third point of view voiced by Koffka (1925). This representative of Gestalt psychology had made the very general claim that one can discern two forms of development: (1) development as maturation (*Wachstum* or *Reifung*); and (2) development as learning (*Lernen*). He further explained that some developmental processes take place relatively uninfluenced by the environment (e.g. learning to use your fingers), while others will not evolve without specific environmental factors being present (e.g. learning to play cards). The former ones he considered to have an innate basis, while the latter have to be acquired. In essence, then, Koffka raised the nature–nurture issue with relation to cognitive development (Koffka, 1925, pp. 28–9). Vygotsky (1935n) was of the opinion that Koffka's point of view was valuable in three respects: (1) it claimed that cognitive development could be based both on maturational processes and on learning through teaching; (2) it stated that these two forms of development were mutually interdependent; and (3) it claimed a broader rule for education in child development. The latter point he elaborated by referring to Koffka's *Gestaltist* structural point of view, which implied that a child learning a specific task at the same time learned a structural principle having a wider field of application. This may imply that teaching a child one specific task raises the child's potential for other activities. In Vygotsky's words the child made "one step in the teaching/learning process [*obuchenie*] and two in cognitive development." Koffka's view, then, implied that teaching may precede cognitive development, promote it, and create new structures (*novoobrazovanija*; or *Neuleis-tungen*). This Vygotsky (1934a, p. 203) considered to be an "infinitely important" and "infinitely valuable" insight.

On a number of occasions Vygotsky (1934a; 1935n) noted that the point of view propagated by Koffka, in a way, returned to Herbart's old idea of the "formal disciplines" (see also chapter 11). The study of these formal disciplines (e.g. Latin, Greek, mathematics) would provide the pupils with the necessary intellectual training, the beneficial effects of which would generalize to all other subjects of the curriculum. Although Herbart's idea worked out in a reactionary way, Vygotsky judged his theories to be more valid than those of his American opponent Thorndike, whose attempts to refute Herbart simply missed the point. Thorndike demonstrated the trivial truth that the learning of any occasionally chosen task will not necessarily influence the learning of another – equally occasionally chosen – task. Moreover, the tasks he used (e.g. learning to distinguish lines of different length) were all in the domain of the lower psychological functions, which was not very surprising in view of Thorndike's associationistic starting point, but the tasks did make his research of little value here. Vygotsky argued that "scientific thought develops dialectically" (1934a, p. 203) and that Herbart's point of view might be valid in the domain of the higher psychological processes. To support this view one would have to show that the learning of specific abilities in one domain transforms the intellectual functioning in other areas. This is what Vygotsky set out to do in his empirical investigations.

The Empirical Background of Vygotsky's Own View

Vygotsky's own views on the relation between school instruction and cognitive development were developed partly as a result of his analysis of different existing views, partly by the application of practical knowledge and considerations, and partly as a result of empirical investigations carried out by his collaborators and students. The study into the development of scientific and spontaneous concepts conducted by his collaborator Shif (which was designed in 1932, carried out in 1933 and 1934, and published in Shif (1935)), provided the major empirical support of his ideas (see chapter 11). However, Vygotsky mentions (1934a) that he also relied on four other investigations, carried out by his students Arsen'eva, Zabolotnova, Kanushina, Chanturija, Efes, and Nejfec. The studies were carried out as master's theses and were never published, so their exact nature and results remain unknown.

The first series of experiments investigated the degree of maturity of those functions on which the teaching of school knowledge should build. Here Vygotsky's students tried to reveal the psychological differences between speaking and writing, finding the differences which were mentioned above and which encouraged Scribner and Cole to carry out their investigations (1981). The essential difficulty of writing is that it requires from the child reflection (*osoznanie*) on and control (*ovladenie*) of his own psychological functioning. These psychological qualities are not present when the child enters school but constitute one of the (unintended) results of the teaching of literacy in school. According to Vygotsky the teaching of grammar may have the same beneficial result. Because these psychological abilities are not present at the entrance of elementary school Vygotsky concluded that instruction builds on psychological functions that have not yet matured.

A second series of experiments aimed to show that instruction in school precedes cognitive development. Vygotsky summarized the results of these experiments by stating that they had shown that the child can always perform a function before he consciously understands and controls it. In this case, therefore, the conscious insight – and probably the statement of some principle in words – in the nature of a performed activity was considered to be an indication of the child's cognitive development. Vygotsky explained that the teacher may faithfully explain a task or concept for six or seven lessons until, suddenly, the child grasps the idea. In his view this showed that (the imaginary curve of) school instruction did not proceed in parallel with (the imaginary curve of) cognitive development and, thus, has its own dynamics. The idea of children performing a task before they grasp the underlying principle seems to anticipate part of the investigations carried out in the Kharkov school.

A third series of experiments was dedicated to a problem similar to Herbart's, but made use of psychologically more complex tasks. These experiments are only alluded to by Vygotsky (1934a). He claimed that they had shown that (1) the psychological basis of the instruction of various subjects (e.g. in mathematics and grammar) was very similar and amounted to the child's mastery of reflection and control of his own functions; (2) instruction will have repercussions for development that are much broader than the restricted area of the subject taught; and (3) all cognitive development in elementary school is interconnected and builds on the two major accomplishments of this period: the mastery of reflection and control.

Finally, a fourth series of experiments was dedicated to the investigation of the potential usefulness of the concept of the zone of proximal development. Apparently, Vygotsky and his students repeatedly tested large groups of children to establish the dynamics of their IQ development. The nature of these studies can be guessed from the scarce information provided in the following paragraph.

Vygotsky formulated his main conclusion regarding these investigations in the sixth chapter of *Thinking and Speech*: that instruction enables a whole series of cognitive transformations and that Herbart's idea of the formal disciplines was, therefore, basically sound (Vygotsky, 1934a, p. 222). He considered the principally new psychological functions developed in the school period to be the twin concepts of reflection and control.

The Zone of Proximal Development

The most detailed description of the concept of the zone of proximal development as Vygotsky envisaged it can be found in the stenogram of a lecture delivered at the Bubnov Pedagogical Institute on December 23, 1933 (Vygotsky, 1933c/1935). In this lecture Vygotsky mentioned that in the past researchers such as Binet and Meumann used to think that one cannot start teaching children unless they have reached a certain level of development. A lot of effort had been expended to establish the lowest possible thresholds from which the teaching of various school subjects might be started. The way to establish these thresholds was to ask the child to independently solve some specified task or test. We now know, however, Vygotsky argued, that there is also an upper boundary; that is, we know that optimal periods exist for the learning of an intellectual skill. The mother tongue, for example, is best learned at a very early age, while mathematics should probably be learned considerably later. Is there a way to establish the optimal periods for learning various intellectual skills? Can we establish a child's potential for instruction in a certain domain? To answer these questions Vygotsky turned to the domain of intelligence testing and the concept of the zone of proximal development.

He discussed this concept in the context of intelligence testing at the entrance of elementary school and in the context of the often observed phenomenon of "regression towards the mean." Vygotsky reminded his audience of the general practice of testing all children before they entered elementary school, dividing them into four groups, of which three were allowed to attend the normal school. These three groups were the children with high (110 and higher), average (between 90 and 110), and low IQ (between 70 and 90). Below an IQ of 70 children were referred to special schools. Vygotsky mentioned the fact that IQ scores had been shown to predict with high degree of accuracy a child's performance in school and he was positive about the practice of referring children to different categories on the basis of their IQ scores: "This rule is now used by the school all over the world, it contains the fundamental wisdom of all paedological investigations carried through at the entrance of school" (Vygotsky, 1933c/1935, p. 37).

Unfortunately, research done by Terman, Burt, and Blonsky had pointed out a mysterious phenomenon: children with an initially high IQ tend to lose and children with low initial IQ tend to gain IQ points in the school period, leaving their rank order relatively unchanged. How should we interpret this phenomenon? Vygotsky was inclined to explain these findings by suggesting that children with low IQ scores at entry to school profited more from schooling than children with high IQ scores: relatively speaking, then, the first group was more successful in elementary school. But why would this be the case? Do children with high initial IQ score gain little because school is badly adjusted to their wants? To answer these questions Vygotsky posited the concept of the zone of proximal development:

> In the investigation of the cognitive development of the child it is usual to think that indicative of the child's intellect is only that which the child can do himself. We give the child a series of tests, a series of tasks of varying difficulty, and by the way and the degree of difficulty up to which the child can solve the task we judge the greater or lesser development of his intellect. It is usual to think that indicative of the degree of development of the child's intellect is the independent, unassisted solving of the task by the child. If we would ask him leading questions or demonstrated to him how to solve the task and the child solved the task after the demonstration, or if the teacher started to solve the task and the child finished it or solved it in cooperation with other children, in short, if the child diverged however so much from the independent solving of the task, then such a solution would already not be indicative of the development of his intellect. (Vygotsky, 1933c/1935, p. 41)

This, at least, is what researchers had tended to think for years, Vygotsky argued. He, evidently, did not agree and proposed to give the child hints and prompts to see how far this could lead the child. He mentioned that "various researchers" had used different ways to do this. In this way it had been found that children with the same mental age – as established in the traditional, independent way – were able to solve problems up to different mental age levels. We, therefore, have little reason to say that they have the same mental age after all: using the hints and prompts some children solved tasks four years above their independent performance, while others hardly profited from the help offered. The difference between independent performance and aided performance, thus, seems to be characteristic of the child:

> The zone of proximal development of the child is the distance between his actual development, determined with the help of independently solved tasks, and the level of the potential development of the child, determined with the help of tasks solved by the child under the guidance of adults and in cooperation with his more intelligent partners. (Vygotsky, 1933c/1935, p. 42)

The level of actual, independent development, Vygotsky maintained, was characteristic of the intellectual skills the child had already mastered: it represented the already matured functions, the results of yesterday. However, the performance of children cooperating with more knowledgeable others was characteristic of their future development: it revealed the results of tomorrow. To substantiate this claim he referred to the results found by "the American investigator McCarthy" with regard to the preschool age group. Vygotsky claimed that McCarthy had shown that three-to five-year-old children can perform some tasks independently and other tasks only under the guidance of or in cooperation with an adult. The children were able independently to perform these latter tasks when they were five to seven years' old. Therefore, Vygotsky concluded that:

> we can judge what will happen with this child between 5 and 7 years (other conditions of development staying the same) . . . In this way the investigation of the zone of proximal development became one of the strongest instruments of paedological investigations, allowing [us] to enhance considerably their effectivity, utility, and fruitfulness, the application of diagnostics of the intellectual development to the solution of the tasks raised by pedagogics, [and] the school. (Vygotsky, 1933c/1935, p. 43)

Having briefly mentioned McCarthy's findings Vygotsky returned to the problem of the relative degree of success of different IQ groups in school. Suppose, he argued, we have one group of children with high IQ scores and another with low scores. Suppose, further, that these groups can be subdivided into two subgroups with a proximal zone of, respectively, two or three years of mental age. We, then, have four possible combinations: high IQ, large zone; high IQ, small zone; low IQ, large zone; and low IQ, small zone:

1	High IQ	Large zone
2	High IQ	Small zone
3	Low IQ	Large zone
4	Low IQ	Small zone

In a large-scale empirical investigation Vygotsky claimed to have found that the dynamics of intellectual development and the degree of relative success are comparable for the first and third, and for the second and fourth groups. This may mean that his findings indicated that children with similar zones of proximal development gained or lost similar quantities of IQ points. The zone of proximal development, therefore, was more important for and predictive of the child's intellectual development than the traditional IQ score.

To show the intricacy of the phenomena discussed, Vygotsky brought in yet another complicating factor. Suppose, he reasoned, that we have a group C of either illiterate children forming part of a group of illiterate children or literate children forming part of a group of literate children. Further, suppose we have another group D of either literate children forming part of a bigger group of illiterate children or illiterate children forming part of a group of literate children (the problem of illiterate children was a very real problem in the Soviet Union at the time). These children can have various IQ scores, which leads us to:

1   High IQ   C (homogeneous (il)literacy)
2   High IQ   D (mixed literacy)
3   Low IQ   C (homogeneous (il)literacy)
4   Low IQ   D (mixed literacy)

Which groups of children are the most similar with regard to the dynamics of intellectual development and their relative success in school? Vygotsky again referred to empirical investigations performed under his guidance and stated that

> The investigation shows, and this time much more significantly and tellingly than in the case of the zone of proximal development, that the similarity appears considerably greater between the first and third, and second and fourth, than between the first and second and the third and fourth groups. This means that for the dynamics of the intellectual development in school and for the progress of the child in the course of school instruction [the] determining [factor] is not so much the size of the IQ in itself, that is, the level of development of the present day, as the relation of the level of preparation and development of the child to the level of the demands made by the school. This last quantity – the level of demands made by the school – in paedology one has now proposed to call the ideal mental age. (Vygotsky, 1933c/1935, p. 46)

Vygotsky considered this concept of "the ideal mental age" to be very important. He noted that different researchers had tried to establish the ideal mental age for various school classes. Presumably, then, these researchers tried to deduce from the demands made in a specific class which mental age was required for successful performance in this class. This required mental age had to stand in some optimal relation to the various mental ages of the children attending the class. Vygotsky mentioned that the relation of the ideal mental age of a given class to the real mental age of the children in that class was the most sensitive measure established by paedologists at the time. If these respective levels differed too much – as in the case of an illiterate child forming part of a literate class or a literate child forming

part of an illiterate class – children were expected to gain little. The same
held when the divergence was too small: instruction – as had been said by
Owell – should call into life, drag behind itself, organize development. But
how was the optimal distance between real and ideal mental age to be
established, and what are the optimal conditions for intellectual progress?
Vygotsky mentioned that various attempts – using units for the child's
mental age, program materials, and school years – had been made to answer
these questions, but that for him the most convincing were some small,
individual case studies. These investigations – carried out by his collaborators – demonstrated that the optimal difference between ideal mental age
level and real mental age level coincided with the zone of proximal development of the child (Vygotsky, 1933c/1935, p. 48). If the child has a zone of
proximal development of two mental age years, then the ideal mental age of
his class should be two years above the child's mental age as independently
measured:

> In this way the analysis of the zone of proximal development becomes not
> only a magnificent means for the prognosis of the fate of the intellectual
> development and the dynamics of the relative success [of the child] in school,
> but also a fine means for the composition of classes . . . the level of intellectual
> development of the child, his zone of proximal development, the ideal
> [mental] age of the class, and the relation between the ideal [mental] age of the
> class and the zone of proximal development . . . [form] the best means to solve
> the problem of the composition of classes. (Vygotsky, 1933c/1935, p. 49)

Vygotsky then returned to the problem that formed the focus of his talk at
the Bubnov Pedagogical Institute. How can we, then, explain the phenomenon of "regression towards the mean" (to put it in an anachronistic way)? Is
it a general law that children with high initial IQ tend to lose, while children
with high initial IQ tend to boost their scores? Vygotsky answered in the
negative, arguing that we should take into consideration the composition of
the school class, etc. But why do we still find the phenomenon as a statistical
law? To explain this Vygotsky first remarked that the IQ is something of a
blunt instrument, saying that it was "a symptom, an indication." The
problem is that we do not know what an IQ score indicates and how what it
indicates, evolved. Vygotsky gave his audience a rather personally grounded
example: some coughs indicate influenza, others tuberculosis! It would be
wrong, therefore, to formulate the general law that coughs should be
treated in such and such way. The same holds true for IQ scores: they reflect
very different backgrounds (see also chapter 9).

Why, then, do the children with high initial IQ scores tend to lose IQ
points in the four years of elementary school? Vygotsky argued that the
reason they excelled was that they came from a privileged background

(Vygotsky, 1933c/1935, p. 51). They had plenty of books and toys at their disposal, their parents read stories to them, etc. Vygotsky remarked that the Binet tests in use were exactly designed to test knowledge resulting from this type of environment. It was no wonder that these children performed well. However, they tended to lose their advantage because

> they get them [the high scores] at the cost of the zone of proximal development, that is, they run through their zone of proximal development earlier, and, therefore, they are left with a relatively small zone of development, as they to some extent already used it. According to the data of my investigation in two schools there were more than 57 per cent of these children. (Vygotsky, 1933c/1935, p. 53)

In essence, then, Vygotsky explained the phenomenon of "regression towards the mean" as a result of the levelling effect of schooling. Because the circumstances at school are more equal children from disadvantaged home backgrounds will gain, while those from privileged homes will tend to lose. However, present research seems to disprove Vygotsky's suggestion, for, if anything, schooling seems to increase the individual differences in competence.

Vygotsky's Pedagogical Optimism and the Prediction of Development

The fact that Vygotsky evolved the concept of the zone of proximal development to explain the dynamics of IQ development was remarkable, as was his predictive use of this concept. The way Vygotsky conceived the measurement of intelligence through IQ testing was, in a way, reminiscent of Binet's original conception. Binet (1909/1973, pp. 125–41) maintained that we can boost our IQ through instruction and rejected the view that intelligence is an immutable inborn quantity.

It is quite clear from several of Vygotsky's remarks (e.g. his claim that the zone of proximal development is "revealing the results of tomorrow;" that establishing this zone is "a magnificent means of prognosis;" and that "we can say what will happen with this child . . . other conditions . . . staying the same") that he considered the measurement of the zone of proximal development to be a means to predict the child's future IQ development. In essence, he suggested the measurement of two quantities – independent performance and aided, joint performance – and claimed that the future development of the former was fully determined by the latter. Children were able to profit from the jointly performed tasks, because of their singular

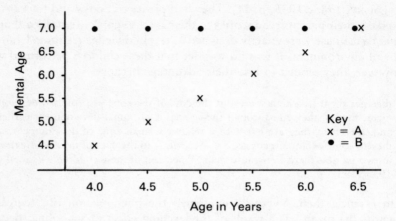

FIGURE 13.1 Predicting the child's future IQ scores on the basis of the measurement of individual and assisted performance

ability to imitate the activities of their more able partners. Referring to McCarthy, Vygotsky maintained that activities that can be imitated by the child will be independently performed in the near future: "Research shows the strictly genetic lawfulness between that which the child can imitate and his mental development" (Vygotsky, 1933n/1984, p. 264). For Vygotsky, then, the dynamics of the child's independently reached IQ scores were fully predictable on the basis of the jointly reached IQ scores. This peculiar view can be pictured in the following way (see figure 13.1).

To be able to predict the child's future cognitive development the investigator should (1) establish the child's independently reached IQ score (in figure 13.1 the child of four years reaches an independent score of 4.5 mental age years (measurement A); the child, therefore, is scoring slightly above the average performance of his age group). The next step is (2) to establish the child's score in joint performance, that is, the child can make use of various hints and prompts and is shown part of the solution, etc. Under this circumstance the child in our example is able to solve the tasks up to a mental age of 7 years' old (measurement B). The child thus has a zone of proximal development of 2.5 mental age years. We now can predict, according to Vygotsky, that in the next 2.5 years our child's independent performance will become progressively better until it has reached the level of the joint performance measured at the age of four. This level will be reached after two and a half years have passed.

The resulting view of cognitive development is rather odd for several, interconnected reasons. First, because Vygotsky, when he spoke of McCarthy's research, suggested that cognitive development proceeds in a linear fashion. A difference of two mental age years between independent and joint performance was expected to have disappeared after two years. This view would be in sharp contradiction with many of Vygotsky's own statements about the dialectics of child development. Secondly, the dynamics of the child's IQ development were pictured by Vygotsky against the background of a static environment. The environment existed in the form of the measurement of the aided or joint performance at one specific point of time and then was disregarded. There is no reason to believe that the child's aided performance at the age of five would be the same as that exhibited at age four. There is no reason, therefore, to believe that some children will have "spent" their zone of proximal development, as Vygotsky clearly suggested. On the contrary, because the environmental conditions have not changed – the adults still play with the child and tutor him – there is every reason to believe that a second measurement at age five would give a higher joint performance score. It is possible that this new zone of proximal development could then be used to predict another independent IQ score for the child at age seven. The examples Vygotsky gave to demonstrate the use of the zone of proximal development suggest that he conceived of the environment as a static background to the dynamically developing child. This, again, was in sharp contradiction with the views he espoused in his various other publications. Also, Vygotsky seemed to suggest that the independent performance of a child will have as its "ceiling" the joint performance. This may be plausible in the case of intelligence tests presented to very young children but when formulated as a general rule it suggests the unfortunate idea that children can never outperform their adult partners, or – to put it even more generally – that the next generation can never transcend the cognitive possibilities of the former. In itself, this idea looms large in any conception which emphasizes, as the cultural-historical theory does, the transfer of cultural knowledge from one generation to the next, but in this particular case it is conspicuously present. The concept of imitation has overtones of noncreative copying mechanisms. Although it is true that Vygotsky tried to avoid such an explanation for children's imitation, by claiming that he was thinking of "intellectual imitation", he did not refer to or provide a fully-fledged theory of imitation that might have solved the problem. Outlines of such theories – which emphasize the selective use and creative combinations of parts of the material presented to the child – had been sketched by Baldwin (1900) and Guillaume (1926/1968).

The Role of Imitation

Why did practically all experts in the field of intelligence testing concentrate their efforts on the child's independent performance? This question was repeatedly raised by Vygotsky in the final years of his life (e.g. Vygotsky, 1933n/1984; 1934a; 1935n). To answer it he referred to a commonly held, yet ill-founded view of the process of imitation. The common misunderstanding was, Vygotsky claimed, the belief that children were capable of imitating anything as if imitation were nothing but a mechanical, automatic process that revealed nothing of the mind of the imitator (Vygotsky, 1933n/1984). To counter this view he might have referred to the detailed studies of imitation carried out by Baldwin and Guillaume, among others. Instead Vygotsky, rather surprisingly, referred to Köhler's (1921) chimpanzee experiments. These investigations had demonstrated that chimpanzees can only imitate those actions that form part of their own repertoire of independently performed actions (Vygotsky, 1933n/1984, p. 263). The general claim that organisms can imitate whatever activity, therefore, is unfounded. Vygotsky assumed that children's imitational capacities are limited in the same sense but at the same time he stressed a fundamental difference between humans and animals in this respect. "The principal difference in the child's imitation is that he can imitate a series of actions that lie far beyond the boundaries of his own possibilities but that are, however, not infinitely large" (Vygotsky, 1934i/1935, p. 13).

In Vygotsky's opinion, then, children can rise above their personal potential, while animals are confined to the zone of actual development. On several occasions he attempted to explain the causes of this fundamental difference. Acknowledging the fact that animals can be taught various behaviors that are not in their normal repertoire he nevertheless denied that this implied that they have a zone of proximal development in any meaningful sense of the word:

> in this case the operation would be performed simply automatically and mechanically like a meaningless habit, and not like an intelligent and sensible decision . . . the animal, even the most intelligent one, cannot develop its intellectual possibilities through imitation or instruction. It cannot acquire anything principally new relative to what it already has in its possession . . . In this sense it may be said that the animal is not able to be taught at all, if we understand teaching in the specifically human sense . . . The animal can only be trained. It can only acquire new habits. It can through exercizes and combinations perfect its intellect, but is not capable of mental development through instruction in the real sense of the word. (Vygotsky, 1934a, pp. 219, 220, 263)

Vygotsky hinted that the difference between humans and animals was based on the difference between insightful learning and trial-and-error learning. One feels that Vygotsky was here looking for a clear-cut distinction between the unintelligent aping of observed behavior on the one hand, and insightful imitation on the other hand. Undoubtedly, examples of rather clumsy mimicking behavior abound in Köhler's descriptions and he did suggest that chimpanzees' imitations are limited (Köhler, 1921, p. 161), but the importance of Köhler's text lay in the fact that he showed that some insightful behavior of chimpanzees is definitely present. It was, therefore, unfortunate that Vygotsky referred to Köhler's work to substantiate the view that the fundamental difference between humans and animals is based on the reliance on insight versus trial-and-error learning. As in other cases (see chapter 9), Vygotsky's attempts to clearly distinguish human and animal behavior lacked clarity.

Vygotsky's reasoning can be summarized as follows. Organisms in general are limited in their capacity for imitation. This was proved by Köhler in the case of chimpanzees. We may assume – and have some practical evidence for this assumption – that the same holds true for humans. However, children are far less limited than other species because they can, to a point, profit from instruction. In contrast to other species, children are capable of intellectual, insightful imitation (Vygotsky, 1934a, p. 263). In the case of children, teaching can evoke and promote their cognitive development.

Vygotsky's interest in the role of imitation may also explain why he once (Vygotsky, 1933e/1966) suggested that play can create the zone of proximal development:

> play also creates the zone of proximal development of the child. In play the child is always behaving beyond his age, above his usual everyday behavior; in play he is, as it were, a head above himself. Play contains in a concentrated form, as in the focus of a magnifying glass, all developmental tendencies; it is as if the child tries to jump above his usual level. The relation of play to development should be compared to the relation between instruction and development ... Play is a source of development and creates the zone of proximal development. (Vygotsky, 1933e/1966, p. 74)

Presumably, Vygotsky was thinking of various types of play in which children imitate adults. In general, he made it very clear that he attached great value to these forms of deferred imitation both for cognitive and emotional development. Of course, these forms of play would not have taken place had the model not been present. In this sense the active imitation of a model in play may stimulate the child's development as much as the imitation that will take place during or following instruction.

The Concept of Sensitive Periods

Establishing the optimal periods for the instruction of specific subjects in school was a task of immense practical importance that had concerned famous pedagogues. One of the most important of these was Montessori, who established empirically the optimal periods for instruction in the pre-school period. She and others (e.g. Drooglever Fortuyn, 1921)[3] had linked the idea of optimal periods for instruction to the concept of sensitive periods elaborated in biology. Although Vygotsky valued the practical recommendations of Montessori, he was rather hesitant to accept the strict analogy between these two concepts. He discussed this issue on two occasions: the first time in a rather neutral fashion (Vygotsky, 1935n) and the second time more critically (Vygotsky, 1934a).

In one text Vygotsky only hinted at the existence of different sensitive periods in the ontogeny of various species (1935n, pp. 22–3). He mentioned the work of the Dutch biologist De Vries (e.g. 1903), who had found that before and after certain periods an organism (more specifically, the plant *Dipsacus sylvestris*) was less sensitive to particular stimuli. As an example Vygotsky related the example of the growth of a queen bee: only during a specific period will the ingestion of a particular food produce a queen bee (see also Drooglever Fortuyn, 1921, pp. 8–9). Vygotsky also introduced the concept of the zone of proximal development as a concept linking up with the idea of sensitive periods in this paper. The connection was, basically, that one cannot wait for environmental interference for indifferent periods: certain developments will not take place, or will take place suboptimally, if the organism is not stimulated at the right time.

A few months later, however, Vygotsky relativized this analogy, seeing at least two differences. First, unlike many pedagogues, Vygotsky did not simply empirically establish the existence of the phenomenon of a child's enhanced capacity to be taught during specific periods but he searched both experimentally and theoretically for an explanation. Establishing the child's performance in joint action, that is, establishing the zone of proximal development, provided "the possibility of elaborating a method for determining these periods" (Vygotsky, 1934a, p. 222). Those tasks should be taught to the child, that he cannot perform independently, but can do in cooperation with others. Vygotsky also warned against drawing a direct biological analogy between De Vries' findings with lower animals and complex processes, such as learning to write. He stated that "Our investigations demonstrated that we are dealing in these periods with processes of the development of higher psychological functions with a purely social nature, which evolve from the cultural development of the child and have coopera-

---

[3]The fact that Vygotsky referred to Drooglever Fortuyn – a Dutch biologist who was little known outside the Netherlands and who was connected with the Montessori school in education – suggests that he met representatives of this school during his stay in Holland in 1925 (see the introduction to part I).

tion and instruction as its source" (Vygotsky, 1934a, p. 223). It is evident, then, that Vygotsky was aware of the biological findings of the time (see also chapter 9), and tried to establish links with them. At the same time, however, his grounding in philosophy made him sensitive to the differences that exist between humans and the other species. The current discussions concerning the validity of ethological findings for child development (e.g. Hinde, 1982; Tinbergen and Tinbergen, 1983; Wilson, 1976) show that this issue has lost little of its topicality.

Conclusion

The work Vygotsky completed concerning the concept of the zone of proximal development and the relation of teaching to cognitive develop-ment is the most well-known aspect of his contribution to psychology. His discussion of the leading role of the social other in children's cognitive development is interesting and its implications are being explored to this very day (e.g. Rogoff and Wertsch, 1984). The specific application of this concept in the context of repeated IQ measurements, however, was rather unfortunate and seems at variance with several basic assumptions of his cultural-historical theory. Rather surprisingly, Vygotsky stated that the concept of the zone of proximal development was not original, a statement that has been eagerly quoted by early and later critics (Kozyrev and Turko, 1936; Rudneva, 1937; Brushlinsky, 1968). He mentioned "Meumann and others," "American investigators," and "the American investigator McCar-thy" as the originators of the concept. However, these references are extremely vague and the present authors have not been able to trace the roots of the concept. The reference to Dorothea McCarthy's work may serve as an example. She showed that normal children who experienced adult speech environments produced generally longer speech samples than children who associated with older children, or peers (McCarthy, 1930, pp. 62–3), and this finding supposedly demonstrated the ability of the more experienced social others to provide children with the "ideal form" of development. Nevertheless, this still seems far removed from the concept of the zone of proximal development as elaborated by Vygotsky.

It could be said that in the final period of his life Vygotsky developed a profound interest in the relation between the teaching/instruction process and mental development. Refuting the views of his colleagues Koffka and Piaget, and relying heavily on the paedological research of his time (with its reliance on mental tests), he developed his own view on this matter. The empirical background of his thinking is, unfortunately, largely unknown (see Shif's research as elaborated in chapter 11 for an exception), but it is clear that whilst Vygotsky's thinking was original, he was indebted to the work of his contemporaries. Although he was conspicuously silent about the main tenets of his cherished cultural-historical theory (see chapters 9 and 16), in the 1930s Vygotsky had once again formed a creative research collective and launched new ideas and in doing so created the Leningrad school of paedology.

14

Emotions: in Search of a New Approach

In the early 1930s Vygotsky turned his attenton to yet another subject within psychology: the study of emotions. For a number of years he worked on a manuscript that dealt with the then popular theories of emotions and their deficits. According to Vygotsky's colleagues and students, several variants of the manuscript with differing titles existed between approximately 1931 and 1933. A version dated 1933 was posthumously found among his papers (Jaroshevsky, 1984, pp. 350–1).

It will come as no surprise to the reader – in view of the fate of many of his other manuscripts – that the study was not published during his lifetime. Attempts by Vygotsky's sister Zinaida Vygodskaja and Luria to publish the manuscript in the mid-1930s also failed (see Luria, 1935b, p. 266, where the manuscript is referred to as "Spinoza and his theory of affection. Prolegomena to the psychology of man (in press))" – and it was only in the late 1960s that the first two short excerpts of Vygotsky's manuscript were published (Vygotsky, 1968; 1970). Finally, fifty years after his death, the manuscript – now called *The Theory of Emotions. A Historical-Psychological Investigation* – was published in its entirety in the sixth volume of the Soviet edition of his collected works (Vygotsky, 1984b).

The major argument of the manuscript was that the existing theories of emotion – in particular the then hotly debated James–Lange theory – were essentially dualistic. For a solution to this dualism Vygotsky turned, rather surprisingly, to Spinoza's philosophy. Of course, the idea of discussing the issue of dualism with respect to the available theories of emotion was not original to Vygotsky. The publication of the James–Lange theory had precipitated a lively debate in both philosophy and psychology and the experts were acutely aware of both the issue of mind–body dualism and the link between modern emotion theories and classical thought (e.g. Irons,

1894, 1895a, 1895b, 1895c; Cannon, 1914; Titchener, 1914). Irons (1895a), for example, anticipated Vygotsky in pointing out the similarities between the James–Lange theory and Descartes' emotion theory put forward in *The Passions of the Soul*.

Vygotsky was well acquainted with this literature and it is difficult to judge exactly which readings may have led him to writing his study. It is likely that he was inspired by his reading of Janet, who devoted a large section of his *From Anxiety to Ecstasy* (Janet, 1929) to various theories of emotion. The theoretical links between Janet's and Vygotsky's writings are important and have been discussed elsewhere (Van der Veer and Valsiner, 1988). Vygotsky definitely made extensive use of the proceedings of the Wittenberg symposium held in the Wittenberg College, Springfield, Ohio, on October 19–23, 1927. This first international symposium on feelings and emotions was attended by several of the leading researchers of that time, among them Karl Bühler, Cannon, Prince, and Washburn. In addition, the papers of international experts – such as Adler, Bekhterev, Claparède, Jaensch, Janet, McDougall, and Stern – were read to the audience (see Reymert, 1928). In dialogue with these modern researchers and reading the Russian translations of Descartes and Spinoza, Vygotsky attempted to develop his own point of view concerning a theory of emotion.

General Outline of the Study

Vygotsky's lengthy manuscript (some 225 pages) had a complex structure, so we will first present the bare outlines of his argument before examining the text closely.

The text began with a detailed discussion of the James–Lange theory of emotion. As is well known, William James and Carl Lange, a Danish physiologist, independently developed a paradoxical theory of emotion. Their theory posited that the physiological changes accompanying emotions (regulated by the autonomic nervous system) – such as trembling and sweating – were the direct result of the perception of a thrilling or threatening stimulus. The "feeling" of the emotion would follow these peripheral reactions. In his *Principles of Psychology* James expressed his hypothesis as follows:

> My theory ... is that *the bodily changes follow directly the perception of the exciting fact, and that our feeling of the same changes as they occur IS the emotion* ... that we feel sorry because we cry, angry because we strike, afraid because we tremble, and not that we cry, strike, or tremble, because we are sorry, angry, or fearful, as the case may be. (James, 1890/1983, pp. 1065–6)

After his presentation of the James–Lange theory, Vygotsky argued that it failed on empirical grounds. He referred to Canon's findings to support this, which demonstrated that (1) if bodily changes do not seem to differ very much from one emotional state to another, how, then, could a person know whether he or she was furious or thrilled? (2) the internal organs are not well supplied with nerves, and internal changes occur therefore too slowly to be a source of emotional feeling; and (3) artificially inducing the bodily changes associated with an emotion does not produce the experience of the true emotion.

All this is, of course, well known and can be found in any textbook. The interesting thing here is that Vygotsky, while using Cannon's findings to criticize the James–Lange theory, did not accept Cannon's thalamus theory as a viable alternative. Cannon's thalamus theory portrayed the thalamic region as the coordinating center of nerve impulses from both the peripheral sense organs and the cortical level of the nervous system. Some emotions might require no coordination with the higher levels of the nervous system, and were thus limited to thalamic control. Others involved integration of both peripheral-thalamic and cortical-thalamic input. The latter usually functioned as an inhibitive control mechanism. The "conflict" of "body" (as exemplified by the peripheral input to the thalamus) and "mind" (cortical-thalamic input) aspects of emotions, Vygotsky reasoned, preserved the mind–body dualism in Cannon's theory of emotions. In this respect, Cannon's theory stayed within the confines of James–Lange's original conception. It still was mainly a physiological theory and did not take into account the psychological aspect of emotional processes. What was needed, Vygotsky argued, was an indepth analysis of the philosophical backgrounds of the James–Lange theory. The principal aim of his study was to present such an analysis. In particular, he attempted to demonstrate that the weaknesses and limitations of the James–Lange theory of emotion might be traced to the influence of Descartes.

Drawing on Irons (1895a), Vygotsky argued that the James–Lange theory was to a great extent equivalent to the theory presented by Descartes in *The Passions of the Soul*. Moreover, Descartes' influence had broader implications: precisely as a result of the way Descartes phrased and solved the mind–body problem the study of psychology had become divided into two camps. The debate between those who propagated psychology as *Naturwissenschaft* (natural science) and those who claimed the possibility of psychology as *Geisteswissenschaft* (hermeneutics) found its origin in Descartes' writings. Thus, the conflict between psychologists who desire to be scientists in the accepted sense common to the natural sciences (studying *behavior*), and psychologists seeking for an understanding of human plans, motives etc. (emphasizing *meaning*) was already present in much of the

French philosopher's work (see chapter 7; Kendler, 1981). It was Vygotsky's conviction that this conflict in psychology was based on an inadequate conceptual basis, and he argued that the germ of a better philosophical analysis could be found in the work of Spinoza.

The structure of the essay, thus, can be summarized as follows. Vygotsky first demonstrated that the James–Lange theory was to a large extent equivalent to Descartes' theory, notably as expressed in the *The Passions of the Soul*. He then proceeded to show that the psychology of emotions – and psychology in general – was hampered by the Cartesian legacy. Finally, he suggested that the study of Spinoza's writings might yield a new and better way of solving the problem of mind–body dualism.

Descartes' Theory of Emotions

In *The Passions of the Soul* Descartes' intention was to explain the nature of passions as a "natural philosopher." He started by describing the bodily processes giving rise to an emotion. For him all sensations were dependent on the nerves, which were "like little threads or tubes coming from the brain and containing, like the brain itself, a certain very fine air or wind which is called the 'animal spirits'" (Descartes, 1649/1985, p. 330). Descartes explained that the so-called spirits are actually extremely small bodies that move very quickly, "like the jets of a flame from a torch." When a person perceives a frightening or startling object, the animal spirits in the sense organs will move through the nerves to the brain, where the pineal gland interacts with the soul. The pineal gland, which is the principal seat of the soul, can be moved by the animal spirits "in as many ways as there are perceptible differences in the objects. But it can also be moved in various different ways by the soul" (Descartes, 1649/1985, p. 341). The soul can move the pineal gland, which causes the animal spirits to move towards the muscles and other parts of the body, thus producing the bodily processes generally connected with an emotion.

From this it may be concluded that Descartes' analysis consists of two parts: (1) an afferent (peripheral) theory of emotion; and (2) an efferent (central) theory of emotion. In the first account we see a purely mechanistic process giving rise to conscious experience only at the ultimate point of a long series of bodily changes. In the second account the soul itself initiates these causal chains. These centripetal and centrifugal (as they were called) parts of Descartes' system can even be in conflict "as the little gland in the middle of the brain can be pushed to one side by the soul and to the other side by the animal spirits ... and these two impulses often happen to be opposed" (Descartes, 1649/1985, p. 346).

Descartes and the James–Lange Theory

Vygotsky focused first on the centripetal aspect of Descartes' theory and compared it with the James–Lange theory of emotion. He observed that in this part of his theory Descartes pictured the passions as having a passive and perceptual character. A frightening object causes the whole process from sense organ up to the pineal gland. There the soul will "perceive" or "feel" (much like a homunculus) the bodily changes. The soul is pictured, therefore, as the ultimate and passive perceiver of the movements of the pineal gland. Exactly the same picture is sketched in the James–Lange theory of emotion, Vygotsky argued. For James and Lange an emotion was the awareness or feeling of visceral changes. James stated, as we saw above, that "the bodily changes follow directly the perception of the existing fact, and that our feeling of the same changes as they occur is the emotion." This means that for both (the afferent part of) Descartes' theory and for the James–Lange theory emotion is equivalent to passive perception (feeling) of bodily changes.

Both the James–Lange theory and the centripetal aspect of Descartes' theory, Vygotsky argued, gave an essentially deterministic and causal account of the origin of emotions and highlighted the description of bodily processes. Such a conception had several implications. For example, it is difficult to conceive of emotional development in ontogenesis. In view of the fact that an emotion is taken to be a process of becoming aware of bodily changes, one would probably have to argue that the nature of these bodily processes changes during ontogenesis. In fact, reasoning from the point of view of the James–Lange theory, one is inclined to consider the primitive emotions (fear, anger) as more real than complex, "higher" emotions (spite, spleen) and to regard development as the decay of these original "childish" emotions. Emotions, at any rate, should be brought under control, for "the chief use of wisdom lies in its teaching us to be masters of our passions" (Descartes, 1649/1985, p. 404). In a Cartesian view, then, the original primitive emotions will either decay, or they will be preserved in their original, primitive state. In the latter case, they ought to come increasingly under the control of the soul. Under no circumstances can the original primitive emotions develop into more refined, higher emotions.

Vygotsky considered this conception to be highly unsatisfactory. In his opinion, human beings are capable of more sophisticated emotions than animals, and adults have a more refined emotional life than children (cf. Elias, 1978). We should, therefore, try to sketch the transition from the first primitive emotions of life to the higher emotional experiences (cf. Averill, 1986). In both the James–Lange theory and Descartes' analysis the emotions were seen as essentially immutable and, therefore, ultimately innate Vygotsky concluded (1984b, p. 273). The lack of a developmental perspective can be explained – at least partially – by the division between mind (soul) and body. It is difficult for a dualist to conceive of the quality of emotions changing gradually as the child's conceptual knowledge and cognitive processes develop. The bodily processes can never develop into higher emotions because higher emotions belong to the realm of the soul. For the same reason it will be difficult to give an account of emotional life that connects the emotions with other psychological processes and consciousness in general.

So far we have seen how Vygotsky attempted to demonstrate the equivalence of Descartes' afferent (centripetal) theory to the James–Lange theory of emotion. His next step was to look for efferent (centrifugal) ideas in this theory. Vygotsky's conclusion was that in James' writings we do not find examples of bodily changes that are caused by the mind. Thus, there would be no purely efferent aspect of the James–Lange theory. He argued, however, that James did half-heartedly accept the possibility of purely intellectual emotions without bodily correlates (Vygotsky, 1984b, p. 250). This may not be entirely correct. The point is that James distinguished between "standard" emotions having a distinct bodily expression, and intellectual, "cerebral" emotions having no such bodily correlates (James, 1884/1984, pp. 127–8). Standard emotions, he argued, could be adequately explained by his theory. James realized that the existence of purely intellectual emotions would invalidate his theory. He even accepted the existence of such mental phenomena but suggested – precisely because of the absence of bodily correlates – that they might better be called judgments or cognitions. James, therefore, solved the problem of intellectual emotions by definition, although he realized that this solution implied "an antagonism . . . between the spirit and the flesh" (James, 1884/1984, pp. 138–40).

Vygotsky, apparently, did not accept James' solution by definition and concluded that here again James' theory coincided with Descartes' theory, for Descartes, too, posited the possibility of "internal emotions which are produced in the soul only by the soul itself" (Descartes, 1649/1985, p. 381). In Vygotsky's opinion the postulation of these "intellectual emotions" was, in a certain sense, inevitable. A purely mechanistic explanation of the passions was clearly inadequate. The exclusive concentration on bodily processes ignored the higher, typically human, qualities of human emotions. These, then, had to be postulated in a way that was not indicative of purely afferent control. Vygotsky's conclusion was that the James–Lange theory coincided to a very large extent with Descartes' analysis in *The Passions of the Soul*.

Mechanistic Causal Explanations

Although a purely efferent theory of emotion cannot be found in James' writings it had, of course, been put forward by other psychologists and philosophers. Vygotsky mentioned Dilthey, Spranger, and Bergson. These thinkers had ridiculed a causal, deterministic approach in psychology: such an approach might be appropriate for the explanation of lower psychophysical processes, such as reflexes, but was definitely inadequate for the explanation of human thought and volition. Vygotsky accepted part of this argument. Although he felt very sympathetic towards Descartes' as well as James–Lange's attempt to explain emotions causally, he did feel that their account was clearly inadequate. He even approvingly referred to Socrates' famous words in *Phaedo*, criticizing a mechanistic world-view:

> It was . . . as if somebody would first say that Socrates acts with reason or intelligence; and then, in trying to explain the causes of what I am doing now, should assert that I am now sitting here because my body is composed of bones and sinews . . . and that the sinews, by relaxing and contracting, make me bend my limbs now, and that this is the cause of my sitting here with my legs bent . . . Yet the real causes of my sitting here in prison are that the Athenians have decided to condemn me, and that I have decided that . . . it is more just if I stay here. (*Phaedo*, 98c–9a)

Vygotsky accepted Socrates' condemnation of mechanistic explanation, particularly as it applied both to Descartes' theory and the James–Lange theory of emotion. However, he did not accept the conclusion, drawn by the proponents of a hermeneutic approach in psychology (Dilthey, Spranger), that any causal explanation in psychology was, therefore, impossible, and that psychology had no other recourse than to rely on hermeneutic procedures. To him the failure of *mechanistic* causal explanation did not imply the logical impossibility of causal explanation of higher psychological processes as such. In fact, Vygotsky argued, both hermeneutic and determinist psychologists shared the same inadequate view of causal explanation. As a result, the former studied the higher psychological processes (considered not to be causally determined, rather they were free like Descartes' description of the soul) while the latter confined themselves to the study of – supposedly causally determined – simple stimulus–response processes (Vygotsky, 1984b, p. 295). This led to "the tragedy of all modern psychology, which consists in the fact that it cannot find a way to understand the real sensible tie between our thoughts and feelings on the one hand, and the activity of the body on the other hand" (Vygotsky, 1984b, p. 265).

Vygotsky's criticism of the James–Lange theory was intriguing and may apply to contemporary theories of emotions as well (Van der Veer and Valsiner, 1989). At any rate, the various problems that Vygotsky raised – such as the mind–body dualism in emotional theories and the lack of a developmental approach – are still among the most topical issues of emotional theory. It is these and other problems that have led modern philosophers and psychologists to look for alternative theoretical conceptions, such as constructionism (see Harré, 1986; Ratner, 1989).

Vygotsky's Search for a Solution

Vygotsky's analysis of the James–Lange theory and his attempt to demonstrate its similarity to Descartes' theory was persuasive. His next step was to attempt to provide an alternative to these explanations. Rather surprisingly, he turned to another great thinker from the past for inspiration. He suggested that the germ of a more acceptable form of causal explanation of emotions might be distilled from Spinoza's *Ethics*. Vygotsky was highly impressed by the writings of the Dutch philosopher whose ideas in his opinion "cut like diamond through glass"[1] (see chapters 1 and 9).

Several factors may have led to Vygotsky's fascination with Spinoza's writings. In the first place, Spinoza opted for a monistic solution of the body–soul problem. Soul and body he considered to be two sides of the same substance. For Spinoza, there was not, on the one hand, a mechanistically determined body, and, on the other a free, undetermined soul. Vygotsky frequently quoted *Ethics*, where it was stated that

> Most writers on the emotions and on human conduct seem to be treating rather of matters outside nature than of natural phenomena following nature's general laws. They appear to conceive man to be situated in nature as a kingdom within a kingdom: for they believe that he disturbs rather than follows nature's order, that he has absolute control over his actions, and that he is determined solely by himself. (Spinoza, 1677/1955, p. 128)

Spinoza disagreed with these theories and wanted to extend the deterministic approach to all human actions and to the realm of the soul. He did not accept the existence of Descartes' free, undetermined soul and refuted his dualism. This attitude was very important to Vygotsky, whose aims were similar (see also chapter 7). In his view an adequate theory of emotion

---

[1]Two of Spinoza's books had been translated into Russian at that time, both before the 1917 revolution: *Ethics* and *Treatise on the Purification of the Intellect*.

should give a meaningful account of the relation between children's lower emotions and adult's higher emotions. Having quoted Spinoza, Vygotsky concluded:

> Therefore it is impossible to cut the enormous field of emotions into two parts, one of which is amenable to the peripheral hypothesis, and the other not. There do not exist feelings which because of a birth privilege belong to the higher class, and at the same time others which because of their very nature can be reckoned among the lower class. The sole difference is a difference in richness and complexity, and all our emotions are capable of ascending all the steps of our sentimental evolution. (Vygotsky, 1984b, p. 279)

One can see from the above that the dualism of Descartes and others was contrary to Vygotsky's developmental, "genetic" approach. Criticizing both the idea of mechanistic causal explanation as well as the idea of hermeneutic understanding, Vygotsky sought a monistic, causal approach in psychology. But what type of causal explanation did he have in mind if it was not mechanistic causality? And how, according to Vygotsky, could the study of Spinoza's work be helpful in conceiving a developmental approach in the study of emotions? Unfortunately, we do not know the answers to these and other questions, since Vygotsky's manuscript is incomplete. It ends with the analysis of Cartesian theory and the constructive discourse on Spinoza was never written.

This lack may be interpreted in different ways. Of course, Vygotsky may not have finished the study for the simple reason that he had other, more pressing things to do, and as we have seen, many unpublished and unfinished manuscripts were found in his private archives. Another, more interesting reason might be that he simply realized that he was on the wrong track: he may have become convinced that no simple answers for the problem of dualism in psychology were to be found in Spinoza's writings. We will try to reconstruct his possible line of thought using Vygotsky's other writings, and point out some potential problems.

In his manuscript Vygotsky repeatedly asserted that there can be none other than a causal explanation in the psychology of emotions, at the same time dismissing the possibility of mechanistic causal explanation. What, then, did he have in mind when speaking about causal explanation? Jaroshevsky, the Soviet historian of psychology, has suggested the following. Jaroshevsky distinguishes three levels of deterministic explanation in the history of science (in Vygotsky, 1984b, p. 346). The first level is mechanistic determinism, characteristic of (part of) Descartes' writings and thinkers like La Mettrie. In this view human behavior is explained by referring to tiny bodies that interact through collision and watches and other automata are the metaphors most frequently used to understand the human being. The second level is biological determinism, which Jaroshevsky sees exemplified in Darwin's writings. Human behavior is here explained by reference to biological explanatory concepts, like "homeostasis," "survival value," "selection," etc. Cannon's thalamus theory can be seen as such a theory. Finally, the third level of explanation is social-historical determinism: human activity is explained by referring to social and cultural influences and by retracing its historical development both in phylogeny and ontogeny. The last type of explanation, Jaroshevsky claims, was typical of Vygotsky and was used by him to construct his cultural-historical theory of the higher psychological processes (see chapter 9).

Accepting the social-cultural theory of mind does not imply that one dismisses the other two levels of explanation in psychology, but it does entail that they should be submitted to social-historical analysis when one is dealing with the specifically human higher psychological processes. Vygotsky claimed that when social and cultural factors come into play the lower processes do not cease to exist but are "superseded" (see Hegel); that is, they are still present and will re-emerge when the higher processes, for one reason or the other, are unable to function (see chapters 4 and 11). For psychology this means that the primary level of analysis and explanation is focused on social and cultural factors. Should explanation on this level fail, then the researcher has to resort to one of the lower levels of explanation. Vygotsky, in particular, attempted to show that the child incorporates cultural tools through language, and that the child's affective and cognitive psychological processes are, therefore, ultimately determined by his social cultural surroundings.

It would seem that modern social-constructionist views of emotion come close to formulating the approach Vygotsky was advocating. Social-constructionism accepts two general classes of (adult) human emotions: (1) emotions that have natural analogs in animals and human infants (such as joy and fear); and (2) emotions that have no such natural analogs (such as anger). Both classes of emotions, however, are mediated by the individual's social consciousness and, therefore, change their nature as the individual's cognitive capacities develop. A child's feeling of jealousy, for example, is qualitatively different from the adult feeling of the same name (see Ratner, 1989, for examples and a lucid account of social-constructionism). This view may well be in harmony with Vygotsky's distinction between higher and lower psychological processes and his view of cognitive development. After all, he frequently argued that children's conceptual development transformed their mental functioning in all respects (see chapter 11). He also interpreted the fact that the emotional feelings of many mental patients change by reference to the cognitive changes that had taken place during their illness.

Can the approach Vygotsky was looking for be found in Spinoza's writings? It is true that Spinoza claimed that there is no principal distinction between (lower) emotional processes and (higher) intellectual processes, and he also believed that both should be explained causally. Spinoza's belief in the unity of soul and body and his espousal of determinism was echoed by Vygotsky's search for a new psychology of emotions. Yet one doubts whether a developmental theory of emotions can benefit from the study of Spinoza's writings, for a developmental perspective seems to be entirely lacking in his work (Calhoun and Solomon, 1984) and Spinoza's writings have a reductionist flavor (Harré, 1986, p. 3). One can also question the value of Vygotsky's solution for the general ontological problem of body and mind. Is his hierarchical theory of mind, in which the lower psychological processes are "superseded" by the higher, really relevant to the ontological problem of mind—body dualism? Is not some form of dualism retained in the distinction between lower and higher psychological processes? These questions remain unanswered. In this chapter we have set ourselves the more modest goal of presenting Vygotsky's "rather naive and strange" (Vygotsky, 1984b, p. 138) attempt to connect classical philosophy and modern psychological research.

Conclusions

In the early 1930s Vygotsky wrote a penetrating analysis of the James–Lange theory of emotions, demonstrating the equivalence of this theory to Descartes' theory of the passions. In order to find an antidote to Cartesian dualism he turned to the works of Spinoza, only to find that the answer did not lie there. However, Vygotsky's own view of the nature and development of emotions was potentially useful and bears a resemblance to modern social-constructionist views of emotions.

15

A Final Word

The last chapter of *Thinking and Speech* gives the best insight available (except for his correspondence) into Vygotsky's personal preferences. Dictated in the final months of his life it contains many references to the poets he loved and to the works of literature and plays he enjoyed, in short to the world of words and masquerades he had loved from his early youth.

The content of this chapter might even be partially reconstructed starting from several of the poetic fragments quoted. For Vygotsky began his last piece of work with a quotation from his acquaintance and favorite poet, Osip Mandel'shtam: "I have forgotten the word I wanted to say and without flesh the thought flies back to its home of shadows." These were lines from a poem published in *Tristia*, the collection of poems that Mandel'shtam had dedicated to Vygotsky in 1922 (see chapter 1).

Near the end of the chapter we find two lines from Gumilyov's poem "The Word" (1921), which complemented Mandel'shtam's: "And like bees in a deserted hive badly smell dead words."[1] For Vygotsky, Gumilyov's lines expressed the idea that words without meaning or sense or without underlying thoughts, smell of death; that is, they are as empty as thoughts without words. Again Vygotsky referred to Mandel'shtam's poem adding to his interpretation of Gumilyov's lines that thoughts not embodied in words would merely be Stygian shadows or "mist, bell sounds and brokenness" (Vygotsky, 1934a, p. 317; cf. Mandel'shtam, 1975, p. 65). These quotations from the two great Acmeist poets thus summarized the subject of Vygotsky's chapter: word and thought presuppose each other, but are distinguishable and interact in exceedingly complex ways, that remind us of the interplay of form and content in literary works (see chapter 2).

[1] The American edition of *Thinking and Speech* (Vygotsky, 1987, p. 284) gives a translation of these lines that is – to put it mildly – not verbatim: "And as the bees which have sunk into their silent Yule season, so do dead words sink."

One need not construe these lines as having a hidden political meaning in order to suppose that Vygotsky, in selecting these quotations, may have wished to make a moral statement. The least one could say is that his literary tastes were in sharp conflict with those of the ruling powers: on May 13, 1934 – when Vygotsky was dictating his chapter – Mandel'shtam was arrested for the first time (for having written a poem that ridiculed Stalin) and he would die in a concentration camp several years later. Gumilyov – the first husband of Akhmatova – had been accused of conspiracy against the Soviet government and shot in 1921. By referring to these authors – even without mentioning their names – Vygotsky demonstrated that he had remained an independent thinker who did not toe the Party line.[2]

Between Words and Thoughts

In his discussion of the relation between words and thoughts Vygotsky relied heavily on the existing linguistic and psychological literature, borrowing various conceptual distinctions embodied therein. Many linguists of that time distinguished between several forms or planes of speech and Vygotsky attempted to organize their different findings into a coherent framework and, above all, to find a consistent developmental interpretation of them.

He started his chapter with the global observation that speech and thinking have different roots. Thinking and speech are connected neither phylogenetically nor ontogenetically. Phylogenetically, for instance, one can point to the problem-solving of animals – thinking without speech – and to their verbal feats – speech without thought. Many years before Vygotsky had spelled out his argument for the existence of periods of preverbal thinking and pre-intellectual speech on several occasions (Vygotsky, 1929e; 1929f; 1929h; see also chapter 9). He reasoned that at some point in time thinking and speech become intertwined and that the ensuing interdependent whole can best be studied through the concept of word-meaning. Vygotsky thought word-meaning embodied "the *unity* of word and

---

[2]Vygotsky seems to have been consistently out of tune with the prescribed literary taste. In the same chapter of *Thinking and Speech* he quoted the *avant-guard* poet Khlebnikov, which was remarkable in 1934 when "socialist realism" had just been declared the official doctrine. In chapter 2 of this book we have already seen that his *The Psychology of Art* was dangerously close to formalism – a literary approach that had already been condemned by Lunarcharsky in 1924 – and that Vygotsky used a story of the emigré writer Bunin to illustrate his own literary views. It may be significant that from 1928 to 1934 – the period in which *avant-guard* literature and formalist ideas were increasingly criticized by the authorities and during which the doctrine of "socialist realism" evolved – Vygotsky did not publish works on art and literature.

thought" (1934, p. 262). In his concept-formation research he had shown that in child development word-meanings undergo a long series of transformations (see chapter 11).

It is interesting to note that Vygotsky now dismissed the Gestalt view of the relation between words and thoughts that he had half-heartedly accepted earlier. In 1934 he claimed that it was fundamentally misleading to compare words to the sticks used by Köhler's apes (see chapter 9) as it equated words with ordinary objects and could do nothing to explain (the development of) word-meanings (Vygotsky, 1934a, p. 266–7).

Having made the very general point about the different origins of thinking and speech Vygotsky started elaborating on the various distinctions between different levels of thought and speech that had been made in the existing literature. It was his aim to demonstrate the differences between thought on the one hand and various forms of speech on the other hand. More specifically, he wished to argue for the fundamental role of inner speech and to show its developmental course.

The first distinction Vygotsky made was that between the internal, semantic plane of speech and the external, auditory plane, for although they form a unity they can be distinguished. Piaget (1924), for example, had demonstrated that even older children can use perfect external speech while not fully understanding the semantic side of their words. Vygotsky also argued that children's language development showed a differential development for the internal and external planes of speech. The development of the semantic plane proceeded from wholes to parts, as children's first thoughts are very global and diffuse and only gradually become differentiated. External speech, on the other hand, would develop from parts to wholes as the child first forms one-word sentences and then speaks longer phrases (Vygotsky, 1934a, p. 270). Even without accepting these – somewhat dubious – concepts of whole and part one has to accept that word and thought are not each other's mirror images. In adult speech one can also distinguish between the internal, semantic and the external, vocal plane. Vygotsky explained that the difference can be seen quite clearly when the psychological and grammatical subject and predicate do not coincide. Thus, in the sentence "The clock has fallen", the subject grammatically speaking is "the clock" and the predicate "has fallen." Psychologically speaking, however, both "the clock" and "has fallen" can be the subject of the utterance depending on the context involved. The sentence could be the answer to both the question "Which objects have fallen?" and to "What happened to the clock?" When answering these questions with the same sentence, "The clock has fallen", its psychological subject will differ.

This distinction between grammatical and psychological subjects and predicates was a very old one and was borrowed from Vossler (1923). In fact, in several places Vygotsky quoted Vossler verbatim (1934a, pp. 272–3; 1987, pp. 251–2)[3] and his references to Paul (1886) and to Uhland's words in the play *Herzog Ernst von Schwaben* were directly taken from Vossler (1923, pp. 105–51). Until now these facts have gone unnoticed, probably because even in the original 1934 edition of *Thinking and Speech* most of the quotation marks were left out. The modern reader is entitled to know, however, that Vygotsky's reasoning about the subtle interactions between the psychological and grammatical planes of speech can be found fully, and in more elaborate form, in Paul (1886, pp. 100–7) and, in particular, in Vossler (1923, pp. 105–51).

Vygotsky showed – again inspired by examples given in Vossler (1923) – the interdependence of the internal and external aspects of speech by pointing out, among other things, a problem that arose in translating a poem from German into Russian. In the poem, by Heine (see Heine, 1968, p. 88) a firtree (*der Fichtenbaum*) is dreaming of a palm (*die Palme*). In the original text the gender of both nouns suggested a heterosexual love affair between the two trees. Unfortunately, the Russian equivalent for firtree happened to be of the wrong gender and Tjutchev in his translation replaced it by a cedar, which has the right gender in Russian, in order to preserve the intended meaning of the poem. This example demonstrated the simple truth that the grammatical properties of words may evoke various shades of meaning that are lost in translation. Vygotsky (1934a, p. 274) concluded that the existence of two planes of speech – an internal plane, or grammar of thought, and an external plane, or grammar of words – was demonstrated sufficiently and that the sense structure may be changed as the internal plane is embodied in the external one and vice versa. He suggested that these two planes are not fully differentiated in early periods of development, since young children and primitive people tend to see names as properties of objects (Vygotsky, 1934a, pp. 274–5).

The Method: Starting from Egocentric Speech

Having clarified the difference between these two planes of speech to his satisfaction, Vygotsky proceeded to investigate the phenomenon of inner speech. For him this was the phenomenon that lay "behind" the plane of semantic speech. It is not clear, however, what "behind" means in this context and the present authors feel that the various conceptual distinctions

---

[3]Unfortunately, in Vygotsky (1987) Vossler became Fasler, Uhland turned into Uland, while the poor duke Ernst von Schwaben became Ernst Shvabskii.

made in his chapter cannot easily be accommodated in one hierarchically structured whole. Instead, we would suggest that the various distinctions partially overlap and in fact sometimes express more or less the same idea. More specifically, it seems that the phenomenon of inner speech can be seen as part of the semantic plane of speech and not necessarily as a phenomenon that is "deeper" in the sense of being closer to thoughts. In the following we will see that other concepts also overlapped.

How should the phenomenon of inner speech be investigated? And what is actually meant by it? This last question can be answered only very vaguely at this stage: for Vygotsky inner speech was not simply speech without sound as Watson claimed, nor was it everything that preceeds the motor act (i.e. the viewpoint of Goldstein). Essentially Vygotsky believed that it was speech for oneself and not speech for others. It was this functional aspect that implied a series of structural properties, which made other definitions of inner speech untenable.

As the adequate method to investigate inner speech, Vygotsky proposed to start from the study of egocentric speech and to infer the properties of inner speech by extrapolation. Of course this appoach presupposed that these phenomena were meaningfully related. Consequently, Vygotsky devoted much space to the arguments that egocentric speech (1) serves the same function as inner speech, that is, to plan our behavior; (2) has a structure similar to that of inner speech; and (3) is, genetically speaking, transformed into inner speech. Once these claims have been substantiated one might use the objectively observable properties of egocentric speech to deduce the properties of inner speech. In this way, following an indirect route, we might be able to lay bare the peculiarities of inner speech, that is, to observe the nonobservable, or – as Vygotsky (1934a, p. 316) put it – "the other side of the moon."

The problem was, of course, that Piaget's (1923) own interpretation of egocentric speech was rather different from Vygotsky's and said nothing of a possible genetic relation to inner speech. In Vygotsky's reading, Piaget's view could be summarized as follows: (1) egocentric speech does not serve any function at all; it simply accompanies the on-going action of the child; (2) the structure of a child's egocentric speech differs from that of adult speech because it is not yet sufficiently socialized; and (3) egocentric speech does not become transformed into inner speech; it simply fades away. Vygotsky remarked that if (2) were true one would expect the structure of egocentric speech to become less differentiated from communicative, socialized speech as the child grows older. Eventually, it would vanish completely, because it had become structurally equivalent to communicative speech. Rather surprisingly, he claimed to have carried out investigations that disproved this theory. Analyzing the structural properties of egocentric speech of children in the age range of three to seven years' old he found that egocentric speech does not become more comprehensible as the child grows older. What is more, Vygotsky claimed that at the age of three egocentric speech did not differ from communicative speech, while at the age of seven it differed 100 percent. This would be a set of intriguing results (curiously enough, no researcher seems to have reinvestigated this issue) that is hard to align with Piaget's assertions. It did accord with Vygotsky's idea of a growing differentiation of two planes of speech, one of which, egocentric speech, would be subsumed and transformed into inner speech, while the other, social speech, would remain evident and serve a communicative function.

Vygotsky's next step was to argue – with Grünbaum (1927) – that egocentric speech although structurally increasingly difficult to understand, still was social speech, that is, speech intended to be heard by others. He pointed out that Piaget's own sketch of egocentric speech seemed to imply this view, for Piaget had observed that (1) egocentric speech often proceeds in the form of collective monologues, that is, in a collective of children; (2) noted that egocentric speech is often accompanied by the illusion of understanding by the recipient; and (3) observed that egocentric speech is external, audible speech. In order to substantiate his alternative interpretation of these findings Vygotsky carried out a number of small experiments. As with the investigation mentioned above they were probably carried out around 1929 in the Krupskaja Academy of Education, but as with that experiment, we are not presented with any raw data, only Vygotsky's summarizing statistics.

The first thing Vygotsky did was to try to undermine the child's idea that others were understanding him. If this would lead to a diminishing number of egocentric utterances that would confirm the idea that the child is indeed addressing others with the aim of being understood. Placing the child in (1) a collective of deaf–mutes or (2) a collective of children speaking a foreign language indeed led to a considerable decrease of egocentric speech. Vygotsky reported that the ratio of egocentric utterances before and after the experimental intervention was 8 : 1. The second experimental intervention Vygotsky introduced was meant to disturb the development of a collective monologue. In order to accomplish this the child was (1) placed in a collective of children unknown to him; (2) forced to play at some distance from the collective; (3) forced to play alone; and (4) forced to play alone and left after some time by the experimenter. Again the result was that the frequency of egocentric utterances decreased. Here the ratio of the number of egocentric utterances in the normal situation compared to that in the strange situations was 6 : 1. Finally, Vygotsky manipulated the possibility of normal, audible speech by introducing a number of restraints. These included (1) placing the child at a distance from the others; (2) having an orchestra play; (3) making loud noises and (4) forbidding the children to speak out loud (only whispering was allowed). Again he found that egocentric speech diminished this time in a ratio of 5.4 : 1.

Vygotsky believed that these findings proved that his interpretation of the function, structure, and fate of egocentric speech was beyond any reasonable doubt (cf. Vygotsky and Luria, 1930a). The child was definitely trying to address the other children and egocentric speech was, therefore, a form of social speech. On the other hand, the developmental curves showed that its structure changed to produce an increasing incomprehensibility. This seemed to imply that part of communicative speech branched off to form egocentric and, eventually, inner speech, which would serve its own functions. More specifically, inner speech would help to plan the subject's behavior, an issue that received little attention in Vygotsky's last chapter.

"The Other Side of the Moon": Inner Speech

Vygotsky claimed that when studying children's egocentric speech he came to the conclusion that inner speech must have very special properties. In itself this was hardly a new idea, for as Watson had already suggested our thoughts (even if registered with the help of a phonograph and thus made audible to the ear of interested government officials) would never be understandable to the outsider. Accepting this comforting thought Vygotsky set out to sketch the peculiarities of inner speech drawing heavily on the existing linguistic literature. In the first place inner speech must have a special syntax: it is fragmented, abbreviated, and shows a tendency towards predicativity, that is, a tendency towards omitting the subject of the utterance.

It is remarkable that Vygotsky did not illustrate the syntax of inner speech by giving examples from protocols of egocentric speech registered in his own research. Instead, he resorted to analogies with ordinary speech. When would we omit the subject of a sentence in ordinary speech? Vygotsky distinguished between (1) the case of answering a question and (2) the more general case of a situation in which the subject of the sentence is known to both speaker and listener. Obviously, when answering a question we will not always fully repeat all the information that the question contained: monosyllabic answers abound in conversations. To illustrate the more general case of shared context Vygotsky quoted Levin's declaration of love to Kitty from Tolstoy's *Anna Karenina*. Levin and Kitty conducted their conversation by only writing down the initials of the words and Vygotsky emphasized the importance of this literary fragment by referring to the fact that it was based on a historical conversation that took place in Tolstoy's own life, although in a recent biography of Tolstoy the credibility of this story – related by the writer and his wife – is considered very doubtful (Wilson, 1988, p. 194). Be that as it may, it is clear that cases of abbreviated speech are frequent in everyday conversations and that they rest on the common knowledge of speaker and listener. From these examples Vygotsky concluded that it is only logical to expect abbreviated speech in inner speech as the speaker and listener are one and all the contextual knowledge is available. In this respect, he argued, inner speech is diametrically opposed to written speech.

Another factor that allows the speaker to use abbreviated speech is intonation: intonation can give one and the same word various shades of meaning. To illustrate this fact Vygotsky (1934a, p. 298) again referred to a literary source. Dostoevsky, in his *Diary of a Writer* told the story of a group of drunkards who communicated with the help of only one – rather indecent – word pronounced in a variety of ways. Referring to this extremely unlikely story Vygotsky argued that normal, dialogical speech can be much more abbreviated than written speech. Thus it seemed that one could, following Humboldt, distinguish between various speech genres – inner speech, dialogical speech, and written speech – which differed in several dimensions. Vygotsky's strategy was to argue that written speech was diametrically opposed to inner speech and to extrapolate several tendencies present in normal and egocentric speech to inner speech. He claimed, for example, that the predicative character of egocentric speech was more outspoken in situations where it more clearly served an intellectual function, that is, when the child was confronted with an unexpected problem. The implication was that inner speech – supposedly serving an exclusively intellectual function – would be completely predicative. Again, however, the reader was shown no protocol fragments to illustrate this finding. It also seems odd that Vygotsky introduced the subject of intonation. The possibilities of intonation distinguish normal speech from written speech but it cannot possibly play a role in inner speech. Introducing this topic, therefore, could only serve the more general purpose of distinguishing different speech genres and was of no use for Vygotsky's aim of characterizing inner speech.

(That Vygotsky did introduce the topic of intonation becomes understandable when we realize that this part of his chapter was based on the Soviet linguist Jakubinsky's (1923/1988) famous paper "On dialogical speech," which dealt with the various factors that play a role in normal dialogical speech. In fact, it is no exaggeration to say that Vygotsky (1934a, pp. 292–304; 1987, pp. 266–75) simply paraphrased the content of Jakubinsky's paper, adding as his own contribution the extrapolation of the findings to the domain of inner speech. It is easy to support this claim, as Vygotsky followed Jakubinsky's line of thought closely and several times quoted him verbatim. For example, Vygotsky's (1934a, pp. 295–8) quotations from and references to Tarde, Polivanov, and Shcherba (see Budagov, 1988) were all present in Jakubinsky (1923/1988, pp. 27–43). Jakubinsky also gave various examples of abbreviation in normal speech (e.g. the case of monosyllabic answers) and explicitly compared written and normal speech. And the fragments from Tolstoy's *Anna Karenina* and Dostoevsky's *Diary of a Writer* are fully quoted in Jakubinsky's paper. Many more examples could be given but the present short list suffices to show Vygotsky's style of working in this chapter. As in the case of his use of Vossler (1923) it was not easy to see this influence: Vygotsky did mention Jakubinsky's name several times but gave no source and never made clear that his reasoning and all of his examples were directly inspired by or taken from Jakubinsky's paper.

Vygotsky continued his reasoning in the chapter by pointing to several peculiarities of the semantics of inner speech. Referring to Paulhan (1928) he claimed that in inner speech sense dominates over meaning or signification. Paulhan had argued that words evoke different tendencies in different individuals and he labeled these tendencies the senses of the word. The senses can be distinguished from the word's signification, that is, those senses that are shared by all individuals. Sense and signification of the word have transient boundaries and Paulhan argued that they can be represented as concentric circles with the smallest circle denoting the signification (Paulhan, 1928, pp. 293–4). One may say, then, that Paulhan's concept of "sense" was roughly equivalent with the personal connotation a given word has for a specific person, while his "signification" roughly coincided with its impersonal dictionary definition. Paulhan gave several examples demonstrating that words may have a personal sense for a person who does not know their dictionary meaning and vice versa. He emphasized that the sense of the words of a text is dependent on the wider context: it can only be grasped by reading the whole passage of a book. Paulhan even went as far as to claim that in the end an adequate understanding of the sense of words requires reading the whole body of work of a writer and a knowledge of his life (1928, pp. 324–7).

Vygotsky thought that this reasoning again implied that inner speech – even if objectively registered – would be incomprehensible to an outsider. For it is obvious that when speaking for oneself the personal meanings or senses will be more prevalent than in the case of speech for others. This may lead to very idiosyncratic word formations and personal idioms or "dialects." He claimed that a tendency towards the development of such "inner dialects" had indeed been observed in his own experiments registering egocentric speech.

We may conclude, then, that inner speech differs in a variety of ways from normal, dialogical speech on the one hand and written speech on the other. All of its peculiarities are rooted in the fact that it is speech not intended to be heard by others. It follows that inner speech is no mirror image, no simple copy of normal speech. The path between thought and the spoken word involves a series of transformations. For Vygotsky the transformation from the spoken word to inner speech and vice versa had been sufficiently clarified. The task that remained was to clarify the relation between inner speech and thoughts.

Thoughts and Motives

Vygotsky continued his line of thought by stating that one and the same thought may be expressed in various ways, as one utterance may stand for various thoughts. Clearly the thought and its verbal expression do not coincide. He illustrated this truth by referring to Stanislavsky's system of recreating the hidden meaning of lines spoken in, for example, Griboedov's *Woe from Wit* and he quoted lines by the poets Tyutchev and Fet about the difficulty of expressing thoughts in words. It seems, that in Vygotsky's view thoughts were identifiable entities that might be expressed in words. Every possible phrasing of the thought, however, was at the same time a completion of the thought in one or the other direction. In order to communicate with others we have to operate with words with their ordinary dictionary meaning, but in doing so the original thought will inevitably be changed and shades of meaning – personal senses – will be lost. Vygotsky summarized this view by stating that

> The thought is not only externally mediated by signs, but also internally by meanings. The whole point is that direct communication of minds is impossible not only physically, but also psychologically. It can only be reached through indirect, mediated ways. This road amounts to the internal mediation of the thought first by meanings, then by words. Therefore the thought can never be equal to the direct meaning of words. The meaning mediates the thought on its road towards verbal expression, that is, the road from thought to the word is a roundabout, internally mediated road. (Vygotsky, 1934a, p. 314)

The present authors read this rather cryptic statement as once again expressing the idea that between the plane of thought and the plane of the spoken word one can find the plane of inner speech where sense dominates over meaning.

Having distinguished the plane of spoken words, the plane of inner speech, and the plane of thought, Vygotsky stated that thoughts can only be understood from an examination of the underlying forces that caused them. All thoughts are born out of emotions, drives, needs, and motivations. It was a thesis he did not develop. In fact, Vygotsky only dealt with it by referring the reader once more to the same analysis by Stanislavsky of Griboedov's *Woe from Wit*, but this time the hidden meanings of words detected by Stanislavsky served to illustrate the idea that each spoken line has an underlying motive. We may conclude, therefore, that Vygotsky's distinguishing between thoughts and their underlying motives remained rather theoretical and was not sufficiently illustrated by example.

Vygotsky believed that he had proved his main argument: that the relation between words and thoughts is not a thing but a process. It is a movement from thought to word and back again. Or, in other words, the "thought is not expressed in the word, but is completed in the word. One might therefore speak of the becoming (the unity of being and non-being) of the thought in the word" (Vygotsky, 1934a, p. 269).

In all generality this conclusion may be accepted and Vygotsky's description of the connection between egocentric speech and inner speech should be considered truly original. It is this part of his argument that has been hotly debated and has generated much research (e.g. Piaget, 1962; Kohlberg, Yaeger, and Hjertholm, 1968; Zivin, 1979).

On Vygotsky's Possible Other Sources: A Connection with Bakhtin?

Vygotsky's general linguistic arguments – e.g. that one can distinguish different forms of speech that are different yet interact; that there is more than the meaning of words; that one can distinguish grammatical and psychological subjects and predicates, etc. – are not original. We have shown how his reasoning was entirely based on the works of Vossler (1923), Jakubinsky (1923/1988), and Paulhan (1928), and it is clear to the present writers that a great deal of Vygotsky's arguments were quite commonplace in the linguistic circles of the 1920s and 1930s.

Of course, our exploration of the linguistic background of Vygotsky's thinking can only be considered a first step and a more thorough investigation of Vygotsky's sources would be rewarding. In this respect Radzikhovsky, the author of the commentaries in the Russian edition of *Thinking and Speech*, has made some interesting observations. As we have done, Radzikhovsky observed that in the seventh chapter of *Thinking and Speech* Vygotsky quoted some literary works via other authors (1982, pp. 488–9). He claimed – without giving his reasons – that Vygotsky took the fragment of Dostoevsky's *Diary of a Writer* from Gornfel'd (1906) (Radzikhovsky, 1982, p. 488; n. 87). As we have seen, this is most certainly wrong: the fragment was quoted via Jakubinsky (1923/1988). Radzikhovsky also made several claims concerning the following two fragments of poetry quoted by Vygotsky in his seventh chapter (1934a, p. 314):

> How can the heart express itself,
> How can the other understand you . . .

and

> Oh, if the soul could express itself without the word!

The first fragment was attributed by Radzikhovsky to Fet and he claimed (Radzikhovsky, 1982, p. 489, n. 92) – again without giving any reasons – that it was quoted by Vygotsky via Bakhtin's *Marxism and the Philosophy of Language* (Bakhtin, 1930/1972). If true, this would prove that Vygotsky knew Bakhtin's work. Radzikhovsky (1982, p. 489; n. 93) attributed the second fragment to Gumilyov's poem "The Word." Unfortunately, this is mistaken. For the first fragment was not written by Fet but comes from Tyutchev's famous poem "Silentium!" (Tyutchev, 1836/1976, pp. 132–3), while the second fragment was not written by Gumilyov, but is part of a poem written by Fet (Fet, 1844/1979, pp. 64–5).

Nevertheless, Radzikhovsky may have been right in pointing to Bakhtin as one of the possible sources of inspiration for Vygotsky. One reason to suppose that Vygotsky read Bakhtin (1930/1972) is that the poetic fragment by Fet given above can be found in Bakhtin (1930/1972, p. 86) as well as another line from Tyutchev's "Silentium!": These lines were quoted there in the context of a discussion that was similar to Vygotsky's. Among other things, Bakhtin argued that the internal thought expressing itself would be changed by the medium used, that is, speech (Bakhtin, 1930/1972, p. 86).

In itself, however, showing that various literary fragments are present in the work of both Vygotsky and Bakhtin without performing a thorough analysis of their texts is hardly sufficient evidence to draw any conclusion about a possible mutual influence. To illustrate the danger of Radzikhovsky's approach, we might point out that the very same fragment of Dostoevsky's *Diary of a Writer* that was present in Jakubinsky (1923/1988), and borrowed by Vygotsky (1934a), was also presented – and for the same purpose – in Bakhtin (1930/1972, p. 106)!

We, thus, conclude that Radzikhovsky's remarks do not demonstrate beyond doubt that Vygotsky consulted Bakhtin's *Marxism and the Philosophy of Language*. We do know that Bakhtin referred to Vygotsky (1925j) in his *Freudianism. A Critical Essay* (Bakhtin, 1927/1983; see also chapter 5), but this fact and the similarities between the writings of both authors can only serve as a starting point for a future investigation about their possible mutual influence.

Another claim made by Radzikhovsky (1982, p. 489; n. 96) is that Vygotsky's quotations from Gumilyov's poem "The Word" (given in the very beginning of this chapter) was borrowed from an article written by Osip Mandel'shtam. Again he gave no reasons for this supposition. The particular article, entitled "On the nature of the word," was published in 1922 as a separate brochure and had the lines from Gumilyov's poem on its cover (see Mandel'shtam, 1922/1987, pp. 280–1). Radzikhovsky's claim may have been partially based on the fact that Mandel'shtam (1922/1987, p. 58) also quoted Tyutchev's famous words from "Silentium!": "How can the heart express itself," "How can the other understand you . . . ." In itself, this would make his rather weak claim somewhat stronger although Tyutchev's poem is very famous and generally known by educated Russians.

In summary we might say Radzikhovsky's (1982) analysis of Vygotsky's sources is not convincing and that at present there are insufficient reasons to suppose that Vygotsky quoted several literary fragments via Bakhtin and/or Mandel'shtam.

Conclusions

The last chapter of *Thinking and Speech* was Vygotsky's final word on issues of scientific interest. Dictated in the spring of 1934 it contained many references to works of literature and to the available linguistic writings. The chapter owed much to Vossler (1923), Jakubinsky (1923/1988), and Paulhan (1928), and, in fact, it could be argued that Vygotsky's sole contribution to the debate on inner and external speech was to extrapolate the findings of these authors to the domain of inner speech. Vygotsky's constructive replications of Piaget's findings on egocentric speech were truly original and it is unfortunate that these were given only very vaguely.

16
Criticisms

With rather few exceptions (e.g. Brushlinsky, 1968), current criticism of Vygotsky's ideas seems to be rare. Modern researchers appear either to accept Vygotsky as an important historical figure whose ideas are relevant to our present-day understanding of the human mind, or to dismiss him as an historical figure whose obsolete ideas now have little relevance. But there is no theoretical debate between adherents and opponents of a Vygotskian view of human development (cf. Brushlinsky, 1988, p. 7; Tulviste, 1988b, p. 5). This is as disappointing as it is surprising, for it would seem that the material for such a debate has been mounting. Many researchers have been trying to replicate and extend different aspects of Vygotskian thinking. Researchers such as Kohlberg, Yaeger, and Hjertholm (1968), Zivin (1979), and Goudena (1983) have investigated the issue of the planning function of egocentric speech. Wertsch (1980; 1981; 1984) studied the topic of dialogical speech in mother–child dyads. Adams et al. (1987), and Van der Veer (1991) replicated the research of artificial attention and memory, and Brown (in Campione et al., 1984; Brown and Ferrara, 1985) investigated the issue of aided performance in the zone of proximal development. Finally, Scribner and Cole (1981) and Tulviste (1988a) investigated the cultural-historical claims about cross-cultural differences in mental makeup. Many more replication studies could be added.

Surprisingly enough, neither these replication studies nor the recent theoretical analyses (e.g. Berg, 1970; Puzyrej, 1986a; Rissom, 1985; Wertsch, 1985) of Vygotsky's work have led to a global appraisal of Vygotsky's endeavor. The one notable exception is, again, Brushlinsky (1968), who, starting from a theoretical framework inspired by Rubinshtejn came to a rather negative evaluation of Vygotsky's accomplishments as a whole. It would seem, then, that the theoretical debate about the validity and fruitfulness of Vygotskian ideas is only at its very beginning, possibly because of a lack of insight in the real historical Vygotsky. The present book is, of course, an attempt to fuel a future debate.

We should not think, however, that the situation was the same in the 1920s and 1930s. In fact, Vygotsky's ideas at times met with very sharp criticism and critics did not hesitate to condemn his theory as a whole. Although many of these criticisms cannot be viewed in isolation from the prevailing ideological views, it is facile to regard these criticisms simply as an expression of "Stalinism" or some other "ism" as many adherents of the Vygotskian paradigm argue. All critique – and it has never been otherwise in any historical period or country – is a mixture of the prevailing ideological views and of fair or unfair scientific criticism, and Vygotsky is not a prototype of the single-minded investigator conducting his research whilst ignoring each and every "ideological" issue. It is true that his writings mostly lacked the empty jargon employed by the likes of Zalkind. It is also true that Vygotsky tended to discuss ideologically sensitive topics in an objective, scientific way. Yet we have seen that he sincerely believed in the utopian ideas of the communist world-view (Vygotsky, 1930w; chapter 3), that he was actively involved in the organizations linked with the Communist Party (chapter 1), and that he attempted to incorporate the communist world-view in his research (e.g. Shif's research in chapter 11). Of course, there was simply no way he could have avoided becoming involved in the continuing ideological debate in Soviet society, even if he had wished to.[1] Vygotsky was one of the many active figures and researchers who at the same time contributed to and were the victims of the maelstrom of Soviet society. In this chapter part of this debate will be presented. Undoubtedly, more material will be found by future historians of psychology but the present overview will give the reader at least some idea of the ideological debates that provided the context in which Vygotsky's ideas were formed and it may enhance insight into the ideological (non-)embeddedness of his views (see also Bubnov, 1936; Frankel, 1930; F., 1936; Ja., 1936, and Markov, 1936).

The Growing Ideological Pressure

Although intellectual freedom in the real sense of the word had never existed in the Soviet Union, the situation grew considerably worse as 1929 approached. The personnel of educational and scientific institutions were more and more frequently subjected to political investigations and purges, which might result in dismissal, imprisonment, or execution. The idea was, of course, "to oust bourgeois academicians of certain institutions in order to

---

[1]Vygotsky participated, for example, in the reactology discussion (cf. Vygotsky, 1931s).

replace them with supporters of the Communist Party" (Graham, 1987, p. 9). That Luria and Leont'ev participated in similar purges should be noted. In the 1920s students awaiting interrogation by the university authorities were pulled out of the line and submitted to Luria's "lie detector" (Joravsky, 1989, p. 249; Levitin, 1982, pp. 156–8; Luria, 1979, pp. 35–6; 201–2; see also chapter 10).

In order to give an idea of the conditions that gradually developed in Soviet academia we can do no better than to quote from the resolution that was published in 1931 in connection with the attack on Kornilov's reactology and his Institute of Experimental Psychology. This resolution ("Itogi diskussii po reaktologicheskoj psikhologii," 1931a; 1931b; 1931c) declared that "the acuteness of the struggle at the scientific front reflects the acuteness of the class struggle in our country." The existing petty bourgeois schools of thought in Western psychology – such as behaviorism, Stern's personalism, and Gestalt psychology – were condemned for their ahistorical, abstract, and, therefore, essentially reactionary nature. Unfortunately – as the resolution continued – remnants of these anti-socialist and subversive ideas were still present in the writings of several would-be Soviet scientists, notably the adherents of Chelpanov and Vygotsky's former teacher Gustav Shpet, the resolution warned. It further declared that it was of the utmost importance to "destroy and annihilate these remnants of bourgeois idealistic theories that formed a direct reflection of the resistance of counter-revolutionary elements of the country against the socialist construction." Several organizational measures were suggested in order to purge psychology of these elements. These included a general examination of the content of text-books used at universities and institutes. The decision was taken to devote more attention to the formation of reliable communist cadres at the universities by demanding that a certain quota of the persons writing their dissertations should be Party members. Moreover, the ideological commitments of the personnel had to be examined thoroughly and the appointment of heads of the staff now required the permission of the "competent Party center." Finally, it was required that students should work for some period at a collective farm, or factory.

These quotations demonstrate that the Party culture, with its fear of dissenting opinions and its demand for a strictly uniform world-view, was being imposed on scientific debates (cf. Jakhot, 1981). More and more frequently researchers were forced to demonstrate their loyalty to the latest ideological point of view. The most common procedure to deal with researchers whose ideology was considered to be suspect, was the organization of public debates where carefully prepared opponents tried to demolish the scientific position of the researcher. Of course, many psychologists pleaded guilty in advance – admitting to ridiculous or simply incomprehensible accusations – in the hope of mitigating the expected sanctions. One of them was Anan'ev who, as the victim of the anti-reactology campaign, recanted in an article in *Psikhologija* and seized the opportunity to try to drag down Vygotsky with him. Quoting Stalin, Anan'ev acknowledged the correctness of the criticisms of his views and asked for more. He now clearly realized the reactionary nature of the reactology he had promoted. However, he had not been the only erring psychologist in the past few years: Vygotsky and Luria, in particular, had espoused incorrect views. Their so-called Marxist approach was in reality an unhappy mixture of behaviorist and psychoanalytic ideas. Anan'ev singled out Vygotsky's and Luria's *Studies in the History of Behavior* (1930a) for its lack of the social-class concept. In this book, Anan'ev said, both history and child development were treated from an abstract sociological point of view, thereby ignoring the concept of social class. Anan'ev added that living in Leningrad he was somewhat cut off from the on-going debates in Moscow and, thus, did not know how far the criticism and self-criticism in the case of Vygotsky and Luria had gone, but he sincerely hoped that his colleagues would repent (Anan'ev, 1931, pp. 341–2).

The editorial board of *Psikhologija* – which included Vygotsky and Luria – apparently was not completely satisfied with Anan'ev's text and remarked in a footnote that while appreciating the change in the theoretical position of one of the main representatives of reflexology they did not agree with his present views.

Anan'ev must have chosen Vygotsky and Luria as the target of his attack because he knew they had been "outlawed" by the "competent Party centers" (he had probably attended Talankin's talk; see below) and would be the victims of one of the public debates yet to come. Indeed, such a debate had been mooted for some time and Vygotsky and Luria had carefully prepared their defense. That this was so is clear in one of the letters Vygotsky wrote to Luria, when the latter was in Samarkand for the first psychological expedition to Central Asia (see chapter 10):

> The discussion is delayed all the time. First, it did not materialize because the discussion about Zalkind intervened, then there was the psychological congress. Not even a date has been fixed now. Apparently it will be held in June. The auspices are the same as with you. Our decision is unshakeable. (Vygotsky in a letter to Luria, dated June 1, 1931)

Several days before this letter was written the first more or less official criticism of Vygotsky's and Luria's theoretical views had been heard. At the First All-Union Congress on Psychotechnics and the Psychophysiology of Labor in Leningrad A. A. Talankin – a member of the Party cell of

Kornilov's Institute and a very active participant in the discussion on reactology – had given a talk entitled "About the turning-point on the psychological front" (Talankin, 1931a). In this talk he criticized practically all existing psychological currents, concentrating on Kornilov's and Bekhterev's ideas. In the published version of his talk a special paragraph was dedicated to "the group of Vygotsky and Luria." Talankin warned against their tendency to uncritically transfer Western psychological theories, such as Freudianism, Gestalt psychology, and the theories of Karl Bühler to Soviet psychology. He continued by criticizing their concept of "instrument" as it was at variance with the concept of "tool" as understood by Marxism. Further, he remarked that Vygotsky's concept of culture was crudely mechanistic, because he understood culture "as the sum of things, instruments, and symbols." Finally, Talankin remarked that

> the cultural-psychological conception of Vygotsky and Luria has to be fought seriously. Thus far it has not been criticized. We have to demonstrate that a Marxist solution of the problem of the development of psychic processes on a historical-labor basis undoubtedly differs radically from the formulation of the problem of development that we see in Vygotsky and Luria. (Talankin, 1931a, p. 15)

Some pages later Talankin (1931a, p. 22) returned to Vygotsky's and Luria's ideas when discussing the concept of labor. Emphasizing Marx' and Engels' idea that it was labor that created man, he criticized *Studies of the History of Behavior* (Vygotsky and Luria, 1930a). In his opinion Köhler's ape, Sultan, reaching for a banana with a stick demonstrated the important role of labor. Why, then, did this concept of labor disappear in Vygotsky's and Luria's treatment of the history of man? It was, no doubt, this criticism that Anan'ev referred to in his article.

Talankin (1931b, pp. 39–40) repeated his talk in a slightly modified form in Kharkov, claiming that Vygotsky and Luria thought of "culture as a system of things that organize the person's behavior. Of course, such a thing-like understanding of culture is a non-Marxist understanding." In the ritual discussions that followed his talk, however, Vygotsky and Luria did not receive much attention ("Diskussija o polozhenii na psikhologicheskom fronte", 1931).

Seen against the background of Talankin's criticims of other psychological approaches the critique of the cultural-historical theory was rather mild. Talankin mentioned, for example, that *Studies of the History of Behavior* contained a lot of interesting material and he began his critical notes by remarking that "the group of Vygotsky and Luria is undoubtedly talented." Vygotsky, who attended Talankin's talk, wrote a letter to Luria in which he said that it had apparently been formally decided that they would be "beaten, but not killed" (*bit', no ne ubivat*) (Vygotsky in a letter to Luria, dated June 1, 1931).

Nevertheless, it had been decided by "the competent Party centers" that the cultural-historical theory was in need of a principled Marxist critique and a public discussion of Vygotsky's ideas was now more than ever unavoidable. This discussion, however, did not take place in 1931.

The Public Debate

It is clear, then, that until 1932 Vygotsky and his co-workers managed to avoid major confrontations with the leading Party ideologues. Of course, some minor frictions were unavoidable. Thus, Kurazov (1931, pp. 108–9) criticized Vygotsky for his "vulgar evolutionary point of view" claiming that in his discussion of Köhler's investigations Vygotsky had not emphasized sufficiently the intellectual differences between human beings and chimpanzees. Further, during the campaign against Kornilov many of the researchers working at his Institute did not escape criticism either. Thus, the cultural-historical theory was labeled "Vygotsky's and Luria's culturological psychology" and the journal *Psikhologija*, whose policy Vygotsky influenced (being a member of its editorial board) was condemned since "it reflected all of the above mentioned anti-Marxist currents on the psychological front and during the whole period of its three-year existence did not distinguish itself from bourgeois journals. A fraction of the editorship of the journal followed a clearly opportunistic line, allowing the acute moments of the class struggle to be concealed by bare formalism" ("Itogi diskussii po reaktologicheskoj psikhologii", 1931a, p. 388).

It was Feofanov (1932), however, who opened the real attack against Vygotsky's ideas with an article in *Pedologija* entitled "The theory of cultural development in paedology as an electric[2] conception that on the whole has idealist roots." Feofanov was experienced in writing this type of article (cf. Feofanov, 1931a; 1931b; 1931c) and had undoubtedly been asked to open the debate. Judging by a footnote his article was intended as the first of a series.

> The editorial board is of the opinion that the so-called "theory of cultural development" requires the most severe Marxist–Leninist criticism as it smuggles in – under the flag of "historical development" – idealist, subjectivist

---

[2]He intended to write "eclectic." It was Talankin (1931b), who first used the word "eclectic" with regard to Vygotsky's approach. All of the later critics repeated this criticism.

conceptions, mixed with mechanistic elements of a "behaviorist" theory. The editorial board is of the opinion that the paper by comrade Feofanov is merely the first step towards such a criticism and represents on the whole just the *formulation* of several of the main problems of the culturological theory. Several of the formulations of the article are incorrect. The present article opens the discussion about the matter in question. (In Feofanov, 1932, p. 21)

Referring to Vygotsky paedology text-books (Vygotsky, 1929n; 1929p; 1930p; 1931h) Feofanov above all tried to find wordings or views that seemed ideologically dubious. Thus he deduced from the fact that Vygotsky often characterized child development with words such as "growth" and claimed that it results in qualitative changes, as dramatic as those which take place in the transformation from chrysalis to butterfly, that the author favored a biologistic approach. And from the fact that Vygotsky often formulated general laws for child development he deduced that the author did not distinguish beween the development of children of workers and bourgeois. It is clear that Feofanov was deliberately distorting Vygotsky's views, since in the books he referred to (e.g. Vygotsky, 1931h, pp. 471–80) Vygotsky paid particular attention to "the adolescent of the working class" (relying heavily on Spranger) and explicitly distinguished between the natural and cultural lines in child development. That Feofanov realized this becomes clear from the fact that he *also* accused Vygotsky of dualism, pointing out that the distinction between natural and cultural periods in child development is wrong as such initial, natural periods did not exist in his view. Here, of course, Feofanov made justified use of Vygotsky's unhappy use of the word "cultural" (see chapter 9). His further remark, that we cannot say with Vygotsky that "primitives" have a natural memory, whereas cultural man has an artificial memory, because both types of memory are the result of development in a specific milieu and as such are artificial, also seems to the point. Feofanov went on to argue that it is misleading to distinguish between development due to the mastering of cultural instruments and development due to the development of nervous tissue: in both cases the cortex develops in interaction with the social milieu. He, thus, ignored Vygotsky's reasons for introducing the concept of the mastery of cultural instruments, that is, the wish to differentiate between animal and human development and to build a bridge between a Marxist view of anthropogeny and contemporary primate research (see chapter 9). Finally, Feofanov criticized Vygotsky's abstract approach, arguing that he had not sufficiently emphasized that child development always takes place in a specific social milieu in a specific historical period. (It is ironic that this criticism was formulated at a time when Vygotsky's co-worker was precisely investigating the influence of social milieu and historical changes in practice (see chapter

10). Apparently, Vygotsky's views were too general: instead of giving us a grand vision of child development as the mastering of cultural instruments, he should have sketched the poor prospects for the proletarian child in a bourgeois society. Instead of describing such cultural tools as mnemonic signs and writing systems he should have focused on hard labour and practice. Vygotsky's views were deemed to be "abstract" and Feofanov concluded that they gave "an incorrect view of the development of the Soviet child" and had "a harmful influence on the practice of our education" (Feofanov, 1932, p. 34).

In the next issue of *Pedologija* Abel'skaja and Neopikhonova (1932) repeated several of Feofanov's criticisms. The topic of their review article – the transcript of a talk given at the Herzen Pedagogical Institute in Leningrad where Vygotsky was teaching at the time – was Heinz Werner's (1925) *Einführung in die Entwicklungspsychologie*, but the authors seized the opportunity to compare Werner's view with Vygotsky's ideas as expressed in *Studies in the History of Behavior* (Vygotsky and Luria, 1930a) and *Paedology of the Adolescent* (Vygotsky, 1931h). Abel'skaja's and Neopikhonova's aim was to criticize Werner for his mistakes and to point out that similar mistakes had been made by "Soviet paedology and psychology," that is, Vygotsky, Luria, and Basov (cf. Luria, 1929b). Thus, when Vygotsky and Luria pointed out the formal similarities between the development of animals, "primitives," and Western children they were repeating Werner's mistake, that is, they ignored the role of the production means and the social-historic conditions and tended to see the three domains of development as organistic. To illustrate Vygotsky's organistic approach the authors repeated Feofanov's criticism of the chrysalis–butterfly metaphor and referred to a text in which Vygotsky – quoting Kretschmer – drew a parallel between the development of the nervous system and the development of the higher psychological functions (1931h, pp. 346–7). Finally, Abel'skaja and Neopikhonova – following Talankin, Anan'ev, and Feofanov – pointed out that Vygotsky's concept of "cultural instrument" was abstract and formal as it was not by any means grounded in a concrete analysis of labor conditions in specific historical periods.

Again, the members of the editorial board of *Pedologija* intervened by adding a footnote, where they stated that Vygotsky's and Luria's "theory of cultural development" did *not* represent "Soviet paedology and psychology," as Abel'skaja and Neopikhonova had mistakingly claimed. Referring to Feofanov's paper and to "the further critical articles ... that will be published in the next issues of our journal" the cultural-historical theory was condemned as suffering from fundamental methodological defects. However, these "further critical articles" were not to be published in *Pedologia* as the journal closed down in 1932 (see chapter 12).

In 1933 the position of Vygotsky and his associates apparently grew worse.

It seems possible to infer from a letter from Vygotsky to Luria (dated March 29, 1933) that some commission was investigating (the ideological content of?) his work, but that Vygotsky believed there would be a chance to continue his work. In another letter Vygotsky mentions that he had been summoned by the leading ideologist Mitin, who suggested they work together: "Maybe, we will find support from this side. I have no more news. When I get to know something, I'll let you know. I am endlessly being interrogated and pulled about" (Vygotsky in a letter to Luria, dated November 21, 1933). Obviously, no help was offered by Mitin and Vygotsky's position does not seem to have improved. The next major public attack on the work of both Vygotsky and Luria that the present authors have been able to find was Razmyslov's (1934) infamous article "On Vygotsky's and Luria's 'cultural-historical theory of psychology.'"

Razmyslov followed the earlier critics in claiming that Vygotsky's cultural-historical theory was too general and did not specify the class background of the children whose development it tried to sketch. Neither did Vygotsky refer to means of production and other important concepts of the Communist world-view. A specific feature of Razmyslov's critique was that he, to a greater degree than Feofanov, attacked the authors of the theory and considerably broadened the "analysis" of their work.

To prove that Vygotsky's key idea of human consciousness as originating in social interaction was faulty, Razmyslov first concisely summarized Marx and Engels' fundamental ideas regarding the development of individual consciousness. Concluding that according to these classics individual consciousness originates in class consciousness, he reproached Vygotsky for his vague talk of "social collectives." To say that individuals appropriate the ideas and skills of the collective of which they form part, as Vygotsky did, reminded him very much of the ideas of the "neopositivists" Durkheim and Lévy-Bruhl. What did Vygotsky mean by saying that each psychological function appears twice, first on the interpsychological, then on the intrapsychological plane? Wasn't this exactly the idea of Durkheim? Razmyslov concluded that:

> Everywhere where it would have been necessary from our point of view to speak about the class, [and] production environment of the child, about the influence of the school, the Pioneer vanguard, and the *Komsomol* movement as bearers of the influence of the Party and the proletariat on the children ... Vygotsky ... simply speaks about the influence of the collective, without deciphering about which collective he is speaking and what he means by "collective." (Razmyslov, 1934, p. 81)

Although Razmyslov erroneously attributed the idea of the inter–intradevelopment of psychological functions to Durkheim (it was borrowed from Durkheim's colleague at the Collège de France, Pierre Janet (see Van der Veer and Valsiner, 1988)) there was some truth to his observations. Vygotsky did indeed take inspiration from Durkheim and Lévy-Bruhl, and his cultural-historical theory did not incorporate the Marxist catchwords on production means, surplus value, etc. In this sense his theory seemed far too much based on a broad current of European thinking (the anthropological and psychological work sketched in chapter 9) to be called a Marxist or Communist theory in the way Razmyslov and his comrades used this term.

Characteristic of Razmyslov's article was that the author did not refrain from quoting very old articles in order to discredit the reputation of their authors. Luria, for example, was criticized for his early psychoanalytic writings and Vygotsky for his early reflexological views. The clear goal of these references was to demonstrate that the authors held ideologically suspect beliefs all their lives, and not just when propagating the cultural-historical theory. It is in this context that Razmyslov's lengthy treatment of Vygotsky's *Pedagogical Psychology* (1926i, see chapter 3) can be understood.

Our claim that Razmyslov simply tried to damage Vygotsky's reputation can easily be illustrated. Quoting Vygotsky's words:

> The psychological nature of the educational [*vospitatel'nyj*] process is completely identical whether we wish to educate [*vospitat'*] a fascist or a proletarian whether we train an acrobat or [create] a good official. Our interest should be in the mechanism of establishing new reactions itself, irrespective of the good these reactions give rise to. (Vygotsky, 1926i, p. 63)

Razmyslov concluded that Vygotsky was not interested in the outcomes of the educational process, a view he considered both politically harmful and scientifically incorrect (1934, p. 84). Of course, Vygotsky had simply been making a technical point explaining – elsewhere in the same passage – that the subdisciplines of general pedagogics or social ethics had to define the *goal* of the educational process, whereas psychology studied its psychological *nature*.

Continuing his attack Razmyslov quoted Vygotsky's ideas, expressed in *Pedagogical Psychology*, about questioning the necessity for, and possible disappearance of formal instruction in schools. Aware that the Central Committee of the Party had recently condemned all ideas of the then prevalent movement against formal schooling for its "anti-Leninist character," Razmyslov triumphantly condemned Vygotsky's ideas which had been written some ten years earlier.

These few examples will suffice to illustrate Razmyslov's style (see also chapter 10). The author concluded that Vygotsky and Luria with their still "little-known" cultural-historical theory "objectively exerted a bourgeois influence on the proletariat," a fact that did not surprise him as Vygotsky and Luria had neglected Lenin's directives (Razmyslov, 1934, pp. 79, 86).

We may conclude, then, that Razmyslov repeated several of the earlier criticisms raised by Talankin, Anan'ev, and Feofanov, adding a critique of Luria's expedition to Central Asia (see chapter 10) and unearthing various ideologically suspect quotations found in Vygotsky's and Luria's early writings. In this way he managed to cast doubt on the ideological reliability of the authors and their theory. In fact the cultural-historical theory was *not* Marxist in the sense ascribed to that word in the early 1930s. Whether it was non-Marxist in a broader sense of the word still remains to be seen.

Posthumous Attacks

The history of Soviet psychology is littered with bizarre events and developments but even against this background it is remarkable that the active criticism of Vygotsky and his theories continued for several years after his death.

It is true that the criticisms of Razmyslov, Anan'ev and others had not convinced Vygotsky's friends and colleagues of his alleged crimes and they continued actively promoting his ideas. Kolbanovsky, the head of the Institute of Experimental Psychology, merits special attention in regard to this. He seems to have defended Vygotsky in Party meetings, and in his sympathetic necrology (Kolbanovsky, 1934c, p. 393) he tried to rebut the accusation that Vygotsky had been an eclectic thinker. His foreword and introductory article in *Thinking and Speech* can also be seen – despite the critique that Kolbanovsky formulated – as an attempt to make Vygotsky's book more palatable for Party ideologists and to make its publication possible (Kolbanovsky, 1934a; 1934b).[3] He presented Vygotsky as one of those "representatives of the non-Party intelligentsia" (Kolbanovsky, 1934a, p. v) who had reached a mature understanding of Marxism-Leninism only after some time. It was in his earlier writings that Vygotsky had made the mistakes of ignoring Piaget's class background (Kolbanovsky, 1934b, p.

---

[3]More than 20 years later, in 1956, Kolbanovsky (1956) introduced Vygotsky to a new readership. Using large parts of his earlier article, he again tried to make Vygotsky acceptable to the ruling party. Whereas in his first article Kolbanovsky (1934c, p. 389) had triumphantly and correctly related Vygotsky's criticism of Pavlov, he now (Kolbanovsky, 1956, p. 105) attempted to demonstrate their fundamental agreement. Reading these two introductions to Vygotsky's work one realizes what fundamental and tragic changes had taken place in Soviet psychology in the intervening years.

xvi) and underestimating the role of the brain. Likewise, it was the younger Vygotsky who had claimed erroneously that speech and thinking have different roots: speech and thinking could not have different roots as Engels (1925) had clearly demonstrated that *both* originated in practical labor activity. Thus, one could claim that some speech is pre-intellectual and some thinking pre-verbal, but one could not contradict Engels' claim about their common origin in labor (Kolbanovsky, 1934b, pp. xvii–xxiv; cf. chapter 9). Finally, in his concept-formation research Vygotsky – claiming that words are instrumental in the formation of real concepts – had tended to ignore the fact that words, too, are the result of labor activity (Kolbanovsky, 1934b, p. xxvii). On the whole, however, Kolbanovsky's judgment of Vygotsky's writings was favorable and he clearly suggested that Vygotsky had recognized his wrong-doings.

Kolbanovsky was not the only one to defend Vygotsky's views. Vygotsky's new collaborators and colleagues in Leningrad also attempted to defend the legacy of their teacher. His student Levina, for example, prepared the lecture series *Foundations of Paedology* (Vygotsky, 1935g) for publication and Zankov, Shif, and El'konin published several other talks under the title *Children's Mental Development in the Process of Education* (Vygotsky, 1935h). Shif (1935) and Konnikova (1935) managed to have their doctoral dissertations published (see chapter 11 and below) and Zankov (1935a) dedicated his book on defectology to his late teacher and colleague. In that same year Blonsky (1935) referred very positively to the work of his fellow paedologist. Finally, in 1936 the brochure *The Diagnostics of Development* (Vygotsky, 1936a; written in 1931) was published on the iniative of Danjushevsky and edited by Levina. Apparently, it was only with the Paedology Decree in 1936 that reference to Vygotsky's writings became definitely impossible (see chapter 12).

Both the article written by Kozyrev and Turko (1936) and Rudneva's (1937) brochure were written under the influence of this decree. Kozyrev and Turko – working at the Herzen Pedagogical Institute in Leningrad where Vygotsky had been teaching – focused their criticisms in particular on those followers of Vygotsky who had formed "the so-called Leningrad school of paedology" (Kozyrev and Turko, 1936, p. 44) and against the theoretical concepts that Vygotsky had elaborated in his Leningrad period (see chapters 11, 12, and 13). They considered Kolbanovsky's (1934a) preface to *Thinking and Speech* to be "far too positive," and it was denounced as being partially responsible for Vygotsky's popularity in Leningrad circles (Kozyrev and Turko, 1936, pp. 44, 49, 54).

One of the concepts developed in Vygotsky's Leningrad period was, of course, the concept of the zone of proximal development. Kozyrev and Turko boldly declared that this concept did no more than repeat the old slogan about the heredity of teachability, "although it is glossed over very skilfully" (1936, p. 47). To prove this they quoted Vygotsky's reasonings about the concept of sensitive zones and the optimal periods for teaching specific skills (see chapter 13). Whilst acknowledging the fact that Vygotsky clearly distinguished between his concept of the zone of proximal development and the concept of the sensitive zones, they pointed out that Vygotsky (1934a, p. 223) nevertheless accepted Montessori's claim that children should learn writing at four or five years' old. Vygotsky thus accepted the existence of optimal periods for the teaching/learning (*obuchenie*) of specific topics. How then, asked Kozyrev and Turko, can the Party hope to liquidate the illiteracy of the adult masses (1936, p. 49)? How can the workers be trained to be the leading Soviet intelligentsia?[4] The authors had to conclude that because of these statements Vygotsky was one of those who claimed the biological inferiority of the working classes.

One can easily see what was the driving force for this accusation (which simply repeated some phrases contained in the Paedology Decree itself). By speaking about optimal periods for the teaching of specific skills Vygotsky acknowledged that some processes of development had to take place in order for instruction to be successful. Some processes had to be in the process of developing – but should not have finished their development – for instruction to be fruitful. But this simple statement – that instruction can come too early, or too late – was already unacceptable in the Soviet Union of that time, for it proved that one "fatalistically" accepted the role of biological determinants of development. In a country that was rapidly heading towards the Lysenko affair this was sufficient proof of a non-scientific approach (cf. Van der Veer, 1990).

Kozyrev and Turko did not judge the rest of *Thinking and Speech* to be much better. Vygotsky's chapter on the different roots of thinking and speech, in particular, was deemed scientifically worthless (following Kolbanovsky, 1934b). In claiming that the actions of the chimpanzee are not connected with its speech, Vygotsky was contradicting not only Engels but

---

[4]These were now rather common questions. The editors of Vygotsky (1935h, p. 53), for example, felt compelled to add a footnote to Vygotsky's chapter on multilingualism in childhood. It was said that "The author does not indicate that the given problem under the conditions of our Union of Soviet republics has paramount political significance. By promoting the right solution of Lenin's Nationalities Policy the mastering of several languages of the nationalities of the USSR also helps to bring them most closely together, to further the growth of brotherly solidarity and the power of our great Union. In addition, for the workers the mastering of foreign languages forms an important means of mastering the contemporary achievements of advanced technology, and also promotes the development of international proletarian solidarity in the struggle against capitalism."

also academician N. Ja. Marr. Quoting several of Marr's statements[5] Kozyrev and Turko (1936, pp. 45, 49) concluded that Vygotsky was not sufficiently knowledgeable in the field of linguistics and had committed grave errors.

The remainder of the article was devoted to Kozyrev's and Turko's attempts to argue that paedology had no right to existence, and to attack the work of several of Vygotsky's students and collaborators. Kozyrev and Turko argued that paedology did not exist by referring to Vygotsky's (1931c, p. 18) example of the memory of a seven-year-old child. Vygotsky had said that a psychologist was interested in the memory process and its regularities but not in the age period of seven years: the phenomena he studied would be used for a deepening of our understanding of the development of memory. A paedologist, however, would be interested in the age period, considering the memory-related phenomena as part of many other data which reveal the peculiarities of this age period. He would use the results of memory tests – comparing them with other results typical for this age period – in order to deepen our understanding of this particular age period (cf. chapter 12). This distinction was considered artificial and unconvincing by Kozyrev and Turko (1936, p. 53), who could not understand what tasks would be left for the pedagogue.

Konnikova and Zankov were the targets of Kozyrev's and Turko's criticism of Vygotsky's students. Zankov (1935b) was criticized for a chapter in which he used Vygotsky's distinction between scientific and everyday concepts (see chapter 11). This distinction itself was denounced as untenable and Zankov's investigation was criticized for its poor methodology. Konnikova's (1935) dissertation on autonomous speech – which was written under the supervision of Levina, then head of the Paedological Faculty of the Herzen Pedagogical Institute – was damned for its many laudatory references to Vygotsky's works.

Enough has been said of Kozyrev's and Turko's article to make its character clear. The authors clearly followed the procedure that now had become distressingly widespread in the Soviet Union: on the premise of a Party directive, the work of an author would be scrutinized for (dis)agreement with that directive's content. The result of this activity is best judged by quoting the critics themselves:

The example of the uncritical reception and extolment of prof. L. S. Vygotsky again underlines *the need for an intensified class vigilance in all domains of*

---

[5]One year later Rudneva (1937, p. 12) was still so impressed by these quotations – which also claimed that speech and thinking originated in labor activity – that she reproduced them, not referring, however, to Kozyrev's and Turko's article.

our scientific knowledge, for in his sabotage work the enemy uses the tiniest
possibilities and does harm where we sometimes do not expect it. (Kozyrev
and Turko, 1936, p. 57; original emphasis)

The reader may wonder what Rudneva (1937) could add to the accusations already made by others and, in fact, in the thirty-two pages of her
peculiar brochure she made ample use of their work. Thus, she repeated the
ideas that Vygotsky was an eclectic thinker ("being an eclectic, he combined
subjective idealism with vulgar materialism;" Rudneva, 1937, p. 6), that he
had propagated incorrect opinions about the roots of speech and thinking,
that he had defended a hereditarian view of mental development, and that
his cultural-historical theory was false ("the slander against worker's children is combined with the imperialists' slander against the colonial peoples
in order to justify the occupation of new territories in the name of 'progress'
and 'culture;'" Rudneva, 1937, p. 28). She, too, criticized the concept of the
zone of proximal development as it seemed to imply that honest adult
communist workers could not become leading Soviet intellectuals. But we
should give credit to Rudneva that she realized the oddness of Vygotsky's
claim concerning the levelling effect of schooling (1937, pp. 17–18) (see
chapter 13).

Unfortunately, her work was at a still lower scientific and moral level
than the writings of the earlier critics. Having mentioned, for example, that
at one time Vygotsky – like many of his colleagues (cf. Blonsky and
Skosyrev, 1935; Luria, 1930b) – was rather fascinated by Jaensch's ideas (cf.
Vygotsky, 1930e), she remarked that "Incidentally, Vygotsky, who, having
been abroad knew his foreign languages well, had to know of the fascist
demagogue Jaensch's zoological hatred of the Soviet Union, of Marxism,
and still he shamelessly dragged this trash into the pages of our press"
(Rudneva, 1937, p. 14).[6]

Rudneva's main aim was to discredit Vygotsky and his followers by
showing that Vygotsky was, first, an adherent of Shul'gin's movement
against formal education (a movement condemned by a Decree of the
Central Committee of the Party on September 3, 1935), and second, a
propagator of paedology, condemned by the Paedology Decree of July 4,
1936. The first accusation was clearly borrowed from Razmyslov and to
illustrate it Rudneva could do no more than repeat his quotations from
Pedagogical Psychology (1937, p. 4). Rudneva, too, condemned Vygotsky's
and Shif's concept-formation research. The distinction between two types of

---

[6]Vygotsky indeed knew about Jaensch's questionable attitude towards the Nazi government and in his brochure against fascism he bitterly attacked his German colleague (cf.
Vygotsky, Giljarovsky, Gurevich, Krol', Shmarjan *et al.*, 1934, pp. 19–28).

concepts was in itself considered worthless and incompatible with the fundamental tenets of dialectical logic. Furthermore, she could not understand the origin of the different levels in concept development. Was Vygotsky defending the "counter-revolutionary" idea of spontaneous development (Rudneva, 1937, p. 9)? Finally, Vygotsky's scientific concepts seemed based on the purely verbal and not rooted in practical labor activity (cf. Leont'ev's similar claims, in Leont'ev, 1935/1983).

Rudneva concluded that Vygotsky's theories were not compatible with the ideas of Marx, Engels, Lenin, Stalin, Kirov, and Zhdanov. She urged others to condemn Vygotsky, "all the more as some of his followers have not yet been disarmed (Luria, Leont'ev, Shif, and others)" (Rudneva, 1937, p. 32).

Conclusions

In 1931 it became clear that Vygotsky could not escape the fate of so many of his colleagues: his writings were to be tested for their ideological reliability. Surprisingly little is known of the concrete details of the attack when it was finally launched. We do not know, for example, whether there have been public meetings exclusively devoted to the discussion of Vygotsky's theories. (According to one story, such a meeting indeed took place and Vygotsky was the first speaker, delivering one of his long and fascinating speeches which left the audience spell-bound. As a result, the officials did not know how to proceed further, as the general atmosphere was clearly not suitable for a frontal attack. After some hesitation it was announced that on this day no further speeches would be delivered and that the second part of the meeting was suspended. The present authors have been unable to verify the truth of this story.) Neither has it been possible to document any published reactions of Vygotsky or Luria to their critics. It seems clear that Vygotsky's later writings changed in response to some of the attacks – references to "primitive" thought, for example, disappeared from his writings – but we have no written account of his defense or counter-attacks. It is evident, though, that they attempted to mitigate the results of the campaign launched against them. Luria, apparently, wrote at least one penitential letter which has been preserved in the archives of the Luria family[7] in response to criticisms published in the journal *Estestvoznanie i Marksizm* (*Natural Science and Marxism*). The defense, however, was to no avail and,

---

[7]This information is based on the very instructive notes to the Soviet edition of Vygotsky's correspondence prepared by A. A. Puzyrej. It is unclear when this correspondence will be published.

after the Paedology Decree, the writings of Vygotsky were prohibited and effectively banned. It was not until 1956 that sections of their (abridged) writings would become available again. Meanwhile, the criticisms leveled against them still exist, awaiting further judgment. It is clear that many of them are simply nonsensical, but others – e.g. the criticism of the concepts of the zone of proximal development and of primitivism – deserve some further thought. These criticisms may have been born of base motives but the motives for statements are not relevant for the judgement of their validity.

One can view this period of Soviet psychology's history from two sides: as the story of the blacklisting of a member of the "non-Party intelligentsia," or as the (far from perfect) beginning of the critical appraisal of his work. We have argued that both points of view can be defended.

Epilogue

The Quest for Synthesis and its Intellectual Interdependency

The over-riding concern evident in Vygotsky's intellectual work is the quest for synthesis, or so we have argued. Throughout his life Vygotsky persistently tried to create novel ideas by way of dialectical synthesis. This was his main focus of interest in human development. However, his dialectical approach did not stop there, for he made a consistent effort to apply a similar method to his own theorizing. In his application of the dialectical approach at both the scientific and meta-scientific levels Vygotsky was indeed remarkably consistent. However, the particular results of that application often remained fragmentary, and his style of discussion of novel ideas creates difficulties for contemporary analysts of his work.

We hope that our description of Vygotsky's life and the history of his ideas explains at least part of the rich complex of reasons why his legacy is heterogeneous in its nature. A young man knowing that he might die any time cannot be expected to take a long time to create a complete system of thought and to support his original ideas with carefully designed long-term empirical research programs. Furthermore, the social conditions under which Vygotsky worked changed rapidly. And last but not least, Vygotsky was primarily a producer of oral narratives rather than written treatises. And this guaranteed an even greater fragmentation of ideas, a great deal of repetition, and a lack of cohesiveness. Many of Vygotsky's interesting ideas are recurrent bursts of novelty in oral discourse, left mostly unfinished. In contrast, many of those aspects of Vygotsky's thinking that are elaborated in great detail (including some empirical investigations) show inconsistencies between the original idea and its specification. For example, the empirical evidence in favour of the "cultural-historical theory" is primarily cross-sectional in its presentation (e.g. of outcomes of the use of "mediating devices" by different age groups), whereas the theory itself claims to concentrate on the processes of development. Furthermore, Vygotsky's theoretical concerns and erudite style changed during his life; in 1924–5 he

Lev Vygotsky.

was critically fascinated by different ideas than in 1933–4. Of course, that personal development was guided by the changes in the intellectual world of the Soviet Union over that short period. The later Vygotsky had experienced a wave of dogmatic criticisms of his work.

Two Perspectives on Criticism: Static and Dialectical

Vygotsky's method used in his critical analysis of the ideas of his contemporaries has created some confusion among contemporary efforts to interpret his work, as is evident in the frequently asked question whether Vygotsky was, or was not, a Marxist. It is easy to see the static nature of this question – it is essentially an effort to classify Vygotsky as a member of one or the other distinct classes of ideological orientation (the common-place mistake of imagining the world can be divided into simple binary categories).

This book makes it clear that Vygotsky cannot be so classified. We have traced Vygotsky's intellectual interdependency with a number of theoretical and philosophical tendencies (among which Marxist/Hegelian dialectical thought was but one – albeit a major one). Furthermore, Vygotsky's dialectical mind applied to all these intellectual ties the "Thesis–Antithesis–Synthesis" scheme. Since this approach is not adopted by contemporary psychology, it is difficult for many psychologists to understand how Vygotsky could be "a Piagetian" in much of his thinking (whilst being highly critical of Piaget in some areas), or how he could appreciate some aspects of Pavlov's reflexology (while subjecting other aspects of it, e.g. physiological reductionism, to severe criticism). Also, although Vygotsky identified himself with the Soviet paedology movement of his time, he nevertheless subjected that movement to a devastating criticism (and re-defined "paedology" for his own purposes). And although he increasingly distanced himself from the new line of research of his time – emphasis on praxis of the Kharkov School – he would not deny that it produced some intellectually valuable new ideas. He could subject Luria's psychoanalytic efforts to severe criticism while continuing to work with him, even joining the Russian Psychoanalytic Society.

Vygotsky's style of criticism has been a major stumbling-block in contemporary interpretations of his work. Perhaps the function of criticism in Vygotsky's intellectual milieu was different from that in international psychology of the 1990s. This difference seems to be predicated on the dialectical world-view of Vygotsky and the lack of a dialectical approach in our own.

A present-day psychologist is most likely to adopt a non-dialectical, "either–or" perspective when determining the "class membership" of one or another approach in psychology. Hence the frequent non-dialectical contrasts between "Piagetian" and "Vygotskian" approaches, or the widespread separation of psychologists into "social" versus "cognitive" categories, which seem to occupy our minds in their meta-psychological activities. Even the existence of an overlap of the two ("social cognition") does not alter the non-dialectical classification of the psychological "mindscape," since the focus of that taxonomy is mostly "book-keeping," rather than synthesizing ideas from opposing camps. For example, how often do we find an analysis of the opposing ideas of behaviorism and cognitivism that is oriented towards transcending *both* these limited perspectives (indeed, the need for a post-cognitivistic psychology does not seem to be expressed in these terms!).

In a direct contrast, for Vygotsky any two opposing directions of thought served as opposites united with one another in the continuous whole – the discourse on ideas. This discourse is expected to lead us to a more adequate understanding of the human psyche, that is, to *transcend* the present state of theoretical knowledge, rather than force the existing variety of ideas into a strict classification of tendencies in the socially constructed scientific discipline of psychology. Hence there was something valuable to learn from exactly those ideas that Vygotsky criticized in the strongest possible terms. Criticisms, for him, did not mean dismissing the opposing viewpoint, but was rather a "marker" on a "mindscape" of ideas that designates the entrance points to intellectual impasses. Especially now, when empiricism dominates psychology, it seems the development of the discipline begins to resemble a random walk from one theoretical impasse to another. Vygotsky's analytic style allowed him to avoid theoretically "dead" directions for empirical efforts – a luxury that the systematization of "theories and systems" in contemporary psychology does not afford. For Vygotsky it was the reasoning against other viewpoints that could lead his ideas to reach a breakpoint for a novel synthesis: a result of his broad knowledge of international psychology. As we have shown, his innovations were often very closely linked with the work of his predecessors and contemporaries, and amounted to minor modifications of those.

The Basis for Novelty Construction: Intellectual Interdependency

If we were to try to understand the processes of scientific creativity from a purely sociogenetic perspective then we would have to accept that no innovative scientist can create any new ideas independently from the collective-cultural processes that surround him, the cultural history in which his life course is embedded, and the particular interpersonal relationships of his life course. Or, in other terms, it is the *intellectual interdependency* of the scientist or artist that sets up the conditions under which novel ideas or expressions can come into being. The epigraph to this book expressed the idea of such interdependency quite concisely. However, the notion should be further elaborated so that many of the details included in the present book can fit into the rather complex canvas we have painted here.

The social world of any cohort of people developing in parallel in a given cultural setting is filled with general concepts that organize the social and personal spheres of people, and facilitate the collective construction of the cultural meanings as those are communicated across generations. These concepts are usually fuzzy as to their exact meanings – allowing their users to "fill them in" with the particular emphases that fit their goals or needs. As an example, let us consider the use of the term "science" (or "scientific") in the discourse of scientists. This term cannot have a simple meaning that remains constant over time and contexts – the uses of that term, ranging from "natural science" or "physical sciences" to areas like "scientific communism" or "political science," demonstrate the heterogeneity of its meaning. If we add to this heterogeneity the variety of uses of the term in psychologists' discourse we bring the matter of the polysemantic nature of general concepts very close home. For instance, Vygotsky's contributions can be labeled as the "core of developmental science" at one (enthusiastic) extreme, while his consistent use of the clinical method and non-use of any statistical methodology can earn his work the label "soft science" at best (dependent upon the evaluator's perspective). Since the psychology of our present time is imbued with the habit of classification of different approaches into different categories of "science" ("basic" versus "applied" science, "true" versus "soft" science, etc.), it is in psychologists' meta-level discourse about their approaches that the mediational nature of fuzzy meanings can be demonstrated.

Through the help of mediating devices (meanings of abstract concepts) both cultural continuity and cultural change are made possible. Furthermore, the fuzziness of these meanings affords variability within the culture at the given time of the development of the society. In other words, heterogeneity of interpretations of the same abstract terms is the rule (rather than exception), as it is functional in the process of development of our knowledge about the world.

But the history of science is also filled with examples of the extreme rigidity of a group of specialists in a given discipline, who hold on to a core idea in a highly compulsive and defensive manner. Compulsive avoidance of the heterogeneity of meanings of concepts in social discourse leads to dogmatic adherence to a particular version of the meaning. The mechanisms for such standardization of terms often have taken the form of in-group–out-group differentiation and social consensus-building within the in-group. The social organization of the scientific enterprise is not different from the social organization of any other institution. Both Vygotsky's appearance in psychology and his disappearance from the list of acceptable psychologists for some decades after his death, provide good examples of the in-group–out-group regulation in Soviet psychology of the time.

However, all the people involved in social discourse are co-constructors of ideas. Their social worlds include a variety of concepts of heterogeneous meanings. The individual makes use of some of these concepts and adjusts their meanings in accordance with the context in which these meanings are to be used. Other concepts may be actively rejected, or merely passed by without their being integrated into the knowledge structure that the individual is constructing. Nevertheless, even in the latter case, the presence of these concepts in the social world of the individual (and his mind) is a relevant part of the "mindscape" that leads to new ideas. The emergence of a new idea takes place within an individual's mind while he is participating in (immediate or deferred) social discourse. Hence the personal achievement of novel ideas is intellectually interdependent with the socially available and culturally organized "raw materials" – concepts with heterogeneous meanings. Intellectual innovation thus necessarily occurs in the social context – both the "means" (meanings) and "needs" (goals set by the individual in the given task setting) are at first suggested to him socially. These may later be transferred into an internal psychological sphere – thus, a Tibetan monk contemplating issues of jealousy in the isolation of his cave is involved in as much a socially constructed endeavour as a psychologist leading a discussion on the same topic at a conference.

Thus, all new ideas are transformations or substitutions of old ones, based on the texture of meanings that is currently surrounding the individual and on which the internalized personal construction of understanding the world is based. In our previous effort to make sense of intellectual interdependency (see Van der Veer and Valsiner, 1988, pp. 61–2) we emphasized the similarity of the creation of novel ideas in psychology to children's construction of knowledge while acting within their environment. The constructive interpretation of the notions of assimilation and accommodation as mutually linked processes of knowledge construction can be taken to elaborate how a particular thinker is intellectually interpedendent with his cultural environment. It is clear that this interdependence entails a bi-directional notion of cultural "transmission," that is, the messages located in the cultural environment are not merely "accepted as they are" by the creative individual, but, rather, analyzed and "reassembled" (in one's system of "personal sense") in novel ways. Hence the individual is a co-constructor of culture rather than a mere follower of the enculturation efforts of the others. Psychologically, individuals always move beyond their cultural backgrounds – with assistance from the latter. The culture is thus a means for the personal co-construction of intellectual development, rather than an external powerful "judge" that either "accepts" or "rejects" the person's thoughts, feelings, and actions, as well as attempts to superimpose itself on the otherwise "free" human beings.

Vygotsky's Intellectual Interdependency

The case of Vygotsky constitutes a complex example of intellectual interdependency. At every period of his active search for understanding of human psychological functioning – from his early interest in how *Hamlet* has an impact upon the audience to the interest in issues of paedology – Vygotsky's thinking demonstrates intricate intellectual interdependence. The preceding chapters of this book discussed these ideas and their roots in the different areas of Vygotsky's intellectual activities. What remains to be accomplished here is to present a general summary of his intellectual interdependence over his life.

Vygotsky's first notable intellectual connections (with dialectical philosophy and literary scholarship) were forged in his school and university years, and enabled him to develop a perspective on the reception of literary works that concentrated upon the interaction between the recipient and the text. The structural nature of any text was a given, and prepared the ground for his later insistence upon structural units for the analysis of psychological phenomena. His interest in the processes of reconstruction of the meaning of the texts in the sense-world of individual recipients guided Vygotsky into the study of complex aesthetic reactions. By coincidence that study complemented the work being done by Kornilov, and Vygotsky joined his Institute. In the social context of the burgeoning activities of intellectuals who cherished the opportunity to build their own new systems of psychology on Marxist grounds, Vygotsky established an interdependency with the Gestalt psychology movement, which was to provide him with much material for further intellectual syntheses. At the same time, his pedagogical interests in the development of retarded and handicapped children kept his interest focused upon the necessity of the social environment assisting individuals' development.

When his professional relationship with Kornilov's reactology and jargon-driven Marxist psychology foundered in about 1926–7, Vygotsky moved towards an integration of his idea of dialectical synthesis (allied with the structural emphasis of Gestalt psychology) on the one hand, and the process of development in special education on the other. Intellectual interdependence with the work of Ach, Adler, Baldwin, Binet, Janet, Köhler, and Werner among psychologists, and Thurnwald and Lévy-Bruhl among anthropologists, was the context within which the cultural-historical theory and its empirical demonstrations were born. His fascination with the possibility that this theoretical and methodological synthesis might be of interest to international psychology is an example of participation in the enterprise of knowledge which does not recognize nationality. Vygotsky was a member of the international psychological community of his time (even if he only left the USSR once), rather than a Soviet psychologist.

Given the changes in the intellectual climate in the USSR, and his increasing interest in paedological and medical issues, Vygotsky's intellectual interdependence took a new form. By committing himself to the study of paedology in the early 1930s, Vygotsky could develop his theories of a link between structural-dynamic dialectics and issues of ontogeny. Thus, an intellectual interdependence with the works of Claparède, Goldstein, Meumann, Montessori, and Piaget was advanced. The international nature of Vygotsky's intellectual linkages was explicit and his critics did not fail to make use of that in the new Slavophilic atmosphere of intolerance, orchestrated by the "Kremlin mountaineer with his thick fingers fatty like worms" (see Mandel'shtam). Vygotsky's looked to the eminent psychologists of other nations for inspiration at a time when Russia was concerned only with the goal of creating a new society. Utopias of that kind may fail, but as people try to create them they set up an interesting social context for the pursuits of individual intellectuals.

Vygotsky's Legacy: Fundamental Contributions to Psychology

During the course of the work on this book, the authors' understanding of Vygotsky's contributions to psychology has developed a great deal. Some of the novel-looking ideas that we always thought to be attributable to Vygotsky transpire to have originated in the minds of his contemporaries. Thus his best-known contributions – the zone of proximal development, the method of the study of concept-formation (the Vygotsky blocks method) as well as the reasoning about concepts, meaning and sense, and the basic sociogenetic perspective – are all reflections on and developments of the original work of his predecessors and contemporaries.

Tracing Vygotsky's contributions to the work of others does not, of course, diminish his relevance for psychology, but rather brings the contributions of his contemporaries out of the shadow of psychology's history. Again, we are confronted with the need to study the history of psychology as of utmost importance for our present-day psychological research efforts, rather than as a separate area of study.

Equally important are those domains of ideas that truly can be seen as the result of Vygotsky's quest for synthesis. We have found amongst Vygotsky's materials a number of hints of ideas, and some half-developed theoretical and methodological directions that could make a fundamental contribution to this discipline if they were advanced further. It is worthwhile to provide a short overview of some basic orientations that were essential to Vygotsky's thinking, and which seem to us to have the potential to contribute to a basic reorganization of contemporary psychology.

First, of course, we would need to reiterate the main theme of this book – that of the *process of dialectical synthesis*. Since his time the notion of synthesis has become almost extinct in psychology, and the term "dialectical" is often used as an umbrella-concept to render vague philosophizing about the human psyche legitimate. Although Vygotsky's discussions of the processes involved in dialectical synthesis were not sufficiently precise, there is no reason why that notion cannot be phrased in specific terms. This is true of any discipline – be it psychology, biology, anthropology, or economics – that deals with the relatively rapid construction of novel forms. Dialectical ideas, made precise and freed from their vague ideological connotations can become a productive tool.

Secondly, Vygotsky's *consistent developmental perspective* stands as a worthwhile contribution to psychology. Throughout its history psychology has limited itself to ontological analyses of psychological phenomena. Explicit efforts to discard that focus in favour of a focus on development have been half-hearted, and have usually led to a reversion to the ontological focus. In some ways, present-day psychology is similar to pre-Darwinian biology, since we are eager to classify and re-classify psychological phenomena, as they exist at a given time, into strictly separable classes (an analog to the classification of natural phenomena by Karl Linné). The question of rules and methods of transformation of one class into another is still rarely asked, and even more rarely answered. In short, the developmental framework that entered biology in the nineteenth century by way of the work of Lamarck, von Baer, Darwin and other leading scientists, is yet to become established in twentieth-century psychology. Vygotsky's consistent emphasis on taking a developmental perspective of psychological phenomena, be they those of child development (ontogenesis) or adults' and apes' problem-solving (microgenesis), is an approach well worth continuing today.

Thirdly, no fundamental contribution to psychology can bypass the issue of general methodology of research. Here, Vygotsky's *method of double stimulation* is worthy of careful scrutiny and further elaboration. Discarding the static ethos of traditional experimental methodology where "effects" of the changes in the "independent variables" upon the selected outcomes measured by "dependent variables" are sought, Vygotsky developed a methodological scheme that introduces the dynamic emergence of novel structures of psychological phenomena as the main focus of empirical investigation. Furthermore, his methodological orientation retains the notion of structured organization of the experimental setting together with the subject's (limited) freedom of re-defining the experimental situation. The notion of "experimental control" is set up by Vygotsky in a methodological framework where the traditional norm of the experimenter's maximum control over what happens in an experiment is retained as a special case, rather than the modal one. The human subject always "imports" into an experimental setting a set of "stimulus-means" (psychological instruments) in the form of signs that the experimenter cannot control externally in any rigid way. Hence, the experimental setting becomes a context of investigation where the experimenter can manipulate its structure in order to trigger (but not "produce") the subject's *construction* of new psychological phenomena.

It is lamentable that this methodological implication of Vygotsky's method of double stimulation has been persistently overlooked since his day, yet, at the same time, outcries about crises in psychology's traditional methodology can be heard from time to time. These speculations about crises have left the methodological foundations of the discipline largely unchanged, and hence it remains unproductive beyond the domain of critical discourse in psychology. But perhaps there is a reason for not taking this half-finished methodological imperative of Vygotsky's and developing it further? Indeed, its implications for scientific methodology are far-reaching, and psychology in general is a highly conservative discipline that does not easily allow for major revolutions within its way of approaching its objects of investigation.

Finally, Vygotsky's consistent *anti-reductionistic stance* can be seen as a major contribution to psychology. Again, he was hardly original in taking this stance, but the social discourse of psychologists in the Soviet Union led him to express that perspective decisively in a number of ways. The refusal to give up the study of higher psychological functions under the challenge of different camps of reductionism was Vygotsky's credo from the beginning to the end of his intellectual work. He believed the human psychological functions are organized hierarchically, and each level of that hierarchy may need to be studied in its specifics; hence the emphasis upon "analysis into units" which should retain the relevant characteristics of the phenomenon in its whole (i.e., the analysis into "minimal *Gestalts*"). It is a perspective to which contemporary psychology in the 1990s needs to return. Of course, Vygotsky did not elaborate this notion in any way, which must be done if it is to become applicable in present-day research. In fact, Vygotsky's refusal to look at the processes of *both* analysis and synthesis (i.e., concentrating only on the latter) in the human mind and conduct may have blocked any productive elaboration of the idea in his thinking. Vygotsky's creativity, like the creativity of any other productive intellectual at any time, had its surprising limitations.

A Continuing Quest for Understanding

The case of Vygotsky is a good illustration of intellectual interdependency in the difficult efforts made by human beings to understand themselves. Vygotsky's main contribution to psychology was to tear down artificially created boundaries between adjacent areas of human culture, and to encode knowledge from different areas into his efforts to overcome the conceptual "crisis" of psychology. In paying tribute to Vygotsky we need not idolize the man, but nor should we deny his creative contributions. Instead, we should recognize his intellectual efforts in the social context of his time. This may help us to remind ourselves of the *pointe* of Bunin's short story that was the key turning point for Vygotsky, encouraging him to enter the complex labyrinth of psychology. As in the case of the young woman's "gentle breath" that generalizes to a basic feeling about the world at large, it is the ethos of the collectively constructed ideas of Vygotsky's time that disseminates in the world of psychology, through our efforts to explore his creativity. History can help us to move forward and we may try to arrive at new syntheses through our own intellectual interdependencies. Vygotsky provided us with several intellectual tools that may prove useful in creating psychology's own zone of proximal development. Such intellectual tools are badly needed, for "it is by instruments and helps that the work is done, which are as much wanted for the understanding as for the hand. And as the instruments of the hand either give motion or guide it, so the instruments of the mind supply either suggestions for the understanding or cautions" (Bacon, 1620/1960, p. 39).

References

Abel'skaja R. and Neopikhonova, O. (1929) The principal problems of psychology in the light of the Gestalt theory. *Voprosy Pedagogiki*, 5/6, 105–29.

Abel'skaja, R. and Neopikhonova, Ja. S. (1932) Problema razvitija v nemetskoj psikhologii i ee vlijanie na sovetskuju pedologiju i psikhologiju. *Pedologija*, 4, 27–36.

Ach, N. (1921) *Über die Begriffsbildung. Eine experimentelle Untersuchung*. Bamberg: C. C. Buchners Verlag.

Achmanova, O. S. and Vygodskaja, Z. S. (1962) *Russko-Anglijskij Slovar'*. Moscow: Gosudarstvennoe Izdatel'stvo Inostrannykh i Nacional'nykh Slovarej.

Adams, A. K., Sciortino-Brudzynski, A. P., Bjorn, K. M., and Tharp, R. G. (1987) Forbidden colors. Vygotsky's experiment revisited. Paper presented at the meeting of the Society for Research on Child Development, Baltimore, Md., April.

Adler, A. (1927) *Praxis und Theorie der Individualpsychologie*. München: Bergmann.

Agol, I. (1928) Neovitalizm i marksizm. *Pod Znamenem Marksizma*, 3, 202–37.

Alcina Franch, J. and Palop Martínez, J. (1988) *Los Incas. El reino del sol*. Madrid: Anaya.

Anan'ev, B. G. (1931) O nekotorykh voprosakh marksistsko-leninskoj rekonstrukcii psikhologii. *Psikhologija*, 3–4, 325–44.

Angelini, A. (1988) *La psicoanalisi in Russia. Dai precursori agli anni Trenta*. Napoli: Liguori Editore.

Anweiler, O. (1964) *Geschichte der Schule und Pädagogik in Russland vom Ende des Zarenreiches biz zum Beginn der Stalin-Aera*. Berlin–Heidelberg: Quelle und Meyer.

Arian', P. (1912) The paedological congress in Brussels. *Vestnik Psikhologii, Kriminal'noj Antropologii, i Pedologii*, 9, 1, 104–9.

Artemov, V. A. (1928) Sovremennaja nemetskaja psikhologija. *Psikhologija*, 1, 66–94.

Averill, J. R. (1986) The acquisition of emotions during adulthood. In R. Harré (ed.), *The Social Construction of Emotions*. Oxford: Basil Blackwell, pp. 98–118.

Bacher, G. (1925) Die Ach'sche Suchmethode in ihrer Verwendung zur Intelligenz-prüfung. Ein Beitrag zur Psychologie des Schwachsinns. *Untersuchungen zur Psychologie, Philosophie und Pädagogik*, 4, 3/4, 209–89.

Bacon, F. (1620/1960) *The New Organon and Related Writings*. New York: Macmillan.

Bakhtin, M. M. (1927/1983) *Frejdizm. Kriticheskij ocherk*. New York: Chalidze Publications.

—— (1930/1972) *Marksizm i filosofija jazyka*. The Hague: Mouton.

Baldwin, J. M. (1900) *Mental Development in the Child and the Race*. New York: Macmillan.

Barash, D. P. (1986) *The Hare and the Tortoise: Culture, Biology and Human Nature*. Harmondsworth: Penguin.

Basov, M. Ja. (1914) The Second All-Russian Congress on Experimental Pedago-gics. *Vestnik Psikhologii, Kriminal'noj Antropologii, i Pedologii*, 11, 1, 77–113.

—— (1930) The problem of world views in paedology. In A. B. Zalkind (ed.), *Psikhonevrologicheskie nauki v SSSR*. Moscow–Leningrad: Gosudarstvennoe Medicinskoe Izdatel'stvo, pp. 157–8.

—— (1931) *Obshchie osnovy pedologii*. Moscow–Leningrad: Gosudarstvennoe Izdatel'stvo.

Bejn, E. S., Vlasova, T. A., Levina, R. E., Morozova, N. G., and Shif, Zh. I. (1983) Posleslovie. In L. S. Vygotsky, *Sobranie sochinenij. Vol. 5: Osnovy defektologii*. Moscow: Pedagogika, pp. 333–420.

Bejn, E. S., Levina, R. E., and Morozova, N. G. (1983) Kommentarii. In L. S. Vygotsky, *Sobranie sochinenij. Vol. 5: Osnovy defektologii*. Moscow: Pedago-gika, pp. 343–57.

Benigni, L. and Valsiner, J. (1985) Developmental psychology without the study of developmental processes. *ISSBD Newsletter*, 4.

Bekhterev, V. M. (1904) *Psikhika i zizhn'*, 2nd edn. St Petersburg: K. L. Rikker.

—— (1921/1992) *Collective Reflexology*, ed. L. H. Strickland and E. Lockwood. in preparation.

Berg, E. E. (1970) L. S. Vygotsky's theory of the social and historical origins of consciousness. PhD thesis. University of Wisconsin.

Berry, J. W. and Dasen, P. R. (eds) (1974) *Culture and Cognition: Readings in Cross-Cultural Psychology*. London: Methuen.

Binet, A. (1894) *Psychologie des grands calculateurs et des joueurs d'échecs*. Paris: Librairie Hachette et Cie.

—— (1909/1973) *Les idées modernes sur les enfants*. Paris: Flammarion.

Binswanger, L. (1922) *Einführung in die Probleme der allgemeinen Psychologie*. Berlin: Springer.

Birilev, A. V. (1924) Svet dlja slepykh i nekotorye voprosy metodiki prepodavanija slepym. In L. S. Vygotsky (ed.), *Voprosy vospitanija slepykh, glukhonemykh i umstvenno otstalykh*. Moscow: Izdatel'stvo SPON NKP.

Bloch, M. (1983) *Marxism and Anthropology*. Oxford: Oxford University Press.

Blonsky, P. P. (1916) *Kurs pedagogiki*. Moscow: Zadruga.

—— (1920) *Reforma nauki*. Moscow: Izdatel'stvo Otdela Narodnogo Proshvesh-chenija.

—— (1921) *Ocherk nauchnoj psikhologii.* Moscow: GIZ.

—— (1922) *Pedagogika.* Moscow: Rabotnik Prosveshchenija.

—— (1925a) Psikhologija kak nauka povedenija. In K. N. Kornilov (ed.), *Psikhologija i marksizm.* Leningrad: Gosizdat, pp. 225–9.

—— (1925b) *Pedologija.* Moscow: Rabotnik Prosveshchenija.

—— (1935) *Pamjat' i myshlenie.* Moscow–Leningrad: Gosudarstvennoe Social'no-Ekonomicheskoe Izdatel'stvo.

Blonsky, P. P. and Skosyrev, V. N. (eds) (1935) *Ejdetizm i shkol'nyj vozrast.* Moscow: Biomedgiz.

Boeselager, W. F. (1975) *The Soviet Critique of Neopositivism.* Dordrecht: Reidel.

Bogdanov, A. A. (1922) *Tektologija.* Berlin: Izdatel'stvo Z. I. Grzhebina.

—— (1925) Uchenie o refleksakh i zagadki pervobytnogo myshlenija. *Vestnik Kommunisticheskoj Akademii,* 10, 67–96.

Bolles, M. M. and Goldstein, K. (1938) A study of the impairment of "abstract behavior" in schizophrenic patients. *Psychiatric Quarterly,* 12, 42–65.

Borovsky, V. M. (1926) O probleme myshlenija v psikhologii povedenija. In K. N. Kornilov (ed.), *Problemy sovremennoj psikhologii.* Leningrad: Gosudarstvennoe Izdatel'stvo, pp. 145–51.

—— (1929a) *Psikhologija s tochki zrenija materialista.* Moscow–Leningrad: Gosizdat.

—— (1929b) Psychology in the USSR. *Journal of General Psychology,* 2, 177–86.

Brainard, P. P. (1930) The mentality of a child compared with that of apes. *Journal of Genetic Psychology,* 37, 268–92.

Brill, R. G. (1984) *International Congress on Education of the Deaf. An Analytical History 1878–1980.* Washington, DC: Gallaudet College Press.

Brown, A. L. and Ferrara, R. A. (1985) Diagnosing zones of proximal development. In J. V. Wertsch (ed.), *Culture, Communication, and Cognition: Vygotskian Perspectives.* Cambridge, Mass: Cambridge University Press, pp. 273–305.

Brushlinsky, A. V. (1968) *Kul'turno-istoricheskaja teorija myshlenija.* Moscow: Vysshaja Shkola.

—— (1988) Uglubljat' fundamental'nye issledovanija, povyshat' kul'turu nauchnykh diskussij. *Voprosy Psikhologii,* 1, 5–8.

Bubnov, A. (1936) O teorii i praktike sovremennoj pedologii. *Srednaja Shkola,* 8, 1–8.

Budagov, R. A. (1988) *Portrety jazykovedov XIX–XXvv.* Moscow: Nauka.

Bühler, Ch. (1929) *Das Seelenleben des Jugendlichen. Versuch einer Analyse und Theorie der psychischen Pubertät.* Jena: Verlag von Gustav Fischer.

Bühler, K. (1918) *Die geistige Entwicklung des Kindes.* Jena: Verlag von Gustav Fischer.

—— (1919) *Abriss der geistigen Entwicklung des Kindes.* Leipzig: Verlag von Quelle und Meyer.

—— (1927) *Die Krise der Psychologie.* Jena: G. Fischer.

Bukharin, N. I. (1924a) On world revolution, our country, culture and so on. *Krasnaja Nov',* 1, 170–88.

—— (1924b) Enchmeniada. In N. I. Bukharin, *Ataka.* Moscow: Gosudarstvennoe Izdatel'stvo, pp. 128–70.

Bunin, I. A. (1916/1984) Legkoe dykhanie. In A. I. Bunin, *Izbrannye sochinenij*. Moscow: Khudozhestvennaja Literatura, pp. 261–5.

Bunzel, R. L. (1966) Introduction. In L. Lévy-Bruhl, *How Natives Think*. New York: Washington Square Press, pp. v–xviii.

Bykhovsky, B. (1923) O metodologicheskikh osnovanijakh psikhoanaliticheskogo uchenija Frejda. *Pod Znamenem Marksizma*. 11/12, 158–77.

—— (1926) Freud's sociological views. *Pod Znamenem Marksizma*, 9/10, 178–94.

Cairns, R. B. (1986) Phenomena lost: Issues in the study of development. In J. Valsiner (ed.), *The Individual Subject and Scientific Psychology*. New York: Plenum, pp. 97–112.

Calhoun, Ch. and Solomon, R. C. (1984) *What is an Emotion? Classic Readings in Philosophical Psychology*. New York: Oxford University Press.

Campione, J. C., Brown, A. L., Ferrara, R. A., and Bryant, N. R. (1984) The zone of proximal development: Implications for individual differences and learning. In B. Rogoff and J. V. Wertsch (eds), *Children's Learning in the "Zone of Proximal Development"*. San Francisco: Jossey-Bass, pp. 77–91.

Cannon, W. B. (1914) Recent studies of bodily effects of fear, rage, and pain. *Journal of Philosophy*, 11, 162–5.

Carotenuto, A. (1984) *A Secret Symmetry*. New York: Pantheon Books.

Chagin, B. A. and Klushin, V. I. (1975) *Bor'ba za istoricheskij materializm v SSSR v 20-e gody*. Leningrad: Nauka.

Chalmers, A. F. (1982) *What is this Thing Called Science?* Queensland: University of Queensland Press.

Chelpanov, G. (1914) The Psychological Institute at Moscow University. *Uchenye zapisski imperatorskogo Moskovskago Universiteta*. Otdel istoriko-filologicheskij, 43, 273–98.

—— (1924) *Psikhologija i marksizm*. Moscow: A. V. Dumnov and Co.

Chuchmarev, Z. N. (1925) Reflexology and reactology as branches of science of human behavior. In K. N. Kornilov (ed.), *Psikhologija i marksizm*. Leningrad: Gosizdat, pp. 199–221.

Cole, M. and Griffin, P. (1980) Cultural amplifiers reconsidered. In D. R. Olson (ed.), *The Social Foundations of Language and Thought*. New York: Norton, pp. 343–64.

Cole, M. and Scribner, S. (1974) *Culture and Thought. A Psychological Introduction*. New York: John Wiley.

Compayré, G. (1903) *L'évolution intellectuelle et morale de l'enfant*. Paris: Alcan.

Conquest, R. (1988) *Zhatva skorbi*. London: Overseas Publications Interchange Ltd.

Crick, F. (1988) *What Mad Pursuit: A Personal View of Scientific Discovery*. London: Penguin.

Dajan, G. (1924) Vtoroj psikhonevrologicheskij s'ezd. *Krasnaja Nov'*, 2, 155–66.

Darwin, Ch. (1965) *The Expression of the Emotions in Man and Animals*. Chicago: University of Chicago Press.

—— (1871/1981) *The Descent of Man, and Selection in Relation to Sex*. Princeton, NJ: Princeton University Press.

—— (1982) *The Origin of Species*. Harmondsworth: Penguin.

Deborin, A. (1928) Ein neuer Feldzug gegen den Marxismus. *Unter dem Banner des Marxismus*, 1/2, 44–67.

Delacroix, H. (1924) *Le language et la pensée*. Paris: Alcan.

Descartes, R. (1649/1985) The passions of the soul. In J. Cottingham, R. Stoothoff, and D. Murdoch (eds), *The Philosophical Writings of Descartes. Vol. 1*. Cambridge: Cambridge University Press, pp. 328–404.

Descoeudres, A. (1914) Couleur, forme ou nombre? *Archives de Psychologie*, 14, 305–41.

De Vries, H. (1905) *Species and Varieties. Their Origin and Mutation*. Chicago–London.

Dewey, E. (1922) *The Dalton Laboratory Plan*. New York: Dutton.

Dewey, J. (1910/1985) How we think. In J. A. Boydston (ed.), *The Middle Works of John Dewey*. 1899–1924. Vol. 6. Carbondale and Edwardsville: Southern Illinois University Press, pp. 177–355.

—— (1915) *Psikhologija i pedagogika myshlenija*. Moscow: Mir.

—— (1929) *Impressions of Soviet Russia and the Revolutionary World*. New York: New Republic.

Diderot, D. (1972) *Lettre sur les aveugles*. Paris: Garnier-Flammarion.

Diskussija o polozhenii na pedologicheskom fronte v obshchestve pedologov-marksistov (1932). *Pedologija*, 4 (24), 94–108.

Diskussija o polozhenii na psikhologicheskom fronte (1931). *Sovetskaja Psikhonevrologija*, 2–3, 24–53.

Driesch, H. (1926) *Grundprobleme der Psychologie. Ihre Krisis in der Gegenwart*. Leipzig: Verlag Emmanuel Reinicke.

Drooglever Fortuyn, A. B. (1921) *De gevoelige periode als een der grondslagen van het Montessori-onderwijs*. Zeist: I. Ploegsma.

Durkheim, E. (1985) *Les formes élémentaires de la vie religieuse. Le système totémique en Australie*. Paris: Quadrige/PUF.

Edinger, L. (1911) *Vorlesungen über den Bau der nervösen Zentralorgane der Menschen und der Tiere*. Leipzig: Quelle und Meyer.

Editorial Board (1931) Necrology of Basov. *Pedologija*, 4, 1–2.

Eibl-Eibesfeldt, I. (1980) *Grundriss der vergleichenden Verhaltensforschung*. München: R. Piper und Co. Verlag.

Elias, N. (1978) *The Civilizing Process: The Development of Manners*. New York: Urizen Books.

Eliasberg, W. (1925) Psychologie und Pathologie der Abstraktion. *Zeitschrift für angewandte Psychologie*, Beiheft 35.

Engels, F. (1925/1978) *Dialektik der Natur*. Berlin: Dietz Verlag.

Ermakov, I. D. (1922) Russland. *Internationale Zeitschrift für Psychoanalyse*, 8, 236–7.

—— (1923) *Etjudy po psikhologii A. S. Pushkina*. Moscow–Petrograd: Gosudarstvennoe Izdatel'stvo.

—— (1924) Russische Psychoanalytische Gesellschaft (Sitzungsbericht). *Internationale Zeitschrift für Psychoanalyse*, 10, 351–2.

Eysenck, H. J. (1985) *Decline and Fall of the Freudian Empire*. Harmondsworth: Viking.

F., G. (1936) O sostojanii i zadachakh psikhologicheskoj nauki v SSSR. *Pod Znamenem Marksizma*, 9, 87–99.

Fet, A. A. (1844/1979) *Stikhotvorenija*. Moscow: Khudozhestvennaja Literatura.

Fejgina, L. K. (1988) Gomel'skij period zhizni L. S. Vygotskogo. In Ja. L. Kolominsky (ed.), *Nauchnoe nasledie L. S. Vygotskogo i aktual'nye problemy obuchenija i vospitanija*. Minsk: Pedagogicheskoe Obshchestvo BSSR, pp. 202–9.

Feofanov, M. P. (1931a) Pedologicheskie elementy sochsorevnovanija i udarnichestvo. *Pedologija*, 1, 9–16.

—— (1931b) Metodologicheskie osnovy shkoly Basova. *Pedologija*, 3, 27–43.

—— (1931c) Izvrashchenije marksizma v psikhologii u prof. Chuchmareva. *Psikhologija*, 3–4, 345–58.

—— (1932) Teorija kul'turnogo razvitija v pedologii kak elektricheskaja koncepcija, imejushchaja v osnovnom idealisticheskie korni. *Pedologija*, 1/2, 21–34.

Fitzpatrick, S. (1970) *The Commissariat of Enlightenment*. Cambridge: Cambridge University Press.

—— (1979) *Education and Social Mobility in the Soviet Union (1921–1934)*. Cambridge: Cambridge University Press.

Frankel, A. (1930) Against eclecticism in psychology and paedology. *Povesteniya Nacional'nostej*, 7–8.

Frankfurt, Ju. V. (1925) On one falsification of Marxism in psychology. *Krasnaja nov'*, 4.

—— (1926) G. V. Plekhanov about the psychophysiological problem. *Pod Znamenem Marksizma*, 6, 37–60.

Freud, S. (1923) The ego and the id. In S. Freud, *On Metapsychology. The Pelican Freud Library. Vol. 11*. Harmondsworth: Penguin, pp. 341–401.

—— (1913/1983) *Totem und Tabu*. Frankfurt am Main: Fischer.

—— (1920/1984) Beyond the pleasure principle. In S. Freud, *On Metapsychology. The Pelican Freud Library. Vol. 11*. Harmondsworth: Penguin, pp. 269–338.

—— (1987) *Zur Psychopathologie des Alltagslebens*. Frankfurt am Main: Fischer.

—— (1989a) *Vvedenie v psikhoanaliz. Lekcii*. Moscow: Nauka.

—— (1989b) *Psikhologija bessoznatel'nogo*. Moscow: Prosveshchenie.

Fridman, B. D. (1925) Osnovnye psikhologicheskie vozrenija Frejda i teorija istoricheskogo materializma. In K. N. Kornivlov (ed.), *Psikhologija i marksizm*. Leningrad: Gosudarstvennoe Izdatel'stvo, pp. 113–59.

Geertz, C. (1973) *The Interpretation of Cultures*. New York: Basic Books.

Gelb, A. and Goldstein, K. (1920) *Psychologischen Analysen hirnpathalogischer Fälle*. Leipiz: Barth.

—— (1925) Über Farbenamnesie nebst Bemerkungen über das Wesen der amnestischen Aphasie überhaupt und die Beziehung zwischen Sprache und dem Verhalten zur Umwelt. *Psychologische Forschung*, 6, 127–86.

Gel'mont, A. M. (1931) For Marxist–Leninist paedology (on the errors of P. P. Blonsky). *Pedologija*, 4, 37–51.

Georgiev, F. (1937) Against behaviorism and reactology. *Pod Znamenem Marksizma*, 1, 163–9.

Gershonov, L., Razmyslov, A. and Shemjakin, F. (1932) O zhurnale "Psikhologija" za 1931 g. *Psikhologija*, 5, 70–7.

Gerver, A. V. (1912) Report of the activities of the Psycho-neurological Institute for 1911. *Vestnik Psikhologii, Kriminal'noj Antropologii, i Pedologii*, 9, 4–5, 120–68.

Geuter, U. (1985) Das Ganze und die Gemeinschaft – Wissenschaftliches und politisches Denken in der Ganzheitspsychologie Felix Kruegers. In C. F. Graumann (ed.), *Psychologie im Nationalsozialismus*. Berlin: Springer-Verlag, pp. 55–87.

Gilbert, M. (1979) *The Jews of Russia*. Jerusalem: Bernstein.

Goldstein, K. (1933) L'analyse de l'aphasie et l'étude de l'essence du langage. *Journal de Psychologie*, 30, 430–96.

—— (1948) *Language and Language Disturbances*. New York: Grune and Stratton.

Goldstein, K. and Gelb, A. (1920) Psychologische Analysen hirnpathologischer Falle auf Grund von Untersuchungen Hirnverletzter. *Zeitschrift für Psychologie*, 83, 1–94.

Goldstein, K. and Katz, S. E. (1937) The psychopathology of Pick's disease. *Archives of Neurology and Psychiatry*, 38, 473–90.

Goldstein, K. and Scheerer, M. (1941) Abstract and concrete behavior. An experimental study with special tests. *Psychological Monographs*, 53, 74–151.

Gornfel'd, A. G. (1906) *Muki slova*. Moscow–Leningrad: Gosizdat.

Goudena, P. P. (1983) *Private Speech. An Analysis of its Social and Self-Regulatory Functions*. PhD thesis. University of Utrecht.

Gould, S. J. (1981) *The Mismeasure of Man*. Harmondsworth: Penguin.

Graham, L. R. (1987) *Science, Philosophy, and Human Behavior in the Soviet Union*. New York: Columbia University Press.

Groos, K. (1921) *Das Seelenleben des Kindes*. Berlin: Verlag von Reuther und Reichard.

Grünbaum, A. A. (1908) Über die Abstraktion der Gleichheit. *Archiv für die gesamte Psychologie*, 12, 340–478.

—— (1927) Die Struktur der Kinderpsyche. *Zeitschrift für pädagogische Psychologie*, 28, 446–63.

Guillaume, P. (1926/1968) *L'imitation chez l'enfant*. Paris: PUF.

Guillaume, P. and Meyerson, I. (1930) Recherches sur l'usage de l'instrument chez les singes. I: Le probleme du détour. *Journal de Psychologie*, 27, 177–236.

—— (1931) Recherches sur l'usage de l'instrument chez les singes. II: L'intermédiaire lié à l'objet. *Journal de Psychologie*, 28, 481–555.

Gumilyov, N. (1921/1988) Slovo. In N. Gumilyov, *Stikhotvoreniya i poemy*. Leningrad: Sovetskyj Pisatel', p. 312.

Haenen, J. (1989) An interview with P. Ja. Gal'perin. *Soviet Psychology*, 27, 3, 7–23.

Hanfmann, E. (1941) A study of personal patterns in an intellectual performance. *Character and Personality*, 9, 315–25.

Hanfmann, E. and Kasanin, J. (1937) A method for the study of concept formation. *Journal of Psychology*, 3, 521–40.

—— (1942) Conceptual thinking in schizophrenia. *Nervous and Mental Disorders*, Monograph 67.

Harré, R. (ed.) (1986) *The Social Construction of Emotions*. Oxford: Basil Blackwell.

Harrower, M. (1983) *Kurt Koffka. An Unwitting Self-Portrait*. Gainesville: University Press of Florida.

Heine, H. (1968) *Buch der Lieder*. Munchen: DTV.

Heller, M. and Nekrich, A. M. (1986) *Utopia in Power. The History of the Soviet Union From 1917 to the Present*. New York: Summit Books.

Hinde, R. A. (1982) *Ethology*. Glasgow: Fontana Paperbacks.

Hobson, J. A. (1990) *The Dreaming Brain*. Harmondsworth: Penguin Books.

Høffding, H. (1892) *Psykologi i omrids paa grundlag af erfaring*. Kobenhavn: Philipsens Forlag.

Hull, C. L. (1920) *Quantitative Aspects of the Evolution of Concepts*. Princeton: Psychological Review Company.

Irons, J. (1894) Prof. James' theory of emotion. *Mind*, 3, 77–97.

—— (1895a) Descartes and modern theories of emotion, *Philosophical Review*, 4, 291–302.

—— (1895b) Recent developments in theory of emotion. *Psychological Review*, 2, 279–84.

—— (1895c) The physical basis of emotion. *Mind*, 4, 92–9.

Itogi diskussii po reaktologicheskoj psikhologii (1931a) *Psikhotekhnika i Psikhofiziologija Truda*, 4–6, 387–91.

Itogi diskussii reaktologicheskoj psikhologii (1931b) *Psikhologija*, 4, 1–12.

Itogi diskussii reaktologicheskoj psikhologii (1931c) *Sovetskaja Psikhonevrologija*, 2–3, 53–9.

Ivanov, V. V. (1986) Commentaries. In L. S. Vygotsky, *Psikhologija iskusstva*. Moscow: Iskusstvo, pp. 492–560.

Ja., G. (1936) Likvidirovat' vrednoe nasledstvo pedologov. *Srednaja Shkola*, 8, 20–23.

Jaensch, E. R. (1923) *Über den Aufbau der Wahrnemungswelt und ihre Struktur im Jugendalter*. Leipzig: Barth.

—— (1925) *Die Eidetik und die typologische Forschungsmethode*. Leipzig: Quelle und Meyer.

Jakhot, I. (1981) *Podavlenie filosofi v SSSR (20–30 gody)*. New York: Chalidze Publications.

Jakubinsky, L. P. (1923/1988) O dialogicheskoj rechi. In L. P. Jakubinsky, *Izbrannye raboty*. Moscow: Nauka.

James, W. (1888/1984) What is an emotion? In C. Calhoun and R. C. Solomon (eds), *What is An Emotion? Classic Readings in Philosophical Psychology*. New York: Oxford University Press, pp. 127–41.

—— (1890/1983) *The Principles of Psychology*. Cambridge, Mass.: Harvard University Press.

—— (1902/1985) *The Varieties of Religious Experience*. Harmondsworth: Penguin Classics.

James, W. and Lange, C. (1922) *The Emotions*. Baltimore: Williams and Wilkins.

Janet, P. (1926) *De l'angoisse à l'extase. Vol. I*. Paris: Alcan.

—— (1929) *De l'angoisse à l'extase. Vol. II*. Paris: Alcan.

Jaroshevsky, M. G. (1984) Posleslovie (Afterword). In L. S. Vygotsky, *Sobranie sochinenij. Tom 6. Nauchnoe nasledstvo*. Moscow: Pedagogika, pp. 329–47.

—— (1987) L. S. Vygotsky as an investigator of the psychology of art. In L. S. Vygotsky, *Psikhologija iskusstva*. Moscow: Pedagogika, pp. 292–323.

—— (1988) Vozvrashchenie Frejda. *Psikhologicheskij Zhurnal*, 9, 6, 129–38.

—— (1989) *Lev Vygotsky*. Moscow: Progress Publishers.

Jaroshevsky, M. G. and Gurgenidze, G. S. (1982) Posleslovie. In L. S. Vygotsky, *Sobranie sochinenij. Tom 1. Voprosy teorii i istorii psikhologii*. Moscow: Pedagogika, pp. 437–58.

Joravsky, D. (1985) Cultural revolution and the fortress mentality. In A. Gleason, P. Kenez, and R. Stites (eds), *Bolshevik Culture*. Bloomington: Indiana University Press, pp. 93–113.

—— (1989) *Russian Psychology. A Critical Analysis*. Oxford: Basil Blackwell.

Jurinets, V. (1924) Frejdizm i marksizm. *Pod Znamenem Marksizma*, 8/9, 51–93.

—— (1925) Psychoanalyse und Marxismus. *Unter dem Banner des Marxismus*, 1, 90–133.

Kafka, G. (1922) Tierpsychologie. In G. Kafka (ed.), *Handbuch der vergleichenden Psychologie. Band 1*. München: Verlag von Ernst Reinhardt, pp. 11–144.

Kasanin, J. and Hanfmann, F. (1938) An experimental study of concept formation in schizophrenia. *American Journal of Psychiatry*, 95, 35–52.

Kätzel, S. (1987) *Marxismus und Psychoanalyse*. Berlin: VEB Deutscher Verlag der Wissenschaften.

Kendler, H. H. (1981) *Psychology: A Science in Conflict*. New York: Oxford University Press.

Kevles, D. J. (1985) *In the Name of Eugenics*. Berkeley: University of California Press.

Klausen, A. M. (1984) *Antropologins historia*. Stockholm: Norsteds.

Kloos, P. (1991) Replication, restudy, and the nature of anthropological fieldwork. In R. van der Veer, M. H. van IJzendoorn, and J. Valsiner (eds), *Reconstructing the Mind. Replicability in Research on Human Development*. New Jersey: Ablex Publishing Company.

Koffka, K. (1924) Introspection and the method of psychology. *British Journal of Psychology*, 15, 149–61.

—— (1925) *Die Grundlagen der psychischen Entwicklung. Eine Einführung in die Kinderpsychologie*. Osterwieck am Harz: A. W. Zickfeldt.

—— (1926a) Die Krisis in der Psychologie. *Die Naturwissenschaften*, 14, 581–6.

—— (1926b) Samonabljudenie i metod psikhologii. In K. Kornilov (ed.), *Problemy sovremennoi psikhologii* (pp. 179–192). Leningrad: GIZ.

—— (1927) Bemerkungen zur Denkpsychologie. *Psychologische Forschung*, 9, 163–83.

—— (1932) Preodolenie mekhanisticheskikh i vitalisticheskikh techenij v sovremennoj psikhologii. *Psikhologija*, 5, 1–2, 59–69.

Kohlberg, L., Yaeger, J. and Hjertholm, E. (1968) Private speech: Four studies and a review of theories. *Child Development*, 39, 691–736.

Köhler, W. (1921) *Intelligenzprüfungen an Menschenaffen*. Berlin: Julius Springer.

—— (1928) Bermerkungen zur Gestalttheorie. *Psychologische Forschung*, 11, 188–234.

—— (1930) *Issledovanie intellekta chelovekopodobnykh obez'jan*. Moscow: Izdatel'stvo Kommunisticheskoj Akademii.

Kolbanovsky, V. N. (1934a) Predislovie redaktora. In L. S. Vygotsky, *Myshlenie i Rech'*. Moscow: Gosudarstvennoe Social'no-Ekonomicheskoe Izdatel'stvo, pp. iii–v.

—— (1934b) Problema myshlenija i rechi v issledovanijakh L. S. Vygotskogo. In L. S. Vygotsky, *Myshlenie i Rech'*. Moscow: Gosudarstvennoe Social'no-Ekonomischeskoe Izdatel'stvo, pp. vi–xxxv.

—— (1934c) Lev Semenovich Vygotsky. *Sovetskaja Psikhotekhnika*, 7, 387–95.

—— (1956) O psikhologicheskikh vzgljadakh L. S. Vygotskogo. *Voprosy Psikhologii*, 5, 104–13.

Kolnaj, A. (1920) *Psychoanalyse und Soziologie*. Leipzig: Quelle und Meyer.

Konnikova, T. E. (1935) *Perekhodnyj etap v razvitii rechi (avtonomnaja rech')*. Phd thesis.

Konorov', M. (1908) Paedology in Russian pedagogical journals. *Vestnik Psikhologii, Kriminal'noj Antropologii, i Gipnotizma*, 5, 2, 76–82.

Korniloff, K. N. (1922) Dynamometrische Methode der Untersuchung der Reaktionen. *Archiv für die gesamte Psychologie*, 42, 59–78. (This article was received by the editor of the journal in 1914, but not published earlier due to the First World War.)

Kornilov, K. N. (1931a) O prirode tipov prostoj reakcii. *Trudy psikhologicheskogo Instituta pri Moskovskom Universitete*, 1, 1, 1–54.

—— (1931b) The dynamometric method in the study of reactions. *Trudy Psikhologicheskogo Instituta pri Moskovskom Universitete*, 1, 1, 269–73.

—— (1914) The new method of the experimental study of will. *Trudy 2-ogo Vserossijskogo s'ezda po eksperimental'noj pedagogike*. Petrograd.

—— (1915) *Detskaja psikhologija*. Moscow.

—— (1921a) Main types of work processes from the perspective of reactology. *Voprosy Truda*, 1.

—— (1921b) *Metodika issledovanija rebenka rannego vozrasta*. Moscow: Gosizdat.

—— (1922a) *Uchenie o reakcijakh cheloveka s psikhologicheskoj tochki zrenija ("reaktologija")*. Moscow: Gosudarstvennoe Izdatel'stvo.

—— (1922b) On the transition from one type of work processes to others from the standpoint of reactology. *Organizacija Truda*, 2, 93–7.

—— (1923a) Contemporary psychology and Marxism. I. *Pod Znamenem Marksizma*, 1, 41–50.

—— (1923b) Contemporary psychology and Marxism. II. *Pod Znamenem Marksizma*, 4–5, 86–114.

—— (1924a) The dialectical method in psychology. *Pod Znamenem Marksizma*, 1, 107–13.

—— (1924b) *Sovremennaja psikhologija i marksizm*. Moscow–Leningrad: Gosizdat.

—— (1925a) *Psikhologija i marksizm*. Leningrad: Gosizdat.

—— (1925b) Psychology and Marxism. In K. N. Kornilov (ed.), *Psikhologija i marksizm*. Leningrad: Gosizdat, pp. 9–24.

—— (1925c) Psychology and Marxism of Professor Chelpanov. In K. N. Kornilov (ed.), *Psikhologija i marksizm*. Leningrad: Gosizdat, pp. 231–42.

—— (1926a) *Problemy sovremennoj psikhologii*. Leningrad: Gosizdat.

—— (1926b) The naive and dialectical materialism in their relationship with the science of human behavior. In K. N. Kornilov (ed.), *Problemy sovremennoj psikhologii*. Leningrad: Gosizdat, pp. 7–19.

—— (1926c) The mechanistic materialism in contemporary psychology (response to V. Struminsky). *Pod Znamenem Marksizma*, 4–5, 185–212.

—— (1927) The contemporary state of psychology in the USSR. *Pod Znamenem Marksizma*, 10–11, 195–217.

—— (1928a) Relative relevance of the methods of scientific investigation in the fields of psychology and paedology from the viewpoint of Marxism. *Psikhologija*, 1, 1, 5–20.

—— (1928b) *Uchebnik psikhologii s tochki zrenija dialekticheskogo materializma*. Leningrad: Gosizdat.

Kornilov, K. N. and Frankfurt, Ju. V. (1929) Objective or Marxist direction in psychology. *Vestnik Kommunisticheskoi Akademii*, Kniga, 35/36, 181–204

Kozulin, A. (1984) *Psychology in Utopia. Toward a Social History of Soviet Psychology*. Cambridge, Mass.: MIT Press.

—— (1985) Georgy Chelpanov and the establishment of the Moscow institute of psychology, *Journal of the History of the Behavioral Sciences*, 21, 23–32.

—— (1990a) *Vygotsky's Psychology. A Biography of Ideas*. Brighton: Harvester Wheatsheaf.

—— (1990b) The concept of regression and Vygotskian developmental theory. *Developmental Review*, 10, 218–238.

Kozyrev, A. V. and Turko, P. A. (1936) "Pedagogicheskaja shkola" professora L. S. Vygotskogo. *Vysshaja Shkola*, 2, 44–57.

Kurazov, I. F. (1931) *Vvedenie v istoricheskuju psikhologiju*. Moscow–Leningrad: Gosudarstvennoe Social'no-Ekonomicheskoe Izdatel'stvo.

Kreppner, K., Valsiner, J. and Van der Veer, R. (forthcoming). *Too Close for Comfort: Some Puzzling Similarities Between the Ideas of William Stern and Lev Vygotsky*.

Kretschmer, E. (1929) *Körperbau und Charakter. Untersuchungen zum Konstitutionsproblem und zur Lehre von den Temperamenten*. Berlin: Verlag von Julius Springer.

Kretschmer, E. (1950) *Medizinische Psychologie*. Stuttgart: Georg Thieme Verlag.

Krop, H. (1988) *Johannes Buridan. De ethiek*. Baarn: Ambo.

Krünegel, M. (1926) Grundfragen der Heilpedagogik zu ihren Grundlegung und Zielstellung. *Zeitschrift für Kinderforschung*, 32.

Kuper, A. (1988) *The Invention of Primitive Society. Transformations of an Illusion*. London: Routledge and Kegan Paul.

La Mettrie, J. O. de (1981) *L'homme machine*. Paris: Denoël/Gonthier.

Lane, H. (1984) *When the Mind Hears: A History of the Deaf*. New York: Random House.

Lange, M. V. (1930) Collective as a factor of behavior. In A. B. Zalkind (ed.),

Psikhonevrologicheskie nauki v SSSR. Moscow–Leningrad: Gosudarstvennoe Medicinskoe Izdatel'stvo, pp. 189–90.

Lapidus, G. W. (1978) Educational strategies and cultural revolution: The politics of Soviet development. In S. Fitzpatrick (ed.), *Cultural Revolution in Russia, 1928–1931.* Bloomington: Indiana University Press, pp. 78–104.

Lazursky, A. F. and Filosofova, L. N. (1916) Natural-experimental schemes of the personality of students. *Vestnik Psikhologii, Kriminal'noj Antropologii, i Pedologii,* 12, 2–3, 97–100.

Leakey, R. E. (1981) *The Making of Mankind.* London: Abacus.

Lebedinsky, M. S. (1932) Problemy nasledstvennosti v psikhologii i metod bliznetsov, *Psikhologija,* 5, 1–2, 163–204.

Lehmann, A. G. L. (1905) Die körperliche Ausserungen psychischen Zustande. III. *Elemente der Psychodynamik.* Leipzig.

Lemaitre, A. (1904) Observations sur le language intérieur des enfants. *Archives de Psychologie,* 4, 1–43.

Lenin, V. I. (1909) *Materializm i empiriokriticism.* Moscow: Izdanie "Zveno".

—— (1922) O znachenii voinstvujushchego materializma. *Pod Znamenem Marksizma.* (See V. I. Lenin, Sobranie sochinenii, 45 (5th edn), pp. 23–33 Moscow:

Leont'ev, A. N. (1930) Razvitie vnutrennoj struktury vysshego povedenija. In A. B. Zalkind (ed.), *Psikhonevrologicheskie nauki v SSSR. Materiali 1 Vsesojuznogo s'ezda po izucheniju povedenija cheloveka.* Moscow–Leningrad: Gosudarstvennoe Medicinskoe Izdatel'stvo, pp. 140–1.

—— (1931) *Razvitie pamjati. Eksperimental'noe issledovanie vysshikh psikhologicheskikh funkcij.* Moscow–Leningrad: Uchpedgiz.

—— (1931/1983) Razvitie vysshikh form zapominanija. In A. N. Leont'ev, *Izbrannye psikhologicheskie proizvedenija. Vol. I.* Moscow: Pedagogika, pp. 31–64.

—— (1932) The development of voluntary attention in the child. *Journal of Genetic Psychology,* 40, 52–81.

—— (1934) L. S. Vygotsky. *Sovetskaja Psikhonevrologija,* 6, 187–90.

—— (1935/1983) Psikhologicheskoe issledovanie rechi. In A. N. Leont'ev, *Izbrannye psikhologicheskie proizvedenija. Tom 1.* Moscow: Pedagogika, pp. 65–75.

—— (1975) *Dejatel'nost', soznanie, lichnost'.* Moscow: Izdatel'stvo Politicheskoj Literatury.

—— (1986) Predislovie. In L. S. Vygotsky, *Psikhologija iskusstva.* Moscow: Iskusstvo, pp. 5–13.

Levina, R. E. (1936) *K psikhologii detskoj rechi v patologicheskikh sluchajakh.* Moscow.

Levina, R. E. and Morozova, N. G. (1984) Vospominanija o L. S. Vygotskom. *Defektologija,* 5, 81–6.

Levit, S. G. (1935) Twin investigations in the USSR. *Character and Personality,* 3, 188–93.

Levitin, K. (1982) *One is Not Born a Personality.* Moscow: Progress Publishers.

Lévy-Bruhl, L. (1910/1922) *Les fonctions mentales dans les sociétés inférieures.* Paris: Alcan.

—— (1922/1976) *La mentalité primitive.* Paris: Retz.

—— (1966) *How Natives Think.* New York: Washington Square Press.

Lewin, K. (1922) Das Problem der Willensmessung und das Grundgesetz der Assoziation. *Psychologische Forschung*, 1, 3/4; 2, 1/2.

—— (1926a) Vorbemerkungen über die psychischen Krafte und Energien und über die Struktur der Seele. *Psychologische Forschung*, 7, 294–329.

—— (1926b) Vorsatz, Wille und Bedürfniss. *Psychologische Forschung*, 7, 330–85.

—— (1926c) Filmaufnamen über: Trieb und Affektausserungen psychopatischer Kinder. *Zeitschrift für Kinderforschung*, 32, 414–47.

—— (1931/1982) Der Übergang von der aristotelischen zur galileischen Denkweise in Biologie und Psychologie. In A. Metraux (ed.), *Kurt–Lewin–Werkausgabe. Band 1. Wissenschaftstheorie*. Bern-Stuttgart: Huber and Klett-Cotta, pp. 233–78.

Lieberman, P. (1984) *The Biology and Evolution of Language*. Cambridge, Mass.: Harvard University Press.

Lindworsky, J. (1931) *Experimentelle Psychologie*. München: Verlag Josef Kösel and Friedrich Pustet.

Lipmann, O. and Bogen, H. (1923) *Naive Physik*. Leipzig: Verlag von Johan Ambrosius Barth.

Luchkov, V. V. and Pevzner, M. S. (1981) Znachenie teorii L. S. Vygotskogo dija psikhologii i defektologii. *Vestnik Moskovskogo Universiteta. Serija 14. Psikhologija*, 4, 60–70.

Luria, A. R. (1922a)   Kasan. *Internationale Zeitschrift für Psychoanalyse*, 8, 390.

—— (1922b) Kasaner Psychoanalytische Vereinigung (Sitzungsbericht). *Internationale Zeitschrift für Psychoanalyse*, 8, 523–5.

—— (1923a) Review of K. Sotonin, Die Temperamente. *Internationale Zeitschrift für Psychoanalyse*, 9, 102–103.

—— (1923b) Review of K. Sotonin, Die Idee der philosophischen Klinik. *Internationale Zeitschrift für Psychoanalyse*, 9, 103–5.

—— (1923c) Kasaner Psychoanalytische Vereinigung (Sitzungsbericht). *Internationale Zeitschrift für Psychoanalyse*, 9, 114–17.

—— (1923d) Kasaner Psychoanalytische Vereinigung (Sitzungsbericht). *Internationale Zeitschrift für Psychoanalyse*, 9, 238–9.

—— (1923e) *Psikhoanaliz v svete osnovnykh tendencij sovremennoj psikhologii*. Kazan.

—— (1923f) Russland. *Internationale Zeitschrift für Psychoanalyse*, 9, 113–14.

—— (1924a) Russische Psychoanalytische Gesellschaft (Sitzungsbericht). *Internationale Zeitschrift für Psychoanalyse*, 10, 113–15.

—— (1924b) Russische Psychoanalytische Gesellschaft (Mitgliederverzeichnis). *Internationale Zeitschrift für Psychoanalyse*, 10, 243.

—— (1925a) Psikhoanaliz, kak sistema monisticheskoj psikhologii. In K. N. Kornilov (ed.), *Psikhologija i marksizm*. Leningrad: Gosudarstvennoe Izdatel'stvo, pp. 47–80.

—— (1925b) Russische Psychoanalytische Vereinigung (Sitzungsbericht). *Internationale Zeitschrift für Psychoanalyse*, 11, 136–7.

—— (1925c) Die Psychoanalyse in Russland. *Internationale Zeitschrift für Psychoanalyse*, 11, 395–8.

—— (1925d) Russische Psychoanalytische Vereinigung (Mitgliederverzeichnis), *Internationale Zeitschrift für Psychoanalyse*, 11, 142.

—— (1926a) Die moderne russische Physiologie und die Psychoanalyse. *Internationale Zeitschrift für Psychoanalyse*, 12, 40–53.

—— (1926b) Russische Psychoanalytische Vereinigung (Sitzungsbericht). *Internationale Zeitschrift für Psychoanalyse*, 12, 125–6.

—— (1926c) Russische Psychoanalytische Vereinigung (Sitzungsbericht). *Internationale Zeitschrift für Psychoanalyse*, 12, 227–9.

—— (1926d) Russland. *Internationale Zeitschrift für Psychoanalyse*, 12, 578.

—— (1926e) Psikhoanaliz kak sistema monisticheskoj psikhologii. In K. N. Kornilov (ed.), *Problemy sovremennoj psikhologii*. Leningrad: Gosizdat, pp. 244–52.

—— (1926f) Principial'nye voprosy sovremennoj psikhologii. *Pod Znamenem Marksizma*, 4–5, 129–39.

—— (1926g) Moskovskij gosudarstvennyj institut eksperimental'noj psikhologii v 1924 godu. In K. N. Kornilov (ed.), *Problemy sovremennoj psikhologii*. Leningrad: Gosizdat, pp. 244–52.

—— (1927a) Russische Psychoanalytische Vereinigung (Mitgliederverzeichnis). *Internationale Zeitschrift für Psychoanalyse*, 13, 137.

—— (1927b) Russland. *Internationale Zeitschrift für Psychoanalyse*, 13, 248–9.

—— (1927c) Russische Psychoanalytische Vereinigung (Sitzungsbericht). *Internationale Zeitschrift für Psychoanalyse*, 13, 266–7.

—— (1928a) Die moderne Psychologie und der dialektische Materialismus. *Unter dem Banner des Marxismus*, 4, 506–24.

—— (1928b) The problem of the cultural behavior of the child. *Journal of Genetic Psychology*, 35, 493–506.

—— (1928c) Psikhologija v opredelenii sledov prestuplenija. *Nauchnoe Slovo*, 3, 79–82; 85–92.

—— (1928d) Psychology in Russia. *The Pedagogical Seminar and Journal of Genetic Psychology*, 35, 347–53.

—— (1928e) Soprjazhennaja motornaja metodika i ee primenenie v issledovannii effektivnykh reackcij. In K. N. Kornilov (ed.), *Problemy sovremennoj psikhologii*. Vol. 3. Moscow: Gosizdat.

—— (1929a) Puti razvitija detskogo myshlenija. *Estestvoznanie i Marksizm*, 2, 97–130.

—— (1929b) Review of H. Werner's *Einführung in die Entwicklungspsychologie*, *Estestvoznamie i Marksizm*, 1, 175–7.

—— (1929c) Review of Kornilov (ed.), 1928; Zalkind (ed.), 1928; and Spielrein (ed.), 1928. *Journal of Genetic Psychology*, 36, 491–6.

—— (1929d/1978) The development of writing in the child. In M. Cole (ed.), *The Selected Writings of A. R. Luria*. New York: M. E. Sharpe, pp. 145–94.

—— (1930a) The new method of expressive motor reactions in studying affective traces. Ninth International Congress of Psychology. *Proceedings and Papers*. New Haven, September 1–7, 1929. Princeton: Psychological Review Company, pp. 294–6.

—— (1930b) Ob odnoj popitke postroit' psikhofiziologii i tipologii lichnosti. Review of W. Jaensch's Grundzüge einer Physiologie und Klinik der psychophysischen Persönlichkeit. *Psikhologija*, 4, 574–82.

—— (1930c) Review of Basov (1928). *Journal of Genetic Psychology*, 37, 176–8.

—— (1930d) Struktura psikhofiziologicheskikh processov i ikh otrazhenie v soprjazhennoj motorike. In A. B. Zalkind (ed.), *Psikhonevrologicheskie nauki v SSSR*. Moscow–Leningrad: Gosudarstvennoe Medicinskoe Izdatel'stvo, pp. 78–9.

—— (1930e) The function of sign in the development of child behavior. In A. B. Zalkind (ed.), *Psikhonevrologicheskie nauki v SSSR*. Moscow–Leningrad: Gosudarstvennoe Medicinskoe Izdatel'stvo, pp. 139–40.

—— (1931a) K problemy nevrodinamicheskogo razvitija rebenka. *Pedologija*, 2, 18–29.

—— (1931b) Psychological expedition to Central Asia. *Science*, 74, 383–4.

—— (1931c) Psychologische Expedition nach Mittelasien. *Zeitschrift für angewandte Psychologie*, 40, 551–2.

—— (1932a) Krizis burzhuaznoj psikhologii. *Psikhologija*, 1/2, 63–88.

—— (1932b) Psychological expedition to Central Asia. *Journal of Genetic Psychology*, 40, 241–2.

—— (1932c) *The Nature of Human Conflicts*. New York: Liveright.

—— (1932d) Psychological expedition to Central Asia. *Journal of Genetic Psychology*, 40, 214–2.

—— (1932/33) (Report from) Russia. *Character and Personality*, 1, 82.

—— (1933a) Puti sovetskoj psikhologii za 15 let. *Sovetskaja Psikhonevrologija*, 1, 25–36.

—— (1933b) The second psychological expedition to Central Asia, *Science*, 78, 191–2.

—— (1934) The second psychological expedition to Central Asia, *Journal of Genetic Psychology*, 44, 255–9.

—— (1934/35) (Report from) Russia. *Character and Personality*, 3, 350–1.

—— (1935a) L. S. Vygotsky. *Character and Personality*, 3, 238–40.

—— (1935b) Professor L. S. Vygotsky (1896–1934). *Journal of Genetic Psychology*, 46, 224–6.

—— (1935c) (Report from) Russia. *Character and Personality*, 3, 350–1.

—— (1936) K voprosu o geneticheskom analize psikhologicheskikh funkcij v svjazi s ikh razvitiem. In *Problemy nervnoj fiziologii i povedenija. Sbornik posvjashchennyj professoru I.S. Beritashvili*. Tbilisi: Izdatel'stvo Gruzinskogo Filiala Akademii Nauk SSSR, pp. 361–7.

—— (1936/7) The development of mental functions in twins. *Character and Personality*, 5, 35–47.

—— (1963) The variability of mental functions as the child develops (based on a comparative study of twins). *Soviet Psychology and Psychiatry*, 1, 17–21.

—— (1971) Towards the problem of the historical nature of psychological processes. *International Journal of Psychology*, 6, 259–72.

—— (1974) *Ob istor26cheskom razvitii poznavatel'nykh processov*. Moscow: Nauka.

—— (1976) *Cognitive Development: Its Cultural and Social Foundations*. Cambridge, Mass.: Harvard University Press.

—— (1977/8) Psychoanalysis as a system of monistic psychology. *Soviet Psychology*, 16, 2, 7–45.

—— (1979) *The Making of Mind*. Cambridge, Mass.: Harvard University Press.

—— (1982) *Etapy projdennogo put'i*. Moscow: Izdatel'stvo Moskovskogo Universiteta.

Luria, A. R. and Artemeva, E. (1970) On two ways of achieving the validity of psychological investigation. *Voprosy Psikhologii*, 3, 106–12.

Luria, A. R. and Judovich, F. Ja. (1956) *Speech and the Development of Psychological Processes* Children. Moscow: Izdatel'stvo APN RFSSR. (English: 1959 in London: Stapl Press.)

Luria, A. R. and I nt'ev, A. N. (1926) Issledovanie ob'ektivnykh simptomov affektivnykh rea . Opyt reaktologicheskogo issledovanija massovogo affekta. In K. N. Kornilo d.), *Problemy sovremennoj psikhologii*. Leningrad: Gosudarstvennoe Izdatel' , pp. 47–100.

Luria, A. R. and Mi ova, A. N. (1936a) Eksperimental'noe razvitie konstruktivnoj dejatel'nosti. ferencial'noe obuchenie odnojajcevykh bliznetsov. In S. G. Levit (ed.), *Trua ediko-geneticheskogo instituta. Tom 4*. Moscow: Mediko-Geneticheskij In , pp. 487–505.

—— (1936b) Eksp iental'noe razvitie vosprijatija metodom diferencirovannogo obuchenija odnc vykh bliznecov. In *Nevrologija i genetika*.

Mandel'shtam, N. 1970) *Vospominanija. Kniga Pervaja*. Paris: YMCA-Press.

Mandel'shtam, O.) *Selected Poems*. Rivers Press.

—— (1922/1987) rode slova. In O. Mandel'shtam, *Slovo i kul'tura*. Moscow: Sovetskij Pisatel 55–67.

Margaraiz, E. and , J. (1925) La structure des récits et l'interpretation des images de Dawi l'enfant. *Archives de Psychologie*. 19, 211–39.

Markarianz, T. (1 Der erste Kongress für experimentelle Pädagogik in Russland. *Zeitschrift Pädagogische Psychologie und Experimentelle Pädagogik*, 12, 175–80.

Markov, V. N. (19 Vosstanovit' polnost'ju v pravakh pedagogiki i pedagogov. *Srednaja Shkola* –19.

Marx, K. (1890/19 *Das Kapital. Kritik der politischen Ökonomie*. Berlin: Dietz Verlag.

M'Comisky, J. G. a orsley, A. R. (1970) A modified form of the Vigotsky test. *British Journal dical Psychology*, 43, 193–6.

McCarthy, D. A.) *The Language Development of the Preschool Child*. Minneapolis, M University of Minnesota Press.

Mead, G. H. (198 he *Individual and the Social Self*. Chicago: University of Chicago Press.

Medvedev, R. A.) *K sudu istorii. Genezis i posledstvija stalinizma*. New York: Alfred A. f.

Meumann, E. (190 telligenz und Wille. Leipzig: Quelle und Meyer.

Miller, M. A. (19 he origins and development of Russian psychoanalysis, 1990–1930. *Jo of the American Academy of Psychoanalysis*, 14, 125–135.

—— (1990) The ion of psychoanalysis and the problem of the unconscious in Russia. *Socia arch*, 57, 875–88.

Mirenova, A. N.) Obuchenie i rost u odnojajtsovykh bliznetsov (OB).

Eksperimental'noe issledovanie po metodu vzaimokontrolja A. Gezella i G. Tompsona. *Psikhologija*, 4, 119–22.

Mitjushin, A. A. (1988) G. Shpet i ego mesto v istorii otechestvennoj psikhologii. *Vestnik Moskovskogo Universiteta. Serija 13. Psikhologija*, 2, 33–42.

Mjasishchev, V. N. (1930) Gestalttheorie i uchenie o refleksakh. In I. Kurazov (ed.), *Refleksologija i smezhynie napravlenija*. Leningrad: Izdanie Gosudarstvennogo Refleksologicheskogo im. V. M. Bekhtereva Instituta po Izucheniju Mozga, pp. 44–70.

Molozhavy, S. S. (1928a) Dialectics in paedology. *Pod Znamenem Marksizma*, 10–11, 229–39.

—— (1928b) The science of the child in its principles and methods. *Pedologija*, 1, 27–39.

—— (ed.), (1929) *Igra i trud v doshkol'nom vozraste*. Moskva-Leningrad: Gosudarstvennoe Izdatel'stvo.

—— (1930a) The principle problems of paedology. In A. B. Zalkind (ed.), *Psikhonevrologicheskie nauki v SSSR*. Moskva–Leningrad: Gosudarstvennoe Medicinskoe Izdatel'stvo, pp. 18–21.

—— (1930b) Paedology at the First Congress on the Study of Human Behavior. *Pedologija*, 3, 329–46.

—— (1930c) The stages of the social formation of the child. In A. B. Zalkind (ed.), *Psikhonevrologicheskie nauki v SSSR*. Moscow–Leningrad: Gosudarstvennoe Medicinskoe Izdatel'stvo, pp. 132–3.

—— (1930d) The problem of class typology of childhood. In A. B. Zalkind (ed.), *Psikhonevrologicheskie nauki v SSSR*. Moscow–Leningrad: Gosudarstvennoe Medicinskoe Izdatel'stvo, pp. 147–8.

Molozhavyj, S. S. and Molozhavaja, E. (1926) *Plan zanjatij kruzhkov po izucheniju rebenka i detskogo kollektiva*. Moscow: NKPS-Transpechat.

—— (1930) Expressive activity as a factor of formation of the child in preschool age. In A. B. Zalkind (ed.), *Psikhonevrologicheskie nauki v SSSR*. Moscow–Leningrad: Gosudarstvennoe Medicinskoe Izdatel'stvo, pp. 163–4.

Molozhavyj, S. S. and Shimkevich, E. (1926) The study of children's collective during play. *Prosveshchenie na Transporte*, 1, 10–15.

Münsterberg, H. (1909) *Psychology and the Teacher*. New York: D. Appleton.

—— (1922) *Grundzüge der Psychotechnik*. Leipzig: Barth.

Murchison, C. (ed.), (1929) *The Psychological Register*. Worcester, MA: Clark University Press.

Na I vsesojuznom s'ezde po izucheniju povedenija cheloveka (1930) *Pedologija*, 2 (8), 290–6.

Na poroge tret'ego goda (1929) *Pedologija*, 4, 458–62.

Nestjuk, N. (1929) The First All-Union Paedological Congress [described] on the pages of Soviet press. *Pedologija*, 1–2, 264–6.

O polozhenii na pedagogicheskom fronte (1931) *Pedologija*, 7–8, 8–11.

Osipova, V. N. (1928) The school of V. M. Bekhterev and paedology. *Pedologija*, 1, 10–26.

—— (1930) Synthesis and analysis in reflexological experiment. In A. B. Zalkind (ed.), *Psikhonevrologicheskie nauki v SSSR*. Moscow–Leningrad: Gosudarstvennoe Medicinskoe Izdatel'stvo, pp. 134–6.

Otchet o dejatel'nosti Psikhologicheskogo Seminaria pri Moskovskom Universiteta za 1907–1913 gody. (1914). *Uchenye zapiski imperatorskogo Moskovskago Universiteta. Otdel istoriko-filologicheskij*, 43, 299–327.

Ovsiankina, M. (1928) Die Wiederaufname unterbrochener Handlungen. *Psychologische Forschung*, 11, 302–79.

Parkhurst, H. (1922) *Education on the Dalton Plan*. New York: Dutton.

Paul, H. (1886) *Principien der Sprachgeschichte*. Halle: Max Niemeyer.

Paulhan, F. (1928) Qu'est-ce que le sens des mots? *Journal de Psychologie*, 25, 289–329.

Pavlov, I. P. (1923) *Dvatsatiletnii opyt ob'ektivnogo izuchenia vyshchei nervnoi deiatel'nosti (povedenia) zhivotnykh*. Leningrad: Gosizdat.

Pervoe predostorezhenie. (1922) *Pravda*, 194, Thursday, August 31, p. 1.

Peterson, M. N. (1930) *Sintaksis russkogo jazyka*. Moscow: Bjuro Zaochnogo Obuchenija pri Pedfake 2-go MGU.

Petrova, A. (1925) "Deti-primitivy". Psikhologicheskij analiz. In M. Gurevich (ed.), *Voprosy pedologii i detskoj psikhonevrologii*. Moscow: Zhizn' i Znanie, pp. 60–92.

Petrovsky, A. V. (1967) *Istorija sovetskoj psikhologii*. Moscow: Prosveshchenie.

Piaget, J. (1921) Une forme verbale de la comparaison chez l'enfant. *Archives de la Psychologie*, 18, 141–72.

—— (1923) *Le language et la pensée chez l'enfant*. Neuchatel: Delachaux et Niestlé.

—— (1924) *Le jugement et le raisonnement chez l'enfant*. Neuchatel: Delachaux et Niestlé.

—— (1926) *La représentation du monde chez l'enfant*. Paris: Librarie Felix Alcan.

—— (1927a) *La causalité physique chez l'enfant*. Paris: Librarie Felix Alcan.

—— (1927b) La première année de l'enfant. *British Journal of Psychology*, 18, 97–120.

—— (1932) *Le jugement moral chez l'enfant*. Paris: Alcan.

—— (1933) Psychologie de l'enfant et l'enseignement de l'histoire. *Bulletin trimestriel de la Conférence Internationale pour l'enseignement de l'histoire*, 2, 8–13.

—— (1962) *Comments on Vygotsky's Critical Remarks*. Cambridge: MIT Press.

Piaget, J. and Rossello, P. (1921) Notes sur les types de description d'images chez l'enfant. *Archives de la Psychologie*, 18, 208–34.

Pinkevitch, A. (1930) *The New Education in the Soviet Republic*. London: Williams and Norgate.

Pinkus, B. (1988) *The Jews of the Soviet Union. The History of a National Minority*. Cambridge: Cambridge University Press.

Pis'mo t. Stalina i metodologicheskaja bditel'nost na pedologicheskom fronte. (1931) *Pedologija*, 5–6 (17–18) 1–2.

Plan Zhurnala *Pedologija* na 1932 g. (1932) *Pedologija*, 1–2, 4–7.

Politzer, G. (1969) *Ecrits 2. Les fondements de la psychologie*. Paris: Editions Sociales.

—— (1974) *Critique des fondements de la psychologie*. Paris: PUF.

Potebnja, A. A. (1922) *Mysl' i jazyk*. Odessa: Gosudarstvennoe Izdatel'stvo Ukrainy.

Premack, D. (1986) *Gavagai! or the Future History of the Animal Language Controversy*. Cambridge, Mass.: MIT Press.

Puzyrej, A. A. (1986a) *Kul'turno-istoricheskaja teorija L. S. Vygotskogo i sovremennaja psikhologij*. Moscow: Izdatel'stvo Moskovskogo Universiteta.

—— (1986b) Neopublikovannaja rukopis' L. S. Vygotskogo. *Vestnik Moskovskogo Universiteta. Serija 14. Psikhologija*, 51–2.

Radzikhovsky, L. A. (1982) Kommentarii. In L. S. Vygotsky, *Sobranie sochinenyj. Tom 2. Problemy obshchej psikhologii*. Moscow: Pedagogika, pp. 480–91.

Ratner, C. (1989) A social constructionist critique of the naturalist theory of emotion. *Journal of Mind and Behavior*, 10, 211–30.

Razmyslov, P. (1934) O "kul'turno-istoricheskoj teorii psikhologii" Vygotskogo i Lurija. *Kniga i Proletarskaja Revoljucija*, 4, 78–86.

Reich, W. (1929) Dialekticheskij materializm i psikhoanaliz. *Pod Znamenem Marksizma*, 7/8, 180–206.

Reisner, M. (1925) Social psychology and Marxism. In K. N. Kornilov (ed.), *Psikhologija i marksizm*. Leningrad: Gosizdat, pp. 25–45.

Révész, G. (1921) Tierpsychologische Untersuchungen. *Zeitschrift für Psychologie*, 88, 130–7.

Reymert, M. L. (1928) *Feelings and Emotions. The Wittenberg Symposium*. Worcester: Clark University Press.

Rezoljucija pedologicheskoj sekcii I vsesojuznogo s'ezda po izucheniju povedenija cheloveka (1930) *Pedologija*, 3, 341–6.

Ribot, T. (1888) *La psychologie de l'attention*. Paris: Alcan (Russian edition 1897).

Richards, G. (1987) *Human Evolution. An Introduction for the Behavioural Sciences*. London: Routledge and Kegan Paul.

Rignano, E. (1928) Die Gestalttheorie. *Psychologische Forschung*, 11, 172–87.

Rimat, F. (1925) Intelligenzuntersuchungen anschliessend an die Ach'sche Suchmethode. *Untersuchungen zur Psychologie, Philosophie und Pädagogik*, 5, 3/4, 1–116.

Rissom, I. (1985) *Der Begriff des Zeichens in den Arbeiten Lev Semenovic Vygotskijs. Die kulturhistorische Konzeption des Zusammenhangs von Spracherwerb und kognitiver Entwicklung*. Göppingen: Kümmerle Verlag.

Rivers, W. H. R. (1901) Primitive color vision. *Popular Science Monthly*, 59, 44–58.

Rogoff, B. and Wertsch, J. V. (eds) (1984) *Children's Learning in the "Zone of Proximal Development"*. San Francisco: Jossey-Bass Inc.

Rudneva, E. I. (1937) *Pedologicheskie isvrashchenija Vygotskogo*. Moscow: Gosudarstvennoe Uchebno-Pedagogicheskoe Izdatel'stvo.

Russell, B. (1946) *A History of Western Philosophy*. London: Allen and Unwin.

Rybnikov, N. A. (1916) *Derevenskij shkol'nik i ego idealy*. Moscow: Zadruga.

—— (1925) *Russkaja pedologicheskaja literatura: sistematicheskij ukazatel'*. Orel: Krasnaja Kniga.

—— (1926) *Slovar' russkogo rebenka*. Moscow: Gosizdat.

—— (ed.) (1927) *Detskaja rech'*. Moscow: Institute of Experimental Psychology.

—— (ed.) (1928) *Skazki i rebenok*. Moscow: Gosizdat.

—— (1928) Predislovie. In N. A. Rybnikov (ed.), *Krug predstavlenij sovremennogo shkol'nika*. Moscow–Leningrad: Rabotnik Prosveshchenija, pp. 3–6.

Sacks, O. (1989) *Seeing Voices. A Journey into the World of the Deaf*. Berkeley: University of California Press.

Sakharov, L. S. (1928) Obrazovanie ponjatij u umstvenno-otstalykh detej (referat). *Voprosy defektologii*, 2, 24–33.

—— (1930) O metodakh issledovanija ponjatij u shkol'nika. *Psikhologija*, 3, 3–33.

Samukhin, N. V., Birenbaum, G. V. and Vygotsky, L. S. (1934) K voprosu o demencii pri bolezni Pika. *Sovetskaja Nevropatologija, Psikhiatrija, Psikhogigiena*, 6, 97–136.

—— (1981) K vosprosu o demencii pri bolezni Pika. (abridged). In *Khrestomatija po patopsikhologii*. Moscow: Izdatel'stvo Moskovskogo Universiteta, pp. 114–49.

Sapir, I. (1926) Frejdizm i marksizm. *Pod Znamenem Marksizma*, 11, 59–87.

—— (1929) Frejdizm, sociologija, psikhologija. *Pod Znamenem Marksizma*, 7/8, 207–36.

Savage-Rumbaugh, E. S. (1986) *Ape Language. From Conditioned Response to Symbol*. Oxford: Oxford University Press.

Scheerer, E. (1980) *Gestalt* psychology in the Soviet Union. *Psychological Research*, 41, 113–32.

—— (1985) Organische Weltanschauung und Ganzheitspsychologie. In C. F. Graumann (ed.), *Psychologie im Nationalsozialismus*. Berlin: Springer Verlag, pp. 15–53.

Schmidt, V. (1924) *Psychoanalytische Erziehung in Sowjetrussland. Bericht über das Kinderheim-Laboratorium in Moskau*. Leipzig: Internationaler Psychoanalytischer Verlag.

—— (1927) Russische Psychoanalytische Vereinigung (Sitzungsbericht). *Internationale Zeitschrift für Psychoanalyse*, 13, 370–1.

—— (1928a) Russische Psychoanalytische Vereinigung. *Internationale Zeitschrift für Psychoanalyse*, 14, 294–5.

—— (1928b) Russische Psychoanalytische Vereinigung. *Internationale Zeitschrift für Psychoanalyse*, 14, 432.

Scribner, S. and Cole, M. (1981) *The Psychology of Literacy*. Cambridge: Harvard University Press.

Semeonoff, B. and Laird, A. J. (1952) The Vigotsky test as a measure of intelligence. *British Journal of Psychology*, 43, 94–102.

Semeonoff, B. and Trist, E. (1958) *Diagnostic Performance Tests*. London: Tavistock Publications.

Semon, R. (1920) *Die Mneme als erhaltendes Prinzip im Wechsel des organischen Geschehens*. Leipzig: Verlag von Wilhelm Engelmann.

Serebrovsky, A. (1928) The experience of qualitative characterization of the process of organic evolution. *Pod Znamenem Marksizma*, 9–10, 215–28.

Sergeeva, A. D. (1974) Blonsky in the N. K. Krupskaja Academy of Communist Education. *Sovetskaja Pedagogika*, 7, 104–9.

Shapiro, S. A. and Gerke, E. D. (1930) Process prisposoblenija k uslovijam sredy v povedenija rebenka. In M. Ja. Basov (ed.), *Ocherednye problemy pedologii*. Moscow–Leningrad: Gosudarstvennoe Izdatel'stvo, pp. 73–111.

Shchelovanov, N. M. (1916) Report of the activities of the Third All-Russian Congress on Experimental Pedagogics. *Vestnik Psikhologii, Kriminal'noj Antropologii, i Pedologii*, 12, 2–3, 2, 93–6.

—— (1929) The history, tasks and methods of work of the clinic of paedology and neuropathology of infancy and of the Division of Development of the State of the reflexological Institute of the Brain. In N. M. Shchelovanov (ed.), *Voprosy geneticheskoj refleksologii i pedologii mladenchestva*, Vol. 1. Moscow–Leningrad: Gosudarstvennoe Medicinskoe Izdatel'stvo, pp. 5–15.

—— (1930) The role of the genetic method in the study of problems of human reflexology. In A. B. Zalkind (ed.), *Psikhonevrologicheskie nauki v SSSR*. Moscow–Leningrad: Gosudarstvennoe Medicinskoe Izdatel'stvo, pp. 130–2.

Shemyakin, F. and Gershonovich, L. (1932) Kak Trotsky i Kautsky revizuyut marksizm v voprosakh psikhologii. *Psikhologija*, 1/2, 3–25.

Shif, Zh. I. (1935) *Razvitie nauchnykh ponjatij u shkol'nika. Issledovanie k voprosu umstvennogo razvitija shkol'nika pri obuchenii obshchestvovedeniju*. Moscow–Leningrad: Gosudarstvennoe Uchebno-Pedagogicheskoe Izdatel'stvo.

Shirvindt, M. L. (1930) Psikhoanaliz. In B. A. Fingert and M. L. Shirvindt (eds), *Osnovnye techenija sovremennoj psikhologii*. Leningrad: Gosizdat.

Shpet, G. (1927) *Vnutrennjaja forma slova*. Moscow: Gosudarstvennaja Akademija Khudozhestvennykh Nauk.

Smedslund, J. (1978) Bandura's theory of self-efficacy: A set of common-sense theorems. *Scandinavian Journal of Psychology*, 19, 1–14.

—— (1979) Between the analytic and the arbitrary: A case study of psychological research. *Scandinavian Journal of Psychology*, 20, 129–40.

Smirnov, A. A. (ed.) (1975) *Razvitie i sovremennoe sostojanie psikhologicheskoj nauki v SSSR*. Moscow: Pedagogika.

Solomon, R. C. (1983) *In the Spirit of Hegel*. New York: Oxford University Press.

Solov'ev, I. M. (1930) Activity and external stimulation. In A. B. Zalkind (ed.), *Psikhonevrologicheskie nauki v SSSR*. Moscow–Leningrad: Gosudarstvennoe Medicinskoe Izdatel'stvo, pp. 71–3.

Spinoza, B. de (1677/1955) *On the Improvement of the Understanding. The Ethics. Correspondence*. Mineola: Dover Publications.

Spisok nauchnykh institutov, zanimajushchikhsja razrabotkoj voprosa o detskom trude, s kratchajshim ukazaniem osnovnykh problem imi razrabatyvaemykh (1929). *Pedologija*, 3, 404–9.

Spranger, E. (1923/1973) Die Frage nach der Einheit der Psychologie. In *Gesammelte Schriften. Band 4*. Heidelberg: Quelle und Meyer, pp. 1–36.

—— (1927) *Psychologie des Jugendalters*. Jena: Fischer Verlag.

Staats, A. W. (1983) *Psychology's Crisis of Disunity*. New York: Praeger.

Stern, W. (1927) *Psychologie der frühen Kindheit bis zum sechsten Lebensjahre*. Leipzig: Quelle und Meyer.

Stern, C. and Stern, W. (1928/1981) *Die Kindersprache. Eine psychologische und sprachtheoretische Untersuchung*. Darmstadt: Wissenschaftliche Buchgesellschaft.

Struminsky, V. (1926) Marxism in contemporary psychology. *Pod Znamenem Marksizma*, 1, 3, 207–33; 2, 4–5, 140–84.

Talankin, A. A. (1931a) O povorote na psikhologicheskom fronte. *Sovetskaja Psikhonevrologija*, 2–3, 8–23.

—— (1931b) O "marksistskoj psikhologii" prof. Kornilova. *Psikhologija*, 4, 1, 24–43.

—— (1932) Protiv men'shevistvuyuschego idealizma v psikhologii. *Psikhologija*, 1/2, 38–62.

Teplov, B. M. (1960) The fight of K. N. Kornilov in 1923–1925 for the reorganization of psychology on the basis of Marxism. In E. I. Ignat'ev (ed.), *Voprosy psikhologii lichnosti*. Moscow.

Thomas, L. V. (1976) Lucien Lévy-Bruhl: l'origine de l'anthropologie moderne. In L. Lévy-Bruhl, *La mentalité primitive*. Paris: Metz, pp. 13–27.

Thurnwald, R. (1922) Psychologie des primitiven Menschen. In G. Kafka (ed.), *Handbuch der vergleichenden Psychologie. Band 1*. München: Verlag von Ernst Reinhardt, pp. 147–320.

Tinbergen, N. and Tinbergen, E. A. (1983) *"Autistic" Children. New Hope for a Cure*. London: Allan and Unwin.

Titchener, E. B. (1941) A historical note on the James-Lange theory of emotion. *American Journal of Psychology*, 25, 427–47.

Tulviste, P. (1988a) *Kul'turno-istoricheskoe razvitie verbal'nogo myshlenija*. Tallinn: Valgus.

—— (1988b) O nekotorykh prichinakh neudovletvoritel'nogo sostojanija sovetskoj psikhologii. *Voprosy Psikhologii*, 2, 5–6.

Tyutchev, F. (1836/1976) Silentium. In D. Obolenskyj, *The Heritage of Russian Verse*. Bloomington: Indiana University Press.

Ukhtomsky, A. (1924) Dominanta i integral'nyj obraz. *Vrachebnaja Gazeta*, 2.

—— (1927) Dominanta kak faktor povedenija. *Vestnik Kommunisticheskoj Akademii*, 22, 215–41.

Upravlenie Psikho-Pedologicheskim Institutom (1908) *Vestnik Psikhologii, Kriminal'noi Antropologii, i Gipnotizma*, 5, 1, 94–6.

Usnadze, D. (1924) Ein experimenteller Beitrag zum Problem der psychologischen Grundlagen der Namengebung. *Psychologische Forschung*, 5, 24–43.

—— (1929) Gruppenbildungsversuche bei vorschulpflichtigen Kindern. *Archiv für die gesamte Psychologie*, 73, 217–48.

—— (1930) Die Begriffsbildung im vorschulpflichtigen Alter. *Zeitschrift für angewandte Psychologie*, 34, 138–212.

Vagner, V. (1901) *Biologicheskii metod v zoopsikhologii*. St Petersburg: Parovaia skoropechatnaia G. Pozharova.

—— (1910) *Biologicheskie osnovania sravnitel'noi psikhologii*, Vol. 1. St Petersburg: M. Wolf.

—— (1913) *Biologicheskie osnovania sravnitel'noi psikhologii (biopsikhologia)*. Vol. 2. *Instinkt i razum*. St Petersburg: M. Wolf.

—— (1923) *Biopsikhologia i smezhnyie nauki*. Leningrad: Obrazovanie.

—— (1925) *Vozniknovenie i razvitie psikhicheskikh sposobnostei, Vypusk 3. Ot refleksov do instinktov.* Leningrad: Nachatki znanii.

—— (1929) *Psikhologicheskie tipy i kollektivnaia psikhologia.* Leningrad: Nachatki znanii.

Valsiner, J. (1988) *Developmental Psychology in the Soviet Union.* Brighton: Harvester Press.

Valsiner, J. and Van der Veer, R. (1988) On the social nature of human cognition. *Journal for the theory of the Behavioral Sciences*, 18, 117–35.

Valsiner, J. and Van der Veer, R. (1992) The encoding of distance: the concept of the "zone of proximal development" and its interpretations. In R. R. Cocking and K. A. Renninger (eds), *The Development and Meaning of Psychological Distance.* Hillsdale, NJ: Erlbaum.

Van der Veer, R. (1984) Early periods in the work of L. S. Vygotskij: The influence of Spinoza. In M. Hedegaard, P. Hakkarainen, and Y. Engeström (eds), *Learning and Teaching on a Scientific Basis.* Aarhus: Psykologisk Institut, pp. 87–98.

—— (1987) From language and thought to thinking and speech. *Journal of Mind and Behavior*, 8, 175–7.

—— (1990) The reform of Soviet psychology: A historical perspective. *Studies in Soviet Thought*, 40, 205–21.

—— (1991) The forbidden colors game. An argument in favor of internalization? In R. van der Veer, M. H. van IJzendoorn and J. Valsiner (eds), *Reconstructing the Mind. Replicability in Research on Human Development.* New Jersey: Ablex Publishing Company.

Van der Veer, R. and Valsiner, J. (1988) Lev Vygotsky and Pierre Janet. On the origin of the concept of sociogenesis. *Developmental Review*, 8, 52–65.

—— (1989) Overcoming dualism in psychology: Vygotsky's analysis of theories of emotion. *Quarterly Newsletter of the Laboratory of Comparative Human Cognition*, 11, 124–31.

Van der Veer, R. and Van IJzendoorn, M. H. (1985) Vygotsky's theory of the higher psychological processes: Some criticisms. *Human Development*, 28, 1–9.

Van der Veer, R., Van IJzendoorn, M. H. and Valsiner, J. (eds) (1991) *Reconstructing the Mind. Replicability in Research on Human Development.* New Jersey: Ablex Publishing Company.

Van IJzendoorn, M. H. and Van der Veer, R. (1984) *Main Currents of Critical Psychology. Vygotsky, Holzkamp, Riegel.* New York: Irvington Publishers.

Varshava, B. E. and Vygotsky, L. S. (1931) *Psikhologicheskij slovar'.* Moscow: Gosudarstvennoe Uchebno-Pedagogicheskoe Izdatel'stvo.

Vidal, F. (1986) Piaget et la psychanalyse: premieres rencontres. *Les Bloc-notes de la Psychanalyse*, 6, 171–89.

—— (1987) Jean Piaget and psychoanalysis. A historical and biographical note (up to the 1930s). In S. Bem and H. Rappard (eds), *Studies in the History of Psychology and the Social Sciences 4.* Leiden: Psychologisch Instituut.

—— (1988a) Freud und Piaget. Jean, "Enkel" von Sigmund. In B. Nitzschke (ed.), *Freud und die akademische Psychologie.* Munchen: Psychologie Verlags Union.

—— (1988b) L'institut Rousseau au temps des passions. *Education et Recherche*, 10, 60–81.

Vnukov, V. A. (1925) Primitivy, ikh socio-biologicheskij smysl. In M. Gurevich (ed.), *Voprosy pedologii i detskoj psikhonevrologii.* Moscow: Zhizn' i Znanie, pp. 93–109.

Vocate, D. R. (1987) *The Theory of A. R. Luria.* Hillsdale: Lawrence Erlbaum.

Volkelt, H. (1914) *Uber die Vorstellungen der Tiere. Ein Beitrag zur Entwicklungspsychologie.* Leipzig: Krueger.

von Wright, G. (1988) *Vetenskapen och förnuftet.* Stockholm: MänPocket.

Vossler, K. (1923) *Gesammelte Aufsatze zur Sprachphilosophie.* München: Verlag der Hochschulbuchhandlung Max Hueber.

Vygodskaja, G. L. and Lifanova, T. M. (1984) Lev Semenovich Vygotsky. In *Vsesojuznaja Konferencija "Aktual'nye problemy istorii psikhologii". Vol. II* (pp. 111–15). Erevan: Izdatel'stvo Erevanskogo Universiteta.

—— (1988) L. S. Vygotsky. Life and work. In *Proceedings of the Seventh European CHEIRON Conference.* Budapest: Hungarian Psychological Association, pp. 733–9.

Vygotsky, L. S. (1915a) Tragedija o Gamlete, prince Datskom, U. Shekspira. Unpublished manuscript. Gomel', August 5–September 12. Family Archives.

—— (1915b) [About Aikhen'wald]. *Novyj put'.*

—— (1916a) Review of A. Belyj, Peterburg. *Novyj put'*, 47, 27–32.

—— (1916b) Review of A. Belyj, Peterburg. *Letopis'*, 12, 327–8.

—— (1916c) Review of V. Ivanov, Borozdy i mezhi. *Letopis'*, 10, 351–2.

—— (1916d) Tragedija o Gamlete, prince Datskom, U. Shekspira. Unpublished manuscript. Moscow, February 14–February 28. Family Archives.

—— (1916e/1986) Tragedija o Gamlete, prince Datskom, U. Shekspira. In L. S. Vygotsky, *Psikhologija iskusstva.* Moscow: Iskusstvo, pp. 336–491.

—— (1916f/1987) Tragedija o Gamlete, prince Datskom, U. Shekspira (excerpt). In L. S. Vygotsky, *Psikhologija isskusstva.* Moscow: Pedagogika, pp. 251–91.

—— (1916g) [About the new theater]. *Letopis'.*

—— (1917a) Review of D. Merezhkovskij, Budet radost'. *Letopis'*, 1, 309–10.

—— (1917b) Review of N. L. Brodsky's review of I. S. Turgenev's poem "Pop". *Letopis'*, 5–6, 366–7.

—— (1917c) [About Shakespeare]. *Novaja Zhizn'.*

—— (1917d) Avodim Khoin. *Novyj Put'*, 11–12, 8–10.

—— (1922a) O metodakh prepodovanija khudozhestvennoj literatury v shkolakh II stupeni. Manuscript.

—— (1922b) [Content unknown]. *Zhizn' Iskusstva.*

—— (1923a) Bol'shoy narodnyj pisatel'. K jubileju Serafimovicha. *Polesskaja Pravda*, 1069, December 9.

—— (1923b) 10 dnej, kotorye potryasli mir. *Polesskaja Pravda*, 1081, December 23.

—— (1923c) Gastroli Maksimova. *Polesskaja Pravda*, 1072, December 13.

—— (1923d) O belorusskoj literature. *Polesskaja Pravda*, 1075, December 16.

—— (1923e) Ob issledovanni processov ponimanija jazyka metodom mnogokratnogo perevoda teksta c odnogo jazyka na drugoj. Unpublished manuscript. Family archives.

—— (1924a) Anketnyj metod psikhologicheskogo issledovanija uchashchikhsja. *Na Putjakh k Novoj Shkole*, 6–7.

—— (1924b) Foreword. In A. F. Lazursky, *Psikhologija obshchaja i eksperimental'naja*. Leningrad: Gosudarstvennoe Izdatel'stvo, pp. 5–23.

—— (1924c) Foreword. In L. S. Vygotsky, *Sobranie sochinenij. Tom 1. Voprosy teorii i istorii psikhologii*. Moscow: Pedagogika, pp. 63–77.

—— (ed.) (1924d) *Voprosy vospitanija slepykh glukhonemykh i umstvenno otstalykh detej*. Moscow: Izdatel'stvo SPON NKP.

—— (1924e) Foreword. In L. S. Vygotsky (ed.), *Voprosy vospitanija slepykh glukhonemykh i umstvenno otstalykh detej*. Moscow: Izdatel'stvo SPON NKP, pp. 3–4.

—— (1924f) K psikhologii i pedagogike detskoj defektivnosti. In L. S. Vygotsky (ed.), *Voprosy vospitanija slepykh glukhonemykh i umstvenno otstalykh detej*. Moscow: Izdatel'stvo SPON NKP, pp. 5–30.

—— (1924g/1974) K psikhologii i pedagogike detskoj defektivnosti. *Defektologija*, 3, 70–6.

—— (1924h/1980) K psikhologii i pedagogike detskoj defektivnosti. (excerpt). In I. Il'jasov and V. Ja. Ljaudis (eds), *Khrestomatija po vozrastnoj i pedagogicheskoj psikhologii*. Moscow: Izdatel'stvo Moskovskogo Universiteta, pp. 24–35.

—— (1924i/1983) K psikhologii i pedagogike detskoj defektivnostio. In L. S. Vygotsky, *Sobranie sochinenij. Tom 5. Osnovy defektologii*. Moscow: Pedagogika, pp. 62–84.

—— (1924j/1983) Defekt i kompensacija. In L. S. Vygotsky, *Sobranie sochinenij. Tom 5. Osnovy defektologii*. Moscow: Pedagogika, pp. 34–49.

—— (1924k/1983) Slepoj rebenok. In L. S. Vygotsky, *Sobranie sochinenij. Tom 5. Osnovy defektologii*. Moscow: Pedagogika, pp. 86–100.

—— (1925a) Review of A. N. Graborov, Vspomogatel'naja shkola. *Narodnoe Prosveshchenie*, 9, 170–1.

—— (1925b/1983) Principy social'nogo vospitanija glukhonemykh detej. In L. S. Vygotsky, *Sobranie sochinenij. Tom 5. Osnovy defektologii*. Moscow: Pedagogika, pp. 101–14.

—— (1925c) Principles of social education for deaf and dumb children in Russia. In *International Conference on the Education of the Deaf*. London: William H. Taylor and Sons, pp. 227–37.

—— (1925d) Principy vospitanija fizicheski defektivnykh detej. *Narodnoe Prosveshchenie*, 1, 112–120.

—— (1925e/1926) Principy vospitanija fizicheski defektivnykh detej. In *Puti vospitanija fizicheski defektivnogo rebenka*. Moscow: Izdatel'stvo SPON NKP, pp. 7–22.

—— (1925f/1983) Principy vospitanija fizicheski defektivnykh detej. In L. S. Vygotsky, *Sobranie sochinenij. Tom 5. Osnovy defektologii*. Moscow: Pedagogika, pp. 49–62.

—— (1925g) Soznanie kak problema psikhologija povedenija. In K. N. Kornilov (ed.), *Psikhologija i marksizm*. Leningrad: Gosudarstvennoe Izdatel'stvo, pp. 175–98.

—— (1925h/1982) Soznanie kak problema psikhologija povedenija. In L. S. Vygotsky, *Sobranie sochinenij. Tom 1. Voprosy teorii i istorii psikhologii*. Moscow: Pedagogika, pp. 78–98.

—— (1925i/1983) Opytnaja proverka novykh metodov obuchenija glukhonemykh detej rechi. In L. S. Vygotsky, *Sobranie sochinenij. Tom 5. Osnovy defektologii.* Moscow: Pedagogika, pp. 322–50.

—— (1925j/1965) *Psikhologija iskusstva.* Moscow: Iskusstvo.

—— (1925k/1986) *Psikhlogija iskusstva.* Moscow: Iskusstvo.

—— (1925l/1986) *Psikhologija iskusstva.* Moscow: Iskusstvo.

—— (1925m/1987) *Psikhologija iskusstva.* Moscow: Iskusstvo.

—— (1926a) *Grafika Bykhovskogo.* Moscow: Sovremennaja Rossija, pp. 5–8.

—— (1926b) Metodika refleksologicheskogo i psikhologicheskogo issledovanija. In K. N. Kornilov (ed.), *Problemy sovremennoj psikhologii.* Leningrad: Gosudarstvennoe Izdatel'stvo, pp. 26–46.

—— (1926c/1982) *Problemy sovremennoj psikhologii.* In L. S. Vygotsky, *Sobranie sochinenij. Tom 1. Voprosy teorii i istorii psikhologii.* Moscow: Pedagogika, pp. 43–62.

—— (1926d) Problema dominantnykh reakcij. In K. N. Kornilov (ed.), *Problemy sovremennoj psikhologii.* Leningrad: Gosudarstvennoe Izdatel'stvo, pp. 100–24.

—— (1926e) O vlijanii rechevogo ritma na dykhanie. In K. N. Kornilov (ed.), *Problemy sovremennoj psikhologii.* Leningrad: Gosudarstvennoe Izdatel'stvo, pp. 169–73.

—— (1926f) Samonabljudenie i metod psikhologii K. Koffka. In K. N. Kornilov (ed.), *Problemy sovremennoj psikhologii.* Leningrad: Gosudarstvennoe Izdatel'stvo, pp. 176–8.

—— (1926g/1972) Samonabljudenie i metod psikhologii K. Koffka. In L. S. Vygotsky, *Samonabljudenie i metod psikhologii K. Koffka.* Moscow: Izdatel'stvo Moskovskogo Universiteta.

—— (1926h/1982) Samonabljudenie i metod psikhologii K. Koffka. In L. S. Vygotsky, *Sobranie sochinenij. Tom 1. Voprosy teorii i istorii psikhologii.* Moscow: Pedagogika, pp. 99–102.

—— (1926i) *Pedagogicheskaja psikhologija.* Moskva: Rabotnik Prosveshchenija.

—— (1926j/1980) *Pedagogicheskaja psikhologija* (excerpt). In I. I. Il'jasov and V. Ja. Ljaudis (eds), *Khrestomatija po vozrastnoj i pedagogicheskoj psikhologii.* Moscow: Izdatel'stvo Moskovskogo Universiteta, pp. 49–53.

—— (1926k) Foreword. In E. Thorndike, *Principy obuchenija, osnovannye na psikhologii.* Moscow: Rabotnik Prosveshchenija, pp. 5–23.

—— (1926l/1982) Foreword. In L. S. Vygotsky, *Sobranie sochinenij. Tom 1. Voprosy teorii i istorii psikhologii.* Moscow: Pedagogika, pp. 176–95.

—— (1926m/1982) Istoricheskij smysl psikhologicheskogo krizisa. In L. S. Vygotsky, *Sobranie sochinenij. Tom 1. Voprosy teorii i istorii psikhologii.* Moscow: Pedagogika, pp. 291–346.

—— (1926n/1983) Istoricheskij smysl psikhologicheskogo krizisa. (excerpt). In *Istorija sovetskoj psikhologii truda.* Moscow: Izdatel'stvo Moskovskogo Universiteta, pp. 58–61.

—— (1926o) *Metody prepodavanija psikhologii. Programma kursa.* Gosudarstvennyj archiv Moskovskoj oblasti, f. 948, op. 1, d. 613, p. 25.

—— (1926p) Review of O. Rule, Psikhika proletarskogo rebenka. Unpublished manuscript. Family archives.

—— (1927a) Biogeneticheskij zakon. *Bol'shaja Sovetskaja Enciklopedija*, 6, 275–9.

—— (1927b) Defekt i sverkhkompensacija. In *Umstvennaja otstalost', slepota i glukhonemota*. Moscow: Doloj Negramotnost', pp. 51–76.

—— (1927c/1983) Defekt i sverkhkompensacija. In L. S. Vygotsky, *Sobranie sochinenij. Tom 5. Osnovy defektologii*. Moscow: Pedagogika, pp. 34–49.

—— (1927d) Review of M. Ja. Basov, Metodika psikhologicheskikh nabljudenij za det'mi. *Narodnyj Uchitel'*, 1, 152.

—— (1927e) Sovremennaja psikhologija i iskusstvo. *Sovetskoe Iskusstvo*, 8, 5–8.

—— (1927f/1977) Instrumental'nyj metod. *Vestnik Moskovskogo Universiteta Ser. 14, Psikhologija*, 2, 89–95.

—— (1927g) Rebenok i detdom. Stat'ja programma-minimum dlja povyshenija kvalifikacii rabotnikov Socvosa. Unpublished manuscript. Family archives.

—— (1928a/1983) Slepoj rebenok. In L. S. Vygotsky, *Sobranie sochinenij. Tom 5. Osnovy defektologii*. Moscow: Pedagogika, pp. 86–100.

—— (1928b) Defekt i kompensacija. *Pedagogicheskaja Enciklopedija. Vol. 2*, 391–2.

—— (1928c) Tri osnovnykh tipa defekta. *Pedagogicheskaja Enciklopedija. Vol. 2*, 392.

—— (1928d) Psikhofiziologicheskaja osnova vospitanija rebenka s defektom. *Pedagogicheskaja Enciklopedija. Vol. 2*, 392–3.

—— (1928e) Social'no-psikhologicheskaja osnova vospitanija rebenka s defektom. *Pedagogicheskaja Enciklopedija. Vol. 2*, 393–4.

—— (1928f) Psikhologicheskie osnovy vospitanija i obuchenija slepogo rebenka. *Pedagogicheskaja Enciklopedija. Vol. 2*, 394–5.

—— (1928g) Psikhologicheskie osnovy vospitanija i obuchenija glukhonemogo rebenka. *Pedagogicheskaja Enciklopedija. Vol. 2*, 395.

—— (1928h) Vospitanie glukhonemykh detej. *Pedagogicheskaja Enciklopedija. Vol. 2*, 395–6.

—— (1928i) Kaleki. *Pedagogicheskaja Enciklopedija. Vol. 2*, 396.

—— (1928j) Bol'nye deti. *Pedagogicheskaja Enciklopedija. Vol. 2*, 396–7.

—— (1928k) Umstvenno otstalye deti. *Pedagogicheskaja Enciklopedija. Vol. 2*, 397–8.

—— (1928l) Rebenok s defektom i normal'nyj. *Pedagogicheskaja Enciklopedija. Vol. 2*, 398.

—— (1928m) Bikheviorizm. *Bol'shaja Medicinskaja Enciklopedija. Vol. 3*, 483–6.

—— (1928n) Voljuntarizm. *Bol'shaja Medicinskaja Enciklopedija. Vol. 5*, 588–9.

—— (1928o) Volja i ee rasstrojstva. *Bol'shaja Medicinskaja Enciklopedija. Vol. 5*, 590–600.

—— (1928p) Problema kul'turnogo razvitija rebenka. *Pedologija*, 1, 58–77.

—— (1928q) Instrumental'nyj metod v pedologii. In *Osnovnye metody pedologii v SSSR*. Moscow, pp. 158–9.

—— (1928r) Itogi z'ezda. *Narodnoe Prosveshchenie*, 2, 56–67.

—— (1928s/1983) Itogi s'ezda. In L. S. Vygotsky, *Sobranie sochinenij. Tom 5. Osnovy defektologii*. Moscow: Pedagogika, pp. 327–8.

—— (1928t) *Pedologija shkol'nogo vozrasta*. Moscow: Izdatel'stvo BZO pri pedfake 2-go MGU.

—— (1928u) K voprosu o dinamike detskogo kharaktera. In *Pedologija i vospitanie*. Moscow: Rabotnik Prosveshchenija, pp. 99–119.

—— (1928v/1983) K voprosu o dinamike detskogo kharaktera. In L. S. Vygotsky, *Sobranie sochinenij. Tom 5. Osnovy defektologii*. Moscow: Pedagogika, pp. 153–65.

—— (1928w) Metodicheskie ukazanija k provedeniju senso-motornogo vospitanija rebenka v shkol'nom vozraste. *Voprosy Defektologii*. 1.

—— (1928x) Na perekrestkakh sovetskoj i zarubezhnoj pedagogiki. *Voprosy defektologii*, 1, 18–26.

—— (1928y) Pamjati V. M. Bekhtereva. *Narodnoe Prosveshchenie*, 2, 68–70.

—— (1928z) Sovremennaja psikhologija i iskusstvo. *Sovetskoe Iskusstvo*, 1, 5–7.

—— (1928aa) Psikhologicheskaja nauka v SSSR. In Volgin, Gordov, and Lupnol (eds), *Obshestvennye nauki v SSSR 1917–1927*. Moscow: Rabotnik: Prosveshchenija, pp. 25–46.

—— (1928ab/1983) Defektologija i uchenie o razvitii i vospitanii nenormal'nogo rebenka. In L. S. Vygotsky, *Sobranie sochinenij. Tom 5. Osnovy defektologii*. Moscow: Pedagogika, pp. 166–73.

—— (1928ac/1983) Metody izuchenija umstvenno otstalogo rebenka. In L. S. Vygotsky, *Sobranie sochinenij. Tom 5. Osnovy defektologii*. Moscow: Pedagogika, pp. 325–6.

—— (1928ad/1983) Moral insanity. In L. S. Vygotsky, *Sobranie sochinenij. Tom 5. Osnovy defektologii*. Moscow: Pedagogika, pp. 150–2.

—— (1928ae/1983) Osnovy raboty s umstvenno otstalymi i fizicheski detektivnymi det'mi. In L. S. Vygotsky, *Sobranie sochinenij. Tom 5. Osnovy defektologii*. Moscow: Pedagogika, pp. 181–70.

—— (1928af/1983) Prenija po dokladam. In L. S. Vygotsky, *Sobranie sochinenij. Tom 5. Osnovy defektologii*. Moscow: Pedagogika, pp. 331–2.

—— (1928ag) Razvitie trudnogo rebenka i ego izuchenija. In *Osnovnye problemy pedologii v SSSR*. Moscow, pp. 132–6.

—— (1928ah/1983k) Razvitie trudnogo rebenka i ego izuchenija. In L. S. Vygotsky, *Sobranie sochinenij. Tom 5. Osnovy defektologii*. Moscow: Pedagogika, pp. 175–80.

—— (1928ai) *Vystuplenie na konferencii po voprosam metodiki prepodovanija v pedagogicheskom tekhnikume. 10 April 1928*. State Archives of the Moscow District, f. 948, op. 1, d. 775, pp. 13–15.

—— (1928aj) *Genezis kul'turnykh form povedenija*. Unpublished manuscript. Family archives.

—— (1928ak) *Lekcii po psikhologii razvitija*. Unpublished manuscript. Family archives.

—— (1928al) *Problema kul'turnogo povedenija rebenka*. Unpublished manuscript. Family archives.

—— (1929a) K voprosu o dlitel'nosti detstva umstvenno otstalogo rebenka. *Voprosy Defektologii*, 2, 8, 111.

—— (1929b/1983) K voprosu o dlitel'nosti detstva umstvenno otstalogo rebenka. In L. S. Vygotsky, *Sobranie sochinenij. Tom 5. Osnovy defektologii*. Moscow: Pedagogika, pp. 328–9.

—— (1929c) Anomalii kul'turnogo razvitija rebenka. *Voprosy Defektologii*, 2, 8, 106–7.

—— (1929d/1983) Anomalii kul'turnogo razvitija rebenka. In L. S. Vygotsky, *Sobranie sochinenij. Tom 5. Osnovy defektologii.* Moscow: Pedagogika, pp. 326–7.

—— (1929e) Geneticheskie korni myshlenija i rechi. *Estestvoznanie i Marksizm*, 1, 106–33.

—— (1929f) Die genetische Wurzeln des Denkens und der Sprache. *Unter dem Banner des Marxismus*, 3, 450–70.

—— (1929g) Genial'nost. *Bol'shaja Medicinskaja Enciklopedija. Vol. 6*, 612–13.

—— (1929h) K voprosu ob intellekte antropoidov v svjazi s rabotami V. Kolera, *Estesvoznanie i Marksizm*, 2, 131–53.

—— (1929i) K voprosu o plane nauchno-issledovatel'skoj raboty po pedologii nacional'nykh men'shinstv. *Pedologii*, 3, 367–77.

—— (1929j) Osnovnye polozhenija plana pedologicheskoj issledovatel'skoj raboty v oblasti trudnogo detstva. *Pedologija*, 3, 333–42.

—— (1929k/1983) Osnovyne polozhenija plana pedologicheskoj issledovatel'skoj raboty v oblasti trudnogo detstva. In L. S. Vygotsky, *Sobranie sochinenij. Tom 5. Osnovy defektologii.* Moscow: Pedagogika, pp. 188–95.

—— (1929l) *Osnovnye problemy sovremennoj defektologii. Tom 1.* Moscow: Trudy 2 MGU.

—— (1929m/1983) *Osnovnye problemy sovremennoj defektologii. Tom I.* In L. S. Vygotsky, *Sobranie sochinenij. Tom 5. Osnovy defektologii.* Moscow: Pedagogika, pp. 6–33.

—— (1929n) *Pedologija junosheskogo vozrasta.* Moscow: Cipkno.

—— (1929o) *Pedologija pionerskogo vozrasta.* Unpublished manuscript. Family archives.

—— (1929p) *Pedologija podrostka. Vol. I.* Moscow: Izdanie Bjuro Zaochnogo Obuchenija pri Pedfake 2 MGU.

—— (1929q) *Pedologija shkol'nogo vozrasta.* Moscow: Izdanie Bjuro Zaochnogo Obuchenija pri Pedfake 2 MGU.

—— (ed.) (1929r) *Predmet i metody sovremennoj psikhologii.* Moscow: Izdanie Bjuro Zaochnogo Obuchenija pri Pedfake 2-go MGU.

—— (1929s) The problem of the cultural development of the child II. *Journal of Genetic Psychology*, 36, 415–34.

—— (1929t) Razvitie aktivnogo vnimanija v detskom vozraste. *Voprosy marksistkoj pedagogiki. Trudy AKV. Tom 1.* Moscow: Uchebno-Pedagogicheskie Izdatel'stvo, pp. 112–42.

—— (1929u/1956) Razvitie aktivnogo vnimanija v detskom vozraste. In L. S. Vygotsky, *Izbrannye psikhologicheskie issledovanija.* Moscow: Izdatel'stvo APN RSFSR, pp. 389–426.

—— (1929v/1976) Razvitie aktivnogo vnimanija v detskom vozraste. In *Khrestomatija po vnimaniju.* Moscow: Izdatel'stvo Moskovskogo Universiteta, pp. 184–299.

—— (1929w) Struktura interesov v perekhodnom vozraste i interesy rabochego podrostka. In *Voprosy pedologii rabochego podrostka.* Moscow: Izdatel'stvo

Instituta Povyshenija Kvalifikacii Pedagogov.

—— (1929x) *Trudnoe Detstvo*. Moscow: Cipkno.

—— (1929y/1983) *Trudnoe Detstvo* (excerpt). In L. S. Vygotsky, *Sobranie sochinenij. Tom 5. Osnovy defektologii*. Moscow: Pedagogika, pp. 137–49.

—— (1929z/1986) Konkretnaja psikhologija cheloveka. *Vestnik Moskovskogo Universiteta Ser 14. Psikhologija*, 1, 15–65.

—— (1929aa) Vystuplenija po dokladom. *Voprosy Defektologii*, 2, 8, 108–12.

—— (1929ab/1983) Vystuplenija po dokladom (abridged). In L. S. Vygotsky, *Sobranie sochinenij. Tom 5. Osnovy defektologii*. Moscow: Pedagogika, pp. 331–2.

—— (1929ac) Review of C. and W. Stern, Die Kindersprache. *Estestvoznanie i Marksizm*, 3, 185–92.

—— (1929ad) Review of N. Dmitrieva, N. Ol'denburg, and L. Perekrestova, Shkol'naja dramaticheskaja rabota na osnove issledovanija detskogo tvorchestva. *Isskustvo v Shkole*, i, 29–31.

—— (1929ae) Review of D. N. Kashkarov, Sovremennye uspekhi zoopsikhologii. *Estestvoznanie i Marksizm*, 3, 209–11.

—— (1929af) Review of S. M. Rives, O merakh pedagogicheskogo vozdejstvija. *Pedologija*, 4, 645–6.

—— (1929ag) *O nekotorykh metodologicheskikh voprosakh*. Archives of the APN SSSR, f. 4, op. 1, ed. khr. 103, pp. 51–2, 73–4.

—— (1929ah) *Ocherk kul'turnogo razvitija normal'nogo i nenormal'nogo rebenka*. Unpublished manuscript. Family archives.

—— (1929ai) *Problema kul'turnogo vozrasta*. Unpublished manuscript. Family archives.

—— (1930a) Biologicheskaja osnova affekta. *Khochu Vse Znat'*, 15–16, 480–1.

—— (1930b) Vydajushchajasja pamjat'. *Khochu Vse Znat'*, 19, 553–4.

—— (1930c) Vozmozhno li simulirovat' vydajushchujusja pamjat'? *Khochu Vse Znat'*, 24, 700–3.

—— (1930d) Strukturnaja psikhologija. In L. Vygotsky, S. Gellershtejn, B. Fingert, and M. Shirvindt (eds), *Osnovnye techenija sovremennoj psikhologii*. Moscow: Gosudarstvennoe Izdatel'stvo, pp. 84–125.

—— (1930e/1972) Strukturnaja psikhologija. In L. Vygotsky, *Strukturnaja psikhologija*. Moscow: Izdatel'stvo Moskovskogo Universiteta.

—— (1930f) Ejdetika. In L. Vygotsky, S. Gellershtejn, B. Fingert, and M. Shirvindt (eds), *Osnovnye techenija sovremennoj psikhologii*. Moscow: Gosudarstvennoe Izdatel'stvo, pp. 178–205.

—— (1930g/1975) Ejdetika. In *Khrestomatija po oshchushcheniju i vosprijatiju*. Moscow: Izdatel'stvo Moskovskogo Universiteta, pp. 275–81.

—— (1930h) Eksperimental'nye issledovanie vysshikh processov povedenija. In A. B. Zalkind (ed.), *Psikhonevrologicheskie nauki v SSSR*. Moscow–Leningrad: Gosudarstvennoe Medicinskoe Izdatel'stvo, pp. 70–1.

—— (1930i) Razvitie vysshikh form povedenija v detskom vozraste. In A. B. Zalkind, *Psikhonevrologicheskie nauki v SSSR*. Moscow–Leningrad: Gosudarstvennoe Medicinskoe Izdatel'stvo, 138–9.

—— (1930j) Kul'turnoe razvitie anomal'nogo i trudno vospituemogo rebenka. In

A. B. Zalkind (ed.), *Psikhonevrologicheskie nauki v SSSR*. Moscow–Leningrad: Gosudarstvennoe Medicinskoe Izdatel'stvo, pp. 195–6.

—— (1930k/1983) Kul'turno razvitie anomal'nogo i trudno vospituemogo rebenka. In L. S. Vygotsky, *Sobranie sochinenij. Tom 5. Osnovy defektologii.* Moscow: Pedagogika, pp. 330–1.

—— (1930l) Novoe v oblasti pedologicheskikh issledovanij. *Detskij Dom*, 7, 22–7.

—— (1930m) O svjazi mezhdu trudovoj dejatel'nost'ju i intellektual'nym razvitiem rebenka. *Pedologija*, 5/6, 588–96.

—— (1930n/1976) O svjazi mezhdu trudovoj dejatel'nost'ju i intellektual'nym razvitiem rebenka. *Defektologija*, 6, 3–8.

—— (1930o/1980) O svjazi mezhdu trudovoj dejatel'nost'ju i intellektual'nym razvitiem rebenka. In I. I. Il'jasov and V. Ja. Ljaudis (eds), *Khrestomatija po vozrastnoj i pedagogicheskoj psikhologii.* Moscow: Izdatel'stvo Moskovskogo Universiteta, pp. 114–20.

—— (1930p) *Pedologija Podrostka. Vol. II.* Moscow: Izdanie Bjuro Zaochnogo Obuchenija pri Pedfake 2 MGU.

—— (1930q/1960) Povedenie zhivotnykh i cheloveka. In L. S. Vygotsky, *Razvitie vysshikh psikhicheskikh funkcij.* Moscow: Izdatel'stvo Pedagogicheskikh Nauk, pp. 397–457.

—— (1930r) Foreword. In B. R. Buckingham, *Issledovanie pedagogicheskogo processa dlja uchitelej.* Moscow: Rabotnik Prosveshchenija, pp. 5–21.

—— (1930s) Foreword. In W. Köhler, *Issledovanie intellekta chelovekopodobnykh obez'jan.* Moscow: Izdatel'stvo Kommunisticheskoj Akademii, pp. i–xxix.

—— (1930t/1982) Foreword. In L. S. Vygotsky, *Sobranie sochinenij. Tom 1. Voprosy teorii i istorii psikhologii.* Moscow: Pedagogika, pp. 210–37.

—— (1930u) Problema vysshikh intellektual'nykh funkcij v sisteme psikhotekhnicheskogo issledovanija. *Psikhotekhnika i Psikhofiziologija Truda*, 3, 374–84.

—— (1930v/1983) Problema vysshikh intellektual'nykh funkcij v sisteme psikhotekhnicheskogo issledovanija. In *Istorija sovetskoj psikhologii truda.* Moscow: Izdatel'stvo Moskovskogo Universiteta, pp. 50–8.

—— (1930w) Socialisticheskaja peredelka cheloveka. *VARNITSO*, 3, 9–10, 36–44.

—— (1930x) *Voobrazhenie i tvorchestvo v detskom vozraste.* Moscow–Leningrad: GIZ.

—— (1930y/1967) *Voobrazhenie i tvorchestvo v detskom vozraste.* In L. S. Vygotsky, *Voobrazhenie i tvorchestvo v detskom vozraste.* Moscow: Prosveshchenie.

—— (1930z/1960) Instrumental'nyj metod v psikhologii. In L. S. Vygotsky, *Razvitie vysshikh psikhicheskikh funkcij.* Moscow: Izdatel'stvo APN RSFSR, pp. 224–34.

—— (1930aa/1982) *Razvitie vysshikh psikhicheskikh funkcij.* In L. S. Vygotsky, *Sobranie sochinenij. Tom 1. Voprosy teorii i istorii psikhologii.* Moscow: Pedagogika, pp. 103–8.

—— (1930ab/1982) O psikhologicheskikh sistemakh. In L. S. Vygotsky, *Sobranie sochinenij. Tom 1. Voprosy teorii i istorii psikhologii.* Moscow: Pedagogika, pp. 109–31.

—— (1930ac) Foreword. In K. Bühler, *Ocherk dukhovnogo razvitija rebenka.* Moscow: Rabotnik Prosveshchenija, pp. 5–26.

—— (1930ad/1982) Foreword. In L. S. Vygotsky, *Sobranie sochinenij. Tom 1. Voprosy teorii i istorii psikhologii.* Moscow: Pedagogika, pp. 196–209.

—— (1930ae) Psikhika, soznanie, bessoznatel'noe. In *Elementy obshchej psikhologii.* Moscow: Izdatel'stvo BZO pri Pedfake 2-go MGU, pp. 48–61.

—— (1930af/1982) Psikhika, soznanie, bessoznatel'noe. In L. S. Vygotsky, *Sobranie sochinenij. Tom 1. Voprosy teorii i istorii psikhologii.* Moscow: Pedagogika, pp. 132–48.

—— (1930ag/1983) K voprosu o rechevom razvitii i vospitanii glukhonemogo rebenka. In L. S. Vygotsky, *Sobranie sochinenij. Tom 5. Osnovy defektologii.* Moscow: Pedagogika, pp. 329–30.

—— 1930ah) Son i snovidenija. In *Elementy obshchej psikhologii.* Moscow: Izdanie Bjuro Zaochnogo Obuchenija pri Pedfake 2-go MGU, pp. 62–75.

—— (1930ai) K probleme razvitija interesov v perekhodnom vozraste. In *Rob-Itnicha osvIta.* Kharkov: Derzh. Vid. Ukr, pp. 63–81.

—— (1930aj) *Vvedenie k materialam sobrannym sotrudnikami instituta nauchnoj pedagogiki. 13 April 1930.* Scientific Archives of the APN SSSR.

—— 1930ak) *Razvitie soznanija v detskom vozraste.* Unpublished manuscript. Family archives.

—— (1931a) K voprosu o pedologii i smezhnykh s neju naukakh. *Pedologija*, 3, 52–8.

—— (1931b) K voprosu o psikhologii i pedologii. *Psikhologija*, 4, 78–100.

—— (1931c) Pedologija i smezhnye s neju nauki. *Pedologija*, 7/8, 12–22.

—— (1931d) Psikhotekhnika i pedologija. *Psikhotekhnika i Psikhofiziologija Truda*, 2–3, 173–84.

—— (1931e) Kollektiv kak faktor razvitija defektivnogo rebenka (1). *Voprosy Defektologii*, 1–2, 8–17.

—— (1931f) Kollektiv kak faktor razvitija defektivnogo rebenka (2). *Voprosy Defektologii*, 3, 3–18.

—— (1931g/1983) Kollektiv kak faktor razvitija defektivnogo rebenka (2). In L. S. Vygotsky, *Sobranie sochinenij. Tom 5. Osnovy defektologii.* Moscow: Pedagogika, pp. 196–218.

—— (1931h) *Pedologija Podrostka. Vol. III.* Moscow–Leningrad: Gosudarstvennoe Uchebno-Pedagogichesko Izdatel'stvo.

—— (1931i/1980) *Pedologija Podrostka. Vol. III* (excerpt). In I. I. Il'jasov and V. Ja. Ljaudis (eds), *Khrestomatija po vozrastnoj i pedagogicheskoj psikhologii.* Moscow: Izdatel'stvo Moskovskogo Universiteta, pp. 138–42.

—— (1931j/1984) *Khrestomatija po vozrastnoj i pedagogicheskoj psikhologii.* (abridged). In L. S. Vygotsky, *Sobranie sochinenij. Tom 4. Detskaja psikhologija.* Moscow: Pedagogika, pp. 5–242.

—— (1931k) Foreword. In A. N. Leont'ev, *Razvitie pamjati.* Moscow–Leningrad: Uchpedgiz, pp. 6–13.

—— (1931l/1982) Foreword. In L. S. Vygotsky, *Sobranie sochinenij. Tom 1.*

Voprosy teorii i istorii psikhologii. Moscow: Pedagogika, pp. 149–55.

—— (1931m/1960) Istorija razvitija vysshikh psikhicheskikh funkcij. In L. S. Vygotsky, *Razvitie vysshikh psikhicheskikh funkcij.* Moscow: Izdatel'stvo APN RSFSR, pp. 13–223.

—— (1931n/1983) Istorija razvitija vysshikh psikhicheskikh funkcij. In L. S. Vygotsky, *Sobranie sochinenij. Tom 3. Problemy razvitija psikhiki.* Moscow: Pedagogika, pp. 5–228.

—— (1931o/1983) K voprosu o kompensatornykh processakh v razvitii umstvenno otstalogo rebenka. In L. S. Vygotsky, *Sobranie sochinenij. Tom 5. Osnovy defektologii.* Moscow: Pedagogika, pp. 115–36.

—— (1931p) Foreword. In Ja. K. Cvejfel', *Ocherki osobennosti povedenija i vospitanija glukhonemogo rebenka.* Moscow–Leningrad: Uchpedgiz, pp. 3–5.

—— (1931q/1983) Foreword. In L. S. Vygotsky, *Sobranie sochinenij. Tom 5. Osnovy defektologii.* Moscow: Pedagogika, pp. 219–21.

—— (1931r) Myshlenie. *Bol'shaja Medicinskaja Enciklopedija, Vol. 19,* 414–26.

—— (1931s) *Vystuplenie. Materialy reaktologicheskoj diskussii.* Archives of the NII of General and Pedagogical Psychology of the APN SSSR, f. 82, op. 1, ed. khr. 11, pp. 5–15.

—— (1931t) *Prakticheskaja dejatel'nost' i myshlenie v razvitii rebenka v svjazi s problemoj politekhnizma.* Unpublished manuscript. Family archives.

—— (1932a) K probleme psikhologii shizofrenii. *Sovetskaja Nevropatologija, Psikhiatrija, Psikhogigiena, 8,* 352–64.

—— (1932b/1956) K probleme psikhologii shizofrenii. In L. S. Vygotsky, *Izbrannye psikhologicheskie issledovanija.* Moscow: Izdatel'stvo APN RSFSR, pp. 481–96.

—— (1932c) Foreword. In A. Gesell, *Pedologija rannogo vozrasta.* Moscow: Uchpedgiz, pp. 3–14.

—— (1932d) Foreword. In J. Piaget, *Rech i myshlenie rebenka.* Moscow–Leningrad: Uchpedgiz, pp. 3–54.

—— (1932e/1960) Sovremennye techenija v psikhologii. In L. S. Vygotsky, *Razvitie vysshikh psikhicheskikh funkcij.* Moscow: Izdatel'stvo APN RSFSR, pp. 458–81.

—— (1932f/1960) Lekcii po psikhologii. In L. S. Vygotsky, *Razvitie vysshikh psikhicheskikh funkcij.* Moscow: Izdatel'stvo APN RSFSR, pp. 235–363.

—— (1932g/1959) Lekcii po psikhologii. (excerpt). *Psikhologija, 3,* 125–34.

—— (1932h/1979) Lekcii po psikhologii. (excerpt). In *Khrestomatija po obshchej psikhologii.* Moscow: Izdatel'stvo Moskovskogo Universiteta, pp. 155–62.

—— (1932i/1982) Lekcii po psikhologii. In L. S. Vygotsky, *Sobranie sochinenij. Tom 2. Problemy obshchej psikhologii.* Moscow: Pedagogika, pp. 363–465.

—— (1932j/1982) O pis'mennoj rechi i.t.d. *Vestnik Moskovskogo Universiteta Ser. 14.* Psikhologija, 1982, 1, 60–7.

—— (1932k) Foreword. In E. K. Gracheva, *Vospitanie i obuchenie gluboko otstalogo rebenka.* Moscow–Leningrad: Uchpedgiz, pp. 3–10.

—— (1932l/1969) Foreword. *Defektologija, 1,* 83–7.

—— (1932m/1983) Foreword. In L. S. Vygotsky, *Sobranie sochinenij. Tom 5. Osnovy defektologii.* Moscow: Pedagogika, pp. 222–30.

—— (1932n) Mladencheskij vozrast (two versions). Unpublished manuscript. Family archives.

—— (1932o/1984) Mladencheskij vozrast. In L. S. Vygotsky, *Sobranie sochinenij. Tom 4. Detskaja psikhologija.* Moscow: Pedagogika, pp. 269–317.

—— (1932p/1984) Rannee detstvo. In L. S. Vygotsky, *Sobranie sochinenij. Tom 4. Detskaja psikhologii.* Moscow: Pedagogika, pp. 340–67.

—— (1933a) K probleme psikhologii shizofrenii. In *Sovremennye problemy shizofrenii.* Moscow: Medgiz, pp. 19–28.

—— (1933b/1981) K probleme psikhologii shizofrenii. In *Khrestomatija po patopsikhologii.* Moscow: Izdatel'stvo Moskovskogo Universiteta, pp. 60–5.

—— (1933c/1935) Dinamika umstvennogo razvitija shkol'nika v svjazi s obucheniem. In L. S. Vygotsky, *Umstvennoe razvitie detej v processe obuchenija.* Moscow–Leningrad: Uchpedgiz, pp. 33–52.

—— (1933d/1935) O pedologicheskom analize pedagogicheskogo processa. In L. S. Vygotsky, *Umstvennoe razvitie detej v processe obuchenija.* Moscow–Leningrad: Uchpedgiz, pp. 116–34.

—— (1933e/1966) Igra i ee rol' v psikhicheskom razvitii rebenka. *Voprosy Psikhologii,* 62–76.

—— (1933f/1968) Problema soznanija. In *Psikhologija grammatiki.* Moscow: Izdatel'stvo Moskovskogo Universiteta.

—— (1933g/1982) Problema soznanija. In L. S. Vygotsky, *Sobranie sochinenij. Tom 1. Voprosy teorii i istorii psikhologii.* Moscow: Pedagogika, pp. 156–67.

—— (1933h/1984) Krizis pervogo goda zhizni. In L. S. Vygotsky, *Sobranie sochinenij. Tom 4. Detskaja psikhologija.* Moscow: Pedagogika, pp. 318–39.

—— (1933i/1984) Krizis trekh let. In L. S. Vygotsky, *Sobranie sochinenij. Tom 4. Detskaja psikhologija.* Moscow: Pedagogika, pp. 368–75.

—— (1933j/1984) Krizis semi let. In L. S. Vygotsky, *Sobranie sochinenij. Tom 4. Detskaja psikhologija.* Moscow: Pedagogika, pp. 376–85.

—— (1933k/1984) Uchenie ob emocijakh. In L. S. Vygotsky, *Sobranie sochinenij. Tom 6. Nauchnoe nasledstvo.* Moscow: Pedagogika, pp. 91–318.

—— (1933l) Foreword. In L. V. Zankov, M. S. Pevzner, and V. F. Schmidt, *Trudnye deti v shkol'noj rabote.* Moscow–Leningrad: Uchpedgiz, pp. 3–4.

—— (1933m/1935) Razvitie zhitejskikh i nauchnykh ponjatij v shkol'nom vozraste. In L. S. Vygotsky, *Umstvennoe razvitie detej v processe obuchenija.* Moscow–Leningrad: Uchpedgiz, pp. 96–115.

—— (1933n/1984) Problema vozrasta. In L. S. Vygotsky, *Sobranie sochinenij. Tom 4. Detskaja psikhologija.* Moscow: Pedagogika, pp. 244–68.

—— (1933o) *Vvodnaja lekcija po vozrastnoj psikhologii.* Archives of the Herzen Pedagogical Institute.

—— (1933p) *Kriticheskie vozrasta.* Archives of the Herzen Pedagogical Institute.

—— (1933q) *Negativnaja faza perekhodnogo vozrasta.* Archives of the Herzen Pedagogical Institute.

—— (1933r) *O perekhodnom vozraste.* Archives of the Herzen Pedagogical Institute.

—— (1933s) *Pedologija doshkol'nogo vozrasta.* Archives of the Herzen Pedagogical Institute.

—— (1933t) *Problema razvitija (absoljutnaja i otnositel'naja uspeshnost')*. Archives of the Herzen Pedagogical Institute.

—— (1933u) *Doshkol'nyj vozrast*. Unpublished manuscript. Family archives.

—— (1933v) *K voprosu o dinamike umstvennogo razvitija normal'nogo i nenormal'nogo rebenka*. Unpublished manuscript. Family archives.

—— (1933w) Ob issledovanii uchebnoj raboty skhol'nika. Unpublished manuscript. Family archives.

—— (1934a) *Myshlenie i rech. Psikhologicheskie issledovanija*. Moscow–Leningrad: Gosudarstvennoe Social'no-Ekonomicheskoe Izdatel'stvo.

—— (1934b/1956) Myshlenie i rech. Psikhologicheskie issledovanija. In L. S. Vygotsky, *Izbrannye psikhologicheskie issledovanija*. Moscow: Izdatel'stvo APN RSFSR, pp. 39–386.

—— (1934c/1977) Myshlenie i rech. Psikhologicheskie issledovanija. (excerpt). *Nauka i Tekhnika*, 6, 6–9.

—— (1934d/1981) Myshlenie i rech. Psikhologicheskie issledovanija. (excerpt). In *Khrestomatija po obshchej psikhologii*. Moscow: Izdatel'stvo Moskovskogo Universiteta, pp. 153–82.

—— (1934e/1982) Myshlenie i rech. Psikhologicheskie issledovanija. In L. S. Vygotsky, *Sobranie sochinenij. Tom 2. Problemy obshchej psikhologii*. Moscow: Pedagogika, pp. 5–361.

—— (1934f) Chapter 4. In L. S. Vygotsky, V. A. Giljarovsky, M. O. Gurevich, M. B. Krol', A. S. Shmarjan, et al. (eds), *Fashizm v psikhonevrologii*. Moscow–Leningrad: Gosudarstvennoe Izdatel'stvo Biologicheskoj i Medicinskoj Literatury, pp. 18–28.

—— (1934g) Teorija umstvennoj otstalosti. In *Umstvenno otstalyj rebenek*. Moscow: Uchpedgiz.

—— (1934h) Thought in schizophrenia. *Archives of Neurology and Psychiatry*, 31, 1063–77.

—— (1934i/1935) Problema obuchenija i umstvennogo razvitija v shkol'nom vozraste. In L. S. Vygotsky, *Umstvennoe razvitie detej v processe obuchenija*. Moscow–Leningrad: Uchpedgiz, pp. 3–19.

—— (1934j/1960) Problema razvitija i raspada vysshikh psikhicheskikh funkcij. In L. S. Vygotsky, *Razvitie vysshikh psikhicheskikh funkcij*. Moscow: Izdatel'stvo APN RSFSR, pp. 364–83.

—— (1934k) Foreword. In K. Koffka, *Osnovy psikhicheskogo razvitija*. Moscow–Leningrad: Gosudarstvennoe Social'no-Ekonomicheskoe Izdatel'stvo, pp. ix–lvi.

—— (1934l/1982) Foreword. In L. S. Vygotsky, *Sobranie sochinenij. Tom 1. Voprosy teorii i istorii psikhologii*. Moscow: Pedagogika, pp. 238–90.

—— (1934m) Psikhologija i uchenie o lokalizacii psikhicheskikh funkcij. In *Pervyj Vseukrainskij s'ezd nevropatologov i psikhiatrov*. Kharkov, pp. 34–41.

—— (1934n/1960) Psikhologija i uchenie o lokalizacii psikhicheskikh funkcij. In L. S. Vygotsky, *Razvitie vysshikh psikhicheskikh funkcij*. Moscow: Izdatel'stvo APN RSFSR, pp. 384–96.

—— (1934o/1982) Psikhologija i uchenie o lokalizacii psikhicheskikh funkcij. In L. S. Vygotsky, *Sobranie sochinenij. Tom 1. Voprosy teorii i istorii psikhologii*. Moscow: Pedagogika, pp. 168–74.

—— (1934p) *Osnovy pedologii*. Moscow: Izdatel'stvo 2-go Moskovskogo Medicinskogo Instituta.

—— (1934q) Mladenchestvo i rannij vozrast. Archives of the Herzen Pedagogical Institute.

—— (1934r) Perekhodnyj vozrast. Archives of the Herzen Pedagogical Institute.

—— (1934s) Myshlenie shkol'nika. Archives of the Herzen Pedagogical Institute.

—— (1934t) Shkol'nyj vozrast. Archives of the Herzen Pedagogical Institute.

—— (1934u) Problema vozrasta. Family archives.

—— (1934v) Slaboumie pri bolezni Pick'a. Family archives.

—— (1934w) Eksperimental'nye issledovanija vospitanija novykh rechevykh refleksov po sposobu svjazyvanija s kompleksami. Family archives.

—— (1934x) Shkol'nyj vozrast. Archives of D. B. El'konin.

—— (1935a) K voprosu o mnogojazychii v detskom vozraste. In L. S. Vygotsky, *Umstvennoe razvitie detej v processe obuchenija*. Moscow–Leningrad: Uchpedgiz, pp. 53–72.

—— (1935b/1980) K voprosu o mnogojazychii v detskom vozraste (excerpt). In I. I. Il'jasov and V. Ja. Ljaudis (eds), *Khrestomatija po vozrastnoj i pedagogicheskoj psikhologii*. Moscow: Izdatel'stvo Moskovskogo Universiteta, pp. 67–72.

—— (1935c/1983) K voprosu o mnogojazychii v detskom vozraste. In L. S. Vygotsky, *Sobranie sochinenij. Tom 3. Problemy razvitija psikhiki*. Moscow: Pedagogika, pp. 329–37.

—— (1935d) Predistorija pis'mennoj rechi. In L. S. Vygotsky, *Umstvennoe razvitie v processe obuchenija*. Moscow–Leningrad: Uchpedgiz, pp. 73–95.

—— (1935e/1980) Predistorija pis'mennoj rechi. In I. I. Il'jasov and V. Ja. Ljaudis (eds), *Khrestomatija po vozrastnoj i pedagogicheskoj psikhologii*. Moscow: Izdatel'stvo Moskovskogo Universiteta, pp. 72–81.

—— (1935f) K voprosu o razvitii ponjatij v shkol'nom vozraste. In Zh. I. Shif, *Razvitie nauchnykh ponjatij u shkol'nika. Issledovanie k voprosu umstvennogo razvitija shkol'nika pri obuchenii obshchestvovedeniju*. Moscow–Leningrad: Gosudarstvennoe Uchebno-Pedagogicheskoe Izdatel'stvo, pp. 3–17.

—— (1935g) *Osnovy pedologii*. Leningrad: Gosudarstvennyj Pedagogicheskij Institut Imeni A. I. Gercena.

—— (1935h) *Umstvennoe razvitie detej v processe obuchenija*. Moscow–Leningrad: Uchpedgiz.

—— (ed.) (1935i) *Umstvenno otstalyj rebenok*. Moscow: Uchpedgiz.

—— (1935j) Problema umstvennoj otstalosti. In L. S. Vygotsky (ed.), *Umstvenno otstalyj rebenok*. Moscow: Uchpedgiz, pp. 3–74.

—— (1935k/1956) Problema umstvennoj otstalosti. In L. S. Vygotsky, *Izbrannye psikhologicheskie issledovanija*. Moscow: Izdatel'stvo APN RSFSR, pp. 453–80.

—— (1935l/1981) Problema umstvennoj otstalosti. (excerpt). In *Khrestomatija po patopsikhologii*. Moscow: Izdatel'stvo Moskovskogo Universiteta, pp. 150–7.

—— (1935m/1983) Problema umstvennoj otstalosti. In L. S. Vygotsky, *Sobranie sochinenij. Tom 5. Osnovy defektologii*. Moscow: Pedagogika, pp. 231–56.

—— (1935n) Obuchenie i razvitie v doshkol'nom vozraste. In L. S. Vygotsky, *Umstvennoe razvitie detej v processe obuchenija*. Moscow–Leningrad: Uchpedgiz.

—— (1935o/1969) Obuchenie i razvitie v doshkol'nom vozraste (abridged). *Sem'ja i Shkola*, 12, 14–16.

—— (1935p/1980) Obuchenie i razvitie v doshkol'nom vozraste (abridged). In *Istorija sovetskoj doshkol'noj pedagogika. Khrestomatija*. Moscow: Prosveshchenie, pp. 241–5.

—— (1936a) *Diagnostika razvitija i pedologicheskaja klinika trudnogo detstva*. Moscow: Izdatel'stvo Eksperimental'nogo Defektologicheskogo Instituta.

—— (1936b/1981) *Diagnostika razvitija i pedologicheskaja klinika trudnogo detstva* (abridged). In *Khrestomatija po patopsikhologii*. Moscow: Izdatel'stvo Moskovskogo Universiteta, pp. 66–80.

—— (1936c/1983) *Diagnostika razvitija i pedologicheskaja klinika trudnogo detstva*. In L. S. Vygotsky, *Sobranie sochinenij. Tom 5. Osnovy defektologii*. Moscow: Pedagogika, pp. 257–311.

—— (1936d) K voprosu o psikhologii tvorchestva aktera. In P. M. Jakobson, *Psikhologija specificheskikh chuvstv aktera*. Moscow: GIZ, pp. 197–211.

—— (1936e/1984) K voprosu o psikhologii tvorchestva aktera. In L. S. Vygotsky, *Sobranie sochinenij. Tom 6. Nauchnoe nasledstvo*. Moscow: Pedagogika, pp. 319–28.

—— (1939) Thought and Speech. *Psychiatry*, 2, 29–54.

—— (1956) *Ibrannye psikhologicheskie issledovanija*. Moscow: Izdatel'stvo APN RSFSR.

—— (1960) *Razvitie vysshikh psikhicheskikh funkcij*. Moscow: Izdatel'stvo APN RSFSR.

—— (1962) *Thought and Language* [excerpt from 1934b]. Cambridge, Mass.: MIT Press.

—— (1965) Psychology and localization of functions. *Neuropsychologia*, 3, 381–6.

—— (1968) O dvukh napravlenijakh v ponimanii prirody emocij v zarubezhnoj psikhologii v nachale 20 veka. *Voprosy Psikhologii*, 2, 149–56.

—— (1970) Spinoza i ego uchenie ob emocijakh v svete sovremennoj psikhonevrologii. *Voprosy Filosofii*, 6, 120–30.

—— (1971) *The Psychology of Art*. Cambridge, Mass.: MIT Press.

—— (1972) Problema vozrastnoj periodizacii detskogo razvitija. *Voprosy Psikhologii*, 2, 114–23.

—— (1982a) *Sobranie sochinenij. Tom 1. Voprosy teorii i istorii psikhologii*. Moscow: Pedagogika.

—— (1982b) *Sobranie sochinenij. Tom 2. Problemy obshchej psikhologii*. Moscow: Pedagogika.

—— (1983a) *Sobranie sochinenij. Tom 3. Problemy razvitija psikhiki*. Moscow: Pedagogika.

—— (1983b) *Sobranie sochinenij. Tom 5. Osnovy defektologii*. Moscow: Pedagogika.

—— (1984a) *Sobranie sochinenij. Tom 4. Detskaja psikhologija*. Moscow: Pedagogika.

—— (1984b) *Sobranie sochinenij. Tom 6. Nauchnoe nasledstvo*. Moscow: Pedagogika.

—— (1986) *Thought and Language* (abridged from 1934b). Cambridge Mass.: MIT Press.

—— (1987) *The Collected Works of L. S. Vygotsky. Vol. 1. Problems of General Psychology.* New York: Plenum Press.

Vygotsky, L. S., Artemov, V. A., Bernshtejn, N. A., Dobrynin, N. F., and Luria, A. R. (1927) *Praktikum po eksperimental'noj psikhologii.* Moscow–Leningrad: GIZ.

Vygotsky, L. S., Artemov, V. A., Dobrynin, N. F., Luria, A. R. (eds) (1927) *Psikhologicheskaja khrestomatija.* Moscow–Leningrad: GIZ.

Vygotsky, L. S., Gellershtejn, S., Fingert, B., and Shirvindt, M. (eds) (1930) *Osnovnye techenija sovremennoj psikhologii.* Moscow: Gosudarstvennoe Izdatel'stvo.

Vygotsky, L. S., Giljarovskij, V. A., Gurevich, M. O., Krol', M. B., Shmar'jan, A. S. et al. (eds) (1934) *Fashizm v psikhonevrologii.* Moscow–Leningrad: Gosudarstvennoe Izdatel'stvo Biologicheskoj i Medicinskoj Literatury.

Vygotsky, L. S. and Leont'ev, A. N. (1932) Foreword. In A. N. Leont'ev, *Razvitie pamjati.* Moscow–Leningrad: Uchpedgiz.

Vygotsky, L. S. and Luria, A. R. (1925a) Foreword. In S. Freud, *Po to storonu principa udovol'stvija.* Moscow: Sovremennye Problemy, pp. 3–16.

—— (1925b/1989) Foreword. In S. Freud, *Psikhologija bessoznatel'nogo.* Moscow: Prosveshchenie, pp. 29–36.

—— (1926) Foreword. In R. Schultz, *Praktika eksperimental'noj psikhologii, pedagogiki i psikhotekhniki.* Moscow: Voprosy Truda, pp. 3–5.

—— (1930a) *Etjudy po istorii povedenija. Obez'jana. Primitiv. Rebenok.* Moscow–Leningrad: Gosudarstvennoe Izdatel'stvo.

—— (1930b) The function and fate of egocentric speech. Ninth International Congress of Psychology. *Proceedings and Papers.* New Haven, September 1–7, 1929. Princeton: Psychological Review Company, pp. 464–50.

—— (1930c) *Tool and Symbol in the Development of the Child.* (Unpublished manuscript submitted for publication in Murchison's *Handbook of Child Psychology,* 2nd edn.)

—— (1930d/1984) Orudie i znak. In L. S. Vygotsky, *Sobranie sochinenij. Tom 6. Nauchnoe nasledstvo.* Moscow: Pedagogika, pp. 6–90.

Walker, S. (1983) *Animal Thought.* London: Routledge and Kegan Paul.

Wallon, H. (1925) *L'enfant turbulent. Recueil d'observations.* Paris: Alcan.

Wallon, H. (1942) *De l'acte à la pensée.* Paris: Flammarion.

Werner, H. (1925) *Einführung in die Entwicklungspsychologie.* Leipzig: J. A. Barth.

Wertsch, J. V. (1980) The significance of dialogue in Vygotsky's account of social, egocentric, and inner speech. *Contemporary Educational Psychology,* 5, 150–62.

—— (1981) Adult–child interaction as a source of self-regulation in children. In S. R. Yussen (ed.), *The Development of Reflection.* New York: Academic Press.

—— (1984) The role of semiotic mediation in Vygotsky's account of higher mental processes. In E. Mertz and R. J. Parmentier (eds), *Semiotic Mediation: Psychological and Sociocultural Perspectives.* New York: Academic Press.

—— (1985) *Vygotsky and the Social Formation of Mind*. Cambridge, Mass.: Harvard University Press.

Wilson, E. O. (1976) *Sociobiology. The New Synthesis*. Cambridge, Mass.: Bellknap Press.

Wilson, A. N. (1988) *Tolstoy*. New York: Fawcett Columbine.

Windholz, G. (1984) Pavlov and the demise of the influence of Gestalt psychology in the Soviet Union. *Psychological Research*, 46, 187–206.

Woolfson, C. (1982) *The Labour Theory of Culture. A Re-examination of Engels' Theory of Human Origins*. London: Routledge and Kegan Paul.

Yates, F. A. (1984) *The Art of Memory*. London: Ark Paperbacks.

Yerkes, R. M. (1916) The mental life of monkeys and apes. A study of ideational behavior. *Behavior Monographs*, 3, 1, New York: Holt.

Yerkes, R. M. and Yerkes, D. M. (1928) Concerning memory in the chimpanzee. *Journal of Comparative Psychology*, 8, 237–71.

Yerkes, R. and Learned, E. W. (1925) *Chimpanzee Intelligence and its Vocal Expression*. Baltimore.

Za marksisto-leninskuju pedologiju! (1931) *Pedologija*, 7–8, 3–7.

Zalkind, A. B. (1924a) Frejdizm i marksizm. *Krasnaja Nov'*, 4.

—— (1924b) *Revoljucija i molodjezh*. Moscow: Izdanie Kommunisticheskogo Universiteta im. Ja. Sverdlova.

—— (1927a) *Osnovnye voprosy pedologii*. Moscow: Rabotnik Prosveshchenija.

—— (1927b) *Zhizn organizma i vnushenie*. Moscow: GIZ.

—— (1929) Psychoneurological sciences in the period of reconstruction. *Pedologija*, 4, 453–62.

—— (1929) The fundamentals and the practice of mental hygiene in adolescence and youth in Soviet Russia. *Mental Hygiene*, 14, 647–9.

—— (1930a) First All-Union Congress on human behaviour. *Pedologija*, 2, 161–4.

—— (1930b) (ed.). *Psikhonevrologicheskie nauki v SSSR: Materialy I vsesojuznogo s'ezda po izucheniju povedenija cheloveka*. Moscow–Leningrad: Gosudarstvennoe Medicinskoe Izdatel'stvo.

—— (1930c) Main characteristics of transitional age. *Pedologija*, 1, 3–25.

—— (1931a) The psychoneurological front and psychological discussion. *Pedologija*, 3, 1–6.

—— (1931b) The differentiation on the paedological front. *Pedologija*, 3, 15, 7–14.

—— (1932) For Marxist–Leninist methodology in paedology: on "Sex Education." *Pedologija*, 1–2, 11–20.

Zaluzhnyj, A. S. (1930) The study of the pioneer-group as a complex organized collective. In A. B. Zalkind (ed.), *Psikhonevrologicheskie nauki v SSSR*. Moscow–Leningrad: Gosudarstvennoe Medicinskoe Izdatel'stvo, pp. 186–8.

Zankov, L. V. (1930a) Active remembering in the mentally retarded child. In A. B. Zalkind (ed.), *Psikhonevrologicheskie nauki v SSSR*. Moscow–Leningrad: Gosudarstvennoe Medicinskoe Izdatel'stvo, pp. 195–6.

—— (1930b) The study of the active remembering. In A. B. Zalkind (ed.), *Psikhonevrologicheskie nauki v SSSR*. Moscow–Leningrad: Gosudarstvennoe Medicinskoe Izdatel'stvo, pp. 73–6.

—— (1935a) *Ocherki psikhologii umstvenno-otstalogo rebenka*. Moscow: Gosudarstvennoe Uchebno-Pedagogicheskoe Izdatel'stvo.

—— (1935b) K voprosu o razvitii myshlenija shkol'nika. In *Novye puti v defektologii*. Leningrad.

Zazzo, R. (1979) *Psychologie et marxisme. La vie et l'oeuvre de Henri Wallon*. Paris: Denoël/Gonthier.

Zeigarnik. B. (1927) Das Behalten erledigter und unerledigter Handlungen. *Psychologische Forschung*, 9, 1–85.

—— (1988) V shkole Kurta Levina. *Voprosy Psikhologii*, 3, 171–9.

Zen'kovsky, V. (1960) *Russkaja pedagogika v XX veke*. Paris: Izdanie Religiozno-pedagogicheskogo kabineta pri Pravoslavnom Bogoslovskom Institute.

Zinov'ev, G. E. (1923) Intelligentsia and revolution. *Pravda*, November 25 and 27.

Zivin, G. (ed.) (1979) *The Development of Self-Regulation Through Private Speech*. New York: John Wiley.

Index of Names

Index of Subjects